Software Metrics

Software Metrics

A Rigorous and Practical Approach

Second Edition

Norman E. Fenton

and

Shari Lawrence Pfleeger

PWS Publishing Company

INTERNATIONAL THOMSON COMPUTER PRESS

I ⓣ P   An International Thomson Publishing Company

London • Bonn • Boston • Johannesburg • Madrid • Melbourne •
Mexico City • New York • Paris • Singapore • Tokyo • Toronto •
Albany, NY • Belmont, CA • Cincinnati, OH • Detroit, MI

Software Metrics: A Rigorous and Practical Approach
Second Edition
Copyright © 1997 Norman E. Fenton and Shari Lawrence Pfleeger

I (T) P A division of International Thomson Publishing Inc.
The ITP logo is a trademark under licence.

The following figures and tables have been reproduced from other sources as indicated: **Figure 7.2:** Conte, S.D., Shen, U.Y., and Dunsmore, H.E. *Software Engineering Metrics and Models*, Benjamin Cummings Publishing Inc.
Figure 8.24: Ince, D.C. and Shepperd, M.J. *An empirical and theoretical analysis of an information flow based system design metric.* Proc. ESEC.
Figures 9.6 and 9.8: Grady, R.B. and Caswell, D.L. *Software Metrics: Establishing a company-wide program.* Reprinted by permission of Prentice Hall, Englewood Cliffs, New Jersey, USA. **Table 2.8:** Seigel, S. and Castellan, N.J. *Nonparametric statistics for the behavioural sciences*, 2nd edition, McGraw-Hill. **Table 11.6** Rock, P. (ed), *Software Reliability Handbook*, Elsevier North Holland.
Table 11.4: Behrens, C.A., *Measuring the productivity of computer systems development activities with function points* IEEE Trans. Software Engineering.

For more information, contact:

International Thomson Computer Press
Berkshire House
168–173 High Holborn
London WC1V 7AA
UK

PWS Publishing Company
20 Park Plaza
Boston
Massachusetts 02116-4324
USA

http://www.itcpmedia.com

British Library Cataloguing-in-Publication Data
A catalogue record for this book is available from the British Library

Library of Congress Cataloging-in-Publication Data
A catalog record for this book is available from the Library of Congress

First printed 1996
Commissioning Editor Samantha Whittaker
Cover Designed by Button Eventures
Typeset by Hodgson Williams Associates, Tunbridge Wells and Cambridge
Printed in the UK by Cambridge University Press, Cambridge

UK ISBN 1-85032-275-9
US ISBN 0-534-95600-9

Contents

PART II: SOFTWARE-ENGINEERING MEASUREMENT

PART III: MEASUREMENT AND MANAGEMENT

Preface

Although not always acknowledged as essential to good software engineering, software metrics play an important role. Measurement is used to assess situations, track progress, evaluate effectiveness, and more. But the gap between how we *do* measure and how we *could* measure is still larger than it should be. A key reason for this gap between potential and practice has been the lack of a coordinated, comprehensive framework for understanding and using measurement. The rigorous measurement framework introduced by the highly successful first edition of *Software Metrics: A Rigorous Approach* in 1991 has helped to advance the role of measurement by inspiring discussion of important issues, explaining essential concepts, and suggesting new approaches for tackling long-standing problems.

As one of the first texts on software metrics, the first edition broke new ground by introducing software engineers to measurement theory, graph-theoretic concepts, and new approaches to software reliability. This second edition brings the coverage of software metrics fully up to date. The book has been comprehensively rewritten and redesigned to reflect changing developments in software metrics, most notably their growing acceptance in industrial practice. This edition stresses the original framework for software metrics, but emphasizes its practical applications. Based on measurement theory and a classification of entities as products, processes, and resources, the framework has been expanded to include notions of process visibility and goal-directed measurement. The theory is liberally supplemented with case studies and examples to illustrate the application of each idea and technique.

The new edition also reflects classroom and industrial feedback about the first edition. Thus, the text now includes extensive case studies, and more worked examples and exercises. Every section of the book has been improved and updated, including new sections on process maturity and measurement, the Goal–Question–Metric paradigm, metrics planning, experimentation, empirical studies, object-oriented metrics, and metrics tools. The book continues to provide an accessible and comprehensive introduction to software metrics, which should be now an essential facet of the software engineering process.

This book is designed to suit several audiences. It is structured as the primary textbook for an academic or industrial course on software metrics and quality assurance. But it is also a useful supplement for any course in software engineering. Because of its breadth, the book is a major reference book for academics and practitioners, as it makes accessible important and interesting results that have appeared only in research-oriented publications. Researchers in software metrics will find special interest in the material reporting new results, and in the extensive annotated bibliography of measurement-related information. Finally, the book offers help to software managers and developers who seek guidance on establishing or expanding a measurement program; they can focus on the practical guidelines for selecting metrics and planning their use.

The book is arranged in three parts. Part I offers the reader a basic understanding of why and how we measure. It examines and explains the fundamentals of measurement, experimentation, and data collection and analysis. Next, Part II explores software engineering measurement in greater detail, with comprehensive information about a range of specific metrics and their uses, illustrated by a wealth of examples and case studies. Finally, Part III provides a management perspective on software measurement, explaining how to plan a measurement program, what has been successful in other organizations, and how measurement can be used to evaluate the effectiveness of techniques and tools. The book also includes an annotated bibliography, a glossary, and answers to selected exercises from the main chapters.

Norman Fenton is a Professor of Computing Science at the Centre for Software Reliability, City University, London, UK.

Shari Lawrence Pfleeger is President of Systems/Software, Washington, DC, a consultancy that specializes in software engineering and technology evaluation.

Acknowledgments

This book has been fashioned and influenced by many people over the last few years. We are especially indebted to Barbara Kitchenham, Bev Littlewood, and Peter Mellor for key contributions to several of the chapters, and for allowing us to embellish their ideas in this new edition. And we thank Tom DeMarco and Tom Gibb for their thorough review of, and insightful comments about, an early version of the manuscript.

Special thanks are also due to the original South Bank Polytechnic METKIT team, notably Martin Bush, Ros Herman, David Mole, Meg Russell, and Robin Whitty, who inspired, sponsored, edited, and corrected the first edition. Other colleagues have given us helpful advice, including Nick Ashley, Richard Bache, Bill Bail, Vic Basili, Sarah Brocklehurst, the Grubstake Group (Albert Baker, Antonia Bertolino, Jim Bieman, Dave Gustafson, Austin Melton, Linda Ott, and Robin Whitty), Tracy Hall, Les Hatton, Bill Hetzel, Gillian Hill, Chuck Howell, Darrel Ince, Agnes Kaposi, Chris Kemerer, Taghi Khoshgoftaar, Bob Lockhart, Bob Malcolm, Tom Maibaum, Steve Minnis, Margaret Myers, Martin Neil, Niklas Ohlsson, Ron Prather, James Robertson, Suzanne Robertson, Gerald Robinson, Terry Rout, Roger Shaw, Martin Shepperd, Claude Stricker, Lorenzo Strigini, Dale Tiller, Alan Todd, Klaas van den Berg, Hans van Vliet, Dave Wright, Marv Zelkowitz, and Horst Zuse. Carol Allen and Basi Isaacs provided clerical support, and Chuck Pfleeger and Stella Page provided valuable technical and emotional support. We also appreciate the efforts of Christof Ebert, Bob Grady, Armstrong Takang, Aimo Torn, Faridah Yahya, and numerous others who have pointed out problems with the first edition that we have corrected here.

We continue to be indebted to the European Commission, whose ESPRIT-funded METKIT and PDCS projects partly supported the writing of the first edition and whose PDCS 2 project partly supported the writing of the second edition; British Telecom Research Laboratories and NATO also supported some of the initial work. We are grateful to the UK Engineering and Physical Sciences Research Council and the UK Department of Trade and Industry, whose DESMET project work forms the core of Chapters 4, 5 and 6, and whose SMARTIE and DATUM projects provided many of the examples used throughout the book.

PART I

FUNDAMENTALS OF MEASUREMENT AND EXPERIMENTATION

1 Measurement: what is it and why do it?

Software measurement, once an obscure and esoteric specialty, has become essential to good software engineering. Many of the best software developers measure characteristics of the software to get some sense of whether the requirements are consistent and complete, whether the design is of high quality, and whether the code is ready to be tested. Effective project managers measure attributes of process and product to be able to tell when the software will be ready for delivery and whether the budget will be exceeded. Informed customers measure aspects of the final product to determine if it meets the requirements and is of sufficient quality. And maintainers must be able to assess the current product to see what should be upgraded and improved.

This book addresses all of these concerns and more. The first six chapters examine and explain the fundamentals of measurement and experimentation, providing you with a basic understanding of why we measure and how that measurement supports investigation of the use and effectiveness of software-engineering tools and techniques. Chapters 7 through 12 explore software engineering measurement in great detail, with information about specific metrics and their uses. Chapters 13, 14 and 15 offer a management perspective on software measurement, explaining current practices and looking ahead toward the future of measurement and metrics. Collectively, the chapters offer broad coverage of all aspects of software-engineering measurement, plus enough depth so that you can apply the metrics to your processes, products and resources. If you are a student, not yet experienced in working on projects with groups of people to solve interesting business or research problems, this book explains how measurement can become a natural and useful part of your regular development and maintenance activities.

This chapter begins with a discussion of measurement in our everyday lives. In the first section, we explain how measurement is a common and necessary practice for understanding, controlling and improving our environment. In this section, you will see why measurement requires rigor and care. In the second section, we describe the role of measurement in software engineering. In particular, we look at how measurement needs are directly related to the goals we set and the questions we must answer when developing our software. Next, we compare software engineering measurement with measurement in other engineering disciplines, and propose specific objectives for software measurement. The last section provides a roadmap to the measurement topics discussed in the remainder of the book.

1.1 MEASUREMENT IN EVERYDAY LIFE

Measurement lies at the heart of many systems that govern our lives. Economic measurements determine price and pay increases. Measurements in radar systems enable us to detect aircraft when direct vision is obscured. Medical system measurements enable doctors to diagnose specific illnesses. Measurements in atmospheric systems are the basis for weather prediction. Without measurement, technology cannot function.

But measurement is not solely the domain of professional technologists. Each of us uses it in everyday life. Price acts as a measure of value of an item in a shop, and we calculate the total bill to make sure the shopkeeper gives us correct change. We use height and size measurements to ensure that our clothing will fit properly. When making a journey, we calculate distance, choose our route, measure our speed, and predict when we will arrive at our destination (and perhaps when we need to refuel). So measurement helps us to understand our world, interact with our surroundings and improve our lives.

1.1.1 *What is measurement?*

These examples present a picture of the variety in how we use measurement. But there is a common thread running through each of the described activities: in every case, some aspect of a thing is assigned a descriptor that allows us to compare it with others. In the shop, we can compare the price of one item with another. In the clothing store, we contrast sizes. And on our journey, we compare distance traveled to distance remaining. The rules for assignment and comparison are not explicit in the examples, but it is clear that we make our comparisons and calculations according to a well-defined set of rules. We can capture this notion by defining measurement formally in the following way:

Measurement is the process by which numbers or symbols are assigned to attributes of entities in the real world in such a way as to describe them according to clearly defined rules.

Thus, measurement captures information about attributes of entities. An **entity** is an object (such as a person or a room) or an event (such as a journey or the testing phase of a software project) in the real world. We want to describe the entity by identifying characteristics that are important to us in distinguishing one entity from another. An **attribute** is a feature or property of an entity. Typical attributes include the area or color (of a room), the cost (of a journey), or the elapsed time (of the testing phase). Often, we talk about entities and their attributes interchangeably, as in "It is cold today" when we really mean that the air temperature is cold today, or "she is taller than he" when we really mean "her height is greater than his height." Such loose terminology is acceptable for everyday speech, but it is incorrect and unsuitable for scientific endeavors. Thus, it is wrong to say that we measure things or that we measure attributes; in fact, we measure attributes of things. It is ambiguous to say that we "measure a room," since we can measure its length, area, or temperature. It is likewise ambiguous to say that we "measure the temperature," since we measure the temperature of a specific geographical location under specific conditions. In other words, what is commonplace in common speech is unacceptable for engineers and scientists.

When we describe entities by using attributes, we often define the attributes using numbers or symbols. Thus, price is designated as a number of dollars or pounds sterling, while height is defined in terms of inches or centimeters. Similarly, clothing size may be "small," "medium" or "large," while fuel is "regular," "premium" or "super." These numbers and symbols are abstractions that we use to reflect our perceptions of the real world. For example, in defining the numbers and symbols, we try to preserve certain relationships that we see among the entities. Thus, someone who is six feet in height is taller than someone who is five feet in height. Likewise, a "medium" T-shirt is smaller than a "large" T-shirt. This number or symbol can be very useful and important. If we have never met Herman but are told that he is seven feet tall, we can imagine his height in relation to ourselves without our ever having seen him. Moreover, because of his unusual height, we know that he will have to stoop when he enters the door of our office. Thus, we can make judgments about entities solely by knowing and analyzing their attributes.

Measurement is a process whose definition is far from clear-cut. Many different authoritative views lead to different interpretations about what constitutes measurement. To understand what measurement is, we must ask a host of questions that are difficult to answer. For example:

- We have noted that color is an attribute of a room. In a room with blue walls, is "blue" a measure of the color of the room?
- The height of a person is a commonly understood attribute that can be measured. But what about other attributes of people, such as intelligence?

Is intelligence adequately measured by an IQ test score? Similarly, wine can be measured in terms of alcohol content ("proof"), but can wine quality be measured using the ratings of experts?

- The accuracy of a measure depends on the measuring instrument as well as on the definition of the measurement. For example, length can be measured accurately as long as the ruler is accurate and used properly. But some measures are not likely to be accurate, either because the measurement is imprecise or because it depends on the judgment of the person doing the measuring. For instance, proposed measures of human intelligence or wine quality appear to have likely error margins. Is this a reason to reject them as bona fide measurements?

- Even when the measuring devices are reliable and used properly, there is margin for error in measuring the best understood physical attributes. For example, we can obtain vastly different measures for a person's height, depending on whether we make allowances for the shoes being worn or the standing posture. So how do we decide which error margins are acceptable and which are not?

- We can measure height in terms of meters, inches or feet. These different scales measure the same attribute. But we can also measure height in terms of miles and kilometers – appropriate for measuring the height of a satellite above earth, but not for measuring the height of a person. When is a scale acceptable for the purpose to which it is put?

- Once we obtain measurements, we want to analyze them and draw conclusions about the entities from which they were derived. What kind of manipulations can we apply to the results of measurement? For example, why is it acceptable to say that Fred is twice as tall as Joe, but not acceptable to say that it is twice as hot today as it was yesterday? And why is it meaningful to calculate the mean of a set of heights (to say, for example, that the average height of a London building is 200 meters), but not the mean of the football jersey numbers of a team?

To answer these and many other questions, we examine the science of measurement in Chapter 2. This rigorous approach lays the groundwork for applying measurement concepts to software engineering problems. However, before we turn to measurement theory, we examine first the kinds of things that can be measured.

1.1.2 Making things measurable

"What is not measurable make measurable".

This phrase, attributable to Galileo Galilei (1564–1642), is part of the folklore of measurement scientists (Finkelstein 1982). It suggests that one of the aims of science is to find ways to measure attributes of things in which we are interested. Implicit in this statement is the idea that measurement makes concepts more visible and therefore more understandable and controllable. Thus, as scientists, we should be creating ways to measure our world; where we can already measure, we should be making our measurements better.

In the physical sciences, medicine, economics, and even some social sciences, we are now able to measure attributes that were previously thought unmeasurable. Whether we like them or not, measures of attributes such as human intelligence, air quality, and economic inflation form the basis for important decisions that affect our everyday lives. Of course, some measurements are not as refined (in a sense to be made precise in Chapter 2) as we would like them to be; we use the physical sciences as our model for good measurement, continuing to improve measures when we can. Nevertheless, it is important to remember that the concepts of time, temperature and speed, once unmeasurable by primitive peoples, are now not only commonplace but also easily measured by almost everyone; these measurements have become part of the fabric of our existence.

To improve the rigor of measurement in software engineering, we need not restrict the type or range of measurements we can make. Indeed, measuring the unmeasurable should improve our understanding of particular entities and attributes, making software engineering as powerful as other engineering disciplines. Even when it is not clear how we might measure an attribute, the act of proposing such measures will open a debate that leads to greater understanding. Although some software engineers may continue to claim that important software attributes like dependability, quality, usability and maintainability are simply not quantifiable, we prefer to try to use measurement to advance our understanding of them.

Strictly speaking, we should note that there are two kinds of quantification: measurement and calculation. **Measurement** is a direct quantification, as in measuring the height of a tree or the weight of a shipment of bricks. **Calculation** is indirect, where we take measurements and combine them into a quantified item that reflects some attribute whose value we are trying to understand. For example, when the city inspectors assign a valuation to a house (from which they then decide the amount of tax owed), they calculate it by using a formula that combines a variety of factors, including the number of rooms, the type of heating and cooling, and the overall floor space. The valuation is a quantification, not a measurement, and its expression as a number makes it more useful than qualitative assessment alone. As we shall see in Chapter 2, we use **direct** and **indirect** to distinguish measurement from calculation.

Sport offers us many lessons in measuring abstract attributes like quality in an objective fashion. Here, the measures used have been accepted universally, even though there is often discussion about changing or improving the measures. In the following examples, we highlight measurement concepts, showing how they may be useful in software engineering:

> **EXAMPLE 1.1:** In the decathlon athletics event, we measure the time to run various distances as well as the length covered in various jumping activities. These measures are subsequently combined into an *overall score*, computed

using a complex weighting scheme that reflects the importance of each component measure. The weights are sometimes changed as the relative importance of an event or measure changes. This score is widely accepted as a description of the athlete's all-round ability. In fact, the winner of the Olympic decathlon is generally acknowledged to be the world's finest athlete.

EXAMPLE 1.2: The England soccer league points system is used to select the best all-round team over the course of a season. In 1981, the points system was changed; a win yielded three points instead of two, while a draw still yielded one point. This change was made to reflect the consensus view that the qualitative difference between a win and a draw was greater than that between a draw and a defeat.

EXAMPLE 1.3: There are no universally-recognized measures to identify the best individual soccer players (although number of goals scored is a fairly accurate measure of quality of a striker). Although many fans and players have argued that player quality is an unmeasurable attribute, this issue was addressed prior to the 1994 World Cup games in the USA. To provide an objective (measurable) means of determining the "man of the match," several new measurements were proposed:

To help FIFA assess the best players, it will be necessary to add to the pitch markings. At ten meter intervals there will be lines both across and down the pitch. This will allow accurate pass yardage, sideways pass yardage, dribble yardage, and heading yardage to be found for each player.

Translated from "Likely changes to the rules for the 1994 World Cup,"
Nouveaux FIFA d'Arbitres (FIFA Referees News), March 1990.

It was suggested that these measurements be added and weighted with the number of goals scored; tackles, saves or interceptions made; frequency and distance of passes (of various types), dribbles and headers. Notice that the proposed new measure of player quality required a change to the physical environment in which the game is played.

It is easy to see parallels in software engineering. In many instances, we want an overall score that combines several measures into a "big picture" of what is going on during development or maintenance. We want to be able to tell if a software product is good or bad, based on a set of measures, each of which captures a facet of "goodness." Similarly, we want to be able to measure an organization's ability to produce good software, or a model's ability to make good predictions about the software-development process. The composite measures can be controversial, not only because of the individual measures comprising it, but also because of the weights assigned.

Likewise, controversy erupts when we try to capture qualitative information about some aspect of software engineering. Different experts have different opinions, and it is sometimes impossible to get consensus.

Finally, it is sometimes necessary to modify our environment or our practices in order to measure something new or in a new way. It may mean using a new tool (to count lines of code or evaluate code structure), adding a new step in a process (to report on effort), or using a new method (to make measurement simpler). In many cases, change is difficult for people to accept; as we will see in later chapters, there are management issues to be considered whenever a measurement program is implemented or changed.

1.2   MEASUREMENT IN SOFTWARE ENGINEERING

We have seen that measurement is essential to our daily lives, and measuring has become commonplace and well-accepted. In this section, we examine the realm of software engineering to see why measurement is needed.

Software engineering describes the collection of techniques that apply an engineering approach to the construction and support of software products. Software engineering activities include managing, costing, planning, modeling, analyzing, specifying, designing, implementing, testing, and maintaining. By "engineering approach,' we mean that each activity is understood and controlled, so that there are few surprises as the software is specified, designed, built, and maintained. Whereas computer science provides the theoretical foundations for building software, software engineering focuses on implementing the software in a controlled and scientific way.

The importance of software engineering cannot be understated, since software pervades our lives. From oven controls to airbags, from banking transactions to air traffic control, and from sophisticated power plants to sophisticated weapons, our lives and the quality of life depend on software. For such a young profession, software engineering has usually done an admirable job of providing safe, useful and reliable functionality. But there is room for a great deal of improvement. The literature is rife with examples of projects that have overrun their budgets and schedules. Worse, there are too many stories about software that has put lives and businesses at risk.

Software engineers have addressed these problems by continually looking for new techniques and tools to improve process and product. Training supports these changes, so that software engineers are better-prepared to apply the new approaches to development and maintenance. But methodological improvements alone do not make an engineering discipline.

1.2.1   *Neglect of measurement in software engineering*

Engineering disciplines use methods that are based on models and theories. For example, in designing electrical circuits we appeal to theories like Ohm's law, which describes the relationship between resistance, current and voltage in the circuit. But the laws of electrical behavior have evolved by using the scientific method: stating a hypothesis, designing and running an experiment to test its truth, and analyzing the results. Underpinning the scientific process is measurement: measuring the variables to differentiate cases, measuring the changes in behavior, and measuring the causes and effects. Once the scientific method suggests the validity of a model or the truth of a theory, we continue to use measurement to apply the theory to practice. Thus, to build a circuit with a specific current and resistance, we know what voltage is required and we use instruments to measure whether we have such a voltage in a given battery.

It is difficult to imagine electrical, mechanical and civil engineering without a central role for measurement. Indeed, science and engineering can be neither effective nor practical without measurement. But measurement has been considered a luxury in software engineering. For most development projects:

1. We fail to set measurable targets for our software products. For example, we promise that the product will be user-friendly, reliable and maintainable without specifying clearly and objectively what these terms mean. As a result, when the project is complete, we cannot tell if we have met our goals. This situation has prompted Tom Gilb to state (Gilb, 1988)

Gilb's Principle of Fuzzy Targets: projects without clear goals will not achieve their goals clearly.

---

2. We fail to understand and quantify the component costs of software projects. For example, most projects cannot differentiate the cost of design from the cost of coding or testing. Since excessive cost is a frequent complaint from many of our customers, we cannot hope to control costs if we are not measuring the relative components of cost.
3. We do not quantify or predict the quality of the products we produce. Thus, we cannot tell a potential user how reliable a product will be in terms of likelihood of failure in a given period of use, or how much work will be needed to port the product to a different machine environment.
4. We allow anecdotal evidence to convince us to try yet another revolutionary new development technology, without doing a carefully controlled study to determine if the technology is efficient and effective. Figure 1.1 shows examples typical of promotional materials for automated software development tools and techniques. But most of the time, these materials are not accompanied by reports of the scientific basis for the claims.

When measurements are made, they are often done infrequently, inconsistently, and incompletely. The incompleteness can be frustrating to those who want to make use of the results. For example, a developer may claim that 80% of all software costs involve maintenance, or that there are on average 55 faults in every 1000 lines of software code. But we are not always told how these results were obtained, how experiments were designed and executed, which entities were measured and how, and what were the realistic error margins. Without this additional information, we remain skeptical and unable to decide whether to apply the results to our own

Figure 1.1: Measurement for promotion

situations. In addition, we cannot do an objective study to repeat the measurements in our own environments. Thus, the lack of measurement in software engineering is compounded by the lack of a rigorous approach.

It is clear from other engineering disciplines that measurement can be effective, if not essential, in making characteristics and relationships more visible, in assessing the magnitude of problems, and in fashioning a solution to problems. As the pace of hardware innovation has increased, the software world has been tempted to relax or abandon its engineering underpinnings and hope for revolutionary gains. But now that software, playing a key role, involves enormous investment of energy and money, it is time for software engineering to embrace the engineering discipline that has been so successful in other areas.

1.2.2   Objectives for software measurement

Even when a project is not in trouble, measurement is not only useful but necessary. After all, how can you tell if your project is healthy if you have no measures of its health? So measurement is needed at least for assessing the status of your projects, products, processes, and resources. Because we do not always know what derails a project, it is essential that we measure and record characteristics of good projects as well as bad. We need to document trends, the magnitude of corrective action, and the resulting changes. In other words, we must control our projects, not just run them. Tom DeMarco, a strong supporter of the need for measurement in software development, asserts that.

"You cannot control what you cannot measure".

(DeMarco, 1982)

There are compelling reasons to consider the measurement process scientifically, so that measurement will be a true engineering activity. Every measurement action must be motivated by a particular goal or need that is clearly defined and easily understandable. That is, it is not enough to assert that we must measure to gain control. The measurement objectives must be specific, tied to what the managers, developers and users need to know. Thus, these objectives may differ according to the kind of personnel involved and at which level of software development and use they are generated. But it is the goals that tell us how the measurement information will be used once it is collected.

Below are examples of the kinds of information needed to understand and control a software development project, separated by manager and developer perspectives:

Managers

- *What does each process cost?* We can measure the time and effort involved in the various processes that comprise software production. For example, we can identify the cost of eliciting requirements, the cost of specifying the system, the cost of designing the system, and the cost of coding and testing the system. In this way, we gain understanding not only of the total project cost but also of the contribution of each activity to the whole.

- *How productive is the staff?* We can measure the time it takes for staff to specify the system, design it, code it, and test it. Then, using measures of the size of specifications, design, code, and test plans, for example, we can determine how productive the staff is at each activity. This information is useful when changes are proposed; the manager can use the productivity figures to estimate the cost and duration of the change.

- *How good is the code being developed?* By carefully recording faults, failures and changes as they occur, we can measure software quality, enabling us to compare different products, predict the effects of change, assess the effects of new practices, and set targets for process and product improvement.

- *Will the user be satisfied with the product?* We can measure functionality by determining if all of the requirements requested have actually been implemented properly. And we can measure usability, reliability, response time, and other characteristics to suggest whether our customers will be happy with both functionality and performance.

- *How can we improve?* We can measure the time it takes to perform each major development activity, and calculate its effect on quality and productivity. Then we can weigh the costs and benefits of each practice to determine if the benefit is worth the cost. Alternatively, we can try several variations of a practice and measure the results to decide which is best; for example, we can compare two design methods to see which one yields the higher quality code.

Engineers

- *Are the requirements testable?* We can analyze each requirement to determine if its satisfaction is expressed in a measurable, objective way. For example, suppose a requirement states that a system must be reliable; the requirement can be replaced by one that states that the mean time to failure must be greater than 15 elapsed hours of CPU time.
- *Have we found all the faults?* We can measure the number of faults in the specification, design, code, and test plans, and trace them back to their root causes. Using models of expected detection rates, this information can help us to decide whether inspections and testing have been effective and whether a product can be released for the next phase of development.
- *Have we met our product or process goals?* We can measure characteristics of the products and processes that tell us whether we have met standards, satisfied a requirement, or met a process goal. For example, certification may require that fewer than 20 failures have been reported per beta-test site over a given period of time. Or a standard may mandate that no module contain more than 100 lines of code. The testing process may require that unit testing must achieve 90% statement coverage.
- *What will happen in the future?* We can measure attributes of existing products and current processes to make predictions about future ones. For example, measures of size of specifications can be used to predict size of the target system, predictions about future maintenance problems can be made from measures of structural properties of the design documents, and predictions about the reliability of software in operational use can be made by measuring reliability during testing.

1.2.3   Measurement for understanding, control and improvement

The lists above show us that measurement is important for three basic activities. First, there are measures that help us to *understand* what is happening during development and maintenance. We assess the current situation, establishing baselines that help us to set goals for future behavior. In this sense, the measurements make aspects of process and product more visible to us, giving us a better understanding of relationships among activities and the entities they affect.

Second, the measurement allows us to *control* what is happening on our projects. Using our baselines, goals and understanding of relationships, we predict what is likely to happen and make changes to processes and products that help us to meet our goals. For example, we may monitor the complexity of code modules, giving thorough review only to those that exceed acceptable bounds.

Third, measurement encourages us to *improve* our processes and products. For instance, we may increase the number or type of design reviews we do, based on measures of specification quality and predictions of likely design quality.

Figure 1.2: Software measurement – resource estimation

No matter how measurements are used, it is important to manage the expectations of those who will make measurement-based decisions. Users of the data should always be aware of the limited accuracy of prediction and of the margin of error in the measurements. As with any other engineering discipline, there is room in software engineering for abuse and misuse of measurement. Figure 1.2 irreverently shows how management can pressure developers to produce precise measures with inadequate models, tools and techniques.

If you are expecting measurement to provide instant, easy solutions to your software engineering problems, be aware of our corollary to DeMarco's rule:

You can neither predict nor control what you cannot measure.

1.3 THE SCOPE OF SOFTWARE METRICS

Software metrics is a term that embraces many activities, all of which involve some degree of software measurement:

- cost and effort estimation
- productivity measures and models
- data collection
- quality models and measures
- reliability models

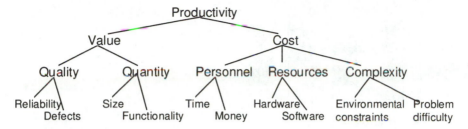

Figure 1.3: A productivity model

- performance evaluation and models
- structural and complexity metrics
- capability-maturity assessment
- management by metrics
- evaluation of methods and tools

Each of these activities will be covered in some detail in later chapters. Our theoretical foundations, to be described in Chapters 2 and 3, will enable us to consider the activities in a unified manner, rather than as diverse, unrelated topics.

The following brief introduction will give you a sense of the techniques currently in use for each facet of measurement. It provides signposts to where the material is covered in detail in later chapters.

1.3.1 Cost and effort estimation

Managers provided the original motivation for deriving and using software measures. They wanted to be able to predict project costs during early phases in the software life-cycle. As a result, numerous models for software cost and effort estimation have been proposed and used. Examples include Boehm's COCOMO model (Boehm, 1981), Putnam's SLIM model (Putnam, 1978) and Albrecht's function points model (Albrecht, 1979). These and other models often share a common approach: effort is expressed as a (pre-defined) function of one or more variables (such as size of the product, capability of the developers and level of reuse). Size is usually defined as (predicted) lines of code or number of function points (which may be derived from the product specification). Cost models and effort prediction are discussed in Chapter 12.

1.3.2 Productivity models and measures

The pressing needs of management have also resulted in numerous attempts to define measures and models for assessing staff productivity during different software processes and in different environments.

Figure 1.3 illustrates an example of the possible components that contribute to overall productivity. It shows productivity as a function of value and cost; each is then decomposed into other aspects, expressed in measurable form. This model is a

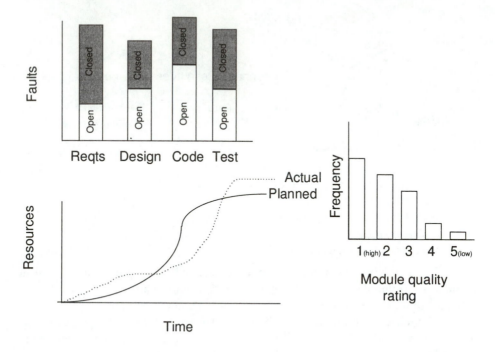

Figure 1.4: Metrics for management

significantly more comprehensive view of productivity than the traditional one, which simply divides size by effort. That is, many managers make decisions based on the rate at which lines of code are being written per person month of effort. This simpler measure can be misleading, if not dangerous (Jones, 1986). Productivity models and measures are covered mainly in Chapter 11.

1.3.3 Data collection

The quality of any measurement program is clearly dependent on careful data collection. But collecting data is easier said than done, especially when data must be collected across a diverse set of projects. Thus, data collection is becoming a discipline in itself, where specialists work to ensure that measures are defined unambiguously, that collection is consistent and complete, and that data integrity is not at risk. But it is acknowledged that metrics data collection must be planned and executed in a careful and sensitive manner. We will see in Chapter 14 how Hewlett-Packard and others have made public the managerial framework that helped to make its corporate metrics program a success.

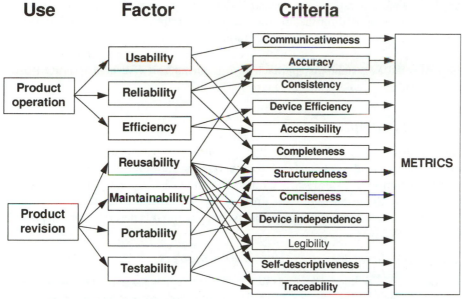

Figure 1.5: Software quality model

Figure 1.4 contains several examples of how the data collected can be distilled into simple charts and graphs that show managers the progress and problems of development. Basili and Weiss have described a general methodology for valid data collection (Basili and Weiss, 1984), while Mellor describes the data collection necessary for reliability assessment (Mellor, 1992). This material is covered in Chapters 5, 6, 10 and 11.

Data collection is also essential for scientific investigation of relationships and trends. We will see in Chapter 4 how good experiments, surveys, and case studies require carefully planned data collection, as well as thorough analysis and reporting of the results.

1.3.4 Quality models and measures

Productivity cannot be viewed in isolation. Without an accompanying assessment of product quality, speed of production is meaningless. This observation has led software engineers to develop models of quality whose measurements can be combined with those of productivity models. For example, Boehm's advanced COCOMO cost-estimation model is tied to a quality model (Boehm *et al.*, 1978). Similarly, the McCall quality model (McCall *et al.*, 1977), commonly called the FCM (Factor Criteria Metric) model, is related to productivity.

These models are usually constructed in a tree-like fashion, similar to Figure 1.5. The upper branches hold important high-level quality factors of software products, such as reliability and usability, that we would like to quantify. Each quality factor is composed of lower-level criteria, such as structuredness and traceability. The criteria are easier to understand and measure than the factors; thus, actual measures (metrics) are proposed for the criteria. The tree describes the pertinent relationships between factors and their dependent criteria, so we can measure the factors in terms of the dependent criteria measures. This notion of divide-and-conquer has been implemented as a standard approach to measuring software quality (ISO 9126). Quality models are described at length in Chapter 9.

1.3.5   Reliability models

Most quality models include reliability as a component factor, but the need to predict and measure reliability itself has led to a separate specialization in reliability modeling and prediction. Littlewood (1988) and others provide a rigorous and successful example of how a focus on an important product quality attribute has led to increased understanding and control of our products. This material is described in Chapter 10.

1.3.6   Performance evaluation and models

Performance is another aspect of quality. Work under the umbrella of performance evaluation includes externally observable system performance characteristics, such as response times and completion rates (Ferrari *et al.,* 1978, 1983; Kleinrock, 1975). Performance specialists also investigate the internal workings of a system, including the efficiency of algorithms as embodied in computational and algorithmic complexity (Garey and Johnson 1979; Harel, 1992). The latter is also concerned with the inherent complexity of problems measured in terms of efficiency of an optimal solution. This material is described in Chapter 7.

1.3.7   Structural and complexity metrics

Desirable quality attributes like reliability and maintainability cannot be measured until some operational version of the code is available. Yet we wish to be able to predict which parts of the software system are likely to be less reliable, more difficult to test, or require more maintenance than others, even before the system is complete. As a result, we measure structural attributes of representations of the software which are available in advance of (or without the need for) execution; then, we try to establish empirically predictive theories to support quality assurance, quality control, and quality prediction. Halstead (1977) and McCabe (1976) are two classic examples of this approach; each defines measures that are derived from suitable representations of source code. This material and more recent developments are described in Chapter 8.

1.3.8   Management by metrics

Measurement is becoming an important part of software project management. Customers and developers alike rely on measurement-based charts and graphs to help them decide if the project is on track. Many companies and organizations define a standard set of measurements and reporting methods, so that projects can be compared and contrasted. This uniform collection and reporting is especially important when software plays a supporting role in the overall project. That is, when software is embedded in a product whose main focus is a business area other than software, the customer or ultimate user is not usually well-versed in software terminology, so measurement can paint a picture of progress in general, understandable terms. For example, when a power plant asks a software developer to write control software, the customer usually knows a lot about power generation and control, but very little about programming languages, compilers or computer hardware. The measurements must be presented in a way that tells both customer and developer how the project is doing. In Chapter 6, we will examine several measurement analysis and presentation techniques that are useful and understandable to all who have a stake in the project's success.

1.3.9 Evaluation of methods and tools

Many articles and books describe new methods and tools that may make your organization or project more productive and your products better and cheaper. But it is difficult to separate the claims from the reality. Many organizations perform experiments, run case studies or administer surveys to help them decide whether a method or tool is likely to make a positive difference in their particular situations. These investigations cannot be done without careful, controlled measurement and analysis. As we will see in Chapter 4, an evaluation's success depends on good experimental design, proper identification of the factors likely to affect the outcome, and appropriate measurement of factor attributes.

1.3.10 Capability maturity assessment

In the 1980s, the US Software Engineering Institute (SEI) proposed a capability maturity model (Humphrey, 1989) to measure a contractor's ability to develop quality software for the US government. This model assessed many different attributes of development, including use of tools, standard practices and more. To use the first version of the model, called a *process maturity assessment*, a contractor answered over 100 questions designed to determine the contractor's actual practices. The resulting "grade" was reported as a five-level scale, from "1" (*ad hoc* development dependent on individuals) to "5" (a development process that could be optimized based on continuous feedback).

There were many problems with the first model, as described by Bollinger and McGowan (Bollinger and McGowan, 1991), and the SEI has since revised its approach. The new model, called a *capability maturity assessment*, is based on key practices that every good contractor should be using. Other organizations, inspired by the SEI's goal, have developed other assessment models, in the hope that such evaluation will encourage improvement and enable organizations to compare and contrast candidate developers.

The notion of evaluating process maturity is very appealing, and we describe in Chapter 3 how process maturity can be useful in understanding what and when to measure. In Chapter 13, we will look at several maturity assessment techniques, including ISO 9000, examining the pros and cons of this type of evaluation.

1.4 SUMMARY

This introductory chapter has described how measurement pervades our everyday life. We have argued that measurement is essential for good engineering in other disciplines; it should likewise become an integral part of software engineering practice. In particular:

- The lessons of other engineering disciplines suggest that measurement must play a more significant role in software engineering.
- Software measurement is not a mainstream topic within software engineering. Rather it is a diverse collection of fringe topics (generally referred to as *software metrics*) that range from models for predicting software project costs at the specification stage to measures of program structure.
- Much software-metrics work has lacked the rigor associated with measurement in other engineering disciplines.
- General reasons for needing software-engineering measurement are not enough. Engineers must have specific, clearly stated objectives for measurement.
- We must be bold in our attempts at measurement. Just because no one has measured some attribute of interest does not mean that it cannot be measured satisfactorily.

We have set the scene for a new perspective on software metrics. To anchor a metrics program on a solid foundation of measurement theory, we turn to the next chapter. This rigorous basis will enable us to implement a scientific and effective approach to constructing, calculating and appropriately applying the metrics that we derive.

1.5 EXERCISES

1 Explain the role of measurement in determining the best players in your favorite sport.
2 How would you begin to measure the *quality* of a software product?
3 Consider some everyday measurements. What entities and attributes are being measured? What can you say about error margins in the measurements? Explain how the measuring process may affect the entity being measured.

4   In this chapter we gave examples of measurement objectives from both managers' and engineers' view points. Now consider the user's viewpoint. What measurement objectives might a software user have?

5   A commonly-used software quality measure in industry is the number of known errors per thousand lines of product source code. Compare the usefulness of this measure for developers and users. What are the possible problems with relying on this measure as the sole expression of software quality?

2 | The basics of measurement

In Chapter 1, we saw how measurement pervades our world. We use measurement every day, to understand, control and improve what we do and how we do it. In this chapter, we examine measurement in more depth, trying to apply general measurement lessons learned in daily activities to the activities we perform as part of software development.

Ordinarily, when we measure things, we do not think about the scientific principles we are applying. We measure attributes such as the length of physical objects, the timing of events, and the temperature of liquids or of the air. To do the measuring, we use both tools and principles that we now take for granted. However, these sophisticated measuring devices and techniques have been developed over time, based on the growth of understanding of the attributes we are measuring. For example, using the length of a column of mercury to capture information about temperature is a technique that was not at all obvious to the first person who wanted to know how much hotter it is in summer than in winter. As we understood more about temperature, materials, and the relationships between them, we developed a framework for describing temperature as well as tools for measuring it.

Unfortunately, we have no comparably deep understanding of software attributes. Nor do we have the associated sophisticated measurement tools. Questions that are relatively easy to answer for non-software entities are difficult for software. For example, consider the following questions:

1. How much must we know about an attribute before it is reasonable to consider measuring it? For instance, do we know enough about "complexity" of programs to be able to measure it?

2. How do we know if we have really measured the attribute we wanted to measure? For instance, does a count of the number of "bugs" found in a system during integration testing measure the quality of the system? If not, what does the count tell us?

3. Using measurement, what meaningful statements can we make about an attribute and the entities that possess it? For instance, is it meaningful to talk about doubling a design's quality? If not, how do we compare two different designs?

4. What meaningful operations can we perform on measures? For instance, is it sensible to compute average productivity for a group of developers, or the average quality of a set of modules?

To answer these questions, we must establish the basics of a theory of measurement. We begin by examining formal measurement theory, developed as a classical discipline from the physical sciences. We see how the concepts of measurement theory apply to software, and we explore several examples to determine when measurements are meaningful and useful. This theory tells us not only when and how to measure, but also how to analyze and depict data, and how to tie the results back to our original questions about software quality and productivity.

2.1   THE REPRESENTATIONAL THEORY OF MEASUREMENT

In any measurement activity, there are rules to be followed. The rules help us to be consistent in our measurement, as well as providing a basis for interpretating data. Measurement theory tells us the rules, laying the groundwork for developing and reasoning about all kinds of measurement. This rule-based approach is common in many sciences. For example, recall that mathematicians learned about the world by defining axioms for a geometry. Then, by combining axioms and using their results to support or refute their observations, they expanded their understanding and the set of rules that govern the behavior of objects. In the same way, we can use rules about measurement to codify our initial understanding, and then expand our horizons as we analyze our software.

However, just as there are several kinds of geometry (for example, Euclidean and non-Euclidean), depending on the set of rules chosen, there are also several theories of measurement. In this book, we present an overview of the *representational* theory of measurement.

2.1.1   *Empirical relations*

The representational theory of measurement seeks to formalize our intuition about the way the world works. That is, the data we obtain as measures should represent attributes of the entities we observe, and manipulation of the data should preserve

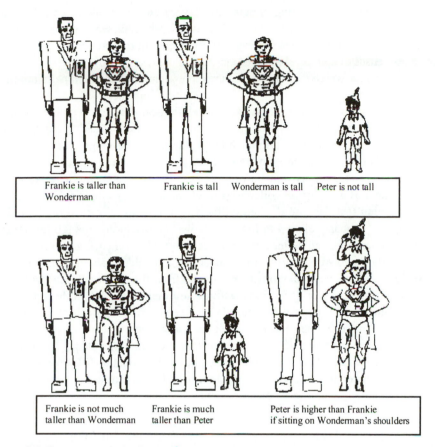

Figure 2.1: Some empirical relations for the attribute "height"

relationships that we observe among the entities. Thus, our intuition is the starting point for all measurement.

Consider the way we perceive the real world. We tend to understand things by comparing them, not by assigning numbers to them. For example, Figure 2.1 illustrates how we learn about height. We observe that certain people are taller than others without actually measuring them. It is easy to see that Frankie is taller than Wonderman who in turn is taller than Peter; anyone looking at this figure would agree with this statement. However, our observation reflects a set of rules that we are imposing on the set of people. We form pairs of people and define a binary relation on them. In other words, "taller than" is a binary relation defined on the set of pairs of people. Given any two people, x and y, we can observe that

- x is taller than y, or
- y is taller than x

Therefore, we say that "taller than" is an **empirical relation** for height.

When the two people being compared are very close in height, we may find a difference of opinion; you may think that Jack is taller than Jill, while we are convinced that Jill is taller than Jack. Our empirical relations permit this difference by requiring only a consensus of opinion about relationships in the real world. A (binary) empirical relation is one for which there is a reasonable consensus about which pairs are in the relation.

We can define more than one empirical relation on the same set. For example, Figure 2.1 also shows the relation "much taller than". Most of us would agree that both Frankie and Wonderman are much taller than Peter (although there is less of a consensus about this relation than "taller than").

Empirical relations need not be binary. That is, we can define a relation on a single element of a set, or on collections of elements. Many empirical relations are unary, meaning that they are defined on individual entities. The relation "is tall" is an example of a unary relation in Figure 2.1; we can say Frankie is tall but Peter is not tall. Similarly, we can define a ternary relationship by comparing groups of three; Figure 2.1 shows how Peter sitting on Wonderman's shoulders is higher than Frankie.

We can think of these relations as mappings from the empirical, real world to a formal mathematical world. We have entities and their attributes in the real world, and we define a mathematical mapping that preserves the relationships we observe. Thus, height (that is, tallness) can be considered as a mapping from the set of people to the set of real numbers. If we can agree that Jack is "taller than" Jill, then any measure of height should assign a higher number to Jack than to Jill. As we shall see later in this chapter, this preservation of intuition and observation is the notion behind the representation condition of measurement.

EXAMPLE 2.1: Suppose we are evaluating the four best-selling word-processing programs: A, B, C, and D. We ask 100 independent computer users to rank these programs according to their functionality, and the results are shown on the left-hand portion of Table 2.1. Each cell of the table represents the percentage of respondents who preferred the row's program to the column's program; for instance, 80% rated program A as having greater functionality than program B. We can use this survey to define an empirical relation "greater functionality than" for word-processing programs; we say that program x has greater functionality than program y if the survey result for cell (x, y) exceeds 60% (we take 60% as representing a significant preference). Thus, the relation consists of the pairs (C, A), (C, B), (C, D), (A, B), (A, D). This set of pairs tells us more than just five comparisons; for example, since C has greater functionality than A, and A in turn has greater functionality than B and D, then C has greater functionality than B and D. Note that neither pair (B, D) nor (D, B) is in the empirical relation; there is no clear consensus about which of B and D has greater functionality.

Table 2.1: Sampling 100 users to express preferences among products A, B, C, and D

	A	B	C	D			A	B	C	D
A	—	80	10	80		A	—	45	50	44
B	20	—	5	50		B	55	—	52	50
C	90	95	—	96		C	50	48	—	51
D	20	50	4	—		D	54	50	49	—

More functionality   *More user-friendly*

Suppose we administer a similar survey for the attribute "user-friendliness", with the results shown on the right-hand side of Table 2.1. In this case, there is no real consensus at all. At best, we can deduce that "greater user-friendliness" is an empty empirical relation. This statement is different from saying that all the programs are equally user-friendly, since we did not specifically ask the respondents about indifference or equality. Our immature understanding of user-friendliness may be the reason that there are no useful empirical relations.

Example 2.1 shows how we can start with simple user surveys to gain a preliminary understanding of relationships. However, as our understanding grows, we can define more sophisticated measures.

EXAMPLE 2.2:   Table 2.2 shows that people had an initial understanding of temperature thousands of years ago. This intuition was characterized by the notion of "hotter than". Thus, for example, by putting your hand into two different containers of liquid, you could feel if one were hotter than the other. No measurement is necessary for this determination of temperature difference. However, people needed to make finer discriminations in temperature. In 1600, the first device was constructed to capture this comparative relationship; the thermometer could consistently assign a higher number to liquids that were "hotter than" others.

Table 2.2: Historical advances in temperature measurement

2000 BC	Rankings, "hotter than"
1600 AD	First thermometer measuring "hotter than"
1720 AD	Fahrenheit scale
1742 AD	Celsius scale
1854 AD	Absolute zero, Kelvin scale

Example 2.2 illustrates an important characteristic of measurement. We can begin to understand the world by using relatively unsophisticated relationships that require no measuring tools. Once we develop an initial understanding and have accumulated some data, we may need to measure in more sophisticated ways and with special tools. Analyzing the results often leads to the clarification and re-evaluation of the

attribute, and yet more sophisticated empirical relations. In turn, we have improved accuracy and increased understanding.

Formally, we define **measurement** as a mapping from the empirical world to the formal, relational world. Consequently, a **measure** is the number or symbol assigned to an entity by this mapping in order to characterize an attribute.

Sometimes, the empirical relations for an attribute are not yet agreed upon, especially when they reflect personal preference. We see this lack of consensus when we look at the ratings of wine or the preference for design technique, for example. Here, the raters have some notion of the attribute they want to measure, but there is not always a common understanding. We may find that what is tasteless or difficult for one rater is delicious or easy for another rater. In these cases, we can still perform a subjective assessment, but the result is not necessarily a measure, in the sense of measurement theory. For example, Figure 2.2 shows several rating formats, some of which you may have encountered in taking examinations or responding to opinion polls. These questionnaires capture useful data. They enable us to establish the basis for empirical relations, characterizing properties so that formal measurement may be possible in the future.

2.1.2   The rules of the mapping

We have seen how a measure is used to characterize an attribute. We begin in the real world, studying an entity and trying to understand more about it. Thus, the real world is the **domain** of the mapping, and the mathematical world is the **range**. When we map the attribute to a mathematical system, we have many choices for the mapping and the range. We can use real numbers, integers, or even a set of non-numeric symbols.

EXAMPLE 2.3:   To measure a person's height, it is not enough simply to specify a number. If we measure height in inches, then we are defining a mapping from the set of people into inches; if we measure height in centimeters, then we have a different mapping. Moreover, even when the domain and range are the same, the mapping definition may be different. That is, there may be many different mappings (and hence different ways of measuring) depending on the conventions we adopt. For example, when we measure height we may or may not allow shoes to be worn, or we may measure people standing or sitting.

Thus, a measure must specify the domain and range as well as the rule for performing the mapping.

EXAMPLE 2.4:   In some everyday situations, a measure is associated with a number, the assumptions about the mapping are well-known, and our terminology is imprecise. For example, we say "Felix's age is 11," or "Felix is 11." In expressing ourselves in this way, we really mean that we are measuring

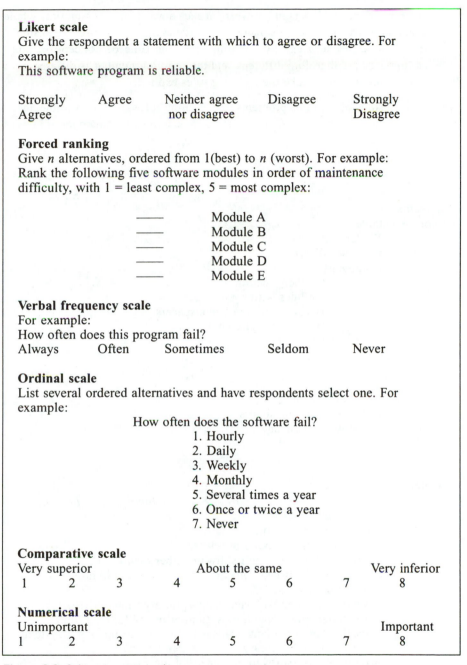

Likert scale
Give the respondent a statement with which to agree or disagree. For example:
This software program is reliable.

| Strongly Agree | Agree | Neither agree nor disagree | Disagree | Strongly Disagree |

Forced ranking
Give *n* alternatives, ordered from 1(best) to *n* (worst). For example: Rank the following five software modules in order of maintenance difficulty, with 1 = least complex, 5 = most complex:

—— Module A
—— Module B
—— Module C
—— Module D
—— Module E

Verbal frequency scale
For example:
How often does this program fail?

| Always | Often | Sometimes | Seldom | Never |

Ordinal scale
List several ordered alternatives and have respondents select one. For example:

How often does the software fail?
1. Hourly
2. Daily
3. Weekly
4. Monthly
5. Several times a year
6. Once or twice a year
7. Never

Comparative scale

| Very superior | | | | About the same | | | Very inferior |
| 1 | 2 | 3 | 4 | 5 | 6 | 7 | 8 |

Numerical scale

| Unimportant | | | | | | | Important |
| 1 | 2 | 3 | 4 | 5 | 6 | 7 | 8 |

Figure 2.2: Subjective rating schemes

age by mapping each person into years in such a way that we count only whole years since birth. But there are many different rules that we can use. For example, the Chinese measure age by counting from the time of conception; their assumptions are therefore different, and the resulting number is different. For this reason, we must make the mapping rules explicit.

We encounter some of the same problems in measuring software. For example, many organizations measure the size of their source code in terms of the number of lines of

Statement type	Include?	Exclude?
Executable		
Non-executable		
Declarations		
Compiler directives		
Comments		
On their own lines		
On lines with source code		
Banners and non-blank spacers		
Blank (empty) comments		
Blank lines		
How produced	Include?	Exclude?
Programmed		
Generated with source code generators		
Converted with automatic translators		
Copied or reused without change		
Modified		
Removed		
Origin	Include?	Exclude?
New work: no prior existence		
Prior work: taken or adapted from		
A previous version, build or release		
Commercial, off-the-shelf software, other than libraries		
Government furnished software, other than reuse libraries		
Another product		
A vendor-supplied language support library (unmodified)		
A vendor-supplied operating system or utility (unmodified)		
A local or modified language support library or operating system		
Other commercial library		
A reuse library (software designed for reuse)		
Other software component or library		

Figure 2.3: Adapted from portion of US Software Engineering Institute checklist for lines-of-code count

code in a program. But the definition of a line of code must be made clear. The US Software Engineering Institute has developed a checklist to assist developers in deciding exactly what is included in a line of code (Park, 1992). Figure 2.3 illustrates part of the checklist, showing how different choices result in different counting rules. Thus, the checklist allows you to tailor your definition of "lines of code" to your needs. We will examine the issues addressed by this checklist in more depth in Chapter 7.

2.1.3   *The representation condition of measurement*

We saw that, by definition, each relation in the empirical relational system corresponds via the measurement to an element in a number system. We want the behavior of the measures in the number system to be the same as the corresponding elements in the real world, so that by studying the numbers, we learn about the real world. Thus, we want the mapping to preserve the relation. This rule is called the representation condition, and it is illustrated in Figure 2.4. That is, the **representation condition** asserts that a measurement mapping M must map entities into numbers and empirical relations into numerical relations in such a way that the empirical relations preserve and are preserved by the numerical relations. In Figure 2.4, we see that the empirical relation "taller than" is mapped to the numerical relation ">". In particular, we can say that

A is taller than B if and only if $M(A)>M(B)$

This statement implies that:

- Whenever Joe is taller than Fred, then M(Joe) must be a bigger number than M(Fred).
- We can map Jill to a higher number than Jack only if Jill is taller than Jack.

EXAMPLE 2.5:   Earlier in this chapter, we noted that there can be many relations on a given set, and we mentioned several for the attribute "height". The representation condition has implications for each of these relations. Consider these examples:

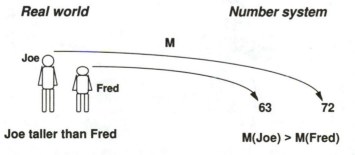

Figure 2.4: Representation condition

For the (binary) empirical relation "taller than", we can have the numerical relation

$$x > y$$

Then, the representation condition requires that for any measure M,

A is taller than B if and only if $M(A) > M(B)$

For the (unary) empirical relation "is tall", we might have the numerical relation

$$x > 70$$

The representation condition requires that for any measure M,

A is tall if and only if $M(A) > 70$

For the (binary) empirical relation "much taller than", we might have the numerical relation

$$x > y + 15$$

The representation condition requires that for any measure M,

A is much taller than B if and only if $M(A) > M(B) + 15$

For the (ternary) empirical relation "x is higher than y if sitting on z's shoulders" we could have the numerical relation

$$0.7x + 0.8z > y$$

The representation condition requires that for any measure M,

A is higher than B if sitting on C's shoulders if and only if

$$0.7M(A) + 0.8M(C) > M(B)$$

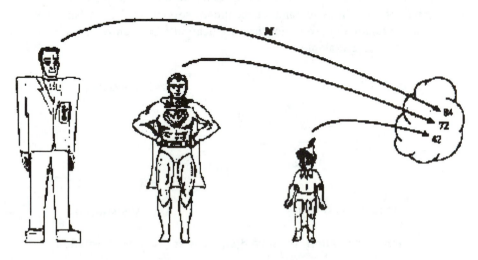

Figure 2.5: A measurement mapping

Consider the actual assignment of numbers M given in Figure 2.5. Wonderman is mapped to the real number 72 (that is, M(Wonderman) = 72), Frankie to 84 (M(Frankie) = 84), and Peter to 42 (M(Peter) = 42). With this particular mapping M, the four numerical relations hold whenever the four empirical relations hold. For example

- Frankie is taller than Wonderman, and M(Frankie) > M(Wonderman).
- Wonderman is tall, and M(Wonderman) = 72 > 70.
- Frankie is much taller than Peter, and M(Frankie) = 84 > 57 = M(Peter)+15. Similarly Wonderman is much taller than Peter and M(Wonderman) = 72 > 57 = M(Peter) + 15
- Peter is higher than Frankie when sitting on Wonderman's shoulders, and $0.7M$(Peter) + $0.8M$(Wonderman) = 87 > 84 = M(Frankie)

Because all the relations are preserved in this way by the mapping, we can define the mapping as a measure for the attribute. Thus, if we think of the measure as a measure of height, we can say that Frankie's height is 84, Peter's is 42, and Wonderman's is 72.

Not every assignment satisfies the representation condition. For instance, if we define the mapping in the following way:

$$M(\text{Wonderman}) = 72$$
$$M(\text{Frankie}) = 84$$
$$M(\text{Peter}) = 60$$

then three of the above relations are satisfied but "much taller than" is not. This is because "Wonderman is much taller than Peter" is not true under this mapping.

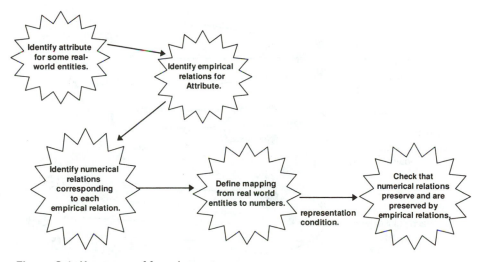

Figure 2.6: Key stages of formal measurement

The mapping that we call a measure is sometimes called a **representation** or **homomorphism**, because the measure represents the attribute in the numerical world. Figure 2.6 summarizes the steps in the measurement process.

There are several conclusions we can draw from this discussion. First, we have seen that there may be many different measures for a given attribute. In fact, we use the notion of representation to define validity: any measure that satisfies the representation condition is a **valid** measure. Second, the richer the empirical relation system, the fewer the valid measures. We consider a relational system to be **rich** if it has a large number of relations that can be defined. But as we increase the number of empirical relations, so we increase the number of conditions that a measurement mapping must satisfy in the representation condition.

> **EXAMPLE 2.6:**   Suppose we are studying the entity "software failures", and we look at the attribute "criticality". Our initial description distinguishes among only three types of failures:
>
> - delayed response
> - incorrect output
> - data loss
>
> where every failure lies in exactly one failure class (based on which outcome happens first). This categorization yields an empirical relation system that consists of just three unary relations: R_1 for delayed response, R_2 for incorrect output, and R_3 for data loss. We assume every failure is in either R_1, R_2 or R_3. At this point, we cannot judge the relative criticality of these failure types; we know only that the types are different.
>
> To find a representation for this empirical relation system in the set of real numbers, we need only choose any three distinct numbers, and then map

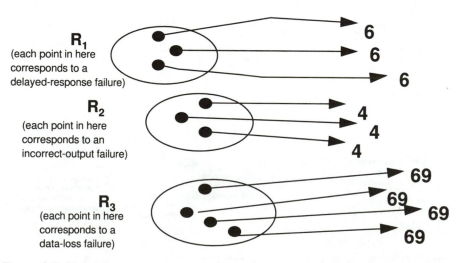

Figure 2.7: Measurement mapping

members from different classes into different numbers. For example, the mapping M, illustrated in Figure 2.7, assigns the mapping as:

$$M(\text{each delayed response}) = 6$$
$$M(\text{each incorrect output}) = 4$$
$$M(\text{each data loss}) = 69$$

This assignment is a representation, because we have numerical relations corresponding to R_1, R_2 and R_3. That is, the numerical relation corresponding to R_1 is the relation "is 6"; likewise, the numerical relation corresponding to R_2 is the relation "is 4", and the numerical relation corresponding to R_3 is the relation "is 69".

Suppose next that we have formed a deeper understanding of failure criticality in a particular environment. We want to add to the above relation system a new (binary) relation, "is more critical than". We now know that each data-loss failure is more critical than each incorrect-output failure and delayed-response failure; each incorrect output failure is more critical than each delayed-response failure. Thus, "x more critical than y" contains all those pairs (x, y) of failures for which either

$$x \text{ is in } R_3 \text{ and } y \text{ is in } R_2 \text{ or } R_1, \text{ or}$$
$$x \text{ is in } R_2 \text{ and } y \text{ is in } R_1$$

To find a representation in the real numbers for this enriched empirical relation system, we now have to be much more careful with our assignment of numbers. First of all, we need a numerical relation to correspond to "more critical than", and it is reasonable to use the binary relation ">". However, it is not enough to simply map different failure types to different numbers. To preserve the new relation, we must ensure that data-loss failures are mapped into a higher number than incorrect-output failures which in turn are mapped to a higher number than delayed-response failures. One acceptable representation is the mapping:

$$M(\text{each delayed response}) = 3$$
$$M(\text{each incorrect output}) = 4$$
$$M(\text{each data loss}) = 69$$

Note that the mapping defined initially in this example would not be a representation, because ">" does not preserve "is more critical than"; incorrect-output failures were mapped to a lower number than delayed-response failures.

There is nothing wrong with using the same representation in different ways, or with using several representations for the same attribute. Table 2.3 illustrates a number of examples of specific measures used in software engineering. In it, we see that examples 1 and 2 in the table give different measures of program length, while examples 9 and 10 give different measures of program reliability. Similarly, the same measure (although of course not the same measurement mapping), *faults found per thousand lines of code (KLOC)*, is used in examples 6, 7 and 8.

Table 2.3: Examples of specific measures used in software engineering

	Entity	Attribute	Measure
1	Completed project	Duration	Months from start to finish
2	Completed project	Duration	Days from start to finish
3	Program code	Length	Number of lines of code (LOC)
4	Program code	Length	Number of executable statements
5	Integration testing process	Duration	Hours from start to finish
6	Integration testing process	Rate at which faults are found	Number of faults found per KLOC (thousand LOC)
7	Tester	Efficiency	Number of faults found per KLOC (thousand LOC)
8	Program code	Quality	Number of faults found per KLOC (thousand LOC)
9	Program code	Reliability	Mean time to failure (MTTF) in CPU hours
10	Program code	Reliability	Rate of occurrence of failures (ROCOF) in CPU hours

How good a measure is faults per KLOC? The answer depends entirely on the entity-attribute pair connected by the mapping. Intuitively, most of us would accept that faults per KLOC is a good measure of the rate at which faults are found for the testing process (example 6). However, it is not such a good measure of efficiency of the tester (example 7), because intuitively we feel that we should also take into account the difficulty of understanding and testing the program under scrutiny. This measure may be reasonable when comparing two testers of the same program, though. Faults per KLOC is not likely to be a good measure of quality of the program code (example 8); if integration testing revealed program X to have twice as many faults per KLOC than program Y, we would probably not conclude that the quality of program Y was twice that of program X.

2.2 MEASUREMENT AND MODELS

In Chapter 1, we discussed several types of models: cost-estimation models, quality models, capability-maturity models, and more. In general, a **model** is an abstraction of reality, allowing us to strip away detail and view an entity or concept from a particular perspective. For example, cost models permit us to examine only those project aspects that contribute to the project's final cost. Models come in many different forms: as equations, mappings, or diagrams, for instance. These show us how the component parts relate to one another, so that we can examine and understand these relationships and make judgments about them.

In this chapter, we have seen that the representation condition requires every measure to be associated with a model of how the measure maps the entities and attributes in the real world to the elements of a numerical system. These models are essential in understanding not only how the measure is derived, but also how to interpret the behavior of the numerical elements when we return to the real world. But we also need models even before we begin the measurement process.

Let us consider more carefully the role of models in measurement definition. Previous examples have made clear that if we are measuring height of people, then we must understand and declare our assumptions to ensure unambiguous measurement. For example, in measuring height, we would have to specify whether or not we allow shoes to be worn, whether or not we include hair height, and whether or not we specify a certain posture. In this sense, we are actually defining a model of a person, rather than the person itself, as the entity being measured. Thus, the model of the mapping should also be supplemented with a model of the mapping's domain – that is, with a model of how the entity relates to its attributes.

> **EXAMPLE 2.7:** To measure length of programs using lines of code, we need a model of a program. The model would specify how a program differs from a subroutine, whether or not to treat separate statements on the same line as distinct lines of code, whether or not to count comment lines, whether or not to count data declarations, and so on. The model would also tell us what to do when we have programs written in a combination of different languages. It might distinguish delivered operational programs from those under development, and it would tell us how to handle situations where different versions run on different platforms.

Process measures are often more difficult to define than product and resource measures, in large part because the process activities are less understood.

> **EXAMPLE 2.8:** Suppose we want to measure attributes of the testing process. Depending on our goals, we might measure the time or effort spent on this process, or the number of faults found during the process. To do this, we need a careful definition of what is meant by the testing process; at the very least, we must be able to identify unambiguously when the process starts and ends. A model of the testing process can show us which activities are included, when they start and stop, and what inputs and outputs are involved.

2.2.1 Defining attributes

When measuring, there is always a danger that we focus too much on the formal, mathematical system, and not enough on the empirical one. We rush to create mappings and then manipulate numbers, without giving careful thought to the relationships among entities and their attributes in the real world. Figure 2.8 presents a whimsical view of what can happen when we hurry to generate numbers without considering their real meaning.

Figure 2.8: Using a suspect definition

The dog in the figure is clearly an exceptionally intelligent dog, but its intelligence is not reflected by the result of an IQ test. It is clearly wrong to *define* the intelligence of dogs in this way. Many people have argued that defining the intelligence of people by using IQ tests is just as problematic. What is needed is a comprehensive set of characteristics of intelligence, appropriate to the entity (so that dog intelligence will have a different set of characteristics from people intelligence) and associated by a model. The model will show us how the characteristics relate. Then, we can try to define a measure for each characteristic, and use the representation condition to help us understand the relationships as well as overall intelligence.

EXAMPLE 2.9: In software development, our intuition tells us that the complexity of a program can affect the time it takes to code it, test it, and fix it; indeed, we suspect that complexity can help us to understand when a module is prone to contain faults. But there are few researchers who have built models of exactly what it means for a module to be complex. Instead, we often assume that we know what complexity is, and we measure complexity without first defining it in the real world. For example, many software developers define program complexity as the cyclomatic number proposed by McCabe and illustrated in Figure 2.9 (McCabe, 1976). This number, based on a graph-theoretic concept, counts the number of linearly independent paths through a program. We will discuss this measure (and its use in testing) in more detail in Chapter 8.

McCabe felt that the number of such paths was a key indicator not just of testability but also of complexity. Hence, he originally called this number, *v*,

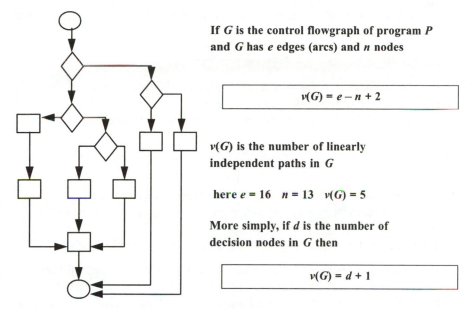

If G is the control flowgraph of program P and G has e edges (arcs) and n nodes

$$v(G) = e - n + 2$$

$v(G)$ is the number of linearly independent paths in G

here $e = 16$ $n = 13$ $v(G) = 5$

More simply, if d is the number of decision nodes in G then

$$v(G) = d + 1$$

Figure 2.9: Computing McCabe's cyclomatic number

the *cyclomatic complexity of a program*. On the basis of empirical research, McCabe claimed that modules with high values of v were those most likely to be fault-prone and unmaintainable. He proposed a threshold value of 10 for each module; that is, any module with v greater than 10 should be redesigned to reduce v. However, the cyclomatic number presents only a partial view of complexity. It can be shown mathematically that the cyclomatic number is equal to one more than the number of decisions in a program, and there are many programs that have a large number of decisions but are easy to understand, code and maintain. Thus, relying only on the cyclomatic number to measure actual program complexity can be misleading. A more complete model of program complexity is needed.

2.2.2   Direct and indirect measurement

Once we have a model of the entities and attributes involved, we can define the measure in terms of them. Many of the examples we have used employ direct mappings from attribute to number, and we use the number to answer questions or assess situations. But when there are complex relationships among attributes, or when an attribute must be measured by combining several of its aspects, then we need a model of how to combine the related measures. It is for this reason that we distinguish direct measurement from indirect.

Direct measurement of an attribute of an entity involves no other attribute or entity. For example, length of a physical object can be measured without reference to any other object or attribute. On the other hand, density of a physical object can be measured only indirectly in terms of mass and volume; we then use a model to show us that the relationship among the three is

$$\text{density} = \frac{\text{mass}}{\text{volume}}$$

Similarly, the speed of a moving object is most accurately measured indirectly using measures of distance and time. Thus, direct measurement forms the building blocks for our assessment, but many interesting attributes are best measured by indirect measurement.

The following direct measures are commonly used in software engineering:

- *Length* of source code (measured by lines of code);
- *Duration* of testing process (measured by elapsed time in hours);
- *Number of defects discovered* during the testing process (measured by counting defects);
- *Time* a programmer spends on a project (measured by months worked).

Table 2.4 provides examples of some indirect measures that are commonly used in software engineering. The most common of all, and the most controversial, is the measure for programmer productivity, because it emphasizes size of output without taking into consideration the code's functionality or complexity. The defect detection efficiency measure is computed with respect to a specific testing or review phase; the total number of defects refers to the total number discovered during the entire product life cycle. The system spoilage measure is routinely computed by Japanese software developers; it indicates how much effort is wasted in fixing faults, rather than in building new code.

Indirect measurement is often useful in making visible the interactions between direct measurements. That is, it is sometimes easier to see what is happening on a project by using combinations of measures. To see why, consider the graph in Figure 2.10.

Table 2.4: Examples of common indirect measures used in software engineering

Programmer productivity	$\dfrac{\text{LOC produced}}{\text{person months of effort}}$
Module defect density	$\dfrac{\text{number of defects}}{\text{module size}}$
Defect detection efficiency	$\dfrac{\text{number of defects detected}}{\text{total number of defects}}$
Requirements stability	$\dfrac{\text{number of initial requirements}}{\text{total number of requirements}}$
Test effectiveness ratio	$\dfrac{\text{number of items covered}}{\text{total number of items}}$
System spoilage	$\dfrac{\text{effort spent fixing faults}}{\text{total project effort}}$

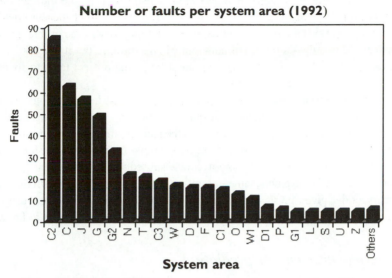

Figure 2.10: Using direct measurement to assess a product (Pfleeger, Fenton, and Page, 1994)

The graph shows the number of faults in each system area of a large, important software system in the UK. From the graph, it appears as if there are five system areas that contain the most problems for the developers maintaining this system. However, Figure 2.11 depicts the same data with one big difference: instead of using

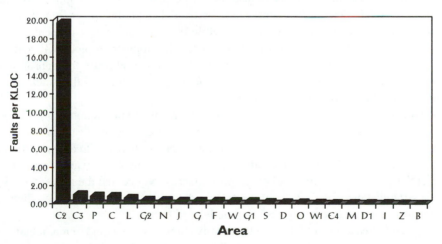

Figure 2.11: Using indirect measurement to assess a product (Pfleeger, Fenton, and Page, 1994)

the direct measurement of faults, it shows fault density (that is, the indirect measure defined as faults per thousand lines of code). From the indirect measurement, it is very clear that one system area is responsible for the majority of the problems. In fact, system area C2 is only 4000 lines of code out of two million, but it is a big headache for the maintainers. Here, indirect measurement helps the project team to focus their maintenance efforts more effectively.

The representational theory of measurement as described in this chapter is initially concerned with direct measurement of attributes. Where no previous measurement has been performed, direct measurement constitutes the natural process of trying to understand entities and the attributes they possess. However, simple models of direct measurement do not preclude the possibility of more accurate subsequent measurement that will be achieved indirectly. For example, temperature can be measured as the length of a column of mercury under given pressure conditions. This measure is indirect because we are examining the column, rather than the entity whose temperature we want to know.

2.2.3   Measurement for prediction

When we talk about measuring something, we usually mean that we wish to assess some entity that already exists. This measurement for assessment is very helpful in understanding what exists now or what has happened in the past. However, in many circumstances, we would like to predict an attribute of some entity that does not yet exist. For example, suppose we are building a software system that must be highly reliable, such as the control software for an aircraft, power plant, or x-ray machine. The software construction may take some time, and we want to provide early assurance that the system will meet reliability targets. However, reliability is defined in terms of operational performance, something we clearly cannot measure before the product is finished. To provide reliability indicators before the system is complete, we can build a model of the factors that affect reliability, and then predict the likely reliability based on our understanding of the system while it is still under development.

Similarly, we often need to predict how much a development project will cost, or how much time and effort will be needed, so that we can allocate the appropriate resources to the project. Simply waiting for the project to end, and then measuring cost and schedule attributes, are clearly not acceptable.

The distinction between measurement for assessment and prediction is not always clear-cut. For example, suppose we use a globe to determine the distance between London and Washington, DC. This indirect measurement helps us to assess how far apart the cities are. However, the same activity is also involved when we want to predict the distance we will travel on a future journey. Notice that the action we take in assessing distance involves the globe as a model of the real world, plus prediction procedures that describe how to use the model.

In general, measurement for prediction always requires some kind of mathematical model that relates the attributes to be predicted to some other attributes that we can measure now. The model need not be complex to be useful.

EXAMPLE 2.10:   Suppose we want to predict the number of pages, m, that will print out as a source code program, so that we can order sufficient paper or estimate the time it will take to do the printing. We could use the very simple model:

$$m = x/a$$

where x is a variable representing a measure of source-code program length in lines of code, and a is a constant representing the average number of lines per page.

Effort prediction is universally needed by project managers.

EXAMPLE 2.11:   A common generic model for predicting the effort required in software projects has the form

$$E = aS^b$$

where E is effort in person months, S is the size (in lines of code) of the system to be constructed, and a and b are constants. We will examine many of these models in Chapter 12.

Sometimes the same model is used both for assessment and prediction, as we saw with the example of the globe, above. The extent to which it applies to each situation depends on how much is known about the parameters of the model. In Example 2.10, suppose a is known to be 55 in a specific environment. If a program exists with a known x, then the indirect measure of hard-copy pages computed by the given formula is not really a prediction problem (except in a very weak sense), particularly if the hard-copy already exists. However, if we had only a program specification, and we wished to know roughly how many hard-copy pages the final implementation would involve, then we would be using the model to solve a prediction problem. In this case, we need some kind of procedure for determining the unknown value of x based on our knowledge of the program specification. The same is true in Example 2.11, where invariably we need some means of determining the parameters a, b, and S based on our knowledge of the project to be developed.

These examples illustrate that the model alone is not enough to perform the required prediction. In addition, we need some means of determining the model parameters, plus a procedure to interpret the results. Therefore, we must think in terms of a prediction system, rather than of the model itself.

A **prediction system** consists of a mathematical model together with a set of prediction procedures for determining unknown parameters and interpreting results (Littlewood, 1988).

EXAMPLE 2.12:   Suppose we want to predict the cost of an automobile journey from London to Bristol. The entity we want to predict is the journey and the attribute is its cost. We begin by obtaining measures (in the assessment sense) of:

- *a*: the distance between London and Bristol;
- *b*: the cost per gallon of fuel, and
- *c*: the average distance we can travel on a gallon of fuel in our car.

Next, we can predict the journey's cost by using the formula

$$cost = ab/c$$

In fact, we are using a prediction system that involves

1. *a model:* that is, the formula *cost = ab/c*;
2. *a set of procedures for determining the model parameters:* that is, how we determine the values *a*, *b*, and *c* – for example, we may consult with the local automobile association, or simply ask a friend;
3. *procedures for interpreting the results:* for example, we may use Bayesian probability to determine likely margins of error.

Using the same model will generally yield different results if we use different prediction procedures. For instance, in Example 2.12, model parameters supplied by a friend may be very different from those supplied by the automobile association. This notion of changing results is especially important when predicting software reliability.

EXAMPLE 2.13:   A well known reliability model is based on an exponential distribution for the time to the ith failure of the product. This distribution is described by the formula

$$F(t) = 1 - e^{-(N-i+1)at}$$

Here, N represents the number of faults initially residing in the program, while a represents the overall rate of occurrence of failures. There are many ways that the model parameters N and a can be estimated, including sophisticated techniques such as Maximum Likelihood Estimation. The details of these prediction systems will be discussed in Chapter 10.

Remember that a model defines an association among attributes. It is possible to have a useful prediction system based on models in which we have not determined the full functional form of the relationship:

EXAMPLE 2.14:   In a major study of software design measures at STC in 1989, Kitchenham and her colleagues confirmed an association between large values of certain program structure and size measurements with large values of measures of fault-proneness, change-proneness, and subjective complexity (Kitchenham *et al.*, 1990). As a result of their study, a special type of prediction system was constructed, having two components:

- a procedure for defining what is meant by a "large" value for each measure;
- a statistical technique for confirming that programs with large values

of size and structure measures were more likely either to have a large number of faults, to have a large number of changes, or to be regarded as complex, compared with programs that did not have large values.

The STC researchers concluded that this procedure can be used to assist project managers in reducing potential project risks by identifying a group of programs or modules that are likely to benefit from additional scrutiny, such as inspection, redesign or additional testing.

Accurate predictive measurement is always based on measurement in the assessment sense, so the need for assessment is especially critical in software engineering. Everyone wants to be able to predict key determinants of success, such as the effort needed to build a new system, or the reliability of the system in operation. However, there are no magic models. The models are dependent on high-quality measurements of past projects (as well as the current project during development and testing) if they are to support accurate predictions. Because software development is more a creative process than a manufacturing one, there is a high degree of risk when we undertake to build a new system, especially if it is very different from systems we have developed in the past. Thus, software engineering involves risk, and there are some clear parallels with gambling.

> Testing your methods on a sample of past data gets to the heart of the scientific approach to gambling. Unfortunately this implies some preliminary spadework, and most people skimp on that bit, preferring to rely on blind faith instead (Drapkin and Forsyth, 1987).

We can replace "gambling" with "software prediction," and then heed the warning. In addition, we must recognize that the quality of our predictions is based on several other assumptions, including the notion that the future will be like the past, and that we understand how data are distributed. For instance, many reliability models specify a particular distribution, such as Gaussian or Poisson. If our new data do not behave like the distribution in the model, our prediction is not likely to be accurate.

2.3 MEASUREMENT SCALES AND SCALE TYPES

We have seen how direct measurement of an attribute assigns a representation or mapping M from an observed (empirical) relation system to some numerical relation system. The purpose of performing the mapping is to be able to manipulate data in the numerical system and use the results to draw conclusions about the attribute in the empirical system. We do this sort of analysis all the time. For example, we use a thermometer to measure air temperature, and then we conclude that it is hotter today than yesterday; the numbers tell us about the characteristic of the air.

But not all measurement mappings are the same. And the differences among the mappings can restrict the kind of analysis we can do. To understand these differences, we introduce the notion of a measurement scale, and then we use the scale to help us understand which analyses are appropriate.

We refer to our measurement mapping, M, together with the empirical and numerical relation systems, as a **measurement scale**. Where the relation systems (that is, the domain and range) are obvious from the context, we sometimes refer to M alone as the scale. There are three important questions concerning representations and scales:

1. How do we determine when one numerical relation system is preferable to another?
2. How do we know if a particular empirical relation system has a representation in a given numerical relation system?
3. What do we do when we have several different possible representations (and hence many scales) in the same numerical relation system?

Our answer to the first question is pragmatic. Recall that the formal relational system to which the scale maps need not be numeric; it can be symbolic. However, symbol manipulation may be far more unwieldy than numerical manipulation. Thus, we try to use the real numbers wherever possible, since analyzing real numbers permits us to use techniques with which we are familiar.

The second question is known as the **representation problem**, and its answer is sought not just by software engineers but by all scientists who are concerned with measurement. The representation problem is one of the basic problems of measurement theory; it has been solved for various types of relation systems characterized by certain types of axioms. Rather than address it in this book, we refer you to the classical literature on measurement theory.

Our primary concern in this chapter is with the third question. Called the **uniqueness problem**, this question addresses our ability to determine which representation is the most suitable for measuring an attribute of interest.

In general, there are many different representations for a given empirical relation system. We have seen that the more relations there are, the fewer are the representations. This notion of shrinking representations can best be understood by a formal characterization of scale types. In this section, we classify measurement scales as one of five major types

- nominal
- ordinal
- interval
- ratio
- absolute

There are other scales that can be defined (such as a logarithmic scale), but we focus only on these five, since they illustrate the range of possibilities and the issues that must be considered when measurement is done.

One relational system is said to be **richer** than another if all relations in the second are contained in the first. Using this notion, the scale types listed above are shown in increasing levels of richness. That is, the richer the empirical relation system, the more restrictive the set of representations, and so the more sophisticated the scale of measurement.

The idea behind the formal definition of scale types is quite simple. If we have a satisfactory measure for an attribute with respect to an empirical relation system (that is, it captures the empirical relations in which we are interested), we want to know what other measures exist that are also acceptable. For example, we may measure the length of physical objects by using a mapping from length to inches. But there are equally acceptable measures in feet, meters, furlongs, miles, and more. In this example, all of the acceptable measures are very closely related, in that we can map one into another by multiplying by a suitable positive constant (such as converting inches to feet by multiplying by $\frac{1}{12}$). A mapping from one acceptable measure to another is called an **admissible transformation**. When measuring length, the class of admissible transformations is very restrictive, in the sense that all admissible transformations are of the form

$$M' = aM$$

where M is the original measure, M' is the new one, and a is a constant. In particular, transformations of the form

$$M' = b + aM \qquad (b \neq 0)$$

or

$$M' = aM^b \qquad (b \neq 1)$$

are not acceptable. Thus, the set of admissible transformations for length is smaller than the set of all possible transformations. We say that the more restrictive the class of admissible transformations, the more **sophisticated** the measurement scale.

2.3.1   Nominal scale

Suppose we define classes or categories, and then place each entity in a particular class or category, based on the value of the attribute. This categorization is the basis for the most primitive form of measurement, the **nominal scale**. Thus, the nominal scale has two major characteristics:

- The empirical relation system consists only of different classes; there is no notion of ordering among the classes.
- Any distinct numbering or symbolic representation of the classes is an acceptable measure, but there is no notion of magnitude associated with the numbers or symbols.

In other words, nominal-scale measurement places elements in a classification scheme. The classes are not ordered; even if the classes are numbered from 1 to n for identification, there is no implied ordering of the classes.

EXAMPLE 2.15:   Suppose that we are investigating the set of all known software faults in our code, and we are trying to capture the location of the faults. Then we seek a measurement scale with faults as entities and "location" as the attribute. We can use a common but primitive mapping to identify the fault location: we denote a fault as "specification", "design" or "code", according to where the fault was first introduced. Notice that this classification imposes no judgment about which class of faults is more severe or important than another. However, we have a clear distinction among the classes, and every fault belongs to exactly one class. This is a very simple empirical relation system. Any mapping, M, that assigns the three different classes to three different numbers satisfies the representation condition and is therefore an acceptable measure. For example, the mappings M_1 and M_2 defined by

$$M_1(x) = \begin{cases} 1 \text{ if } x \text{ is specification fault} \\ 2 \text{ if } x \text{ is design fault} \\ 3 \text{ if } x \text{ is code fault} \end{cases}$$

$$M_2(x) = \begin{cases} 101 \text{ if } x \text{ is specification fault} \\ 2.73 \text{ if } x \text{ is design fault} \\ 69 \text{ if } x \text{ is code fault} \end{cases}$$

are acceptable. In fact, any two mappings, M and M', will always be related in a special way: M' can be obtained from M by a one-to-one mapping. The mappings need not involve numbers; distinct symbols will suffice. Thus, the class of admissible transformations for a nominal scale measure is the set of all one-to-one mappings.

2.3.2   Ordinal scale

The ordinal scale is often useful to augment the nominal scale with information about an ordering of the classes or categories. The ordering leads to analysis not possible with nominal measures. Thus, the **ordinal scale** has the following characteristics:

- The empirical relation system consists of classes that are ordered with respect to the attribute.
- Any mapping that preserves the ordering (that is, any monotonic function) is acceptable.
- The numbers represent ranking only, so addition, subtraction, and other arithmetic operations have no meaning.

However, classes can be combined, as long as the combination makes sense with respect to the ordering.

EXAMPLE 2.16:   Suppose our set of entities is a set of software modules, and the attribute we wish to capture quantitatively is "complexity". Initially, we may define five distinct classes of module complexity: "trivial", "simple", "moderate", "complex" and "incomprehensible". There is an implicit order relation of "less complex than" on these classes; that is, all trivial modules are less complex than simple modules, which are less complex than moderate modules, and so on. In this case, since the measurement mapping must preserve this ordering, we cannot be as free in our choice of mapping as we could with a nominal measure. Any mapping, M, must map each distinct class to a different number, as with nominal measures. But we also must ensure that the more complex classes are mapped to bigger numbers. Therefore, M must be a monotonically increasing function. For example, each of the mappings M_1, M_2 and M_3 is a valid measure, since each satisfies the representation condition.

$$M_1(x) = \begin{cases} 1 \text{ if } x \text{ is trivial} \\ 2 \text{ if } x \text{ is simple} \\ 3 \text{ if } x \text{ is moderate} \\ 4 \text{ if } x \text{ is complex} \\ 5 \text{ if } x \text{ is incomprehensible} \end{cases} \quad M_2(x) = \begin{cases} 1 \text{ if } x \text{ is trivial} \\ 2 \text{ if } x \text{ is simple} \\ 3 \text{ if } x \text{ is moderate} \\ 4 \text{ if } x \text{ is complex} \\ 10 \text{ if } x \text{ is incomprehensible} \end{cases} \quad M_3(x) = \begin{cases} 0.1 \text{ if } x \text{ is trivial} \\ 1001 \text{ if } x \text{ is simple} \\ 1002 \text{ if } x \text{ is moderate} \\ 4570 \text{ if } x \text{ is complex} \\ 4573 \text{ if } x \text{ is incomprehensible} \end{cases}$$

However, neither M_4 nor M_5 is valid:

$$M_4(x) = \begin{cases} 1 \text{ if } x \text{ is trivial} \\ 2 \text{ if } x \text{ is simple} \\ 3 \text{ if } x \text{ is moderate} \\ 4 \text{ if } x \text{ is complex} \\ 5 \text{ if } x \text{ is incomprehensible} \end{cases} \quad M_5(x) = \begin{cases} 1 \text{ if } x \text{ is trivial} \\ 3 \text{ if } x \text{ is simple} \\ 2 \text{ if } x \text{ is moderate} \\ 4 \text{ if } x \text{ is complex} \\ 10 \text{ if } x \text{ is incomprehensible} \end{cases}$$

Because the mapping for an ordinal scale preserves the ordering of the classes, the set of ordered classes $<C_1, C_2, \ldots, C_n>$ is mapped to an increasing series of numbers $<a_1, a_2, \ldots, a_n>$ where a_i is greater than a_j when i is greater than j. Any acceptable mapping can be transformed to any other as long as the series of a_i is mapped to another increasing series. Thus, in the ordinal scale, any two measures can be related by a monotonic mapping, so the class of admissible transformations is the set of all monotonic mappings.

2.3.3   Interval scale

We have seen how the ordinal scale carries more information about the entities than does the nominal scale, since ordinal scales preserve ordering. The interval scale carries more information still, making it more powerful than nominal or ordinal. This scale captures information about the size of the intervals that separate the classes, so that we can in some sense understand the size of the jump from one class to another. Thus, an interval scale can be characterized in the following way:

- An interval scale preserves order, as with an ordinal scale.
- An interval scale preserves differences but not ratios. That is, we know the difference between any two of the ordered classes in the range of the mapping, but computing the ratio of two classes in the range does not make sense.

- Addition and subtraction are acceptable on the interval scale, but not multiplication and division.

To understand the difference between ordinal and interval measures, consider first an example from everyday life.

> **EXAMPLE 2.17:** We can measure air temperature on a Fahrenheit or Celsius scale. Thus, we may say that it is usually 20 degrees Celsius on a summer's day in London, while it may be 30 degrees Celsius on the same day in Washington, DC. The interval from one degree to another is the same, and we consider each degree to be a class related to heat. That is, moving from 20 to 21 degrees in London increases the heat in the same way that moving from 30 to 31 degrees does in Washington. However, we cannot say that it is two-thirds as hot in London as Washington; neither can we say that it is 50% hotter in Washington than in London. Similarly, we cannot say that a 90-degree Fahrenheit day in Washington is twice as hot as a 45-degree Fahrenheit day in London.

There are fewer examples of interval scales in software engineering than of nominal or ordinal.

> **EXAMPLE 2.18:** Recall the five categories of complexity described in Example 2.16. Suppose that the difference in complexity between a trivial and simple system is the same as that between a simple and moderate system. Then any interval measure of complexity must preserve these differences. Where this equal step applies to each class, we have an attribute measurable on an interval scale. The following measures have this property and satisfy the representation condition:

$$M_1(x) = \begin{cases} 1 \text{ if } x \text{ is trivial} \\ 2 \text{ if } x \text{ is simple} \\ 3 \text{ if } x \text{ is moderate} \\ 4 \text{ if } x \text{ is complex} \\ 5 \text{ if } x \text{ is incomprehensible} \end{cases} \quad M_2(x) = \begin{cases} 0 \text{ if } x \text{ is trivial} \\ 2 \text{ if } x \text{ is simple} \\ 4 \text{ if } x \text{ is moderate} \\ 6 \text{ if } x \text{ is complex} \\ 8 \text{ if } x \text{ is incomprehensible} \end{cases} \quad M_3(x) = \begin{cases} 3.1 \text{ if } x \text{ is trivial} \\ 5.1 \text{ if } x \text{ is simple} \\ 7.1 \text{ if } x \text{ is moderate} \\ 9.1 \text{ if } x \text{ is complex} \\ 11.1 \text{ if } x \text{ is incomprehensible} \end{cases}$$

Suppose an attribute is measurable on an interval scale, and M and M' are mappings that satisfy the representation condition. Then we can always find numbers a and b such that

$$M = aM' + b$$

We call this type of transformation an **affine transformation**. Thus, the class of admissible transformations of an interval scale is the set of affine transformations. In Example 2.17, we can transform Celsius to Fahrenheit by using the transformation

$$F = 9/5C + 32$$

Likewise, in Example 2.18, we can transform M_1 to M_3 by using the formula

$$M_3 = 2M_1 + 1.1$$

EXAMPLE 2.19: The timing of an event's occurrence is a classic use of interval scale measurement. We can measure the timing in units of years, days, hours, or some other standard measure, where each time is noted relative to a given fixed event. We use this convention every day by measuring the year with respect to an event (that is, by saying "1998 AD"), or by measuring the hour from midnight. Software development projects can be measured in the same way, by referring to the project's start day. We say that we are on day 87 of the project, when we mean that we are measuring 87 days from the first day of the project. Thus, using these conventions, it is meaningless to say "Project X started twice as early as project Y" but meaningful to say "the time between project X's beginning and now is twice the time between project Y's beginning and now."

On a given project, suppose the project manager is measuring time in months from the day work started: April 1, 1988. But the contract manager is measuring time in years from the day that the funds were received from the customer: January 1, 1989. If M is the project manager's scale and M' the contract manager's scale, we can transform the contract manager's time into the project manager's by using the following admissible transformation:

$$M = 12\ M' + 9$$

2.3.4 Ratio scale

Although the interval scale gives us more information and allows more analysis than either nominal or ordinal, we sometimes need to be able to do even more. For example, we would like to be able to say that one liquid is twice as hot as another, or that one project took twice as long as another. This need for ratios gives rise to the ratio scale, the most useful scale of measurement, and one that is common in the physical sciences. A **ratio scale** has the following characteristics:

- It is a measurement mapping that preserves ordering, the size of intervals between entities, and ratios between entities.
- There is a zero element, representing total lack of the attribute.
- The measurement mapping must start at zero and increase at equal intervals, known as units.
- All arithmetic can be meaningfully applied to the classes in the range of the mapping.

The key feature that distinguishes ratio from nominal, ordinal and interval scales is the existence of empirical relations to capture ratios.

EXAMPLE 2.20: The length of physical objects is measurable on a ratio scale, enabling us to make statements about how one entity is twice as long as another. The zero element is theoretical, in the sense that we can think of an object as having no length at all; thus, the zero-length object exists as a limit of things that get smaller and smaller. We can measure length in inches, feet, centimeters, meters, and more, where each different measure preserves the relations about length that we observe in the real world. To convert from one length measure to another, we can use a transformation of the form $M = aM'$ where a is a constant. Thus, to convert feet F to inches I, we use the transformation $I = 12F$.

In general, any acceptable transformation for a ratio scale is a mapping of the form

$$M = aM'$$

where a is a positive scalar. This type of transformation is called a **ratio transformation**, because it preserves the ratios in M' as they are transformed to M.

EXAMPLE 2.21: The length of software code is also measurable on a ratio scale. As with other physical objects, we have empirical relations like "twice as long". The notion of a zero-length object exists – an empty piece of code. We can measure program length in a variety of ways, including lines of code, thousands of lines of code, the number of characters contained in the program, the number of executable statements, and more. Suppose M is the measure of program length in lines of code, while M' captures length as number of characters. Then we can transform one to the other by computing $M' = aM$, where a is the average number of characters per line of code.

2.3.5   Absolute scale

As the scales of measurement carry more information, the defining classes of admissible transformations have become increasingly restrictive. The absolute scale is the most restrictive of all. For any two measures, M and M', there is only one admissible transformation: the identity transformation. That is, there is only one way in which the measurement can be made, so M and M' must be equal. The **absolute scale** has the following properties:

- The measurement for an absolute scale is made simply by counting the number of elements in the entity set.
- The attribute always takes the form "number of occurrences of x in the entity."
- There is only one possible measurement mapping, namely the actual count.
- All arithmetic analysis of the resulting count is meaningful.

There are many examples of absolute scale in software engineering. For instance, the number of failures observed during integration testing can be measured only in one way: by counting the number of failures observed. Hence, a count of the number of failures is an absolute-scale measure for the number of failures observed during integration testing. Likewise, the number of people working on a software project can be measured only in one way: by counting the number of people.

Because there is only one possible measure of an absolute attribute, the set of acceptable transformations for the absolute scale is simply the identity transformation. The uniqueness of the measure is an important difference between the ratio scale and the absolute scale.

EXAMPLE 2.22: We saw in Example 2.21 that the number of lines of code (LOC) is a ratio-scale measure of length for source code programs. A common mistake is to assume that LOC is an absolute-scale measure of length, because it is obtained by counting. However, it is the attribute (as characterized by empirical relations) that determines the scale type. As we have seen, the length of programs cannot be absolute, because there are many different ways to measure it (such as LOC, thousands of LOC, number of characters, and number of bytes). It is incorrect to say that LOC is an absolute scale measure of program length. However, LOC is an absolute scale measure of the attribute "number of lines of code" of a program. For the same reason, "number of years" is a ratio-scale measure of a person's age; it cannot be an absolute scale measure of age, because we can also measure age in months, hours, minutes, or seconds.

Table 2.5 summarizes the key elements distinguishing the measurement-scale types discussed in this chapter. This table is similar to those found in other texts on measurement. However, most texts do not point out the possible risk of misinterpretation of the Examples column. Since scale types are defined with respect to the set of admissible transformations, we should never give examples of attributes without specifying the empirical relation system that characterizes an attribute. We have seen that as we enrich the relation system for an attribute by preserving more information with the measurement mapping, so we may arrive at a more restrictive (and hence different) scale type. Thus, when Table 2.5 says that the attributes length, time interval, and (absolute) temperature are on the ratio scale, what it really means is that we have developed sufficiently refined empirical relation systems to allow ratio-scale measures for these attributes.

Table 2.5: Scales of measurement

Scale type	Admissible transformations (how measures M and M' must be related)	Examples
Nominal	1–1 mapping from M to M'	Labeling, classifying entities
Ordinal	Monotonic increasing function from M to M', that is, $M(x) \geq M(y)$ implies $M'(x) \geq M'(y)$	Preference, hardness, air quality, intelligence tests (raw scores)
Interval	$M' = aM + b$ $(a > 0)$	Relative time, temperature (Fahrenheit, Celsius), intelligence tests (standardized scores)
Ratio	$M' = aM$ $(a > 0)$	Time interval, length, temperature (Kelvin)
Absolute	$M' = M$	Counting entities

2.4 MEANINGFULNESS IN MEASUREMENT

There is more than just academic interest in scale types. Understanding scale types enables us to determine when statements about measurement make sense. For instance, we have seen how it is inappropriate to compute ratios with nominal, ordinal and interval scales. In general, measures often map attributes to real numbers, and it is tempting to manipulate the real numbers in familiar ways: adding, averaging, taking logarithms, and performing sophisticated statistical analysis. But we must remember that the analysis is constrained by the scale type. We can perform only those calculations that are permissible for the given scale, reflecting the type of attribute and mapping that generated the data. In other words, knowledge of scale type tells us about limitations on the kind of mathematical manipulations that can be performed. Thus, the key question we should ask after having made our measurements is: can we deduce meaningful statements about the entities being measured?

This question is harder to answer than it first appears. To see why, consider the following statements:

1. The number of errors discovered during the integration testing of program X was at least 100.
2. The cost of fixing each error in program X is at least 100.
3. A semantic error takes twice as long to fix as a syntactic error.
4. A semantic error is twice as complex as a syntactic error.

Intuitively, statement 1 seems to make sense, but statement 2 does not; the number of errors may be specified without reference to a particular scale, but the cost of fixing an error cannot be. Statement 3 seems to make sense (even if we think it cannot possibly be true) because the ratio of time taken is the same, regardless of the scale of measurement used. (That is, if a semantic error takes twice as many minutes to repair as a syntactic error, it also takes twice as many hours, seconds or years to repair.) Statement 4 does not appear to be meaningful, and we require clarification. If "complexity" means time to understand, then the statement makes sense. But other definitions of complexity may not admit measurement on a ratio scale; in those instances, statement 4 is meaningless.

Our intuitive notion of a statement's meaningfulness involving measurement is quite distinct from the notion of the statement's truth. For example, the statement "The President of the United States is 125 years old" is a meaningful statement about the age measure, even though it is clearly false. We can define "meaningfulness" in a formal way.

We say that a statement involving measurement is **meaningful** if its truth value is invariant of transformations of allowable scales.

EXAMPLE 2.23: We can examine the transformations to decide on meaningfulness. Consider these statements:

Fred is twice as tall as Jane.
This statement implies that the measures are at least on the ratio scale, because it uses scalar multiplication as an admissible transformation. The statement is meaningful because no matter which measure of height we use (inches, feet, centimeters, etc.), the truth or falsity of the statement remains consistent. In other words, if M and M' are different measures of height, then the statements

$$M(\text{Fred}) = 2M(\text{Jane})$$

and

$$M'(\text{Fred}) = 2M'(\text{Jane})$$

are either both true or both false. This consistency of truth is due to the relationship $M = aM'$ for some positive number a.

The temperature in Tokyo today is twice that in London.
This statement also implies ratio scale but is not meaningful, because we measure (air) temperature only on two scales, Fahrenheit and Celsius. Suppose that the temperature in Tokyo is 40°C and in London 20°C. Then on the Celsius scale, the statement is true. However, on the Fahrenheit scale, Tokyo is 104°F while London is 68°F.

The difference in temperature between Tokyo and London today is twice what it was yesterday.
This statement implies that the distance between two measures is meaningful, a condition that is part of the interval scale. The statement is meaningful, because Fahrenheit and Celsius are related by the affine transformation $F = 9/5C + 32$, ensuring that ratios of differences (as opposed to just ratios) are preserved. For example, suppose yesterday's temperatures on the Celsius scale were 35°C in Tokyo and 25°C (a difference of 10) in London, while today it is 40°C in Tokyo and 20°C in London (a difference of 20). If we transform these temperatures to the Fahrenheit scale, we find that yesterday's temperatures were 95°F in Tokyo and 77°F London (a difference of 18); today's are 104°F in Tokyo and 68°F in London (a difference of 36). Thus, the truth value is preserved with the transformation.

Failure x is twice as critical as failure y.
This statement is not meaningful if we have only an ordinal scale for failure criticality. To see why, suppose we have four classes of failures, $class_i$, for i from 1 to 4 in increasing order of criticality. We can define two mappings, M and M', to be valid ordinal measures as follows:

Failure class	Mapping M	Mapping M'
$class_1$	1	3
$class_2$	3	4
$class_3$	6	5
$class_4$	7	10

Suppose y is in class$_2$ and x in class$_3$. Notice that $M(x) = 6$ and $M(y) = 3$ while $M'(x) = 5$ and $M'(y) = 4$. In this case, the statement is true under M but false under M'.

Meaningfulness is often clear when we are dealing with measures with which we are familiar. But sometimes we define new measures, and it is not as easy to tell if the statements about them are meaningful.

Example 2.24: Suppose we define a crude notion of speed of software programs, and we rank three word processing programs A, B, and C with respect to a single empirical binary relation "faster than". Suppose further that the empirical relation is such that A is faster than B which is faster than C. This notion of program speed is measurable on an ordinal scale, and any mapping M in which $M(A)>M(B)>M(C)$ is an acceptable measure. Now consider the statement "Program A is faster than both programs B and C" where we mean that A is faster than B and A is faster than C. We can show that this statement is meaningful in the following way. Let M and M' be any two acceptable measures. Then we know that, for any pair of programs x and y, $M(x)>M(y)$ if and only if $M'(x)>M'(y)$. Using the scale M, the statement under scrutiny corresponds to

$$M(A) > M(B) \text{ and } M(A) > M(C)$$

which is true. But then

$$M'(A) > M'(B) \text{ and } M'(A) > M'(C)$$

is also true because of the relationship between M and M'.

By similar argument, we can show that the statement "Program B is faster than both programs A and C" is meaningful even though it is false.

However, consider the statement "Program A is more than twice as fast as Program C". This statement is not meaningful. To see why, define acceptable measures M and M' as follows:

$$M(A) = 3; \ M(B) = 2; \ M(C) = 1$$
$$M'(A) = 3; \ M'(B) = 2.5; \ M'(C) = 2$$

Using scale M the statement is true, since $3 = M(A) > 2M(C) = 2$. However, using M' the statement is false. Although the statement seems meaningful given our understanding of speed, the sophistication of the notion "twice as fast" was not captured in our overly-simplistic empirical relation system, and hence was not preserved by all measurement mappings.

The terminology often used in software engineering can be imprecise and misleading. Many software practitioners and researchers mistakenly think that to be meaningful, a measure must be useful, practical, worthwhile, or easy to collect. These characteristics are not part of meaningfulness. Indeed, such issues are difficult to address for any measure, whether it occurs in software or in some other scientific discipline. For example, carbon-dating techniques for measuring the age of fossils may not be practical or easy to do, but the measures are certainly valid and meaningful! Thus, meaningfulness should be viewed as only one attribute of a measure.

2.4.1   Statistical operations on measures

The scale type of a measure affects the types of operations and statistical analyses that can be sensibly applied to the data. Many statistical analyses use arithmetic operators:

$$+, -, \div, \times$$

The analysis need not be sophisticated. At the very least, we would like to know something about how the whole data set is distributed. We use two basic measures to capture this information: measures of central tendency, and measures of dispersion. A **measure of central tendency**, usually called an **average**, tells us something about where the "middle" of the set is likely to be, while a **measure of dispersion** tells us how far the data points stray from the middle.

We have measured an attribute for 13 entities, and the resulting data points in ranked order are:
2, 2, 4, 5, 5, 8, 8, 10 ,11, 11, 11, 15, 16
The **mean** of this set of data (that is, the sum divided by the number of items) is *9.1*
The **median** (that is, the value of the middle-ranked item) is *8*
The **mode** (that is, the value of the most commonly occurring item) is *11*

Figure 2.12: Different ways to compute the central tendency of a set of numbers

Figure 2.12 shows the computation of measures of central tendency for a given set of data. Measures of dispersion include the maximum and minimum values, as well as the variance and standard deviation; these measures give us some indication of how the data are clustered around a measure of central tendency.

But even these simple analytical techniques cannot be used universally. In particular, nominal and ordinal measures do not permit computation of mean, variance and standard deviation. That is, the notion of mean is not meaningful for nominal and ordinal measures.

Example 2.25:   Suppose the data points $\{x_1,..., x_n\}$ represent a measure of understandability for each module in system X, while $\{y_1..., y_m\}$ represent the understandability values for each module in system Y. We would like to know which of the two systems has the higher average understandability. The statement "The average of the x_is is greater than the average of the y_js" must be meaningful; that is, the statement's truth value should be invariant with respect to the particular measure used.

Suppose we assess every module's understandability according to the following classification: trivial, simple, moderate, complex, incomprehensible. In this way, our notion of understandability is representable on an ordinal scale. From this, we can define two valid measures of understandability, M and M', as in Table 2.6.

Table 2.6: Measures of understandability

	trivial	simple	moderate	complex	incomprehensible
M	1	2	3	4	5
M'	1	2	3	4	10

Suppose that X consists of exactly five modules, and the understandability of each is rated as:

x_1	trivial
x_2	simple
x_3	simple
x_4	moderate
x_5	incomprehensible

while Y's seven modules have understandability

y_1	simple
y_2	moderate
y_3	moderate
y_4	moderate
y_5	complex
y_6	complex
y_7	complex

Using M, the mean of the X values is 2.6, while the mean of the Y values is 3.1; thus, the "average" of the Y values is greater than the average of the X values. However, using M', the mean of the X values is 3.6, while the mean of the Y values is 3.1. Since the definition of meaningfulness requires the truth value to be preserved, the mean is not a meaningful measure of central tendency for ordinal scale data.

On the other hand, the median (that is, the middle-ranked item) *is* a meaningful measure of central tendency. Using both M and M', the median of the Y values (in both cases 3) is greater than the median of the X values (in both cases 2). Similarly, if we define M'' as a radically different measure according to Table 2.7, the median of the Y values, 69, is still greater than the median of the X values, 3.8.

Table 2.7: Different measure M''

	trivial	simple	moderate	complex	incomprehensible
M''	0.5	3.8	69	104	500

Example 2.25 confirms that the mean cannot be used as a measure of central tendency for ordinal-scale data. However, the mean is acceptable for interval- and ratio-scale

data. To see why, let $\{x_1,\ldots,x_n\}$ and $\{y_1,\ldots,y_m\}$ be two sets of entities for which some attribute can be measured on a ratio scale. We must show that the statement "The mean of the x_is is greater than the mean of y_js" is meaningful. To do so, let M and M' be two measures for the attribute in question. Then we want to show that the means preserve the relation. In mathematical terms, we must demonstrate that

$$\frac{1}{n}\sum_{i=1}^{n} M(x_i) > \frac{1}{m}\sum_{j=1}^{m} M(y_j) \quad \text{if and only if} \quad \frac{1}{n}\sum_{i=1}^{n} M'(x_i) > \frac{1}{m}\sum_{j=1}^{m} M'(y_j)$$

The ratio scale gives us the extra information we need to show that the assertion is valid. Thanks to the relationship between acceptable transformations for a ratio scale, we know that $M = aM'$ for some $a>0$. When we substitute aM' for M in the above equation, we get a statement that is clearly valid.

The same investigation can be done for any statistical technique, using scale and transformation properties to verify that a certain analysis is valid for a given scale type. Table 2.8 presents a summary of the meaningful statistics for different scale types. The entries are inclusive reading downwards. That is, every meaningful statistic of a nominal scale type is also meaningful for an ordinal-scale type, every meaningful statistic of an ordinal scale type is also meaningful for an interval scale type, and so on. We will return to the appropriateness of analysis when we discuss experimental design and analysis in Chapter 4, and again when we investigate the analysis of software measurement data in Chapter 6.

Table 2.8: Summary of measurement scales and statistics relevant to each (Siegel and Castellan, 1988)

Scale type	Defining relations	Examples of appropriate statistics	Appropriate statistical tests
Nominal	Equivalence	Mode Frequency	Non-parametric
Ordinal	Equivalence Greater than	Median Percentile Spearman r Kendall τ Kendall W	Non-parametric
Interval	Equivalence Greater than Known ratio of any intervals	Mean Standard deviation Pearson product-moment correlation Multiple product-moment correlation	Non-parametric
Ratio	Equivalence Greater than Known ratio of any intervals Known ratio of any two scale values	Geometric mean Coefficient of variation	Non-parametric and parametric

2.4.2   Objective and subjective measures

When measuring attributes of entities, we strive to keep our measurements objective. By doing so, we make sure that different people produce the same measures, regardless of whether they are measuring product, process or resource. This consistency of measurement is very important. Although no measurement is truly objective (because there is always some degree of subjectivity about the entities and attributes) some measures are clearly more subjective than others. Subjective measures depend on the environment in which they are made. The measures can vary with the person measuring, and they reflect the judgment of the measurer. What one judge considers bad, another may consider good, and it may be difficult to reach consensus on attributes such as process, product or resource quality.

Nevertheless, it is important to recognize that subjective measurements can be useful, as long as we understand their imprecision. For example, suppose we want to measure the quality of requirements before we turn the specification over to the test team, who will then define test plans from them. Any of the techniques shown in Figure 2.2 would be acceptable. For example, we may ask the test team to read and rate each requirement on a scale from 1 to 5, where "1" means "I understand this requirement completely and can write a complete test script to determine if this requirement is met," to "5": "I do not understand this requirement and cannot begin to write a test script." Suppose the results of this assessment look like the chart in Table 2.9.

Even though the measurement is subjective, the measures show us that we may have problems with our interface requirements; perhaps the interface requirements should be reviewed and rewritten before proceeding to test plan generation or even to design. It is the general picture that is important, rather than the exactness of the individual measure, so the subjectivity, although a drawback, does not prevent us from gathering useful information about the entity. We will see other examples throughout this book where measurement is far from ideal but still paints a useful picture of what is going on in the project.

2.4.3   Measurement in extended number systems

In many situations we cannot measure an attribute directly. Instead, we must measure it in terms of the more easily understood component attributes of which it is composed. (We sometimes call these components **sub-attributes**.) For example, suppose that

Table 2.9: Results of requirements assessment

Requirement type	1 (good)	2	3	4	5 (bad)
Performance requirements	12	7	2	1	0
Database requirements	16	12	2	0	0
Interface requirements	3	4	6	7	1
Other requirements	14	10	1	0	0

Table 2.10: Transportation attributes

Option	Journey time (hours)	Cost per mile (dollars)
Car	3	1.5
Train	5	2.0
Plane	3.5	3.5
Executive coach	7	4.0

we wish to assess the *quality* of the different types of transport available for traveling from our home to another city. We may not know how to measure quality directly, but we know that quality involves at least two significant sub-attributes, journey time and cost per mile. Hence, we accumulate data in Table 2.10 to describe these attributes.

Intuitively, given two transport types, A and B, we would rank A superior to B (that is, A is of higher quality than B) if

journey time (A) < journey time (B) AND cost per mile (A) < cost per mile (B)

Using this rule with the data collected for each journey type, we can depict the relationships among the candidates as shown in Figure 2.13. In the figure, an arrow from transport type B to transport type A indicates the superiority of A to B. Thus, Car is superior to both Train and Plane because, in each case, the journey time is shorter and the cost per mile is less. The figure also shows us that Car, Train and Plane are all superior to Coach.

Notice that in this relation Train and Plane are incomparable; that is, neither is superior to the other. Train is slower but cheaper than Plane. It would be inappropriate to force an ordering because of the different underlying attributes. We could impose an ordering only if we had additional information about the relative priorities of cost and timing. If cost is more important to us, then Train is preferable; if speed were more important, we would prefer Plane.

Now suppose we wish to use the representation condition to define a measure that characterizes the notion of journey quality given by the above relation system. It is easy to prove that there is no possible measure that is a single-valued real number. For suppose there were. Then Plane would be mapped to some real number $m(\text{Plane})$, while Train would be mapped to some real number $m(\text{Train})$. Exactly one of the following must then be true:

1. $m(\text{Plane}) < m(\text{Train})$
2. $m(\text{Plane}) > m(\text{Train})$
3. $m(\text{Plane}) = m(\text{Train})$

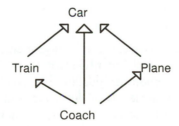

Figure 2.13: Quality relationships based on rule and collected data

If the first statement were true, then the representation condition implies that Plane must be superior to Train. This is false, because Train is cheaper. Similarly, the second statement is false because Train is slower than Plane. But the third statement is also false, since it implies an equality relation that does not exist.

The reason we cannot find a measure satisfying the representation condition is because we are looking at too narrow a number system. When we have genuinely incomparable entities, we have a partial order, as opposed to what is called a strict weak order, so we cannot measure in the set of real numbers $\Re$. (A **strict weak order** has two properties: it is asymmetric and negatively transitive. By **asymmetric**, we mean that if the pair (x, y) is in the relation, then (y, x) is not in the relation. A relation is **negatively transitive** if, whenever (x, y) is in the relation, then for every z, either (x, z) or (z, y) is in the relation.) What we need instead is a mapping into pairs of real numbers, that is, into the set $\Re \times \Re$. In the transport example, we can define a representation in the following way. First, we define a measure m that takes a transport type into a pair of elements:

$$m(\text{Transport}) = (\text{Journey time, Cost per mile})$$

Then we define the actual pairs:

$$m(\text{Car})=(3, \ 1.5)$$
$$m(\text{Train})=(5, \ 2)$$
$$m(\text{Plane})=(3.5, \ 3.5)$$
$$m(\text{Coach})=(7, \ 4)$$

The numerical binary relation over $\Re \times \Re$ that corresponds to the empirical superiority relation is defined as:

$$(x, y) \text{ superior to } (x', y') \text{ if } x{<}x' \text{ and } y{<}y'$$

The numerical relation preserves the empirical relation. It too is only a partial order in $\Re \times \Re$ because it contains incomparable pairs. For example, the pair $(5, 2)$ is not superior to $(3.5, 3.5)$; nor is $(3.5, 3.5)$ superior to $(5, 2)$.

EXAMPLE 2.26: Suppose we wish to assess the quality of four different C compilers. We determine that our notion of quality is defined in terms of two sub-attributes: speed (average KLOC compiled per second) and resource (minimum Kbytes of RAM required). We collect data about each compiler, summarized in Table 2.11.

Using the same sort of analysis as above, we can show that it is not possible to find a measure of this attribute in the real numbers that satisfies the representation condition.

These examples are especially relevant to software engineering. The International Standards Organization has published a standard, ISO 9126, for measuring software quality that explicitly defines software quality as the combination of six distinct sub-attributes. We will discuss the details of this standard in Chapter 9. However, it is important to note here that the standard reflects a widely held view that no single

Table 2.11: Comparing four compilers

	Speed	Resource
A	45	200
B	20	400
C	30	300
D	10	600

real-valued number can characterize such a broad attribute as quality. Instead, we look at n-tuples that characterize a set of n sub-attributes. The same observation can be made for complexity of programs.

EXAMPLE 2.27: Many attempts have been made to define a single, real-valued metric to characterize program complexity. For instance, in Example 2.9, we were introduced to one of the most well-known of these metrics, the cyclomatic number. This number, originally defined by mathematicians on graphs, is the basis of an intuitive notion of program complexity. The number corresponds to an intuitive relation, "more complex than", that allows us to compare program flowgraphs and then make judgments about the programs from which they came. That is, the cyclomatic number is a mapping from the flowgraphs into real numbers, intended to preserve the complexity relation. As we have seen in examining journey quality, if the relation "more complex than" is not a strict weak order, then cyclomatic number cannot be an ordinal-scale measure of complexity. (Indeed, a theorem of measurement theory asserts that a strict weak order is a necessary and sufficient condition for an ordinal scale representation in $\Re$.) We contend that no general notion of complexity can give rise to such an order. To see why, consider the graphs depicted in Figure 2.14. Flowgraph y represents a conditional choice structure, x represents a sequence of two such structures, and z represents a looping construct. Intuitively, it seems reasonable that graph x is more complex than graph y. If "more complex than" produced a strict weak order, we should be able to show that this relation is negatively transitive. That is, we should be able to show that for any z, either x is related to z or z is related to y. But neither of the following statements is obviously true:

$$x \text{ is more complex than } z$$

and

$$z \text{ is more complex than } y$$

Some programmers would argue that x is more complex than z, for instance, while others would say that z is more complex than x; we cannot reach consensus. In other words, some of the graphs are not comparable, so the relation is not a strict weak order and the cyclomatic number cannot be on an ordinal scale. Notice that the cyclomatic number for x is 3, for y is 2, and for z is 2, forcing us to conclude that x should be more complex than z. Thus, the cyclomatic number,

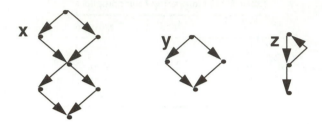

Figure 2.14: Three program flowgraphs

clearly useful in counting the number of linearly independent paths in the program flowgraph, should not be used as a comprehensive measure of complexity.

In spite of theoretical problems, there are many situations when we must combine sub-attributes to impose a strict ranking, and hence an ordinal scale. That is, we need to define a single real-valued number as a measure. For example, if we are buying a coat, we may take into account the price, quality of material, fit, and color. But in the end, we are forced to determine preference. Consciously or subconsciously, we must define some combination of component measures to arrive at a preference ranking.

EXAMPLE 2.28: We want to buy a word-processing program for our home computer. It is likely that the decision will be based on a collection of attributes, such as price, reliability and usability. Since the word processor will be used primarily for letter-writing, we may give price a heavier weighting than reliability when ranking the programs. However, if we are buying a database package for use in a critical air-traffic control system application, it is likely that reliability would get a larger weighting than price.

Other, similar problems can arise. We may need to determine which program is safest, based on a set of criteria. Or we may wish to choose from among a variety of design techniques, based on survey data that captures developer preferences, design quality assessments, and cost of training and tools. Each of these instances presents a problem in making a decision with multiple criteria. There is an extensive literature on multi-criteria decision theory, and the measurement theory that relates to it. We discuss this type of analysis in Chapter 6, when we address data analysis techniques. However, here we must look at how to combine measures in a way that remains true to the spirit of measurement theory.

2.4.4 Indirect measurement and meaningfulness

When we are measuring a complex attribute in terms of simpler sub-attributes, we are measuring indirectly. In doing so, we must adhere to the same basic rules of measurement theory that apply to direct measures. We must pay particular attention to issues of scale types and meaningfulness.

Scale types for indirect measures are similar to those for direct ones. Our concerns include the uniqueness of the representation, as well as the admissible transformations for each scale type. We call an admissible transformation a rescaling, and we define rescaling in the following way. Suppose that we measure each of n sub-attributes with measure M_i. Let M be an indirect measure involving components M_1, M_2, ..., M_n. That is, $M = f(M_1, M_2, ..., M_n)$ for some function f. We say that M' is a **rescaling** of M if there are rescalings M_1', M_2', ..., M_n', of M_1, M_2, ..., M_n respectively, such that $M' = f(M_1', M_2', ..., M_n')$.

Strictly speaking, this defines rescaling in the **wide** sense. Rescaling in the **narrow** sense requires us to verify that $M' = f(M_1, M_2, ..., M_n)$.

EXAMPLE 2.29: Density d is an indirect measure of mass m and volume V. The specific relationship is expressed as

$$d = m/V$$

Every rescaling of d is of the form $d' = \alpha d$ (for $\alpha > 0$). To see why, we must demonstrate two things: that a function of this form is a rescaling, and that every rescaling has this form. For the first part, we have to find rescalings m' and V' of m and V, respectively, such that $\alpha d = m'/V'$. Both m and V are ratio scale measures, so αm and V are acceptable rescalings of m and V respectively. Since

$$\alpha d = \alpha \left(\frac{m}{V} \right) = \frac{\alpha m}{V}$$

therefore we have a rescaling.

To show that every rescaling is of the appropriate form, notice that since m and V are ratio scale measures, every rescaling of m must be of the form $\alpha_1 m$ for some α_1 and every rescaling of V must be of the form $\alpha_2 V$ for some α_2. Therefore, every rescaling of d has the form

$$\frac{\alpha_1 m}{\alpha_2 V} = \frac{\alpha_1}{\alpha_2} \left(\frac{m}{V} \right) = \frac{\alpha_1}{\alpha_2} d = \alpha d \quad \text{(where } \alpha = \frac{\alpha_1}{\alpha_2} \text{)}$$

Now, we can define scale types for indirect scales in exactly the same way as for direct scales. Example 2.29 shows us that the scale for density d is ratio, because all the admissible transformations have the form $d \rightarrow \alpha d$. In the same way, we can show that the scale type for an indirect measure M will generally be no stronger than the weakest of the scale types of the M_is. Thus, if the M_is contain a mixture of ratio, interval, and nominal scale types, then the scale type for M will at best be nominal, since it is weakest.

EXAMPLE 2.30: An indirect measure of testing efficiency T is D/E, where D is the number of defects discovered and E is effort in person months. Here D is an absolute scale measure, while E is on the ratio scale. Since absolute is stronger than ratio scale, it follows that T is a ratio scale measure. Consequently, the acceptable rescalings of T arise from rescalings of E into other measures of effort (person days, person years, etc.).

Many of the measures we have used in our examples are assessment measures. But indirect measures proliferate as prediction measures, too.

EXAMPLE 2.31: In Example 2.11, we saw that many software resource prediction models predict effort E (in person months) by using an equation of the form

$$E = aS^b$$

where S is a measure of software size, and a and b are constants. Some researchers have doubted the meaningfulness of these indirect effort measures. For example, DeMillo and Lipton looked at the Walston and Felix model. Walston and Felix assert that effort can be predicted by the equation

$$E = 5.2S^{0.91}$$

where S is measured in lines of code (Perlis *et al.*, 1981). DeMillo and Lipton contend that the prediction equation is an example of a meaningless measure. They assert that "both E and S are expressed as a ratio scale ... but the measurement is not invariant under the transformation $S \rightarrow \alpha S$ and so is meaningless" (DeMillo and Lipton, 1981). In fact, this argument is relevant only when we consider scales defined in the narrow sense. In the more usual wide sense, it is easy to show that the equation is meaningful and that the scale type for effort is ratio. However, demonstrating scale type and meaningfulness is very different from asserting that the relationship is valid.

Many times, models of effort involve several levels of indirect measurement. That is, an indirect measure is defined to be a combination of other measures, both direct and indirect.

EXAMPLE 2.32: Halstead developed a theory of software physics (discussed in Chapter 3), that defines attributes as combinations of counts of operators and operands. His equation for software effort, E, is

$$E = V/L$$

where V, the program volume, is on a ratio scale, but L, the estimated program level, appears to be only an ordinal scale. Thus, E cannot be a ratio scale. However, Halstead claims that E represents the number of mental discriminations necessary to implement the program, which is necessarily a ratio-scale measure of effort. Therefore, Halstead's effort equation is not meaningful.

The unit in which the measure is expressed can affect the scale of the measure.

EXAMPLE 2.33: Consider another effort measure

$$E = 2.7v + 121w + 26x + 12y + 22z - 497$$

cited by DeMillo and Lipton (DeMillo and Lipton, 1981). E is supposed to represent person months, v is the number of program instructions, and w is a subjective complexity rating. The value of x is the number of internal documents generated on the project, while y is the number of external documents. Finally, z is the size of the program in words. DeMillo and Lipton correctly point out that, as in Example 2.32, effort should be on a ratio scale, but it cannot be ratio in this equation because w, an ordinal measure, restricts E to being ordinal. Thus, the equation is meaningless. However, E could still be an ordinal-scale measure of effort if we drop the pre-condition that E expresses effort in person months.

In this chapter, we have laid a foundation of principles on which to base valid measurement. The next chapter builds on this foundation by introducing a framework for how to choose measures, based on needs and process.

2.5 Summary

Measurement requires us to identify intuitively understood attributes possessed by clearly defined entities. Then, we assign numbers or symbols to the entities in a way that captures our intuitive understanding about the attribute. Thus, direct measurement of a particular attribute must be preceded by intuitive understanding of that attribute. This intuitive understanding leads to the identification of relations between entities. For example, the attribute height for the entity person gives rise to relations like "is tall", "taller than", and "much taller than".

To measure the attribute, we define corresponding relations in some number system; then measurement assigns numbers to the entities in such a way that these relations are preserved. This relationship between the domain and range relationships is called the **representation condition**.

In general, there may be many ways of assigning numbers that satisfy the representation condition. The nature of different assignments determines the scale type for the attribute. There are five well-known scale types: nominal, ordinal, interval, ratio and absolute. The scale type for a measure determines what kind of statements we can meaningfully make using the measure. In particular, the scale type tells us what kind of operations we can perform. For example, we can compute means for ratio-scale measures, but not for ordinal measures; we can compute medians for ordinal-scale measures but not for nominal-scale measures.

Many attributes of interest in software engineering are not directly measurable. This situation forces us to use vectors of measures, with rules for combining the vector elements into a larger, indirect measure. We define scale types for these in a similar way to direct measures, and hence can determine when statements and operations are meaningful.

In the next chapter, we build on this foundation to examine a framework for measurement that helps us to select appropriate measures to meet our needs.

2.6 EXERCISES

1   At the beginning of the chapter, we posed four questions:

   • How much must we know about an attribute before it is reasonable to consider measuring it? For instance, do we know enough about "complexity" of programs to be able to measure it?
   • How do we know if we have really measured the attribute we wanted to measure? For instance, does a count of the number of "bugs" found in a system during integration testing measure the quality of the system? If not, what does the count tell us?
   • Using measurement, what meaningful statements can we make about an attribute and the entities that possess it? For instance, is it meaningful to talk about doubling a design's quality? If not, how do we compare two different designs?
   • What meaningful operations can we perform on measures? For instance, is it sensible to compute average productivity for a group of developers, or the average quality of a set of modules?

   Based on what you have learned in this chapter, answer these questions.

2   i. List, in increasing order of sophistication, the five most important-measurement scale types.
   ii. Suppose that the attribute "complexity" of software modules is ranked as a whole number between 1 and 5, where 1 means "trivial," 2 "simple," 3 "moderate," 4 "complex," and 5 "incomprehensible." What is the scale type for this definition of complexity? How do you know? With this measure, how could you meaningfully measure the *average* of a set of modules?

3   We commonly use ordinal measurement scales. For example, we can use an ordinal scale to rank the understandability of programs as either trivial, simple, moderate, complex or incomprehensible. For each of two other common measurement scale types, give an example of a useful software measure of that type. State exactly which software entity is being measured and which attribute. State whether the entity is a product, process, or resource.

4   Define measurement, and briefly summarize the representation condition for measurement.

5   For the empirical and numerical relation system of Example 2.5, determine which of the following numerical assignments satisfy the representation condition:

i.   M(Wonderman) = 100; M(Frankie) = 90; M(Peter) = 60
ii. M(Wonderman) = 100; M(Frankie) = 120; M(Peter) = 60
iii. M(Wonderman) = 100; M(Frankie) = 120; M(Peter) = 50
iv. M(Wonderman) = 68; M(Frankie) = 75; M(Peter) = 40

6 For the relation systems in Example 2.6, determine which of the following mappings are representations. Explain your answers in terms of the representation condition.

i.   M(each delayed response) = 6; M(each incorrect output) = 6; M(each data-loss) = 69
ii. M(each delayed response) = 1; M(each incorrect output) = 2; M(each data-loss) = 3
iii. M(each delayed response) = 6; M(each incorrect output) = 3; M(each data-loss) = 2
iv. M(each delayed response) = 0; M(each incorrect output) = 1; M(each data-loss) = 0.5

7 Suppose that we could classify every software failure as either a) syntactic, b) semantic, or c) system crash. Suppose additionally that we agree that every system crash failure is more critical than every semantic failure, which in turn is more critical than every syntactic failure. Use this information to define two different measures of the attribute of criticality of software failures. How are these measures related? What is the scale of each?

8 Explain why you would not conclude that the quality of program X was twice as great as program Y if integration testing revealed program X to have twice as many faults per KLOC than program Y.

9 Explain why it is wrong to assert that lines of code is a bad software measure.

10 Explain why neither M_4 nor M_5 is a valid mapping in Example 2.16.

11 In Example 2.18, determine the affine transformations from:

i. M_1 to M_2
ii. M_2 to M_1
iii. M_2 to M_3
iv. M_3 to M_2
v. M_1 to M_3

12 Explain why duration of processes is measurable on a ratio scale. Give some example measures and the admissable transformations that relate them.

13 Determine which of the following statements are meaningful:

i.   The length of Program A is 50.
ii. The length of Program A is 50 executable statements.
iii. Program A took 3 months to write.
iv. Program A is twice as long as Program B.

v.   Program A is 50 lines longer than Program B.

vi. The cost of maintaining program A is twice that of maintaining Program B.

vii. Program B is twice as maintainable as Program A.

viii. Program A is more complex than Program B.

14 Formally, what do we mean when we say that a statement about measurement is meaningful? Discuss the meaningfulness of the following statements:

- "The average size of a Windows application program is about four times that of a similar DOS program."
- "Of the two Ada program analysis tools recommended in the Ada coding standard, tool A achieved a higher average usability rating than tool B." For this example, program usability was rated on a four-point scale:

4: can be used by a non-programmer

3: requires some knowledge of Ada

2: usable only by someone with at least five years' Ada programming experience

1: totally unusable

15 Show that the mean can be used as a measure of central tendency for interval-scale data.

16 Show that, for nominal-scale measures, the median is not a meaningful notion of average, but the mode (that is, the most commonly occurring class of item) is meaningful.

17 Suppose that "complexity" of individual software modules is ranked (according to some specific criteria) as one of the following:

{trivial, simple, moderate, complex, very complex, incomprehensible}

Let M be any measure (in the representation sense) for this notion of complexity, and let S be a set of modules for each of which M has been computed.

i.   You want to indicate the average complexity of the modules in S. How would you do this in a meaningful way? (Briefly explain your choice.)

ii. Explain why it is not meaningful to compute the mean of the Ms. (You should construct a statement involving means that you can prove is not meaningful.)

iii. Give two examples of criteria that might be used to enable an assessor objectively to determine which of the complexity values a given module should be.

State carefully any assumptions you are making.

18 Example 2.26 defines a quality attribute for compilers. Draw a diagram to illustrate the empirical relation of quality. Explain why it is not possible to find a measure for this attribute in the set of real numbers that satisfies the representation condition. Define a measurement mapping into an alternative number system that does satisfy the representation condition.

19 A commonly used indirect measure of programmer productivity P is $P = L/E$, where L is the number of lines of code produced and E is effort in person months. Show that every rescaling of P is of the form $P' = \alpha P$ (for $\alpha > 0$).

20 Show that the Walston–Felix effort equation in Example 2.31 defines a ratio-scale measure.

21 Construct a representation for the relations "greater functionality" and "greater user-friendliness" characterized by Table 2.1.

22 Consider the attribute, "number of bugs found," for software-testing processes. Define an absolute-scale measure for this attribute. Why is "number of bugs found" not an absolute scale measure of the attribute of program correctness?

2.7 FURTHER READING

There is no elementary text book as such on measurement theory. The most readable book on the representational theory of measurement is:

Roberts, F.S., *Measurement Theory with Applications to Decision Making, Utility, and the Social Sciences*, Addison-Wesley, Reading, MA, 1979.

A more formal mathematical treatment of the representational theory of measurement (only for the mathematically gifted) is

Krantz, D.H., Luce, R.D., Suppes, P. and Tversky, A., *Foundations of Measurement*, Volume 1, Academic Press, New York, 1971.

A very good introduction to measurement using non-scientific examples, including attributes like religiosity and aspects of political ideology, may be found in:

Finkelstein, L., "What is not measurable, make measurable," *Measurement and Control*, 15, pp. 25–32, 1982.

Detailed discussions of alternative definitions of meaningfulness in measurement may be found in:

Falmagne, J.-C. and Narens, L., "Scales and meaningfulness of quantitative laws," *Synthese*, 55, pp. 287–325, 1983.

Roberts, F.S., "Applications of the theory of meaningfulness to psychology," *Journal of Mathematical Psychology*, 29, pp. 311–32, 1985.

The origin of the definition of the hierarchy of measurement scale types (nominal, ordinal, interval, and ratio) is the classic paper:

Stevens, S.S., "On the theory of scale types and measurement," *Science*, 103, pp. 677–80, 1946.

A criticism of this basic approach appears in:

Velleman, P.F. and Wilkinson, L., "Nominal, ordinal, interval and ratio typologies are misleading," *The American Statistician*, 47(1), pp. 65–72, February 1993.

Other relevant texts are:

Belton, V., "A comparison of the analytic hierarchy process and a simple multi-attribute utility function," *European Journal of Operational Research*, 26, pp. 7–21, 1986.

Finkelstein, L., "A review of the fundamental concepts of measurement," *Measurement*, 2(1), pp. 25–34, 1984.

Finkelstein, L., "Representation by symbol systems as an extension of the concept of measurement," *Kybernetes*, Volume 4, pp. 215–23, 1975.

Sydenham, P.H. (ed.), *Handbook of Measurement Science*, Volume 1, Wiley, New York, 1982.

Campbell, N.R., *Physics: The Elements*, Cambridge University Press, Cambridge, MA, 1920. Reprinted as *Foundations of Science: The Philosophy of Theory and Experiment*, Dover, New York, 1957.

Ellis, B., *Basic Concepts of Measurement*, Cambridge University Press, 1966.

Kyburg, H.E., *Theory and Measurement*, Cambridge University Press, 1984.

Vincke, P., *Multicriteria Decision Aids*, Wiley, New York, 1992.

Zuse, H., *Software Complexity: Measures and Methods*, De Gruyter, Berlin, 1991.

3 A goal-based framework for software measurement

Chapter 1 described measurement's essential role in good software engineering practice, and Chapter 2 explained a general theory of measurement. In this chapter, we return to software engineering, presenting a conceptual framework for the diverse software-measurement activities that contribute to your organization's software practices. These practices may include not only your usual development and maintenance activities, but also any experiments and case studies you may perform as you investigate new techniques and tools.

The framework presented here is based on three principles: classifying the entities to be examined, determining relevant measurement goals, and identifying the level of maturity that your organization has reached. The first section explores the classification of measures as process, product or resource, and whether the attribute is internal or external. The next section presents the Goal–Question–Metric (GQM) paradigm to tie measurement to the overall goals of the project and process. Then, we show how process maturity and GQM can work hand-in-hand to suggest a rich set of measurements as we measure what is visible in the process. We also look at measurement validation: the process of ensuring that we are measuring what we say we are, so that we satisfy the representation condition introduced in Chapter 2. Finally, we review the major activities of software measurement to see how they relate to the framework presented.

3.1 CLASSIFYING SOFTWARE MEASURES

As we have seen in Chapter 2, the first obligation of any software-measurement activity is identifying the entities and attributes we wish to measure. In software, there are three such classes:

- **Processes** are collections of software-related activities.
- **Products** are any artifacts, deliverables or documents that result from a process activity.
- **Resources** are entities required by a process activity.

A process is usually associated with some timescale. That is, the activities in the process are ordered or related in some way that depends on time, so that one activity must be completed before another can begin. The timing can be explicit, as when design must be complete by October 31, or implicit, as when a flow diagram shows that design must be completed before coding can begin.

Resources and products are associated with the process. Each process activity has resources and products that it uses, as well as products that are produced. Thus, the product of one activity may feed another activity. For example, a design document can be the product of the design activity which is then used as input for the coding activity.

Many of the examples that we use in this book relate to the development process or the maintenance process. But the concepts that we introduce apply to any process: the reuse process, the configuration management process, the testing process, and so on. In other words, measurement activities may focus on any process and need not be concerned only with the comprehensive development process. As we shall see later in this chapter, our choice of measurements depends on our measurement goals.

Within each class of entity, we distinguish between internal and external attributes:

- **Internal attributes** of a product, process or resource are those that can be measured purely in terms of the product, process or resource itself. In other words, an internal attribute can be measured by examining the product, process or resource on its own, separate from its behavior.
- **External attributes** of a product, process or resource are those that can be measured only with respect to how the product, process or resource relates to its environment. Here, the behavior of the process, product or resource is important, rather than the entity itself.

To understand the difference between internal and external attributes, consider a set of software modules. Without actually executing the code, we can determine several important internal attributes: its size (perhaps in terms of lines of code or number of operands), its complexity (perhaps in terms of the number of decision points in the code), and the dependencies among modules. We may even find faults in the code as we read it: misplaced commas, improper use of a command, or failure to consider a particular case. However, there are other attributes of the code that can be measured only when the code is executed: for instance, the number of failures experienced by the user, the difficulty that the user has in navigating among the screens provided, or the length of time it takes to search the database and retrieve requested information. It is easy to see that these attributes depend on the behavior of the code, making them external attributes rather than internal. Table 3.1 provides additional examples of types of entities and attributes.

Managers often want to be able to measure and predict external attributes. For example, the cost-effectiveness of an activity (such as design inspections) or the productivity of the staff can be very useful in ensuring that the quality stays high while the price stays low. Users are also interested in external attributes, since the behavior of the system affects them directly; the system's reliability, usability and portability affect maintenance and purchase decisions. However, external attributes are usually more difficult to measure than internal ones, and they are measured quite late in the development process. For example, reliability can be measured only after development is complete and the system is ready for use.

Moreover, it is sometimes difficult to define the attributes in measurable ways with which everyone agrees. For example, we all want to build and purchase systems of high quality. But we do not always agree on what we mean by quality, and it is often difficult to measure quality in a comprehensive way. Thus, we tend to define these high-level attributes in terms of other, more concrete attributes that are well-defined and measurable. The McCall model introduced in Chapter 1 is a good example of this phenomenon, where software quality is defined as a composite of a large number of narrower, more easily measurable terms.

In many cases, developers and users focus their efforts on only one facet of a broad attribute. For example, some measure quality, an external product attribute, as the number of faults found during formal testing, an internal process attribute. By using internals to make judgments about externals, we can come to misleading conclusions. But there is a clear need for internal attribute measurements to support measurement and decision making about external attributes. One of the goals of software-measurement research is to identify the relationships among internal and external attributes, as well as to find new and useful methods for measuring directly the attributes of interest.

3.1.1 Processes

We often have questions about our software-development activities and processes that measurement can help us to answer. We want to know how long it takes for a process to complete, how much it will cost, whether it is effective or efficient, and how it compares with other processes that we could have chosen, for example. However, only a limited number of internal process attributes can be measured directly. These measures include:

Table 3.1: Components of software measurement

ENTITIES	ATTRIBUTES	
Products	*Internal*	*External*
Specifications	size, reuse, modularity, redundancy, functionality, syntactic correctness, ...	comprehensibility, maintainability, ...
Designs	size, reuse, modularity, coupling, cohesiveness, functionality, ...	quality, complexity, maintainability, ...
Code	size, reuse, modularity, coupling, functionality, algorithmic complexity, control-flow structuredness, ...	reliability, usability, maintainability, ...
Test data	size, coverage level, ...	quality, ...
...	...	...
Processes		
Constructing specification	time, effort, number of requirements changes, ...	quality, cost, stability, ...
Detailed design	time, effort, number of specification faults found, ...	cost, cost-effectiveness,
...		
Testing	time, effort, number of coding faults found, ...	cost, cost-effectiveness, stability, ...
...	...	...
Resources		
Personnel	age, price, ...	productivity, experience, intelligence, ...
Teams	size, communication level, structuredness, ...	productivity, quality, ...
Software	price, size, ...	usability, reliability, ...
Hardware	price, speed, memory size, ...	reliability, ...
Offices	size, temperature, light, ...	comfort, quality, ...
...	...	...

- the duration of the process or one of its activities;
- the effort associated with the process or one of its activities;
- the number of incidents of a specified type arising during the process or one of its activities.

For example, we may be reviewing our requirements to ensure their quality before turning them over to the designers. To measure the effectiveness of the review process, we can measure the number of requirements errors found during specification. Likewise, we can measure the number of faults found during integration testing to determine how well we are doing. And the number of personnel working on the project between May 1 and September 30 can give us insight into the resources needed for the development process.

Many of these measures can be used in combination with other measures to gain a better understanding of what is happening on a project:

EXAMPLE 3.1: During formal testing, we can use the indirect measure

$$\frac{\text{cost}}{\text{number of errors found}}$$

as a measure of the average cost of each error found during the process.

EXAMPLE 3.2: AT&T developers wanted to know the effectiveness of their software inspections. In particular, managers needed to evaluate the cost of the inspections against the benefits received. To do this, they measured the average amount of effort expended per thousand lines of code reviewed. As we will see later in this chapter, this information, combined with measures of the number of faults discovered during the inspections, allowed the managers to perform a cost–benefit analysis.

In some cases, we may want to measure properties of a process which itself consists of a number of distinct processes:

EXAMPLE 3.3: The testing process may be composed of unit testing, integration testing, system testing, and acceptance testing. Each component process can be measured to determine how effectively it contributes to overall testing effectiveness. We can track the number of errors identified in each subprocess, along with the duration and cost of identifying each error, to see if each subprocess is cost-effective.

Cost is not the only process measure we can examine. Controllability, observability and stability are also important in managing a large project. These attributes are clearly external ones. For example, stability of the design process can depend on the particular period of time, as well as on the choice of designers. Attributes such as these may not yet be sufficiently well-understood to enable objective measurement according to the principles described in Chapter 2, so they are often indicated by subjective ratings. However, the subjective or ill-defined observations may form the basis for the empirical relations required for subsequent objective measurement.

We often propose objective measures of external attributes in terms of internal attributes. For example, measures of the effectiveness of code maintenance can be defined in terms of the number of faults discovered and the number of faults corrected. In the AT&T study of Example 3.2, inspection effectiveness was defined as average faults detected per thousand lines of code inspected. In each case, we examine the process of interest and decide what kind of information would help us to understand, control or improve the process. We will investigate process attributes in Chapter 12.

3.1.2 Products

Products are not restricted to the items that management is committed to deliver to the customer. Any artifact or document produced during the software life cycle can be measured and assessed. For example, developers often build prototypes for examination only, so that they can understand requirements or evaluate possible designs; these prototypes may be measured in some way. Likewise, test harnesses that are constructed to assist in system testing may be measured; system size measurements should include this software if they are to be used to determine team productivity. And documents, such as the user guide or the customer specification document, can be measured for size, quality, and more.

3.1.2.1 External product attributes

There are many examples of external product attributes. Since an external product attribute depends on both product behavior and environment, each attribute measure should take these characteristics into account. For example, if we are interested in measuring the reliability of code, we must consider the machine on which the program is run as well as the mode of operational usage. That is, someone who uses a word-processing package only to type letters may find its reliability to be different from someone who uses the same package to merge tables and link to spreadsheets. Similarly, the understandability of a document depends on the experience and credentials of the person reading it; a nuclear engineer reading the specification for power-plant software is likely to rate its understandability higher than a mathematician reading the same document. Or the maintainability of a system may depend on the skills of the maintainers and the tools available to them.

Usability, integrity, efficiency, testability, reusability, portability and inter-operability are other external attributes that we can measure. These attributes describe not only the code but also the other documents that support the development effort. Indeed, the maintainability, reusability and even testability of specifications and designs are as important as the code itself.

3.1.2.2 Internal product attributes

Internal product attributes are sometimes easy to measure. We can determine the size of a product by measuring the number of pages it fills or the number of words it contains, for example. Since the products are concrete, we have a better understanding of attributes like size, effort, and cost. Other internal product attributes are more difficult to measure, because opinions differ as to what they mean and how to measure them. For example, there are many aspects of code complexity, and no consensus about what best measures it. We will explore this issue in Chapter 8.

Because products are relatively easy to examine in an automated fashion, there is a set of commonly used internal attributes. For instance, specifications can be assessed in terms of their length, functionality, modularity, reuse, redundancy, and syntactic correctness. Formal designs and code can be measured in the same way; we can also measure attributes such as structuredness (of control and data flow, for example) as well as module coupling and cohesiveness.

Users sometimes dismiss many of these internal attributes as unimportant, since a user is interested primarily in the ultimate functionality, quality, and utility of the software. However, the internal attributes can be very helpful in suggesting what we are likely to find as the external attributes.

> **EXAMPLE 3.4:**   Consider a software purchase to be similar to buying an automobile. If we want to evaluate a used car, we can perform dynamic testing by actually driving the car in various conditions in order to assess external attributes such as performance and reliability. But usually we cannot make a complete dynamic assessment before we make a purchase decision, because not every type of driving condition is available (such as snowy or slick roads). Instead, we supplement our limited view of the car's performance with measures of static properties (that is, internal attributes) such as water level, oil type and level, brake fluid type and level, tire tread and wear pattern, brake wear, shock type response, fan belt flexibility and wear, and so on. These internal attributes provide insight into the likely external attributes; for example, uneven tire wear may indicate that the tires have been under-inflated, and the owner may have abused the car by not performing necessary maintenance. Indeed, when a car is serviced, the mechanic measures only internal attributes and makes adjustments accordingly; the car is not always driven for any length of time to verify the conditions indicated by the internal attributes. In the same way, measures of internal software product attributes can tell us what the software's performance and reliability may be. Changes to the inspection process, for instance, may be based on measures of faults found, even though the ultimate goal of reliability is based on failures, not faults.

Just as processes may be comprised of subprocesses, there are products that are collections of subproducts.

> **EXAMPLE 3.5:**   A software system design document may consist of a large number of module design documents. Average module size, an attribute of the system design, can be derived by calculating the size of each module. For example, suppose the designs are represented by data-flow diagrams. We can measure size by the number of bubbles in each diagram, and then calculate the comprehensive measure according to Table 3.2.

3.1.2.3   The importance of internal attributes

Many software-engineering methods proposed and developed in the last 25 years provide rules, tools, and heuristics for producing software products. Almost invariably, these methods give structure to the products; it is claimed that this structure makes them easier to understand, analyze, and test. The structure involves two aspects of development:

Table 3.2: Definition of example design measurements

Entity	Entity Type	Attribute	Proposed Measure	Type
Module design document D_i	Product	Size	Number_of_bubbles$_i$	Direct
System design document $\{D_1, \ldots, D_n\}$	Product	Average module size	$1/n \sum_{i=1}^{n}$ Number_of_bubbles$_i$	Indirect

- the development process, since certain products need to be produced at certain stages, and
- the products themselves, since the products must conform to certain structural principles.

In particular, product structure is usually characterized by levels of internal attributes such as modularity, coupling, or cohesiveness.

EXAMPLE 3.6: One of the most widely respected books in software engineering is Brooks' *Mythical Man-Month* (Brooks, 1975). There, Brooks describes the virtues of top-down design:

> A good top-down design avoids bugs in several ways. First, the clarity of structure and representation makes the precise statement of requirements and functions of the modules easier. Second, the partitioning and independence of modules avoids system bugs. Third, the suppression of detail makes flaws in the structure more apparent. Fourth, the design can be tested at each of its refinement steps, so testing can start earlier and focus on the proper level of detail at each step.

> Similarly, the notion of high module cohesion and low module coupling is the rationale for most structured design methods (Yourdon and Constantine, 1979). Designs that possess these attributes are assumed to lead to more reliable and maintainable code.

Brooks and Yourdon assume what most other software engineers assume: that good internal structure leads to good external quality. Although intuitively appealing, the connection between internal attribute values and the resulting external attribute values has rarely been established, in part because (as we shall see in Chapters 4 and 15) it is sometimes difficult to perform controlled experiments and confirm relationships between attributes. At the same time, there is little understanding of measurement validation and the proper ways to demonstrate these relationships. Software measurement can help us to understand and confirm relationships empirically; a key to the success of this analysis is the ability to provide accurate and meaningful measures of internal product attributes.

3.1.2.4 Internal attributes and quality control and assurance

A major reason that developers want to use internal attributes to predict external ones is the need to monitor and control the products during development. For example, knowing the relationship between internal design attributes and failures, we want to be able to identify modules at the design stage whose profile, in terms of measures of internal attributes, shows that they are likely to be error-prone or difficult to maintain or test later on. Figure 3.1 shows an irreverent view of this process.

3.1.2.5 Validating composite measures

"Quality" is frequently used by software engineers to describe an internal attribute of design or code. However, "quality" is multi-dimensional; it does not reflect a single aspect of a particular product.

> **EXAMPLE 3.7:** Consider the "gross national product" (GNP), a measure of all the goods and services produced by a country in a given time period. Economists look at the trend in GNP over time, hoping that it will rise – that the country is becoming more productive. The GNP is a weighted combination of the values of key goods and services produced; the weights reflect the priorities and opinions of the economists defining the measure. The value of individual goods and services can be measured directly, but the GNP itself is an indirect measure.

In the same way that economists want to control the economy and make a country more productive, we want to measure and control the quality of our products, and we usually do so by measuring and controlling a number of internal (structural) product

Figure 3.1: Using internal measures for quality control and assurance

attributes. Without articulating the specific attributes that contribute to the general notion of quality, many people assume that the various cognitive and structural notions of complexity, maintainability, and usability can be captured by a single number, much like GNP. This number should therefore be a powerful indicator of all the attributes which one normally associates with high-quality systems, such as high reliability and high maintainability.

However, this approach ignores the question of whether the component internal attributes are a complete and accurate depiction of the comprehensive one, and whether the weighting is appropriate. Just as economists question whether GNP is valid (does it capture values like beauty and environmental quality?), we must question the validity of measures that paint what may be a partial picture of the attribute of interest. In later chapters, we shall give scrutiny to conventional approaches to measuring size, quality, complexity, and more.

3.1.3   Resources

The resources that we are likely to measure include any input for software production. Thus, *personnel* (individual or teams), *materials* (including office supplies), tools (both software and hardware) and *methods* are candidates for measurement. We measure resources to determine their magnitude (how many staff are working on this project?), their cost (how much are we paying for testing tools?), and their quality (how experienced are our designers?) These measures help us to understand and control the process by telling us how the process is using and changing inputs to outputs. For example, if we are producing poor-quality software, resource measurements may show us that the software quality is the result of using too few people or people with the wrong skills.

Cost is often measured across all types of resources, so that managers can see how the cost of the inputs affects the cost of the outputs. For instance, the division chief may want to know if a large investment in CASE tools is yielding benefits in terms of more productive staff or better quality products. Cost is often defined in terms of its components, so that managers can see which aspects of cost are having the biggest effect.

Productivity is always important, and managers are keen not only to measure it but also to understand how to improve it. Although a measure of staff, productivity is an external resource attribute, since it depends on the underlying development process. That is, a productive worker using one process may become less productive if the process changes. Productivity is usually measured as some form of:

$$\frac{\text{amount of output}}{\text{effort input}}$$

Notice that this resource measure combines a process measure (input) with a product measure (output). The general notion is an economic one, where businesses or markets are judged by comparing what goes in with what comes out. For software development, the measure of output is usually computed as the number of lines of code produced as the final product, while the input measure is the number of person months used to specify, design, code, and test the software. However, the economic analogy is incomplete for software, since the amount of software output is not related to the input in the same way as that in manufacturing. That is, most manufacturing processes involve replication, so that one car is much like another coming off the assembly line. But software development is a creation, not a replication, process, and the relationship between inputs and profits is defined differently. We will explore these ideas in more depth in Chapter 12.

There are many other staff attributes that we can measure, whose values may have an influence on the process or product. For example, the experience, age, or intelligence of a developer may affect the quality of the design or code. Similarly, the size, structure, and communication patterns of the development team are important.

We can also classify and analyze tools and methods. Languages are block-structured or not, object-oriented or not, and so on. Techniques can be rated as manual or automated, and tools can require special training or experience. These attributes of resources help us to understand how to use tools and methods in more effective ways.

No developer has the time to measure and analyze everything. It is important to focus measurement activities on those areas needing the most visibility, understanding, and improvement. In the next section, we present a technique for determining which attributes to measure first.

3.2   DETERMINING WHAT TO MEASURE

Utility is in the eye of the beholder. In other words, a particular measurement is useful only if it helps you to understand the underlying process or one of its resultant products. In turn, recognizing improvement of the process and products can occur only when the project has clearly defined goals for process and products. That is, you cannot tell if you are going in the right direction until you know where you want to go. The Goal–Question–Metric approach (GQM) to process and metrics, first suggested by Basili and his colleagues, has proven to be a particularly effective approach to selecting and implementing metrics (Basili and Weiss, 1984; Basili and Rombach, 1988). To use GQM, you express the overall goals of your organization. Your organization can encompass the entire corporation for which you work, or only the quality assurance group to which you are assigned; the scope of the metrics and goals is up to you and your needs. Then, you generate questions whose answers you must know in order to determine if your goals are being met. Finally, you analyze each question in terms of what measurements you need in order to answer to each question.

Once you have a list of possible measures, you must assess your organization to see whether it is capable of providing useful information for the measurement. For example, if your developers cannot tell when design ends and coding begins, then measuring the duration of the design activity will be impossible. To help you understand when measurement is appropriate for your organization, we introduce the notion of process maturity. The more mature your process, the more that is visible and therefore measurable. This section explains how an understanding of goals can be used to generate suggested metrics for a given project in the context of a process maturity framework.

3.2.1   The Goal–Question–Metric paradigm

Many metrics programs begin by measuring what is convenient or easy to measure, rather than by measuring what is needed. Such programs often fail because the resulting data are not useful to the developers and maintainers of the software. A measurement program can be more successful if it is designed with the goals of the project in mind. The GQM approach provides a framework involving three steps:

1. List the major goals of the development or maintenance project.
2. Derive from each goal the questions that must be answered to determine if the goals are being met.
3. Decide what must be measured in order to be able to answer the questions adequately.

By deriving the measurements in this way, it becomes clear how to use the resulting data. As an example, Figure 3.2 illustrates how several metrics might be generated from a single goal.

Suppose your overall goal is to evaluate the effectiveness of using a coding standard, as shown in Figure 3.2. That is, you want to know if code produced by following the standard is superior in some way to code produced without it. To decide if the standard is effective, you must ask several key questions. First, it is important to know who is using the standard, so that you can compare the productivity of the coders who use the standard with the productivity of those who do not. Likewise, you probably want to compare the quality of the code produced with the standard with the quality of non-standard code.

Once these questions are identified, you must analyze each question to determine what must be measured in order to answer the question. For example, to understand who is using the standard, it is necessary to know what proportion of coders is using the standard. However, it is also important to have an experience profile of the coders, explaining how long they have worked with the standard, the environment, the language, and other factors that will help to evaluate the effectiveness of the standard. The productivity question requires a definition of productivity, which is usually some measure of effort divided by some measure of product size. As shown in the figure, the metric can be in terms of lines of code, function points, or any other metric that will be useful to you. Similarly, quality may be measured in terms of the number of errors found in the code, plus any other quality measures that you would like to use.

In this way, you generate only those measures that are related to the goal. Notice

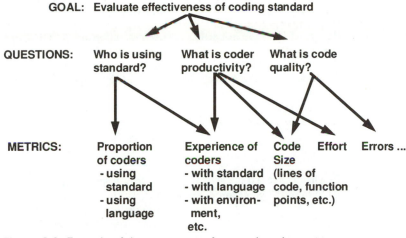

Figure 3.2: Example of deriving metrics from goals and questions

that, in many cases, several measurements may be needed to answer a single question. Likewise, a single measurement may apply to more than one question. The goal provides the purpose for collecting the data, and the questions tell you and your project how to use the data.

EXAMPLE 3.8: AT&T used GQM to help determine which metrics were appropriate for assessing their inspection process (Barnard and Price, 1994). Their goals, with the questions and metrics derived, are shown in Table 3.3.

What is not evident from the GQM tree or table is the model needed to combine the measurements in a sensible way so that the questions can be answered. For example, the tree in Figure 3.2 suggests measuring coder productivity; this attribute may be measured in terms of effort per line of code, but that relationship is not explicit in the tree. Thus, the GQM approach must be supplemented by one or more models that express the relationships among the metrics.

EXAMPLE 3.9: Once AT&T researchers and developers generated the list of metrics in Table 3.3, they specified metrics equations and the data items that describe what the metrics really mean. For instance, the average preparation rate is a function of the total number of lines of code inspected, the preparation time for each inspection, and the number of inspectors. A model of the metric expresses the average preparation rate as an equation. First, the preparation time for each inspection is divided by the number of inspectors; then, the sum over all inspections is calculated and used to normalize the total number of lines of code.

Table 3.3: Examples of AT&T goals, questions and metrics (Barnard and Price, 1994)

Goal	Questions	Metrics
Plan	How much does the inspection process cost?	Average effort per KLOC Percentage of reinspections
	How much calendar time does the inspection process take?	Average effort per KLOC Total KLOC inspected
Monitor and control	What is the quality of the inspected software?	Average faults detected per KLOC Average inspection rate Average preparation rate
	To what degree did the staff conform to the procedures?	Average inspection rate Average preparation rate Average lines of code inspected Percentage of reinspections
	What is the status of the inspection process?	Total KLOC inspected
Improve	How effective is the inspection process?	Defect removal efficiency Average faults detected per KLOC Average inspection rate Average preparation rate Average lines of code inspected
	What is the productivity of the inspection process?	Average effort per fault detected Average inspection rate Average preparation rate Average lines of code inspected

Even when the metrics are expressed as an equation or relationship, the definition is not always clear and unambiguous. The tree does not tell you how to measure a line of code or a function point, only that some measure of code size is needed to answer a question about productivity. Additional work is needed to define each metric. In cases where no objective measure is available, subjective measures must be identified.

In general, typical goals are expressed in terms of productivity, quality, risk, customer satisfaction, and the like, coupled with verbs expressing the need to assess, evaluate, improve, or understand. It is important that the goals and questions be understood in terms of their audience: a productivity goal for a project manager may be different from that for a department manager or corporate director. To aid in generating the goals, questions, and metrics, Basili and Rombach provided a series of templates:

Templates for goal definition

- **Purpose:** To (characterize, evaluate, predict, motivate, etc.) the (process, product, model, metric, etc.) in order to (understand, assess, manage, engineer, learn, improve, etc.) it.

  Example: To *evaluate* the *maintenance process* in order to *improve* it.

- **Perspective:** Examine the (cost, effectiveness, correctness, defects, changes, product measures, etc.) from the viewpoint of the (developer, manager, customer, etc.)

  Example: Examine the *cost* from the viewpoint of the *manager*.

- **Environment:** The environment consists of the following: process factors, people factors, problem factors, methods, tools, constraints, etc.

  Example: The maintenance staff are poorly motivated programmers who have limited access to tools.

Basili and Rombach also provide separate guidelines for defining product-related questions and process-related questions. Steps involve defining the process or product, defining the relevant attributes, and obtaining feedback related to the attributes. What constitutes a goal or question may be vague, and several levels of refinement may be required for certain goals and questions; that is, a goal may first have to be related to a series of subgoals before questions can be derived.

We can relate the GQM templates to the attribute framework introduced earlier in this chapter. A goal or question can be associated with at least one pair of entities and attributes. Thus, a goal is stated, leading to a question that should be answered so that we can tell if we have met our goal; the answer to the question requires that we measure some attribute of an entity (and possibly several attributes of an entity, or several attributes of several entities). The use of the measure is determined by the goals and questions, so that assessment, prediction, and motivation are tightly linked to the data analysis and reporting.

Thus, GQM complements the entity–attribute measurement framework. The results of a GQM analysis are a collection of measurements related by goal tree and overall model. However, GQM does not address issues of measurement scale, objectivity, or feasibility. So the GQM measures should be used with care, remembering the overall goal of providing useful data that can help to improve our processes, products and resources.

3.2.2 *Measurement and process improvement*

Measurement offers visibility into the ways in which the processes, products, resources, methods, and technologies of software development relate to one another. As we have seen, measurements can help us to answer questions about the effectiveness of techniques or tools, the productivity of development activities (such as testing or configuration management), the quality of products, and more. In addition, measurement allows us to define a baseline for understanding the nature and impact of proposed changes. Finally, measurement allows managers and developers to monitor the effects of activities and changes on all aspects of development, so that action can be taken as early as possible to control the final outcome should actual measurements differ significantly from plans. Thus, measurement is useful for:

- understanding
- establishing a baseline
- assessing and predicting

We have seen how these goals can be interpreted using GQM. But measurement is useful only in the larger context of assessment and improvement. Choosing metrics, collecting data, analyzing the results and taking appropriate action require time and resources; these activities make sense only if they are directed at specific improvement goals.

Some development processes are more mature than others, as noted by the Software Engineering Institute's (SEI's) reports on process maturity and capability maturity (Humphrey, 1989; Paulk, 1991). While some organizations have clearly-defined processes, others are more variable, changing significantly with the people who work on the projects. The SEI has suggested that there are five levels of process maturity, ranging from *ad hoc* (the least predictable and controllable) to *repeatable*, *defined*, *managed*, and *optimizing* (the most predictable and controllable); this notion is illustrated in Figure 3.3.

The SEI distinguishes one level from another in terms of key process activities going on at each level. This and other assessment schemes will be discussed in detail in Chapter 14, where we see how measurement supports a variety of improvement models (such as ISO 9000, SPICE and Bootstrap).

But all of these models share a common goal and approach, namely that they use process visibility as a key discriminator among a set of "maturity levels." That is, the more visibility into the overall development process, the higher the maturity and the better managers and developers can understand and control their development and maintenance activities. At the lowest levels of maturity, the process is not well understood at all; as maturity increases, the process is better-understood and better-defined. At each maturity level, measurement and visibility are closely related: a developer can measure only what is visible in the process, and measurement helps to increase visibility. Thus, the five-level maturity scale such as the one employed by the SEI is a convenient context for determining what to measure first and how to plan a measurement program that grows to embrace additional aspects of development and management.

Table 3.4 presents an overview of the types of measurement suggested by each maturity level, where the selection depends on the amount of information visible and available at a given maturity level. Level 1 measurements provide a baseline for comparison as you seek to improve your processes and products; level 2 measurements focus on project management, while level 3 measures the intermediate and final

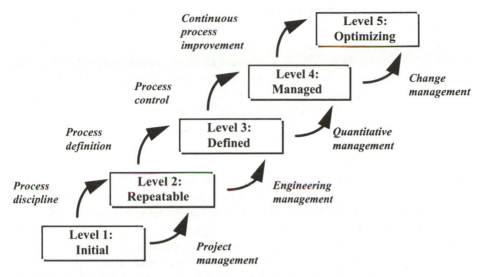

Figure 3.3: The Software Engineering Institute's levels of process maturity

products produced during development. The measurements at level 4 capture characteristics of the development process itself to allow control of the individual activities of the process. A level 5 process is mature enough and managed carefully enough to allow measurements to provide feedback for dynamically changing the process during a particular project's development.

Let us look at each maturity level in more detail.

Level 1: *ad hoc*

The initial level of process maturity is characterized by an *ad hoc* approach to the software-development process. That is, inputs to the process are ill-defined; while outputs are expected, the transition from inputs to outputs is undefined and uncontrolled. Similar projects may vary widely in their productivity and quality characteristics because of lack of adequate structure and control. For this level of

Table 3.4: Overview of process maturity and measurement (Pfleeger and McGowan, 1990)

Maturity level	Characteristics	Type of metrics to use
5. Optimizing	Improvement fed back to the process	Process plus feedback for changing the process
4. Managed	Measured process	Process plus feedback for control
3. Defined	Process defined and institutionalized	Product
2. Repeatable	Process dependent on individuals	Project management
1. Initial	Ad hoc	Baseline

process maturity, it is difficult even to write down or depict the overall process; the process is so reactive and ill-defined that visibility is nil and comprehensive measurement difficult. You may have goals relating to improved quality and productivity, but you do not know what current levels of quality and productivity are. For this level of process maturity, baseline measurements are needed to provide a starting point for measuring improvement as maturity increases. If your organization is at level 1, you should concentrate on imposing more structure and control on the process, in part to enable more meaningful measurement.

Level 2: repeatable

The second process level, called repeatable, identifies the inputs and outputs of the process, the constraints (such as budget and schedule), and the resources used to produce the final product. The process is repeatable in the same sense that a subroutine is repeatable: proper inputs produce proper outputs, but there is no visibility into how the outputs are produced. Asked to define and describe the process, you and your development team can draw no more than a diagram similar to Figure 3.4. This figure shows a repeatable process as a simplified Structured Analysis and Design Technique (SADT) diagram, with input on the left, output on the right, constraints at the top, and resources on the bottom. For example, requirements may be input to the process, with the software system as output. The control arrow represents such items as schedule and budget, standards, and management directives, while the resources arrow can include tools and staff.

Since it is possible to measure only what is visible, Figure 3.4 suggests that project management measurements make the most sense for a repeatable process. That is, since the arrows are all that is visible, we can associate measurements with each arrow in the process diagram. Thus, for a repeatable process, measures of the input might include the size and volatility of the requirements. The output may be measured in terms of system size (functional or physical), the resources as overall staff effort, and the constraints as cost and schedule in dollars and days, respectively.

Level 3: defined

The defined level of maturity (level 3) differs from level 2 in that a defined process provides visibility into the "construct the system" box. At level 3, intermediate activities are defined, and their inputs and outputs are known and understood. This additional structure means that the input to and output from the intermediate activities can be examined, measured, and assessed, since these intermediate products are well-defined and visible. Figure 3.5 shows a simple example of a defined process with three typical activities. However, different processes may be partitioned into more distinct functions or activities.

Because the activities are delineated and distinguished from one another in a defined process, measurement of product attributes should begin no later than level 3. Defects discovered in each type of product can be tracked, and you can compare the defect density of each product with planned or expected values. In particular,

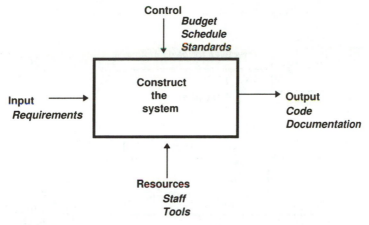

Figure 3.4: A repeatable process (level 2)

early product measures can be useful indicators of later product measures. For example, the quality of the requirements or design can be measured and used to predict the quality of the code. Such measurements use the visibility in the process to provide more control over development: if requirements quality is unsatisfactory, additional work can be expended on the requirements before the design activity begins. This early correction of problems helps not only to control quality but also to improve productivity and reduce risk.

Level 4: managed

A managed process (level 4) adds management oversight to a defined process, as shown in the example process of Figure 3.6. Here, you can use feedback from early project activities (for example, problem areas discovered in design) to set priorities for current activities (for example, redesign) and later project activities (for example, more extensive review and testing of certain code, and a changed sequence for integration). Because you can compare and contrast, the effects of changes in one activity can be tracked in the others. By level 4, the feedback determines how resources are deployed; the basic activities themselves do not change. At this level, you can evaluate the effectiveness of process activities: how effective are reviews?

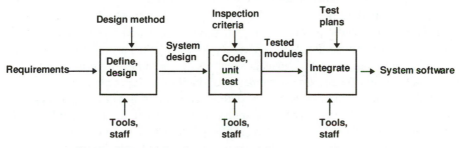

Figure 3.5: A defined process (level 3)

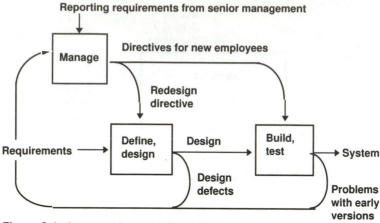

Figure 3.6: A managed process (level 4)

Configuration management? Quality assurance? Defect-driven testing? You can use the collected measures to stabilize the process, so that productivity and quality will match expectations.

A significant difference between levels 3 and 4 is that level 4 measurements reflect characteristics of the overall process and of the interaction among and across major activities. Management oversight relies on a metrics database that can provide information about such characteristics as distribution of defects, productivity and effectiveness of tasks, allocation of resources, and the likelihood that planned and actual values will match.

Level 5: optimizing

An optimizing process is the ultimate level of process maturity; it is depicted in Figure 3.7. Here, measures from activities are used to improve the process, possibly by removing and adding process activities, and changing the process structure dynamically in response to measurement feedback. Thus, the process change can affect the organization and project as well as the process. Results from one or more ongoing or completed projects may also lead to a refined, different development process for future projects. The *spiral model* (Boehm, 1988) is an example of such a dynamically changing process, responding to feedback from early activities in order to reduce risk in later ones.

This tailoring of the process to the situation is indicated in the figure by the collection of process boxes labeled $T_0, T_1, \ldots, T_n$. At time T_0, the process is as represented by box T_0. However, at time T_1, management has the option of revising or changing the overall process. For example, suppose you begin development with a standard waterfall approach. As requirements are defined and design is begun, measurements may indicate a high degree of uncertainty in the requirements. Based on this information, you may decide to change the process to one that prototypes the requirements and the design, so that some of the uncertainty can be resolved before

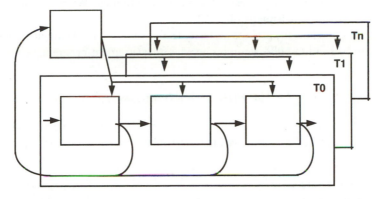

Figure 3.7: An optimizing process (level 5)

you make substantial investment in implementation of the current design. In this way, being able to optimize the process gives you maximum flexibility in development. Measurements act as sensors and monitors, and the process is not only under your control but you can change it significantly in response to warning signs.

The five categories of measurements described here – baseline, project management, product, process for feedback, process for control – are meant to be nested. That is, at a given maturity level, you can collect the measurements for that level and all levels below it. However, it is important to note that process maturity does not involve a discrete set of five possible ratings. Instead, maturity represents relative locations on a continuum from 1 to 5. An individual process is assessed or evaluated along many dimensions, and some parts of the process can be more mature or visible than others. For example, a repeatable process may not have well-defined intermediate activities, but the design activity may indeed be clearly defined and managed. The process-visibility diagrams presented here are meant only to give a general depiction of typical processes. It is essential that you begin any measurement program by examining the process model and determining what is visible. The figures and tables should not proscribe measurement simply because the overall maturity level is a particular integer; if one part of a process is more mature than the rest, measurement can enhance the visibility of that part and help to meet overall project goals, at the same time bringing the rest of the process up to a higher level of maturity. Thus, in a repeatable process with a well-defined design activity, design quality metrics may be appropriate and desirable, even though they are not generally recommended for level 2.

Moreover, it is important to remember that successful metrics programs start small and grow according to the goals and needs of a particular project (Rifkin and Cox, 1991). Your metrics program should begin by addressing the critical problems or goals of the project, viewed in terms of what is meaningful or realistic at the project's maturity level. The process maturity framework then acts as a guideline for how to expand and build a metrics program that not only takes advantage of visibility and maturity but also enhances process improvement activities. We will discuss these issues in more detail in Chapters 13 and 14.

Next, we explain how the process maturity framework, coupled with understanding of goals, can be used to build a comprehensive measurement program.

3.2.3 Combining GQM with process maturity

Suppose you are using the Goal–Question–Metric paradigm to decide what your project should measure. You may have identified at least one of the following high-level goals:

- improving productivity
- improving quality
- reducing risk

Within each category, you can represent the goal's satisfaction as a set of subgoals, each of which can be examined for its implications for resources, products and process. For example, the goal of improving productivity can be represented as several subgoals affecting resources:

- ensuring adequate staff skills
- ensuring adequate managerial skills
- ensuring adequate host software engineering technology

Similarly, to improve productivity using products can mean

- identifying problems early in the life cycle
- using appropriate technology
- reusing previously built products

Next, for each subgoal, you generate questions that reflect the areas of deepest concern. For example, if "improving productivity" is your primary goal, and "ensuring adequate staff skills" is an important subgoal, you create a list of questions that you may be interested in having answered, such as:

1. Does project staffing have the right assortment of skills?
2. Do the people on the project have adequate experience?

Similarly, if you have chosen "improving quality" with a subgoal of "improving the quality of the requirements", then the related questions might include:

1. Is the set of requirements clear and understandable?
2. Is the set of requirements testable?
3. Is the set of requirements reusable?
4. Is the set of requirements maintainable?
5. Is the set of requirements correct?

However, before you identify particular measurements to help you answer these questions, it is useful to determine your process maturity level. Since process maturity suggests that you measure only what is visible, the incorporation of process maturity with GQM paints a more comprehensive picture of what measures will be most useful to you.

For example, suppose you want to answer the question "Is the set of requirements maintainable?" If you have specified a process at level 1, then the project is likely to have ill-defined requirements. Measuring requirements characteristics is difficult at this level, so you may choose to count the number of requirements and changes to those requirements to establish a baseline. If your process is at level 2, the requirements are well-defined and you can collect additional information: the type of each requirement (database requirements, interface requirements, performance requirements, and so on) and the number of changes to each type. At level 3, your visibility into the process is improved, and intermediate activities are defined, with entry and exit criteria for each activity. For this level, you can collect a richer type of measurement: measuring the traceability of each requirement to the corresponding design, code, and test components, for example, and noting the effects of each change on the related components. Thus, the goal and question analysis is the same, but the metric recommendations vary with maturity. The more mature your process, the richer your measurements. In other words, the more mature your process, the more mature your measurements.

Moreover, maturity and measurement work hand in hand. As the measurements provide additional visibility, aiding you in solving project problems, you can use this approach again to expand the measurement set and address other pressing problems. Thus, your measurement program can start small and grow carefully, driven by process and project needs.

Using goals to suggest a metrics program has been successful in many organizations and is well-documented in the literature (Grady and Caswell, 1987; Rifkin, 1991; Pfleeger, 1993). The GQM paradigm, in concert with process maturity, has been used as the basis for several tools that assist managers in designing measurement programs. For example, the ami project, funded by the European Community under its ESPRIT program, has a handbook and tool that suggest the use of both GQM and process maturity (Pulford et al., 1995).

GQM has helped us to understand why we measure an attribute, and process maturity suggests whether we are capable of measuring it in a meaningful way. Together, they provide a context for measurement. Without such a context, measurements can be used improperly or inappropriately, giving us a false sense of comfort with our processes and products. In the next section, we look at the need for care in capturing and evaluating measures.

3.3 Applying the framework

In Chapter 1, we introduced several diverse topics involving software measurement. In particular, we saw how the topics relate to essential software engineering practices. When divorced from any conceptual high-level view of software measurement and its objectives, many of the activities may have seemed unrelated. In this section, we revisit the topics to see how each fits into our unifying framework and to describe some of the issues that will be addressed in later chapters of this book. That is, we look at which processes, products, and resources are relevant in each case, which attributes we are measuring (and whether these are internal or external) , and whether the focus is on assessment or prediction. Using the same topic headings as before, we describe these activities briefly; details will be provided in subsequent chapters.

3.3.1 Cost and effort estimation

Cost and effort estimation focuses on predicting the attributes of cost or effort for the development process. Here, the process includes activities from detailed specification through implementation. Most of the estimation techniques present a model; we examine a popular approach to see how cost and effort estimation is usually done.

> **Example 3.10:** Boehm's original, basic COCOMO model (described in more detail in Chapter 12) asserts that the effort required to develop a software system (measured by E in person months) is related to size (measured by S in thousands of delivered source statements) by the equation
>
> $$E = aS^b$$
>
> where a and b are parameters determined by the type of software system to be developed.
>
> The model is intended for use during requirements capture, when estimates of effort are needed. Thus, to use the technique, we must determine the parameters a and b. Boehm provides three choices for these constants, dependent on the type of software system it is classified to be. We must also determine the size S of the eventual system; since the system has yet to be built, we must predict S in order to predict E.

Thus, it is more correct to view COCOMO as a prediction system rather than as a model. The model is expressed as the equation in Example 3.10, but the prediction system includes the inference procedures for calculating the model's parameters. The calculations involve a combination of calibration based on past history, assessment based on expert judgment, and the subjective rating of attributes. The underlying theory provides various means for interpreting the results based on the choice of parameters. It is ambiguous to talk of *the* COCOMO cost-estimation model, since the same data can produce results that vary according to the particular prediction procedures used. These observations apply to most cost-and-effort estimation models.

Cost models often reflect a variety of attributes, representing all of the entity types. For example, for more advanced versions of COCOMO as well as other cost-estimation approaches, the inference procedures involve numerous internal and external attributes of the requirements specification (a product), together with process and resource attributes subjectively provided by users.

Both basic COCOMO and Albrecht's function point cost-estimation model (described in detail in Chapter 12) assert that effort is an indirect measure of a single product attribute: size. In Albrecht's model, size is measured by the number of function points, derived from and measuring the specifications. Here "size" really means a more specific attribute, namely functionality. In the latest version of COCOMO, called COCOMO 2.0, size is defined in different ways, depending on when during the development process the estimate is being made (Boehm *et al.*, 1995). Early on, size is described in terms of object points that can be derived from a prototype or initial specification. As more is known about the system, function points provide the size measure. When yet more information is available, size is defined as the number of thousands of delivered source statements, an attribute of the final implemented system. Thus, to use the model for effort prediction, you must predict size at the specification phase; that is, using the model involves predicting an attribute of a future product in order to predict effort. This approach can be rather unsatisfactory, since predicting size may be just as hard as predicting effort. In addition, the number of source statements captures only a very narrow view of size, namely length. In Chapter 7, we propose several ways to address these problems.

3.3.2 *Productivity measures and models*

To analyze and model productivity, we must measure a resource attribute, such as personnel (either as teams or individuals) active during particular processes. The most commonly used model for productivity measurement expresses productivity as a fraction: the process output influenced by the personnel divided by personnel effort or cost during the process. In this equation, productivity is viewed as a resource attribute, captured as an indirect measure of a product-attribute measure and a process-attribute measure.

In recent years, productivity has been viewed in a different light. Inspired by Japanese notions of spoilage, where engineers measure how much effort is expended fixing things that could have been put right before delivery, some software engineers compare the cost of fault prevention with the cost of fault detection and correction.

EXAMPLE 3.11: Watts Humphrey has defined a Personal Software Process (PSP) that encourages software engineers to evaluate their individual effectiveness at producing quality code (Humphrey, 1995). As part of the PSP, Humphrey suggests that we capture time and effort information about appraisal, failure and prevention. The appraisal cost is measured as the percentage of development time spent in design and test reviews. The failure cost is the percentage of time spent in compile and test, while the prevention cost is that time spent preventing defects before they occur (in such activities as prototyping and formal specification). The ratio of appraisal cost to failure cost then tells us the relative effort spent in early defect removal. Such notions help us to understand how to improve our productivity.

3.3.3   Data collection

Even the simplest models depend on accurate measures. Often, product measures may be extracted with a minimum of human intervention, since the products can be digitized and analyzed automatically. But automation is not usually possible for process and resource measures. Much of the work involved in data collection is therefore concerned with how to set in place rigorous procedures for gathering accurate and consistent measures of process and resource attributes.

Chillarege and his colleagues at IBM have suggested a scheme for collecting defect information that adds the rigor usually missing in such data capture. In their scheme, the defects are classified orthogonally, meaning that any defect falls in exactly one category (Chillarege *et al.*, 1992). Such consistency of capture and separation of cause allow us to analyze not only the product attributes but also process effectiveness. In Chapter 5, we shall see how quality of data collection affects the quality of data and of subsequent analysis.

3.3.4   Quality models and measures

Quality models usually involve product measurement, as their ultimate goal is predicting product quality. We saw in Chapter 1 that both cost and productivity are dependent on the quality of products output during various processes. The productivity model in Figure 1.5 explicitly considers the quality of output products; it uses an internal process attribute, defects discovered, to measure quality. The quality factors used in most quality models usually correspond to external product attributes. The criteria into which the factors are broken generally correspond to internal product or process attributes. The metrics that measure the criteria then correspond to proposed measures of the internal attributes. In each case, the terms used are general and are usually not well-defined and precise.

Gilb has suggested a different approach to quality. He breaks high-level quality attributes into lower-level attributes; his work is described in Chapter 9 (Gilb, 1988) .

3.3.5   Reliability models

Reliability is a high-level, external product attribute that appears in all quality models. The accepted view of reliability is the likelihood of successful operation during a given period of time. Thus, reliability is a relevant attribute only for executable code. Many people view reliability as the single most important quality attribute to consider, so research on measuring and predicting reliability is sometimes considered a separate sub-discipline of software measurement.

In Chapter 9, we consider proposals to measure reliability using internal process measures, such as number of faults found during formal testing or mean time to failure during testing. It is in that chapter that we describe the pitfalls of such an approach.

As we have seen, many developers observe failures (and subsequent fixes) during operation or testing, and then use this information to determine the probability of the next failure (which is a random variable). Measures of reliability are defined in terms of the subsequent distributions (and are thus defined in terms of process attributes). For example, we can consider the distribution's mean or median, or the rate of occurrence of failures. But this approach presents a prediction problem: we are trying to say something about future reliability on the basis of past observations.

> **EXAMPLE 3.12:** The *Jelinski–Moranda* model for software reliability assumes an exponential probability distribution for the time of the *i*th failure. The mean of this distribution (and hence the mean time to *i*th failure, or MTTF_i) is given by
>
> $$\text{MTTF}_i = \frac{\alpha}{N - i + 1}$$
>
> where N is the number of faults assumed to be initially contained in the program, and $1/\alpha$ represents the size of a fault, that is, the rate at which it causes a failure. (Faults are assumed to be removed on observation of a failure, and each time the rate of occurrence of failures is reduced by $\phi = 1/\alpha$.) The unknown parameters of the model, N and α, must somehow be estimated; this estimation can be done using, for example, Maximum Likelihood Estimation after observing a number of failure times.

In this example, we cannot discuss only the Jelinski–Moranda model; we must specify a prediction system as well. In this case, the prediction system supplements the model with a statistical inference procedure for determining the model parameters, and a prediction procedure for combining the model and the parameter estimates to make statements about future reliability.

3.3.6 *Performance evaluation and models*

Performance evaluation is generally concerned with measuring efficiency, a product attribute. This attribute can involve time efficiency (speed of response or computation for given input) or space efficiency (memory required for given input), but it is more usually the former. Like reliability, efficiency is a product attribute that appears high in the hierarchy of most quality models. Classical performance evaluation (Ferrari, 1978; Ferrari *et al.*, 1983; Kleinrock, 1975) is concerned with measuring the external attribute of efficiency for executable products. You may be tempted to conclude that efficiency can be only an external attribute (like reliability) and that no other type of measurement is possible. However, even when little is known about the compiler and target machine, efficiency can be predicted quite accurately by considering any representation of the source code. In particular, a high-level description of the underlying algorithm is normally enough to determine reasonably good predictors of efficiency of the implemented code; for time efficiency, the prediction is done by first determining key inputs and basic machine operations, and then calculating the number of basic operations required as a function of input size. This area of work (traditionally the staple diet of computer scientists) is called **algorithmic analysis** or **algorithmic complexity**, where complexity is synonymous with efficiency. Viewed with our framework, algorithmic efficiency is an internal attribute that can be measured and used to predict the external attribute of efficiency of executable code.

Computational complexity is closely related and also fits our software measurement framework. Here, we are interested in measuring the inherent complexity of a problem; a problem is synonymous with the requirements specification (a product in our sense), and complexity is synonymous with the efficiency of the fastest algorithm possible to solve the problem. For example, suppose our requirements specification asserts: "For an n-node network with known distances between any pair of nodes, the system must compute the shortest route through the network that visits each node."

This requirements specification seeks a general solution to the so-called traveling-salesman problem, a highly complex task because the underlying problem is known to be in a complexity class called NP-complete. We want to measure the speed of the algorithm; the notions of speed and fast algorithms will be addressed in Chapter 7. In this example, there is no known fast algorithm that will solve the problem, nor is there ever likely to be one.

3.3.7   Structural and complexity metrics

Many high-level quality attributes (that is, external product attributes) are notoriously difficult to measure. For reasons to be made clear in Chapter 7, we are often forced to consider measures of internal attributes of products as weaker substitutes. The Halstead measures are examples of this situation; defined on the source code, the internal measures suggest what the external measures might be. Numerous other measures have been proposed that are defined on graphical models of either the source code or design. By measuring specific internal attributes like control-flow structure, information flow and number of paths of various types, they attempt to quantify those aspects of the code that make the code difficult to understand. Unfortunately, much work in this area has been obfuscated by suggestions that such measures capture directly the external attribute of complexity. In other words, many software engineers claim that a single internal attribute representing complexity can be an accurate predictor of many external quality attributes, as well as of process attributes like cost and effort. We discuss this problem and suggest a rigorous approach to defining structural attributes in Chapter 8.

3.3.8 *Capability-maturity assessment*

As we have seen, the SEI capability-maturity model and its offshoots attempt to capture notions of process visibility: clearly an internal process attribute. But the maturity level has also been interpreted in a very different way, as a resource attribute. An SEI capability-maturity evaluation results in a profile of an organization's typical development process, as described in more detail in Chapter 14. The profile is associated with a score, placing the organization somewhere on the scale between *ad hoc* (1) and optimizing (5). This score is considered by some practitioners to be a rating of the development organization's capability, to be used in evaluating how well-prepared the developers are to build a proposed software product. That is, the maturity score is viewed as an attribute of the contractor, rather than of the contractor's process. For example, the US Air Force has proposed that contractors be rated at least level 3 on the SEI scale in order to be considered for bidding on Air Force-funded development work.

3.3.9 *Management by metrics*

Managers often use metrics to set targets for their development projects. These targets are sometimes derived from best practice, as found in a sample of existing projects.

> **EXAMPLE 3.13:** The US Department of Defense analyzed US government and industry performance, grouping projects into low, median and best-in-class ratings. From their findings, the analysts recommended targets for Defense Department-contracted software projects, along with indicated levels of performance constituting management malpractice, shown in Table 3.5. That is, if a project demonstrates that an attribute is below the malpractice level, then something is seriously wrong with the project.
>
> Defect-removal efficiency is a process measure, while defect density, requirements creep (that is, an increase or change from the original set of

Table 3.5: Quantitative targets for managing US defense projects (NetFocus, 1995)

Item	Target	Malpractice level
Defect removal efficiency	> 95%	< 70%
Original defect density	< 4 per function point	> 7 per function point
Slip or cost overrun in excess of risk reserve	0%	> 10%
Total requirements creep (function points or equivalent)	< 1% per month average	> 50%
Total program documentation	< 3 pages per function point	> 6 pages per function point
Staff turnover	1–3% per year	> 5% per year

requirements) and program documentation are product measures. Cost overrun and staff turnover capture resource attributes.

Notice that the measures in Example 3.13 are a mixture of measurement types. Moreover, none of the measures is external. That is, none of the measures reflects the actual product performance as experienced by the user. This situation illustrates the more general need for managers to understand likely product quality as early in the development process as possible. But, as we shall see in later chapters, unless the relationship between internal and external attributes is well-understood, such management metrics can be misleading.

3.3.10 Evaluation of methods and tools

Often, organizations consider investing in a new method or tool but hesitate because of uncertainty about cost, utility, or effectiveness. Sometimes the proposed tool or method is tried first on a small project, and the results are evaluated to determine if further investment and broader implementation are in order. For example, we saw in Example 3.6 that AT&T used goals and questions to decide what to measure in evaluating the effectiveness of its inspections.

> **EXAMPLE 3.14:** The results of the AT&T inspection evaluation are summarized in Table 3.6. For the first sample project, the researchers found that 41% of the inspections were conducted at a rate faster than the recommended rate of 150 lines of code per hour. In the second project, the inspections with rates below 125 found an average of 46% more faults per KLOC than those with faster rates. This finding means either that more faults can be found when inspection rates are slower, or that finding more faults causes the inspection rate to slow. Here, the metrics used to support this analysis are primarily process metrics.

These examples show us that it takes all types of attributes and metrics – process, product and resource – to understand and evaluate software development.

Table 3.6: Code inspection statistics from AT&T (Barnard and Price, 1994)

Metric	First sample project	Second sample project
Number of inspections in sample	27	55
Total KLOC inspected	9.3	22.5
Average LOC inspected (module size)	343	409
Average preparation rate (LOC/hour)	194	121.9
Average inspection rate (LOC/hour)	172	154.8
Total faults detected (observable and non-observable) per KLOC	106	89.7
Percentage of reinspections	11	0.5

3.3.11   A mathematician's view of metrics

In Chapter 2, we discussed the theory of measurement, explaining that we need not use the term "metric" in our exposition. There is another, more formal, reason for using care with the term. In mathematical analysis, a *metric* has a very specific meaning: it is a rule used to describe how far apart two points are. More formally, a **metric** is a function *m* defined on pairs of objects *x* and *y* such that $m(x, y)$ represents the distance between *x* and *y*. Such metrics must satisfy certain properties:

- $m(x, x) = 0$ for all *x*: that is, the distance from a point to itself is 0;
- $m(x, y) = m(y, x)$ for all *x* and *y*: that is, the distance from *x* to *y* is the same as the distance from *y* to *x*;
- $m(x, z) < m(x, y) + m(y, z)$ for all *x*, *y* and *z*: that is, the distance from *x* to *z* is no larger than the distance measured by stopping through an intermediate point.

There are numerous examples where we might be interested in "mathematical" metrics in software:

> **EXAMPLE 3.15:**   Fault-tolerant techniques like *N*-version programming are popular for increasing the reliability of safety-critical systems. The approach involves developing *N* different versions of the critical software components independently. Theoretically, by having each of the *N* different teams solving the same problem without knowledge of what the other teams are doing, the probability that all the teams, or even of the majority, will make the same error is kept small. When the behavior of the different versions differs, a voting procedure accepts the behavior of the majority of the systems. The assumption, then, is that the correct behavior will always be chosen.
>
> However, there may be problems in assuring genuine design independence, so we may be interested in measuring the level of diversity between two designs, algorithms or programs. We can define a metric *m*, where $m(P_1, P_2)$ measures the diversity between two programs P_1 and P_2. In this case, the entities being measured are products. Should we use a similar metric to measure the level of diversity between two methods applied during design, we would be measuring attributes of process entities.

> **EXAMPLE 3.16:**   We would hope that every program satisfies its specification completely, but this is rarely the case. Thus, we can view program correctness as a measure of the extent to which a program satisfies its specification, and define a metric $m(S, P)$ where the entities *S* (specification) and *P* (program) are both products.

To reconcile these mathematically precise metrics with the framework we have proposed, we can consider pairs of entities as a single entity. For example, having produced two programs satisfying the same specification, we consider the pair of programs to be a single product system, itself having a level of diversity. This approach is consistent with a systems view of N-version programming. Where we have implemented N versions of a program, the diversity of the system may be viewed as an indirect measure of the pairwise program diversity.

3.4 SOFTWARE MEASUREMENT VALIDATION

The very large number of software measures in the literature aims to capture information about a wide range of attributes. Even when you know which entity and attribute you want to assess, there are many measures from which to choose. Finding the best measure for your purpose can be difficult, as candidates measure or predict the same attribute (such as cost, size, or complexity) in very different ways. So it is not surprising when managers are confused by measurement: they see different measures for the same thing, and sometimes the implications of one measure lead to a management decision opposite to the implications of another! One of the roots of this confusion is the lack of software-measurement validation. That is, we do not always stop to ensure that the measures we use actually capture the attribute information we seek.

The formal framework presented in Chapter 2 and in this chapter leads to a formal approach for validating software measures. The validation approach depends on distinguishing measurement from prediction, as discussed in Chapter 2. That is, we must separate our concerns about two types of measuring:

- **Measures** or **measurement systems** are used to assess an existing entity by numerically characterizing one or more of its attributes.
- **Prediction systems** are used to predict some attribute of a future entity, involving a mathematical model with associated prediction procedures.

Informally, we say that a *measure* is **valid** if it accurately characterizes the attribute it claims to measure. On the other hand, a *prediction system* is **valid** if it makes accurate predictions. So not only are measures different from prediction systems, but the notion of validation is different for each. Thus, to understand why validation is important and how it should be done, we consider measures and prediction systems separately.

3.4.1 Validating prediction systems

Validating a prediction system in a given environment is the process of establishing the accuracy of the prediction system by empirical means; that is, by comparing model performance with known data in the given environment.

Thus, validation of prediction systems involves experimentation and hypothesis-testing, as we shall see in Chapter 4. Rather than being a mathematical proof, validation involves confirming or refuting a hypothesis.

This type of validation is well accepted by the software engineering community. For example, researchers and practitioners use data sets to validate cost-estimation or reliability models. If you want to know whether COCOMO is valid for your type of development project, you can use data that represent that type of project and assess the accuracy of COCOMO in predicting effort and duration.

The degree of accuracy acceptable for validation depends on several things, including the person doing the assessment. We must also consider the difference between **deterministic** prediction systems (we always get the same output for a given input) and **stochastic** prediction systems (the output for a given input will vary probabilistically) with respect to a given model.

Some stochastic prediction systems are more stochastic than others. In other words, the error bounds for some systems are wider than in others. Prediction systems for software cost estimation, effort estimation, schedule estimation and reliability are very stochastic, as their margins of error are large. For example, Boehm has stated that under certain circumstances the COCOMO effort-prediction system will be accurate to within 20%; that is, the predicted effort will be within 20% of the actual effort value. An **acceptance range** for a prediction system is a statement of the maximum difference between prediction and actual value. Thus, Boehm specifies 20% as the acceptance range of COCOMO. Some project managers find this range to be too large to be useful for planning, while other project managers find 20% to be acceptable, given the other uncertainties of software development. Where no such range has been specified, you must state in advance what range is acceptable before you use a prediction system.

EXAMPLE 3.17:   Sometimes the validity of a complex prediction system may not be much greater than that of a very simple one. For example, it has been shown that if the weather tomorrow in Austria is always predicted to be the same as today's weather, then the predictions are accurate 67% of the time. The use of sophisticated computer models increases this accuracy to just 70%!

In Chapter 10, we present a detailed example of how to validate software-reliability prediction systems using empirical data.

3.4.2   Validating measures

Measures used for assessment are the measures discussed in Chapter 2. We can turn to measurement theory to tell us what validation means in this context:

Validating a software measure is the process of ensuring that the measure is a proper numerical characterization of the claimed attribute by showing that the representation condition is satisfied.

EXAMPLE 3.18:   We want to measure the length of a program in a valid way. Here, "program" is the entity and "length" the attribute. The measure we choose must not contradict any intuitive notions about program length.

Specifically, we need both a formal model that describes programs (to enable objectivity and repeatability) and a numerical mapping that preserves our intuitive notions of length in relations that describe the programs. For example, if we concatenate two programs P_1 and P_2, we get a program $P_1; P_2$ whose length is the combined lengths of P_1 and P_2. Thus, we expect any measure m of length always to satisfy the condition

$$m(P_1; P_2) = m(P_1) + m(P_2)$$

If program P_1 has a greater length than program P_2, then any measure m of length must also satisfy

$$m(P_1) > m(P_2)$$

We can measure program length by counting lines of code (in the carefully defined way we describe in Chapter 7). Since this count preserves these relationships, lines of code is a valid measure of length. We will also describe a more rigorous length measure in Chapter 7, based on a formal model of programs.

This type of validation is central to the representational theory of measurement. That is, we want to be sure that the measures we use reflect the behavior of entities in the real world. If we cannot validate the measures, then we cannot be sure that the decisions we make based on those measures will have the effects we expect. In some sense, then, we use validation to make sure that the measures are defined properly and are consistent with the entity's real-world behavior.

3.5 SOFTWARE MEASUREMENT VALIDATION IN PRACTICE

The software-engineering community has always been aware of the need for validation. As new measures are proposed, it is natural to ask whether the measure captures the attribute it claims to describe. But in the past, validation has been a relaxed process, sometimes relying on the credibility of the proposer, rather than on rigorous validation procedures. That is, if someone of stature says that measure X is a good measure of complexity, then practitioners and researchers begin to use X without question. Or software engineers adopt X after reading informal arguments about why X is probably a good measure. This situation can be remedied only by reminding the software community of the need for rigorous validation.

An additional change in attitude is needed, though. Many researchers and practitioners assume that validation of a measure (in the measurement-theory sense) is not sufficient. They expect the validation to demonstrate that the measure is itself part of a valid prediction system.

EXAMPLE 3.19: Many people use lines of code as a measure of software size. The measure has many uses: it is a general size measure in its own right, it can be used to normalize other measures (like number of faults) to enable comparison, and it is input to many compound measures such as productivity (measured as effort divided by lines of code produced). But some software engineers claim that lines of code is not a valid software measure because it is not a good predictor of reliability or maintenance effort.

Thus, a measure must be viewed in the context in which it will be used. Validation must take into account the measurement's purpose; a measure may be valid for some uses but not for others.

3.5.1   A more stringent requirement for validation

As we have seen with lines of code, it is possible for a measure to serve both purposes: to measure an attribute in its own right, and to be a valuable input to a prediction system. But a measure can be one or the other without being both. We should take care not to reject as invalid a reasonable measure just because it is not a predictor. For example, there are many internal product attributes (such as size, structuredness, and modularity) that are useful and practical measures, whether or not they are also part of a prediction system. If a measure for assessment is valid, then we say that it is **valid in the narrow sense** or is **internally valid**.

However, many process attributes (such as cost), external product attributes (such as reliability) and resource attributes (such as productivity) play a dual role. We say that a measure is **valid in the wide sense** if it is both

1. internally valid; and
2. a component of a valid prediction system.

Suppose we wish to show that a particular measure is valid in the wide sense. After stating a hypothesis that proposes a specific relationship between our measure and some useful attribute, we must conduct an experiment to test the hypothesis, as described in Chapter 4. Unfortunately, in practice the experimental approach is not often taken. Instead, the measure is claimed to be valid in the wide sense by demonstrating a statistical correlation with another measure. For example, a measure of modularity might be claimed to be valid or invalid on the basis of a comparison with known development costs. This validation is claimed even though there is no demonstrated explicit relationship between modularity and development costs! In other words, our measure cannot be claimed to be a valid measure of modularity simply because of the correlation with development costs. We require a model of the relationship between modularity and development costs, showing explicitly all the factors interconnecting each. Only then can we judge whether measuring modularity is the same as measuring development cost.

This type of mistake is common in software engineering, as well as in other disciplines. Engineers forget that statistical correlation does not imply cause and effect. For example, suppose we propose to measure obesity using inches, normally a length measure. We measure the height and weight of each of a large sample of people, and we show that height correlates strongly with weight. Based on that result, we cannot say that height is a valid measure of obesity, since height is only one of several factors that must be taken into account; heredity and body fat percentages play a role, for instance. In other words, just because height correlates with weight does not mean that height is a valid measure of weight or obesity. Likewise, there may be a statistical correlation between modularity and development costs, but that does not mean that modularity is the key factor determining development cost.

It is sometimes possible to show that a measure is valid in the wide sense without a stated hypothesis and planned experiment. Available data can be examined using techniques such as regression analysis; the measure may be consistently related (as shown by the regression formula) to another variable. However, this approach is subject to the same problems as the correlation approach. It requires a model showing how the various factors interrelate. Given our poor understanding of software, this type of validation appears fraught with difficulty. Nevertheless, many software engineers continue to use this technique as their primary approach to validation.

The many researchers who have taken this approach have not been alone in making mistakes. It is tempting to measure what is available and easy to measure, rather than to build models and capture complex relationships. Indeed, speaking generally about measurement validation, Krantz asserts:

> A recurrent temptation when we need to measure an attribute of interest is to try to avoid the difficult theoretical and empirical issues posed by fundamental measurement by substituting some easily measured physical quantity that is believed to be strongly correlated with the attribute in question: hours of deprivation in lieu of hunger; skin resistance in lieu of anxiety; milliamperes of current in lieu of aversiveness, etc. Doubtless this is a sensible thing to do when no deep analysis is available, and in all likelihood some such indirect measures will one day serve very effectively when the basic attributes are well understood, but to treat them now as objective definitions of unanalyzed concepts is a form of misplaced operationalism.
>
> Little seems possible in the way of careful analysis of an attribute until means are devised to say which of two objects or events exhibits more of the attribute. Once we are able to order the objects in an acceptable way, we need to examine them for additional structure. Then begins the search for qualitative laws satisfied by the ordering and the additional structure.
>
> (Krantz *et al.*, 1971)

Neither we nor Krantz claim that measurement and prediction are completely separate issues. On the contrary, we fully support the observation of Kyburg:

> If you have no viable theory into which X enters, you have very little motivation to generate a measure of X.
>
> (Kyburg, 1984)

However, we are convinced that our initial obligation in proposing measures is to show that they are valid in the narrow sense. Good predictive theories follow only when we have rigorous measures of specific, well-understood attributes.

3.5.2 Validation and imprecise definition

In Example 3.18, we noted that lines of code (LOC) is a valid measure of program length. However, LOC has not been shown convincingly to be a valid measure of complexity. Nor has it been shown to be part of an accurate prediction system for complexity. The fault lies not with the LOC measure but with the imprecise definition of complexity. Although complexity is generally described as an attribute that can affect reliability, maintainability, cost, and more, the fuzziness surrounding its definition presents a problem in complexity research. Chapter 8 explores whether complexity can ever be defined and measured precisely.

The problems with complexity do not prevent LOC from being a useful measure for purposes other than length. For example, if there is a stochastic association between a large number of lines of code and a large number of unit-testing errors, this relationship can be used in choosing a testing strategy and in reducing risks.

Many studies have demonstrated a significant correlation between LOC and the cyclomatic number. The researchers usually suggest that this correlation proves that the cyclomatic number increases with size; that is, larger code is more complex code. However, careful interpretation of the measures and their association reveals only that the number of decisions increases with code length, a far less profound conclusion. Chapter 8 contains more detailed discussion of validation for both the McCabe and Halstead measures.

3.5.3 How not to validate

New measures are sometimes validated by showing that they correlate with well-known, existing measures. Li and Cheung present an extensive example of this sort (Li and Cheung, 1987). This approach is appealing because:

- It is generally assumed that the well-known existing measure is valid, so that a good correlation means that the new measure must also be valid.
- This type of validation is straightforward, since the well-known measure is often easy to compute; automated tools are often available for computation.
- If the management is familiar with the existing measures, then the proposed measures have more credibility.

Well-known measures used in this way include Halstead's suite of software science measures, McCabe's cyclomatic number, and lines of code. However, although these may be valid measures of very specific attributes (such as number of decisions for cyclomatic number, and source-code program length for lines of code), they have not been shown to be valid measures of attributes such as cognitive complexity, correctness, or maintainability. Thus, we must take great care in validating by comparison with existing measures. We must verify that the qualities associated with the existing measures have been demonstrated in the past.

There is much empirical evidence to suggest that measures such as Halstead's suite and McCabe's cyclomatic number are associated with development and maintenance effort and faults. But such correlations do not imply that the measures are good predictors of these attributes. The many claims made that Halstead and McCabe measures have been validated are annulled by studies showing that the correlations with process data are no better than using a simple measure of size, such as lines of code (Hamer and Frewin, 1982).

There is a more compelling scientific and statistical reason why we must be wary of the correlate-against-existing-measures approach. Unstructured correlation studies run the risk of identifying spurious associations. Using the 0.05 significance level, we can expect a significant but spurious correlation 1 in 20 times by chance. Thus, if you have 5 independent variables and look at the 10 possible pairwise correlations, there is a 0.5 (1 in 2) chance of getting a spurious correlation. In situations like this, if we have no hypothesis about the reason for a relationship, we can have no real confidence that the relationship is not spurious. Courtney and Gustafson examine this problem in detail (Courtney and Gustafson, 1993).

3.5.4 Choosing appropriate prediction systems

To help us formulate hypotheses necessary for validating the predictive capabilities of measures, we divide prediction systems into the following classes:

- **Class 1:** using internal attribute measures of early life-cycle products to predict measures of internal attributes of later life-cycle products. For example, measures of size, modularity, and reuse of a specification are used to predict size and structuredness of the final code.
- **Class 2:** using early life-cycle process attribute measures and resource-attribute measures to predict measures of attributes of later life-cycle processes and resources. For example, the number of faults found during formal design review is used to predict cost of implementation.
- **Class 3:** using internal product-attribute measures to predict process attributes. For example, measures of structuredness are used to predict time to perform some maintenance task, or number of faults found during unit testing.
- **Class 4:** using process measures to predict later process measures. For example, measures of failures during one operational period are used to predict likely failure occurrences in a subsequent operational period. In examples like this, where an external product attribute (reliability) is effectively defined in terms of process attributes (operational failures), we may also think of this class of prediction systems as using process measures to predict later external product measures.

Notice that there is no class of prediction system using internal structural attributes to predict external and process attributes. We doubt whether there will ever be such a class of generally accepted prediction system. In theory, it is always possible to construct products that appear to exhibit identical external attributes but which in fact vary greatly internally.

However, we usually assume that certain internal attributes that result from modern software-engineering techniques (such as modularization, low coupling, control and data structuredness, information hiding and reuse) will generally lead to products exhibiting a high degree of desirable external attributes like reliability and maintainability. Thus, programs and modules that have poor values of desirable internal attributes (such as large, unstructured modules) are likely (but not certain) to have more faults and take longer to produce and maintain. We return to this issue in Chapter 8.

3.6 SUMMARY

This chapter presents a framework to help us to discuss what to measure and how to use the measures appropriately. The key points to remember are the following:

- All entities of interest in software can be classified as either processes, products, or resources. Anything we may wish to measure is an identifiable attribute of these.
- Attributes are either internal or external. Although external attributes (such as reliability of products, stability of processes, or productivity of resources) tend to be the ones we are most interested in measuring, we cannot do so directly. We are generally forced to use indirect measures of internal attributes.
- The Goal–Question–Metric paradigm is a useful approach for deciding what to measure. Since managers and practitioners have little time to measure everything, the GQM approach allows them to choose those measures that relate to the most important goals or the most pressing problems.
- The GQM approach creates a hierarchy of goals to be addressed (perhaps decomposed into subgoals), questions that should be answered in order to know if the goals have been met, and measurements that must be made in order to answer the questions. The technique considers the perspective of the people needing the information and the context in which the measurements will be used.
- Process maturity must also be considered when deciding what to measure. If an entity is not visible in the development process, then it cannot be measured. Five levels of maturity, ranging from *ad hoc* to optimizing, can be associated with the types of measurements that can be made.
- GQM and process maturity must work hand-in-hand. By using GQM to decide what to measure and then assessing the visibility of the entity, software engineers can measure an increasingly richer set of attributes.
- Many misunderstandings and misapplications of software measurement would be avoided if people thought carefully about the above framework. Moreover, this framework highlights the relationships among apparently diverse software measurement activities.

- Measurement is concerned not only with assessment (of an attribute of some entity that already exists) but also with prediction (of an attribute of some future entity). We want to be able to predict attributes like the cost and effort of processes, as well as the reliability and maintainability of products. Effective prediction requires a prediction system: a model supplemented with a set of prediction procedures for determining the model parameters and applying the results.
- The validation approach described in this chapter guides you in determining precisely which entities and attributes have to be considered for measurement. In this sense, it supports a goal-oriented approach.
- Software measures and prediction systems will be neither widely used nor respected without a proper demonstration of their validity. However, commonly accepted ideas and approaches to validating software measures bear little relation to the rigorous requirements for measurement validation in other disciplines. In particular, formal validation requirements must first be addressed before we can tackle informal notions such as usefulness and practicality.
- The formal requirement for validating a measure involves demonstrating that it characterizes the stated attribute in the sense of measurement theory.
- To validate a prediction system formally, you must first decide how stochastic it is (that is, determine an acceptable error range), and then compare performance of the prediction system with known data points. This comparison will involve experiments, such as those described in Chapter 4.
- Software measures that characterize specific attributes do not have to be shown to be part of a valid prediction system in order to be valid measures. A claim that a measure is valid because it is a good predictor of some interesting attribute can be justified only by formulating a hypothesis about the relationship and then testing the hypothesis.

3.7   EXERCISES

1   For each entity listed in Table 3.1, find at least one way in which environmental considerations will influence the relevant external attributes.

2   What different product, process or resource attributes might the following measure?:

    i.   the number of faults found in program P using a set of test data created specifically for P;

    ii.   the number of faults found in program P using a standard in-house set of test data;

    iii.   the number of faults found in program P by programmer A during one hour.

3   Check the dictionary definitions of the following measures as a basis for validation: (i) candlepower, (ii) decibel, (iii) horsepower, (iv) lightyear, (v) span.

4   Look at the four classes of prediction systems on page 110. To which of the four classes do the following prediction systems belong?: (i) the COCOMO model (Example 3.10), (ii) the Jelinski–Moranda reliability model (Example 3.12), (iii) stochastic systems, (iv) coupling as a predictor of program errors.

5   Explain briefly the idea behind the GQM paradigm. Is it always the right approach for suggesting what to measure? Suppose you are managing a software-development project for which reliability is a major concern. A continual stream of anomalies is discovered in the software during the testing phase, and you suspect that the software will not be of sufficient quality by the shipping deadline. Construct a GQM tree that helps you to make an informed decision about when to ship the software.

6   Suppose that a software producer considers software quality to consist of a number of attributes, including reliability, maintainability, and usability. Construct a simple GQM tree corresponding to the producer's goal of improving the quality of the software.

7   Your department manager asks you to help improve the maintainability of the software that your department develops. Construct a GQM tree to identify an appropriate set of measures to assist you in this task.

8   Suppose your development team has as its goal "improve effectiveness of testing". Use the GQM approach to suggest several relevant questions and measures that will enable you to determine if you have met your goal.

9   Our confidence in a prediction system depends in part on how well we feel we understand the attributes involved. After how many successful predictions would you consider the following validated?

   i.   a mathematical model to predict the return time of Halley's comet to the nearest hour;
   ii.   a timetable for a new air service between London and Paris;
   iii. a system that predicts the outcome of the spinning of a roulette wheel;
   iv.   a chart showing how long a bricklayer will take to erect a wall of a given area.

3.8   FURTHER READING

The COCOMO model is interesting to study, because it is a well-documented example of measurement that has evolved as goals and technology have changed. The original COCOMO approach is described in:

> Boehm, B.W., *Software Engineering Economics*, Prentice Hall, Englewood Cliffs, NJ, 1981.

An overview of the revision to COCOMO is in:

> Boehm, B.W., Clar, B., Horowitz, E., Westland, C., Madachy, R. and Selby, R,."Cost models for future software life cycle processes: COCOMO 2.0," *Annals of Software Engineering* 1(1), pp. 1–30.

The first paper to mention GQM is:

> Basili, V.R., and Weiss, D.M., "A method for collecting valid software engineering data," *IEEE Transactions on Software Engineering*, 10(6), pp. 728–38, 1984.

More detail and examples are provided in:

> Basili, V.R. and Rombach, H.D., "The TAME project: Towards improvement-oriented software environments," *IEEE Transactions on Software Engineering*, 14(6), pp. 758–73, 1988.

Despite its widespread appeal, GQM is not without its critics. These texts argue strongly against GQM on grounds of practicality.

> Bache, R. and Neil, M., "Introducing metrics into industry: a perspective on GQM," in *Software Quality Assurance and Metrics: A Worldwide Perspective* (eds: N.E. Fenton, R.W. Whitty, Y. Iizuka), International Thomson Press, pp. 59–68, 1995.
> Hetzel, W.C., *Making Software Measurement Work: Building an Effective Software Measurement Program*, QED Publishing Group, Wellesley, MA, 1993.

Researchers at IBM have produced a good analysis of fault categorization. The structure and its application are described in:

> Chillarege, R., Bhandari, I.S., Chaar, J.K., Halliday, M.J., Moebus, D.S., Ray B.K., and Wong, M.-Y., "Orthogonal defect classification: A concept for in-process measurements," *IEEE Transactions on Software Engineering*, 18(11), pp. 943–56, 1992.

For a good example of industry needs, look at the NetFocus newsletter. This newsletter describes the derivation of a metrics "dashboard" that depicts a small number of key measures. The dashboard is to be used by project managers to "drive" a software-development project, telling the manager when the products are ready for release to the customer.

> NetFocus: Software Program Managers Network, number 207, Department of the Navy (US), January 1995.

Correlation is often used to "validate" software measures. The paper by Courtney and Gustafson shows that use of correlation analysis on many metrics will inevitably throw up spurious "significant" results.

Courtney, R.E. and Gustafson D.A., "Shotgun correlations in software measures," *Software Engineering Journal*, 8(1), pp. 5–13, 1993.

4 Empirical investigation

Software engineers have many questions to answer. The test team wants to know which technique is best for finding faults in code. The maintainers seek the best tool to support configuration management. Project managers try to determine what types of experience make the best programmers or designers, while designers look for models that are good at predicting reliability. To answer these and other questions, we often rely on the advice and experience of others, which is not always based on careful, scientific research (Fenton, Pfleeger, and Glass, 1994). As a software practitioner, it is important to make key decisions or assessments in an objective and scientific way. We know from previous chapters that measurement plays a crucial role in assessing scientifically our current situation and in determining the magnitude of change when we manipulate our environment. In this chapter, we explain the assessment techniques available and describe which to use in a given situation.

Suppose you are a software practitioner trying to evaluate a technique, method or tool. You can use three main types of assessment to answer your questions: *surveys*, *case studies* and *formal experiments*. The chapter begins by introducing you to each type, explaining how to decide which is appropriate for the investigation you want to undertake. Next, it focuses on key issues in experimental design, enabling you to understand how the design supports your decision making. That is, the concepts will help you to determine whether an experiment is appropriate for your evaluation, to design the experiment, and to derive meaningful results from it. Finally, the chapter looks at how to design and perform case studies.

We cannot design the specific experiment or case study for you, but we provide guidelines about what to consider in designing your own. The techniques described and the situations used as examples are limited to those most likely to aid software development and maintenance decisions. Thus, there are experimental designs and situations not addressed; in those cases, you are referred to more general texts on statistics and experimental design for the broader, more generally applicable information.

4.1   FOUR PRINCIPLES OF INVESTIGATION

Suppose your managers or colleagues have proposed the use of a new tool, technique, or method. You have decided to investigate the tool, technique, or method in a scientific way, rather than rely on "common wisdom." Your scientific investigation is likely to involve a survey, a case study, or a formal experiment. This section addresses the differences among these types of investigations, giving examples of situations in which each might be appropriate.

4.1.1   Choosing an investigative technique

A **survey** is a retrospective study of a situation to try to document relationships and outcomes. Thus, a survey is always done after an event has occurred. You are probably most familiar with social science surveys, where attitudes are polled to determine how a population feels about a particular set of issues, or a demographer surveys a population to determine trends and relationships. Software engineering surveys are similar, in that they poll a set of data from an event that has occurred to determine how the population reacted to a particular method, tool, or technique, or to determine trends or relationships.

> **EXAMPLE 4.1:**   Your organization may have used an object-oriented language for the first time. After the object-oriented project is complete, you may perform a survey to capture the size of the code produced, the effort involved, the number of faults and failures, and the project duration. Then, you may compare these figures with those from projects using procedural languages to see if object orientation led to improvements over the standard situation.

When performing a survey, you have no control over the situation at hand. That is, because it is a retrospective study, you can record a situation and compare it with similar ones. But you cannot manipulate variables as you do with case studies and experiments.

Both case studies and formal experiments are usually not retrospective. You decide in advance what you want to investigate and then plan how to capture data to support your investigation. A **case study** is a research technique where you identify key factors that may affect the outcome of an activity and then document the activity: its inputs,

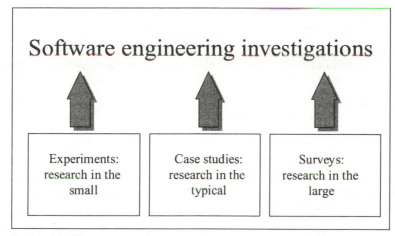

Figure 4.1: Three types of investigation

constraints, resources, and outputs. By contrast, a **formal experiment** is a rigorous, controlled investigation of an activity, where key factors are identified and manipulated to document their effects on the outcome. Figure 4.1 illustrates that formal experiments, case studies, and surveys are three key components of empirical investigation in software engineering. They are not the only types of investigation. Other methods, including feature analysis, are not addressed in this book; their descriptions are available in social science research textbooks, and in a series of columns by Kitchenham (Kitchenham, 1996).

Kitchenham, Pickard and Pfleeger note that the differences among the research methods are also reflected in their scale (Kitchenham, Pickard, and Pfleeger, 1995). By their nature, since formal experiments require a great deal of control, they tend to be small, involving small numbers of people or events. We can think of experiments as "research in the small." Case studies usually look at a typical project, rather than trying to capture information about all possible cases; these can be thought of as "research in the typical." And surveys try to poll what is happening broadly over large groups of projects: "research in the large."

Several general guidelines can help you decide whether to perform a survey, case study, or a formal experiment. The first step is deciding whether your investigation is retrospective or not. If the activity you are investigating has already occurred, you must perform a survey or case study. If the activity has yet to occur, you may choose between a case study and a formal experiment.

The central factor in this choice is the level of control needed for a formal experiment. If you have a high level of control over the variables that can affect the outcome, then you can consider an experiment. If you do not have that control, an experiment is not possible; a case study is the preferred technique. But the level of control satisfies the technical concerns; you must also address the practical concerns of research. It may be possible but very difficult to control the variables, either because of the high cost of doing so, or the degree of risk involved. For example, safety-

Table 4.1: Factors relating to choice of research technique

Factor	Experiments	Case studies
Level of control	High	Low
Difficulty of control	Low	High
Level of replication	High	Low
Cost of replication	Low	High

critical systems may entail a high degree of risk in experimentation, and a case study may be more feasible.

The other key aspect to consider is the degree to which you can replicate the basic situation you are investigating. For instance, suppose you want to investigate the effects of language on the resulting software. Can you develop the same project multiple times using a different language each time? If replication is not possible, then you cannot do a formal experiment. However, even when replication is possible, the cost of replication may be prohibitive. Table 4.1 summarizes these concerns. The table is read across and up. For example, if the study you want to do has a low replication cost, then an experiment is more appropriate than a case study. Similarly, if you have no control (that is, the difficulty of control is high), then you should consider a case study.

As Kitchenham, Pickard and Pfleeger point out, a formal experiment is especially useful for investigating alternative methods of performing a particular, self-standing task (Kitchenham, Pickard, and Pfleeger, 1995). For instance, you can perform an experiment to determine if VDM is better than statecharts for specifying a set of requirements. Here, the self-standing task can be isolated from the rest of the development process, but the task is still embedded in the usual way the code is developed. Also, the self-standing task can be judged immediately, so that the experiment doesn't delay project completion. On the other hand, a case study may be preferable to a formal experiment if the process changes caused by the independent variables are wide-ranging, requiring the effects to be measured at a high level and across too many dependent variables to control and measure.

All three research techniques involve careful measurement. In this chapter, we focus primarily on formal experiments and case studies. However, we encourage you to become familiar with all three types of investigation, as each makes a valuable contribution to the body of software engineering knowledge.

4.1.2   Stating the hypothesis

Before you decide on how to investigate, the first step in your investigation is deciding what you want to investigate. That goal helps you to decide which type of research technique is most appropriate for your situation. The goal for your research can be expressed as a hypothesis you want to test. That is, you must specify what it is that you want to know. The **hypothesis** is the tentative theory or supposition that you think explains the behavior you want to explore. For example, your hypothesis may be "Using the Cleanroom method produces better-quality software than using the SSADM method." Whether you examine past records to assess what happened when a particular group used each method (a survey), evaluate a "snapshot" of your organization as it is using Cleanroom (a case study) or do a carefully controlled comparison of those using Cleanroom with those using SSADM (a formal experiment), you are testing to see if the data you collect will confirm or refute the hypothesis you have stated.

Wherever possible, you should try to state your hypothesis in quantifiable terms, so that it is easy to tell whether the hypothesis is confirmed or refuted.

> **EXAMPLE 4.2:**   Rather than saying "Using the Cleanroom method produces better-quality software than using the SSADM method", you can define "quality" in terms of the defects found and restate the hypothesis as "Code produced using the Cleanroom method has a lower number of defects per thousand lines of code than code produced using the SSADM method."

It is important to recognize that quantifying the hypothesis often leads to the use of surrogate measures. That is, in order to identify a quantity with a factor or aspect you want to measure (for example, quality), you must measure the factor indirectly using something associated with that factor (for example, defects). Because the surrogate is an indirect measure, there is danger that a change in the surrogate is not the same as a change in the original factor. For example, defects (or lack thereof) may not accurately reflect the quality of the software: finding a large number of defects during testing may mean that testing was very thorough and the resulting product is nearly defect-free, or it may mean that development was sloppy and there are likely to be many more defects left in the product. (We will return to this issue in Chapter 9.) Similarly, delivered lines of code may not accurately reflect the amount of effort required to complete the product, since that measure does not take into account issues like reuse or prototyping. Therefore, along with a quantifiable hypothesis, you should document the relationship between the measures and the factors they intend to reflect. In particular, you should strive for quantitative terms that are as direct and unambiguous at possible.

4.1.3   Maintaining control over variables

Once you have an explicit hypothesis, you must decide what variables can affect its truth. Then, for each variable identified, you must decide how much control you have over it. Knowing what you control is essential, since the key discriminator between experiments and case studies is the degree of control over behavioral events and the variables they represent. A case study is preferable when you are examining events where relevant behaviors cannot be manipulated.

> **EXAMPLE 4.3:**   If you are investigating the effect of a design method on the quality of the resulting software, but you have no control over who is using which design method, then you probably want to do a case study to document the results. Experiments are done when you can manipulate behavior directly,

precisely, and systematically. Thus, if you can control who uses the Cleanroom method, who uses SSADM, and when and where they are used, then an experiment is possible. This type of manipulation can be done in a "toy" situation, where events are organized to simulate their appearance in the real world, or in a "field" situation, where events are monitored as they actually happen.

This difference between case studies and formal experiments can be stated more rigorously by considering the notion of a state variable. A **state variable** is a factor that can characterize your project and influence your evaluation results. Sometimes, state variables are called **independent variables**, because they can be manipulated to affect the outcome. The outcome, in turn, is evidenced by values of the dependent variable; that is, the **dependent variable** is one whose value is affected by changing one or more independent variables.

Examples of state variables include the application area, the system type, or the developers' experience with the language, tool, or method. In a formal experiment, you identify the variables and sample over them. This phrase means that you select projects exhibiting a variety of characteristics possible for your organization and design your research so that more than one value will be taken for each characteristic. You aim for coverage, so that you have an instance for each possibility or possible combination.

> **EXAMPLE 4.4:** Suppose your hypothesis involves the effect of language on the quality of the resulting code. "Language" is a state variable, and an ideal experiment would involve projects where many different languages would be used. You would design your experiment so that the projects involved represent as many languages as possible.

In a case study, you sample from the state variable, rather than over it. This phrase means that you select a value of the variable that is typical for your organization and its projects. In Example 4.4, a case study might involve choosing a language that is usually used on most of your projects, rather than trying to choose a set of projects to cover as many languages as possible.

Thus, a state variable is used to distinguish the "control" situation from the "experimental" one in a formal experiment. When you cannot differentiate control from experiment, you must do a case study instead of a formal experiment. You may consider your current situation to be the control, and your new situation to be the experimental one; a state variable tells you how the experimental differs from the control.

> **EXAMPLE 4.5:** Suppose you want to determine whether a change in programming language can affect the productivity of your project. Then language is a state variable. If you currently use FORTRAN to write your programs and you want to investigate the effects of changing to Ada, then you can designate FORTRAN to be the control language and Ada to be the

experimental one. The values of all other state variables should stay the same (for example, application experience, programming environment, type of problem, and so on), so that you can be sure that any difference in productivity is attributable to the change in language. This type of experiment was carried out at NASA's Goddard Space Flight Center to support the decision to move from FORTRAN to Ada. The experiments revealed that productivity in Ada did not exceed FORTRAN until the third use of Ada, when programmers began to use Ada as it was intended to be used.

4.1.4   *Making your investigation meaningful*

There are many areas of software engineering that can be analyzed using surveys, case studies, and experiments. One key motivator for using a formal experiment rather than a case study or survey is that the results of an experiment are usually more generalizable. That is, if you use a survey or case study to understand what is happening in a certain organization, the results apply only to that organization (and perhaps to organizations that are very similar). But because a formal experiment is carefully controlled and contrasts different values of the controlled variables, its results are generally applicable to a wider community and across many organizations. In the examples below, we will see how each of these investigations can help to answer a variety of questions.

4.1.4.1   Confirming theories and "conventional wisdom"

Many techniques and methods are used in software engineering because "conventional wisdom" suggests that they are the best approaches. Indeed, many corporate, national and international standards are based on conventional wisdom. For example, many organizations use standard limits on structural measures or rules of thumb about module size to "assure" the quality of their software; they insist that the cyclomatic number be ten or less, or they restrict module size to 200 lines of code. However, there is very little quantitative evidence to support claims of effectiveness or utility of these and many other standards, methods, or tools. Case studies and surveys can be used to confirm the truth of these claims in a single organization, while formal experiments can investigate the situations in which the claims are true generally. Thus, formal experiments can be used to provide a context in which certain standards, methods, and tools are recommended for use.

4.1.4.2   Exploring relationships

Software practitioners are interested in the relationships among various attributes of resources and software products. For example:
- How does the project team's experience with the application area affect the quality of the resulting code?
- How does the requirements quality affect the productivity of the designers?

• How does the design structure affect the maintainability of the code?

The relationship can be suggested by a case study or survey. For instance, a survey of completed projects may reveal that software written in Ada has fewer faults than software written in other languages. Clearly, understanding and verifying these relationships is crucial to the success of any future project. Each relationship can be expressed as a hypothesis, and a formal experiment can be designed to test the degree to which the relationship holds. Usually, many factors are kept constant or under control, and the value of one attribute is carefully varied to observe the effects of the changes. As part of the experiment's design, the attributes are clearly defined, consistently used, and carefully measured.

> **EXAMPLE 4.6:** Suppose you want to explore the relationship between programming language and productivity. Your hypothesis may state that certain types of programming languages (for example, object-oriented languages) make programmers more productive than other types (for example, procedural languages). A careful experiment would involve measuring not only the type of language and the resulting productivity but also controlling other variables that might affect the outcome. That is, a good experimental design would ensure that factors such as programmer experience, application type, or development environment were controlled so that they would not confuse the results. After analyzing the outcome, you would be able to conclude whether or not programming language affects programmer productivity.

4.1.4.3 Evaluating the accuracy of models

Models (as part of prediction systems) are often used to predict the outcome of an activity or to guide the use of a method or tool. For example, size models such as function points suggest how large the code may be, and cost models predict how much the development or maintenance effort is likely to cost. Capability-maturity models guide the use of techniques such as configuration management or the introduction of testing tools and methods. Formal experiments can confirm or refute the accuracy and dependability of these models and their generality by comparing the predictions with the actual values in a carefully controlled environment.

Models present a particularly difficult problem when designing an experiment or case study, because their predictions often affect the outcome. That is, the predictions become goals, and the developers strive to meet the goal, intentionally or not. This effect is common when cost and schedule models are used, and project managers turn the predictions into targets for completion. For this reason, experiments evaluating models can be designed as "double-blind" experiments, where the participants do not know what the prediction is until after the experiment is done. On the other hand, some models, such as reliability models, do not influence the outcome, since reliability measured as mean time to failure cannot be evaluated until the software is ready for use in the field. Thus, the time between consecutive failures cannot be "managed" in the same way that project schedules and budgets are managed.

4.1.4.4 Validating measures

Many software measures have been proposed to capture the value of a particular attribute. For example, several measures claim to measure the complexity of code. As we saw in Chapter 3, a measure is said to be "valid" if it reflects the characteristics of an attribute under differing conditions. Thus, suppose code module X has complexity measure C. The code is augmented with new code, and the resulting module X' is now perceived to be much more difficult to understand. If the complexity measure is valid, then the complexity measure C' of X' should be larger than C. In general, a study can be conducted to test whether a given measure appropriately reflects changes in the attribute it is supposed to capture.

As we have seen, validating measures is fraught with problems. Often, validation is performed by correlating one measure with another. But surrogate measures used in this correlation can mislead the evaluator. It is very important to validate using a second measure which is itself a direct and valid measure of the factor it reflects. Such measures are not always available or easy to measure. Moreover, the measures used must conform to human notions of the factor being measured. For example, if system A is perceived to be more reliable than system B, then the measure of reliability of A should be larger than that for system B; that is, the perception of "more" should be preserved in the mathematics of the measure. This preservation of relationship means that the measure must be objective and subjective at the same time: objective in that it does not vary with the measurer, but subjective in that it reflects the intuition of the measurer (as we saw in Chapter 2).

4.2 PLANNING FORMAL EXPERIMENTS

Suppose you have decided that a formal experiment is the best investigative technique for the questions you want to answer. Formal experiments, like software development itself, require a great deal of care and planning if they are to provide meaningful, useful results. This section discusses the planning needed to define and run a formal experiment, including consideration of several key characteristics of the experiment.

4.2.1 Procedures for performing experiments

There are several steps to carrying out a formal experiment:

- conception
- design
- preparation
- execution
- analysis
- dissemination and decision making

We discuss each of these steps in turn.

4.2.1.1 Conception

The first step is to decide what you want to learn more about, and define the goals of your experiment. The conception stage includes the type of analysis described earlier, to ensure that a formal experiment is the most appropriate research technique for you to use. Next, you must state clearly and precisely the objective of your study. The objective may include showing that a particular method or tool is superior in some way to another method or tool. Alternatively, you may wish to show that, for a particular method or tool, differences in environmental conditions or quality of resources can affect the use or output of the method or tool. No matter what you choose as your objective, it must be stated so that it can be clearly evaluated at the end of the experiment. That is, it should be stated as a question you want to answer. Then, the next step is to design an experiment that will provide the answer.

4.2.1.2 Design

Once your objective is clearly stated, you must translate the objective into a formal hypothesis, as described in the previous section. Usually, there are two hypotheses described: the null hypothesis and the experimental (or alternative) hypothesis. The **null hypothesis** is the one that assumes that there is no significant difference between two treatments (that is, between two methods, tools, techniques, environments, or other conditions whose effects you are measuring) with respect to the dependent variable you are measuring (such as productivity, quality, or cost). The **alternative hypothesis** posits that there is a significant difference between the two treatments.

> **EXAMPLE 4.7:** Suppose you want to find out if the Cleanroom technique of developing software produces code of higher quality than your current development process. Your hypotheses might be formulated as follows:
>
> - **Null hypothesis:** there is no difference in code quality between code produced using Cleanroom and code produced using our current process.
> - **Alternative hypothesis:** the quality of code produced using Cleanroom is higher than the quality of code produced using our current process.

It is always easy to tell which hypothesis is to be the null hypothesis and which the alternative. The distinguishing characteristic involves statistical assumptions: the null hypothesis is assumed to be true unless the data indicates otherwise. Thus, the experiment focuses on departures from the null hypothesis, rather than on departures from the alternative hypothesis. In this sense, "testing the hypothesis" means determining whether the data are convincing enough to reject the null hypothesis and accept the alternative as true. Later in this chapter, we will see how statistics can be used to decide when to accept or reject the hypothesis.

Hypothesis definition is followed by the generation of a formal design to test the hypothesis. The experimental design is a complete plan for applying differing experimental conditions to your experimental subjects so that you can determine how the conditions affect the behavior or result of some activity. In particular, you want to plan how the application of these conditions will help you to test your hypothesis and answer your objective question.

To see why a formal plan or design is needed, consider Example 4.8:

Example 4.8: You are managing a software-development organization. Your research team has proposed the following objective for an experiment: "We want to determine the effect of using the C++ language on the quality of the resulting code." The problem as stated is far too general to be useful. You must ask specific questions, such as

1. How is quality to be measured?
2. How is the use of C++ to be measured?
3. What factors influence the characteristics to be analyzed? For example, will experience, tools, design techniques, or testing techniques make a difference?
4. Which of these factors will be studied in the investigation?
5. How many times should the experiment be performed, and under what conditions?
6. In what environment will the use of C++ be investigated?
7. How should the results be analyzed?
8. How large a difference in quality will be considered important?

These are just a few of the questions that must be answered before the experiment can begin.

There is formal terminology for describing the components of your experiment. In addition to being useful when consulting with a statistician, this terminology encourages you to consider all aspects of the experiment, so that it is completely planned to ensure useful results. The new method or tool you wish to evaluate (compared with an existing or different method or tool) is called the **treatment**. You want to determine if the treatment is beneficial in certain circumstances. For example, you may want to choose between two techniques, depending on their effect on the quality of the resulting product.

Your experiment will consist of a series of tests of your methods or tools, and the experimental design describes how these tests will be organized and run. In any individual test run, only one treatment is used. An individual test of this sort is sometimes called a **trial**, and the **experiment** is formally defined as the set of trials. Sometimes, your experiment can involve more than one treatment, and you want to compare and contrast the differing results from the different treatments. The **experimental objects** or **experimental units** are the objects to which the treatment is being applied. Thus, a development or maintenance project can be your experimental object, and aspects of the project's process or organization can be changed to affect the outcome. Or, the experimental objects can be programs or modules, and different methods or tools can be used on those objects.

EXAMPLE 4.9:   If you are investigating the degree to which a design-related treatment results in reusable code components, you may consider design components as the experimental objects.

At the same time, you must identify who is applying the treatment; these people are called the **experimental subjects**. The characteristics of the experimental subjects must be clearly defined, so that the effects of differences among subjects can be evaluated in terms of the observed results.

When you are comparing using the treatment to not using it, you must establish a **control object**, which is an object not using or being affected by the treatment. The control provides a baseline of information that enables you to make comparisons. In a case study, the control is the environment in which the study is being run, and it already exists at the time the study begins. In a formal experiment, the control situation must be defined explicitly and carefully, so that all the differences between the control object and the experimental object are understood.

The **response variables** (or dependent variables) are those factors that are expected to change or differ as a result of applying the treatment. In Example 4.8 above, quality may be considered as a composite of several attributes: the number of defects per thousand lines of code, the number of failures per thousand hours of execution time, and the number of hours of staff time required to maintain the code after deployment, for example. Each of these is considered a response variable. In contrast, as we noted earlier, state (or independent variables) are those factors that may influence the application of a treatment and thus indirectly the result of the experiment. We have seen that state variables usually describe characteristics of the developers, the products, or the processes used to produce or maintain the code. It is important to define and characterize state variables so that their impact on the response variables can be investigated. But state variables can also be useful in defining the scope of the experiment and in choosing the projects that will participate.

EXAMPLE 4.10:   Use of a particular design technique may be a state variable. You may decide to limit the scope of the experiment only to those projects that use Ada for a program design language, rather than investigating Ada on projects using any design technique. Or you may choose to limit the experiment to projects in a particular application domain, rather than considering all possible projects.

Finally, as we saw earlier, state variables (and the control you have over them) help to distinguish case studies from formal experiments.

The number of and relationships among subjects, objects, and variables must be carefully described in the experimental plan. The more subjects, objects, and variables, the more complex the experimental design becomes and often the more difficult the analysis. Thus, it is very important to invest a great deal of time and care in designing your experiment, rather than rush to administer trials and collect data. Later in this chapter, we address in more detail the types of issues that must be identified and planned in a formal experimental design. In many cases, the advice in this section should be supplemented with the advice of a statistician, especially when many subjects and objects are involved. Once the design is complete, you will know what experimental factors (that is, response and state variables) are involved, how many subjects will be needed, from what population they will be drawn, and to what conditions or treatments each subject will be exposed. In addition, if more than one treatment is involved, the order of presentation or exposure will be laid out. Criteria for measuring and judging effects will be defined, as well as the methods for obtaining the measures.

4.2.1.3 Preparation

Preparation involves readying the subjects for application of the treatment. For example, preparation for your experiment may involve purchasing tools, training staff, or configuring hardware in a certain way. Instructions must be written out or recorded properly. If possible, a dry run of the experiment on a small set of people may be useful, so that you are sure that the plan is complete and the instructions understandable.

4.2.1.4 Execution

Finally, the experiment can be executed. Following the steps laid out in the plan, and measuring attributes as prescribed by the plan, you apply the treatment to the experimental subjects. You must be careful that items are measured and treatments are applied consistently, so that comparison of results is sensible.

4.2.1.5 Analysis

The analysis phase has two parts. First, you must review all the measurements taken to make sure that they are valid and useful. You organize the measurements into sets of data that will be examined as part of the hypothesis-testing process. Second, you analyze the sets of data according to the statistical principles described at the end of this chapter. These statistical tests, when properly administered, tell you if the null hypothesis is supported or refuted by the results of the experiment. That is, the statistical analysis gives you an answer to the original question addressed by the research.

4.2.1.6 Dissemination and decision making

At the end of the analysis phase, you will have reached a conclusion about how the different characteristics you examined affected the outcome. It is important to document your conclusions in a way that will allow your colleagues to duplicate your experiment and confirm your conclusions in a similar setting. To that end, you must document all of the key aspects of the research: the objectives, the hypothesis, the experimental subjects and objects, the response and state variables, the treatments, and the resulting data. Any other relevant documentation should be included:

instructions, tool or method characteristics (for example, version, platform, vendor), training manuals, and more. You must state your conclusions clearly, making sure to address any problems experienced during the running of the experiment. For example, if staff changed during project development, or if the tool was upgraded from one version to another, you must make note of that.

The experimental results may be used in three ways. First, you may use them to support decisions about how you will develop or maintain software in the future: what tools or methods you will use, and in what situations. Second, others may use your results to suggest changes to their development environment. The others are likely to replicate your experiment to confirm the results on their similar projects. Third, you and others may perform similar experiments with variations in experimental subjects or state variables. These new experiments will help you and others to understand how the results are affected by carefully controlled changes. For example, if your experiment demonstrates a positive change in quality by using C++, others may test to see if the quality can be improved still further by using C++ in concert with a particular C++-related tool or in a particular application domain.

4.2.2 Principles of experimental design

Useful results depend on careful, rigorous and complete experimental design. In this section, we examine the principles that you must consider in designing your experiment. Each principle addresses the need for simplicity and for maximizing information. Simple designs help to make the experiment practical, minimizing the use of time, money, personnel, and experimental resources. An added benefit is that simple designs are easier to analyze (and thus are more economical) than complex designs. Maximizing information gives you as complete an understanding of your experimental conditions and results as possible, enabling you to generalize your results to the widest possible situations.

Involved in the experimental design are two important concepts: experimental units and experimental error. As noted above, an **experimental unit** is the experimental object to which a single treatment is applied. Usually, you apply the treatment more than once. At the very least, you apply it to the control group as well as at least one other group that differs from the control by a state variable. In many cases, you apply the treatment many times to many groups. In each case, you examine the results to see what the differences are in applying the treatments. However, even when you keep the conditions the same from one trial to another, the results can turn out to be slightly different.

> **EXAMPLE 4.11:** You are investigating the time it takes for a programmer to recognize faults in a program. You have seeded a collection of programs with a set of known faults, and you have asked a programmer to find as many faults as possible. Today you give the same programmer a different but equivalent program with different but equivalent seeded faults, but the programmer takes more time today to find the set of faults as he or she took yesterday.

To what is this variation attributable? **Experimental error** describes the failure of two identically treated experimental units to yield identical results. The error can reflect a host of problems:

- errors of experimentation
- errors of observation
- errors of measurement
- the variation in experimental resources
- the combined effects of all extraneous factors that can influence the characteristics under study but which have not been singled out for attention in the investigation

Thus, in Example 4.11, the differences may be due to such things as:

- the programmer's mind wandered during the experiment
- the timer measured elapsed time inexactly
- the programmer was distracted by loud noises from another room
- the programmer found the faults in a different sequence today than yesterday
- faults that were thought to be equivalent are not
- programs that were thought to be equivalent are not

The aim of a good experimental design is to control for as many variables as possible, both to minimize variability among participants and to minimize the effects of irrelevant variables (such as noise in the next room or the order of presentation of the experiment). Ideally, we would like to eliminate the effects of other variables so that only the effects of the independent variables are reflected in the values of the dependent variable. That is, we would like to eliminate experimental error. Realistically, this complete elimination is not always possible. Instead, we try to design the experiment so that the effects of irrelevant variables are distributed equally across all the experimental conditions, rather than allowing them to inflate artificially (or bias) the results of a particular condition. In fact, statisticians like whenever possible to measure the extent of the variability under "normal circumstances."

The three major principles described below, replication, randomization, and local control, address this problem of variability by giving us guidance on forming experimental units so as to minimize experimental error. We consider each of these in turn.

4.2.2.1 Replication

Replication is the repetition of the basic experiment. That is, replication involves repeating an experiment under identical conditions, rather than repeating measurements on the same experimental unit. This repetition is desirable for several reasons. First, replication (with associated statistical techniques) provides an estimate of experimental error that acts as a basis for assessing the importance of observed differences in an independent variable. That is, replication can help us to know how much confidence we can place in the results of the experiment. Second, replication enables us to estimate the mean effect of any experimental factor.

It is important to ensure that replication does not introduce the confounding of effects. Two or more variables are said to be **confounded** if it is impossible to separate their effects when the subsequent analysis is performed.

> **EXAMPLE 4.12:** Suppose you want to compare the use of a new tool with your existing tool. You set up an experiment where programmer A uses the new tool in your development environment, while programmer B uses the existing tool. When you compare measures of quality in the resulting code, you cannot say how much of the difference is due to the tools because you have not accounted for the difference in the skills of the programmers. That is, the effects of the tools (one variable) and the programmers' skills (another variable) are confounded. This confounding is introduced with the replication when the repetition of the experiment does not control for other variables (like programmer skills).

> **EXAMPLE 4.13:** Similarly, consider the comparison of two testing techniques. A test team is trained in test technique X and asked to test a set of modules. The number of defects discovered is the chosen measure of the technique's effectiveness. Then, the test team is trained in test technique Y, after which they test the same modules. A comparison of the number of defects found with X and with Y may be confounded with the similarities between techniques or a learning curve in going from X to Y. Here, the sequence of the repetition is the source of the confounding.

For this reason, the experimental design must describe in detail the number and kinds of replications of the experiments. It must identify the conditions under which each experiment is run (including the order of experimentation), and the measures to be made for each replicate.

4.2.2.2 Randomization

Replication makes possible a statistical test of the significance of the results. But it does not ensure the validity of the results. That is, we want to be sure that the experimental results clearly follow from the treatments that were applied, rather than from other variables. Some aspect of the experimental design must organize the experimental trials in a way that distributes the observations independently, so that the results of the experiment are valid. **Randomization** is the random assignment of subjects to groups or of treatments to experimental units, so that we can assume independence (and thus validity) of results. Randomization does not guarantee independence, but it allows us to assume that the correlation on any comparison of treatments is as small as possible. In other words, by randomly assigning treatments to experimental units, you can try to keep some treatment results from being biased by sources of variation over which you have no control.

For example, sometimes the results of an experimental trial can be affected by the time, the place, or unknown characteristics of the participants. These uncontrollable factors can have effects that hide or skew the results of the controllable variables. To spread and diffuse the effects of these uncontrollable or unknown factors, you can assign the order of trials randomly, assign the participants to each trial randomly, or assign the location of each trial randomly, whenever possible.

> **EXAMPLE 4.14:**   Consider again the situation in Example 4.13. Suppose each of 30 programmers is trained to perform both testing techniques. We can randomly assign 15 of the programmers to use technique X on a given program, and the remaining 15 can use technique Y on the same program.

A key aspect of randomization involves the assignment of subjects to groups and treatments. If we use the same subjects in all experimental conditions, we say that we have a **related within-subjects design**; this is the situation described in Example 4.14. However, if we use different subjects in different experimental conditions, we have an **unrelated between-subjects design**; we would be using this type of design if we used X to test one program and Y to test another. If there is more than one independent variable in the experiment, we can consider the use of same or different subjects separately for each of the variables. (We will describe this issue in more detail later on.)

Earlier, we mentioned the need for protecting subjects from knowing the goals of the experiment; we suggested the use of double-blind experiments to keep the subjects' actions from being affected by variable values. This technique is also related to randomization. It is important that researchers do not know who is to produce what kind of result, lest the information bias the experiment.

Thus, your experimental design should include details about how you plan to randomize assignment of subjects to groups or of treatments to experimental units, and how you plan to keep the design information from biasing the analytical results. In cases where complete randomization is not possible, you should document the areas where lack of randomization may affect the validity of the results. In later sections, we shall see examples of different designs and how they involve randomization.

4.2.2.3   Local control

As noted earlier, one of the key factors that distinguishes a formal experiment from a case study is the degree of control. **Local control** is the aspect of the experimental design that reflects how much control you have over the placement of subjects in experimental units and the organization of those units. Whereas replication and randomization ensure a valid test of significance, local control makes the design more efficient by reducing the magnitude of the experimental error. Local control is usually discussed in terms of two characteristics of the design: blocking and balancing the units.

Blocking means allocating experimental units to blocks or groups so the units within a block are relatively homogeneous. The blocks are designed so that the predictable variation among units has been confounded with the effects of the blocks. That is, the experimental design captures the anticipated variation in the blocks by grouping like varieties, so that the variation does not contribute to the experimental error.

EXAMPLE 4.15: You are investigating the comparative effects of three design techniques on the quality of the resulting code. The experiment involves teaching the techniques to twelve developers and measuring the number of defects found per thousand lines of code to assess the code quality. It may be the case that the twelve developers graduated from three universities. It is possible that the universities trained the developers in very different ways, so that being from a particular university can affect the way in which the design technique is understood or used. To eliminate this possibility, three blocks can be defined so that the first block contains all developers from university X, the second block from university Y, and the third block from university Z. Then, the treatments are assigned at random to the developers from each block. If the first block has six developers, you would expect two to be assigned to design method A, two to B, and two to C, for instance.

Balancing is the blocking and assigning of treatments so that an equal number of subjects is assigned to each treatment, wherever possible. Balancing is desirable because it simplifies the statistical analysis, but it is not necessary. Designs can range from being completely balanced to having little or no balance.

In experiments investigating only one factor, blocking and balancing play important roles. If the design includes no blocks, then it must be completely randomized. That is, subjects must be assigned at random to each treatment. A balanced design, with equal numbers of subjects per treatment, is preferable but not necessary. If one blocking factor is used, subjects are divided into blocks and then randomly assigned to each treatment. In such a design, called a **randomized block design**, balancing is essential for analysis. Thus, this type of design is sometimes called a **complete balanced block design**. Sometimes, units are blocked with respect to two different variables (for example, staff experience and program type) and then assigned at random to treatments so that each blocking variable combination is assigned to each treatment an equal number of times. In this case, called a **Latin Square**, balancing is mandatory for correct analysis.

Your experimental design should include a description of the blocks defined and the allocation of treatments to each. This part of the design will assist the analysts in understanding what statistical techniques apply to the data that results from the experiments. More detail about the analysis can be found in Chapter 6.

4.2.3   Types of experimental designs

There are many types of experimental designs. It is useful to know and understand the several types of designs that you are likely to use in software engineering research, since the type of design constrains the type of analysis that can be performed and therefore the types of conclusions that can be drawn. For example, there are several ways to calculate the F-statistic for an analysis of variance (explained in Chapter 6); the choice of calculation depends on the experimental design, including the number of variables and the way in which the subjects are grouped and balanced. Similarly, the measurement scale of the variables constrains the analysis. Nominal scales simply divide data into categories and can be analyzed by using statistical tests such as the Sign test (which looks at the direction of a score or measurement); on the other hand, ordinal scales permit rank ordering and can be investigated with more powerful tests such as Wilcoxon (looking at the size of the measurement differences). Parametric tests such as analysis of variance can be used only on data that are at least of an interval scale.

The sampling also enforces the design and constrains the analysis, as we will see in Chapter 6. For example, the amount of random variance should be equally distributed among the different experimental conditions if parametric tests are to be applied to the resulting data. Not only does the degree of randomization make a difference to the analysis, but also the distribution of the resulting data. If the experimental data are normally or near-normally distributed, as shown in Figure 4.2, then you can use parametric tests. However, if the data are not normally distributed, or if you do not know what the distribution is, nonparametric methods are preferable; examples of distributions that are not normal are shown in Figure 4.3.

Many investigations involve more than one independent variable. In addition, the experiment invokes changes in the dependent variable as one or more of the independent variables changes. An independent variable is called a **factor** in the experimental design.

EXAMPLE 4.16:   A study to determine the effects of experience and language on the productivity of programmers has two factors: experience and language. The dependent variable is productivity.

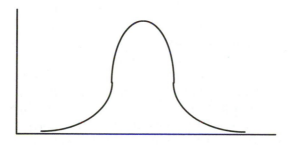

Figure 4.2: A normal distribution

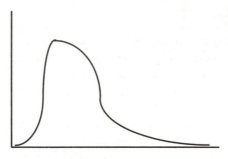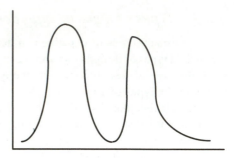

Figure 4.3: Examples of non-normal distributions: the distribution on the left is skewed, while that on the right is bimodal.

Various values or classifications for each factor are called the **levels** of the factor. Levels can be continuous or discrete, quantitative or qualitative. In Example 4.16, we may choose to measure experience in years of experience as a programmer; then each integer number of years can be considered a level. If the most experienced programmer in the study has eight years of experience, and if there are five languages in the study, then the first factor has eight levels and the second factor five.

There are several types of factors, reflecting such things as treatments, replications, blocking, and grouping. This chapter does not tell you what factors should be included in your design. Neither does it prescribe the number of factors nor the number of levels. Instead, it explains how the factors can be related to each other, and how the levels of one factor are combined with the levels of another factor to form the treatment combinations. The remainder of this section explains how to derive a design from the number of factors and levels you want to consider in your investigation.

Most designs in software engineering research are based on two simple relations between factors: crossing and nesting; each is discussed separately.

4.2.3.1 Crossing

The design of an experiment can be expressed in a notation that reflects the number of factors and how they relate to the different treatments. Expressing the design in terms of factors, called the **factorial design**, tells you how many different treatment combinations are required. Two factors, A and B, in a design are said to be **crossed** if each level of each factor appears with each level of the other factor. This relationship is denoted $A \times B$. The design itself is illustrated with three levels in Figure 4.4, where a_i represents the levels of factor A and b_j the levels of factor B. The figure's first row indicates that you must have a treatment for level 1 of A occurring with level 1 of B, of level 1 of A occurring with level 2 of B, and of level 1 of A with level 3 of B. The first column shows that you must have a treatment for level 1 of B occurring with each of the two levels of A. A crossed design with n levels of the first factor and m levels of the second factor will have nm cells, with each cell representing a particular situation. Thus, Figure 4.4 has two levels for A and three for B, yielding six possible treatments in all. In the previous example, the effects of language and experience on productivity can be written as an 8×5 crossed design, requiring 40 different treatment

	Factor B		
	Level 1	**Level 2**	**Level 3**
Factor A — Level 1	$a_1\, b_1$	$a_1\, b_2$	$a_1\, b_3$
Level 2	$a_2\, b_1$	$a_2\, b_2$	$a_2\, b_3$

Figure 4.4: Example of a crossed design

combinations. This design means that your experiment must include treatments for each possible combination of language and experience. For three factors, A, B and C, the design $A \times B \times C$ means that all combinations of all the levels occur.

4.2.3.2   Nesting

Factor B is **nested** within factor A if each meaningful level of B occurs in conjunction with only one level of factor A. The relationship is depicted as $B(A)$, where B is the nested factor and A is the nest factor. A two-factor nested design is depicted in Figure 4.5, where, like Figure 4.4, there are two levels of factor A and three levels of factor B. Now B is dependent on A, and each level of B occurs with only one level of A. That is, B is nested within A.

To understand nesting, and to see how crossing differs from nesting, consider again the effects of language and experience on productivity. In this case, let factor A

Factor A					
Level 1			**Level 2**		
Factor B			Factor B		
Level 1	**Level 2**	**Level 3**	**Level 1**	**Level 2**	**Level 3**
$a_1\, b_1$	$a_1\, b_2$	$a_1\, b_3$	$a_2\, b_1$	$a_2\, b_2$	$a_2\, b_3$

Figure 4.5: Example of a nested design

be the language, and B be the years of experience *with a particular language*. Suppose A has two levels, COBOL and Pascal, and B separates the programmers into those with less than two years of experience with the language and those who have more. For a crossed design, we would have four cells for each language. That is, we would have the following categories:

- COBOL programmers with less than two years of experience with COBOL (a_1b_1)
- COBOL programmers with less than two years of experience with Pascal (a_1b_3)
- COBOL programmers with at least two years of experience with COBOL (a_1b_2)
- COBOL programmers with at least two years of experience with Pascal (a_1b_4)
- Pascal programmers with less than two years of experience with COBOL (a_2b_1)
- Pascal programmers with less than two years of experience with Pascal (a_2b_3)
- Pascal programmers with at least two years of experience with COBOL (a_2b_2)
- Pascal programmers with at least two years of experience with Pascal (a_2b_4)

The eight categories are generated because we are examining experience with each language type, rather than experience in general. However, with a nested design, we can take advantage of the fact that the two factors are related. As depicted in Figure 4.6, we need only consider four treatments with a nested design, rather than eight; treatments a_1b_3, a_1b_4, a_2b_1 and a_2b_2 are not used. Thus, nested designs take advantage of factor dependencies, and they reduce the number of cases to be considered.

Nesting can involve more than two factors. For example, three factors can be nested as $C(B(A))$. In addition, more complex designs can be created as nesting and

Factor A: Language			
Level 1: COBOL		Level 2: Pascal	
<2 years experience with COBOL	≥2 years experience with COBOL	<2 years experience with Pascal	≥2 years experience with Pascal
a_1b_1	a_1b_2	a_2b_3	a_2b_4

Figure 4.6: Nested design for language and productivity example

crossing are combined.

There are several advantages to expressing a design in terms of factorials.

1. Factorials ensure that resources are used most efficiently.
2. Information obtained in the experiment is complete and reflects the various possible interactions among variables. Consequently, the experimental results and the conclusions drawn from them are applicable over a wider range of conditions than they might otherwise be.
3. The factorial design involves an implicit replication, yielding the related benefits in terms of reduced experimental error.

On the other hand, the preparation, administration, and analysis of a complete factorial design is more complex and time-consuming than a simple comparison. With a large number of treatment combinations, the selection of homogeneous experimental units is difficult and can be costly. And some of the combinations may be impossible or of little interest to you, wasting valuable resources. For these reasons, the remainder of this section explains how to choose an appropriate experimental design for your situation.

4.2.4   Selecting an experimental design

As seen above, there are many choices for how to design your experiment. The ultimate choice depends on two things: the goals of your investigation and the availability of resources. The remainder of this section explains how to decide which design is right for your situation.

4.2.4.1   Choosing the number of factors

Many experiments involve only one variable or factor. These experiments may be quite complex, in that there may be many levels of the variable that are compared (for example, the effects of many types of languages, or of several different tools). One-variable experiments are relatively simple to analyze, since the effects of the single factor are isolated from other variables that may affect the outcome. However, it is not always possible to eliminate the effects of other variables. Instead, we strive to minimize the effects, or at least distribute the effects equally across all the possible conditions we are examining. For example, techniques such as randomization aim to prevent variability among people from biasing the results.

But sometimes the absence of a second variable affects performance in the first variable. That is, people act differently in different circumstances, and you may be interested in the variable interactions as well as in individual variables.

> **EXAMPLE 4.17:**   You are considering the effects of a new design tool on productivity. The design tool may be used differently by designers who are well-versed in object-oriented design from those who are new to object-oriented design. If you were to design a one-factor experiment by eliminating the effects of experience with object-oriented design, you would get an incomplete (and

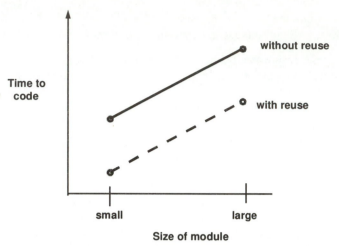

Figure 4.7: No interaction between factors

probably incorrect) view of the effects of the tool. It is better to design a two-factor experiment that incorporates both use of the tool and designer experience. That is, by looking at the effects of several independent variables, you can assess not only the individual effects of each variable (known as the **main effect** of each variable) but also any possible interactions among the variables.

To see what we mean by interaction, consider the reuse of existing code. Suppose your organization has a repository of code modules that is made available to some of the programmers but not all. You design an experiment to measure the time it takes to code a module, distinguishing small modules from large. When the experiment is complete, you plot the results, separating the times for those who reused code from the times of those who did not. This experiment has two factors: module size and reuse. Each factor has two levels; module size is either small or large, and reuse is either present or absent. If the results of your experiment resemble Figure 4.7, then you can claim that there is no interaction between the two factors.

Notice that the lines in Figure 4.7 are parallel; the parallelism is an indication that the two variables have no effect on each other. Thus, an individual line shows the main effect of the variable it represents. In this case, each line shows that the time to code a module increases with the size of the module. In comparing the two lines, we see that reuse reduces the time to code a module, but the parallel lines indicate that size and degree of reuse do not change the overall trend. However, if the results resemble Figure 4.8, then there is indeed interaction between the variables, since the lines are not parallel. Such a graph may result if there is considerable time spent searching through the repository. For a small module, it may actually take more time to scan the repository than to code the module from scratch. For large modules, reuse is better than writing the entire module, but there is still significant time eaten up in working with the repository. There is interaction between size of module and reuse of code.

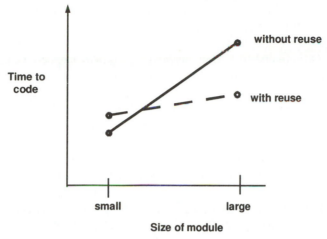

Figure 4.8: Interaction between factors

There is far more information available from the two-factor experiment than there would have been from two one-factor experiments. The latter would have confirmed that the time to code increases with the size of the module, both with and without reuse. But the two-factor experiment shows the relationship between the factors as well as the single-factor results. In particular, it shows that, for small modules, reuse may not be warranted. In other words, multiple-factor experiments offer multiple views of the data and enlighten us in ways that are not evident from a collection of single-factor experiments.

Another way of thinking about whether to use one factor or more is to decide what kind of comparison you want to make. If you are examining a set of competing treatments, you can use a single-factor experiment. For example, you may want to investigate three design methods and their effects on quality. That is, you apply design methods *A*, *B*, and *C* to see which yields the highest-quality design or code. Here, you do not have other variables that may interact with the design method.

On the other hand, you may want to investigate treatment combinations, rather than competing treatments. For example, instead of looking just at design methods, you want to analyze the effects of design methods in conjunction with tool assistance. Thus, you are comparing design method *A* with tool assistance to design method *A* without tool assistance, as well as design method *B* with tool assistance and without tool assistance. You have a two-factor experiment: one factor is the design method, and the other is the absence or presence of tool assistance. Your experiment tests $n_1 + n_2$ different treatments, where n_1 is the number of levels in factor 1, and n_2 is the number of levels in factor 2.

4.2.4.2   Factors versus blocks

Once you decide on the number of factors appropriate for your experiment, you must determine how to use blocking to improve the experiment's precision. However, it is not always easy to tell when something should be a block instead of a factor. To see how to decide, we continue to use the example of staff experience with software design, described in Example 4.17.

In many experiments, we suspect that the experience of the subjects will affect the outcome. One option in the experimental design is to treat experience as a blocking factor, as described earlier. To do this, we can assess the experience of the designers in terms of the number of years each has had experience with design. We can match staff with similar experience backgrounds and then assign staff randomly to the different treatments. Thus, if we are investigating design methods A and B, each block will have at least two subjects of approximately equal experience; within each block, the subjects are assigned randomly to methods A and B.

On the other hand, if we treat experience as a factor, we must define levels of experience and assign subjects in each level randomly to the alternative levels of the other factor. In the design example, we can classify designers as having high and low experience (the two levels of experience); then, within each group, subjects are assigned at random to design method A or B.

To determine which approach (factor or block) is best, consider the basic hypothesis. If we are interested in whether design A is better than design B, then experience should be treated as a blocking variable. However, if we are interested in whether the results of using design methods A and B are influenced by staff experience, then experience should be treated as a factor. Thus, as described before, if we are not interested in interactions, then blocking will suffice; if interactions are important, then multiple factors are needed.

In general, then, we offer the following guidelines about blocking:

- If you are deciding between two methods or tools, then you should identify state variables that are likely to affect the results and sample over those variables using blocks to ensure an unbiased assignment of experimental units to the alternative methods or tools.
- If you are deciding among methods or tools in a variety of circumstances, then you should identify state variables that define the different circumstances and treat each variable as a factor.

In other words, use blocks to eliminate bias; use factors to distinguish cases or circumstances.

4.2.4.3 Choosing between nested and crossed designs

Once you have decided on the appropriate number of factors for your experiment, you must select a structure that supports the investigation and answers the questions you have. As we shall see, this decision is often more complicated in software engineering than in other disciplines, because assigning a group not to use a factor may not be sensible or even possible. That is, there are hidden effects that must be made explicit, and there are built-in biases that must be addressed by the structure of the experiment. In addition, other issues can complicate this choice.

Suppose that a company wants to test the effectiveness of two design methods, *A* and *B*, on the quality of the resulting design, with and without tool support. The company identifies twelve projects to participate in the experiment. For this experiment, we have two factors: design method and tool usage. The first factor has two levels, *A* and *B*, and the second factor also has two levels, use of the tool and lack of use. A crossed design makes use of every possible treatment combination, and it would appear that a crossed design could be used for this experiment.

As shown in Figure 4.9, the twelve projects are organized so that three projects are assigned at random to each treatment in the design. Consider the implications of the design as shown. Any project has been assigned to any treatment. However, unless the tools used to support method *A* are exactly the same as the tools used to support method *B*, the factor levels for tool usage are not comparable within the two methods. In other words, with a crossed design such as this, we must be able to make sense of the analysis in terms of interaction effects. We should be able to investigate down columns (in this example, does tool usage make a difference for a given method?) as well as across rows (in this example, does method make a difference with the use of a given tool?). With the design in Figure 4.9, the interaction between method and tool usage (across rows) is not really meaningful. The crossed design yields four different treatments based on method and tool usage that allow us to identify which treatment produces the best result. But the design does not allow us to make statements about the interaction between tool usage and method type.

We can look at the problem in a different way by using a nested design, as shown in Figure 4.10. Although the treatment cells appear to be the same when looking at the figures, in fact the nested design is analyzed differently from the crossed design (a one-way analysis of variance, as opposed to a two-way analysis of variance), so there is no risk of meaningless interaction effects, as there was with the crossed design.

Crossed		Design method	
		Method A	Method B
Tool usage	Not used	Projects 1, 2, and 3	Projects 7, 8, and 9
	Used	Projects 4, 5, and 6	Projects 10, 11, and 12

Figure 4.9: Crossed design for design methods and tool usage

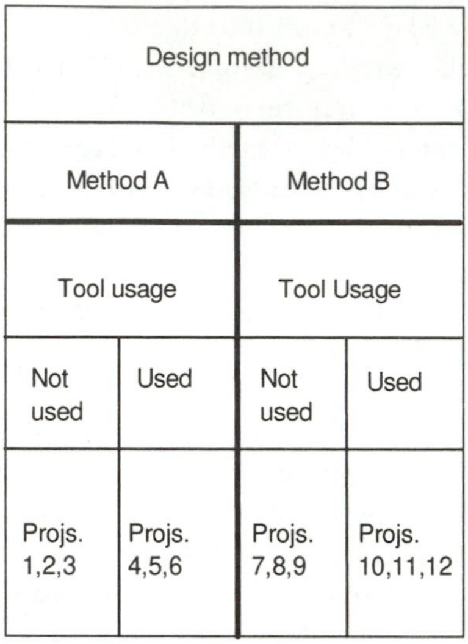

Design method			
Method A		Method B	
Tool usage		Tool Usage	
Not used	Used	Not used	Used
Projs. 1,2,3	Projs. 4,5,6	Projs. 7,8,9	Projs. 10,11,12

Figure 4.10: Nested design for design methods and tool usage

This difference in analysis approach will be discussed in more detail in Chapter 6.

Thus, a nested design is useful for investigating one factor with two or more conditions, while a crossed design is useful for looking at two factors, each with two or more conditions. This rule of thumb can be extended to situations with more than two factors. However, the more factors, the more complex the resulting analysis. For the remainder of this chapter, we focus on at most two factors, as most situations in software-engineering research will involve only one or two factors, with blocking and randomization used to ameliorate the effects of other state variables.

Figure 4.11 summarizes some of the considerations explained so far. Its flowchart helps you to decide on the number of factors, whether to use blocks, and whether to consider a crossed or nested design.

However, there are other, more subtle issues to consider when selecting a design. Let us examine two more examples to see what kinds of problems may be hidden in an experimental design. Consider first the crossed design described by Figure 4.12. The design shows an experiment to investigate two factors: staff experience and design-method type. There are two levels of experience, high and low, and two types of design method. The staff can be assigned to a project after the project's status is determined by a randomization procedure. Then, the project can be assigned to a treatment combination. This example illustrates the need to randomize in several ways, as well as the importance of assigning subjects and treatments in an order that makes sense to the design and the goals of the experiment.

Figure 4.13 is similar to Figure 4.12, except that it is examining method usage, as opposed to method type. In this case, it is important to define exactly what is meant by "not used." Unlike medicine and agriculture, where "not used" means the use of a placebo or the lack of treatment with a chemical, "not used" in software engineering

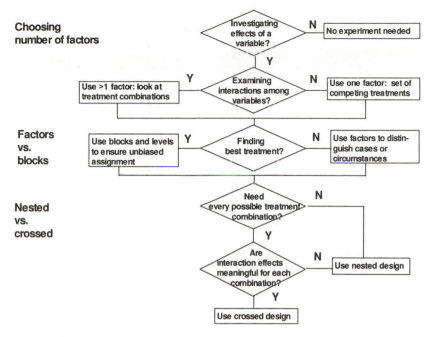

Figure 4.11: Flowchart for choosing design

may be difficult or impossible to control. If we tell designers not to use a particular method, they are likely to use an alternative method rather than no method at all. The alternative method may be hidden, based on how they were trained or what experience they have, rather than an explicitly defined and well-documented other method. In this case, the design is inappropriate for the goals of the experiment. However, if the goal of the experiment is to assess the benefit of a tool to support the given method, then the design is sufficient.

Crossed		Design method	
		Method A	Method B
Staff experience	Low	Projects 1, 2, and 3	Projects 7, 8, and 9
	High	Projects 4, 5, and 6	Projects 10, 11, and 12

Figure 4.12: Crossed design for method types and staff experience

Crossed		Design method	
		Used	Not used
Staff experience	Low	Projects 1, 2, and 3	Projects 7, 8, and 9
	High	Projects 4, 5, and 6	Projects 10, 11, and 12

Figure 4.13: Crossed design for method usage and staff experience

4.2.4.4 Fixed and random effects

Some factors allow us to have complete control over them. For example, we may be able to control what language is used to develop a system, or what processor the system is developed on. But other factors are not easy to control, or are pre-determined; staff experience is an example of this type of factor. The degree of control over factor levels is an important consideration in choosing an experimental design. A **fixed-effects model** has factor levels or blocks that are controlled. A **random-effects model** has factor levels or blocks that are random samples from a population of values.

> **EXAMPLE 4.18:** If staff experience is used as a blocking factor to match subjects of similar experience prior to assigning them to a treatment, then the actual blocks are a sample of all possible blocks, and we have a random-effects model. However, if staff experience is defined as two levels, low and high, the model is a fixed-effects model.

The difference between fixed- and random-effects models affects the way the resulting data are analyzed. For completely randomized experiments, there is no difference in analysis. But for more complex designs, the difference affects the statistical methods needed to assess the results. If you are not using a completely randomized experiment, you should consult a statistician to verify that you are planning to use techniques appropriate to the type of effects in your model.

The degree of randomization also affects the type of design that is used in your experiment. You can choose a crossed design when subjects can be assigned to all levels (for each factor) at random. For example, you may be comparing the use of a tool (in two levels: using the tool and not using the tool) with the use of a hardware platform (using a Sun, a PC, or a Macintosh, for instance). Since you can assign developers to each level at random, your crossed design allows you to look for interaction between the tool and the platform. On the other hand, if you are comparing tool usage and experience (low level of experience versus high level of experience), then you cannot assign people at random to the experience category; a nested design is more appropriate here.

4.2.4.5   Matched- or same-subject designs

Sometimes, economy or reality prevents us from using different subjects for each type of treatment in our experimental design. For instance, we may not find enough programmers to participate in an experiment, or we do not have enough funds to pay for a very large experiment. We can use the same subjects for different treatments, or we can try to match subjects according to their characteristics in order to reduce the scale and cost of the experiments. For example, we can ask the same programmer to use tool A in one situation and then tool B in another situation. The design of matched- or same-subject experiments allows variation among staff to be assessed and accounts for the effects of staff differences in analysis. This type of design usually increases the precision of an experiment, but it complicates the analysis.

Thus, when designing your experiment, you should decide how many and what type of subjects you want to use. For experiments with one factor, you can consider testing the levels of the factor with the same subjects or with different subjects. For two or more variables, you can consider the question of same-or-different separately for each variable. To see how, suppose you have an experimental design with four different treatments, generated by a crossed design with two factors. If different subjects are used for each treatment (that is, for each of both variables), then you have a completely unrelated between-subjects design. Alternatively, you could use the same subjects (or subjects matched for similar values of each level) and subject them to all four treatments; this is a completely related within-subjects design. Finally, you can use the same subjects for one factor but different subjects for the other factor to yield a mixed between- and within-subjects design.

4.2.4.6   Repeated measurements

In many experiments, one measurement is made for each item of interest. However, it can be useful to repeat measurements in certain situations. Repeating a measurement can be helpful in validating it, by assessing the error associated with the measurement process. We explain the added value of repeated measurements by describing an example.

Figure 4.14 depicts the results of an experiment involving one product and three developers. Each developer was asked to calculate the number of function points in the product at each of three different times during development: after the specification was completed, after the design was finished, and after the code was done. Thus, in the figure, there are three points marked at each of the three estimation times. For example, at specification, the three developers produced slightly different function point estimates, so there are three distinct points indicated above "specification" on the x-axis. The figure shows that there were two kinds of variation in the data that resulted. The horizontal variation indicates the variation over time, while the vertical differences at each measurement time indicates the variation due to the differences

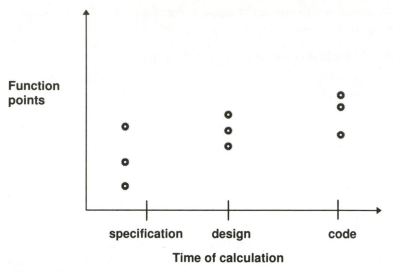

Figure 4.14: Repeated measurements on function point calculations

among the developers. Clearly, these repeated measurements add value to the results of the experiment, but at the cost of the more complex analysis required. The horizontal variation helps us to understand the error about the line connecting the means at each measurement time, and the vertical error helps us to understand observational error.

As you can see, there are many issues to consider when choosing a design for your experiment. In the next section, we look at case studies, to see how their design differs from experiments.

4.3 PLANNING CASE STUDIES

When you choose to perform a case study, many of the issues to be considered are the same as those for an experiment. In this section, we examine some of the differences and describe the steps to follow.

Every case study requires conception, design, preparation, execution, analysis, dissemination, and decision making, just as with an experiment. The hypothesis-setting is particularly important, as it guides what you measure and how you analyze the results. The projects you select for inclusion in your study must be chosen carefully, to represent what is typical in your organization or company.

A case study usually compares one situation with another: the results of using one method or tool with the results of using another, for example. To avoid bias and make sure that you are testing the relationship you hypothesize, you can organize your study in one of three ways: sister project, baseline, or random selection.

4.3.1 Sister projects

Suppose your organization is interested in modifying the way it performs code inspections. You decide to perform a case study to assess the effects of using a new inspection technique. To perform such a study, you select two projects, called **sister projects**, each of which is typical of the organization and has similar values for the state variables that you have planned to measure. For instance, the projects may be similar in terms of application domain, implementation language, specification technique, and design method. Then, you perform inspections the current way on the first project, and the new way on the second project. By selecting projects that are as similar as possible, you are controlling as much as you can. This situation allows you to attribute any differences in result to the difference in inspection technique.

4.3.2 Baselines

If you are unable to find two projects similar enough to be sister projects, you can compare your new inspection technique with a general **baseline**. Here, your company or organization gathers data from its various projects, regardless of how different one project is from another. In addition to the variable information mentioned above, the data can include descriptive measures, such as product size, effort expended, number of faults discovered, and so on. Then, you can calculate measures of central tendency and dispersion on the data in the database, so you have some idea of the "average" situation that is typical in your company. Your case study involves completing a project using the new inspection technique, and then comparing the results with the baseline. In some cases, you may be able to select from the organizational database a subset of projects that is similar to the one using the new inspection technique; again, the subset adds a degree of control to your study, giving you more confidence that any differences in result are caused by the difference in inspection technique.

4.3.3 Random selection

Sometimes, it is possible to partition a single project into parts, where one part uses the new technique while the other does not. Here, the case study resembles a formal experiment, because you are taking advantage of randomization and replication in performing your analysis. It is not a formal experiment, however, because the project was not selected at random from among the others in the company or organization. In this case, you randomly assign the code components to either the old inspection technique or the new. As with an experiment, the randomization helps to reduce the experimental error and balance out the confounding factors.

This type of case study design is particularly useful for situations where the method being studied can take on a variety of values. For example, you may want to determine whether preparation time affects the effectiveness of the inspections. You record the preparation time as well as component size and faults discovered. You can then investigate whether increased preparation time results in a higher detection rate.

Once you have chosen an investigative technique and run your experiment, case study or survey, the resulting data can be analyzed. Chapter 5 discusses data collection, and Chapter 6 explains how to select appropriate analysis techniques. Chapter 15 examines the state of empirical research in software engineering; in that chapter, we look at several examples (good and bad) of case studies, surveys and experiments that have been reported in the literature.

4.4 SUMMARY

We have described the key activities necessary for designing an investigation in software engineering. We began by explaining how to choose an appropriate research technique to fit the goals of your project. In particular, you saw how to state your hypothesis and determine how much control you need over the variables involved. If control is not possible, then a formal experiment is not possible; a case study may be a better approach. If the study is retrospective, then a survey may be done.

Next, we explained the principles of formal experimentation. We listed the six stages of an experiment: conception, design, preparation, execution, analysis, and dissemination. The design of an experiment was discussed in some detail. In particular, we pointed out that you must consider the need for replication, randomization and local control in any experiment that you plan to perform. We showed you how you can think of your design in terms of two types of relationships between factors (crossing and nesting), and we described several issues to be considered when selecting an appropriate design.

Finally, we looked at several possible designs for case studies: sister projects, organizational baselines, and random selection.

4.5 EXERCISES

1. Why it is not always possible to apply the principle of random assignment in experiments involving people?

2. How might the principle of blocking be used in an experiment studying the effectiveness of a course of instruction on the productivity of software programmers?

3. Your company is not a software company, but it is beginning to acknowledge the role software plays in the different company products. If you were to create a company baseline for use in case studies, what variable information would you try to capture?

4. You are about to begin a large project that uses new tools, techniques, and languages for building a mission-critical product. Your company president wants to know if the new tools, techniques and languages should become company standards if the product is a success. Explain how you might assess the product's

success, and what considerations you should make in designing the assessment exercise.

4.6 FURTHER READING

Curtis was probably the first to address the need for measurement and experimentation in software engineering:

Curtis, B., "Measurement and experimentation in software engineering," *Proceedings of the IEEE*, 68(9), pp. 1144–57, 1980.

Basili and his colleagues produced one of the first papers to point out the need for a rigorous experimentation framework in software engineering:

Basili, V.R., Selby, R.W., and Hutchens, D.H., "Experimentation in software engineering," *IEEE Transactions on Software Engineering*, 12(7), pp. 733–43, 1986.

Similar papers exists for informations systems research:

Cheon, M.J., Grover, V., and Sabherwal, R., "The evolution of empirical research in information systems: A study in information systems maturity," *Information and Management*, 24, North Holland, pp. 107–9, 1993.

Galliers, R.D., "Choosing appropriate information systems research approaches: A revised taxonomy," in *Information Systems Research: Contemporary Approaches and Emergent Traditions* (eds H.E. Nissen, H.K. Klein, and R. Hirshheim), Elsevier Science Publishers, B.V. (North Holland), pp. 327–45, 1991.

The following papers scrutinize particular software-engineering approaches or the general investigative technique used in research:

MacDonnell, S.G., "Rigor in software complexity measurement experimentation," *Journal of Systems and Software*, 16, pp. 141–9, 1991.

Shen, V.Y., Conte S.D., and Dunsmore, H.E., "Software science revisited: A critical analysis of the theory and its empirical support," *IEEE Transactions on Software Engineering*, 9(2), pp. 155–65, 1983.

Swanson, E.B. and Beath, C.M., "The use of case study data in software management research," *Journal of Systems and Software*, 8, pp. 63–71, 1988.

Kitchenham, B., Pickard L., and Pfleeger, S.L., "Case studies for method and tool evaluation," *IEEE Software*, 12(4), pp. 52–62, 1995.

Vessey I., and Weber, R., "Research on structured programming: An empiricist's evaluation," *IEEE Transactions on Software Engineering*, 10(4), pp. 397–407, 1984.

Wynekoop, J.L., and Conger, S.A., "A review of computer-aided software engineering research methods," in *Information Systems Research: Contemporary Approaches and Emergent Traditions* (eds H.E. Nissen, H.K. Klein, and R. Hirshheim), Elsevier Science Publishers, B.V. (North Holland), pp. 301–25, 1991.

Zweben, S.H., Edwards, S.H., Weide, B.W., and Hollingsworth, J.E., "The effects of layering and encapsulation on software development cost and quality," *IEEE Transactions on Software Engineering*, 21(3), pp. 200–8, 1995.

Fenton, N., Pfleeger, S.L., and Glass, R.L., "Science and substance: A challenge to software engineers," *IEEE Software*, July 1994.

There are several good books addressing experimentation in general. Cook and Campbell discuss many of the issues involved in doing experiments where it is difficult to control all the variables. The other books address statistics and experimental design.

Cook, T.D. and Campbell, D.T., *Quasi-experimentation: Design and analysis issues for field settings*, Houghton-Mifflin, Boston, MA, 1970.

Lee, W., *Experimental Design and Analysis*, Freeman, San Francisco, CA, 1975.

Green, J. and d'Oliveira, M., *Units 16 & 21 Methodology Handbook (part 2)*, Open University, Milton Keynes, England, 1990.

Ostle, B. and Malone, L.C., *Statistics in Research*, 4th edn, Iowa State University Press, Ames, IA, 1988.

Cochran, W.G., *Sampling Techniques*, 2nd edn, Wiley, New York, 1963.

Campbell, D.T. and Stanley, J., *Experimental and Quasi-Experimental Designs for Research*, Rand McNally, Chicago, IL, 1966.

5 Software-metrics data collection

Including contributions from the first edition by Peter Mellor
(City University)

We saw in Chapter 3 that measurements should be tied to business, project, product, and process goals, so that we know what questions we are trying to answer with our measurement program. And Chapter 4 showed us how to frame questions as hypotheses, so that we can perform measurement-based formal investigations to help us understand the answers. But having the right measures is only part of a measurement program. Software measurement is only as good as the data that are collected and analyzed. In other words, we cannot make good decisions with bad data.

> "Data should be collected with a clear purpose in mind. Not only a clear purpose but a clear idea as to the precise way in which they will be analysed so as to yield the desired information. It is astonishing that men, who in other respects are clearsighted, will collect absolute hotchpotches of data in the blithe and uncritical belief that analysis can get something out of it."
>
> (Moroney, 1950)

In this chapter, we ask ourselves what constitutes good data, and we present guidelines and examples to show how data collection supports decision making. In particular, we focus on the terminology and organization of data related to software quality, including faults and failures, to show how planning and modeling are needed before data collection can begin. We also discuss issues related to collecting data on effort, size, duration, and cost.

5.1   WHAT IS GOOD DATA?

Chapters 2 and 3 explained that measures should be well-defined and valid: that our measures should reflect the attributes we claim they do. But even when we have a well-defined measure that maps a real-world attribute to a formal, relational system in appropriate ways, we need to ask several questions about the data:

- *Are they correct?* **Correctness** means that the data were collected according to the exact rules of definition of the metric. For example, if a lines of code count is supposed to include everything but comments, then a check for correctness assures us that no comments were counted. Similarly, a measure of process duration is correct if time is measured from the beginning of one specified activity and ends at the completion of another specified activity.
- *Are they accurate?* **Accuracy** refers to the difference between the data and the actual value. For example, time measured using an analog clock may be less accurate than time measured using a digital one.
- *Are they appropriately precise?* **Precision** deals with the number of decimal places needed to express the data. For instance, activity duration need not be reported in hours, minutes, and seconds; hours or days are usually sufficient. Likewise, it is not necessary to calculate the mean cyclomatic number to several decimal places; since cyclomatic number expresses one plus the number of decisions in a module, fractions of a decision to several decimals places are meaningless.
- *Are they consistent?* Data should be **consistent** from one measuring device or person to another, without large differences in value. Thus, two evaluators should calculate the same or similar function-point values from the same requirements document. Similarly, when the same data value is computed repeatedly over time, the data should be captured in the same way. For example, we often measure the growth in size of a product over time, especially during maintenance. We want to be sure that the size measure is calculated the same way each time, so that the resulting measures are comparable.
- *Are they associated with a particular activity or time period?* If so, then the data should be time-stamped, so that we know exactly when they were collected. This association of values allows us to track trends and compare activities.
- *Can they be replicated?* We saw in Chapter 4 that data are often collected to support surveys, case studies and experiments. These investigations are frequently repeated under different circumstances, and the results compared. At the very least, project histories and study results are stored in a historical database, so that baseline measures can be established and organizational goals set. Unless the data collection from one study can be replicated on others, this amalgamation is impossible.

Thus, it is very important to assess the quality of data and data collection before data collection begins. Your measurement program must specify not only what metrics to use, but also what precision is required, what activities and time periods are to be associated with data collection, and what rules govern the data collection (such as whether a particular tool will be used to capture the data).

Of critical importance is the definition of the metric. Terminology must be clear and detailed, so that all involved understand what the metric is and how to collect it. The next section examines how we define software metrics in ways that support data collection and analysis.

5.2   How to Define the Data

There are really two kinds of data with which we are concerned. As illustrated by Figure 5.1, raw data results from the initial measurement of process, product or resource. But there is also a refinement process, extracting essential data elements from the raw data so that analysts can derive values about attributes.

To see the difference, consider the measurement of developer effort. The raw effort data may consist of weekly timesheets for each staff member working on a project. To measure the effort expended on the design so far, we must select all relevant timesheets and add up the figures. This refined data is still a direct measurement of effort. But we may derive other, indirect measures as part of our analysis: average effort per staff member, or effort per design component, for example.

Deciding what to measure is the first step. We must specify which direct measures are needed, and also which indirect measures may be derived from the direct ones. Sometimes, we begin with the indirect measures. From a GQM analysis, we understand which indirect measures we want to know; from those, we must determine which direct measures are required to calculate them.

Most organizations are different, not only in terms of their business goals but also in terms of their corporate cultures, development preferences, staff skills, and more. So a GQM analysis of apparently similar projects may result in different metrics at different companies. That is exactly why GQM is preferable to adopting a "one-size-fits-all" standard measurement set. Nevertheless, most organizations share similar problems. Each is interested in software quality, cost and schedule. As a result, most developers collect metrics information about quality, cost, and duration. In this section, we learn about the importance of data definition by examining possible definitions for these attributes and related measures.

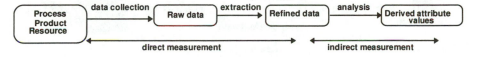

Figure 5.1: The role of data collection in software measurement

5.2.1 The problem with problems

No software developer consistently produces perfect software the first time. Thus, it is important for developers to measure aspects of software quality. Such information can be useful for determining

- how many problems have been found with a product;
- how effective are the prevention, detection, and removal processes;
- whether the product is ready for release to the next development stage or to the customer;
- how the current version of a product compares in quality with previous or competing versions.

The terminology used to support this investigation and analysis must be precise, allowing us to understand the causes as well as the effects of quality assessment and improvement efforts. In general, we talk about problems, but Figure 5.2 depicts some of the components of a problem's cause and symptoms, expressed in terms consistent with IEEE standard 729 (IEEE, 1983).

A **fault** occurs when a human error results in a mistake in some software product. That is, the fault is the encoding of the human error. For example, a developer might misunderstand a user-interface requirement, and therefore create a design that includes the misunderstanding. The design fault can also result in incorrect code, as well as incorrect instructions in the user manual. Thus, a single error can result in one or more faults, and a fault can reside in any of the products of development.

On the other hand, a **failure** is the departure of a system from its required behavior. Failures can be discovered both before and after system delivery, as they can occur in testing as well as in operation. It is important to note that we are comparing actual system behavior with required behavior, rather than with specified behavior, because faults in the requirements documents can result in failures, too.

In some sense, you can think of faults and failures as inside and outside views of the system. Faults represent problems that the developer sees, while failures are problems that the user sees. Not every fault corresponds to a failure, since the conditions under which a fault results in system failure may never be met. This case is easiest to see if you consider fault-containing code that is never executed, or that is not executed enough to increment a counter past unacceptable bounds.

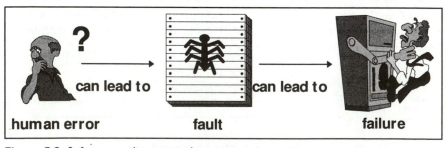

Figure 5.2: Software quality terminology

During both test and operation, we observe the behavior of the system. When undesirable or unexpected behavior occurs, we report it as a failure. The reliability of a software system is defined in terms of failures observed during operation, rather than in terms of faults; usually, we can infer little about reliability from fault information alone. Thus, the distinction between failures and faults is very important. Systems containing many faults may be very reliable, because the conditions that trigger the faults may be very rare. Unfortunately, the relationship between faults and failures is poorly understood; it is the subject of a great deal of software-engineering research. We shall return to this issue in Chapters 9 and 10 when we discuss in more depth how to measure software quality.

One of the problems with problems is that the terminology is not uniform. If an organization measures its software quality in terms of faults per thousand lines of code, it may be impossible to compare the result with the competition if the meaning of "fault" is not the same. The software engineering literature is full of differing meanings for the same terms. Below are just a few examples of how researchers and practitioners differ in their usage of terminology.

- To many organizations, **errors** often mean faults. There is also a separate notion of "processing error," which can be thought of as the system state that results when a fault is triggered but before a failure occurs (Laprie, 1992). This particular notion of error is highly relevant for software fault tolerance (which is concerned with how to prevent failures in the presence of processing errors).
- **Anomalies** usually mean a class of faults that are unlikely to cause failures in themselves but may nevertheless eventually cause failures indirectly. In this sense, an anomaly is a deviation from the usual, but it is not necessary wrong. For example, deviations from accepted standards of good programming practice (such as use of non-meaningful variable names) are often regarded as anomalies.
- **Defects** normally refer collectively to faults and failures. However, sometimes a defect is a particular class of fault. For example, Mellor uses "defect" to refer to faults introduced prior to coding (Mellor, 1986).
- **Bugs** refer to faults occurring in the code.
- **Crashes** are a special type of failure, where the system ceases to function.

Until terminology is the same, it is important for you to define your terms clearly, so that they are understood by all who must supply, collect, analyze, and use the data. Often, differences of meaning are acceptable, as long as the data can be translated from one framework to another.

We also need a good, clear way of describing what we do in reaction to problems. For example, if an investigation of a failure results in the detection of a fault, then we make a **change** to the product to remove it. A change can also be made if a fault is detected during a review or inspection process. In fact, one fault can result in multiple changes to one product (such as changing several sections of a piece of code) or multiple changes to multiple products (such as a change to requirements, design, code, and test plans).

In this book, we describe the observations of development, testing, system operation, and maintenance problems in terms of failures, faults, and changes. Whenever a problem is observed, we want to record its key elements, so that we can then investigate causes and cures. In particular, we want to know the following:

- **Location:** where did the problem occur?
- **Timing:** when did it occur?
- **Symptom:** what was observed?
- **End result:** which consequences resulted?
- **Mechanism:** how did it occur?
- **Cause:** why did it occur?
- **Severity:** how much was the user affected?
- **Cost:** how much did it cost?

The eight attributes of a problem have been chosen to be (as far as possible) mutually independent, so that proposed measurement of one does not affect measurement of another. (This mutual independence applies only to the initial measurement. Analysis of data may reveal, for example, that severity of effect is correlated with location of fault within the product. However, this is something which is discovered after classification, and not something which is assumed when faults are classified.) This characteristic of the attributes is called **orthogonality**. Orthogonality can also refer to a classification scheme within a particular category. For example, cost can be recorded as one of several pre-defined categories, such as "low" (under $100 000), "medium" (between $100 000 to $500 000) and "high" (over $500 000). However, in practice, attempts to over-simplify the set of attributes sometimes result in non-orthogonal classifications. When this happens, the integrity of the data collection and metrics program can be undermined, because the observer does not know in which category to record a given piece of information.

> **EXAMPLE 5.1:** Some organizations try to provide a single classification for software faults, rather than using the eight components suggested above. Here, one attribute is sometimes regarded as more important than the others, and the classification is a proposed ordinal scale measure for this single attribute. Consider the following classification for faults, based on severity:
>
> - major
> - minor
> - negligible
> - documentation
> - unknown
>
> This classification is not orthogonal; for example, a documentation fault could also be a major problem, so there is more than one category in which the fault can be placed. The non-orthogonality results from confusing severity with location, since the described fault is located in the documentation but has a severe effect.

Table 5.1: Fault classifications used in Eurostar control system (Riley 1995)

Cause	Category
error in software design	category not applicable
error in software implementation	initialization
error in test procedure	logic/control structure
deviation from functional specification	interface (external)
hardware not configured as specified	interface (internal)
change or correction induced error	data definition
clerical error	data handling
other (specify)	computation
	timing
	other (specify)

When the scheme is not orthogonal, the developer must choose which category is most appropriate. It is easy to see how valuable information is lost or misrepresented in the recording process.

EXAMPLE 5.2:   Riley describes the data collection used in the analysis of the control system software for the Eurostar train (the high-speed train used to travel from Britain to France and Belgium via the Channel tunnel) (Riley, 1995). In the Eurostar software problem-reporting scheme, faults are classified according to only two attributes, cause and category, as shown in Table 5.1. Note that "cause" includes notions of timing and location. For example, an error in software implementation could also be a deviation from functional specification, while an error in test procedure could also be a clerical error. Hence, Eurostar's scheme is not orthogonal and can lead to data loss or corruption.

On the surface, our eight-category report template should suffice for all types of problems. However, as we shall see, the questions are answered very differently, depending on whether you are interested in faults, failures or changes.

5.2.2   Failures

A failure report focuses on the external problems of the system: the installation, the chain of events leading up to the failure, the effect on the user or other systems, and the cost to the user as well as the developer. Thus, a typical failure report addresses each of the eight attributes as shown in Figure 5.3. Let us examine each of these categories more closely.

Location is usually a code (for example, hardware model and serial number, or site and hardware platform) that uniquely identifies the installation and platform on which the failure was observed. The installation description must be interpreted according to the type of system involved. For example, if software is embedded in an automatic braking system, the "installation" may move about. Similarly, if the system is distributed, then the terminal at which a failure is observed must be identified, as well as the server to which it was online.

Failure report

Location: such as installation where failure was observed

Timing: CPU time, clock time or some temporal measure

Symptom: type of error message or indication of failure

End result: description of failure, such as "operating system crash," "services degraded," "loss of data," "wrong output," "no output"

Mechanism: chain of events, including keyboard commands and state data, leading to failure

Cause: reference to possible fault(s) leading to failure

Severity: reference to a well-defined scale, such as "critical," "major," "minor"

Cost: cost to fix plus cost of lost potential business

Figure 5.3: Failure report

Timing has two, equally important aspects: real time of occurrence (measured on an interval scale), and execution time up to the occurrence of failure (measured on a ratio scale).

The **symptom** category explains what was observed, as distinct from the **end result**, which is a measure of the consequences. For example, the symptom of a failure may record that the screen displayed a number that was one greater than the number entered by the operator; if the larger number resulted in an item's being listed as "unavailable" in the inventory (even though one was still left), that symptom belongs in the "end result" category.

EXAMPLE 5.3: The IEEE standard classification for software anomalies (IEEE, 1992) proposes the following classification of symptoms. The scheme can be quite useful, but it blurs the distinction between symptom and end result:

- operating system crash
- program hang-up
- program crash
- input problem
  - correct input not accepted
  - wrong input accepted
  - description incorrect or missing
  - parameters incomplete or missing
- output problem
  - wrong format
  - incorrect result/data
  - incomplete/missing
  - spelling/grammar
  - cosmetic
- failed required performance
- perceived total product failure

- system error message
- other
- service degraded
- loss of data
- wrong output
- no output

End result refers to the consequence of the failure. Generally, "end result" requires a (nominal scale) classification that depends on the type of system and application. For instance, the end result of a failure may be any of the following:

- operating system crash
- application program aborted
- service degraded
- loss of data
- wrong output
- no output

Mechanism describes how the failure came about. This application-dependent classification details the causal sequence leading from the activation of the source to the symptoms eventually observed. This category may also characterize what function the system was performing or how heavy the workload was when the failure occurred. Unraveling the chain of events is part of diagnosis, so often this category is not completed at the time the failure is observed.

Cause is also part of the diagnosis (and as such is more important for the fault form associated with the failure). Cause involves two aspects: the type of trigger and the type of source (that is, the fault that caused the problem). The trigger can be one of several things, such as:

- physical hardware failure
- operating conditions
- malicious action
- user error
- erroneous report

while the actual source can be faults such as these:

- physical hardware fault
- unintentional design fault
- intentional design fault
- usability problem

For instance, the cause can involve a CASE statement with no code to handle the drop-through condition (the source), plus a situation (the trigger) where the listed cases were not satisfied.

The cause category is often cross-referenced to fault and change reports, so that the collection of reports paints a complete picture of what happened (the failure report), what caused it (the fault reports), and what was done to correct it (the change reports). Then, post-mortem analysis can focus on how to prevent such problems in the future, or at least catch them earlier in the development process.

Severity describes how serious the failure's end result was for the service required from the system. For example, failures in safety-critical systems are often classified for severity as follows (Riley, 1995):

- **Catastrophic** failures involve the loss of one or more lives, or injuries causing serious and permanent incapacity.
- **Critical** failures cause serious permanent injury to a single person but would not normally result in loss of life to a person of good health. This category also includes failures causing environmental damage.
- **Significant** failures cause light injuries with no permanent or long-term effects.
- **Minor** failures result neither in personal injury nor in a reduction to the level of safety provided by the system.

Severity may also be measured in terms of cost to the user.

Cost to the system provider is recorded in terms of how much effort and other resources were needed to diagnose and respond to the failure. This information may be part of diagnosis and therefore supplied after the failure occurs.

Sometimes, a failure occurs several times before it is recognized and recorded. In this case, a ninth category can be useful. **Count** captures the number of failures that occurred in a stated time interval.

> **EXAMPLE 5.4:** In the 1980s, problems with a radiation-therapy machine (the Therac 25) were discovered, and the description of the problems and their software causes are detailed in an article by Leveson and Turner (Leveson and Turner, 1993). Mellor used the above framework to analyze the first of these failures, in which patients died as a result of a critical design failure of the Therac 25 (Mellor, 1992). The Therac administered two types of radiation therapy: X-ray and electron. In X-ray mode, a high-intensity beam struck a tungsten target, which absorbed much of the beam's energy and produced x-rays. In electron mode, the Therac's computer retracted the metal target from the beam path while reducing the intensity of the radiation by a factor of 100. The sequence of a treatment session was programmed by an operator using a screen and keyboard; the Therac software then performed the treatment automatically. In each of the accidents that occurred, the electron beam was supposed to be at a reduced level but instead was applied full-strength, without the tungsten target in place. At the same time, the message "Malfunction 54" appeared on the monitor screen. Diagnosis revealed that the use of the up-arrow key to correct a typing mistake by the operator activated a fault in the software, leading to an error in the system which scrambled the two modes of operation.

Applying our failure framework to the 1986 accident which caused the death, six months later, of Mr V. Cox, the failure report might look like this:

- **Location:** East Texas Cancer Center in Tyler, Texas, USA.
- **Timing (1):** March 21 1986, at whatever the precise time that "Malfunction 54" appeared on the screen.
- **Timing (2):** total number of treatment hours on all Therac 25 machines up to that particular time.
- **Symptom (1):** "Malfunction 54" appeared on screen.
- **Symptom (2):** classification of the particular program of treatment being administered, type of tumor, etc.
- **End result:** strength of beam too great by a factor of 100.
- **Mechanism:** use of the up-arrow key while setting up the machine led to the corruption of a particular internal variable in the software.
- **Cause (1):** (trigger) unintentional operator action.
- **Cause (2):** (source type) unintentional design fault.
- **Severity:** critical, as injury to Mr Cox was fatal.
- **Cost:** effort or actual expenditure by accident investigators.

The failure is classed as "critical," rather than "catastrophic," in accordance with several safety guidelines that (unfortunately) require the loss of several lives for catastrophic failure.

Remember that only some of the eight attributes can usually be recorded at the time the failure occurs. These are:

- location
- timing
- symptom
- end result
- severity

The others can be completed only after diagnosis, including root cause analysis. Thus, a data collection form for failures should include at least these five categories.

When a failure is closed, the precipitating fault in the product has usually been identified and recorded. However, sometimes there is no associated fault. Here, great care should be exercised when closing the failure report, so that readers of the report will understand the resolution of the problem. For example, a failure caused by user error might actually be due to a usability problem, requiring no immediate software fix but perhaps changes to the user manual, or recommendations for enhancement or upgrade. Similarly, a hardware-related failure might reveal that the system is not resilient to hardware failure, but no specific software repair is needed.

Sometimes, a problem is known but not yet fixed when another, similar failure occurs. It is tempting to include a failure category called "known software fault," but such classification is not recommended because it affects the orthogonality of the classification. In particular, it is difficult to establish the correct timing of a failure if one report reflects multiple, independent events; moreover, it is difficult to trace the sequence of events causing the failures. However, it is perfectly acceptable to cross-reference the failures, so the relationships among them are clear.

The need for cross-references highlights the need for forms to be stored in a way that allows pointers from one form to another. A paper system may be acceptable, as long as a numbering scheme allows clear referencing. But the storage system must also be easily changed. For example, a failure may initially be thought to have one fault as its cause, but subsequent analysis reveals otherwise. In this case, the failure's "type" may require change, as well as the cross-reference to other failures.

The form storage scheme must also permit searching and organizing. For example, we may need to determine the first failure due to each fault for several different samples of trial installations. Because a failure may be a first manifestation in one sample, but a repeat manifestation in another, the storage scheme must be flexible enough to handle this.

5.2.3 Faults

A failure reflects the user's view of the system, but a fault is seen only by the developer. Thus, a fault report is organized much like a failure report but has very different answers to the same questions. It focuses on the internals of the system, looking at the particular module where the fault occurred and the cost to locate and fix it. A typical fault report interprets the eight attributes as shown in Figure 5.4.

Again, we investigate each of these categories in more detail.

In a fault report, **location** tells us which product (including both identifier and version) or part of the product (subsystem, module, interface, document) contains the fault. The IEEE Standard Classification for Software Anomalies (IEEE, 1992) provides a high-level classification that can be used to report on location:

- specification
- code
- database
- manuals
- plans and procedures
- reports
- standards/policies

Often, more detail is needed, to pinpoint exactly where the fault occurred. Again, the IEEE standard can offer help. For example, specification can be classified in more detail as:

- requirements
- functional
- preliminary design
- detailed design
- product design
- interface

Fault report
Location: within-system identifier, such as module or document name
Timing: phases of development during which fault was created, detected, and corrected
Symptom: type of error message reported, or activity which revealed fault (such as review)
End result: failure caused by the fault
Mechanism: how source was created, detected, corrected
Cause: type of human error that led to fault
Severity: refer to severity of resulting or potential failure
Cost: time or effort to locate and correct; can include analysis of cost had fault been identified during an earlier activity

---

Figure 5.4: Fault report

- database
- implementation

Timing relates to the three events that define the life of a fault:

1. when the fault is created;
2. when the fault is detected;
3. when the fault is corrected.

Clearly, this part of the fault report will need revision as a causal analysis is performed. It is also useful to record the time taken to detect and correct the fault, so that product maintainability can be assessed.

The **symptom** classifies what is observed during diagnosis or inspection. The IEEE standard on software anomalies (IEEE, 1992) provides a useful and extensive classification that we can use for reporting the symptom. We list the categories in Table 5.2.

The **end result** is the actual failure caused by the fault. If separate failure or incident reports are maintained, then this entry should contain a cross-reference to the appropriate failure or incident reports.

Mechanism describes how the fault was created, detected, and corrected. Creation explains the type of activity that was being carried out when the fault was created (for example, specification, coding, design, maintenance). Detection classifies the means by which the fault was found (for example, inspection, unit testing, system testing, integration testing), and correction refers to the steps taken to remove the fault or prevent the fault from causing failures.

Cause explains the human error that led to the fault. Although difficult to determine in practice, the cause may be described using a classification suggested by Collofello and Balcom (Collofello and Balcom, 1985):

- **communication:** imperfect transfer of information
- **conceptual:** misunderstanding
- **clerical:** typographical or editing errors

Table 5.2: Classification of fault types (IEEE, 1992)

Logic problem
            Forgotten cases or steps
            Duplicate logic
            Extreme conditions neglected
            Unnecessary function
            Misinterpretation
            Missing condition test
            Checking wrong variable
            Iterating loop incorrectly

Computational problem
            Equation insufficient or incorrect
                Missing computation
                Operand in equation incorrect
                Operator in equation incorrect
                Parentheses used incorrectly
            Precision loss
                Rounding or truncation fault
                Mixed modes
            Sign convention fault

Interface/timing problem
            Interrupts handled incorrectly
            I/O timing incorrect
                Timing fault causes data loss
            Subroutine/module mismatch
                Wrong subroutine called
                Incorrectly-located subroutine call
                Non-existent subroutine called
                Inconsistent subroutine arguments

Data handling problem
            Initialized data incorrectly
            Accessed or stored data incorrectly
                Flag or index set incorrectly
                Packed/unpacked data incorrectly
                Referenced wrong data variable
                Data referenced out of bounds
            Scaling or units of data incorrect
            Dimensioned data incorrectly
                Variable type incorrect
                Subscripted variable incorrectly
            Scope of data incorrect

Data problem
            Sensor data incorrect or missing
            Operator data incorrect or missing
            Embedded data in tables incorrect or missing
            External data incorrect or missing
            Output data incorrect or missing
            Input data incorrect or missing

Documentation problem

           Ambiguous statement
           Incomplete item
           Incorrect item
           Missing item
           Conflicting items
           Redundant items
           Confusing item
           Illogical item
           Non-verifiable item
           Unachievable item

Document quality problem

           Applicable standards not met
           Not traceable
           Not current
           Inconsistencies
           Incomplete
           No identification

Enhancement

           Change in program requirements
              Add new capability
              Remove unnecessary capability
              Update current capability
           Improve comments
           Improve code efficiency
           Implement editorial changes
           Improve usability
           Software fix of a hardware problem
           Other enhancement

Failure caused by a previous fix
Other problem

Severity assesses the impact of the fault on the user. That is, severity examines whether the fault can actually be evidenced as a failure, and the degree to which that failure would affect the user.

The **cost** explains the total cost of the fault to system provider. Much of the time, this entry can be computed only by considering other information about the system and its impact.

The optional **count** field can include several counts, depending on the purpose of the field. For example, count can report the number of faults found in a given product or subsystem (to gauge inspection efficiency), or the number of faults found during a given period of operation (to assist in reliability modeling).

EXAMPLE 5.5: We return to the Therac problem described in Example 5.4 (Leveson and Turner, 1993). The fault causing the failure we discussed may be reported in the following way:

- **Location:** product is the Therac 25; the subsystem is the control software. The version number is an essential part of the location. The particular module within the software is also essential.
- **Timing:** the fault was created at some time during the control software's development cycle.
- **Symptom:** the category and type of software fault that were the root cause of the failure.
- **End result:** "Malfunction 54," together with a radiation beam that was too strong.
- **Mechanism:** creation: during code development; detection: diagnosis of operational failure; correction: the immediate response was to remove the up-arrow key from all machines and tape over the hole!
- **Cause:** this is discussed at length in Leveson and Turner (1993).
- **Severity:** critical, even though not all of the "Malfunction 54" failures led to injury.
- **Cost:** the cost to the Therac manufacturers of all investigations of all the failures, plus corrections.

Again, the failure is classified as critical rather than catastrophic, because only one life was lost.

5.2.4 Changes

Once a failure is experienced and its cause determined, the problem is fixed through one or more changes. These changes may include modifications to any or all of the development products, including the specification, design, code, test plans, test data, and documentation. Change reports are used to record the changes and track the products most affected by them. For this reason, change reports are very useful for evaluating the most fault-prone modules, as well as other development products with unusual numbers of defects. A typical change report may look like Figure 5.5.

The **location** identifies the product, subsystem, component, module, or subroutine affected by a given change. **Timing** captures when the change was made, while **end result** describes whether the change was successful or not. (Sometimes changes have unexpected effects and have to be redone; these problems are discovered during regression or specialized testing.)

Changes are made for one of four reasons. The change may be **corrective**, in that it is correcting a fault that has been discovered in one of the software products. Or it may be **adaptive**: the system changes in some way (the hardware is changed, or some part of the software is upgraded), and a given product must be adapted to preserve functionality and performance. Changes also occur for **preventive** maintenance, when developers discover faults by combing the code to find faults before they become failures. And finally, developers sometimes make **perfective** changes, rewriting documentation or comments, or renaming a variable or routine in the hope of clarifying

---

Change report

Location: identifier of document or module changed

Timing: when change was made

Symptom: type of change

End result: success of change, as evidenced by regression or other testing

Mechanism: how and by whom change was performed

Cause: corrective, adaptive, preventive, or perfective

Severity: impact on rest of system, sometimes as indicated by an ordinal scale

Cost: time and effort for change implementation and test

Figure 5.5: Change report

the system structure so that new faults are not likely to be introduced as part of other maintenance activities. The **cause** entry in the change report is used to capture one of these reasons for change: corrective, adaptive, preventive, or perfective maintenance.

The **cost** entry explains the cost to the system developer of implementing a change. The expense includes not only the time for the developer to find and fix the system but also the cost of doing regression tests, updating documentation, and returning the system to its normal working state.

A **count** field may be used to capture the number of changes made in a given time interval, or to a given system component.

EXAMPLE 5.6: As reported by Sheldon and colleagues (Sheldon *et al.*, 1992), a US Air Force project kept track of the faults it found and the phase in the life-cycle when they were corrected. Figure 5.6 shows two pie charts. The first depicts the different types of faults that were encountered, and the second shows that most were not corrected until system integration and flight test. Notice that over 40% of the faults were due to requirements translation or incomplete requirements, but only 9% of them were fixed during the requirements analysis and specification phase. This profile of changes suggests that the project waited until too late in the life cycle to find and fix faults; steps should have been taken much earlier to verify and validate the requirements.

5.3 HOW TO COLLECT DATA

Since the production of software is an intellectual activity, the collection of data requires human observation and reporting. Managers, systems analysts, programmers, testers, and users must record raw data on forms. This manual recording is subject to bias (deliberate or unconscious), error, omission, and delay. Automatic data capture is therefore desirable, and sometimes essential, such as in recording the execution time of real-time software.

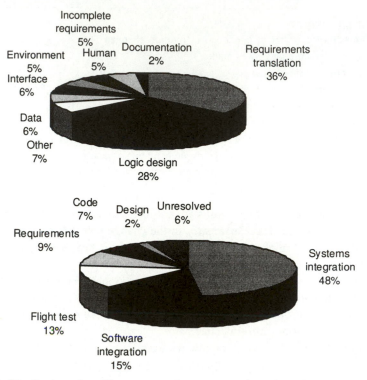

Figure 5.6: Distribution of problem type and correction phase for US Air Force project (Sheldon *et al.*, 1992)

Unfortunately, in many instances, there is no alternative to manual data collection. To ensure that the data are accurate and complete, we must plan our collection effort before we begin to measure and capture data. Ideally we should:

- keep procedures simple;
- avoid unnecessary recording;
- train staff in the need to record data and in the procedures to be used;
- provide the results of data capture and analysis to the original providers promptly and in a useful form that will assist them in their work;
- validate all data collected at a central collection point.

This last point is especially important. Basili and Weiss examined data from NASA's Goddard Space Flight Center in Maryland (Basili and Weiss, 1984). They found that half of the data collected was corrupted in some way and therefore not useful for analysis.

Planning for data collection involves several steps. First, you must decide which products to measure, based on your GQM analysis. You may need to measure several products that are used together, or you may measure one part or subsystem of a larger system.

EXAMPLE 5.7: Ultimately, faults of all types have to be traced to some system component, such as a program, function, unit, module, subsystem, or the system itself. If the measurement program is to enable management to take action to prevent problems, rather than waiting for problems to happen, it is vital that these components be identified at the right level of granularity. This ability to focus on the locus of a problem is a critical factor for your measurement program's success. For example, software development work at a large British computer manufacturer was hampered by not having data amalgamated at high levels. The software system had a large number of very small modules, each of which had no faults or very few faults. At this level of granularity, it was impossible to identify trends in the fault locations. However, by combining modules according to some rule of commonality (for example, similar function, same programmer, or linkage by calling routines), it may have been possible to see patterns not evident at lower levels. In other words, it was of little use to know that each program contained either 0 or 1 known fault, but it was of great interest to see that, for example, a set of 25 programs implementing a single function had 15 faults, whereas a similar set of programs implementing another function had no faults. Such information suggested to management that the first, more fault-prone function, be subject to greater scrutiny.

In this example, the level of granularity of collection was too fine. Of course, lowering the granularity can be useful, too. Suppose that your objective is to monitor the fault density of individual modules. That is, you want to examine the number of faults per thousand lines of code for each of a given set of modules. You will be unable to do this if your data collection forms associate faults only with subsystems, not with individual modules. In this case, the level of granularity in your data collection is too coarse for your measurement objectives. Thus, determining the level of granularity is essential to planning your data collection activities.

The next step in planning data collection is making sure that the product is under configuration control. We must know which version(s) of each product we are measuring.

EXAMPLE 5.8: In measuring reliability growth, we must decide what constitutes a "baseline" version of the system. This baseline will be the system to which all others will be compared. To control the measurement and evaluate reliability over time, the changed versions must have a multi-level version numbering scheme, including a "mark" number that changes only when there is a major functional enhancement. Minor version numbers track lesser changes, such as the correction of individual faults.

The GQM analysis suggests which attributes and measures you would like to evaluate. Once you are committed to a measurement program, you must decide exactly which attributes to measure and how indirect measures will be derived. This will determine what raw data will be collected, and when.

EXAMPLE 5.9: We saw in Chapter 3 that Barnard and Price used GQM to determine what measures they wanted to investigate in evaluating inspection effectiveness (Barnard and Price, 1994). They may have had limited resources, so they may have captured only a subset of the metrics initially, focusing first on the ones supporting the highest-priority goals. Once their metrics were chosen, they defined carefully exactly which direct and indirect measures were needed. For example, they decided that defect-removal efficiency is the percentage of coding faults found by code inspections. To calculate this indirect metric, they needed to capture two direct metrics: total faults detected at each inspection, and total coding faults detected overall. Then, they defined an equation to relate the direct measures to the indirect one:

$$\text{Defect\_removal\_efficiency} = 100 \times \frac{\sum_{i-1}^{N} \text{total\_faults\_detected}_i}{\text{total\_coding\_faults\_detected}}$$

The direct and indirect measures may be related by a measurement model, defining how the metrics relate to one another. Equations such as the one in Example 5.9 are useful models. Sometimes, graphs or relationship diagrams are used to depict the ways in which metrics are calculated or related.

Once the set of metrics is clear, and the set of components to be measured has been identified, you must devise a scheme for identifying each entity involved in the measurement process. That is, you must make clear how you will denote products, versions, installations, failures, faults, and more on your data-collection forms. This step enables you to proceed to form design, including only the necessary and relevant information on each form. We will look at forms more closely in section 5.3.1.

Finally, you must establish procedures for handling the forms, analyzing the data, and reporting the results. Define who fills in what, when, and where, and describe clearly how the completed forms are to be processed. In particular, set up a central collection point for data forms, and determine who is responsible for the data each step of the way. If no one person or group has responsibility for a given step, the data collection and analysis process will stop, as each developer assumes that another is handling the data. Analysis and feedback will ensure that the data are used, and useful results will motivate staff to record information.

5.3.1 Data collection forms

The data collection form encourages collecting good, useful data. The form should be as self-explanatory as possible, and should include the data required for analysis and feedback. Regardless of whether the form is to be supplied on paper or computer, the form design should allow the developer to record both fixed-format data and free-format comments and descriptions. Boxes and separators should be used to enforce formats of dates, identifiers and other standard values. Pre-printing data that is the same on all forms (for example, a project identifier), will save effort and avoid

CDIS FAULT REPORT	S.P0204.6.10.3016

ORIGINATOR:	Joe Bloggs
BRIEF TITLE:	Exception 1 in dps_c.c line 620 raised by NAS

FULL DESCRIPTION   Started NAS endurance and allowed it to run for a few minutes. Disabled the active NAS link (emulator switched to standby link), then re-enabled the disabled link and CDIS exceptioned as above. (I think the re-enabling is a red herring.)   (during database load)

ASSIGNED FOR EVALUATION TO: DATE:

CATEGORISATION: 0 ① 2 3 Design Spec Docn
SEND COPIES FOR INFORMATION TO:
EVALUATOR: _Awd_   DATE: 8/7/92

CONFIGURATION ID	ASSIGNED TO	PART
dpo_s.c		

COMMENTS: dpo_s.c appears to try to use an invalid CID, instead of rejecting the message. AWJ

ITEMS CHANGED

CONFIGURATION ID	IMPLEMENTOR/DATE	REVIEWER/DATE	BUILD/ISSUE NUM	INTEGRATOR/DATE
dpo_s.c v.10	AWJ 8/7/92	MAR 8/7/92	6.120	RA 8-7-92

COMMENTS:

CLOSED

FAULT CONTROLLER: DATE: 9/7/92

Figure 5.7: Problem report form used for air-traffic control support system

mistakes. Figure 5.7 shows an actual form used by a British company in reporting problems for an air-traffic control support system. (Notice that it is clearly designed to capture failure information, but it is labeled as a fault report!)

As we have seen, many measurement programs have objectives that require information to be collected on failures, faults, and changes. Section 5.3.1.1 presents a case study of a project whose specific objective was to monitor software reliability. The project developed several data-collection forms, including separate ones for each failure, fault, and change. We leave it as an exercise for you to determine whether the data collection forms have all the attributes we have suggested in this chapter.

5.3.1.1   Case study

Table 5.3 depicts an index for a suggested comprehensive set of forms for collecting data to measure reliability (and other external product attributes). Each form has a three-character mnemonic identifier. For example, "FLT" refers to the fault record, while "CHR" is a change record. These forms are derived from actual usage by a

Table 5.3: Data collection forms for software reliability evaluation

Identifier	Title
PVD	Product version
MOD	Module version
IND	Installation description
IRP	Incident report
FLT	Fault record
SSD	Subsystem version
DOD	Document issue
LGU	Log of product use
IRS	Incident response
CHR	Change record

large software-development organization. As we describe each set of forms, you can decide if the forms are sufficient for capturing data on a large project.

Some fields are present on all or most of the forms. A coded project identifier is used so that all forms relevant to one project can be collected and filed together. The name and organization of the person who completes each form must be identified so that queries can be referred back to the author in case of question or comment. The date of form completion must be recorded and distinguished from the date of any failures or other significant events. The identifier and product version must always be recorded, and a single project may monitor several products over several successive versions. For example, the installation description form may record the delivery and withdrawal of several successive versions of a product at a given installation, while the log of product use may record the use of several different products at the same terminal or workstation.

The product version, subsystem version, module version and document issue forms identify a product version to be measured: all its component subsystems, modules, and documents, together with their version or issue numbers. They are used to record when the product or component enters various test phases, trial, and service. Previous versions, if any, may be cross-referenced. Some direct product measures (such as size) are recorded; sometimes, the scales used for some associated process measures are also captured. Each subsystem version and module version description form should cross-reference the product version or higher-level subsystem version, to define a hierarchical product structure. Similarly, the document issue description should identify the product version of which the particular issue of the document is part. Together, this set of forms provides a basis for configuration control.

The installation document identifies a particular installation on which the product is being used and measured. It records the hardware type and configuration, and the delivery date for each product version.

The log of product use records the amount the product is used on a given installation. Separate records must be kept for each product version, and each record must refer to a particular period of calendar time, identified by a date; for example, the period can be described by the date of the end of the week. Total product use in successive periods on all installations or terminals can then be extracted as discussed above. This form may be used to record product use on a single central installation, or adapted for use at an individual terminal on a distributed system.

The incident report form has fields corresponding to the attributes listed in the sample failure report at the beginning of this chapter. Each incident must be uniquely identified. The person who completes the form will usually identify it uniquely among those from a particular installation. When the report is passed to the central collection point, a second identifier may be assigned, uniquely identifying it within the whole project.

The incident response report is returned to the installation from the central collection point following investigation of the incident's cause. If the wrong diagnosis is made, there may be a request for further diagnostic information, and several responses may be combined into one report. This report includes the date of response, plus other administrative information. After a response, the incident may be still open (under investigation) or closed (when the investigation has reached a conclusion). A response that closes an incident records the conclusion and refers to the appropriate fault record.

The fault record records a fault found when inspecting a product or while investigating an incident report. Each fault has a unique identifier. Note that a given fault may be present in one or more versions of the product, and may cause several incidents on one or more installations. The fields in this report correspond to those in the fault report recommended earlier in this chapter. Finally, the change record captures all of the fields described in the recommended change report early in the chapter.

Thus, the collection of ten forms includes all aspects of product fault, failure, and change information. Most organizations do not implement such an elaborate scheme for recording quality information. Scrutinize these descriptions to determine if any data elements can be removed. At the same time, determine if there are data elements missing. We will return to the need for these measures in Chapter 10, where we discuss software reliability in more depth.

5.4 WHEN TO COLLECT DATA

It is clear that data-collection planning must begin when project planning begins, and that careful forms, design and organization are needed to support good measurement. The actual data collection takes place during many phases of development. For example, some data relating to project personnel can be collected at the start of the project (for example, qualifications or experience) while other data collection, such as effort, begins at project start and continues through operation and maintenance.

On the other hand, counts of the numbers of specification and design faults in various intermediate products and product components can be collected as inspections are performed. Because there are several kinds of inspections, there may be several inspection-related measurement activities. For example, inspection-related fault information is generally recorded after high-level design, low-level design and coding of each subsystem or module. Data about faults found by inspections and tests should therefore be recorded consistently so that the relative effectiveness of these activities can be determined. Similarly, data about changes made to enhance the product, as opposed to correct faults, can be collected as enhancements are performed.

In general, data should be collected at the beginning of the project to establish initial values, and then again as the initial values change to reflect activities and resources being studied. It is essential that the data-collection activities become part of the regular development process. If developers do not know when they are supposed to be measuring, the measurement will not occur. Thus, it is helpful to compare a model of the normal development process with a list of desired measurements, and then map the measurements directly to the process model. In this way, if something needs to be measured and there is no obvious place to collect the data, the process can be modified to enable measurement. Likewise, if there is a process activity that is important and should be analyzed, the measurement list can be appended to address it.

EXAMPLE 5.11: Pfleeger and Theofanos assisted the US Department of Defense in deciding what to measure in its reuse program (Theofanos and Pfleeger, 1992). They began by capturing the reuse activities in a process model, as shown in Figure 5.8. The four key subprocesses included domain evolution, producing components, consuming components, and library management, where domain evolution involves identifying domains that are likely to provide reusable components.

This process model raised many questions. Notice, for instance, that the process model is completely separate from day-to-day development and maintenance. If this model is to show a programmer how reuse is to work, it must also integrate the regular development activities. When are programmers supposed to fit in reuse? Especially in an organization with a standard process, the reuse managers must demonstrate how reuse is related to development; without such integration, reuse will never become a natural part of development, and reuse activities will stop when incentives are withdrawn or priorities change.

Figure 5.9 illustrates how measures derived from a GQM analysis were mapped to the process. Each metric was assigned a number, and the process model was annotated to show where in the process the measurement would be made. However, the who, when, and how were not specified.

The process of associating metrics with the reuse process raised issues and led to revisions of the process, the questions, and the measurements. For example, the source of component quality information had to be clarified, and the nature of the quality measures redefined. Moreover, the mapping led to questions about responsibility: who fixes a broken component? and can there be more than one version of a component?

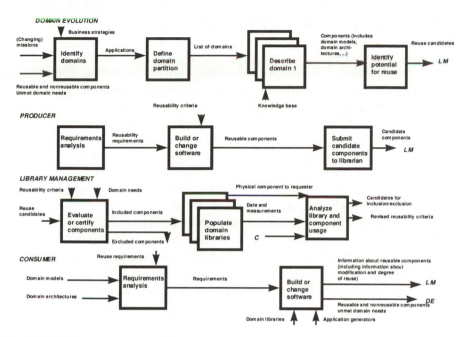

Figure 5.8: Reuse process model

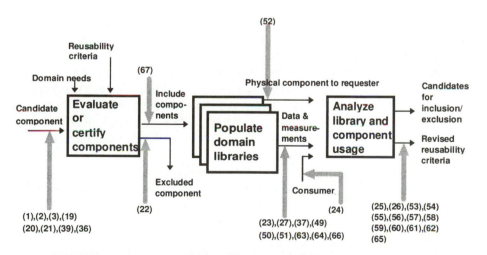

Figure 5.9: Partial process mapping: library management

We have seen how to decide what to collect and how to define it, how to plan the collection, how to design the forms, and how to map the measures to the process. Once we have captured the data, we must store it in a way that supports analysis and feedback.

5.5   HOW TO STORE AND EXTRACT DATA

Raw software-engineering data should be stored on a database, set up using a database-management system (DBMS). An automated tool for organizing, storing, and retrieving data, a DBMS has many advantages over both paper records and computer-stored "flat" files. Languages are available to define the data structure, insert, modify and delete data, and extract refined data. Constraints, such as checks on cross-references among records, can be defined to ensure consistency of data. Formats, ranges, valid values, and more can be checked automatically as they are input.

Several research projects have attempted to define an all-purpose data model or "schema" for software-engineering data (Comer *et al.*, 1987; Ross, 1989). The danger in attempting to define so general a model is that it may be large, cumbersome, and may not yield useful measures, as Moroney warned at the beginning of this chapter. In fact, all such projects reported in the software-engineering literature have found it necessary to adapt the data model to suit particular sets of data. Given a good GQM analysis, so that certain attributes need not be measured (and hence certain raw data need not be collected), general data structures and collection procedures need to be modified, not only to omit what is unnecessary, but also to redefine cross-references to ensure the consistency of what remains.

5.5.1   Raw database structure

We return to the case study of forms presented earlier. Consider a database structure intended to store the contents of the forms listed in Table 5.3. This database will support analysis of system reliability based on reported failure data.

Figure 5.10 depicts a database structure that supports this reliability measurement. In the figure, each box is a table in the database, and an arrow denotes a many-to-one mapping from one table to another. Thus, given an entity in the source table, we can uniquely identify one, and only one, associated entity in the target table. A double arrow means that there is at least one entity in the source table that maps to every entity in the target.

The mappings define the constraints that preserve the logical consistency of the data. For example, every fault recorded must be present in some product being measured. (Here, text in bold refers to table names.)

We can interpret the diagram in the following way:

- **Product** is a table of the products being measured, and **product version** is a table of all baseline product versions.
- **Installation** contains a list of all installations on which these product versions are run, and **product version installation** records the availability of a baseline version of a product on an installation, with its times of delivery and withdrawal.

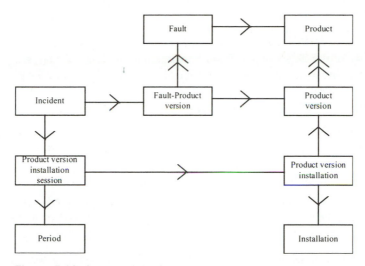

Figure 5.10: Suggested database structure

- **Period** defines the start and end of each of several successive periods of calendar time, covering the time during which a product is being measured.
- **Product version installation session** records the start and end calendar times of each session of using a given version of a product on a given installation, with the amount of use measured during the session. Each session lies wholly within one **period**.
- **Fault** records each fault detected in one or more versions of a product, together with its associated measurements.
- **Fault product version** is a table of fault-identifier/product-version pairs, each of which denotes that the given fault is present on the given version of the product.
- **Incident** is a table of all failures recorded while using a version of a product on a given installation, with various measurements, particularly calendar time of occurrence.

The constraints defined by this structure ensure consistency of data only, but they can help to detect incompleteness and inaccuracy. For example, when the timing of an **incident** is found outside the interval defined by the start and end of an associated **product version installation session**, the database may indicate that a record is missing from the **product version installation session**, or that a time of occurrence has been incorrectly entered in **incident**.

Notice that **incident** refers to **fault product version**. This mapping means that even when failures are not due to a product design fault, or when no causal fault can be found, they must still have a "pseudo-fault" assigned. It may be necessary to update the cross-reference as a result of investigation.

5.5.2   Extracting data

Once the database is designed and populated with data, we must find ways to take advantage of the data's organization in extracting the data for analysis. Suppose we have reliability data organized as described in section 5.5.1, and we want to generate a measure of reliability for a single baseline version of a single product over all installations. We can follow these steps:

1.   Select every **incident** that cross-references the given **product version**.
2.   Group the resulting **incident** records by the **fault** to which they refer, and sort each group by time of occurrence.
3.   Remove all but the first **incident** in each group.
4.   Count the remaining **incident** records within each **period**.
5.   Sum the product use recorded in **product version installation session** for all sessions within each **period**.

The result is a list of pairs of numbers: a count of faults first detected, and a measure of the total use of the given product version, in each successive calendar time period.

This structure is highly flexible and, provided the necessary measurements have been recorded properly, will permit the extraction of sets of refined data for various other kinds of analysis. For example, we can measure usability by analyzing counts of first detections of faults classified as usability problems. We can also extract effort to diagnose faults in order to calculate a measure of maintainability.

In Chapter 6, we take advantage of the fruits of our data collection. We turn to a discussion of data analysis.

5.6   SUMMARY

We have seen in this chapter that the success or failure of any metrics program depends on its underlying data-collection scheme. Chapter 3 showed us how the precise data to be collected is determined by the particular objectives for measurement; there is no universal set of data that can be prescribed. Thus, knowing if your goals are met requires careful collection of valid and complete data.

Data collection should be simple and non-obtrusive, so that developers and maintainers can concentrate on their primary tasks, with data collection playing a supporting role. Because quality is a universal concern, almost all measurement programs require data collection about software problems and their resolution. We distinguish among, and record information about, several types of problems: faults, failures and changes. For each class of entity, we consider measuring a number of different attributes, namely:

- **Location:** where is the entity?
- **Timing:** when did it occur?
- **Symptom:** what was observed?

- **End result:** which consequences resulted?
- **Mechanism:** how did it occur?
- **Cause:** why did it occur?
- **Cost:** how much was incurred by the developer?
- **Count:** how many entities were observed?

Data collection requires a classification scheme, so that every problem is placed in a class, and no two classes overlap. Such a scheme, called an orthogonal classification, allows us to analyze the types and sources of problems, so that we can take action to find and fix problems earlier in the life cycle.

It is important that system components be identified at appropriate levels of granularity. For some projects, this means that we collect subsystem data, while for others it means that we must look at each module carefully. Often, the granularity required means that we are dealing with large amounts of data. For this reason, and for consistency of counting, we should automate our data collection, or at least generate uniform data-collection forms. The collected data should be stored in an automated database, and the results should be reported back to the developers as soon as possible, so that they can use the findings to improve product and process.

5.7 EXERCISES

1. Define the notions of error, fault and failure in software.
2. Below is the severity classification for problems discovered in a large air-traffic control system. Discuss the quality of the classification; in particular, are there problems with orthogonality?

Category 1: operational system critical
- corruption or loss of data in any stage of processing or presentation, including database;
- inability of any processor, peripheral device, network, or software to meet response times or capacity constraints;
- unintentional failure, halt, or interruption in the operational service of the system or the network for whatever reason;
- failure of any processor or hardware item or any common failure mode point within the quoted mean time between failures that is not returned to service within its mean time to repair.

Category 2: system inadequate
- non-compliance with or omission from the air-traffic control operational functions as defined in the functional or system specifications;
- omission in the hardware, software or documentation (including testing records and configuration management records) as detected in a physical configuration audit;

- any Category 1 item that occurs during acceptance testing of the development and training system configurations.

Category 3: system unsatisfactory
- non-compliance with or omission from the non-air-traffic-control support and maintenance functions as defined by the functional or system specifications applicable to the operational, development and training systems;
- non-compliance with standards for deliverable items including documentation;
- layout or format errors in data presentation that do not affect the operational integrity of the system;
- inconsistency or omission in documentation.

3 Your company is developing the software for a telephone switching system for a single client. This very large system is delivered to the customer in phased releases. The customer occasionally observes system failures, such as loss of availability, loss of specific services, or erroneous services. There are two testing phases at which it is possible to gather additional failure data internally: integration testing and system testing. An attempt must be made to fix all failures, whether observed by the user or in test. Devise the necessary forms for a data-collection scheme that has to take account of the following:

- There are rigid reliability requirements for the system.
- There are wide variations in the ability to fix failures occurring in certain parts of the system (one of the project manager's major concerns).
- Your change control procedure has to be auditable.

4 Table 5.3 lists a series of forms to support software reliability measurement. Figure 5.10 depicts a database to organize the information included in these forms. Describe in detail the data elements of each form, and discuss which database tables should contain each element.

5 A software-development company has a metrics program in which the following specific measures are collected for each separate development project:

- total effort (in person years);
- total number of lines of code;
- total number of faults recorded during testing.

  i.   Describe three objectives that could sensibly be addressed by this set of measures. In each case, describe the goal that is to be addressed and how the metrics may enable you to understand and meet your goal. State clearly any limitations or reservations you might have about using this particular set of measures for the stated purposes.

 ii.   Each development project is divided up into modules which, depending on their functionality and criticality, may be specified, designed, and tested using different techniques. For example, some modules are subject to no specific quality-assurance techniques, while others may be formally specified, formally reviewed, and subject to several different testing strategies. What modest additions or changes would you make to the metrics program in order to be able assess the effectiveness of the different software quality-assurance methods?

6   Your company has been asked to build a Patient Observation and Control System, based on the following specification.

Patient Observation and Control System (POCS)

POCS is intended to improve the efficiency of intensive care, providing a better level of customer service while reducing the cost of trained medical staff required to operate it. Sensors attached to the patient will monitor all vital signs: heartbeat, respiration, blood pressure, temperature, and brain activity. The set of parameters to be recorded will vary from patient to patient. For example, a diabetic patient will require blood sugar level measurements in addition to the usual signs, and brain activity should not be recorded for an Arsenal football supporter, to avoid false indications of brain-death.

Drugs will be administered intravenously by pumps that are controlled by the system. The operation of these pumps and the dosage administered are also recorded. The signals from the sensors and pumps are concentrated at the Parameter Analysis Node (PAN) beside the bed. Complete data is held for the past hour on a local file, and essential information only (deviation of vital signs from normal values) is transmitted via a communications link to the nurse's station, where the Breakdown of Essential Data (BED) software displays the status of each patient on a monitor screen, and sounds an alarm to call the nurse to the bedside if necessary. If an emergency arises, a signal will be sent to the junior doctor's paging device. During quiet periods, a signal (to which the doctor must respond by pressing a button on the device) will be sent to the paging device at random intervals to prevent the doctor's falling asleep. If a cardiac arrest is detected, the cardiac team will be automatically alerted. In the case where the customer is a private patient, the senior consultant will also be paged.

i.   What are the three most important dependability attributes of POCS, and why?

ii.   What data would you record about any failure that occurred during the operation of POCS to enable you to measure the three dependability attributes selected in (i)?

iii. In addition to data about failures, what other types of data would you need in order to measure the attributes chosen in (i), and how would you record them?

iv. Describe five modes of POCS failure that could arise from the activation of latent software faults. In each case, state to which dependability attribute that mode of failure is relevant, and how its end result and severity are classified.

7 You are a consultant who builds software for the transportation industry. In the Edward the Confessor pub (known locally as the "Ted the Grass") in Stevenage one night, you happen to get into conversation with Big Mick, the owner of a local taxi firm. Over a pint or three, he outlines to you his requirement for a computer system to assist him in his business. The Stevenage Compute-a-cab Automated Management System (SCAMS) will control the running of Mick's taxis. In particular, it will automate the selection of routes and communication with the control room, to minimize voice radio communication. (At the moment, Mick's taxis are controlled by radio, and many of the drivers are inexperienced and do not have "the knowledge" of the layout of the town, particularly in outlying areas. The controllers therefore spend a lot of time guiding drivers to their destinations by referring to the map on the wall.)

Mick needs a "control and management" system (CAM) in the control room, to communicate via a digital radio link with a "computer on taxi" system (COT) on board each taxi. CAM will maintain a database of the location and status of every taxi. (For example, a taxi may be classified as waiting on rank, on way to pick up, waiting at pick-up location, on way to destination, arrived at destination, returning to base, or taking a tea break.) On receipt of a phone call from a prospective client, a controller will enter the pick-up location in the system, and COM will respond with the identification number of the taxi that can get there most quickly, plus an estimated time of arrival (ETA). If the ETA is acceptable to the client, CAM will signal the appropriate COT. If the driver responds with an "accept" message, the booking is confirmed, and CAM will direct the driver to the pick-up location. After the driver signals "customer picked up," CAM will transmit directions to the destination and, after the "at destination" signal, calculate the fare, inform the driver of the amount received, and record it on the accounts database.

COT will communicate with CAM, and display its directions to the driver. It will transmit back to CAM the status indicated by the driver. If a robbery is attempted, the driver can press a silent alarm, causing the COT to transmit an emergency signal both to CAM and to the police station.

Ideally, the location of each taxi will be determined by a Global Positioning System (GPS) receiver, but it is also possible for the driver to report location directly. The calculation of journey times by CAM requires a geographical database of the town, available by lease from Stevenage Borough Council, which already uses one for managing road repairs.

The next morning, you vaguely recall that you promised Mick a very dependable software system for SCAMS for a highly competitive price, but unfortunately you cannot remember exactly how dependable you promised the software would be; you also cannot remember what price you quoted. Before you meet Mick again and commit yourself to a written contract, you must think seriously about the dependability requirements for the proposed system.

i. Describe five ways in which the proposed SCAMS system could fail due to a software fault. In each case, imagine that you had just received a report of a failure due to that fault during the operation of SCAMS. State what data you would measure and record for that failure.

ii. Accounting for various modes of failure, state which dependability attributes are important for SCAMS, and suggest a reasonable quantitative target. Give reasons for your answer.

iii. What data you would collect during a trial of SCAMS in order to be able to measure the dependability attributes you have identified above, and convince Mick that the system was adequately dependable?

8 The proposed IEEE standard anomaly report form (IEEE,1992) contains the following fields. Comment on the completeness and utility of the form.
- anomaly report number
- date entered
- originator
- project
- computer
- program
- command
- title
- activity
- phase
- symptom
- repeatability
- product condition
- customer value
- actual cause
- source
- type
- resolution
- schedule impact
- severity
- priority
- estimated time to fix: program, documentation, test
- actual time to fix: program, documentation, test

9 Examine the "fault" report form of Figure 5.7. Using the guidelines for data collection discussed in this chapter, suggest changes to the form that would

improve data quality and help you to make better decisions about the data. For each suggested change, explain why the change will help.

5.8 Further reading

The definitions and attributes of failures, faults, and changes in this chapter are based on those in Peter Mellor's 1992 article, which also provides some further examples of how well-known failures fit into this framework. Mellor's terminology is consistent with the IEEE standard, listed below. The framework is essentially the same as that in the British draft standard, BS 5760, which provides comprehensive coverage concentrating on reliability assessment. For a detailed description of database structure for software reliability data, see Mellor's 1986 article.

> British Standards Institute, *Guide to Assessment of Reliability of Systems Containing Software*, British Standards Institute, Draft DD198 (to become BS5760 part 8), 1991.
> Mellor, P., "Field monitoring of software maintenance," *Software Engineering Journal*, 1(1), pp. 43–9, 1986.
> Mellor, P., "Failures, faults and changes in dependability measurement," *Information and Software Technology*, 34(10), pp. 640–54, 1992.
> IEEE Standard 729: *"Glossary of software engineering terminology,"* IEEE Computer Society Press, 1983.

The IEEE draft standard on quality (IEEE, 1992) provides a comprehensive set of classifications for software faults, and also contains some useful templates for various data-collection forms.

> IEEE P1044, *A Standard Classification for Software Anomalies* (draft), IEEE Computer Society Press, 1992a.

Laprie's book contains a set of definitions of terms relevant to dependability assessment, notably faults, errors and failures. The framework is applicable to systems generally. However, when restricted to software, the definitions correspond to those presented in this chapter.

> Laprie, J.-C. (ed.), *Dependability: Basic Concepts and Terminology*, Springer-Verlag, 1992.

Examples of several data-collection forms may be found in the British Standard, and in Grady's books about the measurement program at Hewlett-Packard.

> Grady, R.B. and Caswell, D., *Software Metrics: Establishing a Company-wide Program*, Prentice Hall, Englewood Cliffs, NJ, 1987.
> Grady, R.B., *Practical Software Metrics for Project Management and Process Improvement*, Prentice Hall, Englewood Cliffs, NJ, 1992.

For a comprehensive analysis of the Therac 25 accidents discussed in Example 5.4, Leveson and Turner's article is compelling reading.

Leveson, N.G. and Turner, C.S., "An investigation of the Therac-25 accidents," *IEEE Computer*, pp. 18–41, July 1993.

A full account of the change and maintenance process introduced in Section 5.2.4 may be found in Pfleeger's book.

Pfleeger, S.L., *Software Engineering: The Production of Quality Software*, 2nd edn, Macmillan, New York, 1991.

6 Analyzing software- measurement data

Including contributions from the first edition by
Barbara Kitchenham (University of Keele)

6.1 INTRODUCTION

In Chapter 4, we introduced general techniques for designing experiments and case studies. Then, in Chapter 5, we explained the importance of good data gathering to support rigorous investigation. In this chapter, we turn to the analysis of the data.

Data analysis involves several activities and assumptions:

- We have a number of measurements of one or more attributes from a number of software entities (products, processes, or resources). We call the set of measurements a **data set** or a **batch**.
- We expect the software items to be comparable in some way. For example, we may compare modules from the same software product by examining the differences or similarities in the data. Or, we may look at several tasks from the same project to determine what the data tell us about differences in resource requirements. Similarly, we can compare several projects undertaken by the same company to see if there are some general lessons we can learn about quality or productivity.

- We wish to determine the characteristics of the attribute values for items of the same type (usually we look at measures of central tendency and measures of dispersion), or the relationships between attribute values for software items of the same or different types.

To perform the analysis, we use statistical techniques to describe the distribution of attribute values, as well as the relationship between or among attributes. That is, we want to know what a picture of the data looks like: how many very high values, how many very low values, and how the data progress from low to high. And we want to know if we can express relationships among some attribute values in a mathematical way. Thus, the purpose of the data analysis is to make any patterns or relationships more visible, so that we can use the patterns and relationships to make judgments about the attributes we are measuring.

We begin our discussion of analysis by looking at several classical statistical techniques. In the first section, we explain why some statistical methods must be treated with caution when we apply them to software-measurement data. Then, we present some simple methods for exploring software measurements. In the next section, we turn to the relationships among attributes and how we can use analysis techniques to describe them. Several advanced techniques can be helpful in understanding software, and we discuss two of them: multi-attribute utility theory (including the analytical hierarchy process) and outranking methods. Finally, we end the chapter with a reminder of how statistical tests relate to the number of groups you are analyzing.

6.2 ANALYZING THE RESULTS OF EXPERIMENTS

After you have collected the relevant data (based on the framework we presented in earlier chapters), you must analyze it in an appropriate way. This section describes the items you must consider in choosing the analysis techniques. We discuss typical situations in which you may be performing an experiment, and what technique is most appropriate for each situation. Specific statistical techniques are described and used in the discussion. We assume that you understand basic statistics, including the following notions:

- measures of central tendency
- measures of dispersion
- distribution of data
- Student's t-test
- F-statistic
- Kruskal–Wallis test
- level of significance
- confidence limits

Other statistical tests are described here in overview, but the details of each statistical approach (including formulae and references to other statistical textbooks) can be found in standard statistical textbooks, including Caulcutt (1991), Chatfield (1993), Dobson (1990), and Draper and Smith (1966). However, you need not be a statistical expert to read this chapter; you can read about techniques to learn of the issues involved and types of problems addressed. Moreover, many of the commonly used spreadsheet and statistical packages analyze and graph the data automatically; your job is to choose the appropriate test or technique.

There are three major items to consider when choosing your analysis techniques: the nature of the data you collected, why you performed the experiment, and the type of experimental design you used. We consider each of these in turn.

6.2.1   The nature of the data

In previous chapters, we have considered data in terms of its measurement scale and its position in our entity-and-attribute framework. To analyze the data, we must also look at the larger population represented by the data, as well as the distribution of that data.

6.2.1.1   Sampling, population, and data distribution

The nature of your data will help you to decide what analysis techniques are available to you. Thus, it is very important for you to understand the data as a sample from a larger population of all the data you could have gathered, given infinite resources. Because you do not have infinite resources, you are using your relatively small sample to generalize to that larger population, so the characteristics of the population are important.

From the sample data, you must decide whether measured differences reflect the effects of the independent variables, or whether you could have obtained the result solely through chance. To make this decision, you use a variety of statistical techniques, based in large degree on the sample size and the data distribution. That is, you must consider the large population from which you could have selected experimental subjects and examine how your smaller sample relates to it.

In an experiment where we measure each subject once, the sample size is simply the number of subjects. In other types of experiments where we measure repeatedly (that is, the repeated-measures designs discussed in Chapter 4), the sample size is the number of times a measure is applied to a single subject. The larger the sample size, the more confident we can be that observed differences are due to more than just chance variation. As we have seen in Chapter 4, experimental error can affect our results, so we try to use large samples to minimize that error and increase the likelihood that we are concluding correctly from what we observe. In other words, if the sample size is large enough, we have confidence that the sample of measurements adequately represents the population from which it is drawn.

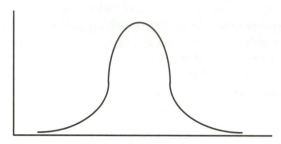

Figure 6.1: The normal distribution

Thus, we must take care in differentiating what we see in the sample from what we believe about the general population. **Sample statistics** describe and summarize measures obtained from a finite group of subjects, while **population parameters** represent the values that would be obtained if all possible subjects were measured. For example, we can measure the productivity of a group of programmers before and after they have been trained to use a new programming language; an increase in productivity is a sample statistic. But we must examine our sample size, population distribution, experimental design, and other issues before we can conclude that productivity will increase for any programmers using the new language.

As we have seen in Chapter 2, we can describe the population or the sample by measures of central tendency (mean, median, and mode) and measures of dispersion (such as variance and standard deviation). These characteristics tell us something about how the data are distributed across the population or sample. Many sets of data are distributed normally, or according to a Gaussian distribution, and have a bell-shaped curve similar to the graph shown in Figure 6.1. By definition, the mean, median, and mode of such a distribution are all equal, and 96% of the data occurs within three standard deviations of the mean.

For example, the data represented by the histogram of Figure 6.2 is sometimes called "normal" because it resembles the bell-shaped curve. As the sample gets bigger, we would expect its graph to look more and more bell-shaped.

You can see in the figure that the data are evenly distributed about the mean, which is a significant characteristic of the normal distribution. But there are other distributions where the data are skewed, so that there are more data points on one

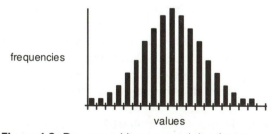

Figure 6.2: Data resembling a normal distribution

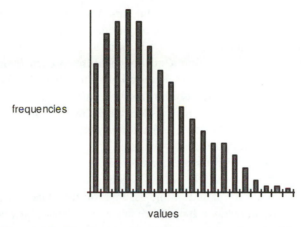

Figure 6.3: Distribution where data are skewed to the left

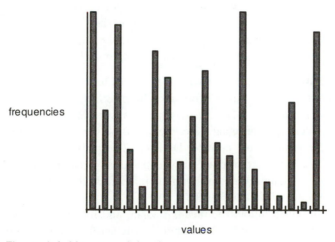

Figure 6.4: Non-normal distribution

side of the mean than another. For example, as you can see in Figure 6.3, most of the data are on the left-hand side, and we say that the distribution is skewed to the left.

There are also distributions that vary radically from the bell-shaped curve, such as the one shown in Figure 6.4. As we shall see, the type of distribution determines the type of analysis we can perform.

6.2.1.2   The distribution of software measurements

Let us see how common software-engineering data "measure up" to being normally distributed. In earlier chapters, we mentioned that many common statistical operations and tests are not meaningful for measures that are not on an interval or ratio scale. Unfortunately, many software measures are only ordinal. This scale results from our wanting to use measures that categorize and rank. For example, we create categories of failure severity, so that we can tell if most of our system failures are trivial, rather than life-threatening. Similarly, we ask our users to rate their satisfaction with the system, or ask designers to assign a quality measure to each requirement before design begins. Such ordinal measures do not allow us to calculate means and standard deviations, as those are suitable only for interval, ratio and absolute data. Thus, we must take great care in choosing analysis techniques that are appropriate to the data we are collecting. (And as we saw in Chapter 5, we may collect data based on the type of analysis we want to do.)

In addition to measurement scale considerations, we must also think about the way in which data are gathered. As we have seen in Chapter 4, many statistical tests and analysis techniques are based on the assumption that data sets are made up of measurements drawn at random. Indeed, we design our data-collection techniques to encourage this randomization and representation, although it is not always possible. Moreover, even when software measurements are on a ratio scale and are selected randomly, the underlying distribution of the general population of data is not always normal. Frequently, the datasets are discrete and non-negative, skewed (usually towards the left), and usually include a number of very large values.

Let us examine these problems more carefully by looking at examples of two real data sets.

Example 6.1: Consider the data sets in Tables 6.1a and 6.1b. Both contain measures of project and product information from commercial software systems. Data set 1 includes all of the data that was available from a particular environment during a particular time interval; it is typical of the project-level data used for project cost control. Data set 2 reflects attributes of all the procedures in a particular product subsystem and is typical of component-level data. This second data set includes various internal product measures that will be described in detail in Chapter 8.

In a normal distribution, the mean, median, and mode of the data are the same. We can use this information to tell us whether the example data sets are normally distributed or not. If, for each attribute of Table 6.1, we compare the mean with the median, we see in Table 6.2 that the median is usually considerably smaller than the mean. Thus, the data are not normally distributed.

There are several other techniques for assessing whether a distribution is normal; some are described by Kitchenham (1992). Until we know something about our data, we must be very cautious about the use of techniques which assume an underlying normal distribution. When we do not know anything about the distribution, there are a number of approaches to dealing with our lack of knowledge:

- We can use robust statistics and non-parametric methods. **Robust statistical methods** are descriptive statistics that are resilient to non-normality. That is, regardless of whether the data are normally distributed or not, robust methods yield meaningful results. On the other hand, **non-parametric**

Table 6.1a: Data set 1

Project effort (months)	Project duration (months)	Product size (lines of code)
16.7	23.0	6050
22.6	15.5	8363
32.2	14.0	13 334
3.9	9.2	5942
17.3	13.5	3315
67.7	24.5	38 988
10.1	15.2	38 614
19.3	14.7	12 762
10.6	7.7	13 510
59.5	15.0	26 500

Table 6.1b: Data set 2

Module size	Module fan-out	Module fan-in	Module control flow paths	Module faults
29	4	1	4	0
29	4	1	4	2
32	2	2	2	1
33	3	27	4	1
37	7	18	16	1
41	7	1	14	4
55	1	1	12	2
64	6	1	14	0
69	3	1	8	1
101	4	4	12	5
120	3	10	22	6
164	14	10	221	11
205	5	1	59	11
232	4	17	46	11
236	9	1	38	12
270	9	1	80	17
549	11	2	124	16

Table 6.2a: Summary statistics for data set 1

Statistic	Effort	Duration	Size
Mean	26.0	15.2	16 742
Median	18.3	14.8	13 048
Standard deviation	21.3	5.1	13 281

Table 6.2b: Summary statistics for data set 2

Statistic	Size	Fan-out	Fan-in	Paths	Faults
Mean	133.3	5.6	5.8	40	5.9
Median	69	4	1	14	4.0
Standard deviation	135.6	3.5	7.9	57.0	5.8

statistical techniques take into account the fact that the data are not normal; they allow us to test various hypotheses about the data set without relying on the properties of the normal distribution. In particular, non-parametric techniques often use properties of the ranking of the data.

- We can attempt to transform our basic measurements into a scale in which the measurements conform more closely to the normal distribution. For example, when investigating relationships between project effort and product size, it is quite common to transform to the logarithmic scale. Whereas the original data are not normally distributed, the logarithms of the data are.

- We can attempt to determine the true underlying distribution of the measurements and use statistical techniques appropriate to that distribution.

EXAMPLE 6.2: Mayer and Sykes looked at the relationship between lines of code per module and the number of decisions contained in each module. They found a very good fit for two different data sets using the negative binomial distribution (Mayer and Sykes, 1989).

6.2.1.3 Statistical inference and hypothesis testing

The distribution type plays a big part in how we make inferences from our data. Statistical inference is the process of drawing conclusions about the population from observations about a sample. The process and its techniques depend on the distribution of the data. As we have noted above, parametric statistical techniques apply only when the sample has been selected from a normally distributed population; otherwise, we must use non-parametric techniques. In both cases, the techniques are used to determine if the sample is a good representation of the larger population. For example, if we perform an experiment to determine the increase in productivity of programmers, as described in Example 4.17, we can calculate a mean productivity and standard deviation. Statistical inference tells us whether the average productivity for any programmer using the new language is likely to be the same as the average productivity of our sample.

The logic of statistical inference is based on the two possible outcomes that can result from any statistical comparison:

1. that the measured differences observed in the course of the experiment reflect simple chance variation in measurement procedures alone (that is, there is no real difference between treated subjects and untreated ones), or

2. that the measured differences indicate the real treatment effects of the independent variable(s).

The first case corresponds to our statement of the null hypothesis; there is no change. Statisticians often denote the null hypothesis as H_0. The second case is the alternative hypothesis, often written as H_1. The purpose of statistical analysis is to see whether the data justify rejecting H_0. The rejection of H_0 does not always mean the acceptance of H_1; there may be several alternative hypotheses, and rejection of

Table 6.3: Results of hypothesis testing

State of the world	Decision: Accept H_0	Decision: Reject H_0
H_0 is true	Correct decision Probability = $1 - \alpha$	Type I error Probability = α
H_0 is false	Type II error Probability = α	Correct decision Probability = $1 - \alpha$

H_0 means simply that more experimentation is needed to determine which alternative hypothesis is the best explanation of the observed behavior.

We emphasize that statistical analysis is directed only at whether we can reject the null hypothesis. In this sense, our data can disprove the alternative hypothesis in light of empirical evidence (that is, the data support the null hypothesis because there is no compelling evidence to reject it), but we can never prove it. In many sciences, a large body of empirical data is amassed, wherein each case rejects the same null hypothesis; then, we say loosely that this evidence "confirms", "suggests", or "supports" the alternative hypothesis, but we have not proven the hypothesis to be fact.

The statistical technique applied to the data yields the probability that the sample represents the general population; it provides the confidence we can have in this result and is called the **statistical significance** of the test. Usually referred to as the alpha (α) level, acceptable significance is agreed upon in advance of the test and often α is set at 0.05 or 0.01. That is, an experiment's results are not considered to be significant unless we are sure that there is at least a 0.95 or 0.99 probability that our conclusions are correct.

Of course, there is no guarantee of certainty. Accepting the null hypothesis when it is actually false is called a **Type II error**. Conversely, incorrectly rejecting the null hypothesis is a **Type I error**. Viewed in this way, the alpha level is the probability of committing a Type I error, as shown in Table 6.3.

We have seen how a normal distribution is continuous and symmetric about its mean, yet software data are often discrete and not symmetric. If you are not sure whether your data are normal or not, you must assume that they are not, and use techniques for evaluating non-normal data.

In the examples that follow, we consider both normal and non-normal cases, depending on the type of data. The examples mention specific statistical tests, descriptions of which are at the end of this chapter, and additional information can be found in standard statistical textbooks. Many of these statistical tests can be computed automatically by spreadsheets, so you need not master the underlying theory to use them; it is important only to know when the tests are appropriate for your data.

6.2.2   *Purpose of the experiment*

In Chapter 4, we noted two major reasons to conduct a formal investigation, whether it be an experiment, case study, or survey:

- to confirm a theory
- to explore a relationship

Each of these requires analysis carefully designed to meet the stated objective. In particular, the objective is expressed formally in terms of the hypothesis, and the analysis must address the hypothesis directly. We consider each one in turn, mentioning appropriate analysis techniques for each objective; all of the techniques mentioned in this section will be explained in more detail later in this chapter.

6.2.2.1 Confirming a theory

Your investigation may be designed to explore the truth of a theory. The theory usually states that use of a certain method, tool, or technique (the treatment) has a particular effect on the subjects, making it better in some way than another treatment (usually the existing method, tool, or technique). For example, you may want to investigate the effect of the Cleanroom technique (which we will describe in Chapter 10) by comparing it with your existing testing methods. The usual analysis approach for this situation is **analysis of variance**. That is, you consider two populations, the one that uses the old technique and the one that uses the new, and you do a statistical test to see if the difference in treatment results is statistically significant. You analyze the variance between the two sets of data to see if they come from one population (and therefore represent the same phenomenon) or two (and therefore may represent different phenomena). The first case corresponds to accepting the null hypothesis, while the second corresponds to rejecting the null hypothesis. Thus, the theory is not proven; instead, the second case provides empirical evidence that suggests some reason for the difference in behavior.

There are two cases to consider: normal data and non-normal data. If the data come from a normal distribution and you are comparing two groups, you can use tests such as the **Student's *t*-test** to analyze the effects of the two treatments. If you have more than two groups to compare, a more general analysis of variance test, using the *F* **statistic**, is appropriate. Both of these are described in most statistics books.

> **EXAMPLE 6.3:** You are investigating the effect on productivity of the use of a new tool. You have two groups that are otherwise equal except for use of the tool: group *A* is using the existing method (without the tool), while group *B* is using the tool to perform the designated task. You are measuring productivity in terms of thousands of delivered source code instructions per month, and the productivity data come from a normal distribution. You can use a Student's *t*-test to compare group *A*'s productivity data with group *B*'s to see if the use of the tool has made a significant change in productivity.

> **EXAMPLE 6.4:** On the other hand, suppose you want to investigate whether the Cleanroom technique yields higher-quality code than your current testing technique. Your null hypothesis is stated as "Code developed and tested using

the Cleanroom technique has the same number of defects per hundred lines of code as code developed using current testing techniques."

You collect data on number of defects per line of code (a measure of defect density) for each of two groups, and you seek an analysis technique that will tell you whether or not the data support the hypothesis. Here, the data on defects per line of code are not normally distributed. You can analyze the defect data by ranking it (for example, by ranking modules according to their defect density) and using the **Kruskal–Wallis test** to tell you if the mean rank of the Cleanroom modules is lower than that of the non-Cleanroom data.

6.2.2.2 Exploring a relationship

Often, an investigation is designed to determine the relationship among data points describing one variable or across multiple variables. For example, you may be interested in knowing the normal ranges of productivity or quality on your projects, so that you have a baseline to compare for the future. A case study may be more appropriate for this objective, but you may want to answer this question as part of a larger experiment. There are three techniques to use to answer questions about a relationship: box plots, scatter plots (or scatter diagrams), and correlation analysis.

A **box plot** can depict for you a summary of the range of a set of data. It shows you where most of the data are clustered and where any outlier data may be. Whereas a box plot shows information about one variable, a **scatter plot** depicts the relationship between two variables. By viewing the relative positions of pairs of data points, you can visually determine the likelihood of an underlying relationship between the variables. You can also identify data points that are atypical, because they are not organized or clustered in the same way as the other data points.

Correlation analysis goes a step further than a scatter diagram by using statistical methods to confirm whether there is a true relationship between two attributes. Correlation analysis can be done in two ways: by generating measures of association that indicate the closeness of the behavior of the two variables, or by generating an equation that describes that behavior.

> **Example 6.5:** You are investigating the relationship between number of control paths (c) in a module and the number of defects (d) identified in the module. A statistical analysis of these two variables can yield a measure of association, between -1 and 1, that indicates whether a high number of control paths usually means a large number of defects. That is, the **measure of association** is 1 if there is a perfect positive linear relationship between the two variables, -1 if there is a perfect negative linear relationship, and 0 if there is no relationship. If you want to be able to predict the number of defects from the number of control paths, then the measure of association is insufficient; correlation analysis techniques (such as **linear regression**) can generate an equation of the form:
>
> $$d = \alpha c + \beta$$

(where α and β are constants) to permit such prediction. The equation represents the line of best fit for the data.

When measures of association are sufficient, it is important to know if the data are normally distributed or not. For normally distributed values, a **Pearson correlation coefficient** is a measure of association that indicates whether or not the two variables are highly correlated. For non-normal data, you must rank the data and use the **Spearman rank correlation coefficient** as a measure of association. An alternative for non-normal data is the **Kendall robust correlation coefficient**, which investigates the relationships among pairs of data points and can identify partial correlations. If the ranking contains a large number of tied values (that is, repeats of the same value, so that they rank the same), a **chi-squared (χ^2) test on a contingency table** can be used to test the association between the variables.

When you need to understand the nature of the association as well, you can use **linear regression** to generate an equation to describe the relationship between two variables you are examining. This technique produces a line that minimizes the sum of the squares of the residuals. That is, linear regression minimizes the distance from the line to the points off the line, so it keeps the line as close as possible to the data points. For more than two variables, **multivariate regression** can be used.

The data to which regression is applied do not need to be normally distributed. However, regression techniques assume that the residuals (the distance from each point to the line) are normally distributed. When they are not, two techniques can be used instead of standard regression. **Theil's robust regression** uses the slopes of a carefully defined set of lines to determine the slope of the regression line. Or, the data points can be transformed to a closer-to-normal distribution by viewing their **logarithms**, rather than the data points themselves; then, regression is applied to the new data to generate a formula, and conversion back to non-logarithmic variables completes the process.

6.2.3   Design considerations

The investigation's design must be considered in choosing the analysis techniques. At the same time, the complexity of analysis can influence the design chosen, as noted earlier. Multiple groups usually require use of the F statistic with a full-blown analysis of variance, rather than a simple Student t-test with two groups. For complex factorial designs with more than two factors, more sophisticated tests of association and significance are needed. Statistical techniques can be used to account for the effects of one set of variables on others, or to compensate for timing or learning effects. These techniques are beyond the scope of this book, and you should consult a statistician for help with this type of design.

6.2.4   Decision tree

To help you understand when to use one analysis technique or another, we have constructed a decision tree, shown in Figure 6.5, to take into account the major

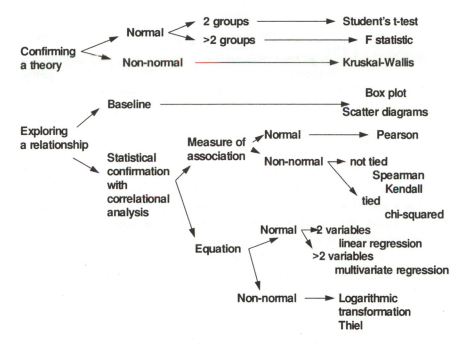

Figure 6.5: Decision tree for analysis techniques

considerations discussed in this section. The decision tree is to be read from left to right. Beginning with the objective of your investigation, move along the branch that fits your situation until you reach a leaf node with the appropriate analysis technique(s).

6.3   EXAMPLES OF SIMPLE ANALYSIS TECHNIQUES

There are many robust techniques that are useful with software measurement data, regardless of the distribution. You need not be a statistician to understand and use them, and you can implement them using simple spreadsheets or statistical packages. The previous section outlined several approaches, based on the reasons you are performing your investigation. In this section, we look at some of the techniques in more detail.

6.3.1   Box plots

Since software-measurement data sets are often not normally distributed, and since the measurements may not be on a ratio scale, it is important to remember that it is more appropriate to use the median and quartiles to define the central location and spread of the component values, rather than the more usual mean and variance. These robust statistics can be presented in a visual form called a **box plot**, as shown in

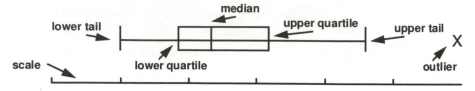

Figure 6.6: Drawing a box plot

Figure 6.6. Box plots are constructed from three summary statistics: the median, the upper quartile, and the lower quartile.

The **median** is the middle-ranked item in the data set. That is, the median is the value m for which half the values in the data set are larger than m and half are smaller than m. The **upper quartile** u is the median of the values that are more than m, and the **lower quartile** l is the median of the values which are less than m. Thus, l, m and u split the data set into four parts. We define the **box length**, d, to be the distance from the upper quartile to the lower; thus, $d = u - l$. Next, we define the **tails** of the distribution; these points represent the theoretical bounds between which we are likely to find all the data points if the distribution is normal. The theoretical upper tail value is the point $u + 1.5d$, and the lower tail value is $u - 1.5d$. These theoretical values must then be truncated to the nearest actual data point to avoid meaningless concepts (such as negative lines of code) and to demonstrate the essential asymmetry of skewed datasets. Values outside the upper and lower tails are called **outliers**; they are shown explicitly on the box plot, and they represent data points that are unusual in some way.

We can use the box plot to tell us if the data set is skewed by looking at the relative positions of the median, the quartiles, and the tails. If the data set is symmetric about the median, the median will be positioned in the center of the box, and the tail lengths (that is, the length from the quartile to the tail point) will be equal. However, if the data set is skewed, the median will be offset from the center of the box and the tail lengths will be unequal.

To see how box plots are used, we apply them to data set 2 of Table 6.1. Figure 6.7 shows the result.

> **EXAMPLE 6.6:** The lines of code values in Table 6.1b are arranged in ascending order. The median is the ninth value: 69. The lower quartile is the fifth value: 37. The upper quartile is the thirteenth value: 205. Thus, the box length is 168. Notice that the construction of the box plot is more difficult for an even number of observations; there, you must take the average of two values when there is no "middle" value. Hoaglin describes this procedure in more detail (Hoaglin, Mosteller and Tukey, 1983). It is clear that the box plot in Figure 6.7 is strongly skewed to the left.

Box plots are simple to compute and draw, and they provide a useful picture of how the data are distributed. The outliers are especially important when you are looking for abnormal behaviors.

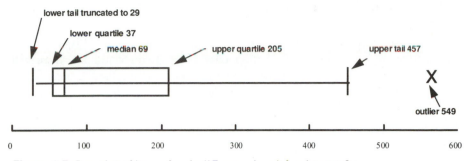

Figure 6.7: Box plot of lines of code (17 procedures) for data set 2

EXAMPLE 6.7:   Figure 6.8 shows box plots for measures taken on 17 software systems. Each system provided three measures: thousands of lines of code (KLOC), average module size in LOC (MOD), and the number of faults found per KLOC (fault density, or FD). The top box plot illustrates KLOC, the middle MOD, and the bottom FD. Each identifies outliers with respect to the measure it is depicting.

Notice that MOD and FD have exactly the same outliers! Systems D, L, and A have abnormally high fault densities, and they also have unusual module sizes: D and A have abnormally low MOD, while L has abnormally high MOD. Further investigation must identify more clearly the relationship between MOD and FD, but the initial data seem to confirm the widely held belief that a system should be composed of modules that are neither too small nor too large.

System	KLOC	MOD	FD
A	10	15	36
B	23	43	22
C	26	61	15
D	31	10	33
E	31	43	15
F	40	57	13
G	47	58	22
H	52	65	16
I	54	50	15
J	67	60	18
K	70	50	10
L	75	96	34
M	83	51	16
N	83	61	18
P	100	32	12
Q	110	78	20
R	200	48	21

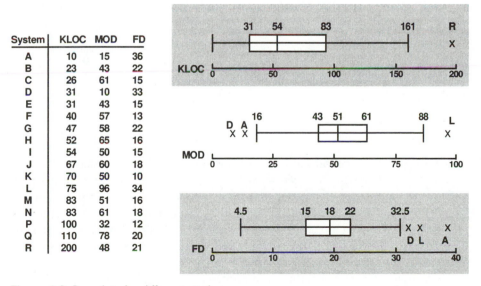

Figure 6.8: Box plots for different attributes

The outliers in the KLOC box plot seem to be unrelated to those in fault density.

In general, since the outliers represent unusual behavior, quality-assurance staff can use box plots to identify the modules that should be tested or inspected first. In this example, we might want to examine all systems whose MOD values are outliers in the box plot, since these modules are the ones most likely to be fault prone.

Thus, box plots point us to abnormal or unusual behavior. On the other hand, they can also help us to see what is usual or normal.

EXAMPLE 6.8:   We often analyze system test fault-density (defined as the number of faults discovered during system test divided by some measure of product size) on past projects to identify the fault-density norm for an organization or product line. We can calculate the likely number of system test faults expected for a new product entering system test by multiplying the median value of the fault density by the actual product size measure. Then, we can define an acceptable range to be between the upper and lower quartiles, and use it to monitor the results of system test.

Many developers seek to implement statistical quality control on software development. For this kind of control, it is too stringent to restrict the identification of potential problem components to those that are outliers. A compromise solution is to review quickly those components with values greater than the upper quartile; then, give greater scrutiny to the components with values greater than the upper quartile plus the box length. Components identified by these criteria are considered to be **anomalies** rather than outliers.

These examples make clear the utility of box plots in

- providing norms for planning purposes;
- summarizing actual measurements for the purposes of project monitoring; and
- identifying software items with unusual values for quality control and process evaluation.

6.3.2   Scatter plots

We saw the utility of box plots in visualizing what is happening in a dataset. The box plot hides most of the expected behavior and shows us instead what is unusual. Another useful depiction of data is a **scatter plot**. Here, we simply graph all the data to see what the patterns or trends may be. For example, the graph in Figure 6.9 contains a point for each of the ten projects in data set 1 of Table 6.1. The abscissa (or x-axis) is labeled from 1 to 10 for the project number, the ordinate (or y-axis) shows the effort, and there is one point for each measurement in the data set.

We can see from the graph that most of the projects require less than 40 person months of effort, but two require a great deal more. Such information raises many

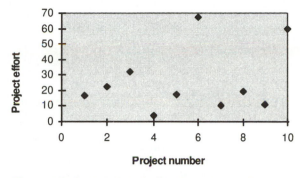

Figure 6.9: Scatter plot of effort from data set I

questions, and often we want to know the relationship between one attribute (such as effort in this example) and others (such as size). Unlike box plots, scatter plots allow us to look at more than one attribute at a time.

In Chapter 4, we saw many reasons for wanting to investigate the relationships among attribute values. For instance, understanding relationships is necessary when, for planning purposes, we wish to predict the future value of an attribute from some known value(s) of the same or different attributes. Likewise, quality control requires us to identify components having an unusual combination of attribute values.

When we are interested in the relationship between two attributes, a scatter plot offers a visual assessment of the relationship by representing each pair of attribute values as a point in a Cartesian plane.

EXAMPLE 6.9:   Figure 6.10 is a scatter plot of effort (measured in person months) against size (measured in thousands of lines of code) for data set 1 in Table 6.1. This plot shows us that there appears to be a general relationship between size and effort, namely that effort increases with the size of the project.

However, there are a few points that do not support this general rule. For instance, two projects required almost 40 person months to complete, but one

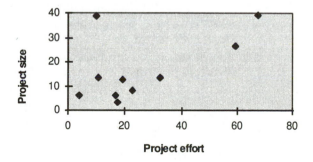

Figure 6.10: Scatter plot of project effort against project size for data set I

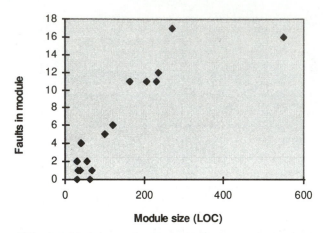

Figure 6.11: Scatter plot of module faults against module size for data set 2

was 10 KLOC, while the other was 68. The scatter plot cannot explain this situation, but it can suggest hypotheses that we can then test with further investigation.

EXAMPLE 6.10: Similarly, Figure 6.11 is a scatter plot of the module data shown in data set 2 of Table 6.1. Here, module size (measured in lines of code) is graphed against the number of faults discovered in the module. That is, there is a point in the scatter plot for each module in the system. Again, the plot shows a trend, in that the number of faults usually increases with the module size. However, again we find one point that does not follow the rule: the largest module does not appear to have as many faults as might have been expected.

Thus, scatter plots show us both general trends and atypical situations. If a general relationship seems to be true most of the time, we can investigate the situations that are different and determine what makes the projects or products anomalous. The general relationship can be useful in making predictions about future behavior, and we may want to generate an estimating equation to project likely events (we will see examples of this in Chapter 12). Similarly, we may project likely anomalies to control problems by taking action to avert their behavior or by minimizing their effects.

For obvious reasons, scatter plots are not helpful for more than three variables, unless you evaluate relationships for all possible pairs and triples. Such partitioning of the problem does not give you a good overview of the behavior that interests you.

6.3.3 Control charts

Another helpful technique is a **control chart**, which helps you to see when your data are within acceptable bounds. By watching the data trends over time, you can decide whether to take action to prevent problems before they occur. To see how control charts work, consider first some non-software examples. Many processes have a normal variation in a given attribute. For instance, steel manufacturers rarely make a one-inch nail that is exactly one inch long; instead, they set tolerances, and a one-inch nail can be a very small fraction above or below an inch in length and still be acceptable. We would expect the actual length values to be randomly distributed about the mean of one inch, and 95% of the nails would have lengths falling within two standard deviations of the one-inch mean. Similarly, the voltage in a 220-volt electrical outlet is rarely exactly 220 volts; instead, it ranges in a band around 220 volts, and appliances are designed to work properly within that small band (but may fail to work if the voltage drops too low or jumps too high).

In the same way, there are parts of the software process that can be expected to behave in a random way, and we can use the control limits to warn us when a value is unusual. We use the values of two standard deviations above and below the mean as guidelines; if a value falls outside these boundaries, then the behavior is unexpected, and we want to investigate why.

Consider the data in Table 6.4. Here, we have information about the ratio between preparation hours and inspection hours for a series of design inspections. We calculate the mean and standard deviation of the data, and then two control limits. The **upper control limit** is equal to two standard deviations above the mean, while the **lower control limit** is two standard deviations below the mean (or zero, if a negative control limit is meaningless). The control limits act as guidelines for understanding when the data are within random statistical variation and when they represent unusual behavior. In this sense, control charts are similar to box plots.

To visualize the behavior of the data, we construct a graph called a **control chart**. The graph shows the upper control limit, the mean, and the lower control limit. As you can see in Figure 6.12, the data are plotted so that we can see when they are getting close to or exceeding the control limits. In the figure, the data stay within the

Table 6.4: Selected design inspection data (Schulmeyer and McManus, 1987)

Component number	Preparation hours/ inspection hours
1	1.5
2	2.4
3	2.2
4	1.0
5	1.5
6	1.3
7	1.0
Mean	1.6
Standard deviation	0.5
Upper control limit (UCL)	2.6
Lower control limit (LCL)	0.4

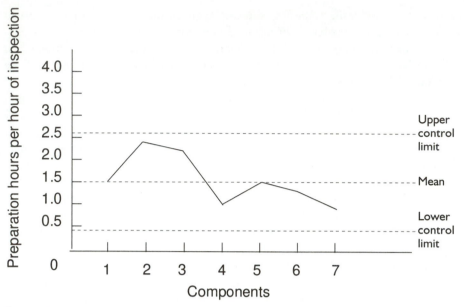

Figure 6.12: Inspection control chart showing hours of preparation per hour of inspection (Humphrey, 1989)

control limits. Thus, the preparation hours per hour of inspection are within what we would expect of random variation. However, if the data were to exceed the control limits, we would take action to bring them back under control – that is, back within the band between the upper and lower control limits. In this example, exceeding the upper control limit means that too much preparation is being done, or not enough time is being spent during inspection; if the value is below the lower control limit, then not enough preparation is being done, or too much time is being spent during inspection. Even when data do not exceed the control limits, action can be taken when the trend veers toward the edge of the acceptable band, so that behavior is drawn back toward the middle.

6.3.4 Measures of association

Scatter plots examine the behavior of two attributes, and sometimes we can determine that the two attributes are related. But evidence of a relationship between two attributes does not constitute proof of causality. That is, just because a change in one attribute seems usually to provoke a predictable change in the other, we do not know for certain that similar changes will take place in the future. However, there are statistical techniques that can help us evaluate the likelihood that the relationship seen in the past will be seen again in the future. We call these techniques **measures of association**, and the measures are supported by statistical tests that check whether the association is significant.

For normally distributed attribute values, the **Pearson correlation coefficient** is a valuable measure of association. Suppose we want to examine the association between two attributes, x and y. For instance, we saw in Example 6.10 that x could be the size of a module, while y is the number of faults found in the module. If the data set of xs is normally distributed (or nearly) and so is the dataset of ys, then we can form pairs (x_i, y_i), where there are i software items and we want to measure the association between x and y. The total number of pairs is n, and for each attribute, we calculate the mean and variance. We represent the mean of the xs by m_x, and the mean of the ys by m_y. Likewise, var(x) is the variance of the set of xs, and var(y) the variance of the y's. Finally, we calculate

$$r = \sum_{i=1}^{n} \frac{(x_i - m_x)(y_i - m_y)}{\sqrt{n \, \text{var}(x) \, \text{var}(y)}}$$

The value of r, called the correlation coefficient, varies from -1 to 1. When r is 1, then x and y have a perfect positive linear relationship; that is, when x increases, then so does y in equal linear steps. Similarly, -1 indicates a perfect negative linear relationship (that is, when x increases, y decreases linearly), and 0 indicates no relationship between x and y (that is, when x increases, y is just as likely to increase as to decrease). Statistical tests can be used to check whether a calculated value of r is significantly different from zero at a specified level of significance; in other words, computation of r must be accompanied by a test to indicate how much confidence we should have in the association.

However, as we have noted before, most software measurements are not normally distributed and usually contain atypical values. In fact, the data set in Example 6.10 is not from a normal distribution, so the Pearson correlation coefficient is not recommended for it. In these cases, it is preferable to use robust measures of association and non-parametric tests of significance. One approach to the problem is the use of a robust correlation coefficient; other approaches, including contingency tables and the chi-squared test, are discussed in standard statistical textbooks.

6.3.5 Robust correlation

The most commonly-used robust correlation coefficient is **Spearman's rank correlation coefficient**. It is calculated in the same way as the Pearson correlation coefficient, but the x and y values are based on ranks of the attributes, rather than raw values. That is, we place the attribute values in ascending order and assign 1 to the smallest value, 2 to the next smallest, and so on. If two or more raw values are equal, each is given the average of the related rank values.

> **EXAMPLE 6.11:** The two smallest modules in dataset 2 have 29 lines of code. In a ranking, each module is assigned the rank of 1.5, calculated as the average of ranks 1 and 2.

Kendall's robust correlation coefficient τ varies from -1 to 1, as Spearman's, but the underlying theory is different. The Kendall coefficient assumes that, for each two pairs of attribute values, (x_i, y_i) and (x_j, y_j), if there is a positive relationship between the attributes, then when x_i is greater than x_j, then it is likely that y_i is greater than y_j. Similarly, if there is a negative relationship, then when x_i is greater than x_j, it is likely that y_i is less than y_j. Kendall's τ is based on assessing all of pairs of vectors (in a data set of points) and comparing positive with negative indications.

Kendall's correlation coefficient is important because it can be generalized to provide partial correlation coefficients. These partial values are useful when the relationship between two attributes may in fact be due to the relationship between both attributes and a third attribute. (See Seigel and Castellan's statistics book for an explanation of partial coefficients and their use (Siegel and Castellan, 1988).)

The rank correlation coefficients are intended to be resilient both to atypical values and to non-linearity of the underlying relationship, as well as not being susceptible to the influence of very large values.

EXAMPLE 6.12: Tables 6.5 and 6.6 contain the values of the Pearson, Spearman and Kendall correlation coefficients for various attribute pairs from data sets 1 and 2 in Table 6.1. Notice that, in both tables, the robust correlations (that is, the Spearman and Kendall values) are usually less than the Pearson correlations. This difference in correlation value is caused by the very large values in both datasets; these large values tend to inflate the Pearson correlation coefficient but not the rank correlations.

Notice, too, that we have calculated some of the correlations both with and without some of the atypical values, as identified by scatter plots earlier in this

Table 6.5: Correlation coefficients for data set 1

Type	Effort v. size	Effort v. size (atypical items removed)	Effort v. duration	Effort v. duration (atypical items removed)
Pearson	0.57	0.91	0.57	0.59
Spearman	0.46	0.56	0.48	0.50
Kendall	0.33	0.67	0.38	0.65

Table 6.6: Correlation coefficients for data set 2

Type	LOC v. faults	LOC v. faults (atypical removed)	Paths v. faults	Paths v. faults (atypical removed)	FO v. faults	FI v. faults
Pearson	0.88	0.96	0.68	0.90	0.65	−0.11
Spearman	0.86	0.83	0.80	0.79	0.54	0.02
Kendall	0.71	0.63	0.60	0.62	0.58	0.02

chapter. It appears that the rank correlation coefficients are reasonably resilient to atypical values. Moreover, the relationship between control flow paths and faults in a module is non-linear, but the rank correlations are not affected by it.

Table 6.5, reflecting data set 1, shows that, in general, all the correlation coefficients were susceptible to the gross outliers in the data. So although the rank correlation coefficients are more reliable for software-measurement data than the Pearson correlation, they can be misleading without visual inspection of any supposed relationship.

Example 6.12 includes a practice common to data analysis: eliminating atypical data points. Sometimes, a scatter plot or correlational analysis reveals that some data illustrate behavior different from the rest. It is important to try to understand what makes these data different. For example, each point may represent a project, and the unusual behavior may appear only in those projects done for a particular customer, X. With those data points removed, the behavior of the rest can be analyzed and used to predict likely behavior on future projects done for customers other than X. However, it is not acceptable to remove data points only to make the associations look stronger; there must be valid reasons for separating data into categories and analyzing each category separately.

6.3.6 Linear regression

Having identified a relationship using box plots, scatter plots, or other techniques, and having evaluated the strength of the association between two variables, our next step is expressing the nature of the association in some way. Linear regression is a popular and useful method for expressing an association as a linear formula. The linear regression technique is based on a scatter plot. Each pair of attributes is expressed as a data point, (x_i, y_i), and then the technique calculates the line of best fit among the points. Thus, our goal is to express attribute y, the dependent variable, in terms of attribute x, the independent variable, in an equation of the form:

$$y = a + bx$$

To see how this technique works, consider again the scatter plot of Figure 6.10. We can draw a line roughly to estimate the trend we see, showing that effort increases as size increases; this line is superimposed on the scatter plot in Figure 6.13.

The theory behind linear regression is to draw a line from each data point vertically up or down to the trend line, representing the vertical distance from the data point to the trend. In some sense, the length of these lines represent the discrepancy between the data and the line, and we want to keep this discrepancy as small as possible. Thus, the line of "best fit" is the line that minimizes these distances.

The mathematics required to calculate the slope, b, and intercept, a, of this "best fit" line are straightforward. The discrepancy for each point is called the **residual**, and the formula for generating the linear regression line minimizes the sum of the squares of the residuals. We can express the residual for a given data point as

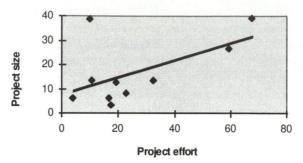

Figure 6.13: Plot of effort against size for data set I, including line to show trend

$$r_i = y_i - a - bx_i$$

Minimizing the sum of squares of the residuals leads to the following equations for a and b:

$$b = \frac{\sum(x_i - m_x)(y_i - m_y)}{\sum(x_i - m_x)^2}$$

$$a = m_y - bm_x$$

The least-squares technique makes no assumptions about the normality of the distribution of either attribute. However, to perform any statistical tests relating to the regression parameters (for example, we may want to determine if the value of b is significantly different from 0), it is necessary to assume that the residuals are distributed normally. In addition, the least-squares approach must be used with care when there are many large or atypical values; these data points can distort the estimates of a and b.

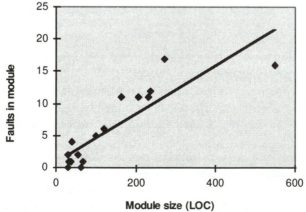

Figure 6.14: Module size against faults, including linear regression line

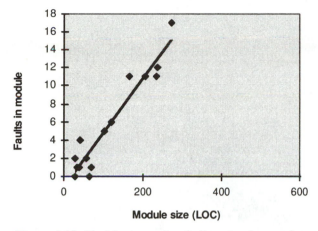

Figure 6.15: Module size against faults, using data set 2 minus largest module

EXAMPLE 6.13: Figure 6.14 shows the scatter plot of module size against faults from data set 2 in Table 6.1. Imposed on the scatter plot is the line generated by linear regression. Notice that there are several values in the dataset that are far from the line, including the point representing the largest module. If we remove the data point for the largest module, the regression line changes dramatically, as shown in Figure 6.15. The remaining data points are much closer to the new line.

After fitting a regression line, it is important to check the residuals to see if any are unusually large. We can plot the residual values against the corresponding dependent variable in a scatter plot. The resulting graph should resemble an ellipsoidal cloud of points, and any outlying point (representing an unusual residual) should be clearly visible, as shown in Figure 6.16.

6.3.7 Robust regression

There are a number of robust linear-regression approaches, and several statistical textbooks (see Sprent (1989), for example) describe them. For instance, Theil proposed estimating the slope of the regression line as the median of the slopes of all lines joining pairs of points with different values. For each pair (x_i, y_i) and (x_j, y_j), the slope is

$$b_{ij} = \frac{y_j - y_i}{x_j - x_i}$$

If there are n data points and all the x_i are different, then there are $n(n - 1)/2$ different values for b_{ij}, and b is estimated by the median value. It is also possible to determine the confidence limits for this estimate.

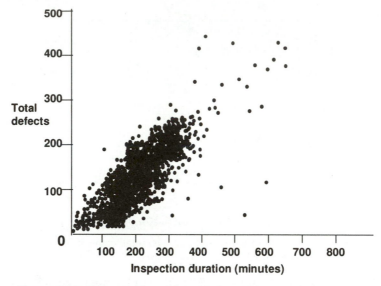

Figure 6.16: A scatter plot with residuals noted

Theil suggested estimating the intercept, a, as the median of all the values

$$a_i = y_i - bx_i$$

EXAMPLE 6.14: We can apply Theil's method to the relationship between size and effort represented by data set 1, and we generate the equation

$$\text{effort(months)} = 8.869 + 1.413 \text{ size(KLOC)}$$

This equation is quite similar to the regression line obtained by least squares when the atypical value is removed. However, the confidence limits on the estimate of the slope range from -0.22 to 2.13 (at the 0.05 level of significance) which includes 0. Thus, we must conclude that the robust technique implies that the relationship between effort and size is not significant.

6.3.8 Multivariate regression

The regression methods we have considered so far have focused on determining a linear relationship between two attributes. Each has involved the use of the least squares technique. This technique can be extended to investigate a linear relationship between one dependent variable and two or more independent variables; we call this **multivariate linear regression**. However, we must be cautious when considering a large number of attributes, because:

- It is not always possible to assess the relationship visually, so we cannot easily detect atypical values.
- Relationships among the dependent variables can result in unstable equations. For example, most size and structure attributes are correlated, so it is

dangerous to include several size and structure measures in the same multivariate regression analysis.
* Robust multivariate regression methods can be quite complicated.

For multivariate linear regression, we recommend using least-squares analysis but avoiding the use of many correlated dependent variables. Be sure to analyze the residuals to check for atypical data points (that is, data points having very large residuals).

6.4   MORE ADVANCED METHODS

There are many other statistical methods for analyzing data. In this section, we consider several advanced methods that can be useful in investigating relationships among attributes: classification tree analysis, transformations, multivariate data analysis and multi-criteria decision aids.

6.4.1   *Classification tree analysis*

Many statistical techniques deal with pairs of measures. But often we want to know which measures provide the best information about a particular goal or behavior. That is, we collect data for a large number of measures, and we want to know which ones are the best predictors of the behavior in a given attribute. A statistical technique called **classification tree analysis** can be used to address this problem. This method, applied successfully by Porter and Selby on NASA Software Engineering Laboratory data, allows large sets of metrics data to be analyzed with respect to a particular goal (Porter and Selby, 1990).

> **EXAMPLE 6.15:**   Suppose you have collected data on a large number of code modules, and you want to determine which of the metrics are the best predictors of poor quality. You define poor quality in terms of one of your measures; for instance, you may say that a module is of poor quality if it has more than three faults. Then, a classification tree analysis generates a decision tree to show you which of the other measures are related to poor quality. The tree may look like the one in Figure 6.17, which suggests that if a module is between 100 and 300 lines of code and has a cyclomatic number of at least 15, then it may have a large number of faults. Likewise, if the module is over 300 lines of code, has had no design review, and has been changed at least five times, then it too may have a large number of faults. This technique is useful for shrinking a large number of collected measures to a smaller one, and for suggesting design or coding guidelines. In this example, the tree suggests that, when resources are limited, design reviews may be restricted to large modules, and code reviews may be advisable for large modules that have been changed a great deal.

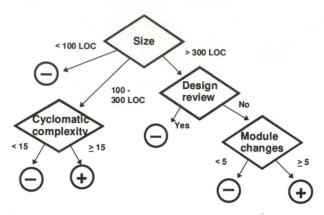

Figure 6.17: Classification tree

6.4.2 Transformations

Sometimes it is difficult to understand the behavior of data in their original form, but much easier if the data are transformed in some way to make the behavior more visible. We noted earlier that it is sometimes possible to transform non-normal data into normal data by applying a logarithmic function. In general, a **transformation** is a mathematical function applied to a measurement. The function transforms the original data set into a new data set. In particular, if a relationship between two variables appears to be non-linear, it is often convenient to transform one of the attributes in order to make the relationship more linear.

EXAMPLE 6.16: Figure 6.18 is a scatter plot of some of the data from data set 2 in Table 6.1. Here, we have graphed the structure of each module, as measured by control flow paths, against the number of faults found in the

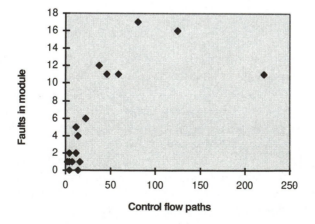

Figure 6.18: Structure graphed against faults, from data set 2

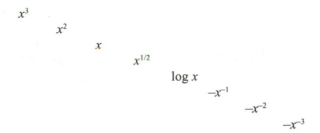

Figure 6.19: Tukey's ladder

module. The relationship between faults and number of paths appears to be non-linear and therefore not suitable for analysis using linear regression.

There are many choices for transformation. Tukey suggested a "ladder" from which to decide on an appropriate transformation function (Mosteller and Tukey, 1977). The ladder consists of a sequence of transformation functions (Figure 6.19).

We begin by positioning ourselves at the x value of the ladder. If we seem to have a curved rather than linear relationship between two attributes, we use the ladder as follows:

- If the relationship looks positive and convex (as in Figure 6.18), we may transform either the independent variable by going down the ladder (that is, using a square-root transformation), or the dependent variable by going up the ladder (that is, using a square transformation).
- If the relationship looks positive and concave, we may transform either the independent variable by going up the ladder, or the dependent variable by going down.

If it is important to obtain an equation for predicting the dependent variable, we recommend transforming the independent variable, so that the dependent variable is in the correct scale.

EXAMPLE 6.17: Figure 6.20 is a graph of the data depicted in Figure 6.18, except that the square root of the control flow paths is plotted, rather than the raw data of data set 2. The relationship of the transformed data to the module faults is clearly more linear for the transformed data than for the raw data. In fact, the relationship obtained using the raw data accounts for only 46% of the variation of the dependent variable, whereas the relationship obtained using the transformed data accounts for 68% of the variation.

There are many other reasons for transforming data. For example, data are often transformed to cope with relationships of the form:

$$y = ax^b$$

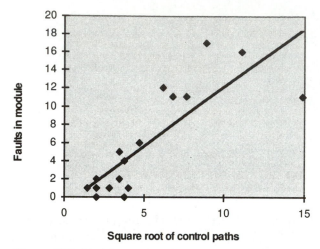

Figure 6.20: Module structure (transformed) plotted against faults

where x and y are two attributes, a is a coefficient, and b is an exponent. We can use logarithms to generate a linear relationship of the form:

$$\log (y) = \log (a) + b \log (x)$$

Then, $\log(a)$ and b can be estimated by applying the least squares technique to the transformed attribute values. The logarithmic transformation is used frequently to investigate the relationship between project effort and product size, or between project effort and project duration, as we shall see in Chapter 12. However, we must take care in the judgments we make from such transformed data. Plotting relationships on a log–log scale can give a misleading impression of the variability in the raw data. To predict effort (as opposed to log(effort)), you should plot an appropriate line on the untransformed scatter plot.

EXAMPLE 6.18: The relationship between effort and duration for data set 1 is depicted in Figure 6.21. A linear relationship is not significant for the raw data. However, when we transform the data using the logarithm of each attribute, the result is the scatter plot of Figure 6.22. This figure shows the linear regression line, which is significant after using the log–log transformation.

6.4.3   Multivariate data analysis

There are several different techniques that can be applied to data involving many variables. In this section, we look at three related techniques. **Principal component analysis** is used to simplify a set of data by removing some of the dependencies among variables. **Cluster analysis** uses the principal components that result, allowing us to group modules or projects according to some criterion. Then, **discriminant**

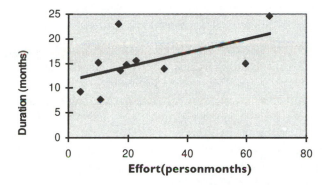

Figure 6.21: Effort plotted against duration, from data set I

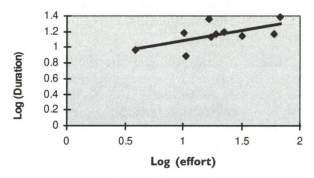

Figure 6.22: Logarithm of effort plotted against logarithm of duration

analysis derives an assessment criterion function that distinguishes one set of data from another; for instance, the function can separate data that are error-prone from data that is not.

6.4.3.1 Principal component analysis

Often, we measure a large set of attributes where some subset of the attributes consists of data that are related to one another. For example, the size of a project affects the amount of effort required to complete it, so size and effort are related. Suppose we want to predict project duration. If we use both size and effort in a duration-prediction equation, we may predict a longer time period than is really required, because we are (in a sense) double-counting; the duration suggested by the size measures may also be represented in our effort value. We must take care to ensure that the variables contributing to our equation are as independent of one another as possible.

In general, if we want to investigate the relationship among several attributes, we want to be sure that subsets of related attributes do not present a misleading picture. **Principal component analysis** generates a linear transformation of a set of correlated attributes, such that the transformed variables are independent. In the process, it simplifies and reduces the number of measures with which we must deal. Thus, we begin with n measures x_i, and our analysis allows us to obtain n new variables of the form

$$y_i = a_{i1}x_1 + a_{i2}x_2 + \ldots + a_{in}x_n$$

The technique identifies values for the a_{ij} and determines the contribution of y_i to the overall variability of the set of transformed variables.

Although the process creates as many transformed variables as there were original variables, we can reduce the number of variables by examining the variability in the relationship. We need fewer transformed variables to describe the variability of the dataset than we had originally, because the attributes that are virtually identical will contribute to a single variable on the new scale. The analysis indicates what proportion of the total variability is explained by each transformation. The transformation accounting for the most variability is called the **first principal component**, the transformation accounting for the next largest amount is called the second principal component, and so on. Principal components that account for less than 5% of the variability are usually ignored.

> **EXAMPLE 6.19:** During the first phase of the Software Certification Programme in Europe (SCOPE), 39 software metrics related to maintainability were collected from modules produced by five industrial software projects. A principal component analysis reduced the set to six, accounting for just under 90% of the variation. Size alone explained almost 57% of the variation. In other words, more than half of the variation in the maintainability measure was explained by changes to the size measure (Neil, 1992).

Principal component analysis is available in most statistical packages (such as GLIM (NAG, 1985)) because it is useful for several purposes:

- to identify the underlying dimensionality of a set of correlated variables;
- to allow a set of correlated variables to be replaced by a set of non-correlated variables in multivariate regression analysis;
- to assist in outlier detection: each set of attribute values for a software item can be transformed into one or more new variables (that is, the principal components); if the first principal component is plotted against the second, there will be no relationship; however, points that are very distant from the central mass of points are regarded as anomalies.

> **EXAMPLE 6.20:** Table 6.7 shows the results of a principal component analysis performed on the four structure and size variables of data set 2. The variables were normalized prior to performing the analysis (that is, transformations were applied, so that each variable had mean 0 and standard deviation 1). The table shows the correlation between each of the original variables and the transformed variables. It also indicates the percentage of the variability accounted for by each component. The analysis suggests that the four original variables can be represented adequately by the first three

Table 6.7: Correlations between principal components and the normalized variables for data set 2 size and structure measures

Original	Principal component 1	Principal component 2	Principal component 3	Principal component 4
LOC	0.81	−0.13	0.57	0.02
Fan-out	0.92	0.06	−0.28	0.27
Fan-in	−0.10	0.99	0.12	0.03
Path	0.92	0.15	−0.21	−0.28
% variation explained	59.1	24.4	11.5	3.9

transformed variables (that is, the first three principal components). It also shows that the first principal component is related to lines of code, fan-out and paths, since the correlation coefficients are positive and high. Similarly, the second principal component is related to fan-in, and the third principal component is related to lines of code.

6.4.3.2 Cluster analysis

Cluster analysis can be used to assess the similarity of modules in terms of their measurable characteristics. It assumes that modules with similar attributes will evidence similar behavior. First a principal components analysis is performed, producing a reduced set of principal components that explain most of the variation in the behavior being investigated. For example, we saw in Example 6.19 that the behavior, maintainability, was explained by six principal components. Next, cluster analysis specifies the behavior by separating it into two categories, usually exhibiting the behavior and not; in Example 6.19, we can think of the categories as "easy to maintain" or "not easy to maintain."

There are many cluster algorithms available with statistics packages. For instance, SPSS-X includes a powerful method called "quick cluster" (Neil, 1992). These algorithms can be used much as box plots were used for single variables: to cluster the data and identify outliers or unusual cases.

6.4.3.3 Discriminant analysis

Discriminant analysis allows us to separate data into two groups and to determine to which of the two groups a new data point should be assigned. The technique builds on the results of a cluster analysis to separate the two groups. The principal components are used as discriminating variables, helping to indicate to which group a particular module is most likely to belong.

The groups generated by a cluster analysis sometimes have overlap between them. Discriminant analysis reduces this overlap by maximizing the variation between clusters and minimizing the variation within each cluster.

6.4.4 *Multi-criteria decision aids*

Most of the techniques we have presented so far are based on classical statistical methods. In this section, we present some newer ways of addressing data analysis, especially when decision makers must solve problems by taking into account several different points of view. In other words, we have assumed so far that the goal of measurement is clear, but there are times (as we saw in Chapter 3) when some people interpret goals differently from others. We need to be able to analyze data and draw conclusions that address many different interpretations of the same goal, even when the interpretations conflict. Thus, rather than "solving" a problem by finding a universal truth or law exhibited by the data, we need instead to find a subjective problem resolution that is consistent and satisfies all parties involved, even if it is not optimal in the mathematical sense.

To understand why this situation is common in software measurement, consider a software system that is being built to meet requirements about safety or reliability. Data are collected to help answer the question "Is this software safe?" but the interpretation of "safe" can differ from one person to another, and it is not always clear that we have sufficient evidence to answer the question. Moreover, we often have to balance several considerations. We may ask "which option provides the most reliability for the least cost?" and we must make decisions that reflect our priorities when there is no clear-cut "best" answer.

Multi-criteria decision aids can help us to address such questions. They draw heavily on methods and results in operations research, measurement theory, probability, fuzzy sets, the theory of social choice, and expert systems. In the 1980s and 1990s, multi-criteria decision aids made great strides, and several computer-based tools have been developed to implement the methods. More information can be found in Vincke (1992).

In this section, we begin with the basic concepts of multi-criteria decision making. Then, we examine two classes of methods that have received a great deal of attention: multiple-attribute utility theory (including the analytical hierarchy process), and outranking methods. The latter is far less stringent than the former, and it allows for more realistic assumptions. Our examples are presented at a very high level, so that you can see how the concepts and techniques are applied to software engineering problems. But these techniques are quite complex, and the details are beyond the scope of this book. The end of this chapter suggests other sources for learning the techniques in depth.

6.4.4.1 Basic concepts of multi-criteria decision making

We often have a general question to answer, and that question is really composed of a set of more specific decision problems. For example, it is not enough to ask, "How do we build a system that we know is safe?" We must ask an assortment of questions, such as:

- Which combination of development methods is most appropriate to develop a safe system in the given environment?
- How much effort should be spent on each of a set of agreed-upon testing techniques in order to assure the safety of this system?
- Which compiler is most appropriate for building a safe system under these conditions?
- What is considered valid evidence of safety, and how do we combine the evidence from different subsets or sources to form a complete picture?
- Which of a set of possible actions should we take after system completion to assess the system safety?

In each case, we have a set of actions, A, to be explored during the decision procedure. A can include objects, decisions, candidates, and more. For instance, in the first question above, A consists of all combinations of mutually compatible methods selected from some original set. An enumeration of A might consist of combinations such as:

- (Z specification, correctness proofs)
- (Z specification, SSADM design)
- (VDM specification, VDM formal verification, proof)
- (SADT)
- (Specification from Visual BASIC rapid prototyping, incremental development)

and so on. Once we have a set of actions, we define a **criterion**, g, to be a function from the set of actions to a totally ordered set, T. That T is **totally ordered** means that there is a relation R on pairs of elements of T that satisfies four properties:

1. R is **reflexive**: for each element x in T, the pair (x, x) is in R.
2. R is **transitive**: if (x, y) and (y, z) are in R, then (x, z) must be in R.
3. R is **antisymmetric**: if (x, y) and (y, x) are in R, then x must equal y.
4. R is **strongly complete**: for any x and y in T, either (x, y) is in R or (y, x) is in R.

These conditions guarantee that any action can be compared to any other action using a relation on T. We can use the total ordering to compare software-engineering techniques, methods, and tools.

EXAMPLE 6.21: Suppose A is a set of verification and validation techniques used on a software project. We can define a criterion that maps A to the set of real numbers by defining g as follows: for each element a of A,

$g(a)$ = the total effort in person months devoted to using technique a

This measure gives us information about experience with each element of A. Alternatively, we can define another criterion, g', to be a mapping to the set of non-negative integers, so that we can compare the effectiveness of two techniques:

$g'(a)$ = the total number of faults discovered when using technique a

We can also have criteria that map to sets that are not numbers. For example, define the set T to be {poor, moderate, good, excellent}, representing categories of ease of use. Then we can define a criterion that maps each element of A to an element of T that represents the ease of use for a particular technique, as rated subjectively by an expert. In this example, T is totally ordered, since

$$\text{poor} < \text{moderate} < \text{good} < \text{excellent}$$

Suppose we consider a family of criteria defined on a set of actions, A. If the family is **consistent** (in a way that is described more fully in Roy (1990)), then a multi-criteria decision problem can be any one of the following:

- to determine a subset of A considered to be best with respect to the family of criteria (the **choice problem**);
- to divide A into subsets according to some norms (the **sorting problem**);
- to rank the actions of A from best to worst (the **ranking problem**).

To address these problems, a decision maker must compare each pair actions, a and b, in one of three ways:

1. strict preference for one of the actions;
2. indifference to either action;
3. refusal or inability to compare the actions.

Each of these choices defines a relation between a and b, and the set of all such relations forms a **preference structure** on A. We can also define a **preference relation**, S, using only conditions 1 and 2: a is related to b if and only if either a is strictly preferred to b, or there is indifference between the two. A classic problem of decision optimization is to define a numerical function that preserves S. In other words, we want to define a function, f, from the set A to some number system, N, that satisfies both of these conditions:

$$f(a) > f(b) \text{ if and only if } a \text{ is strictly preferred to } b$$
$$f(a) = f(b) \text{ if and only if there is indifference between } a \text{ and } b$$

This function may look familiar to you, as it is a mathematical way of describing the representation condition, introduced in Chapter 2. In multi-criteria decision making, a key problem is optimizing f. Here, "optimization" means that f must satisfy the stated conditions in a way that optimizes one or more attributes of the elements of A, such as cost or quality. When N is the set of real numbers, then no such function f exists if there are two actions that are incomparable. Unfortunately, there are many real-world situations where incomparabilities exist; we can include the incomparabilities by mapping to other types of number systems, such as vectors of real numbers, as we did in Chapter 2.

When we can preserve the preference structure by mapping to the real numbers, then we can rank the actions from best to worst, with possible ties when there is indifference between two actions; this mapping is called the **traditional model**. Such a relation is called a **complete preorder**. If there are no ties, then the preference structure is a **complete order**. Any criterion for which the underlying preference structure is a complete preorder is called a **true criterion**.

In the traditional model, indifference must be transitive; that is, if there is indifference between a and b, and indifference between b and c, then there must be indifference between a and c. However, sometimes this condition is not realistic, as when there are "sensibility thresholds" below which we are indifferent; multi-criteria decision making can be extended to cover this case, but here we focus on the traditional model and assume transitivity.

Suppose a and b are possible actions, and we have a set of n criteria $\{g_i\}$. We say that a **dominates** b if $g_i(a) \geq g_i(b)$ for each i from 1 to n. An action is said to be **efficient** if it is strictly dominated by no other action.

EXAMPLE 6.22: We are considering eight compilers, P1 through P8, to select one for use in a safety-critical application. There are four criteria that govern the selection: cost (measured in dollars), speed (measured in number of statements compiled per minute on a standardized set of test data), accuracy and ease of use. The latter two criteria are measured on an ordinal scale of integers from 0 to 3, where 0 represents "poor", 1 represents "fair", 2 represents "good", and 3 represents "very good". Table 6.8 contains the results of the ratings for each criterion. To ensure that the dominance relation holds, we have changed the sign of the values for cost. In this example, we see that:

- P2 dominates P1
- P5 dominates both P4 and P6
- P3, P7, and P8 dominate no other package
- P2, P5, P3, P7, and P8 are efficient

The first task in tackling a multi-criteria decision problem is reducing the set of actions to a (probably smaller) subset of efficient actions. We may find that there is only one efficient action, in which case that action is the simple solution to our problem. However, more often the dominance relation is weak, and multi-criteria decision activities involve enriching the dominance relation by considering all relevant information.

To do this, we consider a vector formed by evaluating all of the criteria for a given action. That is, for each action, a, we form a vector $<g_1(a), g_2(a), ..., g_n(a)>$. Then the collection of all of these n-tuples is called the **image** of A. In Example 6.22, the image of A is the set of eight 4-tuples that correspond to the rows in Table 6.8. For each i from 1 to n, we can identify the (not necessarily unique) action a_i^* in A that is best according to the criterion g_i. The **ideal point** is the point $(z_1, z_2, ..., z_n)$, where $z_i = g_i(a_i^*)$. For instance, the ideal point in Example 6.23 is $(-900, 3000, 3, 2)$.

We can apply all of the criteria to each ideal point, so that we compute all possible $G_{ij} = g_j(a_i^*)$. The $n \times n$ matrix formed by the G_{ij} is called the **payoff matrix**; this

Table 6.8: Ratings for each software package against four criteria

Software package	g_1: cost	g_2: speed	g_3: accuracy	g_4: ease of use
P1	−1300	3000	3	1
P2	−1200	3000	3	2
P3	−1150	3000	2	2
P4	−1000	2000	2	0
P5	−950	2000	2	1
P6	−950	1000	2	0
P7	−900	2000	1	0
P8	−900	1000	1	1

matrix is unique only if each criterion achieves its maximum at only one action. The diagonal of a payoff matrix is the ideal point.

EXAMPLE 6.23: There are two different payoff matrices for the actions and criteria in Example 6.22:

$$M = \begin{bmatrix} a_1^* = P8 & -900 & 1000 & 1 & 1 \\ a_2^* = P2 & -1200 & 3000 & 3 & 2 \\ a_3^* = P2 & -1200 & 3000 & 3 & 2 \\ a_4^* = P3 & -1150 & 3000 & 2 & 2 \end{bmatrix}$$

$$M' = \begin{bmatrix} a_1^* = P7 & -900 & 2000 & 1 & 0 \\ a_2^* = P3 & -1150 & 3000 & 2 & 2 \\ a_3^* = P1 & -1300 & 3000 & 3 & 1 \\ a_4^* = P2 & -1200 & 3000 & 3 & 2 \end{bmatrix}$$

For a given payoff matrix, the **nadir** is the point whose ith coordinate is the minimum of the values in the ith column. In Example 6.23, the nadir for matrix M is (−1200, 1000, 1, 1); for M', the nadir is (−1300, 2000, 1, 0).

These concepts can be used to help solve the multi-criteria decision problem. For instance, it can be shown that a positive linear combination of criteria always yields an efficient action, and that efficient actions can be characterized as those that minimize a certain distance (called the **Tchebychev distance**) to a point that slightly dominates the ideal point. Parametric optimization techniques can then be used to determine efficient actions.

However, there are often more constraints on the problem than these. For instance, in Table 6.8, we see that, although P3 is $50 more expensive, its accuracy is greater than that of P2. Our decision makers may believe that it is worth paying the extra money to increase the accuracy. Such observations are called **substitution rates of criteria**; they allow us to add a particular amount to one criterion to compensate for a loss of one unit of another criterion. Although the assignment of substitution rates is subjective, the technique allows us to insert subjectivity in a controlled way, and to be consistent in applying our subjective judgments.

Suppose that, because of the safety-criticality of the application, the decision makers prefer to pay a lot more for a package to get the highest degree of accuracy, no matter what the speed or ease of use. In this situation, two of the criteria (namely, speed and accuracy) are said to be **preferentially independent**.

6.4.4.2 Multi-attribute utility theory

Multi-attribute utility theory (MAUT) takes these constraints into account, providing another approach to organizing the subjective judgments that decision makers want to insert into their process for choosing from among several alternatives. MAUT assumes that a decision maker want to maximize a function of various criteria. Two types of problems present themselves:

- **The representation problem:** what properties must be satisfied by the decision-maker's preferences so that they can be represented by a function with a prescribed analytical form?
- **The construction problem:** how can the maximization function be constructed, and how can we estimate its parameters?

Most MAUT research to address these questions has concentrated on the case where there is uncertainty (so that probabilities are used) and the criteria are true criteria.

> **EXAMPLE 6.24:** Suppose we are given four criteria for assessing which verification and validation techniques should be used on a software module; these criteria are described in Table 6.9.
>
> A decision maker rates four techniques, and the results are shown in Table 6.10. To define a utility function, U, that is a sum of functions U_i on each g_i, we have several choices. One possibility is to define each U_i to be a transformation onto the unit interval, $[0, 1]$. For instance, we may define:
>
> U_1(little) = 0.8 U_1(moderate) = 0.5 U_1(considerable)= 0.2 U_1(excessive) = 0
> U_2(bad) = 0 U_2(reasonable) = 0.1 U_2(good) = 0.3 U_2(excellent) = 0.6
> U_3(no) = 0.2 U_3(yes) = 0.7
> $U_4(x) = 1/x$

Table 6.9: Criteria for assessing verification and validation techniques

Criterion	Measurement scale
g_1: Effort required	{little, moderate, considerable, excessive}
g_2: Coverage	{bad, reasonable, good, excellent}
g_3: Tool support	{no, yes}
g_4: Ranking of usefulness by expert	{1, 2, ..., n} where n is number of techniques

Table 6.10: Evaluation of four verification and validation techniques

Technique	g_1	g_2	g_3	g_4
Code inspection	considerable	excellent	no	1
Formal proof	excessive	good	no	2
Static analysis	moderate	bad	yes	4
Black box testing	little	good	no	3

Thus, for any technique, we rate the availability of tool support as having greater utility than excellent coverage, and we rate the greatest utility to be ranked top by an expert. The final result can be evaluated by summing the functions for each technique:

U(inspection) = 0.2 + 0.6 + 0.2 + 1 = 2
U(proof) = 0 + 0.3 + 0.2 + 0.5 = 1
U(static analysis) = 0.5 + 0 + 0.7 + 0.25 = 1.45
U(black box) = 0.8 + 0.3 + 0.2 + 0.33

It is easy to see that the criteria in Table 6.9 are non-orthogonal. In an ideal situation, the criteria should be recast into an orthogonal set, so that the relative importance of each is clear and sensible. However, in many situations, politics prevent us from deriving this orthogonal set. Nevertheless, MAUT helps us to impose order and consistency on the situation. Sometimes, the act of applying MAUT makes the decision maker more aware of the need for orthogonality, and the criteria are changed. Otherwise, MAUT helps to generate a reasonable decision when the "best" is not possible.

The analytic hierarchy process (AHP) is a popular MAUT technique developed by Saaty; (Saaty, 1980) contains details of the technique, including many examples of its application. AHP begins by representing the decision problem as a hierarchy graph, where the top node is the main problem objective and the bottom nodes represent actions. At each level of the hierarchy, a decision maker makes a pairwise comparison of the nodes from the viewpoint of their contribution to each of the higher-level nodes to which they are linked. The pairwise comparison involves **preference ratios** (for actions) or **importance ratios** (for criteria), evaluated on a particular numerical scale. Then, the "value" of each node is calculated, based on computing the eigenvalues of the matrix of pairwise comparisons. Each action's global contribution to the main objective is calculated by aggregating the weighted average type. A software package called Expert Choice supports use of AHP.

AHP has been used in dependability assessment (Auer, 1994), and Vaisanen and colleagues have applied it to a safety assessment of programmable logic components (Vaisanen et al., 1994). AHP was also used to help NASA choose from among several strategies for improving a safety feature of the space shuttle (Frank, 1995).

6.4.4.3 Outranking methods

MAUT can be very valuable, resulting in a ranking of actions from best to worst. However, this richness of result is bought at the expense of very strong assumptions that are unrealistic in many situations. For many problems, we do not need such strong results, so we can do without the strong assumptions. However, the dominance relation alone is generally too weak to be useful. Outranking methods seek to enrich the dominance relation without having to make the strong assumptions of MAUT.

An **outranking relation** is a binary relation on a set of actions defined in the following way. Suppose a and b are two actions. Given what is known about the decision maker's preferences, the quality of the valuations of the actions, and the nature of the problem, if there are enough arguments to decide that a is at least as good as b and no essential reason to refute that statement, then we say that a is related to b. This definition is informal, and published outranking methods differ according to the way it is formalized. No matter the definition, the outranking relation is not necessarily complete nor transitive (Roy, 1990).

Any outranking method has two steps:

1. building the outranking relation;
2. exploiting the relation with regard to the chosen problem statement.

To give you an idea of how outranking works, we present a brief example, using the **Electre I** method.

EXAMPLE **6.25**: Table 6.11 lists four criteria for assessing combinations of verification and validation techniques. For instance, action 1 might involve formal proof followed by code inspection, while action 2 might be formal proof plus static code analysis. Each criterion must map onto a totally ordered set, and each is assigned a weight, indicated by the number in parentheses. For example, the weight of the first criterion is 5.

For each ordered pair of actions (a, b), we compute a **concordance index** by adding the weights of all criteria g_i for which $g_i(a)$ is greater than $g_i(b)$. Thus, for the pair $(1, 2)$, action 1 is at least as good as action 2 with respect to all but the first criterion, so we sum the weights $(4 + 3 + 3)$ to yield a concordance index of 10. The full set of concordance indices is shown in Table 6.12. In a sense, this table is the "first draft" of the preference structure (that is, the outranking relation), and we say that a is preferable to b if the concordance index for (a, b) is larger than for (b, a).

Next, we restrict the structure by defining a **concordance threshold**, t, so that a is preferred to b only if the concordance index for (a, b) is at least as large as t. Suppose t is 12. Then, according to Table 6.12, action 2 is still preferable to action 1, but we no longer have preference of action 1 to action 7 because the concordance index for $(1, 7)$ is not large enough.

We further refine the preference structure to include other constraints. For instance, suppose that for criterion g_1 (effort required) we never allow action a to outrank action b if $g_1(a)$ is excessive and $g_1(b)$ is little. In other words, regardless of the values of the other criteria, b is so superior to a with respect to g_1 that we veto its being outranked by a. In general, we handle this situation by defining a **discordance set** for each criterion, containing the ordered pairs of

Table 6.11: Criteria for assessing combined verification and validation techniques

Action	g_1: effort required (weight = 5)	g_2: potential for detecting critical faults (weight = 4)	g_3: coverage achieved (weight = 3)	g_4: tool support (weight = 3)
1	excessive	excellent	good	yes
2	considerable	excellent	average	yes
3	considerable	good	good	yes
4	moderate	good	good	no
5	moderate	good	average	yes
6	moderate	reasonable	good	yes
7	little	reasonable	average	no

values for the criterion for which the outranking is refused.

For example, let us define:

$D_1 = \{(\text{excessive, little}), (\text{considerable, little})\}$
$D_2 = \{(\text{moderate, excellent})\}$
$D_3 = D_4 = \{\}$

Then we can define the outranking relation by saying that one action outranks another provided that its concordance index is at least as large as the threshold, and provided that for each criterion, the preference is not vetoed by the discordance set. The full outranking relation for the example is shown in Figure 6.23.

Finally, we exploit this relationship to find a subset of actions that is optimal with respect to the outranking. In graph theory, such a set (of nodes) is called a *kernel*. There are several graph-theoretic techniques for determining kernels, thus enabling us to find the best course of action, given our constraints. From Figure 6.23, we can see that there are three kernels, namely $\{2, 4, 7\}$ and $\{2, 5, 7\}$; the actions 4 and 5 are considered to be tied.

Table 6.12: Concordance indices

	1	2	3	4	5	6	7
1	–	10	10	10	10	10	10
2	12	–	12	7	10	7	10
3	11	11	–	11	10	10	10
4	8	8	12	–	12	12	10
5	8	11	12	12	–	12	10
6	11	11	11	11	11	–	10
7	5	8	5	8	8	9	–

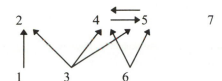

Figure 6.23: Graph of outranking relation –
an arc from node *x* to node *y* indicates that *y*
outranks *x*

6.5 OVERVIEW OF STATISTICAL TESTS

This chapter has mentioned several statistical tests that can be used to analyze your data. We have presented several techniques in terms of the type of relationship we seek (linear, multivariate, and so on), but our choice of technique must also take into account the number of groups being compared, the size of the sample, and more. In this section, we describe a few statistical tests, so that you can see how each one is oriented to a particular experimental situation. The section is organized in terms of sample and experiment type, as summarized in Table 6.13.

6.5.1 One-group tests

In a one-group design, measurements from one group of subjects are compared with an expected population distribution of values. These tests are appropriate when an experimenter has a single set of data with an explicit null hypothesis concerning the value of the population mean. For example, you may have sampled the size of each of a group of modules, and you hypothesize that the average module size is 200 lines of code.

For normal distributions, the parametric test is called the *t*-test (or, equivalently, the Student's *t*-test, single sample *t*-test, or one-group *t*-test). Because the mean of the data is involved, the test is appropriate only for data that are on the interval scale or above.

There are several alternatives for non-parametric data:

6.5.1.1 Binomial test

The binomial test should be used when:

1. the dependent variable can take only two distinct, mutually-exclusive and exhaustive values (such as "module has been inspected" and "module has not been inspected"); and
2. the measurement trials in the experiment are independent.

6.5.1.2 Chi-squared test for goodness of fit

The chi-squared test is appropriate when:

Table 6.13: Examples of statistical tests

Sample type	Nominal	Ordinal	Interval	Ratio
One sample	Binomial	Kolmogorov–Smirnov		Single-sample
	Chi-square	One-sample runs		*T*-test
		Change point		
Two related samples	McNemar change	Sign test	Permutation	Matched groups *T*-test
		Wilcoxon signed ranks		
Two independent samples	Fisher exact	Median test	Permutation	Population
	Chi-square	Wilcoxon–Mann–Whitney		
		Robust rank order		
		Kolmogorov–Smirnov 2-sample		
		Siegel–Tukey		
K related samples	Cochran *Q*-test	Friedman 2-way ANOVA		Within-groups ANOVA
		Page test (ordered alternatives)		
K independent samples	Chi-squared	Kruskal–Wallis 1-way ANOVA		Between-groups
		Jonckheere test		ANOVA

1. the dependent variable can take two or more distinct, mutually exclusive, and exhaustive values (such as "module has fewer than 100 lines of code", "module has between 100 and 300 lines of code", and "module has more than 300 lines of code");
2. the measurement trials in the experiment are independent; and
3. none of the categories has an observed or expected frequency of less than five occurrences.

6.5.1.3 Kolmogorov–Smirnov one-sample test

This test assumes that the dependent measure is a continuous, rather than discrete, variable. It assesses the similarity between an observed and an expected cumulative frequency distribution.

6.5.1.4 One-sample runs test

This test determines if the results of a measurement process follow a consistent sequence, called a **run**. For example, it can be used in analyzing the reasons for system downtime, to determine if one particular type of hardware or software problem is responsible for consecutive system crashes. The test assumes that the successive measurement trials are independent.

6.5.1.5 Change-point test

This test determines whether the distribution of some sequence of events has changed in some way. It assumes that the observations form an ordered sequence. If, at some point in the distribution of observed measures, a shift in the median (or middle) score has occurred, the test identifies the change point.

6.5.2 Two-group tests

Single-sample designs and tests are often used to decide if the results of some process are straying from an already known value. However, these designs are not appropriate when an experimentally established comparison is required.

Two-group designs allow you to compare two samples of dependent measures drawn from related or matched samples of subjects (as in a within-subjects design), or from two independent groups of subjects (as in a between-subjects design). The appropriate statistical test depends on whether the samples are independent or related in some way.

6.5.2.1 Tests to compare two matched or related groups

The parametric *t*-test for matched groups applies when the dependent measurement is taken under two different conditions, and when one of the following additional conditions has been met:

1. the same subject is tested in both conditions (that is, a within-subjects or repeated-measures design has been used); or
2. subjects are matched according to some criterion (that is, a matched-groups design has been used); or
3. pre-screening has been used to form randomized blocks of subjects (that is, a randomized block design has been used).

This test assumes that:

- subjects have been randomly selected from the population (when different subjects have been used in each condition, assignment to the conditions should be random); and
- if fewer than 30 pairs of dependent measures are available, the distribution of the differences between the two scores should be approximately normal.

Like the single-sample *t*-test, this test also requires measurement data to be at least on the interval scale.

Non-parametric alternatives to this test include the McNemar change test, the sign test, and the Wilcoxon signed ranks test. The **McNemar change test** is useful for assessing change on a dichotomous variable, after an experimental treatment has been administered to a subject. For example, it can be used to assess whether programmers switch preferences for language type after receiving training in procedural and object-oriented techniques. The test assumes that the data are frequencies that can be classified in dichotomous terms.

The **sign test** is applied to related samples when you want to establish that one condition is greater than another on the dependent measure. The test assumes that the dependent measure reflects a continuous variable (such as experience) rather than categories. For example, you may use this test to determine whether a particular type of programming construct is significantly easier to implement on a given system.

The **Wilcoxon signed ranks test** is similar to the sign test, taking into account the magnitude as well as the direction of difference; it gives more weight to a pair that shows a large difference than to a pair that shows a small difference.

6.5.2.2 Tests to compare two independent groups

The parametric test appropriate for independent groups or between-subjects designs is the *t*-test for differences between population means. This test is applied when there are two groups of different subjects that are not paired or matched in any way. The test assumes that:

1. subjects have been randomly selected from the population and assigned to one of the two treatment conditions;
2. if fewer than 30 subjects are measured in each group, the distribution of the differences between the two scores should be approximately normal; and
3. the variance, or spread, of scores in the two population groups should be equal or homogeneous.

As before, the data must be measured on at least an interval scale to be suitable for this test. Several non-parametric alternatives to this test are available; they are described in most statistics books.

6.5.3 Comparisons involving more than two groups

Suppose you have measured an attribute of *k* groups, where *k* is greater than two. For example, you are comparing the productivity rates of ten projects, or you want to look at a structural attribute for each of 50 modules. Here, the appropriate statistical analysis technique is an **analysis of variance** (ANOVA). This class of parametric techniques is suitable for data from between-subjects designs, within-subjects designs, and designs that involve a mixture of between- and within-subjects treatments. Complementary non-parametric tests are available but are beyond the scope of this book; some are listed in Table 6.13.

ANOVA results tell you whether at least one statistically significant difference exists somewhere within the comparisons drawn by the analysis. Statistical significance in an ANOVA is reflected in the *F* statistic that is calculated by the procedure. When an *F* statistic is significant, you then apply multiple comparisons tests to determine which levels of a factor differ significantly from the others.

As we noted in Chapter 4, when your experimental design is complex, it is best to consult a statistician to determine which analysis techniques are most appropriate. Because the techniques require different types of data and control, it is sensible to lay out your analysis plans and methods *before* you begin your investigation; otherwise, you risk collecting data that is insufficient or inappropriate for the analysis you need to do.

6.6 SUMMARY

Data sets of software attribute values must be analyzed with care, because software measures are not usually normally distributed. We have presented several techniques here that address a wide variety of situations: differing data distributions, varying measurement scales, varying sample sizes, and differing goals. In general, it is advisable to:

- describe a set of attribute values using box plot statistics (based on median and quartiles) rather than on mean and variance;
- inspect a scatter plot visually when investigating the relationship between two variables;
- use robust correlation coefficients to confirm whether or not a relationship exists between two attributes;
- use robust regression in the presence of atypical values to identify a linear relationship between two attributes, or remove the atypical values before analysis;
- always check the residuals by plotting them against the dependent variable;
- use Tukey's ladder to assist in the selection of transformations when faced with non-linear relationships;
- use principal component analysis to investigate the dimensionality of data sets with large numbers of correlated attributes.

It is also helpful to consider using more advanced techniques, such as multi-criteria decision aid, to help you choose a "good" solution, rather than the "best" solution, subject to the constraints on your problem. But most important, we have demonstrated that your choice of analysis technique must be governed by the goals of your investigation, so that you can support or refute the hypothesis you are testing.

6.7 EXERCISES

1. Why are statistics necessary? Why can't experimenters just look at the data and decide for themselves what is important? On the other hand, which is more important: a) the results of a statistical test; or b) the results of the intra-ocular significance test (that is, when the effect leaps out and hits you between the eyes)?

2. Can a comparison that does not achieve statistical significance still be important?

3. Suppose that three years ago the software-development manager introduced changes to the development practices at your company which were supposed to ensure that more time was spent upfront on projects, rather than coding. Suppose you have the data of Table 6.14 giving actual effort in person days by software development phase for the last five projects (in chronological order). Provide an appropriate graphical representation for the manager so that she can see whether the changes have had an effect.

Table 6.14: Example data for Question 3

	Project 1	Project 2	Project 3	Project 4	Project 5
Requirements	120	100	370	80	410
Specification	320	240	490	140	540
High-level design	30	40	90	40	60
Detailed design	170	190	420	120	340
Coding	1010	420	1130	250	1200
Testing	460	300	580	90	550

4   Construct a box plot for the paths measure in data set 2 of Table 6.1.

5   'Draw the scatter plot of the LOC and the path measures for the modules in data set 2 of Table 6.1. Are there any unusual values?

6   Obtain the Spearman rank correlation coefficient and the Pearson correlation coefficient for paths and LOC for data set 2 of Table 6.1. Why do you think the rank correlation is larger than the Pearson correlation? (Hint: look at the scatter plot produced for Exercise 5.)

7   Using a statistical package or spreadsheet, calculate the least-squares regression line for faults against lines of code for all the modules in data set 2 of Table 6.1. Calculate the residuals and plot the residual against the dependent variable (lines of code). Can you identify any outlying points?

8   If you have access to an appropriate statistical package, do a principal component analysis of the normalized LOC, fan-out, fan-in, and paths measures from data set 2 of Table 6.1. Produce a scatter plot of the first principal component against the second and identify the atypical values.

9   What result do you think you would get if you did a principal component analysis on the raw rather than the normalized size and structure measures in data set 2 of Table 6.1? If you have a statistical package, perform a principal component analysis on the raw size and structure data and see if the results confirm your opinion.

10   Company X runs a large software system S that has been developed in-house over a number of years. The company collects information about software defects discovered by users of S. During the regular maintenance cycle, each defect is traced to one of the nine subsystems of S (labeled with letters A through I), each of which is the responsibility of a different team of programmers. Table 6.15 summarizes information about new defects discovered during the current year:

Suppose you are the manager of system S.

i.   Compute the defect density for each subsystem.

ii.   Use simple outlier analysis to identify unusual features of the system.

iii.   What conclusions can you draw from your outlier analysis?

iv.   What are the basic weaknesses of the metrics data as currently

Table 6.15: Defects discovered and size

System	A	B	C	D	E	F	G	H	I
Defects	35	0	95	35	55	40	55	40	45
Size (KLOC)	40	100	5	50	120	70	60	100	40

collected?

v.   What simple additions or changes to the data-collection strategy would significantly improve your diagnostic capability?

11   Table 6.16 contains three measures for each of seventeen software modules. LOC is the number of lines of code in the module, CFP the number of control flow paths in the module, and Faults the number of faults found in the module. Construct a box plot for each of the three measures, and identify any outliers. What conclusions can you draw? What recommendations can you make to address the problems you have discovered?

12   Table 6.17 contains metrics from 17 software systems under investigation: total number of thousands lines of code for the system (KLOC), average module size (MOD) measured in lines of code, and total number of faults found per thousand lines of code (FD). Construct a box plot for each metric, and identify any outliers.

Table 6.16: Software-module measures

Module	LOC	CFP	Faults
A	15	4	0
B	28	6	15
C	40	2	10
D	60	26	1
E	60	14	0
F	95	18	15
G	110	12	9
H	140	12	6
I	170	54	6
J	180	36	20
K	185	28	14
L	190	32	20
M	210	54	15
N	210	46	18
P	270	128	58
Q	400	84	59
R	420	120	43

Table 6.17: Software-system metrics

System	KLOC	MOD	FD
A	10	15	36
B	23	43	22
C	26	61	15
D	31	10	33
E	31	43	15
F	40	57	13
G	47	58	22
H	52	65	16
I	54	50	15
J	67	60	18
K	70	50	10
L	75	96	34
M	83	51	16
N	83	61	18
P	100	32	12
Q	110	78	20
R	200	48	21

6.8 FURTHER READING

There are several good books on statistics and their application.

Hoel, P.G., *Introduction to Mathematical Statistics*, 3rd edn, Wiley, New York, 1962.
Caulcutt, R., *Statistics in Research and Development*, Chapman & Hall, London, 1991.
Chatfield, C., *Statistics for Technology*, Chapman & Hall, London, 1993.

The book by Siegel and Castellan is a classic text on nonparametric statistics.

Siegel, S. and Castellan, N.J., Jr, *Nonparametric Statistics for the Behavioral Sciences*, 2nd edn, McGraw-Hill, New York, 1988.

For descriptions of box plots and other exploratory data analysis, consult Hoaglin, Mosteller, and Tukey.

Hoaglin, D.C., Mosteller, F. and Tukey, J.W., *Understanding Exploratory Data Analysis*, Wiley, New York, 1983.

Sometimes, you have two data sets representing the same situation. Each is different from the other, in terms of distribution, mean, or variance, but both were collected with reasonable care. This problem arises frequently but is rarely discussed in standard statistical texts; Barford explains how to tell which is the better data set for answering your questions.

Barford, N.C., *Experimental Measurements: Precision, Error and Truth*, Addison-Wesley, Reading, MA, 1967.

For an excellent overview of MCDA, you should consult:

Vincke, P., *Multicriteria Decision Aid*, Wiley, New York, 1992.

Additional references on multi-attribute analysis methods are:

Roy, B., "Decision aid and decision making,' *European Journal of Operational Research*, 45, pp. 324–31, 1990.
Saaty, T., *The Analytic Hierarchy Process*, McGraw-Hill, New York, 1980.

PART II
SOFTWARE-ENGINEERING MEASUREMENT

7 Measuring internal product attributes: size

The first part of this book laid the groundwork for measuring and evaluating software products, processes, and resources. Now, we turn to the actual measurement, to see which metrics we can use and how they are applied to software-engineering problems. In the next four chapters, we look at the products themselves. Here and in Chapter 8, we focus on internal product attributes; Chapters 9 and 10 will turn to external attributes. Then, Chapter 11 looks at resource attributes, and we examine ways to measure productivity, teams, and tools. In Chapter 12, we consider the notion of process attributes, investigating examples of predicting process outcome early in the life cycle.

We saw in Chapter 3 that internal product attributes describe software products (including documents) in a way that is dependent only on the product itself. The most obvious and useful such attribute is the **size** of a software system, which can be measured statically, without having to execute the system. In this chapter, we look at different ways to measure the size of any development product. We start by reviewing current approaches to size measurement, highlighting the pitfalls of the traditional one-dimensional approach. Next, we identify and discuss a number of specific, important aspects of size, namely **length** (physical size), **functionality** (in terms of what the user actually gets), and **complexity** (of the underlying problem that the software is solving). We also consider **reuse** (the extent to which the software is genuinely new), as it is usually expressed in terms of the size of reused product. For each of these attributes, we describe a range of appropriate measures.

7.1 ASPECTS OF SOFTWARE SIZE

Each product of software development is a physical entity; as such, it can be described in terms of its size. Since other physical objects are easily measurable (by length, volume, mass, or other standard measure), measuring the size of software products should be straightforward, relatively simple and consistent with measurement-theory principles. However, in practice, size measurement presents great difficulties. Notions such as effort, functionality, complexity, redundancy, and reuse are bound up in the measures people select and in the way they are used. Simple measures of size are often rejected because they do not adequately reflect:

- **effort:** they fail to take account of redundancy and complexity;
- **productivity:** they fail to take account of true functionality and effort;
- **cost:** they fail to take account of complexity and reuse.

For example, Conte, Dunsmore, and Shen assert that:

> "... there is a major problem with the lines-of-code measure: it is not consistent because some lines are more difficult to code than others....One solution to the problem is to give more weight to lines that have more "stuff" in them."
>
> (Conte, Dunsmore, and Shen, 1986)

Rejecting simple size measures on these grounds reflects a misunderstanding of the basic measurement principles discussed in Chapter 2. Those who reject a measure because it does not provide enough information may be expecting too much of a single measure. Consider the following analogy:

> **EXAMPLE 7.1:** If human size is measured as a single attribute, say height, then we can use it to predict whether or not a person would bump his or her head when entering a doorway. This application of the definition makes height a useful measure. However, we cannot use height effectively by itself to determine whether a person is obese.

Similarly, if we measure software code size as the number of lines of code, for instance, the fact that it is not useful in measuring quality does not negate its value in predicting the amount of space it requires in a file.

> **EXAMPLE 7.2:** If human size is measured in terms of two attributes, say height and weight, then we can use it to determine (on the basis of empirical understanding) whether a person is obese. However, we cannot use it effectively to determine how fast such a person can run nor how intelligent the person might be.

Likewise, models that define an attribute in terms of several internal attributes may be useful, even if they are not complete. As we have seen in Chapter 3, the measures and models are derived from the goals set for them, and applying them to different goals does not invalidate them for their original purpose.

Ideally, we want to define a set of attributes for software size analogous to human height and weight. That is, we want them to be **fundamental**, so that each attribute captures a key aspect of software size. We suggest that software size can be described with three such attributes:

- length
- functionality
- complexity

Length is the physical size of the product, and **functionality** measures the functions supplied by the product to the user. **Complexity** can be interpreted in different ways, depending on our perspective.

- **Problem complexity** (also called **computational complexity** by computer scientists) measures the complexity of the underlying problem.
- **Algorithmic complexity** reflects the complexity of the algorithm implemented to solve the problem; in some sense, this type of complexity measures the **efficiency** of the software, and we prefer to use this term.
- **Structural complexity** measures the structure of the software used to implement the algorithm. For example, we look at control flow structure, hierarchical structure and modular structure to extract this type of measure.
- **Cognitive complexity** measures the effort required to understand the software.

To understand complexity, we look at efficiency and problem complexity in this chapter; we save our discussion of structural complexity for Chapter 8. (We do not consider cognitive complexity in this book; more information is provided in the social science literature.)

To see how the complexity of the software differs from the complexity of the underlying problem being solved, consider that there are many ways to create a very complex solution to a very simple problem.

We also identify the degree of **reuse** as an aspect of size, since it measures how much of a product was copied or modified from a previous version of an existing product. This concept is important when size is provided as input to effort, cost and productivity models.

Remember that one of the purposes of measuring size is to use early product measures to predict subsequent product and process measures. For this reason, we want to measure the size of specifications and designs as well as of final code. However, there has been more research addressed to code measurement than to early product measurement. As of this writing, the state of the art of size measurement is that:

1. there is some consensus on measuring length of programs but not of specifications or designs;
2. there is some work ongoing to measure functionality of specifications (which applies equally to designs and programs); but

3. there is very little work on measuring complexity, other than that which has been done under the umbrella of computational complexity (and which has remained almost untouched by the software-engineering community).

We examine each of these aspects of size in turn.

7.2 LENGTH

There are three major development products whose size would be useful to know: the specification, the design, and the code. Measuring the length of the specification can be a useful indicator of how long the design is likely to be, which in turn is a predictor of code length. Similarly, length of the early products may indicate the amount of effort needed for production of the later ones.

7.2.1 Code

Code can be produced in several ways. The most traditional approach is to use a procedural language. But there are other alternatives, such as object orientation and visual programming, that make traditional measurement difficult.

7.2.1.1 Traditional code measures

The most commonly used measure of source code program length is the number of lines of code (LOC), introduced in Chapter 2. But some lines of code are different from others. For example, many programmers use spacing and blank lines to make their programs easier to read. If lines of code are being used to estimate programming effort, then a blank line does not contribute the same amount of effort as a line implementing a difficult algorithm. Similarly, comment lines improve a program's understandability, and they certainly require some effort to write. But they may not require as much effort as the code itself. Many different schemes have been proposed for counting lines, each defined with a particular purpose in mind, so there are many ways to calculate lines of code for a given program. Without a careful model of a program, coupled with a clear definition of a line of code, confusion reigns. We must take great care to clarify what we are counting and how we are counting it. In particular, we must explain how each of the following is handled:

- blank lines
- comment lines
- data declarations
- lines that contain several separate instructions

Jones reports that one count can be as much as five times larger than another, simply because of the difference in counting technique (Jones, 1986).

> **EXAMPLE 7.3:** There is some general consensus that blank lines and comments should not be counted. Conte, Dunsmore, and Shen define a line of

code as any line of program text that is not a comment or blank line, regardless of the number of statements or fragments of statements on the line. This definition specifically includes all lines containing program headers, declarations, and executable and non-executable statements (Conte, Dunsmore, and Shen, 1986). Grady and Caswell report that Hewlett-Packard defines a line of code as a non-commented source statement: any statement in the program except for comments and blank lines (Grady and Caswell, 1987).

The Hewlett-Packard definition of a line of code is the most widely accepted. To stress the fact that a line of code according to this definition is actually a non-commented line, we use the abbreviation NCLOC, sometimes also called effective lines of code (ELOC). The model associated with this definition views a program as a simple file listing, with comments and blank lines removed, giving an indication of the extent to which it is self-documented.

In a sense, valuable length information is lost when this definition is used. In many situations, program length is important in deciding how much computer storage is required for the source code, or how many pages are required for a printout. Here, the program length must reflect the blank and commented lines. Thus, NCLOC is not a valid measure (in the sense of Chapter 3) of total program length; it is a measure of the uncommented length. Uncommented length is a reasonable and useful attribute to measure, but only when it addresses appropriate questions and goals. If we are relating length with effort from the point of view of productivity assessment, then uncommented length may be a valid input. But even here, there is room for doubt, as uncommented length carries with it an implicit assumption that comments do not entail real programming effort and so should not be considered.

As a compromise, we recommend that the number of comment lines of program text (CLOC) be measured and recorded separately. Then we can define:

$$\text{total length (LOC)} = \text{NCLOC} + \text{CLOC}$$

and some useful indirect measures follow. For example, the ratio:

$$\frac{\text{CLOC}}{\text{LOC}}$$

measures the density of comments in a program.

EXAMPLE 7.4: A large UK organization has written the code for a single application in two different kinds of COBOL. Although the code performs the same kinds of functions, the difference in comment density is striking, as shown in Table 7.1.

As a single measure of program length, LOC may be preferable to NCLOC, and it is certainly easier to measure automatically. In general, it may be useful to gather both measures.

Other code length measures try to take into account the way code is developed and run. Some researchers and practitioners acknowledge that sometimes programs

Table 7.1: Comment density by language type

	Number of programs	Total lines of code	Comment density
Batch COBOL	335	670 000	16%
CICS COBOL	273	507 000	26%

are full of data declarations and header statements, and there is very little code that actually executes. For some purposes (such as testing), it is important to know how much executable code is being produced. Here, they prefer to measure the number of executable statements (ES). This measure counts separate statements on the same physical line as distinct. It ignores comment lines, data declarations, and headings.

Other developers recognize that the amount of code delivered can be significantly different from the amount of code actually written. Drivers, stubs, prototypes, and "scaffolding" for development and testing may be written by the programming team, but these programs are discarded when the final version is tested and turned over to the customer. Here, the developers want to distinguish the amount of delivered code from the amount of developed code. The number of delivered source instructions (DSI) captures this aspect of length; it counts separate statements on the same physical line as distinct, and it ignores comment lines. However, unlike executable statements, DSI includes data declarations and headings as source instructions.

Clearly, the definition of code length is influenced by the way in which it is to be used. Some organizations use length to compare one project with another, to answer questions such as:

- What is our largest/smallest/average project?
- What is our productivity?
- What are the trends in project length over time?

Other organizations measure length only within a project team, asking:

- What is the largest/smallest/average module length?
- Does module length influence the number of faults?

The US Software Engineering Institute has developed a set of guidelines to help you in deciding how to measure a line of code in your organization (Park, 1992). It takes into account the use of automatic code generators, distinguishes physical lines of code from logical ones, and allows you to tailor the definition to your needs.

EXAMPLE 7.5: The Software Engineering Institute did a pilot study of the use of its guidelines at the Defense Information Systems Agency (Rozum and Florac, 1995). The checklist was used to decide that a lines-of-code count would include the following:

- all executable code
- non-executable declarations and compiler directives

but no comments or blank lines. The checklist also requires the user to specify how the code was produced, and the pilot project included all code that was:

* programmed
* generated with source code generators
* converted with automatic translators
* copied or reused without change
* modified

But code that was removed from the final deliverable was not counted.

The checklist takes into account the origin of code, so that code that was new work or adapted from old work was counted, as was local library software and reuse library software. However, code that was furnished by the government or a vendor was not included in the count.

Figure 7.1 presents an example of a simple program. A large number of practitioners were asked to count independently (that is, without conferring or seeking clarification) the "number of lines of code" in the program. Some of the various valid answers are shown in Table 7.2.

Thus, even with a small program, the difference between least and most compact counting methods can be a factor of 5:1, as observed in practice by Jones. When other length measures are used, the same variations are encountered:

number of executable statements: ranges from 6 to 20
number of characters: ranges from 236 to 611

There are other alternatives to lines of code for measuring code length.

Maurice Halstead made an early attempt to capture notions of size and complexity beyond the counting of lines of code (Halstead, 1976). Although his work has had a lasting impact, Halstead's software science measures provide an example of confused and inadequate measurement.

EXAMPLE 7.6:   Halstead's software science attempted to capture attributes of a program that paralleled physical and psychological measurements in other

Table 7.2: Independent counts of lines of code

30	count of the number of physical lines (including blank lines)
24	count of all lines except blank lines and comments
20	count of all statements except comments (statements taking more than one line count as only one line)
17	count of all lines except blank lines, comments, declarations, and headings
13	count of all statements except blank lines, comments, declarations, and headings
6	count of only the executable statements, not including exception conditions

```
with TEXT_IO; use TEXT_IO;
procedure Main is

    —This program copies characters from an input
    —file to an output file. Termination occurs
    —either when all characters are copied or
    —when a NULL character is input

    Nullchar, Eof: exception;
    Char: CHARACTER;
    Input_file, Output_file, Console: FILE_TYPE;
Begin
    loop
        Open (FILE => Input_file, MODE => IN_FILE,
                         NAME => "CharsIn");
        Open (FILE => Output_file, MODE =>OUT_FILE,
                         NAME => "CharOut");
        Get (Input_file, Char);
        if END_OF_FILE (Input_file) then
                raise Eof;
        elseif Char = ASCII.NUL then
                raise Nullchar;
        else
                    Put(Output_file, Char);
        end if;
    end loop;
exception
    when Eof => Put (Console, "no null characters");
    when Nullchar => Put (Console, "null terminator");
end Main
```

Figure 7.1: A simple program

disciplines. He began by defining a program P as a collection of tokens, classified as either operators or operands. The basic metrics for these tokens were:

$$\mu_1 = \text{number of unique operators}$$
$$\mu_2 = \text{number of unique operands}$$

$$N_1 = \text{total occurrences of operators}$$
$$N_2 = \text{total occurrences of operands}$$

For example, the FORTRAN statement

$$A(I) = A(J)$$

has one operator (=) and two operands (A(I) and A(J)).

The **length** of P is defined to be $N = N_1 + N_2$, while the **vocabulary** of P is $\mu = \mu_1 + \mu_2$. The **volume** of a program, akin to the number of mental comparisons needed to write a program of length N, is

$$V = N \times \log \mu$$

The **program level** of a program P of volume V is

$$L = V^*/V$$

where V^* is the potential volume – the volume of the minimal size implementation of P. The inverse of level is the **difficulty**:

$$D = 1/L.$$

According to Halstead's theory, we can calculate an estimate $\hat{L}$ of L as

$$\hat{L} = \frac{1}{D} = \frac{2}{\mu_1} \times \frac{\mu_2}{N_2}$$

Likewise, the estimated program length is

$$\hat{N} = \mu_1 \times \log \mu_1 + \mu_2 \times \log \mu_2.$$

The effort required to generate P is given by

$$E = \frac{V}{\hat{L}} = \frac{\mu_1 N_2 N \log \mu}{2 \mu_2}$$

where the unit of measurement of E is elementary mental discriminations needed to understand P. These relationships are based on those reported in the psychology literature. There, a psychologist named John Stroud claimed that the human mind is capable of making a limited number, β, of elementary discriminations per second. He asserted that $5 \le \beta \le 20$. Halstead claimed that $\beta = 18$, and hence the required programming time T for a program of effort E is

$$T = E/18 \text{ seconds}$$

Some researchers have reported finding a relationship between N and the number of errors in a module, but the theory behind Halstead's measures has been questioned repeatedly (Coulter, 1983; Hamer and Frewin, 1982).

Figure 7.2 is a worked example of the application of Halstead's concepts to a short FORTRAN program (derived from an example in Conte, Dunsmore, and Shen (1986)).

The software-science approach in Example 7.6 illustrates several different software-measurement problems. The metrics are presented in the literature as a definitive collection, with no corresponding consensus on the meaning of attributes such as volume, difficulty, or program level. In other words, the relationship between the empirical relational system (that is, the real world) and the mathematical model is unclear. Further, Halstead gives no real indication of the relationships among different components of his theory. And we cannot tell if he is defining measures or prediction systems.

Using the conceptual framework described in Chapter 3, we can discuss Halstead's metrics in more depth. The focus of Halstead's measurements is a product: the source code for an imperative language. Four internal attributes are measured, and each is measured on an absolute scale: the number of distinct operators, μ_1 (corresponding to the source-code attribute "having operators"), the number of distinct operands, μ_2, and total number of respective occurrences of these, N_1 and N_2.

The formula $N = N_1 + N_2$ is a proposed measure of the internal program attribute of **length**. From the perspective of measurement theory, N is a reasonable measure of the

```
SUBROUTINE SORT (A,N)
INTEGER A(100),N,I,J,SAVE,M
C ROUTINE SORTS ARRAY A INTO DESCENDING ORDER
IF (N.LT.2) GO TO 40
DO 30 I=2,N
M=I-1
DO 20 J=1,M
IF (A(I).GT.A(J)) GO TO 10
GO TO 20
10 SAVE=A(I)
A(I)=A(J)
A(J)=SAVE
20 CONTINUE
30 CONTINUE
40 RETURN
END
```

$$N = N_1 + N_2 = 93$$
$$S_s = N / L_c \sim 93 / 7 \sim 3$$
$$\mu = \mu_1 + \mu_2 = 27$$
$$V = N \times \log \mu = 93 \times 4.75 = 442$$
$$V^* = 11.6$$
$$L = V^* / V = 11.6 / 442 = 0.026$$
$$D = 1 / L = 38.5$$
$$\hat{L} = \frac{1}{D} = \frac{2}{\mu_1} \times \frac{\mu_2}{N_2} = 2 / 14 \times 13 / 42 = 0.044$$
$$E = \frac{V}{\hat{L}} = 442 / 0.044 = 10045$$
$$T = E / \beta = 10045 / 18 = 558 \text{ seconds} = 10 \text{ minutes}$$

Thus, according to Halstead, the sample FORTRAN program requires about 11.6 mental comparisons and should take approximately 10 minutes to code.

Figure 7.2: A worked example of the application of Halstead's concepts

length of the actual code (without comments), since it does not contradict any intuitively understood relations among programs and their lengths. A similar argument applies to the formula for the internal program attribute of vocabulary. The program attribute **volume** is supposed to correspond to the amount of computer storage necessary for a uniform binary encoding; the assumption of a uniform encoding on an arbitrary machine suggests that this measure should be viewed as an internal attribute.

Thus Halstead has proposed reasonable measures of three internal program attributes that reflect different views of size. However, the Halstead approach becomes problematic when we examine the remaining measures, which are nothing more than generally unvalidated (and some would argue intuitively implausible) prediction systems in which the prediction procedures are not properly articulated. For example, consider the equations for effort, E, and time, T. These variables are predicted measures of attributes of the process of implementing the program (although it is not made clear at which stage after requirements capture the process is assumed to start). There is a further serious problem with E, since this proposed measurement scale leads to contradictions involving meaningful statements about effort (the attribute being measured). We discuss this problem and the validation of Halstead's measures further in Chapter 12.

To define length differently, we have two other alternatives to explore, both of which are acceptable on measurement theory grounds as ratio measures:

1. We can measure length in terms of the number of bytes of computer storage required for the program text. This approach has the advantage of being on the same scale as the normal measure of size for object code. It is at least as well understood as LOC, and it is very easy to collect.

2. We can measure length in terms of the number of characters (CHAR) in the program text, another easily-collected measure. For example, most modern word processors compute this count routinely for any text file. (Both the UNIX™ and VMS™ operating systems have the command **wc<filename>** to compute it.)

Because these length measures, as well as lines of code, are on the ratio scale, we can rescale any one measure in terms of any other by multiplying by a suitable (empirical) constant.

EXAMPLE 7.7: If α is the average number of characters per line of program text, then we have the rescaling

$$CHAR = \alpha \, LOC$$

which expresses a stochastic relationship between LOC and CHAR. Similarly, we can use any constant multiple of the proposed measures as an alternative valid length measure. Thus, we can use KLOC (thousands of lines of code) or KDSI (thousands of delivered source instructions) to measure program size.

So far, we have assumed that one line of code is much like another. However, many people argue that a line of code is dependent on language; a line of APL or LISP is very different from a line of BASIC, C++ or Ada. Some practitioners use conversion factors, so that a module of k lines of APL code is considered to be equivalent to αk lines of C code, for some appropriate α. This conversion is important if you must use LOC to measure functionality and effort, rather than just length.

7.2.1.2 Dealing with non-textual or external code

There is another aspect of language dependence that causes a problem. Most code measures assume that software code consists purely of text. Up to about 1990, this assumption was almost invariably true. However, the advent of visual programming and windowing environments (and to a lesser extent object orientation and fourth-generation languages) is changing dramatically our notions of what a software program is.

EXAMPLE 7.8: In the Visual Basic™ programming environment, you can create a sophisticated Windows program, complete with menus, icons, and graphics, with almost no code in the traditional sense. For example, the executable code to produce a scroll bar is constructed automatically after you point at a scroll bar object in the programming environment. You need to write code only to perform the specific actions that result from, say, a click on a specific command button.

In an environment like the one described in Example 7.8, it is not at all clear how you would measure length of your "program." The traditional code length may be negligible, compared to the "length" of the objects provided by the environment and other graphics objects. Thus, a program with just five handwritten BASIC statements can easily generate an executable program of 200 Kb.

These new approaches to programming raise two separate measurement issues:

1. How do we account in our length measures for objects that are not textual?
2. How do we account in our length measures for components that are constructed externally?

Issue 1 is relevant not just for code developed in new programming environments, but also for traditional specification and design documents, and we address this partially in the next section. Issue 2 is an aspect of reuse, and we address it later in this chapter.

Object-oriented development also suggests new ways to measure length. Pfleeger found that a count of objects and methods led to more accurate productivity estimates than those using lines of code (Pfleeger, 1989). Others have reported size measures in terms of objects and methods, too. Lorenz found in his research at IBM that the average class contained 20 methods, and the average method size was 8 lines of code for Smalltalk and 24 for C++. The class contains 6 object attributes or instance variables (Lorenz, 1993).

He also notes that size differs with system and application type. For example, prototype classes have 10 to 15 methods, each with five to ten lines of code, whereas production classes have 20 to 30 methods, each with 10 to 20 lines of code. C++ systems require two to three times more code than do Smalltalk systems.

Williams, at the Space Telescope Science Institute in Baltimore, Maryland, has studied the size of object-oriented software as part of a larger study identifying key factors in measuring functionality and productivity. He recommends using the number of classes, functions, and class interactions to express size (Williams, 1994).

7.2.2   Specifications and designs

Appearing early in the life cycle, specification and design documents usually combine text, graphs, and special mathematical diagrams and symbols. The nature of the presentation depends on the particular style, method, or notation used. When measuring code size, it is customary to identify an atomic object to count (lines of code, executable statements, source instructions, characters or objects and methods, for example). However, a specification or design can consist of both text and diagrams, suggesting at least two types of atomic objects that are incommensurate with respect to length.

We can enforce comparability artificially by defining a page as an atomic object, so that both text and diagrams are composed of a number of sequential pages. Thus, the number of pages measures length for arbitrary types of documentation; it is the most frequently used in industry.

However, we can view length as a composite measure, just as we decompose size. A document may consist of both text and diagrams, where the diagrams have a uniform syntax (such as "labeled digraphs," "data-flow diagrams," or "Z schemas"). Then we can define an acceptable length measure in terms of a pair of numbers representing text length and diagram length. In other words, we define appropriate atomic objects for the different types of diagrams and symbols.

EXAMPLE 7.9:   There are several clear ways to handle well-known methods:

1.   The atomic objects for data-flow diagrams are *processes* (bubbles nodes), *external entities* (box nodes), *data stores* (line nodes) and *data flows* (arcs).
2.   The atomic entities for algebraic specifications are *sorts*, *functions*, *operations*, and *axioms*.
3.   The atomic entities for Z schemas are the various lines appearing in the specification. These lines form part of either a *type declaration* or a (non-conjunctive) *predicate* (Spivey, 1993).

DeMarco's structured analysis and system specification approach is expressed in terms of atomic components (DeMarco, 1978). At the specification stage, there are three system views leading to four types of diagrams and six atomic objects that DeMarco calls **primitives**. Table 7.3 describes the relationship among views, diagrams, and objects.

Table 7.3: Structured analysis components

View	Diagram	Atomic objects
Functional	Data-flow diagram	Bubbles
	Data dictionary	Data elements
Data	Entity relation diagram	Objects, relations
State	State transition diagram	States, transitions

However, DeMarco does not explicitly propose any length measures in terms of these primitives. As we shall see later in this chapter, he defines instead a measure for functionality.

7.2.3 Predicting length

Since source code is relatively easy to analyze, and length (particularly of source code) is a well-studied attribute that is required by many prediction models, it is desirable to predict length as early as possible in the life cycle.

> **EXAMPLE 7.10:** Halstead suggested a prediction system for LOC based on his own measure of length, N. He proposed that for programming language K, there is a constant c_K such that for any program P, an estimate of the LOC in P is N/c_K. When K is FORTRAN, c_K is approximately 7. For instance, a FORTRAN program having Halstead length $N = 70$ should contain approximately 10 LOC. In the example FORTRAN program in Figure 7.2, $N = 93$, so LOC should be approximately 13. In fact it is 16, so 13 is a reasonable estimate.

It is intuitively appealing to predict length by relating the length of later life-cycle products to the length of earlier ones. In particular, length may be predicted by considering the median **expansion ratio** from specification (or design) length to code length on similar projects.

> **EXAMPLE 7.11:** We can use the size of design to predict the size of the resulting code. The design-to-code expansion ratio is
>
> $$\frac{\text{size of design}}{\text{size of code}}$$
>
> At the module-design phase, length (expressed as LOC) may be estimated from the formula:
>
> $$LOC = \alpha \sum_{i=1}^{m} S_i$$
>
> where S_i is the size of module i (measured in terms of the components of the design notation, as discussed above), m is the number of modules, and α is the design-to-code expansion ratio recorded on previous projects using the same design and code conventions.

Many researchers have tried to establish an empirical relationship between the length of program code and the length of program documentation. Walston and Felix observed that:

$$D = 49L^{1.01}$$

where D is the length of documentation measured in pages, and L is length of program code measured in KLOC (Walston and Felix, 1977). Such observations may not be universal, as they depend on organizational and contractual requirements and conventions. But they can form the basis of a useful rule of thumb. For more accurate predictions, data must be collected for specific environments.

There is an obvious benefit in having good, stable length measures for all life-cycle documents. With careful data collection, we can determine and express more accurate relationships between length measures at different phases of the life cycle, using them to improve our predictions.

7.3 REUSE

Program generators, fourth-generation languages, windowing environments, and other labor-saving techniques take advantage of the repetitiveness of some of our tasks. We need not write another sort routine or sensor-monitoring software if we have them expressed in other products. We regularly use operating systems, compilers, database management systems, and libraries of mathematical routines, rather than writing our own. This reuse of software (including requirements, designs, documentation, and test data and scripts as well as code) improves our productivity and quality, allowing us to concentrate on new problems, rather than continuing to solve old ones again. For example, Table 7.4 summarizes the effects of reuse on two divisions of Hewlett-Packard. However, traditional notions of productivity, measured as size of output divided by effort expended, must be adjusted to accommodate this reuse. We must include in our size measurement some method of counting (but not overcounting) the reused products.

Counting reused code is not as simple as it sounds. It is difficult to define formally what we mean by reused code. We sometimes reuse whole programs without modification, but more often we reuse some unit of code (a module, function, or procedure). And we often modify that unit to some extent. However we account for reused code, we want to distinguish a module with one modified line from a module with 100 modified lines. Thus, we consider the notion of **extent of reuse**, measured on an ordinal scale by NASA/Goddard's Software Engineering Laboratory in the following way (Software Productivity Consortium, 1995).

1. **Reused verbatim:** the code in the unit was reused without any changes.
2. **Slightly modified:** fewer that 25% of the lines of code in the unit were modified.

Table 7.4: Quality, productivity, and time-to-market profiles for reuse projects (Lim, 1994)

Organization	Manufacturing productivity	San Diego technical graphics
Quality	51% defect reduction	24% defect reduction
Productivity	57% increase	40% increase
Time to market	data not available	42% reduction

3. **Extensively modified:** 25% or more of the lines of code were modified.
4. **New:** none of the code comes from a previously constructed unit.

The classification can be simplified and reduced to two levels, **new** (levels 3 and 4) or **reused** (levels 1 and 2).

> **EXAMPLE 7.12:** Typical FORTRAN projects at the Software Engineering Laboratory include 20% reused lines of code, while typical Ada projects include 30% reused lines (Software Productivity Consortium, 1995).

For a given program, we can define size in terms of total size and proportion of reuse at the different levels.

> **EXAMPLE 7.13:** Hatton reports a high degree of reuse at Programming Research Ltd, where reuse was encouraged as part of a larger program to eliminate troublesome language constructs from company products (Hatton, 1995). The reuse ratio is computed for each product as the proportion of reused lines out of the total number of lines. Table 7.5 illustrates the reuse ratio for Programming Research products.

Hewlett-Packard considers three levels of code: new code, reused code, and leveraged code. In this terminology, reused code is used as is, without modification, while leveraged code is existing code that is modified in some way. The Hewlett-Packard reuse ratio includes both reused and leveraged code as a percentage of total code delivered. The chart in Figure 7.3 illustrates the degree of reuse on six firmware products at Hewlett-Packard (Lim, 1994).

7.4 FUNCTIONALITY

Many software engineers argue that length is misleading, and that the amount of **functionality** inherent in a product paints a better picture of product size. In particular, those who generate effort and duration estimates from early development products often prefer to estimate functionality rather than physical size. As a distinct attribute, functionality captures an intuitive notion of the amount of function contained in a delivered product or in a description of how the product is supposed to be.

Table 7.5: Reuse of code at Programming Research Ltd (Hatton, 1995)

Product	Reusable lines of code	Total lines of code	Reuse ratio (%)
QAC	40 900	82 300	50
QA FORTRAN	34 000	73 000	47
QA Manager (X)	18 300	50 100	37
QA Manager (Motif)	18 300	52 700	35
QA C++	40 900	82 900	49
QA C Dynamic	11 500	30 400	38

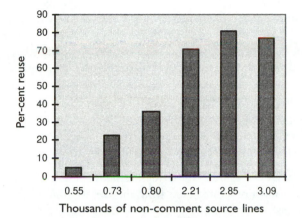

Figure 7.3: Reuse at Hewlett-Packard (the bars represent six different firmware projects)

There have been several serious attempts to measure functionality of software products. We examine three approaches in this chapter: Albrecht's function points, DeMarco's specification weight, and the COCOMO 2.0 approach to object points. Each of these measures was derived as part of a larger effort to supply size information to a cost or productivity model, based on measurable early products, rather than estimates of lines of code.

All three approaches measure the functionality of specification documents, but each can also be applied to later life-cycle products to refine the size estimate and therefore the cost or productivity estimate. Indeed, our intuitive notion of functionality tells us that if a program P is an implementation of specification S, then P and S should have the same functionality.

None of the three approaches to functionality adheres to the rigorous view of measurement that we have described. As we discuss each method, we indicate where the problems are and how they might be addressed rigorously. However, the current lack of rigor should not prevent us from using and refining the current approaches, as functionality is a very important product attribute. Moreover, these methods have been used to good effect in a number of industrial applications.

7.4.1 Albrecht's approach

Albrecht's effort estimation method was largely based on the notion of function points. As their name suggests, **function points** are intended to measure the amount of functionality in a system as described by a specification. We can compute function points without forcing the specification to conform to the prescripts of a particular specification model or technique.

To compute the number of function points, FP, we first compute an unadjusted function point count, UFC. To do this, we determine from some representation of the software the number of items of the following types:

- **External inputs:** those items provided by the user that describe distinct application-oriented data (such as file names and menu selections). These items do not include inquiries, which are counted separately.
- **External outputs:** those items provided to the user that generate distinct application-oriented data (such as reports and messages, rather than the individual components of these).
- **External inquiries:** interactive inputs requiring a response.
- **External files:** machine-readable interfaces to other systems.
- **Internal files:** logical master files in the system.

EXAMPLE 7.14: Figure 7.4 describes a simple spelling checker. To compute the unadjusted function-point count from this description, we can identify the following items:

- the two external inputs: *document filename, personal dictionary-name*
- the three external outputs: *misspelled word report, number-of-words-processed message, number-of-errors-so-far message*
- the two external inquiries: *words processed, errors so far*
- the two external files: *document file, personal dictionary*
- the one internal file: *dictionary*

Next, each item is assigned a subjective "complexity" rating on a three-point ordinal scale: "simple", "average", or "complex". Then, a weight is assigned to the item, based on Table 7.6.

In theory, there are 15 different varieties of items (three levels of complexity for each of the five types), so we can compute the unadjusted function-point count by multiplying the number of items in a variety by the weight of the variety and summing over all fifteen:

$$\text{UFC} = \sum_{i=1}^{15} \left((\text{Number of items of variety } i) \times \text{weight}_i \right)$$

EXAMPLE 7.15: Consider the spelling checker introduced in Example 7.14. If we assume that the complexity for each item is average, then the unadjusted function count, UFC, is

$$\text{UFC} = 4A + 5B + 4C + 10D + 10E = 61$$

If instead we learn that the dictionary file and the misspelled word report are considered complex, then

$$\text{UFC} = 4A + (5 \times 2 + 7 \times 1) + 4C + 10D + 10E = 63$$

To complete our computation of function points, we calculate an **adjusted function point count**, FP, by multiplying UFC by a **technical complexity factor**, TCF. This factor involves the 14 contributing factors listed in Table 7.7.

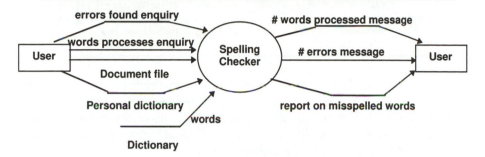

> **Spell-Checker Spec** The checker accepts as input a document file and an optional personal dictionary file. The checker lists all words not contained in either of these files. The user can query the number of words processed and the number of spelling errors found at any stage during processing.

A = # external inputs = 2, B =# external outputs = 3, C = # inquiries = 2,
D = # external files = 2, E = # internal files = 1

Figure 7.4: Computing basic function-point components from specification

Each component or sub-factor in the table is rated from 0 to 5, where 0 means the sub-factor is irrelevant, 3 means it is average, and 5 means it is essential to the systems being built. Although these integer ratings form an ordinal scale, the values are used as if they were a ratio scale, contrary to the principles we introduced in Chapter 2. Also, we find it curious that the "average" value of 3 is not the median value.

The following formula combines the 14 ratings into a final technical complexity factor:

$$\text{TCF} = 0.65 + 0.01 \sum_{i=1}^{14} F_i$$

This factor varies from 0.65 (if each F_i is set to 0) to 1.35 (if each F_i is set to 5). The final calculation of function points multiplies the unadjusted function-point count by the technical complexity factor:

$$\text{FP} = \text{UFC} \times \text{TCF}$$

Table 7.6: Function point complexity weights

Item	Simple	Weighting factor average	Complex
External inputs	3	4	6
External outputs	4	5	7
External inquiries	3	4	6
External files	7	10	15
Internal files	5	7	10

Table 7.7: Components of the technical complexity factor

F_1 Reliable back-up and recovery	F_2 Data communications
F_3 Distributed functions	F_4 Performance
F_5 Heavily used configuration	F_6 Online data entry
F_7 Operational ease	F_8 Online update
F_9 Complex interface	F_{10} Complex processing
F_{11} Reusability	F_{12} Installation ease
F_{13} Multiple sites	F_{14} Facilitate change

EXAMPLE 7.16: To continue our function-point computation for the spelling checker in Example 7.14, we evaluate the technical complexity factor. After having read the specification in Figure 7.3, it seems reasonable to assume that $F_3, F_5, F_9, F_{11}, F_{12}$, and F_{13} are 0, that F_1, F_2, F_6, F_7, F_8, and F_{14} are 3, and that F_4 and F_{10} are 5. Thus we calculate the TCF as

$$TCF = 0.65 + 0.01(18 + 10) = 0.93$$

Since UFC is 63, then

$$FP = 63 \times 0.93 = 59$$

Function points can form the basis for an effort estimate.

EXAMPLE 7.17: Suppose our historical database of project measurements reveals that it takes a developer an average of two person days of effort to implement a function point. Then we may estimate the effort needed to complete the spelling checker as 118 person days (that is, 59 FPs multiplied by 2 person days each).

But function points are also used in other ways as a size measure. For example, we can express defect density in terms of defects per function point. They are also used in contracts, both to report progress and to define payment. For instance, Onvlee claims that 50–60% of software contracts in the Netherlands have their costs tied to a function-points specification (Onvlee, 1995). In other words, many companies write software contracts to include a price per function point, and others track project completion by reporting the number of function points specified, designed, coded, and tested.

Albrecht proposed function points as a technology-independent measure of size. But there are several problems with the function-points measure, and users of the technique should be aware of its limitations.

1. **Problems with subjectivity in the technology factor:** Since the TCF may range from 0.65 to 1.35, the unadjusted function point count can be changed by ±35%. Thus, the uncertainty inherent in the subjective sub-factor ratings can have a significant effect on the final function-point value.

2. **Problems with double-counting:** Symons investigated the use of function points and noted that it is possible to account for internal complexity twice:

in weighting the inputs for the unadjusted function-point count, and again in the TCF (Symons, 1988). Even if the evaluator is careful in separating these two complexity-related inputs, double-counting can occur in the use to which the final function-point count is put. For example, the TCF includes sub-factors such as performance requirements and processing complexity, characteristics often used in cost models. However, if function points are used as a size input to a cost model that rates performance and complexity separately, these adjustment factors are counted twice. Packages such as *Before You Leap* uses function points as a front-end size estimator for a COCOMO cost estimation; here, double-counting is possible.

3. **Problems with counter-intuitive values:** In addition, the sub-factor ratings lead to TCF values that are counter-intuitive. For instance, when each F_i is "average" and rated 3, we would expect TCF to be 1; instead, the formula yields 1.07. Albrecht included the TCF as a means of improving resource predictions, and the TCF accentuates both internal system complexity and complexity associated with the user-view functionality. It may be preferable to measure these concepts separately.

4. **Problems with accuracy:** Kitchenham and Känsälä's research reveals that the TCF does not significantly improve resource estimates (Kitchenham and Känsälä, 1993). Similarly, Jeffery and his colleagues have shown that the UFC seems to be no worse a predictor of resources than the adjusted FP count (Jeffery, Low and Barnes, 1993). So the TCF does not seem useful in increasing the accuracy of prediction. Recognizing this, many function point users restrict themselves to the UFC.

5. **Problems with early life-cycle use:** function-point calculation requires a full software system specification; a user requirements document is not sufficient. Thus, one of the major goals of this measure is not met (ISQAA, 1989).

6. **Problems with changing requirements:** Function points are an appealing size measure in part because they can be recalculated as development continues. They can also be used to track progress, in terms of number of function points completed. However, if we compare a function-point count generated from an initial specification with the count obtained from the resulting system, we sometimes find an increase of 400 to 2000% (Kemerer, 1993). This difference may be due not to the function point calculation method but rather to "creeping elegance," where new, non-specified functionality is built into the system as development progresses. However, the difference occurs also because the level of detail in a specification is coarser than that of the actual implementation. That is, the number and complexity of inputs, outputs, enquiries, and other function point-related data will be underestimated in a specification because they are not well-understood or articulated early in the project. Thus, calibrating function point relationships based on actual projects in your historical database will not always produce equations that are useful for predictive purposes

(unless the function points were derived from the original system specification, not the system itself).

7. **Problems with differentiating specified items:** Because evaluating the input items and technology factor components involves expert judgment, the calculation of function points from a specification cannot be completely automated. To minimize subjectivity and ensure some consistency across different evaluators, organizations (such as the International Function Point User Group) often publish detailed counting rules that distinguish inputs and outputs from enquiries, to define what constitutes a "logical master file", and so on. However, there is still great variety in results when different people compute function points from the same specification (ISQAA, 1989).

8. **Problems with technology dependence:** Function points are not independent of the system analysis and design method used. For example, Verner and Tate used function points in estimating the functionality of systems developed using fourth-generation languages (4GLs). They found that accuracy improved when the function-point input items were tailored to the types of inputs handled by 4GLs. Similar results were reported by Ratcliffe and Rollo when they investigated the use of function points with Jackson System Development. Thus, counting rules for function points may require adjustment to the particular methods being used (Verner and Tate, 1988; Ratcliffe and Rollo, 1990).

9. **Problems with application domain:** Function points have been used successfully in data-processing applications, the domain for which they were originally developed. But their use for real-time and scientific applications is controversial. Two cost-estimation tools, SPR (using feature points, a variation on function points) and ASSET-R, include extensions to enable function points to apply to real-time and scientific applications. However, the effectiveness of these extensions has not been independently assessed and reported in the literature.

10. **Problems with subjective weighting:** Symons notes that the choice of weights for calculating unadjusted function points was determined subjectively from IBM experience. These values may not be appropriate in other development environments (Symons, 1988).

11. **Problems with measurement theory:** Kitchenham, Pfleeger, and Fenton have proposed a framework for evaluating measurements, much like the framework presented in Chapters 2 and 3. They apply the framework to function points, noting that the function-point calculation combines measures from different scales in a manner that is inconsistent with measurement theory. In particular, the weights and TCF ratings are on an ordinal scale, while the counts are on a ratio scale, so the linear combinations in the formula are meaningless. They propose that function points be viewed as a vector of several aspects of functionality, rather than as a single number (Kitchenham, Pfleeger, and Fenton, 1995).

Several attempts have been made to address some of these problems. The International Function Point User Group meets regularly to discuss function points and their applications, and they publish guidelines with counting rules. The organization also trains and tests estimators in the use of function points, with the goal of increasing consistency of interpretation and application. Others have redefined function points to some extent. For example, Symons has developed an improved function-point-like measure based on "logical transactions," similar to input-processing-output transactions. His measure, called **Mark 2 function points**, includes weighted counts of logical transactions (Symons, 1988).

In general, the community of function-point users is especially careful about data collection and analysis. If function points are used with care, and if their limitations are understood and accounted for, they can be more useful than lines of code as a size or normalization measure. As use of function points is modified, evaluated, and reported in the literature, we can monitor the success of the changes.

7.4.2 COCOMO 2.0 approach

As we will see in detail in Chapter 12, COCOMO is a model for predicting effort from a formula whose main independent variable is size. In investigating alternatives to lines of code as a size input for a revised COCOMO, Boehm and his colleagues selected function points for use when the system is completely specified. However, they sought a size measure that could be used even earlier in development, when feasibility is being explored and prototypes built. They selected **object points** for this early size measure in COCOMO 2.0. The object-point approach is a synthesis of the procedure suggested by Kauffman and Kumar (Kauffman and Kumar, 1993) and productivity data reported by Banker and colleagues (Banker, Kauffman, and Kumar, 1994).

To compute object points, an initial size measure is generated by counting the number of screens, reports, and third-generation language components that will be involved in the application. It is assumed that these objects are defined in a standard way as part of an integrated computer-assisted software-engineering environment (ICASE). Next, each object is classified as simple, medium, or difficult, much as are function points. Table 7.8 contains guidelines for this classification.

The number in each cell is weighted according to Table 7.9. The weights reflect the relative effort required to implement an instance of that complexity level.

As with function points, the weighted instances are summed to yield a single object-point number. Then, the procedure differs from function points in that reuse is taken into account, since the object points are intended for use in effort estimation. Assuming that $r\%$ of the objects will be reused from previous projects, the number of new object points is calculated to be

$$\text{New object points} = (\text{object points}) \times (100 - r)/100$$

To use this number for effort estimation, COCOMO 2.0 determines a productivity rate (that is, new object points per person month) from a table based on developer experience and capability, coupled with ICASE maturity and capability.

7.4.3   DeMarco's approach

DeMarco proposes a functionality measure based on his structured analysis and design notation (DeMarco, 1978). These **bang metrics** (now called **specification weight metrics**) involve two measures: one for "function strong" systems, and another for "data strong" systems (DeMarco, 1982).

The **function bang** measure is based on the number of functional primitives (that is, the number of lowest-level bubbles) in a data-flow diagram, as noted in Table 7.3. The basic functional-primitive count is weighted according to the type of functional primitive and the number of data tokens used by the primitive. The **data bang** measure is based on the number of entities in the entity-relationship model. The basic entity count is weighted according to the number of relationships involving each entity. Although the measures are specific to DeMarco's notation, they can easily be adapted for other structured analysis techniques. This dependence may actually be an advantage; unlike function points, bang may be defined formally, and its computation can be automated within CASE tools that support the methodology.

The bang measures have not been subjected to any independent validation. However, they are likely to become more important now that CASE tools can generate

Table 7.8: Object point complexity levels (Boehm *et al.*, 1995)

	For screens		
	Number and source of data tables		
Number of views contained	Total < 4 (<2 server, <2 client)	Total < 8 (2–3 server, 3–5 client)	Total 8+ (>3 server, >5 client)
<3	simple	simple	medium
3–7	simple	medium	difficult
8+	medium	difficult	difficult

	For reports		
	Number and source of data tables		
Number of sections contained	Total < 4 (<2 server, <2 client)	Total < 8 (2–3 server, 3–5 client)	Total 8+ (>3 server, >5 client)
0 or 1	simple	simple	medium
2 or 3	simple	medium	difficult
4+	medium	difficult	difficult

Table 7.9: Complexity weights for object points

Object type	Simple	Medium	Difficult
Screen	1	2	3
Report	2	5	8
3GL component	–	–	10

the values automatically. Where specification and design share common constructs (such as entity-relationship diagrams), bang can be used to measure specification functionality and compare it with design functionality.

7.5 COMPLEXITY

Some of the functionality measures try to adjust for the complexity of the problem being addressed by the requirements specification. For example, Albrecht's TCF is supposed to be a measure of the underlying problem. But a problem can have more than one solution, and the solutions can vary in their approaches and therefore in their complexity. Thus, as we noted at the beginning of this chapter, the complexity of a solution can be considered as a separate component of size, and it can be expressed in a more objective way.

Ideally, we would like the complexity of the solution to be no greater than the complexity of the problem, but that is not always the case. Let us informally define the **complexity of a problem** as the amount of resources required for an optimal solution to the problem. Then **complexity of a solution** can be regarded in terms of the resources needed to implement a particular solution.

We can view solution complexity as having at least two aspects:

- **time complexity:** where the resource is computer time, and
- **space complexity:** where the resource is computer memory.

To understand how to measure and express complexity in this way, we begin by measuring the **efficiency** of a solution. Since each solution is based on an algorithm, we look at algorithmic efficiency.

7.5.1 Measuring algorithmic efficiency

Computer science has traditionally incorporated measurement in its study and comparison of algorithms. Whenever a new algorithm is proposed to solve an important problem, we try to determine how much time or memory is required for implementation.

EXAMPLE **7.18:** Consider the binary search, an algorithm for searching an ordered list (such as a telephone directory) for a single item (such as a specific name); the algorithm is depicted in Figure 7.5. It instructs us .to begin by examining the middle item in the list. If this item is the one we seek, then we are done. If it is not, then we compare our sought-for item with this middle item; the sought-for item is either lower or higher. (We use an appropriate ordering of the set in which we are searching. For instance, if we are looking in a telephone directory, then we use alphabetical order; if we are searching a list of integers, then we use the natural ordering of the integers.)

If the item we seek is lower than the middle item, then we know that our sought-for item cannot appear in any part of the list after the middle item. Thus, we disregard the second half of the list, that is, the list beyond the middle item. Similarly, if our sought-for item is higher than the middle item, we can disregard the first half of the list. We cast off this disregarded half and consider the remainder of the list as the new list to search. Then, we repeat the procedure with this smaller list, continuing to "divide and conquer" by comparing with the middle item and discarding half the list. In this way, we either find the item or exhaust the process (in which case, the item we seek is not in the list).

Suppose that we begin with a list containing 256 elements, and we seek a particular item using a binary search. Then the search must end after at most eight steps, that is, after we have performed at most eight comparisons of our item with a "middle" item. In general, for a list of n elements, the binary search algorithm terminates after at most $\log_2 n$ comparisons. Contrast this with the most naive searching algorithm, in which we examine the list from start to

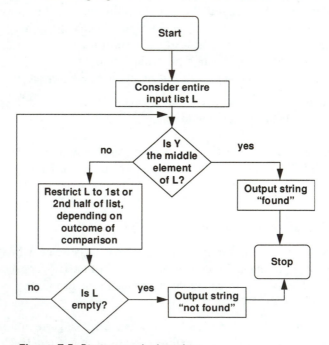

Figure 7.5: Binary search algorithm

finish, comparing our item with the next until we find a match. In the worst case, where the item we seek is at the end of the list, we need n comparisons.

In Example 7.18, the maximum number of comparisons required is an internal attribute of the algorithm. It is dependent neither on the way the algorithm is implemented in a particular programming language, nor on the machine on which it will run. Intuitively, we can agree that the binary search algorithm is a more efficient algorithm than the naive algorithm.

Standard texts on computational complexity (Aho, Hopcroft, and Ullman, 1974; Harel, 1992) provide a comprehensive discussion of how to compute algorithmic efficiency for specific algorithms. Rather than duplicate this work, we view algorithmic efficiency from the perspective of measurement theory. Although we restrict the discussion to measuring time efficiency, it applies equally to memory efficiency.

7.5.1.1 Measuring efficiency

Suppose we want to evaluate the time efficiency of a given computer program. We can measure its time efficiency by running the program through a particular compiler on a particular machine with a particular input, measuring the actual processing time required. For instance, we may find that, for a specific input X, our program runs in 23.6 nanoseconds on machine M with compiler C.

Interpreted in this way, efficiency is an external product measure. We measure it indirectly in terms of the time of a particular process. This approach is rather unsatisfactory, because its dependence on external factors causes us to lose sight of the original product. It may be difficult to differentiate one environment from another, and therefore the effects of the environment may be confounded with the effects of the program, as we noted in Chapter 4. Moreover, comparing the efficiency of different programs in this way does not yield particularly enlightening results.

To measure the product more directly, we abstract and simplify. In general, we can model a program or detailed design in terms of its underlying algorithm. That is, we treat the program or design as we would any other subject for measurement, and we express it more formally.

Next, we identify a small number of types of primitive arithmetic operations relevant to the algorithm. For example, in the searching algorithm of Example 7.18, the *comparison* was the only operation of significant interest. The same is true of sorting algorithms; however, in multiplication algorithms, *addition* is the key operation.

Using this information, we can measure efficiency in terms of the number of operations required for a given input. Notice that we are measuring the product, not the process. The measure is no longer machine- or even implementation-dependent, but it is still input-specific with respect to the algorithm. However, this view of efficiency as an external product attribute still fails to capture any intuitive attribute associated with comparative efficiency of algorithms.

To refine our approach, we note that, for most problems, the inputs may be characterized by a single size parameter, n.

EXAMPLE 7.19: In searching algorithms, our input consists of two things: a list of items and a single item to be sought. However, the efficiency of the algorithm depends only on the list length, not on any characteristic of the single item. Thus, the list length characterizes the problem, and we can consider the parameter n as a candidate size measure. This established, we note that the maximal number of primitive operations required by any search algorithm is a function of the input size n. In the case of the binary search, this function is $\log_2 n$. That is, given a list of size n, we must perform at most $\log_2 n$ comparisons.

Thus, we can measure the efficiency of searching or sorting algorithms as the function $f(n)$ representing the maximum number of primitive operations required for an input list of size n.

EXAMPLE 7.20: The Heapsort sorting algorithm has efficiency $n \log_2 n$ (Knuth, 1973).

EXAMPLE 7.21: The naive searching algorithm, described in Example 7.18, has efficiency n. Consider a variation of the naive algorithm; instead of comparing the item we seek with successive items in the list, we add a checking mechanism and compare our item with both the ith and $(i+1)^{st}$ items. That is, we begin by comparing our item with the first and second items in the list, then with the second and third, then the third and fourth, and so on. This new algorithm has efficiency $2n$.

We now have a "measure" of efficiency that appears to depend neither on the machine nor on the input. But is it a true measurement in the sense of our framework in Chapter 2? To determine the answer, we must identify the relations that are captured and the numerical relation system in which they are found.

Let F be the set of all functions of n. Then F contains, for example n, $2n$, $\log_2 n$ and n^2. We must define a relation ">" on F that corresponds to the empirical relation "more efficient". It is not immediately clear which pairs are in this relation. For example, although it is clear that $n < n^2$, how do we compare an n^2 algorithm with a $100n$ algorithm? The former is more efficient for all inputs $n < 100$, but for larger n the latter is more efficient.

Consider the two algorithms in Example 7.21. One has efficiency n and the other $2n$; intuitively, we want the relation we define to indicate that $n < 2n$. However, recall that we are concerned with the time efficiency of algorithms. In terms of time required for the algorithm, an n algorithm is not really much better; the $2n$ algorithm will always run at least as fast as an algorithm of time efficiency n if we run it on a machine whose primitive operations execute twice as fast. Moreover, if we execute the algorithms on the same machine, although the n algorithm is always faster, for large input n the rate at which it is faster is constant.

On the other hand, consider the difference between an n and an n^2 algorithm, or between an n algorithm and a $\log_2 n$ algorithm (like binary search); in these cases, one algorithm is clearly and always faster than the other. We want to be able to say that a $\log_2 n$ algorithm is clearly more efficient than an n algorithm, and an n algorithm is clearly more efficient than an n^2 algorithm but that there is no significant difference between an n and $2n$ algorithm with respect to efficiency. To formalize this intuitive idea, we introduce big-O notation.

7.5.1.2 Big-O notation

A precise mathematical formalism, called **big-O notation**, allows us to define an order relation on functions; this in turn permits us to define a relation to characterize efficiency. Intuitively, we derive the big-O form of a function $f(n)$ by finding the dominating term of $f(n)$ and then ignoring constant multiples.

EXAMPLE 7.22: Consider the function

$$f(n) = 3n^2 + 2n + 26$$

The dominating term of $f(n)$ is $3n^2$. Ignoring the constant, 3, leaves us with n^2. Thus, we say that $f(n)$ is "big-O n^2," written as $O(n^2)$.

EXAMPLE 7.23: If

$$f(n) = 2n$$

then $f(n)$ is $O(n)$.

EXAMPLE 7.24: If $f(n)$ is $3 \log n + 2$, then it is $O(\log n)$.

Figure 7.6 illustrates how some functions have values that slowly approach a particular value but never reach it. In the figure, as the x value increases, the y value, calculated as $1/x$, gets smaller and smaller, approaching 0 but never actually equaling 0. We call this almost- but never-reached value an **asymptote**, and the function exhibits **asymptotic behavior**. Figure 7.7 illustrates the asymptotic behavior of several other commonly used functions.

Big-O notation captures this behavior. When n is large, the big-O term expresses the general shape of the curve, which adjusts only slightly when the full $f(n)$ is depicted. More formally, we can view $O(g)$ as the set of functions that asymptotically dominate the function g. Because each $O(g)$ is a set, there is a well-defined partial order over its elements, usually expressed as normal set inclusion.

EXAMPLE 7.25: It can be shown that the following strict containments hold:

$$O(1) \subset O(\log n) \subset O(n) \subset O(n \log n) \subset O(n^2) \subset O(c^n) \subset O(n!)$$

$$O(n^i) \subset O(n^j) \text{ for all } i < j$$

$$O(n^i) \subset O(c^n) \text{ for all integers } i$$

Some of the big-O sets are sufficiently common to merit special names. For example, if:

- $f(n)$ is $O(1)$, then we say f has **constant complexity**;
- $f(n)$ is $O(\log n)$, then we say f has **logarithmic complexity**;
- $f(n)$ is $O(n)$ then we say f has **linear complexity**;

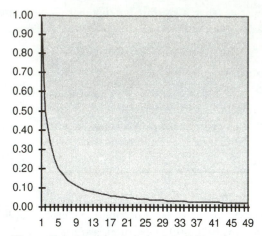

Figure 7.6: Asymptotic behavior of $1/x$

- $f(n)$ is $O(n^2)$ then we say f has **quadratic complexity**;
- $f(n)$ is $O(c^n)$, where $c > 1$, then we say f has **exponential complexity**.

Using this notation and terminology, we can define the **efficiency** of algorithm A to be $O(f(n))$ where, for input size n, algorithm A requires at most $O(f(n))$ operations in the worst case.

EXAMPLE 7.26:   The Bubble Sort sorting algorithm has order $O(n^2)$ in the worst case. That is, for a list of n elements, the algorithm requires at most $O(n^2)$ comparison operations to sort the list. The Mergesort algorithm has order $O(n \log n)$ in the worst case. The Quicksort has an average case complexity of $O(n \log n)$ but a worst case of $O(n^2)$.

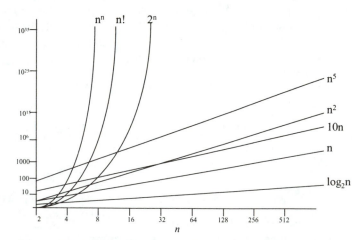

Figure 7.7: Asymptotic behavior of several common functions

This defines a true measure of algorithmic efficiency. The numerical relation system is the set N consisting of all the $O(g)$s; the empirical relation "more efficient" is mapped to the relation "set inclusion".

Using this definition of efficiency, we circumvent the problems we have encountered in comparing algorithms. With our formal definition of efficiency and our set inclusion relation, both the n and $2n$ algorithms are mapped to $O(n)$ – they are equivalent, since (as we have shown informally) each asymptotically dominates the other. On the other hand, the n algorithm is by definition more efficient than the n^2 algorithm, since $O(n) \subset O(n^2)$; this relationship mirrors reality, since no matter how much we speed up the execution time of the primitive operations for a machine running the n^2 algorithm, for sufficiently large input it will still always run slower than the n algorithm. It is in this sense that Harel asserts that the big-O notation is robust – that is, truly machine-independent (Harel, 1992). We can express his meaning in terms of measurement theory: algorithmic efficiency is a true measure, since it preserves the representation condition for an intuitively understood attribute.

Big-O notation also preserves other interesting relations derived from efficiency on the class of algorithms. For example, we have an intuitive understanding of whether or not an algorithm is feasible. This empirical, unary relation may be mapped to the relation "polynomially bounded". Any big-O set that is included in a set $O(n^i)$ for some i is said to be **polynomially bounded**. There is a qualitative difference between those algorithms that are polynomially bounded and those that are not. (The latter are at least exponential.) For the former, it may be possible to implement the algorithm for large input; for the latter, it will never be possible.

7.5.1.3 Predicting efficiency

Our measure of algorithmic efficiency is an accurate predictor of the external view of efficiency of a subsequent implementation of the algorithm.

> **EXAMPLE 7.27:** Suppose we implement the Heapsort sorting algorithm in a machine environment where comparison operations are performed at the rate of 2^{20} per second. If we sort a list of $n = 2^{25}$ items, then we know that any implementation will require $n \log_2 n$ comparisons; that is, we need at least 25×2^{25} comparisons. Thus, the response time must be at least 800 seconds (that is, 13.3 minutes).

We say "at least 800 seconds" in the above example because this is the computation time that we know must be consumed in the worst case; additionally, there may be computation time associated with other parts of the processing. Normally, other processing is incidental, but in certain cases it may be significant. Suppose, for example, that a particular searching algorithm assumes implicitly that the input list is in a certain format; for instance, the items may consist only of uppercase letters and be of a specific length. If the actual input is not of this form, our program may have to reformat the list, which may be more time-consuming than the sorting itself.

7.5.2 Measuring problem complexity

By formally defining it with big-O notation, efficiency measures (as an internal attribute) any software product that can be modeled as an algorithm, such as a program or a low-level design. This approach also provides us with a means of measuring the complexity of a problem.

Suppose that an algorithm for solving all instances of a particular problem requires $f(n)$ computations. We say that $f(n)$ is **asymptotically optimal** if, for every other algorithm with complexity g that solves the problem, f is $O(g)$. We can define the **complexity of a given problem** as big-O of the asymptotically optimal algorithm for the problem's solution.

> **EXAMPLE 7.28:** The problem of searching a sorted list for a single item can be shown to have complexity $O(\log n)$, meaning that the theoretically fastest algorithm necessary to solve the problem requires at least $\log n$ primitive computations (namely pairwise comparisons) for a list of n elements. As we saw in Example 7.18, Binary Sort is an algorithm which meets the lower bound.

> **EXAMPLE 7.29:** The problem of sorting lists into order has complexity $O(n \log n)$, meaning that the theoretically fastest algorithm necessary to solve this problem requires at least $n \log n$ primitive operations. Heapsort is an example of a sorting algorithm that is optimal in the sense of meeting this lowest bound.

A problem having a polynomially-bound solution is said to be **feasible**. The class of all feasible problems is called P; that is, any feasible solution is said to lie in P. From the above examples, we know that both searching and sorting are in P.

However, there is a huge class of important problems for which feasibility is unknown; we do not know whether they lie in P. For example, we do not know if the traveling-salesman problem (mentioned in Chapter 3) is feasible. Such problems are characterized by the fact that, although they seem to admit no feasible solution, there are easy methods (polynomially bounded algorithms) to check a proposed solution. For instance, for the traveling-salesman problem, there is no known polynomial algorithm that will always determine if the shortest route is less than some threshold figure, but there is a polynomial algorithm that will determine in general whether a proposed route is less than the threshold figure. This class of problems is called NP, with the subset of hardest problems being called NP-**complete**. It is strongly conjectured that $P \neq NP$ (that is, there are no polynomial solutions to problems in NP).

The hierarchy of complexity classes of which P, NP, and NP-complete are examples, together with the relations between classes, constitute a measurement system for problem complexity.

> **EXAMPLE 7.30:** The traveling-salesman problem has complexity NP-complete. This designation means (among other things) that it is strongly conjectured that there is no feasible algorithm (one that will terminate in a

reasonable amount of time) for its solution, even though any proposed solution can be checked easily.

Using this hierarchy, we assert that the traveling-salesman problem is more complex than the sorting problem, which is in turn more complex than the searching problem.

In general, it is quite difficult to discover the computational complexity of a given problem. However, several books (for example, Aho, Hopcroft, and Ullman (1974), and Garey and Johnson (1979)) catalogue problems of known complexity. If you are given an algorithmic problem to solve, you should first attempt to determine if the problem (or something similar) has been tackled before. If it has, and if there is a known efficient solution, then use it. For example, if you must solve a problem based on sorting lists, you would be foolish not to employ a well-known algorithm like Heapsort or Quicksort.

If the problem is known to be *NP*-complete, such as the traveling-salesman problem, then it would be foolish to attempt to find a complete solution. Since the greatest minds of the twentieth century agree that no acceptable algorithm is possible (although this has never been proved), your best approach is either to negotiate a weaker version of the problem, obtain a partial solution to the original problem, or to derive an approximate solution.

7.6 SUMMARY

Internal product attributes are important, and measuring them directly allows us to assess early products and predict likely attributes of later ones. In this chapter, we have seen that product size can be measured in many ways. We can think of size as being composed of at least three aspects: length, functionality, and complexity. In many ways, code length is the easiest to measure; it can be expressed in terms of lines of code, number of characters, and more. But we must take into account the dependence of code size measures on language, degree of reuse, and other factors. We can measure the length of specifications and other documents in alternate ways, such as counting pages or number of requirements. Object-oriented products can be measured in terms of numbers of objects and methods.

Functionality can be derived from specifications by using function points, object points, or DeMarco's specification weight (bang); development products available later in the life cycle can be measured, too, and compared with earlier estimates. Measures of both functionality and length can be used to normalize other measures, such as expressing defect density in terms of defects per line of code or per function point. And progress and productivity can be tracked in terms of size or functionality of product.

Complexity is difficult to measure, and we must distinguish between complexity of the problem and complexity of the solution we implement. One aspect of complexity is efficiency. We have presented a theory that allows us to define true measures of the efficiency (as an internal attribute) of software products (namely, anything which can be modeled as an algorithm, such as a program or low-level design). This approach also provides us with a measure of the computational complexity of the initial problem.

7.7 Exercises

1. Recall several programs you have written in a particular programming language. Can you rank them according to length, functionality, and problem complexity? Is the ranking harder to perform if the programs are written in different languages?

2. How is the stochastic relationship

$$CHAR = \alpha \; LOC$$

similar to this formula?

$$time = distance/speed$$

Manipulating the formula allows speed to be expressed as an indirect measure, a ratio of distance and time. Is a similar manipulation meaningful for the LOC relationship?

3. It is important to remember that "prediction' is not "prescription." How might a development policy that all programming staff produce 50 lines of documentation per thousand LOC prove inappropriate?

4. Consider the following informal statement of requirements for a system:

> The system processes various commands from the operator of a chemical plant. The most important commands are:
>
> - calculate and display average temperature for a specified reactor for the day period;
> - calculate and display average pressure for a specified reactor for the day period;
> - calculate and display a summary of the temperature and pressure averages.
>
> The operator can also choose to send the results to an urgent electronic bulletin board if necessary.

Compute both the unadjusted and adjusted function-point count for this system, stating carefully any assumptions you are making.

5. For the specification in Figure 7.4, experiment with different possible values of TCF and different complexity weightings to see how FP may vary from the value 59 in Example 7.16. Assess how this variation would scale up for systems involving hundreds or thousands of inputs, outputs, and interfaces.

6. Suppose algorithms A and B require respectively n^2 and 2^n steps for an input of size n. For a machine that can perform 10^9 floating point operations per second

(1 GigaFLOP), calculate the largest input which A and B can solve within 1 second, 1 hour, 1 year, 1 century, etc. (Recall that 2^{10} is approximately 10^3, 1 day approximately 8×10^4 seconds, 1 year approximately 3×10^7 seconds, and the age of the universe approximately 13 billion years.)

7 Explain very briefly (five lines at most) the idea behind Albrecht's function points measure. List the main applications of function points, and compare function points with the lines-of-code measure.

8 (Exam question)

i.   What do function points measure and what are the major drawbacks?
ii. Give three examples of how you might use the function-point measure in quality control or assurance (stating in each case why it might be preferable to some simpler alternative measure).
iii. Consider the following specification of a simple system for collecting student course marks or grades.

The course-marks system enables lecturers to enter student marks for a pre-defined set of courses and students on those courses. Thus, marks can be updated, but the lecturers cannot change the basic course information, as the course lists are the responsibility of the system administrator. The system is menu-driven, with the lecturer selecting from a choice of courses and then a choice of operations. The operations include:

a) enter coursework marks
b) enter exam marks
c) compute averages
d) produce letter grades
e) display information (to screen or printer)

The information displayed is always a list of the students together with all the known marks, grades, and averages.

Compute the number of function points in this system, stating carefully the assumptions you are making.

9 Look back at the Halstead measures defined in Example 7.9. Consider ways in which the effort and program level measures differ from the concept of problem complexity in Examples 7.24 through 7.28. In particular, compare the likely size of a naive program for the traveling-salesman problem to the size of a program based on sophisticated optimization techniques. How do these sizes relate to Halstead's potential volume?

7.8 FURTHER READING

DeMarco's book discusses many of the reasons why we need to measure size early in the development process. He also introduces the notions of function bang and data bang, now called specification weight.

DeMarco, T., *Controlling Software Projects*, Yourdon Press, New York, 1982.

The Software Engineering Institute has published a technical report containing extensive checklists to guide you in deciding what to include when measuring a line of code.

Park, R., "Software size measurement: A framework for counting source statements," CMU/SEI-92-TR-20, Software Engineering Institute Technical Report, Pittsburgh, PA, 1992.

The latest definition of function-point measurement is available from the International Function Point User Group (IFPUG), which holds meetings annually. There are many national function point user groups, including in the US, UK and the Netherlands. Information about the use of object points with COCOMO is reported at annual COCOMO user-group meetings, often held at the Software Engineering Institute in Pittsburgh, Pennsylvania.

For details of measuring algorithmic efficiency and computational complexity, see Harel's book.

Harel, D., *Algorithmics*, 2nd edn, Addison-Wesley, Reading, MA, 1992.

Garey and Johnson have written the definitive text and reference source for computational complexity.

Garey, M.R. and Johnson, D.S., *Computers and Intractability*, Freeman, San Francisco, CA, 1979.

8 Measuring internal product attributes: structure

We have seen how size measures can be useful in many ways: as input to prediction models, as a normalizing factor, as a way to express progress during development, and more. But there are other useful internal product attributes. Because practitioners and researchers think there may be a link between the structure of products and their quality, many are trying to measure the structural properties of software. In other words, the structure of requirements, design, and code may help us to understand the difficulty we sometimes have in converting one product to another (as, for example, implementing a design as code), in testing a product (as in testing code or validating requirements, for instance) or in predicting external software attributes from early internal product measures. Although the structural measures vary in what they measure and how they measure it, they are often (and misleadingly) called "complexity" metrics.

We begin by describing several distinct classes of structural measures. Then, in Section 8.2 we look in more detail at software control-flow structure. In Section 8.3, we turn to measures that are based on the information and data-flow structure (including metrics for object-oriented designs), and finally to data structure. We end the chapter with a discussion of how to compare general complexity measures.

8.1 TYPES OF STRUCTURAL MEASURES

The size of a development product tells us a lot about the effort that went into creating it. All other things being equal, we would like to assume that a large module takes longer to specify, design, code, and test than a small one. But experience shows us that such an assumption is not valid; the structure of the product plays a part, not only in requiring development effort but also in how the product is maintained. Thus, we must investigate characteristics of product structure, and determine how they affect the outcomes we seek. In this chapter, we focus primarily on code measures, but many of the concepts and measures introduced here can be applied to other development products.

Although the structure of a module is sometimes termed its complexity, there are in fact several aspects of structure or complexity, each playing a different role. We can think of structure as having at least three parts:

1. control-flow structure
2. data-flow structure
3. data structure

The **control flow** addresses the sequence in which instructions are executed in a program. This aspect of structure reflects the iterative and looping nature of programs. Whereas size counts an instruction just once, control flow makes more visible the fact that an instruction may be executed many times as the program is actually run.

Data flow follows the trail of a data item as it is created or handled by a program. Many times, the transactions applied to data are more complex than the instructions that implement them; data-flow measures depict the behavior of the data as it interacts with the program.

Data structure is the organization of the data itself, independent of the program. When data elements are arranged as lists, queues, stacks, or other well-defined structures, the algorithms for creating, modifying, or deleting them are more likely to be well-defined, too. So the structure of the data tells us a great deal about the difficulty involved in writing programs to handle the data, and in defining test cases for verifying that the programs are correct. Sometimes a program is complex due to a complex data structure rather than complex control or data flow.

We discuss each of these aspects of structure in turn.

8.2 CONTROL-FLOW STRUCTURE

A great deal of software metrics work has been devoted to measuring the control-flow structure of imperative language programs or algorithms. The control flow measures are usually modeled with **directed graphs**, where each node (or point) corresponds to a program statements, and each arc (or directed edge) indicates the flow of control from one statement to another. We call these directed graphs **control-flow graphs** or **flowgraphs**.

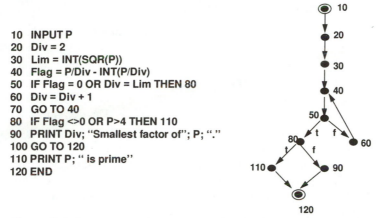

```
10  INPUT P
20  Div = 2
30  Lim = INT(SQR(P))
40  Flag = P/Div - INT(P/Div)
50  IF Flag = 0 OR Div = Lim THEN 80
60  Div = Div + 1
70  GO TO 40
80  IF Flag <>0 OR P>4 THEN 110
90  PRINT Div; "Smallest factor of"; P; "."
100 GO TO 120
110 PRINT P; " is prime"
120 END
```

Figure 8.1: A program and its corresponding flowgraph

Figure 8.1 presents a simple example of a program, A, and a reasonable interpretation of its corresponding flowgraph, $F(A)$. We say "reasonable interpretation" because it is not always obvious how to map a program A to a flowgraph $F(A)$. The flowgraph is a good model for defining measures of control-flow structure, because it makes explicit many of the structural properties of the program. The nodes enumerate the program statements, and the arcs make visible the control patterns.

There are many flowgraph-based measures, some of which are incorporated into static analysis and CASE tools. Many measures try to characterize a desirable (but possibly elusive) notion of structural complexity and preserve our intuitive feelings about complexity: if m is a structural measure defined in terms of the flowgraph model, and if program A is structurally "more complex" than program B, then the measure $m(A)$ should be greater than $m(B)$. In Chapter 2, we noted some theoretical problems with this simplistic approach. There are practical problems as well; since the measures are often based on very specific views of what constitutes good structure, there may be differing opinions about good structured programming.

To avoid this problem, we introduce an approach for analyzing control-flow structure that is independent of any particular view of structured programming. We can also use this technique to describe and differentiate views of structured programming. The technique enables us to show that any program has a uniquely defined structural decomposition into primitive components. In the following sections, we show that this decomposition (which can be generated automatically) may be used to define a wide range of structural measures. These unifying principles objectively make clear the assumptions about structuredness inherent in each measure's definition. Most importantly, we show how the decomposition can be used to generate measures of specific attributes, such as those relating to test coverage. The decomposition is at the heart of many static analysis tools and reverse engineering tools.

8.2.1 Flowgraph model of structure

We begin our discussion by reviewing graph-related terminology. Recall that a **graph** consists of a set of points (or nodes) and line segments (or edges). In a **directed graph**, each edge is assigned a direction, indicated by an arrowhead on the edge. This directed edge is called an **arc**.

Thus, directed graphs are depicted with a set of nodes, and each arc connects a pair of nodes. We write an arc as an ordered pair, $<x, y>$, where x and y are the nodes forming the endpoints of the arc, and the arrow indicates that the arc direction is from x to y. The arrowhead indicates that something flows from one node to another node. The **in-degree** of a node is the number of arcs arriving at the node, and the **out-degree** is the number of arcs that leave the node. We can move from one node to another along the arcs, as long as we move in the direction of the arrows. A **path** is a sequence of consecutive (directed) edges, some of which may be traversed more than once during the sequence. A **simple path** is one in which there are no repeated edges. (The computing terminology is different from that used by graph theorists. The latter usually refer to a "walk" instead of a path, and a "path" instead of a simple path.)

> **EXAMPLE 8.1:** In Figure 8.1, the node labeled "50" has in-degree 1 and out-degree 2. The following sequence S of edges is a path:
>
> $<30, 40> <40, 50> <50, 60> <60, 40> <40, 50> <50, 80>$
>
> However, S is not a simple path, since it repeats edge $<40, 50>$.

A **flowgraph** is a directed graph in which two nodes, the **start node** and the **stop node**, obey special properties: the stop node has out-degree zero, and every node lies on some path from the start node to the stop node.

In drawing flowgraphs, we distinguish the start and stop nodes by encircling them. (Flowgraphs are examples of **finite state machines**. In general, a finite state machine may have many start and stop nodes (states); the convention is to draw a circle around such nodes.) Flowgraph nodes with out-degree equal to 1 are called **procedure nodes**; all other nodes (except the stop node) are termed **predicate nodes.**

> **EXAMPLE 8.2:** In the flowgraph of Figure 8.1, the nodes labeled 50 and 80 are predicate nodes. All the other nodes (except the stop node) are procedure nodes.

When we model program control structure, certain flowgraphs occur often enough to merit special names. Figure 8.2 depicts those flowgraphs that correspond to the basic control constructs in imperative language programming.

For example, the P_2 flowgraph represents the construct **sequence**, where a program

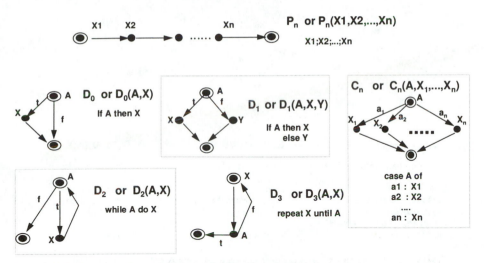

Figure 8.2: Common flowgraphs from program structure models

consists of a sequence of two statements. (The sequence statement P_2 is a special case of a sequence of n statements P_n. Another special instance of P_n is the case $n = 1$, which represents a program consisting of a single statement.) Beneath the name of each construct in the figure, we have written an example of Pascal program code for that construct. For instance, the example Pascal code for the D_0 construct is the *if-then* statement. Not all imperative languages have built-in constructs for each of the control constructs shown here, nor is the particular code for the constructs unique.

EXAMPLE 8.3: Figure 8.2 contains an example of the *repeat-until* statement. An alternate expression for that construct is:

```
10 X
If A then goto 20 else goto 10
20 end
```

The flowgraph model for this program is identical to D_3 in Figure 8.2.

Strictly speaking, a flowgraph is "parameterized" when we associate with it the actual code that it represents. For example, the notation $D_2(A, X)$ (meaning D_2 with parameters A and X) is an explicit denotation of the construct *while A do X*. Sometimes, for convenience, we refer only to the unparameterized names like D_2, meaning the generic *while-do* control construct.

Most imperative programs have built-in control constructs for the flowgraphs in Figure 8.2, but the same is not true for the control constructs shown in Figure 8.3. (We shall soon see that the reasons for this difference are more dogmatic than rational.) In theory, each of these additional constructs can be implemented using *goto* statements. For example, the two-exit loop construct L_2 is equivalent to:

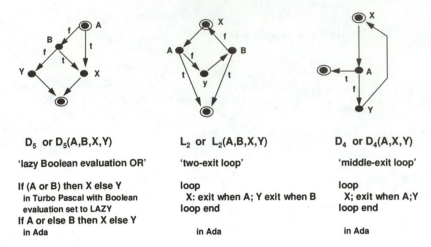

D_5 or D_5(A,B,X,Y)	L_2 or L_2(A,B,X,Y)	D_4 or D_4(A,X,Y)
'lazy Boolean evaluation OR'	'two-exit loop'	'middle-exit loop'

If (A or B) then X else Y in Turbo Pascal with Boolean evaluation set to LAZY If A or else B then X else Y in Ada	loop X: exit when A; Y exit when B loop end in Ada	loop X; exit when A;Y loop end in Ada

Figure 8.3: Flowgraphs for less common control constructs

```
10 X;
If A then goto end;
Y;
If B then goto end
else goto 10;
end
```

There are many possible variations of the constructs in Figure 8.3. For example, a variation on D_5 is the *if-and-then-else* construct, as well as more complex conditions like:

$$\text{if } (A \text{ or } B \text{ or } C) \text{ then } X \text{ else } Y,$$
$$\text{if } ((A \text{ or } B) \text{ and } (B \text{ or } C)) \text{ then } X \text{ else } Y$$

However, all of the flowgraphs in Figure 8.2 and Figure 8.3 have an important common property that makes them suitable as "building blocks" for structured programming. To understand it, we must define formally the ways that we can build flowgraphs.

8.2.1.1 Sequencing and nesting

There are just two legitimate operations we can use to build new flowgraphs from old: **sequencing** and **nesting**. Both have a natural interpretation in terms of program structure.

Let F_1 and F_2 be two flowgraphs. Then the **sequence of F_1 and F_2** is the flowgraph formed by merging the stop node of F_1 with the start node of F_2. The resulting flowgraph is written in one of three notations:

$$F_1 ; F_2$$
$$Seq\ (F_1, F_2)$$
$$P_2\ (F_1, F_2)$$

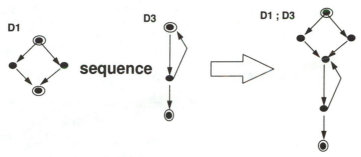

Figure 8.4: Applying the sequence operation

EXAMPLE 8.4: Figure 8.4 shows the result of forming the sequence of the D_1 and D_3 flowgraphs.

The flowgraph sequence operation corresponds to the sequence operation (also called **concatenation**) in imperative language programming. In fact, the flowgraph operation preserves the program operation in the following way. Suppose A and A' are two blocks of program code. Recall that, in general, the flowgraph model of a program A is denoted $F(A)$. Then:

$$F(A \; ; A') = F(A) \; ; F(A')$$

Thus, the flowgraph of the program sequence is equal to the sequence of the flowgraphs.

Let F_1 and F_2 be two flowgraphs. Suppose F_1 has a procedure node x. Then the **nesting of F_2 on to F_1 at x** is the flowgraph formed from F_1 by replacing the arc from x with the whole of F_2. The resulting flowgraph is written as:

$$F_1 (F_2 \text{ on } x)$$

Alternatively, we write $F_1(F_2)$ when there is no ambiguity about the node onto which the graph is nested.

EXAMPLE 8.5: Figure 8.5 shows the result of nesting the D_3 flowgraph onto the D_1 flowgraph.

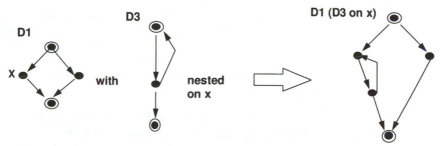

Figure 8.5: Applying the nesting operation

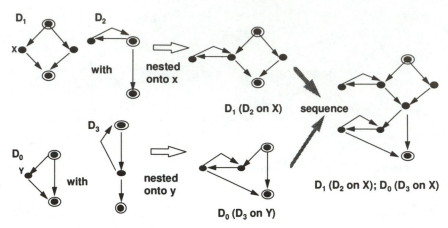

Figure 8.6: Combining the sequence and nesting operations

EXAMPLE 8.6: Figure 8.6 shows the construction of a flowgraph from a number of nesting and sequence operations.

The flowgraph nesting operation corresponds to the operation of procedure substitution in imperative language programming. Specifically, consider a program A in which the procedure A' is called by a parameter x. Then:

$$F(A \text{ with } A' \text{ substituted for } x) = F(A) (F(A') \text{ on } x)$$

Thus, the flowgraph of the program substitution is equal to the nesting of the flowgraphs.

In general, we may wish to nest n flowgraphs $F_1, ..., F_n$ onto n respective procedure nodes $x_1, ..., x_2$. The resulting flowgraph is written as

$$F(F_1 \text{ on } x_1, F_2 \text{ on } x_2, ..., F_n \text{ on } x_n.)$$

In many of our examples, the actual nodes onto which we nest is of no importance, and so we write: $F(F_1, F_2, ..., F_n)$.

Our examples describe graphs that are constructed by using sequencing and nesting constructs. We can sometimes reverse the process, decomposing a flowgraph into smaller pieces that are related by sequencing and nesting. However, there are some graphs that cannot be decomposed that way.

Formally, we say that **prime flowgraphs** are flowgraphs that cannot be decomposed non-trivially by sequencing or nesting.

The building blocks of our approach to control structure analysis and measurement are these prime flowgraphs:

EXAMPLE 8.7: Each of the flowgraphs in Figure 8.2 and Figure 8.3 is prime. The flowgraph on the right-hand side of Figure 8.5 is not prime, because it decomposes as $D_1(D_3)$. In other words, it is constructed by nesting one flowgraph, D_3, onto another, D_1. Similarly, the flowgraph on the right-hand side of Figure 8.4 is not prime, because it decomposes as a sequence of D_1 followed by D_3.

8.2.1.2 The generalized notion of structuredness

Most popular definitions of structured programming assert that a program is structured if it can be composed using only a small number of allowable constructs. Normally, these constructs must be only **sequence**, **selection** and **iteration**. The rationale can be traced back to a classic result of Böhm and Jacopini, demonstrating that every algorithm may be implemented using just these constructs (Böhm and Jacopini, 1966). Some authors have argued (wrongly, in light of Example 8.3) that this statement is equivalent to asserting that a program is structured if it is written without any use of the *goto* statement.

We want to be able to assess an individual program and decide whether or not it is structured; the informal definition of structured programming offers us no help in answering this question. Ideally, we should be able to answer it by considering the flowgraph alone. However, to do so, we need a definition of structuredness that supports many different views, and a mechanism for determining the level of structuredness in an arbitrary flowgraph.

To form this definition, we must introduce more terminology involving a family S of prime flowgraphs. We say that a family of graphs is **S-structured** (or, more simply, that the family members are **S-graphs**) if it satisfies the following recursive rules:

1. Each member of S is S-structured.
2. If F and F' are S-structured flowgraphs, then so are
    a) $F;F'$
    b) $F(F')$ (whenever nesting of F' onto F is defined).
3. No flowgraph is an S-structured graph unless it can be shown to be generated by a finite number of applications of the above steps.

Notice that, by definition, the members of S are themselves S-structured. We call these the **basic S-graphs**, and they correspond to the building blocks we seek. Since this definition is quite general, it permits you to choose which building blocks define your notion of structuredness.

EXAMPLE 8.8: For $S = \{P_1\}$, the set of S-structured graphs is the set $\{P_1, P_2, \ldots, P_n, \ldots\}$.

EXAMPLE 8.9: For $S = \{D_1, D_2\}$, Figure 8.7 shows examples of various S-structured graphs.

The definition allows us to nominate, for any particular development environment, a set of legal control structures (represented by the basic S-graphs) suited for particular applications. Then, by definition, any control structure composed from this nominated set will be "structured" in terms of this local standard; in other words, the set derived from the basic S-graphs will be S-structured.

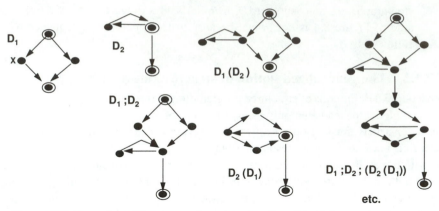

Figure 8.7: Examples of S-structured graphs when $S = \{D_1, D_2\}$

EXAMPLE 8.10:   Let $S^D = \{P_1, D_0, D_2\}$. Then the class of S^D-graphs is the class of flowgraphs commonly called (in the literature of structured programming) the **D-structured** (or sometimes just **structured**) graphs. Stated formally, the Böhm and Jacopini result asserts that every algorithm can be encoded as an S^D-graph. Although S^D is sufficient in this respect, it is normally extended to include the structures D_1 (*if-then-else*) and D_3 (*repeat-until*).

For reasons that have been discussed extensively elsewhere, it is now common to accept a larger set than S^D as the basis for structured programming. For example, there are very powerful arguments for including all of the primes in Figure 8.3. Ada and Modula-2 have specific constructs for these primes, whereas Pascal does not. Thus, in Ada and Modula-2, the set of structured programs includes the set of S-graphs where:

$$S = \{P_1, D_0, D_1, D_2, D_3, D_4, C_n \text{ (for all } n), L_2\}$$

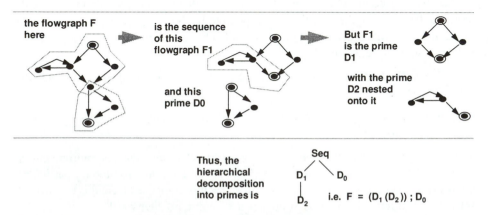

Figure 8.8: Deriving the decomposition tree of a flowgraph

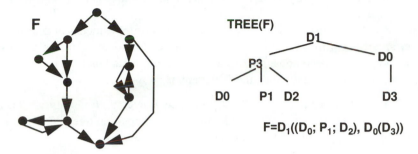

$$F=D_1((D_0; P_1; D_2), D_0(D_3))$$

Figure 8.9: A flowgraph and its decomposition tree

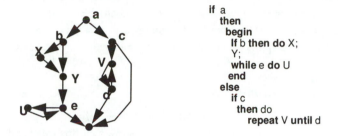

```
if a
  then
    begin
      If b then do X;
      Y;
      while e do U
    end
  else
    if c
      then do
        repeat V until d
```

Figure 8.10: The flowgraph of Figure 8.9 in terms of its program structure

8.2.1.3 Prime decomposition

A result of Fenton and Whitty (1986) tells us that we can associate with any flowgraph a **decomposition tree** to describe how the flowgraph is built by sequencing and nesting primes. Figure 8.8 illustrates how a decomposition tree can be determined from a given flowgraph.

Figure 8.9 presents another example, where a flowgraph is shown with its prime decomposition tree.

To understand this prime decomposition, consider the programming constructs that correspond to the named primes. By expanding TREE(*F*) in Figure 8.9 we can recover the program text as shown in Figure 8.10.

Not only can we always decompose a flowgraph into primes, but we can be assured that the decomposition is always unique:

Prime decomposition theorem: Every flowgraph has a unique decomposition into a hierarchy of primes.

The proof of the theorem (Fenton and Whitty, 1986) provides a constructive means of determining the unique decomposition tree. For large flowgraphs, it is impractical to perform this computation by hand, but there are tools available commercially that do it automatically.

The prime decomposition theorem provides us with a simple means of determining whether an arbitrary flowgraph is S-structured or not for some family of primes S. We just compute the decomposition tree and look at the node labels; if every node is either a member of S or a P_n, then the flowgraph is an S-graph.

> **EXAMPLE 8.11:**   If $S = \{D_1, D_2\}$, then the flowgraph F in Figure 8.9 is not an S-graph, because one of the nodes in the decomposition tree is D_3. However, F is an S^D-graph, where $S^D = \{D_0, D_1, D_2, D_3\}$.

Every flowgraph must be S-structured for some family S (namely, where S is the set of distinct primes found in the decomposition tree); the question is whether any members of S are considered to be "non-structured." The decomposition theorem shows that every program has a quantifiable degree of structuredness characterized by its decomposition tree. The only structures that cannot be decomposed in any way at all are primes. So unless the whole flowgraph is prime, it can be decomposed to a certain extent.

8.2.2   Hierarchical measures

The uniquely defined prime decomposition tree is a definitive description of the control structure of a program. In this section, we show that this tree is all we need to define a very large class of interesting measures. We are able to define many measures because they can be described completely in terms of their effect on primes and the operations of sequence and nesting.

> **EXAMPLE 8.12:**   Suppose we wish to measure formally the intuitive notion of "depth of nesting" within a program. Let the program be modeled by a flowgraph, F; we want to compute α, the depth of nesting of F. We can express α completely in terms of primes, sequence, and nesting:
>
> - **Primes:** the depth of nesting of the prime P_1 is zero, and the depth of nesting of any other prime F is equal to one. Thus, $\alpha(P_1) = 0$, and if F is a prime $\neq P_1$, then $\alpha(F) = 1$.
> - **Sequence:** the depth of nesting of the sequence $F_1, \ldots, F_n$ is equal to the maximum of the depth of nesting of the F_is. Thus: $\alpha(F_1; \ldots; F_n) = \max(\alpha(F_1), \ldots, \alpha(F_n))$.
> - **Nesting:** the depth of nesting of the flowgraph $F(F_1, \ldots, F_n)$ is equal to the maximum of the depth of nesting of the F_i plus one because of the extra nesting level in F. Thus: $\alpha(F(F_1, \ldots, F_n)) = 1 + \max(\alpha(F_1), \ldots, \alpha(F_n))$.
>
> Next, consider the flowgraph F in Figure 8.9. We know that $F = D_1((D_0; P_1; D_2), D_0(D_3))$, so we compute:
>
> $$\begin{aligned} \alpha(F) &= \alpha(D_1((D_0; P_1; D_2), D_0(D_3))) \\ &= 1 + \max(\alpha(D_0; P_1; D_2), \alpha(D_0(D_3))) \qquad \text{(nesting rule)} \end{aligned}$$

$$= 1 + \max(\max(\alpha(D_0), \alpha(P_1), \alpha(D_2)), 1+ \alpha(D_3)) \quad \text{(sequence rule}$$
$$\text{and nesting rule)}$$
$$= 1 + \max(\max(1, 0, 1), 2)$$
$$= 1 + \max(1, 2)$$
$$= 3$$

Next, assume that S is an arbitrary set of primes. We say a measure m is a **hierarchical measure** if it can be defined on the set of S-graphs by specifying:

- $m(F)$ for each $F \in S$ (we call this rule M_1);
- the sequencing function(s) (we call this rule M_2);
- the nesting functions h_F for each $F \in S$ (we call this rule M_3).

As we saw in Example 8.12, we may automatically compute a hierarchical measure for a program once we know rules M_1, M_2, M_3 and the decomposition tree.

The **uniqueness** of the prime decomposition implies that an S-graph can be constructed in only one way. Thus, we can construct new hierarchical measures simply by assigning a value $m(F)$ to each prime and a value to the sequence and nesting functions; in other words, we construct our own rules M_1, M_2 and M_3. However, rather than generate arbitrary and artificial hierarchical measures in this way, we wish instead to show that many existing measures, plus many measures of specific intuitive structural attributes, are indeed hierarchical.

EXAMPLE 8.13: In Chapter 8, we discussed some of the problems involved in defining the lines-of-code measure unambiguously. Given the theory we have presented so far in this chapter, we define a formal length measure, v, that captures unambiguously the number of statements in a program when the latter is modeled by a flowgraph.

$M_1: v(P_1) = 1$ and for each prime $F \neq P_1, v(F) = n + 1$ where n is the number of procedure nodes in F

$$M_2: v(F_1; \ldots; F_n) = \sum v(F_i)$$

$$M_3: v(F(F_1, \ldots, F_n)) = 1 + \sum v(F_i) \text{ for each prime } F \neq P_1$$

Condition M_1 asserts that the length of a procedure node (which will generally correspond to a statement having no control flow) will be 1. The length of a prime with n procedure nodes (which will generally be a control statement involving n non-control statements) is $n+1$. This mapping corresponds to our intuitive notion of length. The sequence and nesting functions given in M_2 and M_3 respectively are equally non-controversial.

To see how this measure works, we apply it to flowgraph F in Figure 8.9:

$$v(F) = v(D_1((D_0; P_1; D_2), D_0(D_3)))$$
$$= 1 + v(D_0; P_1; D_2) + v(D_0(D_3))) \quad \text{(nesting rule)}$$
$$= 1 + (v(D_0) + v(P_1) + v(D_2)) + (1+ v(D_3)) \quad \text{(sequence rule}$$
$$\text{and nesting rule)}$$
$$= 1 + (3 + 1 + 2) + (1 + 2)$$
$$= 10$$

Table 8.1: Some hierarchical measures

Number of nodes measure n

M_1: $n(F)$ = number of nodes in F for each prime F

M_2: $n(F_1;\ldots;F_n) = \sum n(F_i) - k + 1$

M_3: $n(F(F_1,\ldots,F_n)) = n(F) + \sum n(F_i) - 2k$ for each prime F

Number of edges measure e

M_1: $e(F)$ = number of edges in F for each prime F

M_2: $e(F_1;\ldots;F_n) = \sum e(F_i)$

M_3: $e(F(F_1,\ldots,F_n)) = e(F) + \sum e(F_i) - n$ for each prime F

The 'largest prime' measure κ: (first defined in Fenton (1985))

M_1: $\kappa(F)$ = number of predicates in F for each prime F

M_2: $\kappa(F_1;\ldots;F_n) = \max(\kappa(F_1),\ldots,\kappa(F_n))$

M_3: $\kappa(F(F_1,\ldots,F_n)) = \max(\kappa(F),\kappa(F_1),\ldots,\kappa(F_n))$ for each prime F

Number of occurrences of named primes measure p

M_1: $p(F) = 1$ if F is named prime, else 0

M_2: $p(F_1;\ldots;F_n) = \sum p(F_i)$

M_3: $p(F(F_1,\ldots,F_n)) = p(F) + \sum p(F_i)$

D-structured measure d
(This nominal scale measure yields the value 1 if the flowgraph is D-structured and 0 if it is not)

M_1: $d(F) = 1$ for $F = P_1, D_0, D_1, D_2, D_3$ and 0 otherwise

M_2: $d(F_1;\ldots;F_n) = \min(d(F_1),\ldots,d(F_n))$

M_3: $d(F(F_1,\ldots,F_n)) = \min(d(F),d(F_1),\ldots,d(F_n))$

Once a hierarchical measure has been characterized in terms of the rules M_1, M_2, and M_3, then we have all the information we need to calculate the measure for all S-graphs. We also have a constructive procedure for calculating measures using this information together with the prime decomposition tree. This technique is used by both the *QUALMS* and *Prometrix* tools to compute measures. Some other simple but important hierarchical measures that capture very specific properties are shown in Table 8.1.

Many flowgraph-based measures have been proposed, and which are claimed to measure "complexity" in the general sense described in Example 2.27 and in Section 3.3.7. Many of these measures are hierarchical, so they can be defined easily within our framework. By viewing each of them in the context of the three necessary and sufficient rules, M_1, M_2, and M_3, we can see how such measures may be computed automatically. Furthermore, we can see easily what level of subjectivity has crept into the definition of the measure, and we can compare it with the notion of complexity in the real, empirical world that the measure is trying to capture.

In particular, we can isolate three aspects of subjectivity in the measure's definition, namely:

1. What is the "complexity" of the distinguished primes?
2. What is the "complexity" of sequencing?
3. What is the "complexity" of nesting on to a given prime?

The remainder of this section applies this analysis to several popular measures of "complexity."

8.2.2.1 McCabe's cyclomatic complexity measure

As we noted in Chapter 2, McCabe proposed that program complexity be measured by the cyclomatic number of the program's flowgraph (McCabe, 1976). For a program with flowgraph F, the **cyclomatic number** is calculated as

$$v(F) = e - n + 2$$

where F has e arcs and n nodes. The cyclomatic number actually measures the number of **linearly independent** paths through F, and an explanation of this term and its implications can be found in Appendix 8.10.3. This measure is objective and useful when counting linearly independent paths, but it is not at all clear that it paints a complete or accurate picture of program complexity. To see why, let us examine v as a hierarchical measure.

For reasons detailed in Appendix 8.3, we know that, for any flowgraph F,

$$v(F) = 1 + d$$

where d is the number of predicate nodes in F. Thus v can be defined as a hierarchical measure in the following way:

M_1: $v(F) = 1 + d$ for each prime F, where d is the number of predicates
M_2: $v(F_1; \ldots; F_n) = \sum_{i=1}^{n} v(F_i) - n + 1$ for each n
M_3: $v(F(F_1, \ldots, F_n)) = v(F) + \sum_{i=1}^{n} v(F_i) - n$ for each prime F

Thus, if v is a measure of "complexity," it follows that:

1. The "complexity" of primes is dependent only on the number of predicates contained in them.
2. The "complexity" of sequence is equal to the sum of the complexities of the components minus the number of components plus one.
3. The "complexity" of nesting components on a prime F is equal to the complexity of F plus the sum of the complexities of the components minus the number of components.

From a measurement theory perspective, it is extremely doubtful that any of these assumptions corresponds to intuitive relations about complexity. Thus, v cannot be used as a general complexity measure. However, the cyclomatic number is a useful indicator of how difficult a program or module will be to test and maintain. In this context, v could be used for quality assurance. In particular, McCabe has suggested that, on the basis of empirical evidence, when v exceeds 10 in any one module, the module may be problematic.

EXAMPLE 8.14: Grady reported a study at Hewlett-Packard, where cyclomatic number was computed for each module of 850 000 lines of FORTRAN code. The investigators discovered a close relationship between a module's cyclomatic number and the number of updates required. After examining the effects of cost and schedule on modules with more than three updates, the study team concluded that 15 should be the maximum cyclomatic number allowed in a module (Grady, 1994).

EXAMPLE 8.15: The quality assurance procedure for the software in the Channel Tunnel rail system requires that a module be rejected if its cyclomatic number exceeds 20 or if it has more than 50 statements, as determined by the Logiscope tool (Bennett, 1994).

8.2.2.2 McCabe's essential complexity measure

McCabe also proposed a measure to capture the overall level of structuredness in a program. For a program with flowgraph F, the **essential complexity** ev is defined as:

$$ev(F) = v(F) - m$$

where m is the number of subflowgraphs of F that are D-structured primes (that is, either D_0, D_1, D_2, or D_3) (McCabe, 1976). (McCabe actually refers to these curiously as "proper one-entry one-exit subflowgraphs".)

The flowgraph F in Figure 8.11 has a single D-structured prime subflowgraph, namely the D_2 construct on the right. Thus, $m = 1$, and $v(F) = 5$, yielding $ev(F) = 4$.

McCabe asserts that essential complexity indicates the extent to which the flowgraph can be "reduced" by decomposing all those subflowgraphs that are D-primes. In this way, essential complexity is supposed to measure the cyclomatic number of what remains after you decompose all the structured subflowgraphs. The essential complexity of a D-structured program is one, since only a P_n is left after decomposing all the structured primes.

Figure 8.11: Flowgraph with essential complexity 4

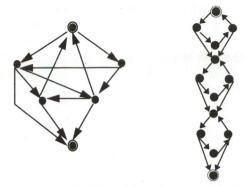

Figure 8.12: A "spaghetti" prime and a sequence of L_2 primes

EXAMPLE **8.16:** The flowgraph on the left of Figure 8.12 is a truly unstructured "spaghetti" prime. Its essential complexity is 6, the same as its cyclomatic number. On the other hand, the flowgraph on the right is the sequence of three L_2 constructs. Since none is a D-prime, then according to McCabe's definition this flowgraph is non-reducible; therefore, its essential complexity should be the same as its cyclomatic number, namely 7.

When a flowgraph is not D-structured, it is not at all clear that the definition of essential complexity corresponds to any natural intuition about structural complexity. For example, in Figure 8.12, the flowgraph on the right has a higher essential complexity value than the spaghetti structure on the left. This unusual circumstance happens because essential complexity is additive on sequences, except when the sequential components are D-structured. Another counter-intuitive feature of essential complexity occurs when a non-structured prime is nested onto a structured prime; the cyclomatic number of the structured prime is added to the overall essential complexity (because the structured prime is not a proper subflowgraph). This phenomenon is present in the flowgraph of Figure 8.11, where there is a D_0 at the highest level.

A more intuitive notion of essential complexity may simply be the cyclomatic number of the largest prime in the decomposition tree. This approach is similar to the largest prime metric described in Table 8.1.

8.2.2.3   Other structural complexity measures

To rectify the perceived shortcomings of v as a "complexity" measure, other measures have been proposed to take into account nesting levels and the different structure of primes. Most of these measures also can be constructed within the hierarchical framework in a manner that sheds considerable light on their assumptions.

Example **8.17:** Bache has proposed a set of axioms to characterize a specific notion of control flow complexity (Bache, 1990). He has also developed a family of measures, the **VINAP measures**, that preserve these axioms; that is, they satisfy the hypothesized representation condition for the attribute. Bache's axioms and the hierarchical definition of the VINAP measures are described in Appendix 8.10.2. A similar set of properties was proposed by Lakshmanan and colleagues (Lakshmanan, Jayaprakesh, and Sinha, 1991). The VINAP measures have been automated in the QUALMS and Prometrix tools. A number of empirical studies have been performed using them, showing that VINAP is a more reliable indicator of the external attribute of maintainability than other proposed complexity metrics. In particular, modules whose VINAP value is greater than 100 are likely to be maintenance nightmares (Neil and Bache, 1993). Consequently, Bache suggests that, as part of a quality assurance procedure, modules having values below 50 or above 100 should be thoroughly rechecked.

EXAMPLE 8.18:   Woodward and colleagues proposed the knot measure to capture an aspect of complexity (Woodward, Hessell, and Hedley,1979). The underlying model for this measure of program control flow structure is the program listing. Control-flow lines are then added, as shown in Figure 8.13. The **knot measure** is defined as the total number of points at which control-flow lines cross. In the FORTRAN program fragment of Figure 8.13, there are three knots.

We discuss two examples (from Basili and Hutchens (1983) and from Prather (1984)) in Appendix 8.10.1.

8.2.3   Test coverage measures

Many researchers approach the problem of complexity from the view of needing to understand how the module works. But there are other aspects of complexity that reflect a different perspective. In particular, the structure of a module is related to the difficulty we find in testing it. We turn now to the application of control structure and decomposition for calculating the minimum number of test cases required to implement a test strategy.

We begin with definitions and assumptions. Suppose that program P has been produced for a known specification S. To test P, we run it with an input i and check to

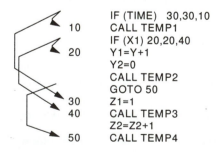

Figure 8.13: Source code documentation annotated with control-flow lines

see that the output for *i* satisfies the specification for *i*. We can formalize this procedure by defining a **test case** to be a pair, (*i*, *S*(*i*)). We are interested in whether *S*(*i*), the expected output, is equal to *P*(*i*), the actual output.

EXAMPLE 8.19:   Suppose *P* is a program produced to meet the following specification, *S*:

The inputs to the program are exam scores expressed as percentages. The outputs are comments, generated according to the following rules:

- For scores under 45, the program outputs "fail".
- For scores between 45 and 80 inclusive, the program outputs "pass".
- For scores above 80, the program outputs "pass with distinction" .

Any input other than a numeric value between 0 and 100 should produce the error message "invalid input."

A set of five test cases for *P* is:

> (40, "fail"),
> (60, "pass"),
> (90, "pass with distinction"),
> (110, "invalid input"),
> (fifty, "invalid input")

Suppose that on input "40," program *P* outputs "fail." Then we say that *P* is correct on that input. If, for the input "110," the program *P* outputs "pass with distinction," then *P* fails on this input; the correct output should have been the error message "invalid input."

There are many different strategies for testing software, and there is no consensus among software engineers about which approach is best in a given situation. Test strategies fall into two categories:

- **Black-box (or closed-box) testing**, in which the test cases are derived from the specification or requirements without reference to the code itself or its structure.
- **White-box (or open-box) testing**, in which the test cases are selected based on knowledge of the internal program structure.

When a white-box test strategy is pursued, test cases are often selected so that every program statement is executed at least once, an approach involving statement coverage. In terms of the program flowgraph, statement coverage is addressed by finding a set of paths such that every node lies on at least one path.

EXAMPLE 8.20:   Figure 8.14 contains a program written to meet the specification *S* of Example 8.19. We can achieve 100% statement coverage for this program by choosing just two the test cases: one with input "90," and one with input "40." For "90," the program executes the path <ABDEFG>. For

```
A   Input(score);
B   If score < 45
C       then print ('fail')
D       else print ('pass');
E   If score > 80
F       then print ('with distinction');
G   End
```

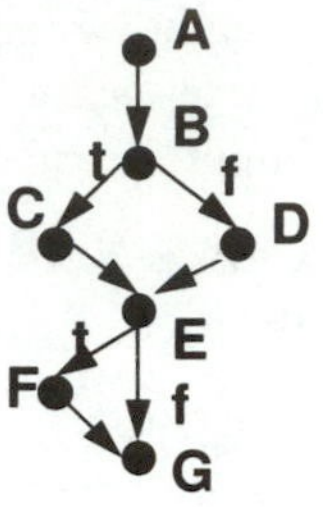

Figure 8.14: A simple program and corresponding flowgraph

"40," the program executes the path <ABCEG>. Thus, C is covered in the second case, and all the other nodes are covered in the first case, so we have complete statement coverage.

An alternative white-box strategy is to select test cases so that every program branch is executed at least once. This approach, called **branch** (or **edge**) **coverage**, means finding a set of paths such that every edge lies on at least one path.

EXAMPLE 8.21: The set of test cases selected in Example 8.20 satisfies branch as well as statement coverage. However, this will not always be true. In the same program the two paths ABCEFG and ABDEFG satisfy 100% statement coverage, but fail to cover the edge EG.

The most exhaustive white-box testing strategy is to select test cases such that every possible program path is executed at least once. This approach is called **path coverage**. In terms of the program flowgraph, path coverage means computing every single path through the flowgraph. This strategy, although appealing in theory, is normally impossible in practice. If the program has even a single loop, then path coverage can never be achieved because a loop gives rise to an infinite number of paths.

In fact, there is a basic impediment to any white-box strategy: **infeasible paths**. An **infeasible path** is a program path that cannot be executed for any input. In practice, infeasible paths can appear in even the simplest of programs.

EXAMPLE 8.22: In the program of Figure 8.14, the path ABCEFG is infeasible. To see why, notice that node C is executed only when the score is less than 45, while node F is executed only when the score is more than 80. Thus, no input score can cause the program to execute both nodes C and F.

The existence of infeasible paths can mean that, in practice, we may not be able to achieve 100% coverage for any white-box strategy (even statement coverage).

Numerous other white-box strategies have been proposed (see Beizer (1990) for a thorough account). In particular, researchers have tried to define strategies so that:

1. they are more comprehensive than statement and branch coverage (in the sense of requiring more test cases); and
2. the number of test cases required is finite even when there are loops.

EXAMPLE **8.23:** **Simple path testing** (Prather, 1987) is a strategy requiring the execution of every simple path (that is, every path which does not contain the same edge more than once).

EXAMPLE **8.24:** McCabe's **structured** (or linearly-independent-path) **testing** was defined in McCabe (1976). It requires that a minimum set of linearly independent paths through the program flowgraph be executed. (The full details are provided in Appendix 8.10.3). This strategy is the rationale for McCabe's cyclomatic number, which is equal to the number of test cases required to satisfy the strategy.

EXAMPLE **8.25:** Woodward, Hedley, and Hessell (1980) describes a testing strategy that requires each LCSAJ (Linear Code Sequence And Jump) construct in the program flowgraph to be executed. An **LCSAJ** is a series of program statements that are executed sequentially in line order, until a transfer of control results in a jump to another line of code. More than one linear sequence can start from a given line, provided the sequence stops (with a jump) at a different line. Each LCSAJ can be characterized by three nodes:

1. the start of the linear sequence of executable statements;
2. the end of the linear sequence; and
3. the target to which control flow is transferred at the end of the linear sequence.

For example, in Figure 8.14: ABC, ABD, BCEF, BCEG, BDEF, and BDEG are LCSAJs.

EXAMPLE **8.26:** Bache and Mullerburg define a strategy called "visit-each-loop" testing. It requires a set of paths such that:

- branch coverage is satisfied; and
- for every loop, there are paths for which control flows both straight past the loop and around the loop at least once (Bache and Mullerburg, 1990).

We have already noted one problem with white-box testing strategies (namely, infeasible paths). In practice, there are two other important obstacles:

1. **No white-box strategy on its own (even 100% path coverage when feasible) can guarantee adequate software testing**. Consider, for example, the program in Figure 8.14 which implements the specification in Example 8.19. The path ABDEFG correctly outputs "distinction" when the input is "90." However, the correct output for one execution does not mean that every execution of the path ABDEFG is correct. For instance, the input score "110" also executes the path ABDEFG, but the program wrongly outputs "pass with distinction" when it should be producing "invalid input."
2. **Knowing the set of paths that satisfies a particular strategy does not tell you how to create test cases to match the paths.** This problem is difficult to solve; however, some commercial testing tools provide assistance.

Associated with every testing strategy are two important measures: the **minimum number of test cases**, and the **test effectiveness ratio**. Bache and Mullerberg call these the **testability measures** (Bache and Mullerberg, 1990).

8.2.3.1 Minimum number of test cases

It is not enough for a test team to choose a test strategy. Before testing starts, the team members must also know the minimum number of test cases needed to satisfy the strategy for a given program. This information helps them to plan their testing, both in terms of generating data for each test case but also in understanding how much time testing is likely to take. Figure 8.15 illustrates, for some of the white-box strategies described above, a minimal set of paths that satisfies the strategy. The flowgraph has a node corresponding to each statement. If a branch has no node on it, then the branch models a program in which no statement appears on that branch. For instance, the portion of the graph labeled with 3, 4 and 5 represents an *if-then* statement, rather than an *if-then-else* statement. `When statement coverage is the testing strategy, the branch labeled 4 does not have to be covered. Thus, the minimum number of test cases required for the branch coverage strategy in Figure 8.15 is four.

The decomposition theorem can help us to compute the minimum number of test cases. A test case corresponds to a path through the flowgraph F. So to calculate the minimum number of test cases, we must compute the minimum number of paths, $m(F)$, required to satisfy the strategy. We can compute $m(F)$ from the decomposition tree as long as we know how to compute $m(F)$ for the primes as well as for sequence and nesting.

Appendix 8.10.4 supplies tables of relevant values for the various testing strategies. we have restricted the definition to a reasonable set of primes, which will be sufficient for most programs. If other primes are discovered in the decomposition tree, then

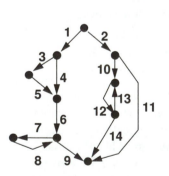

All paths (infinite number)
<2 11>, <2 10 12 14>, <2 10 12 (13 12)^n 14>, <1 3 5 6 9>,
<1 4 6 9>, <1 3 5 6 (7 8)^n 9>, <1 4 6 (7 8)^{n}9>   (any n>0)

Visit-each-loop (7)
<2 11>, <2 10 12 14>, <2 10 12 13 12 14>, <1 3 5 6 9>,
<1 3 5 6 7 8 9>, <1 4 6 9>, <1 4 6 7 8 9>

Simple paths (6)
<2 11>, <2 10 12 14>, <1 3 5 6 9>,
<1 3 5 6 7 8 9>, <1 4 6 9>, <1 4 6 7 8 9>

Linearly independent paths (6)
<2 11>, <2 10 12 14>, <2 10 12 13 12 14>, <1 3 5 6 9>,
<1 3 5 6 7 8 9>, <1 4 6 9>, <1 4 6 7 8 9>

Branch (4)
<2 11>, <2 10 12 13 12 14>, <1 3 5 6 9>, <1 4 6 7 8 9>

Statement (2)
<2 10 12 14>, <1 3 5 6 7 8 9>

Figure 8.15: Paths required to satisfy various white-box testing strategies (number in brackets represents the minimal number of paths required for that strategy)

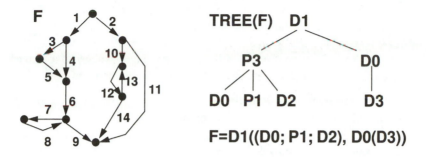

$m(F) = m(D1((D0; P1; D2), D0(D3))$

$\quad = m((D0; P1; D2)) + m(D0(D3))$ formula for nesting on D1

$\quad = m(D0)m(P1)m(D2) + m(D3) + 1$ sequence formula and D0 nesting formula

$\quad = 2 \times 1 \times 2 + 2 + 1 = 7$

Figure 8.16: Computing minimal number of test cases required for 'visit-each-loop' strategy

their values must be added. Figure 8.16 illustrates the computation of the minimum test case number for the "visit-each-loop" strategy.

The tables in Appendix 8.10.4 help us to compute the various test coverage measures for arbitrary flowgraphs:

EXAMPLE 8.27: For the flowgraph in Figure 8.16, we compute the minimum number of test cases m for statement coverage using the tables in Appendix 8.4:

$$
\begin{aligned}
m(F) &= m(D_1(D_0;P_1;D_2),(m(D_0(D_3))) \\
&= m(D_0;P_1;D_2) + m(D_0(D_3)) \\
&= \max(m(D_0),m(P_1),m(D_2)) + m(D_3) \\
&= \max(1,1,1) + 1 = 2
\end{aligned}
$$

EXAMPLE 8.28: Bertolino and Marre note several problems with using some of the strategies and the lower bound to drive test case selection (Bertolino and Marre, 1996). For example, if a complex program is enclosed in a loop, then theoretically it is possible to satisfy branch coverage with a single path. In this case, the lower bound of one test case is not very meaningful, because it is unlikely that the single path required will be both feasible and obvious to construct. Thus, they propose a more practical strategy, based on finding a set of paths that provide reasonable coverage (in a very intuitive sense) which are much more likely to be feasible. The authors provide a hierarchical definition of the minimum number of paths needed to satisfy their testing strategy.

8.2.3.2 Test effectiveness ratio

For a given program and a set of cases to test it, we would like to know the extent to which the test cases satisfy a particular testing strategy.

EXAMPLE 8.29: Suppose we are testing the program in Figure 8.14, and we have run two test cases with input scores "60" and "90." The test cases traverse two paths, ABDEG and ABDEFG, covering 6 of the 7 statements, 7 of the 9 edges, and 2 of the 4 paths in the program. Thus, we say that statement coverage is 86%, branch coverage is 78%, and path coverage is 50%.

We can define these percentages formally. Let T be a testing strategy that requires us to cover a class of objects (such as paths, simple paths, linearly independent paths, LCSAJs, edges or statements). For a given program and set of test cases, the **test effectiveness ratio** TER$_T$ is defined as

$$\text{TER}_T = \frac{\text{number of } T \text{ objects exercised at least once}}{\text{total number of } T \text{ objects}}$$

Some commercial tools, notably LDRA TESTBED, compute various test effectiveness ratios when presented with a program and a set of test cases. The standard UNIX utility *lint* computes the TERs for statement and branch coverage testing of C programs.

EXAMPLE 8.30: Using TESTBED on actual test data used on commercial systems, Mike Hennell has made alarming observations about test effectiveness. For example, for the modest statement coverage strategy, most managers assume a TER of 100% can be achieved routinely. However, the actual TER is typically no better than 40%. The typical TER for branch coverage is lower still, providing objective evidence that most software is not tested as rigorously as we like to think.

In certain cases, the denominator of the TER is precisely the minimum number of test cases required for the strategy (and hence can be computed using the decomposition approach). In particular, path testing, visit-each-loop testing, independent path testing, and simple path testing have this property.

8.3 MODULARITY AND INFORMATION FLOW ATTRIBUTES

So far, we have examined attributes of individual modules. Measures of these are sometimes called **intra-modular measures**. (Although the measures in Section 8.2 were intra-modular, many of them have inter-modular derivatives. For example, for a group of related modules we could consider the mean length, median depth of nesting, median VINAP measure, etc.) Next, we look at collections of modules, either at the design stage or when the program is implemented in code. It is the inter-module dependencies that interest us, and measures of these attributes are called **inter-modular measures**. We restrict our discussion to design (unless we note otherwise), as the design structure is usually carried through to the code.

8.3.1   Models of modularity and information flow

Although there is no standard definition of a module, we can rely on the one suggested by Yourdon:

a **module** is a contiguous sequence of program statements, bounded by boundary elements, having an aggregate identifier (Yourdon and Constantine, 1979).

This deliberately vague definition permits a liberal interpretation. Thus, a module can be any object that, at a given level of abstraction, you wish to view as a single construct. We insist additionally that a module is (at least theoretically) separately compilable. Thus, for example, in Turbo Pascal, anything that has been declared as a program, unit, procedure, or function may be considered a module.

To describe inter-modular attributes, we build models to capture the necessary information about the relationships between modules. Figure 8.17 contains an example of a diagrammatic notation capturing the necessary details about designs (or code). This type of model describes the information flow among modules; that is, it explains which variables are passed between modules.

When measuring some attributes, we need not know the fine details of a design, so our models suppress some of them. For example, instead of examining variables, we may need to know only whether or not one module calls (or depends on) another module. In this case, we use a more abstract model of the design, a directed graph known as the **module call-graph**. A call-graph is not a flowgraph, as it has no circled start or stop node. An example is shown in Figure 8.18. Usually, we assume that the call-graph has a distinguished root node, corresponding to the highest-level module and representing an abstraction of the whole system.

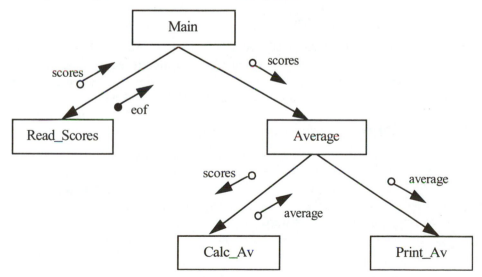

Figure 8.17: Design charts

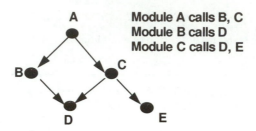

Figure 8.18: Module call-graph

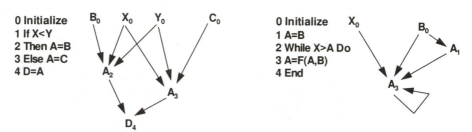

Figure 8.19: Bieman's Data Dependency Graph model of information flow

For intra-modular attributes, we consider models that capture the relevant details about information flow inside a module. Specifically, we look at the dependencies among data. Bieman's Data Dependency Graph (DDG) is a model of information flow supporting this kind of measurement (Bieman and Debnath, 1985). For instance, Figure 8.19 shows two simple program fragments and their corresponding DDG models.

8.3.2   Global modularity

"Global modularity" is difficult to define, because there are many different views of what modularity means. For example, consider **average module length** as an intuitive measure of global modularity. As defined by any of the measures in Chapter 7, module length is on a ratio scale, so we can meaningfully consider average module length for a software system in terms of the mean length of all modules. Boehm cautions us to distinguish this type of measure from "complexity" or "structuredness":

> "A metric was developed to calculate the average size of program modules as a measure of structuredness. However, suppose one has a software product with n 100-statement control routines and a library of m 5-statement computational routines, which would be considered well structured for any reasonable values of m and n. Then, if $n = 2$ and $m = 98$, the average module size is 6.9, while if $m = 10$ and $n = 10$, the average module size is 52.5 statements."

> (Boehm *et al.,* 1978)

Hausen suggests that we describe global modularity in terms of several specific views of modularity (Hausen, 1989), such as:

M_1 = modules/procedures
M_2 = modules/variables

Both Hausen's and Boehm's observations suggest that we focus first on specific aspects of modularity, and then construct more general models from them.

8.3.3   Morphology

Yourdon and Constantine have analyzed what contributes to good design, and they suggest several ways to view design components and structure. They use the notion of **morphology** to refer to the "shape" of the overall system structure when expressed pictorially. Morphological characteristics such as "width" and "depth" can then be used to differentiate good designs from bad (Yourdon and Constantine, 1979). Let us consider designs expressed in terms of **dependency graphs**, and determine which morphological characteristics of the graphs present important information about design quality. Here, we use an edge to connect two nodes if there is a defined dependence between the nodes. For instance, if a node represents a module and one module calls the other, then we connect the two corresponding nodes with an edge (similar to a call-graph, but without directed edges). Similarly, if one module passes data to another, then we can connect the corresponding nodes with an edge.

Many morphological characteristics are measurable directly, including the following:

- **size:** measured as number of nodes, number of edges, or a combination of these
- **depth:** measured as the length of the longest path from the root node to a leaf node
- **width:** measured as the maximum number of nodes at any one level
- **edge-to-node ratio:** can be considered a connectivity density measure, since it increases as we add more connections among nodes.

Examples of these measures are illustrated in Figure 8.20.

If the likely length of each code module can be predicted within reason during design, then a number of quality assurance guidelines can be derived from the design morphology measures.

These measures are not restricted to dependency graphs. They are generally applicable to most graph-type models, and we shall apply them in Chapter 12 to evaluate project management structures.

8.3.4   Tree impurity

The graphs in Figure 8.21 represent different system structures that might be found in a typical design. They exhibit properties that may help us to judge design quality. We say that a graph is **connected** if, for each pair of nodes in the graph, there is a path between the two. All of the graphs in Figure 8.21 are connected. The **complete**

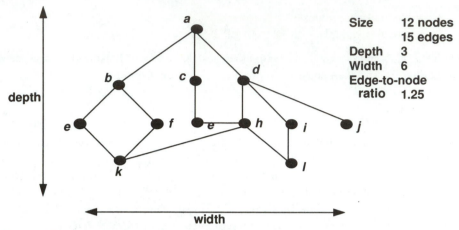

Figure 8.20: A design and corresponding morphology measures

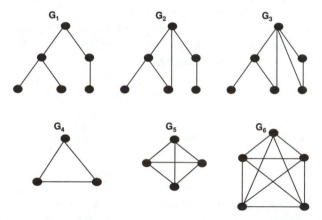

Figure 8.21: Dependency graphs with varying degrees of tree impurity

graph, K_n, is a graph with n nodes, where every two nodes are connected directly by a single edge, so there are $n(n-1)/2$ edges. Graphs G_4, G_5, and G_6 in Figure 8.21 are complete graphs with three, four, and five nodes, respectively. The graph G_1 in Figure 8.21 is called a **tree,** because it is a connected graph having no **cycles** (that is, no path that starts and ends at the same node). None of the other graphs is a tree, because each contains at least one cycle.

Examining the trees in a graph tells us much about the design. Ince and Hekmatpour suggest that:

> The more a system deviates from being a pure tree structure towards being a graph structure, the worse the design is...
>
> ...it is one of the few system design metrics (here "metric" is synonymous with our term "attribute") to have been validated on a real project.

> (Ince and Hekmatpour, 1988)

Thus, we seek to create a measure, called **tree impurity**, to tell us how far a given graph deviates from being a tree. In what follows we restrict our attention to undirected graphs.

To define tree impurity, we first describe several properties of graphs and trees. A tree with n nodes always has n-1 edges. For every connected graph G, we can find at least one subgraph that is a tree built on exactly the same nodes as G; such a tree is called a **spanning subtree**. A **spanning subgraph** G' of a graph G is built on the same nodes of G, but with a minimum subset of edges so that any two nodes of G' are connected by a path. (Thus, a graph may have more than one spanning subgraph.) Intuitively, the tree impurity of G increases as the difference between G and G' increases. We want to make our definition formal, ensuring that it is consistent with principles of measurement theory. Any measure m of tree impurity must satisfy at least four properties:

Property 1: $m(G) = 0$ if and only if G is a tree.

In other words, a graph that is actually a tree has no tree impurity. Thus, for example, any measure m of tree impurity must record $m(G_1) = 0$ for G_1 in Figure 8.21.

Property 2: $m(G) > m(G')$ if G differs from G' only by the insertion of an extra edge (representing a call to an existing procedure).

This property states that if we add an edge to a graph, then the resulting graph has greater tree impurity than the original. Thus, we have $m(G_3) > m(G_2)$ in Figure 8.21.

Property 3:   Let A denote the number of edges in G and N the number of nodes in G. Similarly let A' denote the number of edges in G' and N' the number of nodes in G'. Then if $N > N'$ and $A - N + 1 = A' - N' + 1$ (that is, the spanning subtree of G has more edges than the spanning subtree of G', but in both cases the number of edges additional to the spanning tree is the same) then $m(G) < m(G')$.

This property formalizes our intuitive understanding that we must take account of size in measuring deviation from a tree. Consider the two graphs G_2 and G_4 in Figure 8.21. Each has a single edge additional to its spanning subtree. However, since the spanning subtree of G_4 is smaller, we have an intuitive feeling that its tree impurity should be greater – a single deviation represents a greater proportional increase in impurity.

Property 4:   For all graphs G, $m(G) \leq m(K_N) = 1$ where N = number of nodes of G and K_N is the complete graph of N nodes.

This property says that, of all the graphs with n nodes, the complete graph has maximal tree impurity. Since it is reasonable to assume that tree impurity can be measured on a ratio scale, we can consider our measure to map to some number between 0 and 1, with the complete graph measuring 1, the worst impurity.

EXAMPLE 8.31:   We can define a measure of tree impurity that satisfies all four properties:

$$m(G) = \frac{\text{number of edges more than the spanning tree}}{\text{maximal number of edges more than the spanning tree}}$$

In a complete graph, the number of edges is computed as:

$$e = \frac{n(n-1)}{2}$$

where e is the number of edges in G and n is the number of nodes. Since the number of edges in a spanning tree is always $n - 1$, the maximum number of edges more than the spanning tree is:

$$\frac{n(n-1)}{2} - (n-1) = \frac{(n-1)(n-2)}{2}$$

The actual number of edges more than the spanning subtree must be $e - n + 1$, so our formal equation for the tree impurity measure is

$$m(G) = \frac{2(e-n+1)}{(n-1)(n-2)}$$

We leave it as an exercise to check that m satisfies the 4 properties.

Applying the measure m to the graphs in Figure 8.21, we find that:

$$m(G_2) = 1/10, \ m(G_3) = 1/5 \text{ and } m(G_4) = 1.$$

The measure m of Example 8.31 has been applied to graphs of a system design to characterize its tree impurity. Results suggest a relationship between tree impurity and poor design. Thus m may be useful for quality assurance of designs. System designs should strive for a value of m near zero, but not at the expense of unnecessary duplication of modules. As with all measures of internal attributes, m should be viewed in context with other quality measures, rather than judged by itself.

It is important to note that the measure in Example 8.31 is not the only proposed measure of tree impurity; others appear in the Exercises at the end of the chapter.

8.3.5 Internal reuse

In Chapter 7, we mentioned the need to consider and measure reuse when looking at system size. In that context, we viewed reuse as the proportion of a system that had been constructed outside of or external to the project. In this chapter, we consider reuse in a different sense. We call **internal reuse** the extent to which modules are reused within the same product.

This informal definition leads to a more formally defined measure. Consider the graph in Figure 8.22, where each node represents a module, and two nodes are connected by an edge if one module calls the other. The graph shows that module M_5 is reused, in the sense that it is called by both M_2 and M_3. However, the graph model does not give us information about how many times a particular module calls another

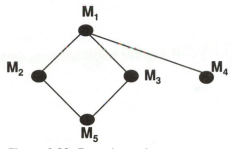

Figure 8.22: Example graph

module. Thus, M_3 is not shown to be reused at all, but it may in fact be called several times by module M_1. If we think of module reuse solely as whether one module is called by another, then this graph model is sufficient.

Suppose we want to define a measure of this type of reuse. The first two properties for a tree density measure should also apply to a reuse measure. Similarly, property 4 seems reasonable, but we must drop the provision that $m(K_N) = 1$. However, property 3 is not applicable, but its converse may be a desirable property.

Yin and Winchester have proposed a simple measure of internal reuse, r, that satisfies properties 1, 2, and 4 plus the converse of 3. Called the **system design measure**, it is defined by

$$r(G) = e - n + 1$$

where G has e edges and n nodes (Yin and Winchester, 1978). Thus, the design measure is equal to the number of edges additional to the spanning subtree of G.

EXAMPLE 8.32: Applying this reuse measure to the graphs in Figure 8.21, we find that

$$r(G_1) = 0, r(G_2) = 1, r(G_3) = 2, r(G_4) = 1, r(G_5) = 3, r(G_6) = 6.$$

This measure is crude as a reuse measure; not only does it take no account of possible different calls from the same module, it also takes no account of the size of the reused components. However, it gives an idea of the general level of internal reuse in a system design. Along with morphology measures and tree impurity, it helps to paint a quantifiable overall picture of the system structure. Empirical evidence is needed to determine the optimal balance between tree impurity and reuse.

8.3.6 *Coupling*

In the early 1970s, researchers at IBM questioned the meaning of "good design." In a landmark paper, Stevens, Myers, and Constantine proposed several new notions of design structure that could help designers and programmers to evaluate design quality (Stevens, Myers, and Constantine, 1974). In this section and the next, we discuss two of these concepts: coupling and cohesion.

Coupling is the degree of interdependence between modules (Yourdon and Constantine, 1979). Usually, coupling is an attribute of pairs of modules, rather than of the design as a whole. The entire set of modules in the design exhibits **global coupling**, which can be derived from the coupling among the possible pairs.

There are no standard measures of coupling. Yet, from the viewpoint of measurement theory, coupling satisfies some of the basic prerequisites for measurement. In particular, there are several well-established empirical relations involving coupling that suggest at least an ordinal scale of measurement. Given modules x and y, we can create an ordinal classification for coupling by defining six relations on the set of pairs of modules.

- **No coupling relation R_0:** x and y have no communication; that is, they are totally independent of one another.
- **Data coupling relation R_1:** x and y communicate by parameters, where each parameter is either a single data element or a homogeneous set of data items that incorporate no control element. This type of coupling is necessary for any communication between modules.
- **Stamp coupling relation R_2:** x and y accept the same record type as a parameter. This type of coupling may cause interdependency between otherwise-unrelated modules.
- **Control coupling relation R_3:** x passes a parameter to y with the intention of controlling its behavior; that is, the parameter is a flag.
- **Common coupling relation R_4:** x and y refer to the same global data. This type of coupling is undesirable; if the format of the global data must be changed, then all common-coupled modules must also be changed.
- **Content coupling relation R_5:** x refers to the inside of y; that is, it branches into, changes data in, or alters a statement in y.

The relations are listed from least dependent at the top to most dependent at the bottom, so that $R_i > R_j$ for $i > j$. We say that x and y are **loosely coupled** if i is 1 or 2, and they are **tightly coupled** if i is 4 or 5.

To model module coupling, we use a directed graph with more detail than a call-graph but less than the full module structure chart. The nodes correspond to the modules, and there may be more than one arc between two nodes. Each arc from a node x to a node y represents coupling between modules x and y; specifically, each arc is labeled by a pair (i, j), where i represents the coupling relation R_i, and j is the number of times the given type of coupling occurs between x and y.

EXAMPLE 8.33: Figure 8.23 is a small example of a coupling-model graph. It represents a system of four modules, where modules M_1 and M_2 share two common record types, module M_1 passes to module M_3 a parameter that acts as a flag in M_3, and module M_2 branches into module M_4 and also passes two parameters that act as flags in M_4.

Fenton and Melton have shown that a valid (in the measurement theory sense) ordinal scale measure c of coupling between modules x and y is:

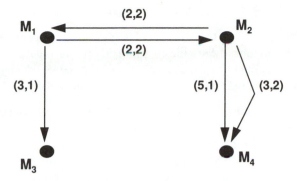

Figure 8.23: Coupling model graph

$$c(x, y) = i + \frac{n}{n+1}$$

where i is the number corresponding to the worst coupling relation R_i between x and y, and n is the number of interconnections between x and y (Fenton and Melton, 1990).

Using the pairwise modular measure, we can define C, a measure of global coupling of a system S consisting of modules $D_1, \ldots, D_n$, in the following way:

$C(S)$ is the median value of the set $\{c(D_i, D_j): 1 \le i < j \le n\}$

Global coupling is, in some sense, the overall level of connectivity in a system.

Few other measures of coupling have been proposed. However, Troy and Zweben identify a range of different counts that can be derived from a design's structure chart; they suggest that each contributes in some way to coupling (Troy and Zweben, 1981). Most of the proposed counts view coupling as a property of an individual module, rather than pairs, so that coupling captures the extent to which a given module is coupled to others. Their measures include:

- the maximum number of interconnections per module;
- the average number of interconnections per module;
- the total number of interconnections per module;
- the number of modules accessing control interconnections;
- the number of data structure interconnections to the top-level module.

These measures are useful in their own right. But Troy and Zweben did not propose specific measures to assess coupling itself, so they were unable formally to test their own hypothesis about the importance of an optimal level of design coupling. Their study concluded that coupling is one of the most important attributes affecting the quality of designs. Our formal measures of coupling allow us to quantify coupling precisely. Further research is needed to apply the measures c and C above to their hypothesis using their data. In fact, for given environments and based on empirical data, practitioners should be able to set optimal levels for the structural measures.

8.3.7   Cohesion

The **cohesion** of a module is the extent to which its individual components are needed to perform the same task. As with coupling, there are no standard measures of cohesion. However, Yourdon and Constantine proposed classes of cohesion that provide an ordinal scale of measurement (Yourdon and Constantine, 1979).

- **Functional:** the module performs a single well-defined function.
- **Sequential:** the module performs more than one function, but they occur in an order prescribed by the specification.
- **Communicational:** the module performs multiple functions, but all on the same body of data (which is not organized as a single type or structure).
- **Procedural:** the module performs more than one function, and they are related only to a general procedure affected by the software.
- **Temporal:** the module performs more than one function, and they are related only by the fact that they must occur within the same timespan.
- **Logical:** the module performs more than one function, and they are related only logically.
- **Coincidental:** the module performs more than one function, and they are unrelated.

These categories of cohesion are listed from most desirable (functional) to least desirable. However, a module may exhibit more than one type of cohesion. For example, a large module may compute functions that are related temporally, but it may also compute totally unrelated functions, exhibiting both temporal and coincidental cohesion. Consequently, we categorize a module by its least desirable type of cohesion. For this example, we say that the module's cohesion is coincidental.

Many traditional design methods seek an appropriate balance between low coupling and high cohesion; that is, high cohesion (preferably functional) and low coupling are desirable. The more recent trend towards languages and methods that support abstract data type encapsulation as modules (hence the designation "modular" languages) at first sight appears to contradict the traditional philosophy. By encapsulating an abstract data type as a module, we characterize it in terms of the operations it may perform on certain objects. Such a module may perform several different functions, but they are all related in the sense that they characterize the abstract data type precisely. For example, a module encapsulating the abstract data type "stack" should perform precisely those functions we associate with a stack of objects, namely *create*, *is-empty*, *pop*, *push*, and so on.

Modules such as these form a special category, and Macro and Buxton have extended the cohesion classification to include it. They say a module has **abstract cohesion** precisely when it is an abstract data type, and they claim that abstract cohesion is even stronger than functional cohesion (Macro and Buxton, 1987). We prefer to think of abstract cohesion as a different notion of cohesion altogether, in the sense that it addresses cohesion of data rather than cohesion of function. We can define various levels of module data cohesion (of which the strongest is an abstract data type), just as we have made explicit the various levels for cohesion of function.

There is no obvious measurement procedure for determining the level of cohesion in a given module. However, we can get a rough idea by writing down a sentence to describe the module's purpose. A good designer should already have done so, but a module with low cohesion is unlikely to have been produced by a good designer! If it is impossible to describe its purpose in a single sentence, then the module is likely to have coincidental cohesion. If the sentence contains words such as "initialize," then the module is likely to have temporal cohesion. Suppose the sentence contains a verb not followed by a specific object, such as "generate output," or "edit files." Then the module probably has logical cohesion. When the descriptive sentence contains words relating to time (such as "first," "then," "after"), then the module is likely to have sequential cohesion. Finally, if the sentence is compound or contains more than one verb, then the module is almost certainly performing more than one function and so is likely to have sequential or communicational cohesion.

Although cohesion is an intra-modular attribute, a simple inter-modular measure of cohesion may be defined by:

$$\text{Cohesion ratio} = \frac{\text{number of modules having functional cohesion}}{\text{total number of modules}}$$

We have presented a simple, ordinal-scale measure of cohesion. More sophisticated intra-module cohesion measures (based on the notion of data slices) are described by Bieman and Ott (Bieman and Ott, 1994).

8.3.8   Information flow

Much of our discussion so far has concerned the notion of **information flow** between modules. For example, each type of coupling corresponds to a particular type of information flowing through the module. Researchers have attempted to quantify other aspects of information flow, including:

- the total level of information flow through a system, where the modules are viewed as the atomic components (an inter-modular attribute); and
- the total level of information flow between individual modules and the rest of the system (an intra-modular attribute).

Let us examine Henry and Kafura's information flow measure, a well-known approach to measuring the total level of information flow between individual modules and the rest of a system (Henry and Kafura, 1981). To understand the measurement, consider the way in which data move through a system. We say a **local direct flow** exists if either:

1. a module invokes a second module and passes information to it; or
2. the invoked module returns a result to the caller.

Similarly, we say that a **local indirect flow** exists if the invoked module returns information that is subsequently passed to a second invoked module. A **global flow** exists if information flows from one module to another via a global data structure.

Using these notions, we can describe two particular attributes of the information flow. The **fan-in** of a module M is the number of local flows that terminate at M, plus the number of data structures from which information is retrieved by M. Similarly, the **fan-out** of a module M is the number of local flows that emanate from M, plus the number of data structures that are updated by M.

Based on these concepts, Henry and Kafura measure information flow "complexity" as

Information flow complexity(M) = length$(M) \times$ ((fan-in$(M) \times$ (fan-out$(M))^2$

Figure 8.24 shows an example of how this measure is calculated from a design's modular structure.

The Henry–Kafura measure, one of the earliest proposed measures to be applicable during design, has received considerable attention. It was the subject of a major validation study using industrial software, in the sense that its prediction ability was investigated. Henry and Kafura established a correlation with their measure and maintenance change data for the UNIX™ operating system; those modules with excessively high values for information flow complexity were well-known by the maintenance staff as being the source of many serious problems.

Henry and Kafura justify the multiplication of fan-in and fan-out in their measure by noting that modules with either a low fan-in or low fan-out are, in a sense, isolated from the system and hence have low "complexity." From a measurement theory

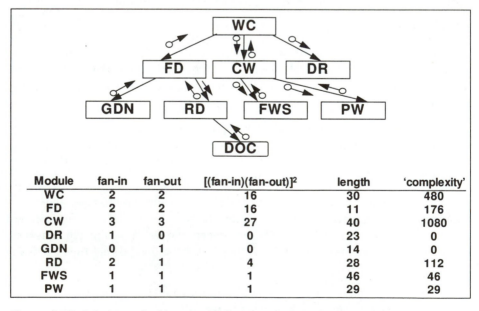

Module	fan-in	fan-out	[(fan-in)(fan-out)]²	length	'complexity'
WC	2	2	16	30	480
FD	2	2	16	11	176
CW	3	3	27	40	1080
DR	1	0	0	23	0
GDN	0	1	0	14	0
RD	2	1	4	28	112
FWS	1	1	1	46	46
PW	1	1	1	29	29

Figure 8.24: Calculating the Henry and Kafura measure of information flow complexity

perspective, we question the basis for this action. In particular, we are concerned about the lack of "complexity" for many modules, as the multiplication leads to a value of zero "complexity" for any module in which either the fan-in or fan-out is zero.

Shepperd studied the Henry–Kafura measure in depth (Shepperd and Ince, 1990). He performed a number of independent studies to validate the measure in the prediction system sense as well as in the measurement-theory sense. As a result, Shepperd has identified a number of theoretical problems with the measure. Some arise from the informal definitions of the model and the notion of indirect flows, which make it difficult to produce the model required to compute the measure. He also questions the distinction between local and global flows and the fact that module reuse is penalized; each instance of reuse is counted as a separate information flow. To address some of these problems, Shepperd proposed the following refinements:

- Recursive module calls should be treated as normal calls.
- Any variable shared by two or more modules should be treated as a global data structure.
- Compiler and library modules should be ignored.
- Indirect local flow should be counted across only one hierarchical level. Indirect flows should be ignored, unless the same variable is both imported and exported by the controlling module.
- No attempt should be made to include dynamic analysis of module calls.
- Duplicate flows should be ignored.
- Module length should be disregarded, as it is a separate attribute.

Thus, the Shepperd refinement to the Henry–Kafura information flow measure for a module M is:

$$\text{Shepperd complexity}(M) = ((\text{fan-in}(M) \times (\text{fan-out}(M))^2$$

Shepperd claims that his measure is an improvement over the original:

> A feature of our new metrics is that they eliminate the blurring of information and control flow that is an unfortunate by-product of their [Henry and Kafura's] original measure, and concentrate purely on information flow.

The hybrid nature of the original Henry–Kafura measure contradicts measurement theory, which demands the characterization of specific attributes. Shepperd's refinements attempt to capture a specific view of information flow structure, and are thus consistent with measurement theory. His empirical validation studies examined how closely the measures correlate with a specific process measure, namely development time. Interestingly, the relationship between development time and the Henry–Kafura measure was not significant for Shepperd's data, but Shepperd's pure-information flow-structure measure is significantly related. Thus, the level of information flow (as measured by Shepperd's measure) is closely correlated with development time. This result supports our view that predictors are more likely to be accurate if they involve measures of specific attributes.

8.3.9 Information flow – test coverage measures

We have discussed the use of control flow in white-box testing, noting the utility of measuring the minimum number of test cases required to satisfy a given strategy. Now, we look at the role of data flow, or of a combination of data and control flow.

Most data-flow testing strategies focus on the program paths that link the definition and use of variables. Such a path is called a **du-path**. We distinguish between:

- variable uses within computations (**c-uses**)
- variable uses within predicates or decisions (**p-uses**)

Figure 8.25 illustrates *du*-paths and describes the *c*-uses, *p*-uses, and definitions for each of the basic blocks of code.

The most stringent and theoretically effective data-flow strategy is to find enough test cases so that every *du*-path lies on at least one program path executed by the test cases; this is called the **all *du*-paths strategy**. Weaker testing strategies involve all *c*-uses, all *p*-uses, all defs and all uses.

Rapps and Weyuker note that, although the all *du*-paths strategy is the most discriminating, it requires a potentially exponential number of test cases (Rapps and Weyuker, 1985). Specifically, if t is the number of conditional transfers in a program, then in the worst case there are 2^t *du*-paths. Despite this characteristic, empirical evidence suggests that *du*-paths testing is feasible in practice, and that the *minimal number of paths P* required for all *du*-paths testing is a very useful measure for quality-assurance purposes.

EXAMPLE 8.34: The worst case scenario for the all *du*-paths criterion in Figure 8.25 is 8 tests. Yet, in this case P is 3, because the set of *du*-paths can be covered by just 3 paths:

<s,1,2,3,4,2,3,4,2,6,t>, <s,1,2,3,5,2,3,5,2,6,t>, <s,1,2,6,t>

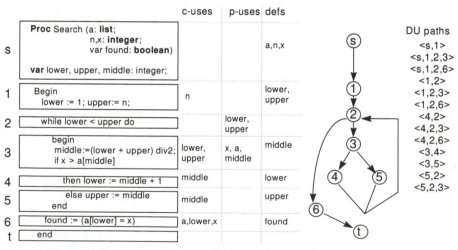

Figure 8.25: Example program and its *du*-paths

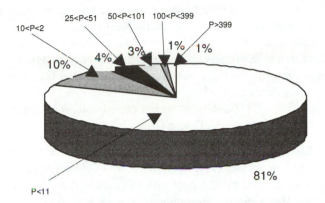

Figure 8.26: Bieman–Schultz results. *P* represents the number of complete paths required to satisfy the all *du*-paths strategy.

EXAMPLE 8.35: Figure 8.26 summarizes the results of an empirical study of the all *du*-paths strategy. Bieman and Schultz looked at a commercial system consisting of 143 modules. For each module, they computed *P*, the minimum number of paths required to satisfy all *du*-paths. Bieman and Schultz found that, for 81% of all modules, *P* was less than 11, and in only one module was *P* prohibitively large. Thus, the strategy seems to be practical for almost all modules. Moreover, Bieman and Schultz noted that the module with excessively high *P* was known to be the "rogue" module of the system (Bieman and Schultz, 1992). Thus, *P* may be a useful quality assurance measure, especially when used with outlier analysis as discussed in Chapter 6. To assure quality, we may want to review (and, if necessary, rewrite) those few modules with infeasible values of *P*, since it is likely that they are overly complex.

8.4 OBJECT-ORIENTED METRICS

The rise in popularity of object-oriented methods raises questions about how we measure object oriented structures. Early measures for object orientation focused on cost and effort prediction (Pfleeger, 1989; Pfleeger and Palmer, 1990), and size was the only internal attribute addressed. Many of the design measures presented so far in this chapter are derived from traditional design techniques; some, such as coupling and cohesion, can be interpreted easily for object-oriented approaches (Pfleeger, 1991), but others have been developed specifically for object orientation.

Chidamber and Kemerer have suggested measures for object-oriented systems, and we discuss them in depth (Chidamber and Kemerer, 1994). The basis for the empirical relation systems in the Chidamber–Kemerer work is the set of "ontological principles" proposed by Bunge and later applied to object-oriented systems by Yand and Weber. (Bunge, 1979; Yand and Weber, 1990) In this work, the world is viewed as being composed of **substantial individuals** that possess a finite set of **properties**. Collectively, a substantial individual and its properties constitute an **object**. A **class** is a set of objects that have common properties, and a **method** is an operation on an object that is defined as part of the declaration of the class.

Attributes such as coupling, cohesion, object complexity, scope of properties are then defined in Bunge's "ontological" terms.

> **EXAMPLE 8.36:** In Bunge's terminology, two objects are coupled if and only if at least one of them acts upon the other. X is said to act upon Y if the history of Y is affected by X, where history is defined as the chronologically ordered states that a substantial individual traverses in time.

Chidamber and Kemerer use these notions to define a number of metrics that are claimed to relate to some of these attributes:

Metric 1: weighted methods per class (WMC)

This metric is intended to relate to the notion of complexity. For a class C with methods $M_1, M_2, ..., M_n$, weighted respectively with "complexity" $c_1, c_2, ..., c_n$, the measure is calculated as

$$\text{WMC} = \sum_{i=1}^{n} c_i$$

Metric 2: depth of inheritance tree (DIT)

In an object-oriented design, the application domain is modeled as a hierarchy of classes. This hierarchy can be represented as a tree, called the **inheritance tree**. The nodes in the tree represent classes, and for each such class, the DIT metric is the length of the maximum path from the node to the root of the tree. This measure relates to the notion of scope of properties. DIT is a measure of how many ancestor classes can potentially affect this class.

Metric 3: number of children (NOC)

This metric relates to a node (class) of the inheritance tree. It is the number of immediate successors of the class.

Metric 4: coupling between object classes (CBO)

For a given class, this measure is defined to be the number of other classes to which the class is coupled.

Metric 5: response for class (RFC)

This measure captures the size of the response set of a class. The response set of a class consists of all the methods called by local methods. RFC is the number of local methods plus the number of methods called by local methods.

Metric 6: lack of cohesion metric (LCOM)

The cohesion of a class is characterized by how closely the local methods are related to the local instance variables in the class. LCOM is defined as the number of disjoint (that is, non-intersecting) sets of local methods.

Li and Henry used these six metrics plus several others, including some simple size metrics (such as the number of attributes plus the number of local methods), to determine whether object-oriented metrics could predict maintenance effort. For the weights in Metric 1 (WMC), they used cyclomatic number. On the basis of an empirical study using regression analysis, they concluded that these measures are indeed useful. In particular, they claim that the Chidamber–Kemerer metrics "contribute to the prediction of maintenance effort over and beyond what can be predicted using size metrics alone" (Li and Henry, 1993).

While the use of object-oriented metrics looks promising, there is as yet no widespread agreement on what should be measured in object-oriented systems and which metrics are appropriate. Indeed, Churcher and Shepperd criticized the Chidamber–Kemerer metrics on the grounds that there is as yet no consensus on the underlying attributes. For example, they argue that even the notion of "methods per class" is ambiguous (Churcher and Shepperd, 1995).

Still, these measures can be useful when restricted to locally specified, commonly accepted definitions of the underlying terms. For example, Lorenz reports that the analysis of object-oriented code at IBM has led to several recommendations about design, including maximum sizes for number of methods per class, and restrictions on the number of different message types sent and received (Lorenz, 1993).

8.5 DATA STRUCTURE

We have seen how information flow (sometimes also called data flow) can be measured, so that we have some sense of how data interact with a system or module. However, there have been few attempts to define measures of actual data items and their structure. In this section, we examine possible data-structure measures to see what they can tell us about system products.

In principle, measuring data structure should be straightforward. As with control flow and data flow, we can consider both local and global measures. Locally, we want to measure the amount of structure in each data item. Unfortunately, there has been little work in this area. Elliott has used a graph-theoretic approach to analyze and measure properties of individual data structures, using the same kind of decomposition that we saw for control structure (Elliott, 1988). He viewed the simple data types (such as integers, characters, and Booleans) as primes, and then considered the various operations that enable us to build more complex data structures (such as the operation of forming an array of a given type). Data structure measures can then be defined hierarchically in terms of values for the primes and values associated with the various operations. Van den Berg used a similar approach to measure the structure of function definitions in functional programming languages (van den Berg and van den Broek, 1995).

Globally, we want to capture the "amount of data" for a given system. An intuitively reasonable measure for this attribute is a count of the total number of (user-defined) variables. We have already seen a similar measure, namely Halstead's μ_2 (number of distinct operands), which is computed as:

μ_2 = number of variables + number of unique constants + number of labels

We can use μ_2 as our data measure, or Halstead's measure N_2, the total number of occurrences of operands.

Boehm also addressed the general problem of measuring the amount of data in a system when he constructed the COCOMO model (Boehm, 1981). He notes that a traditional measure like "number of classes of items in the databases" is poorly defined; the lack of precision has led to data measures that range from 3 to 1 000 000 for very similar systems. To solve this problem, Boehm defines the ratio:

$$D/P = \frac{\text{Database size in bytes or characters}}{\text{Program size in DSI}}$$

where DSI is the number of delivered source instructions.

Using this measure, Boehm has derived a simple ordinal-scale measure called DATA, used as one of the COCOMO cost drivers, to measure amount of data. The definition of this measure and its relative multiplicative effect on cost is shown in Table 8.2.

EXAMPLE 8.37:   According to the COCOMO multipliers in Table 8.2, the cost of a project is increased by 16% when DATA is rated "very high." On the other hand, the cost reduces to 94% of the nominal cost when DATA is "low."

The overall "complexity" of a system cannot be depicted completely without measures of data structure; control-flow measures can fail to identify complexity when it is hidden in the data structure.

EXAMPLE 8.38:   Figure 8.27 presents two functionally equivalent programs that are coded quite differently. Program A has a high control-flow structural complexity (for example, its cyclomatic number is 7), whereas program B is a simple sequence of statements (and its cyclomatic number is 1). The major difference between the two is that the control-flow "complexity" in A has been

Table 8.2: Boehm's measure DATA

DATA	multiplier
Low ($D/P < 10$)	0.94
Nominal ($10 \leq D/P < 100$)	1.00
High ($100 \leq D/P) < 1000$)	1.08
Very high ($D/P \geq 1000$)	1.16

Program A

```
10 If score >= 80 Then Print " Grade A": GOTO 70
20 If score >= 70 Then Print " Grade B": GOTO 70
30 If score >= 60 Then Print " Grade C": GOTO 70
40 If score >= 50 Then Print " Grade D": GOTO 70
50 If score >= 40 Then Print " Grade E": GOTO 70
60 If score< 40    Then Print " Grade F": GOTO 70
70 END
```

Program B

```
10 DIM A$(11)
20 A$(10) = " Grade A"
30 A$(9) = " Grade A"
40 A$(8) = " Grade A"
50 A$(7) = " Grade B"
60 A$(6) = " Grade C"
70 A$(5) = " Grade D"
80 A$(4) = " Grade E"
90 A$(3) = " Grade F"
100 A$(2) = " Grade F"
120 A$(1) = " Grade F"
130 A$(0) = " Grade F"
140 I = Int (score / 10)
140 Print A$(I)
150 END
```

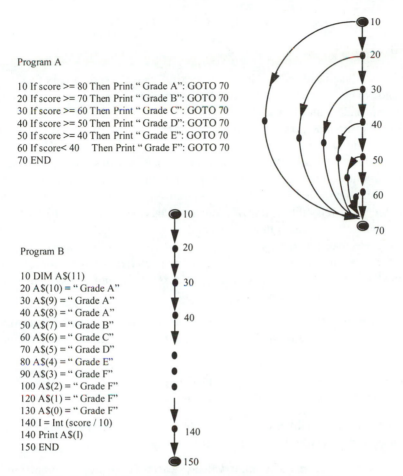

Figure 8.27: Functionally equivalent programs with vastly different control-structure complexity. (This example is derived from a note by R.A. Humphreys that appeared in a newsletter issued by the Centre for Software Reliability.)

transferred to the data structure of B. Whereas A has a single data item of simple type (integer), B requires an 11-dimensional array of character strings, and an integer variable. If we wish to define data-structure measures along the lines suggested above, we might assign a value of 1 to a simple integer or character type, a multiplicative value of 2 to the operation of forming strings, and a multiplicative value of 2 (times number of entries) to the operation of forming an array. In this case, program A has a single data item whose measure is 1, whereas B has two data items, one whose measure is 1, and one whose measure is 44. Thus, the data-structure measure characterizes the difference between A and B in a way not captured by control-flow structure. Although these data structure measures have not been validated empirically, they demonstrate the way in which data-structure complexity can be captured.

8.6 DIFFICULTIES WITH GENERAL "COMPLEXITY" MEASURES

We have discussed the need for viewing "complexity" as the combination of several attributes, and we have shown the importance of examining each attribute separately, so that we can understand exactly what it is that is responsible for the overall "complexity." Nevertheless, practitioners and researchers alike find great appeal in generating a single, comprehensive measure to express "complexity." The single measure is expected to have powerful properties, being an indicator of such diverse notions as comprehensibility, correctness, maintainability, reliability, testability, and ease of implementation. Thus, a high value for "complexity" should indicate low comprehensibility, low reliability, and so on. Sometimes this measure is called a "quality" measure, as it purportedly relates to external product attributes such as reliability and maintainability. Here, a high "quality" measure suggest a low-quality product.

The danger in attempting to find measures to characterize a large collection of different attributes is that often the measures address conflicting goals, counter to the representational theory of measurement.

> **Example 8.39:** Suppose we define a measure, M, that characterizes the quality of people. If M existed, it would have to satisfy at least the following conditions:
>
> $M(A) > M(B)$ whenever A is stronger than B and
> $M(A) > M(B)$ whenever A is more intelligent than B
>
> The fact that some highly intelligent people are very weak physically ensures that no M can satisfy both these properties.

Example 8.39 illustrates clearly why single-valued measures of software "complexity" are doomed to failure. Consider, for example, the list of properties in Table 8.3. Proposed by Weyuker, they are described as properties that should be satisfied by any good "complexity" metric (Weyuker, 1988). In the table, P, Q, R denote any program blocks.

Zuse has used the representational theory of measurement to prove that some of these properties are contradictory; they can never all be satisfied by a single-valued measure (Zuse, 1992).

> **EXAMPLE 8.40:** We can see intuitively why Properties 5 and 6 in Table 8.3 are mutually incompatible. Property 5 asserts that adding code to a program cannot decrease its complexity. This property reflects the view that program size is a key factor in its complexity. We can also conclude from Property 5 that low comprehensibility is not a key factor in complexity. This statement is made because it is widely believed that, in certain cases, we can understand a program more easily as we see more of it. Thus, while a complexity measure M based primarily on size should satisfy property 5, a complexity measure M

Table 8.3: Weyuker's properties for any software complexity metric M

Property 1:	There are programs P and Q for which $M(P) \neq M(Q)$.
Property 2:	If c is a non-negative number, then there are only finitely many programs P for which $M(P) = c$.
Property 3:	There are distinct programs P and Q for which $M(P) = M(Q)$.
Property 4:	There are functionally equivalent programs P and Q for which $M(P) \neq M(Q)$.
Property 5:	For any program bodies P and Q, we have $M(P) \leq M(P;Q)$ and $M(Q) \leq M(P;Q)$.
Property 6:	There exist program bodies P, Q, and R such that $M(P) = M(Q)$ and $M(P;R) \neq M(Q;R)$.
Property 7:	There are program bodies P and Q such that Q is formed by permuting the order of the statements of P and $M(P) \neq M(Q)$.
Property 8:	If P is a renaming of Q, then $M(P) = M(Q)$.
Property 9:	There exist program bodies P and Q such that $M(P) + M(Q) < M(P;Q)$.

based primarily on comprehensibility cannot satisfy property 5.

On the other hand, Property 6 asserts that we can find two program bodies of equal complexity which, when separately concatenated to a same third program, yield programs of different complexity. Clearly this property has much to do with comprehensibility and little to do with size.

Thus, properties 5 and 6 are relevant for very different, and incompatible, views of complexity. They cannot both be satisfied by a single measure that captures notions of size and low comprehensibility. The above argument is not formal. However, Zuse reinforces the incompatibility; he proves formally that while Property 5 explicitly requires the ratio scale for M, Property 6 explicitly excludes the ratio scale.

Cherniavsky and Smith also offer a critique of Weyuker's properties (Cherniavsky and Smith, 1991). They define a code-based "metric" that satisfies all of Weyuker's properties but, as they rightly claim, is not a sensible measure of complexity. They conclude that axiomatic approaches may not work.

Cherniavsky and Smith have correctly found a problem with the Weyuker axioms. But they present no justification for their conclusion about axiomatic approaches in general. They readily accept that Weyuker's properties are not claimed to be complete. But what they fail to observe is that Weyuker did not propose that the axioms were sufficient; she only proposed that they were necessary. The Cherniavsky and Smith "metric" is not a real measure in the sense of measurement theory, since it does not capture a specific attribute. Therefore, showing that the "metric" satisfies a set of axioms necessary for any measure proves nothing about real measures.

These problems could have been avoided by heeding a basic principle of measurement theory: defining a numerical mapping does not in itself constitute measurement. Software engineers often use the word "metric" for any number extracted from a software entity. But while every measure is a metric, the converse is certainly not true. The confusion in analyses such as Cherniavsky and Smith's or Weyuker's arises from wrongly equating these two concepts, and from not viewing the problem from a measurement-theory perspective.

8.7 SUMMARY

It is widely believed that a well-designed software product is characterized largely by its internal structure. Indeed, the rationale behind most software-engineering methods is to ensure that software products are built with certain desirable structural attributes. Thus, it is important to know how to recognize and measure these attributes, since they may provide important indicators of key external attributes, such as maintainability, testability, reusability, and even reliability.

We have described how to perform measurements of what are generally believed to be key internal structural attributes, including modularity, coupling, cohesion, tree impurity, reuse, and information flow. These attributes are relevant for design documents as well as code. Indeed, knowing these attributes, we can identify components that are likely to be difficult to implement, test, and maintain.

We looked in detail at control-flow attributes of programs. We showed how every program is built up in a unique way from so-called prime structures, which are the building blocks of structured programming. A program's structure can therefore be characterized objectively in terms of its prime decomposition, which may be automatically computed by tools like QUALMS and Prometrix. Most measures of internal attributes of programs (including test coverage measures), together with most "complexity" measures, can be computed easily once we know a program's prime decomposition. These measures are called hierarchical. The prime decomposition is a definitive representation of the control structure of a flowgraph; it can also be used as the basis for optimal restructuring of code, and hence as a reverse-engineering tool.

It is unrealistic to expect that general complexity measures (of either the code or system design) will be good predictors of many different attributes. Complexity is an intuitive attribute that includes the specific internal attributes discussed in this chapter. Rather than seek a single measure, we should identify specific attributes of interest and obtain accurate measures of them; in combination, we can then paint an overall picture of complexity.

8.8 EXERCISES

1   Show that there are valid flowgraphs in which not every node lies on a simple path from start to stop. (Hint: consider one of the flowgraphs in Figure 8.3.)

2   The following sets of edges form flowgraphs on five nodes, labeled from 1 to 5. Draw the flowgraphs using the conventions of Figure 8.2. Which of the flowgraphs are primes? For those that are not, represent the flowgraphs by expressions using sequencing and nesting applied to the flowgraphs of Figure 8.2.

   i.   edges (1, 2), (2, 3), (3, 4), (4, 3), (3, 5)
   ii.   edges (1, 2), (2, 3), (1, 4), (3, 4), (4, 3), (3, 5)
   iii. edges (1, 2), (2, 3), (3, 2), (3, 4), (4, 3), (2, 5)
   iv.   edges (1, 2), (2, 3), (2, 5), (3, 4), (4, 1)

3   Draw the decomposition trees for each flowgraph in Exercise 2.
4   Draw three flowgraphs that have equal cyclomatic number but which seem intuitively to rank differently in terms of structural complexity. What actual structural attributes are contributing to "complexity" in your examples? Find hierarchical measures that capture these attributes. (Hint: Example 8.7 and the largest prime in Table 8.1 are likely candidates.)
5   Consider the FORTRAN program shown in Figure 7.2. Compute the knot value.
6   Give a hierarchical definition of the knot count measure.
7   Read about the Harrison–Magel scope measure in Harrison and Magel (1981a). Which program attribute is this measuring? Is it an improvement on McCabe's cyclomatic number?
8   For each hierarchical measure in Table 8.1, calculate the value of the measure for the flowgraph in Figure 8.15.
9   Look at the program in Figure 8.14. How many feasible paths are there for this program? Define a set of test cases that gives you 100% coverage of all the feasible paths.
10 Use the tables in Appendix 8.10.4 to compute the branch coverage measure for the flowgraph in Figure 8.15.
11 Show that the measure m defined in Example 8.31 satisfies the four properties of tree impurity. Compute the measure m for the graphs G_1, G_5 and G_6 in Figure 8.21.
12 A measure of tree impurity proposed by Ince and Hekmatpour is given in Ince and Hekmatpour (1988):

$$m(G) = \sum_{n \in G} (\text{id}(n))^2$$

   where n represents a node of G, and $\text{id}(n)$ is the in-degree of node n. Show that this measure fails to satisfy properties 1 and 3.
13 Yin and Winchester define a family of system design measures, $C_i = e_i - n_i + 1$, where e_i is the number of arcs up to level i, and n_i is the number of nodes up to level i. Taking i to be the last level, they define tree impurity m_2 of the whole design G by $m_2(G) = e - n + 1$, where e is the total number of edges and n is the

total number of nodes of G. Show that properties 1 and 2 are satisfied by m_2 but not property 3 (Yin and Winchester, 1978).

14 Explain why the converse of property 3 in section 8.3.4 is reasonable for the attribute *private reuse*. Show that the Yin and Winchester measure r satisfies the four proposed properties.

15 Compute the Yin and Winchester measure for the graph in Figure 8.20.

16 Propose a precise definition of the cohesion ratio measure that could be automated for a particular high-level programming language such as C or Pascal.

17 What is the rationale behind squaring the product of fan-in and fan-out in the Henry–Kafura measure? (Hint: examine the effect of squaring in the example in Figure 8.24.)

18 Compute the global coupling measure C for the graph in Figure 8.23.

19 Below is a list of measures that can be applied to program bodies. In each case, determine which of the Weyuker properties hold:

- LOC
- cyclomatic number
- is-D-structured
- Henry–Kafura measure
- function points

20 What do you understand by the notions of i) module cohesion and ii) coupling between modules? Describe briefly four different types of coupling, presenting them in ascending order of what you feel to be the strongest type of coupling.

21 "A good design should exhibit high module cohesion and low module coupling." Briefly describe what you understand this assertion to mean.

22 McCabe's cyclomatic number is a classic example of a software metric. Which software entity and attribute do you believe it really measures?

23 Explain briefly the principles behind the statement coverage testing strategy.

24 Describe the difference between black-box and white-box testing. Explain why exhaustive path testing is generally infeasible by giving an example using a flowgraph.

25 What is a prime flowgraph? Give examples of two prime flowgraphs that are not building blocks of the traditional *D*-structured programming, but that are (in a sense you should explain briefly) natural control constructs.

26 By considering the formal definition of *D*-structured programs in terms of prime flowgraphs, deduce that the procedure in Figure 8.28 is *D*-structured.

27 The algorithm in Figure 8.29 describes a simple control system. What can you say about the structuredness of this algorithm?

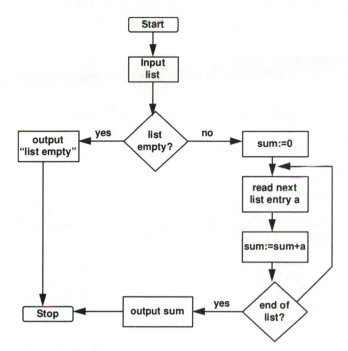

Figure 8.28: Example procedure

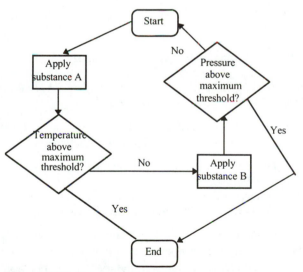

Figure 8.29: Simple control system

8.9 FURTHER READING

Many of the measures introduced in this chapter rely on an understanding of graph theory. Wilson and Watlin's book provides a standard and accessible reference to graph theory concepts and techniques.

Wilson, R.J. and Watkins, J.J., *Graphs: An Introductory Approach*, Wiley, New York, 1990.

Prather and Giulieri present the first discussion of flowgraph decomposition, and Linger, Mills, and Witt offer a related approach.

Prather, R.E. and Giulieri, S.G., "Decomposition of flowchart schemata," *Computer Journal*, 24(3), pp. 258–62, 1981.
Linger, R.C., Mills, H.D. and Witt, R.L., *Structured Programming: Theory and Practice*, Addison-Wesley, Reading, MA, 1979.

More detailed accounts of our particular approach to prime decomposition may be found in the Fenton–Kaposi and Fenton–Whitty articles. We have shortened and simplified the discussion in this chapter. Readers who wish to see proofs and more of the underlying theory required, such as for constructing static analysis tools, should consult these references.

Fenton, N.E. and Kaposi, A.A., "Metrics and software structure," *Journal of Information and Software Technology*, pp. 301–20, July 1987.
Fenton, N.E. and Whitty, R.W., "Axiomatic approach to software metrication through program decomposition," *Computer Journal* 29(4), pp. 329–39, 1986.

A comprehensive treatment of the generalized theory of structuredness can be found in these publications:

Fenton, N.E., Whitty, R.W., and Kaposi, A.A., "A generalized mathematical theory of structured programming," *Theoretical Computer Science*, 36, pp. 145–71, 1985.
Fenton, N.E. and Hill, G., *Systems Construction and Analysis: A Mathematical and Logical Approach*, McGraw-Hill, New York, 1992.

A large number of other structural complexity measures are analyzed using the prime decomposition approach by Bache, and in Whitty and Lockhart.

Bache, R., *Graph Theory Models of Software*, PhD thesis, South Bank University, London SE1 0AA, 1990.
Whitty, R.W. and Lockhart, R., *Structural metrics*, ESPRIT 2 project COSMOS, document GC/WP1/REP/7.3, Goldsmiths College, London, 1990.

Van den Broek and van den Berg generalize the prime decomposition of flowgraphs by allowing arbitrary decomposition operations. They also describe a flowgraph-type model for functional programs and apply the theory of decomposition as described in this chapter.

van den Berg, K.G. and van den Broek, P.M., "Static analysis of functional programs," *Information and Software Technology*, 37(4), pp. 213–24, 1995.

van den Broek, P.M. and van den Berg, K.G., "Generalised approach to software structure metrics," *Software Engineering Journal*, 10(2), pp. 61–8, 1995.

Prather discusses hierarchical measures in depth. In particular, he notes that, for all the well-known metrics, there was a uniformity in the way the nesting functions were defined; they were defined independently of particular primes. In the light of this, Prather defines the subclass of **recursive measures** to correspond to those measures for which there exists a uniform nesting function. Prather has asked whether there are any interesting measures that are hierarchical but not recursive. His affirmative answer is provided by the example of the "number of paths" metric discussed in this chapter. Prather provides a full definition of this measure, whereas we have defined it only for a small family of primes.

Prather, R.E., "On hierarchical software metrics," *Software Engineering Journal*, 2(2), pp. 42–5, 1987.

The following papers discuss axiomatic type properties that should be satisfied by so-called complexity metrics. Melton and his colleagues restrict their discussion to control-flow structure and adopt a measurement-theory-type approach by defining a partial order on flowgraphs. The partial order preserves an intuitive notion of "more complex than". Lakshmanan and colleagues also restrict their properties to control-flow measures.

Lackshmanan, K.B., Jayaprakesh, S., and Sinha, P.K., "Properties of control-flow complexity measures," *IEEE Transactions on Software Engineering*, 17(12), pp. 1289–95, 1991.

Melton, A.C., Bieman, J.M., Baker, A., and Gustafson, D.A., "Mathematical perspective of software measures research," *Software Engineering Journal*, 5(5), pp. 246–54, 1990.

Weyuker, E.J., "Evaluating software complexity measures," *IEEE Transactions on Software Engineering*, SE-14(9), pp. 1357–65, 1988.

Bieman and Ott define a range of intra-modular measures of functional cohesion based on the notion of data slices. This paper is also especially interesting from our perspective, because the authors discuss the scale properties of their measures using measurement theory.

Bieman, J.M. and Ott, L.M., "Measuring functional cohesion," *IEEE Transactions on Software Engineering*, 20(8), pp. 644–57, 1994.

In this chapter, we have discussed several attempts to define a general "complexity" measure. Other well-known hybrid complexity measures are described in the following papers:

Chapin, N., "A measure of software complexity," *Proceedings of the National Computer Conference*, pp. 995–1002, 1977.

Harrison, W.A. and Magel, K.I., "A complexity measure based on nesting level," *ACM SIGPLAN Notices*, 16(3), pp. 63–74, 1981.

Oviedo, E.I., "Control flow, data flow, and program complexity," *Proceedings of*

COMPSAC 80, pp. 146–52, IEEE Computer Society Press, New York, 1980.

Stetter, F., "A measure of program complexity," *Computer Languages*, 9(3), pp. 203–10, 1984.

Zuse provides a comprehensive review of almost every control structure measure appearing in the literature from the viewpoint of measurement theory.

Zuse, H., *Software Complexity: Measures and Methods*, De Gruyter, Berlin, 1991.

Bertolino and Marre have written an excellent paper that explains the practical problems with the branch coverage metric and proposes an alternative metric for branch coverage. The theoretical minimum number of paths for this strategy is more closely aligned to minimum number of practically feasible paths. The paper also shows how the metric can be formulated using the prime decomposition approach.

Bertolino, A. and Marre, M., "How many paths are needed for branch testing?," *Journal of Systems and Software*, 1996.

Beizer's book on testing provides a thorough account of many structural testing strategies. This book is also interesting because of its serious measurement content. For example, the author addresses the issue of theoretical minimum and maximum numbers of paths needed for different strategies.

Beizer, B., *Software Testing Techniques*, Van Nostrand, 1990.

Rapps and Weyuker provide an extensive account of data-flow testing strategies. An excellent account of these strategies may also be found in Bieman and Schultz.

Bieman, J.M. and Schultz, J.L., "An empirical evaluation (and specification) of the all-*du*-paths testing criterion," *Software Engineering Journal*, 7(1), pp. 43–51, 1992.

Rapps, S. and Weyuker, E.J., "Selecting software test data using data flow information," *IEEE Transactions on Software Engineering,* 11(4), pp. 367–75, 1985.

Chidamber and Kemerer provide the most serious study on metrics for object-oriented design, and their work is supported by some empirical data. They also present a good survey of other object-oriented metrics.

Chidamber, S.R. and Kemerer, C.F., "A metrics suite for object oriented design," *IEEE Transactions on Software Engineering*, 20(6), pp. 47–98, 1994.

Many other recent papers suggest measurements for object-oriented development. An example of one is the paper by Abreu and Carapuca.

Abreu, F.B. and Carapuca, R., "Candidate metrics for object-oriented software within a taxonomy framework," *Journal of Systems and Software*, 23(1), pp. 87–96, July 1994.

An excellent online catalogue of publications relevant to object-oriented metrics is maintained by Robin Whitty at the following World Wide Web site:

www.sbu.ac.uk/~csse/publications/OOMetrics.html

8.10 APPENDICES TO CHAPTER 8

Appendix 8.10.1 Some recursive "complexity" measures

The Basili–Hutchens measure $SynC$

This is defined with respect to a family S of primes (Basili and Hutchens, 1983).

M_1:
$$SynC(F) = \begin{cases} 1 + \log_2(k+1) & \text{if } f \in S \\ 2(1 + \log_2(k+1)) & \text{otherwise} \end{cases}$$

for each prime F, where k is the number of predicates in F. (Thus although the "complexity" of the primes is still just a function of the number of predicates it contains, those primes which are *not* in S, i.e. the "unstructured primes are accorded twice the "complexity" of a similar sized prime in S.)

M_2:
$$SynC(F_1;\ldots;F_n) = \sum_{i=1}^{n} SynC(F_i) \text{ for each } n$$

Thus the complexity of sequence is additive, i.e. equal to the sum of the complexities of the parts.

M_3:
$$SynC(F(F_1,\ldots,F_n)) = SynC(F) + 1.1 \sum_{i=1}^{n} SynC(F_i) \text{ for each prime } F$$

Nesting has a multiplicative complexity factor of 1.1, and the contribution of F itself to the function is additive.

Prather's measure μ

defined in Prather (1984) for S^D-graphs where $S^D = \{P_1, D_1, D_2\}$:

M_1: $\mu(P_1) = 1, \mu(D_1) = 2, \mu(D_2) = 2$

M_2: $\mu(F_1;\ldots;F_n) = \sum_{i=1}^{n} \mu(F_i)$ for each n

Thus, the complexity of sequence is additive.

M_3: $\mu(D_1(F_1, F_2)) = \mu(D_1)\max(\mu(F_1), \mu(F_2))$ $\mu(D_2(F_1)) = \mu(D_2)\mu(F_1)$

The complexity of nesting is multiplicative.

Appendix 8.10.2 Bache's axioms and the VINAP measures

Axioms for a measure μ of general control structure:

Let F, G, H be prime flowgraphs ($\neq P_1$) and suppose $\mu(H) > \mu(G)$:

$$F \neq P_1 \Rightarrow \mu(F) > \mu(P_1)$$
$$\mu(F;G) > \max\{\mu(F), \mu(G)\}$$
$$(F;G) = \mu(G;F)$$
$$\mu(F;H) > \mu(F;G)$$
$$\mu(F(F_1 \text{ on } a)) = \mu(F(F_1 \text{ on } b))$$
$$\mu(F(H, F_2, \ldots, F_n)) > \mu(F(G, F_2, \ldots, F_n))$$
$$\mu(H(F)) > \mu(G(F))$$
$$\mu(F(G)) > \mu(F;G)$$
$$\mu(H(G)) > \mu(G(H))$$

The VINAP measures are known to satisfy all the axioms. All elements of the family of VINAP measures have the same functions for sequencing and nesting. Only the value of the primes differs. The measure is defined in terms of the depth of nesting measure α. Full details may be found in (Bache, 1990).

Appendix 8.10.3 McCabe's testing strategy

I. Background

In a **strongly connected graph G**, for any nodes x, y there is a path from x to y and vice versa. Each path can be represented as an n-tuple where n is the number of nodes. For example, in the Graph G of Figure 8.30 each path can be represented as a 6-tuple (vector with 6 components):

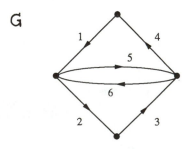

Figure 8.30: A strongly connected graph

$$< 1, 2, 3, 4 > = (1\ 1\ 1\ 1\ 0\ 0)$$
$$< 1, 5, 6, 2, 3, 4, 1 > = (2\ 1\ 1\ 1\ 1\ 1)$$
$$< 1, 5, 4 > = (1\ 0\ 0\ 0\ 1\ 1) \text{ etc.}$$

That is, the ith position in the vector is the number of occurrences of edge i.

A **circuit** is a path that begins and ends at the same node, e.g. $< 1, 2, 3, 6, 5, 4 >$.

A **cycle** is a circuit with no node (other than the starting node) included more than once, e.g. $< 1, 2, 3, 4 >$ and $< 5, 6 >$.

A path p is said to be a **linear combination** of paths $p_1, ..., p_n$ if there are integers $a_1, ..., a_n$ such that $p = \sum a_i p_i$ in the vector representation, e.g. path $< 1, 2, 3, 4, 1, 5, 6 >$ is a linear combination of paths $< 1, 2, 3, 4 >$ and $<1, 5, 6 >$ since

$$(2\ 1\ 1\ 1\ 1\ 1) = (1\ 1\ 1\ 1\ 0\ 0) + (1\ 0\ 0\ 0\ 1\ 1)$$

As another example, let:
$$a = < 1, 2, 3, 4 > = (1\ 1\ 1\ 1\ 0\ 0)$$
$$b = < 5, 6 > = (0\ 0\ 0\ 0\ 1\ 1)$$
$$c = < 1, 5, 4 > = (1\ 0\ 0\ 1\ 1\ 0)$$
$$d = < 2, 3, 6 > = (0\ 1\ 1\ 0\ 0\ 1)$$

Then
$$a + b - c = d \tag{*}$$

A set of paths is **linearly independent** if no path in the set is a linear combination of any other paths in the set. Thus $\{ a, b, c \}$ is linearly independent, but $\{ a, b, c, d \}$ is not by virtue of (*).

A **basis set** of cycles is a maximal linearly independent set of cycles. In a graph of e edges and n nodes, the basis has $e - n + 1$ cycles. Although the size of the basis is invariant, its content is not. For example, for the graph G above:

$$\{ a, b, c \}, \{ a, b, d \}, \{ b, c, d \}, \{ a, c, d \}$$

are different basis sets of cycles. Every path is a linear combination of basis cycles.

II. Strategy

Any flowgraph can be transformed into a strongly connected graph by adding an edge from stop node to start node. Figure 8.31 shows how we transform a flowgraph to obtain the same graph as that of Figure 8.30.

McCabe's test strategy is based on choosing a basis set of cycles in the resulting graph G.

As we have seen above, the number of these is $v(G)$. (McCabe's "cyclomatic complexity") satisfying

$$v(G) = e - n + 1$$

Since the original flowgraph has had one edge added, the formula for computing $v(G)$ for an arbitrary flowgraph G with e edges and n nodes is:

$$v(G) = e - n + 2$$

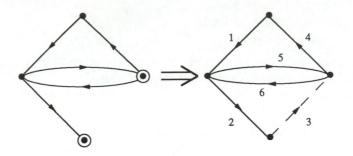

Figure 8.31: Transforming a flowgraph into a strongly connected graph

The idea is that these cycles are "representative" of all the paths since every path is a linear combination of basis cycles. In the example, one possible basis set of cycles is:

$$\{ <4, 1, 2, 3>, <6, 5, >, <6, 2, 3> \}$$

Unfortunately these do not correspond to paths through the flowgraph (because of the artificial introduction of edge 3) which is what we need for a structural testing strategy. We thus have to derive the "smallest" associated paths. These are:

$$<4, 1, 2>, <6, 5, 6, 2>, <6, 2>$$

Note that a different basis set of cycles such as

$$\{ <6, 5>, <6, 2, 3>, <4, 1, 5> \}$$

leads to a different set of testing paths:

$$<6, 5, 6, 2>, <6, 2>, <4, 1, 5, 6, 2>$$

We can also show that if all predicate nodes have out-degree 2 then $v(G) = d + 1$ where d is the number of predicate nodes in G. For if there are p procedure nodes, then $n = p + d + 1$ since the nodes of G are: the procedure nodes, the predicate nodes, plus a single stop node. Now $e = p + 2d$ since each procedure node contributes 1 to the total number of edges and each predicate node contributes 2. Thus $e - n + 2 = (p + 2d) - (p + d + 1) = d - 1$.

Appendix 8.10.4   Computing test coverage measures

Measurement value for primes

Test strategy	P_1	D_0	D_1	C_n	D_2	D_3	D_4	L_2
All-path testing	1	2	2	n	–	–	–	–
Visit-each-loop path testing	1	2	2	n	2	2	2	4
Simple path testing	1	2	2	n	2	1	1	2
Branch testing	1	2	2	n	1	1	1	2
Statement testing	1	1	2	n	1	1	1	1

Sequencing function

Test strategy	$F_1;\ldots;F_n$
All-path testing	$\prod_{i=1}^{n} \mu(F_i)$
Visit-each-loop path testing	"
Simple path testing	"
Branch testing	$\max(\mu(F_1),\ldots,\mu(F_n))$
Statement testing	"

Nesting function

Test strategy	$D_1(F_1,F_2)$	$C_n(F_1,\ldots,F_n)$	$D_0(F)$	$D_2(F)$
All-path testing	$\mu(F_1)+\mu(F_2)$	$\sum_{i=1}^{n}\mu(F_i)$	$\mu(F)+1$	–
Visit-each-loop path testing	"	"	"	$\mu(F)+1$
Simple path testing	"	"	"	"
Branch testing	"	"	"	1
Statement testing	"	"	$\mu(F)$	1

Test strategy	$D_3(F)$	$D_4(F_1,F_2)$	$L_2(F_1,F_2)$
All path testing	–	–	–
Visit-each-loop path testing	$\mu(F)+\mu(F)^2$	$\mu(F_1)+\mu(F_1)^2\,\mu(F_2)$	$1+\mu(F_1)+\mu(F_1)\mu(F_2)+\\ \mu(F_1)^2\,\mu(F_2)$
Simple path testing	$\mu(F)$	$\mu(F_1)$	$1+\mu(F_1)+\mu(F_1)\times\mu(F_2)$
Branch testing	1	1	2
Statement testing	1	1	1

9 Measuring external product attributes

A principal objective of software engineering is to improve the quality of software products. But quality, like beauty, is very much in the eyes of the beholder. In the philosophical debate about the meaning of software quality, proposed definitions include:

- fitness for purpose
- conformance to specification
- degree of excellence
- timeliness

However, from a measurement perspective, we must be able to define quality in terms of specific software product attributes of interest to the user. That is, we want to know how to measure the extent to which these attributes are present in our software products. This knowledge will enable us to specify (and set targets for) quality attributes in measurable form.

In Chapter 3, we defined external product attributes as those that can be measured only with respect to how the product relates to its environment. For example, if the product is software code, then its reliability (defined in terms of the probability of failure-free operation) is an external attribute; it is dependent on both the machine environment and the user. Whenever we think of software code as our product and we investigate an external attribute that is dependent on the user, we inevitably are dealing with an attribute synonymous with a particular view of quality (that is, a quality attribute). Thus, it is no coincidence that the attributes considered in this chapter relate to some popular views of software quality.

In Chapter 8, we considered a range of internal attributes believed to affect quality in some way. Many practitioners and researchers measure and analyze internal attributes because they may be predictors of external attributes. There are two major advantages to doing so. First, the internal attributes are often available for measurement early in the life cycle, whereas external attributes are measurable only when the product is complete (or nearly so). Second, internal attributes are often easier to measure than external ones.

The objective of this chapter is to focus on a small number of especially important external attributes and consider how they may be measured. Where relevant, we indicate the relationships between external and internal attributes. We begin by considering several general software quality models, each of which proposes a specific set of quality attributes (and internal attributes) and their interrelationships. We use the models to identify key external attributes of interest, including **reliability**, **maintainability**, and **usability**. Given the increasing use of software in systems that are crucial to our life and health, software reliability is particularly important. Because reliability has received a great deal of scrutiny from practitioners and researchers, spawning a rich literature about its measurement and behavior, we postpone our discussion of it until Chapter 10, where we present a detailed account. In this chapter, we focus primarily on how usability and maintainability may be measured.

9.1 MODELING SOFTWARE QUALITY

Because quality is really a composite of many characteristics, the notion of quality is usually captured in a model that depicts the composite characteristics and their relationships. Many of the models blur the distinction between internal and external attributes, making it difficult for us to understand exactly what quality is. Still, the models are useful in articulating what people think is important, and in identifying the commonalities of view. In this section, we look at some very general models of software quality that have gained acceptance within the software engineering community. By extracting from them several common external attributes of general interest, we show how the models and their derivatives may then be tailored for individual purpose.

In Chapter 1, we introduced the notion of describing quality by enumerating its component characteristics and their interrelationships. Figure 1.5 presented an example of such a quality model. Let us now take a closer look at this type of model to see how it has been used by industry and what we can learn from the results.

9.1.1 Early models

Both McCall and Boehm have described quality using a decompositional approach (McCall, 1977; Boehm *et al.*, 1978). Figure 9.1 presents Boehm's view of quality's components, while Figure 9.2 illustrates how McCall viewed quality.

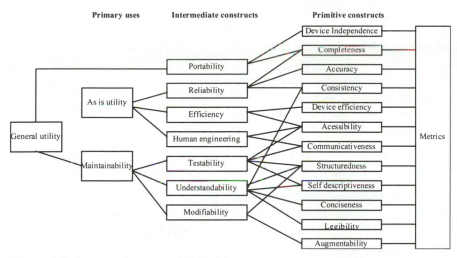

Figure 9.1: Boehm software quality model

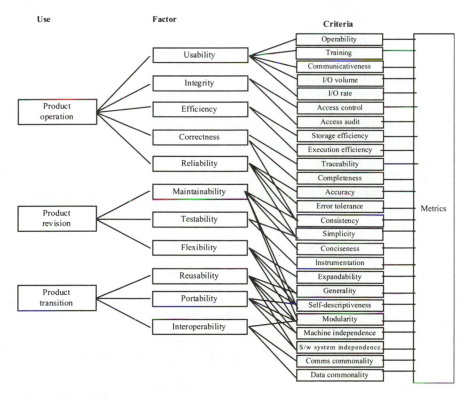

Figure 9.2: McCall software quality model

In models such as these, the model-builders focus on the final product (usually the executable code), and identify key attributes of quality from the user's perspective. These key attributes, called **quality factors**, are normally high-level external attributes like "reliability", "usability", and "maintainability". But they may also include several attributes that arguably are internal, such as "testability" and "efficiency". Each of the models assumes that the quality factors are still at too high a level to be meaningful or to be measurable directly. Hence, they are further decomposed into lower-level attributes called **quality criteria**.

EXAMPLE 9.1: In McCall's model, the factor "reliability" is composed of the criteria "consistency", "accuracy", "error-tolerance" and "simplicity".

Sometimes the quality criteria are internal attributes, such as "structuredness" and "modularity", reflecting the developers' belief that the internal attributes have an effect on the external quality attributes. A further level of decomposition is required, in which the quality criteria are associated with a set of low-level, directly measurable attributes (both product and process) called **quality metrics**. For instance, Figure 9.3 shows how maintainability can be described by three criteria and four metrics, forming a complete decomposition. (This structure has been adapted from a draft IEEE standard for quality metrics (IEEE 1989)).

This presentation is helpful, as we may use it to monitor software quality in two different ways:

- **The fixed model approach:** we assume that all important quality factors needed to monitor a project are a subset of those in a published model. To control and measure each attribute, we accept the model's associated criteria and metrics and, most importantly, the proposed relationships among factors, criteria and metrics. Then, we use the data collected to determine the quality of the product.

- **The "define your own quality model" approach:** we accept the general philosophy that quality is composed of many attributes, but we do not adopt

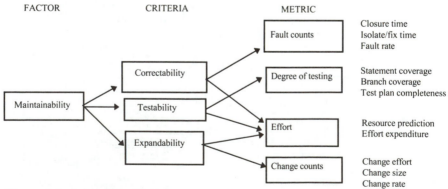

Figure 9.3: A decomposition of maintainability

a given model's characterization of quality. Instead, we meet with prospective users to reach a consensus on which quality attributes are important for a given product. Together, we decide on a decomposition (possibly guided by an existing model) in which we agree on specific measures for the lowest-level attributes (criteria) and specific relationships between them. Then, we measure the quality attributes objectively to see if they meet specified, quantified targets.

The Boehm and McCall models are typical of fixed quality models. Although it is beyond the scope of this book to provide a detailed and exhaustive description of fixed model approaches, we present a small picture of how such a model can be used.

EXAMPLE 9.2: The McCall model, depicted in Figure 9.2, includes 41 metrics to measure the 23 quality criteria generated from the quality factors. Measuring any factor requires us first to consider a checklist of conditions that may apply to the requirements (R), the design (D), and the implementation (I). The condition is designated "yes" or "no," depending on whether or not it is met. To see how the metrics and checklists are used, consider measuring the criterion "completeness" for the factor "correctness". The checklist for completeness is:

1. unambiguous references (input, function, output) [R, D, I];
2. all data references defined, computed, or obtained from external source [R, D, I];
3. all defined functions used [R, D, I];
4. all referenced functions defined [R, D, I];
5. all conditions and processing defined for each decision point [R, D, I];
6. all defined and referenced calling sequence parameters agree [D, I];
7. all problem reports resolved [R, D, I];
8. design agrees with requirements [D];
9. code agrees with design [I].

Notice that there are six conditions that apply to requirements, eight to design and eight to implementation. We can assign a 1 to a "yes" answer and 0 to a "no", and we can compute the completeness metric in the following way to yield a measure that is a number between 0 and 1:

$$\frac{1}{3}\left(\frac{\text{Number of yes for R}}{6} + \frac{\text{Number of yes for D}}{8} + \frac{\text{Number of yes for I}}{8}\right)$$

Since the model tells us that "correctness" depends on "completeness", "traceability" and "consistency", we can calculate analogous measures for the latter two. Then, the measure for "correctness" is the mean of their measures:

$$\text{correctness} = \frac{x + y + z}{3}$$

where x, y and z are the metrics for **completeness**, **traceability** and **consistency**, respectively. In this example, all of the factors are weighted the same. However, it is possible to use different weightings, so that the weights reflect importance, cost, or some other consideration important to the evaluator.

The McCall model was originally developed for the US Air Force, and its use is promoted within the US Department of Defense for evaluating software quality. But there are many other standard (and competing) measures in the Department of Defense, and no single set has been adopted as a department-wide standard.

9.1.2 Define-your-own models

The define-your-own-model approach has been pioneered by Gilb and by Kitchenham and Walker. Gilb's method can be thought of as "design by measurable objectives;" it complements his philosophy of evolutionary development. The software engineer delivers the product incrementally to the user, based on the importance of the different kinds of functionality being provided. To assign priorities to the functions, the user identifies key software attributes in the specification. These attributes are described in measurable terms, so the user can determine whether measurable objectives (in addition to the functional objectives) have been met. An example of this approach is illustrated in Figure 9.4. This simple but powerful technique can be used to good effect on projects of all sizes. It is the antithesis of the more traditional "big-bang" development approach, where an entire system is delivered in one go, and there are no priorities assigned to the several functions.

The COQUAMO (COnstructive QUAlity MOdel) approach of Kitchenham and Walker extended Gilb's ideas and supported them with automated tools as part of an ESPRIT (European Community) project (Kitchenham and Walker, 1989). We shall apply this model later in the chapter, when we examine usability issues.

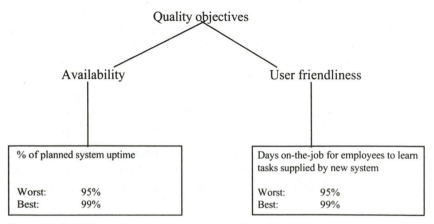

Figure 9.4: Gilb's attribute expansion approach

9.1.3   The ISO 9126 standard quality model

For many years, the user community sought a single model for depicting and expressing quality. The advantage of a universal model is clear: it makes easier the comparison of one product with another. In 1992, a derivation of the McCall model was proposed as the basis for an international standard for software quality measurement. Called *Software Product Evaluation: Quality Characteristics and Guidelines for their Use*, the standard is more commonly referenced by its assigned standard number, *ISO 9126* (ISO 1991). In the standard, software quality is defined to be: "The totality of features and characteristics of a software product that bear on its ability to satisfy stated or implied needs." Then quality is decomposed into six factors:

- functionality
- reliability
- efficiency
- usability
- maintainability
- portability

The standard claims that these six are comprehensive; that is, any component of software quality can be described in terms of some aspect of one or more of the six factors. In turn, each of the six is defined as a "set of attributes that bear" on a relevant aspect of software, and each can be refined through multiple levels of subcharacteristics.

> **EXAMPLE 9.3:** In ISO 9126, "reliability" is defined as "A set of attributes that bear on the capability of software to maintain its level of performance under stated conditions for a stated period of time", while "portability" is defined as "A set of attributes that bear on the capability of software to be transferred from one environment to another."

An annex of ISO 9126 contains examples of possible definitions of subcharacteristics at the first level. However, this annex is not an official part of the International Standard. Attributes at the second level of refinement are left completely undefined. Some software engineers have argued that, since the characteristics and subcharacteristics are not properly defined, ISO 9126 does not provide a conceptual framework within which comparable measurements may be made by different parties with different views of software quality, such as users, vendors, and regulatory agencies. Moreover, the definitions of well-studied attributes such as "reliability" differ from other, well-established standards.

The standard defines a process for evaluating software quality; the process model is illustrated in Figure 9.5. Numerous companies use the ISO 9126 model and framework to support their quality evaluations (Fenton *et al.*, 1995). Thus, despite criticisms, the standard is an important milestone in the development of software quality measurement.

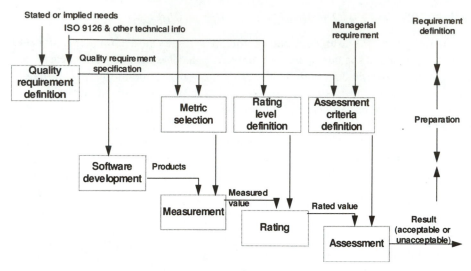

Figure 9.5: ISO 9126 Evaluation process model (ISO, 1991)

9.2 MEASURING ASPECTS OF QUALITY

Many software engineers base their quality assessments on measures defined for a specific purpose, separate from any formal quality model. These definitions often reflect the use to which the software will be put, or the realities of testing a system. For example, certain systems have stringent requirements for **portability** (the ability to move an application from one host environment to another) and **integrity** (the assurance that modifications can be made only by authorized users). The user or practitioner may offer simple definitions of these terms, such as:

$$\text{Portability} = 1 - \frac{ET}{ER}$$

where ET is a measure of the resources needed to move the system to the target environment, and ER is a measure of the resources needed to create the system for the resident environment. Gilb recommends that the onus for setting measurable targets for these attributes should lie with the user.

Measuring many of the quality factors described in formal models, including McCall's and Boehm's, is dependent on subjective ratings. Although objective measures are preferable, subjectivity is better than no measurement at all. However, those performing the rating should be made aware of the need for consistency, so that variability is limited wherever possible.

9.2.1 Defects-based quality measures

Software quality measurement using the decomposition approach clearly requires careful planning and data collection. Proper implementation even for a small number of quality attributes uses extra resources that managers are often reluctant to commit. In many situations, we need only a rough measure of overall software quality based on existing data and requiring few resources. For this reason, many software engineers think of software quality in a much narrower sense, where quality is considered only to be a lack of defects. Here, "defect" is interpreted to mean a known error, fault, or failure, as discussed in Chapter 5.

9.2.1.1 Defect density measures

A *de facto* standard measure of software quality is **defect density**. For a given product (that is, anything from a small program function to a complete system), we can consider the defects to be of two types: the **known defects** that have been discovered through testing, inspection, and other techniques, and the **latent defects** that may be present in the system but of which we are as yet unaware. Then, we can define the **defect density** as:

$$\text{defect density} = \frac{\text{number of known defects}}{\text{product size}}$$

Product size is usually measured in terms of lines of code or one of the other length measures described in Chapter 7; some organizations (notably in the financial community) use function points as their size measure. The defect density measure is sometimes incorrectly called a defect rate.

EXAMPLE **9.4:** Grady reports the results from a number of different studies that measured the number of defects per thousands of non-comment source statements (KNCSS). Figure 9.6 shows how the defect density can vary by an order of magnitude (Grady, 1987).

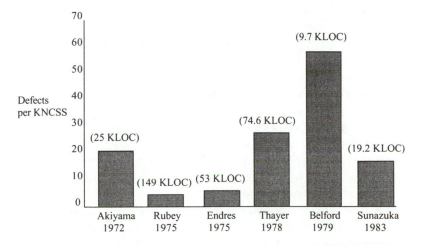

Figure 9.6: Reported defect densities (figures in brackets are the actual system size in KLOC)

Defect density is certainly an acceptable measure to apply to your projects, and it provides useful information. However, before using it, either for your own internal quality assurance purposes or to compare your performance with others, you must remember the following:

1. As discussed in Chapter 5, there is no general consensus on what constitutes a defect. A defect can be either a fault discovered during review and testing (which may potentially lead to an operational failure), or a failure that has been observed during software operation. In published studies, defect counts have included:

   - post-release failures
   - residual faults (that is, all faults discovered after release)
   - all known faults
   - the set of faults discovered after some arbitrary fixed point in the software life cycle (for example, after unit testing)

   The terminology differs widely among studies; fault rate, fault density and failure rate are used almost interchangeably. Thus, to use defect density as a comparative measure, you must be sure that all parties are counting the same things in the same ways.

2. The implication of the phrase "defect rate" is that the number of defects is being recorded with respect to a measure of time (such as operational time or clock time). This measure can be very important. For example, when recording information about operational failures, a defect rate can be calculated based on inter-failure times. In this case, the defect rate, defined with respect to time, is an accurate measure of reliability. However, many studies capture size information but present it as part of a defect rate. Here, "size" is being used as a surrogate measure of time (usually when time is considered to be too difficult to record). Be sure that when you evaluate a study's results, you separate the notion of defect rate from defect density.

3. As discussed in Chapter 7, there is no consensus about how to measure software size in a consistent and comparable way. Unless defect densities are consistently calculated using the same definition of size, the results across projects or studies are incomparable.

4. Although defect density is a product measure in our sense, it is derived from the process of finding defects. Thus, defect density may tell us more about the quality of the defect finding and reporting process than about the quality of the product itself.

5. Even if we were able to know exactly the number of residual faults in our system, we would have to be extremely careful about making definitive statements about how the system will operate in practice. Our caution is based on two key findings:

- It is difficult to determine in advance the seriousness of a fault.
- There is great variability in the way systems are used by different users, and users do not always use the system in the ways expected or intended. Thus, it is difficult to predict which faults are likely to lead to failures, or to predict which failures will occur often.

The dramatic difference in rate of failure occurrence has been highlighted by Adams, who examined IBM operating system data.

> **EXAMPLE 9.5:** Adams at IBM examined data on nine software products, each with many thousands of years of logged use worldwide (Adams, 1984). He recorded the information shown in Table 9.1, relating detected faults to their manifestation as observed failures. For example, the table shows that for product 4, 11.9% of all known defects led to failures that occur on average every 160 to 499 years of use.
>
> Adams discovered that about a third of all detected faults lead to the "smallest" types of failures, namely those that occur on average every 5000 years (or more) of run-time. Conversely, a small number of faults (less than 2%) cause the most common failures, namely those occurring at least once every five years of use. In other words, a very small proportion of the faults in a system can lead to most of the observed failures in a given period of time; most faults in a system are benign, in the sense that in the same given period of time they will not lead to failures. A summary of the data is shown in Figure 9.7, which classifies faults by their "size" (measured as their mean time to failure (MTTF)).

The Adams data suggest that it is quite possible to have products with a very large number of defects failing very rarely, if at all. Such products are certainly high-quality, but their quality is not reflected in a measure based on defect counts. It follows that finding (and removing) large numbers of faults may not necessarily lead

Table 9.1: Adams' data: fitted percentage defects – mean time to problem occurrence in years.

Product	1.6 years	5 years	16 years	50 years	160 years	500 years	1600 years	5000 years
1	0.7	1.2	2.1	5.0	10.3	17.8	28.8	34.2
2	0.7	1.5	3.2	4.5	9.7	18.2	28.0	34.3
3	0.4	1.4	2.8	6.5	8.7	18.0	28.5	33.7
4	0.1	0.3	2.0	4.4	11.9	18.7	28.5	34.2
5	0.7	1.4	2.9	4.4	9.4	18.4	28.5	34.2
6	0.3	0.8	2.1	5.0	11.5	20.1	28.2	32.0
7	0.6	1.4	2.7	4.5	9.9	18.5	28.5	34.0
8	1.1	1.4	2.7	6.5	11.1	18.4	27.1	31.9
9	0.0	0.5	1.9	5.6	12.8	20.4	27.6	31.2

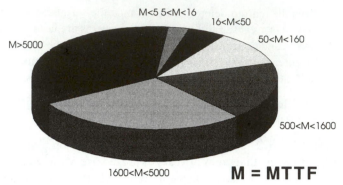

Figure 9.7: Adams' data: faults classified by mean time to failure

to improved reliability, as reliability measures are based on failure data, not fault data. It also follows that a very accurate residual fault density (or even rate) prediction may be a very poor predictor of operational reliability.

Despite these and other serious problems with using defect density, we understand the need for such a measure and the reason it has become a *de facto* standard in industry. Commercial organizations argue that they avoid many of the problems with the measure by having formal definitions that are understood and applied consistently in their own environment. But what works for a particular organization may not transfer to other organizations, so cross-organizational comparisons are dangerous. Nevertheless, organizations are hungry both for benchmarking data and for predictive models of defect density. To meet these goals, we must make cross-project comparisons and inferences. We have seen in Chapter 4 that good experimental design can help us to understand when such comparison makes sense. In Chapter 15, we will examine several empirical models that have been used for predicting defect densities. Here, we turn to what is known about defect density benchmarks; without such knowledge, we cannot interpret the results of any predictive models.

9.2.1.2 Reported evidence of defect densities

Companies are (for obvious reasons) extremely reluctant to publish data about their own defect densities, even when they are relatively low. The few published references we found tend to be reported about anonymous third parties, and in a way that makes independent validation impossible. Nevertheless, company representatives seem happy to quote numbers at conferences and in the gray literature. Notwithstanding the difficulty of determining either the validity of the figures or exactly what was measured and how, there is some consensus on the following: in the USA and Europe, the average defect density (based on number of known post-release defects) appears to be between 5 and 10 per KLOC (Dyer, 1992). Japanese figures seem to be significantly lower (usually below 4 per KLOC), but this figure may be misleading, because only the top companies report their results (Nakimura, 1992). A well-known article on February 11, 1991 in *Business Week* presented results of an extensive study comparing

Table 9.2: Measurement data (including defect density) from an Italian company

Indicators	Project A	Project B	Project C
Estimated effort (person hours)	330	1488	2920
Actual effort (person hours)	350	1452	2920
Work (new developed NCSS)	4 642	11 199	32 254
Size (delivered NCSS)	21 252	220 646	227 049
Defect density (defects/ KLOC)	0.22	1.25	0.25
Testing effort (% on the global effort)	41	56	not available
Productivity (work/person months)	2 122	1 234	1 767

similar state-of-the-art American and Japanese software companies. The average number of defects per KLOC post delivery (for the first 12 months) was 4.44 for the American software but only 1.96 for the Japanese. Most software engineers consider a (delivered) defect density of below 2 per KLOC to be very good. Thus, the figures reported by Bazzana and his colleagues, shown in Table 9.2, are likely to represent state-of-the-art projects (Bazzana *et al.*, 1995).

In one of the more revealing of the published papers, Daskalantonakis reports that Motorola's *six sigma quality goal* is to have "no more than 3.4 defects per million of output units from a project" (Daskalantonakis, 1992). This target translates to an exceptionally low defect density of 0.0034 per KLOC. The paper seems to suggest that the actual defect density lay between 1 and 6 per KLOC on projects in 1990, a figure that was decreasing sharply by 1992.

Of course, even the holy grail of zero-defect software may not actually mean that very high quality has been achieved. For example, Cox reports that at Hewlett-Packard, a number of systems that recorded zero post-release defects turned out to be those systems that were simply never used (Cox, 1991). A related phenomenon is the great variability of defect densities within the same system (as confirmed in the Adams study). In our own study of a major commercial system, a 1.7 million LOC system was divided into 28 subsystems whose median size was 70 KLOC. There were 481 distinct user-reported faults for one year, yielding a very low total defect density of around 0.3 per KLOC. However, 80 faults were concentrated in the subsystem which was by far the smallest (4 KLOC), and whose fault density was therefore a very high 20 per KLOC (Pfleeger, Fenton, and Page, 1994).

Wohlwend and Rosenbaum have presented information about a software process improvement program at Schlumberger. For the system under study, the defect density dropped from 0.22 per KNCSS (for 400 000 NCSS) to 0.13 per KNCSS (for 700 000 NCSS), where NCSS means Non-Comment Source Statements (which tend to be somewhat lower than the more common LOC). However, it is not clear from their study how these low defect densities compare to typical systems at Schlumberger (Wohlwend and Rosenbaum, 1994).

This handful of published studies concentrates on user-detected defects; in other words, the defect densities are really failures per unit of size. There are inevitably many dormant software faults that have not yet led to such failures. Work by Hatton and Roberts gives us an idea of the extent of such faults (and hence the extent to which they could change the magnitude of the defect density); after analyzing millions of lines of code with a static code analyzer, they reported that about 6 in every 1000 lines of commercially released FORTRAN code contain statically detectable faults (Hatton and Roberts, 1994). These faults include anomalies such as overwriting DO loop variables through a calling sequence, or relying on uninitialized variables to always contain appropriate values. On the basis of further, extensive analysis of commercial software, Hatton reports similar defect densities in typical C code (Hatton, 1994).

Benchmarking is also performed using function points as a size measure, rather than lines of code. Jones reports the benchmarking figure of 1.75 coding defects per function point, which he says is based on large amounts of data from different commercial sources (Jones, 1991).

In Chapter 15, we will describe various empirical studies that involved measuring defect densities. In particular, we will look at the effect on defect density of various product and process attributes, and see the extent to which we can predict defect density once these attributes are known.

9.2.1.3 Other quality measures based on defect counts

Defect density is not the only useful defect-based quality measure. For many years, Japanese companies have defined quality in terms of **spoilage**. Specifically, they compute it as

$$\text{system spoilage} = \frac{\text{time to fix post-release defects}}{\text{total system development time}}$$

For example, Tajima and Matsubara described quality improvements at Hitachi in terms of this measure. The results are displayed in Figure 9.8, which confirms that Hitachi has been collecting software metrics data since 1976 (Tajima and Matsubara, 1981).

Inglis describes a set of "standard software quality measures used at AT&T Bell

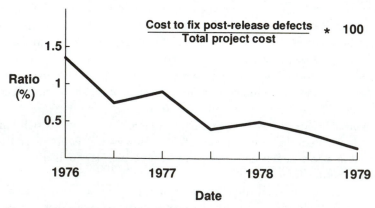

Figure 9.8: Quality improvements at Hitachi

Laboratories," all of which are derived from defects data collection (Inglis, 1985):

- cumulative fault density – faults found internally
- cumulative fault density – faults found by customers
- total serious faults found
- mean time to close serious faults
- total field fixes
- high-level design review errors per KNCSL
- low-level design errors per KNCSL
- code inspection errors per inspected KNCSL
- development test and integration errors found per KNCSL
- system test problems found per developed KNCSL
- first application test site errors found per developed KNCSL
- customer found problems per developed KNCSL.

Clearly, some of these measures require careful data collection.

Assuming that appropriate data-collection procedures are in place, all of the defect-based measures we have discussed may be used for general monitoring purposes and for establishing baselines. In the absence of measures of specific quality attributes, we strongly recommend that these kinds of measures be used. However, it is also important to be aware of the dangers of misinterpreting and misusing these measures. The drawback with using low "defect" rates as if they were synonymous with quality is that, in general, the presence of defects may not lead to subsequent system quality problems. In particular, software faults do not necessarily lead to software failures. Only failures are seen by users, so perceived quality reflects only failure information. As we saw with startling clarity from the Adams study, a preoccupation with faults can paint a misleading picture of quality.

9.2.2   Usability measures

As developers, we sometimes focus on implementing functionality, without much regard for how the user will actually be interacting with the system. The usability of the system plays a big role, not only in customer satisfaction but also in terms of additional functionality and life-cycle costs. Boehm defines usability as follows:

> **Usability** of a software product is the extent to which the product is convenient and practical to use (Boehm *et al.*, 1978).

Our intuitive view of usability is sometimes called *user-friendliness*. Although usability has received widespread attention within the software community, there are few agreed measures that capture our intuitive meaning. However, we can use the definition of software reliability as an analogy and define usability formally as:

> The probability that the operator of a system will not experience a user interface problem during a given period of operation under a given operational profile.

Here, the operational profile represents the way in which we expect the user to interact with the system over time. Computing a measure like this requires extensive and careful data collection in order to formulate a probability distribution for user interface problems. Collecting this data is almost impossible in practice, so we seek a simpler approach. One popular technique is to look for internal characteristics that we think lead to good usability. For example, we often assume that evidence of good usability includes:

- well-structured manuals
- good use of menus and graphics
- informative error messages
- help functions
- consistent interfaces

Unfortunately, we know of no explicit relationships between these internal attributes and the external notion of usability, so the artifacts of good usability do not help us in defining it.

Thus, although we can measure the internal attributes (for example, by counting the number of help screens and error messages, or measuring the structuredness of user manuals), we cannot define them to be measures of usability, just as we could not define structural complexity measures to be measures of quality. In the literature, we find that proposed measures of usability encompass both measures of internal attributes (believed to affect particular views of usability) and measures of particular views of (the external attribute of) usability.

9.2.2.1   External view of usability

Next, we try to decompose usability into more fundamental attributes so that we can measure them. Following Gilb's approach, we can identify these measurable attributes of usability, each of which must be assessed by the user on a particular type of product:

- **Entry level:** this attribute could be measured in terms of experience with similar classes of applications (especially pertinent for popular applications such as word-processing systems or spreadsheets), or simply age (in the case of, for example, a junior school teaching program).
- **Learnability:** this attribute could be measured, for example, in terms of speed of learning; one measure might be hours of training required before independent use is possible.
- **Handling ability:** this attribute could be measured in terms of speed of working when trained, or errors made when working at normal speed.

  EXAMPLE 9.6:   The COQUAMO approach provides automated support for setting targets for and measuring usability (Kitchenham and Pickard, 1987). The system provides a set of templates to be filled in. A completed template for usability is shown in Table 9.3.

Table 9.3: COQUAMO usability template

Classification	general quality: application dependent
Level required	high
Associated qualities	
– synonyms	learnability, operability, user friendliness
– related concepts	understandability
Definition 1	ease with which users can learn to use system
Explosion 1.1	average time for specific classes of user to achieve specific level of competence with system
Measuring units	days
Measuring tool/data source	survey forms and results of survey
Measurement conditions	new graduate intake
	number of people required for test is 20
Worst case	8
Planned level	4
Best case	2
Current level	10
Justification	improvements specifically requested by XYZ
Consequences of failure	cost

This view of usability is concerned with the effort required for learning and operating the system. Although this approach does not produce definitive, objective measures, clear measurable objectives can be set, and we can decide whether the objectives have been met.

The MUSiC project was specifically concerned with defining measures of software usability (Bevan, 1995). The project proposed a number of user performance measures; for instance, **task effectiveness** is defined as

$$\text{task effectiveness} = \frac{\text{quantity} \times \text{quality}}{100}\%$$

The measure tries to capture the notion that the effectiveness with which a user carries out a task has two components: **quantity** of task completed, and **quality** of the goals achieved. Both quantity and quality are measured as percentages. For example, suppose the desired goal is to transcribe a two-page document into a specified format. We could measure quantity as the proportion of transcribed words to original words, and quality as the proportion of non-deviations from the specified format. If we then manage to transcribe 90% of the document, with 3 out of 10 deviations, the task effectiveness is 63%.

The other MUSiC user performance measures are:

$$\text{temporal efficiency} = \frac{\text{effectiveness}}{\text{task time}}$$

$$\text{productive period} = \frac{\text{task time} - \text{unproductive time}}{\text{task time}} \times 100\%$$

$$\text{relative user efficiency} = \frac{\text{user efficiency}}{\text{expert efficiency}} \times 100\%$$

However, the performance view of usability is not the whole story. It fails to capture any notion of user satisfaction, convenience or ease of use. The most direct way to measure user satisfaction is to survey actual users and record the proportion who "like to work with the product." The MUSiC project developed an internationally standardized 50-item questionnaire (taking ten minutes to complete) to assess user satisfaction. This *software usability measurement inventory* (SUMI) provides an overall assessment and usability profile that breaks the overall assessment down into five attributes: effect, efficiency, helpfulness, control and learnability.

9.2.2.2   Internal attributes affecting usability

With the exception of the counting measures, such as number of help screens and menu options, most proposed measures of usability based on internal attributes are actually measures of text structure. These in turn are claimed to be measures of text readability or comprehensibility. Again we have an instance of measures of internal attributes being claimed to be measures of an external attribute; it is claimed that when the measures are applied to user manuals and error messages, they measure usability. However, their use is suspect, and we do not recommend them.

Card's is the only study of which we are aware that attempts specifically to relate an internal view with the external view of usability (Card, Moran, and Newell, 1980). The work relates a user's known key-stroke level to his or her handling ability, measured by the time it will take the user to carry out a task.

9.2.3   *Maintainability measures*

Most software is exercised repeatedly, and some of us are responsible for the upkeep of delivered software. Both before and during this maintenance period, software measurement can be extremely valuable. We want our software to be easy to understand, enhance, or correct; if it is, we say that our software is **maintainable**, and measurements during development can tell us the likelihood that we will meet this goal. Once the software is delivered, measurements can guide us during the maintenance process, so that we can evaluate the impact of a change, or assess the relative merits of several proposed changes or approaches.

We noted in Chapter 5 that maintenance involves several types of changes. The change may be corrective, in that it is correcting a fault that has been discovered in one of the software products. Thus, **corrective maintenance** involves finding and fixing faults. Or the change may be adaptive: the system changes in some way (the hardware is changed, or some part of the software is upgraded), and a given product must be adapted to preserve functionality and performance. Implementing these changes is called **adaptive maintenance**. Changes also occur for preventive reasons; developers discover faults by combing the code to find faults before they become failures. Thus, maintainers are also involved in **preventive maintenance**, where they fix problems before the user sees them. And finally, developers sometimes make perfective changes, rewriting documentation or comments, or renaming a variable or routine in the hope of clarifying the system structure so that new faults are not likely to be introduced as part of other maintenance activities. This **perfective maintenance** differs somewhat from preventive, in that the maintainers are not looking for faults; they are looking for situations that may lead to misinterpretation or misuse. Perfective maintenance may also involve the addition of new functionality to a working, successful system (Pfleeger, 1991).

Maintainability is not restricted to code; it is an attribute of a number of different software products, including specification and design documents, and even test plan documents. Thus, we need maintainability measures for all of the products that we hope to maintain. As with usability, there are two broad approaches to measuring maintainability, reflecting external and internal views of the attribute. Maintainability is an external product attribute, because it is clearly dependent not only on the product, but also on the person performing the maintenance, the supporting documentation and tools, and the proposed usage of the software. The external and more direct approach to measuring maintainability is to measure the maintenance process; if the process is effective, then we assume that the product is maintainable. The alternative, internal approach is to identify internal product attributes (for example, those relating to the structure of the product) and establish that they are predictive of the process measures. We stress once again that, although the internal approach is more practical since the measures can be gathered earlier and more easily, we can never define maintainability solely in terms of such measures.

9.2.3.1 External view of maintainability

Suppose we seek measures to characterize the ease of applying the maintenance process to a specific product. All four types of maintenance activity (corrective, adaptive, preventive, and perfective) are concerned with making specific changes to a product; for simplicity, we refer simply to making changes, regardless of the intent of the change. Once the need for a change is identified, the speed of implementing that change is a key characteristic of maintainability. We can define a measure called **mean time to repair** (MTTR), sometimes measured alternatively as the median time to repair; it is the average time it takes the maintenance team to implement a change and restore the system to working order. Many measures of maintainability are expressed in terms of MTTR.

To calculate this measure, we need careful records of the following information:

- problem recognition time
- administrative delay time
- maintenance tools collection time
- problem analysis time
- change specification time
- change time (including testing and review)

EXAMPLE **9.7:** Figure 9.9 illustrates the mean time to repair the various subsystems for software at a large British firm. This information was useful in

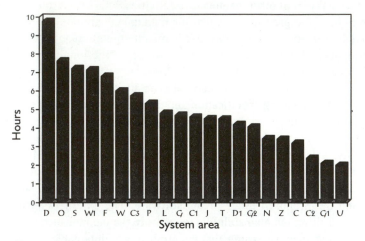

Figure 9.9: Mean time to repair fault, shown by system area

identifying subsystems causing the most problems, and in planning preventive maintenance activities (Pfleeger, Fenton, and Page, 1994).

Other (environment-dependent) measures may be useful if the relevant data are collected and available:

- ratio of total change implementation time to total number of changes implemented
- number of unresolved problems
- time spent on unresolved problems
- percentage of changes that introduce new faults
- number of modules modified to implement a change.

All of these measures in concert paint a picture of the degree of maintenance activity and the effectiveness of the maintenance process. An actual measure of maintainability can be derived from these component measures, tailored to the goals and needs of the organization.

EXAMPLE 9.8: Gilb's approach to measuring quality attributes, introduced in Figure 9.4, is particularly useful for maintainability. Table 9.4 illustrates his suggestions for decomposing maintainability into seven aspects, each of which reveals useful information about overall maintainability. More information about the particular measures can be found in Gilb (1988).

9.2.3.2 Internal attributes affecting maintainability

Numerous measures of internal attributes have been proposed as indicators of maintainability. In particular, a number of the "complexity" measures described in Chapter 8 have been correlated significantly with levels of maintenance effort. As

Table 9.4: Gilb's approach to measuring maintenance

MAINTAINABILITY

SCALE = minutes/NCLOC maintained/year
TEST = logged maintenance minutes for system/ estimated NCLOC
WORST(new code, created by new process) = 0.2 minutes/NCLOC/year
WORST(old code, existing now) = 0.5 minutes/NCLOC/year
PLAN(new code) = 0.1 minutes/NCLOC/year (based on Fagan's inspection
                experience)
PLAN(old code) = 0.3 minutes/NCLOC/year
REFERENCE = estimate based on 5000 programs, average 5000 NCLOC/program,
                70% of 250 programmers in maintenance

we have noted previously, correlation with a characteristic does not make something a measure of that characteristic, so we continue to separate the structural measures from maintainability measures. Nevertheless, some of the structural measures can be used for "risk avoidance" with respect to maintainability. There is a clear intuitive connection between poorly structured and poorly documented products and the maintainability of the implemented products that result from them.

To determine which measures (relating to specific internal attributes) most affect maintainability, we must gather them in combination with external maintainability measures. On the basis of accumulated evidence, we may, for example, identify a particular module having measurably poor structure. We cannot say that such a module will inevitably be difficult to maintain. Rather, past experience tells us that modules with the identified profile have had poor maintainability, so we should investigate the reasons for the given module's poor structure and perhaps restructure it. (There may be other options, such as changing the documentation or enhancing the error-handling capabilities.)

EXAMPLE 9.9: Many organizations investigate the relationship between cyclomatic number and maintenance effort. Based on past history, they develop structural guidelines for code development. The most well-known such guideline is McCabe's; he suggests that no module be allowed a cyclomatic number above 10 (McCabe, 1976).

EXAMPLE 9.10: Porter and Selby have used a statistical technique called classification tree analysis to identify those product measures that are the best predictors of interface errors likely to be encountered during maintenance (Porter and Selby, 1990). The decision tree that results from the classification analysis of their dataset suggests cut-off measures based on past history:

- Between four and eight revisions during design and at least 15 data bindings suggest likely interface errors.
- Interface problems are likely in a module whose primary function is file management where there have been at least nine revisions during design.

These suggestions are particular to the dataset, and are not intended to be general guidelines for any organization. However, the technique can be applied to any database of measurement information, as we saw in Chapter 6.

Cyclomatic number and other simple measures are usually insufficient by themselves as indicators of maintainability, as they capture a very limited view of the software's structure. Many researchers have investigated bounds for a number of more sophisticated measures. The VINAP measure introduced in Chapter 8 is particularly sensitive to identifying maintainability problems through overall poor structure. On the basis of empirical evidence, Bache has proposed a VINAP value of 100 as an upper bound for an individual module.

While measures of internal structural attributes may be important indicators of likely maintenance "hot spots," the correlations do not make explicit the nature of the relationship between the structural attributes and maintainability. However, several models have been proposed to describe such relationships.

EXAMPLE 9.11:   Belady and Lehman have suggested that:

$$M = p + K \exp^{c-d}$$

where M is the total effort expended on maintenance, p is the productive effort, K is an empirical constant, c is a measure of complexity associated with poor design/documentation, and d is a measure of degree of familiarity with the software (Belady and Lehman, 1976).

This model was not validated using empirical data, so it represents only the basis for further investigation. Such models, once validated according to the principles introduced in Chapter 2, can be used to build a crude prediction system in a specific environment, and perhaps to suggest "empirical laws" that might apply to a broader segment of the maintenance community.

For textual products, readability is believed to be a key aspect of maintainability. In turn, the internal attributes determining the structure of documents are considered to be important indicators of readability. The most well-known readability measure is Gunning's **Fog Index** F, defined by:

$$F = 0.4 \times \frac{\text{number of words}}{\text{number of sentences}} + \text{percentage of words of three or more syllables}$$

The measure is supposed to correspond roughly with the number of years of schooling a person would need in order to be able to read a passage with ease and understanding. For large documents, the measure is normally calculated on the basis of an appropriate sample of the text. The Fog Index is sometimes specified in contracts; documentation must be written so that it does not exceed a certain Fog Index level, making it relatively easy for the average user to understand (Gunning, 1968).

There are other readability measures that are specific to software products, such as source code.

EXAMPLE 9.12: De Young and Kampen defined the readability R of programs as:

$$R = 0.295a - 0.499b + 0.13c$$

where a is the average normalized length of variables (where "length of variable" is the number of characters in a variable), b is the number of lines containing statements, and c is McCabe's cyclomatic number. The formula was derived using regression analysis of data about subjective evaluation of readability (De Young and Kampen, 1979).

9.3 SUMMARY

The external attributes that interest us are synonymous with aspects of software quality that, in combination, present a comprehensive picture of quality. Most practitioners focus on reliability, maintainability, and usability, with debate continuing about what other components of quality may be important. However, users and developers can agree among themselves how to measure a particular attribute that interests them. Normally, this measurement involves decomposing an attribute into measurable components, sometimes guided by published quality models or standards. The models make specific assumptions about relationships among attributes. Although it is relatively easy to compute measures using models, the measures are heavily dependent on subjective assessments. However, in the absence of process data and a clearer understanding of the meaning of software quality, we rely on these measures.

A different but popular view equates quality with few defects. Under certain circumstances, defect-based measures can be useful, but we cannot assume that they are always accurate indicators of quality as perceived by the user. Their limitation rests in the fact that software defects discovered during testing, review or compilation may not lead to failures in operation. Thus, high defect levels do not always indicate low quality, and low defect levels may not mean high quality. Nevertheless, defect-based measures provide a powerful basis for baselining and monitoring quality changes.

Measuring maintainability inevitably involves monitoring the maintenance process, capturing process measures such as the time to locate and fix faults. Some internal attribute measures, notably the structural measures described in Chapter 8, may be used as indicators of likely maintainability. Usability must involve assessing people who use the software, and we described several external approaches to usability measurement. There are no internal attributes that obviously predict usability.

9.4 EXERCISES

1. In this chapter, we described three measurable attributes of usability: entry level, learnability, and handling ability. For each one, propose a type of software product for which the attribute could be considered inappropriate.

2. Software-engineering practices are intended to lead to software products with certain desirable quality attributes. For products that might be used in safety-critical environments, dependability is a particularly important requirement. Briefly describe three key attributes of software dependability. List three other quality attributes that might generally be expected to result from good software-engineering practice.

3. The most commonly used software quality measure in industry is the number of faults per thousand lines of product source code. Compare the usefulness of this measure for developers and users. List some possible problems with this measure.

4. Suppose you have overall responsibility for a number of ongoing software projects (some of which are being beta-tested). There are wide quality variations among the projects, and you have available the following measures for each project:

   - mean time to failure
   - mean time to repair reported defects
   - total number of user-reported failures
   - total number of defects found during system testing
   - total number of changes made during development
   - maximum cyclomatic number
   - total project overspend/underspend
   - average number of function points produced per month of programmer effort.

   Discuss the relative merits of these measures for purposes of comparison. Are there any other measures (that are relatively straightforward to collect) that might help you?

5. Compute the Fog Index for:

   - this book and
   - a recent document of your own.

6. Comment on how Gunning's interpretation of the index corresponds to your intuitive perception.

9.5 FURTHER READING

Kaposi and Kitchenham review the popular software quality models and describe an alternative approach.

> Kaposi, A.A. and Kitchenham, B.A., "The architecture of systems quality," *Software Engineering Journal,* 2(1), pp. 2–8, 1987.

Davis and a collection of graduate students describe several simple measures of understandability in the context of measuring the quality of software requirements specifications.

> Davis, A. *et al.*, "Identifying and measuring quality in a software requirements specification," *Proceedings of the First International Software Metrics Symposium*, Baltimore, Maryland, IEEE Computer Society Press, pp. 141–52, 1993.

A special issue of the *Software Quality Journal* (volume 4(2), June 1995) is devoted to software usability assessment.

A recent attempt to define models of maintenance effort (using regression analysis) based on measures of internal attributes is described in:

> Coleman, D., Ash, D., Lowther, B. and Oman, P., "Using metrics to evaluate software system maintainability," *IEEE Computer*, pp. 44–9, August 1994.

A special issue of IEEE Software (volume 13(1), January 1996) addresses the issues of software quality. In particular, it examines what we mean by quality, how we measure it, and how it relates to business value. The introductory article by Kitchenham and Pfleeger reviews the software quality models, and the point-counterpoint pages look at the effects of quality standards.

10 Software reliability: measurement and prediction

Including contributions from the first edition by
Bev Littlewood (City University)

All of the software quality models discussed in Chapter 9 identified software reliability as a key high-level attribute. So it is not surprising that software reliability has been the most extensively studied of all the quality attributes. Quantitative methods for its assessment date back to the early 1970s, evolving from the theory of hardware reliability. In this chapter, we describe these methods, highlighting their limitations as well as their benefits. Building on this work, we describe a state-of-the art approach to software reliability assessment that can provide us with truly accurate predictive measures, providing we have been able to collect data about past failures.

We begin by introducing the basics of reliability theory. Then we address what has become known as the **software-reliability growth problem**: estimating and predicting the reliability of a program as faults are identified and attempts made to fix them. In the approach described here, no individual technique is singled out for unreserved recommendation from the many that have been proposed over the years. We explain in some detail that we reserve judgment, because empirical observation suggests that no such technique has been able consistently to give accurate results over different data sources. Instead, we emphasize the need to examine the accuracy of the actual reliability measures, obtained from several techniques in a particular case, with a view to selecting the one (if any) that yields trustworthy results.

It is important to note that no current methods can feasibly assure software systems with ultra-high reliability requirements. However, the techniques we describe apply to the vast majority of the systems we build: those with relatively modest reliability requirements. Our suggested approach is more computationally intensive than simply adopting a single technique, and it involves some novel statistical techniques. However, we explain the new methods intuitively, and you can apply the methods in practice by using commercially available software tools. The result is reliability measures that are known to be trustworthy, so this approach is well worthwhile.

10.1 BASICS OF RELIABILITY THEORY

The theory of software reliability has its roots in the more general theory of systems and hardware reliability; the hardware approaches are described in many textbooks (Barlow and Proschan, 1975; Catuneaunu and Mihalache, 1989). We apply many of the basic concepts of this general theory to software-reliability problems in the discussion in this chapter.

The basic problem of reliability theory is to predict when a system will eventually fail. In hardware reliability, we are normally concerned with component failures due to physical wear; they can be caused, for example, by corrosion, shock or over-heating. Such failures are probabilistic in nature; that is, we usually do not know exactly when something will fail, but we know that the product eventually will fail, so we can assign a probability that the product will fail at a particular point in time. For example, suppose we know that a hose eventually will dry out, and that the average usage time for the hose is three years. In other words, we can expect that some time around the three-year mark, the hose will begin to leak. The probability of failure of the hose does not go from 0 on day 1094 (one day short of three years) to 1 on day 1095; rather, the probability may start at 0 on day 1 and then increase slowly as we approach the three-year mark. We can graph these daily probabilities over time, and the shape of the curve depends on the characteristics of the hose that affect the failure: the materials, pressure, usage, and so on. In this way, we build a model to describe the likely failure.

The same approach applies in software. We build a basic model of component reliability and create a **probability density function** (pdf) f of time t (written $f(t)$) that describes our uncertainty about when the component will fail.

> **EXAMPLE 10.1:** Suppose we know that a component has a maximum life span of 10 hours. In other words, we know it is certain to fail within 10 hours of use. Suppose also that the component is equally likely to fail during any two time periods of equal length within the 10 hours. Thus, for example, it is just as

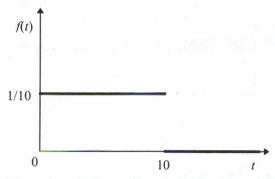

Figure 10.1: Uniform pdf

likely to fail in the first two minutes as in the last two minutes. Then we can illustrate this behavior with the pdf $f(t)$ shown in Figure 10.1. The function $f(t)$ is defined to be 1/10 for any t between 0 and 10, and 0 for any $t > 10$. We say it is **uniform** in the interval of time from $t = 0$ to $t = 10$. (Such an interval is written [0, 10].) In general, for any x we can define the **uniform pdf** over the interval [0, x] to be $1/x$ for any t in the interval [0, x] and 0 elsewhere. Of special interest (for technical reasons) later in this chapter is the pdf that is uniform on the interval [0, 1].

The uniform distribution in Example 10.1 has a number of limitations for reliability modeling. For example, it applies to components only where the failure time is bounded (and where the bound is known). In many situations, no such bound exists, and we need a pdf that reflects the fact that there may be an arbitrarily long time to failure.

EXAMPLE 10.2:   Figure 10.2 illustrates an unbounded pdf that reflects the notion that the failure time occurs purely randomly (in the sense that the future is statistically independent of the past). The function is expressed as the exponential function

$$f(t) = \lambda e^{-\lambda t}$$

In fact, the exponential function follows inevitably from the randomness assumption. As you study reliability, you will see that the exponential is central to most reliability work.

Having defined a pdf $f(t)$, we can calculate the probability that the component fails in a given time interval [t_1, t_2]. Recall from calculus that this probability is simply the area under the curve between the endpoints of the interval. Formally, we compute the area by evaluating the integral:

$$\text{Probability of failure between time } t_1 \text{ and } t_2 = \int_{t_1}^{t_2} f(t)dt$$

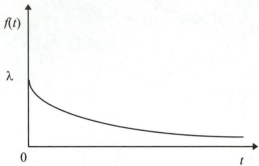

Figure 10.2: Pdf $f(t) = \lambda e^{-\lambda t}$

EXAMPLE 10.3:   For the pdf in Example 10.1, the probability of failure from time 0 to time 2 hours is 1/5. For the pdf in Example 10.2, the probability of failure during the same time interval is:

$$\int_0^2 \lambda e^{-\lambda t} dt = \left[-e^{-\lambda t} \right]_0^2 = 1 - e^{-2\lambda}$$

When $\lambda = 1$, this value is equal to 0.63; when $\lambda = 3$, it is equal to 0.998.

It follows from our definition that the probability of failure at any specific instance of time t is 0, because the time interval has length 0.

Usually, we want to know how long a component will behave correctly before it fails. That is, we want to know the probability of failure from time 0 (when the software first begins operation) to a given time t. The **distribution function** (also called the **cumulative density function**) $F(t)$ is the probability of failure between time 0 and t, expressed as:

$$F(t) = \int_0^t f(t) dt$$

We say that a component **survives** until it fails the first time, so that we can think of survival as the opposite concept to failure. Thus, we define the **reliability function** (also called the **survival function**) $R(t)$ as

$$R(t) = 1 - F(t)$$

This function generates the probability that the component will function properly (that is, without failure) up to time t. If we think of t as the "mission" time of a component, then $R(t)$ is the probability that the component will survive the mission.

EXAMPLE 10.4:   Consider the pdf that is uniform over the interval [0, 1] (as described in Example 10.1). Then $f(t) = 1$ for each t between 0 and 1, and:

$$F(t) = \int_0^t f(t) dt = \int_0^t 1 dt = \left[t \right]_0^t = t$$

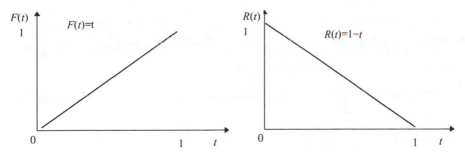

Figure 10.3: Distribution function and reliability function for uniform [0, 1] density function

for each t between 0 and 1. The graphs of both $F(t)$ and $R(t)$ are shown in Figure 10.3.

EXAMPLE 10.5: The distribution function $F(t)$ for the pdf of Example 10.2 is:

$$F(t) = \int_0^t \lambda e^{-\lambda t} dt = \left[-e^{-\lambda t} \right]_0^t = -e^{-\lambda t}$$

Thus,

$$R(t) = e^{-\lambda t}$$

which is the familiar exponential reliability function. Both $F(t)$ and $R(t)$ are shown in Figure 10.4.

Clearly, any one of the functions $f(t)$, $F(t)$, or $R(t)$ may be defined in terms of the others. If T is the random variable representing the yet-to-be-observed time to failure, then any one of these functions gives a complete description of our uncertainty about T. For example:

$$P(T > t) = R(t) = 1 - F(t)$$

where P stands for the probability function. The equation tells us that the probability that the actual time to failure will be greater than a given time t is equal to $R(t)$ or $1 - F(t)$. Thus, having any one of these functions allows us to compute a range of specific reliability measures.

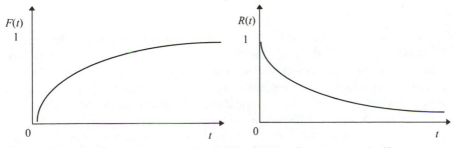

Figure 10.4: Distribution function and reliability function for exponential pdf

The **mean time to failure (MTTF)** is the mean of the probability density function, also called the **expected value** of T (written as $E(T)$). We can compute the mean of the pdf $f(t)$ as

$$E(T) = \int tf(t)dt$$

EXAMPLE 10.6: For the pdf in Example 10.1, the MTTF is 5 hours. The MTTF for the pdf in Example 10.5 is $1/\lambda$.

The **median time to failure** is the point in time t at which the probability of failure after t is the same as the probability of failure before t. It follows that we can calculate its value by finding the m satisfying $F(m) = 1/2$.

EXAMPLE 10.7: For the pdf of Example 10.1, the median time to failure is 5 hours. For the pdf of Example 10.2, we find the median time to failure by solving the following equation for m:

$$\frac{1}{2} = F(m) = \int_0^m \lambda e^{-\lambda t} dt = 1 - e^{-\lambda m}$$

Rearranging this equation gives us:

$$m = \frac{1}{\lambda} \log_e 2$$

So, for example, when $\lambda = 1$, we have $m = 0.69$; when $\lambda = 2$, we have $m = 0.35$.

In some sense, the median time to failure gives us a "middle value" that splits the interval of failure possibilities in two equal parts. We can also consider a given interval, and calculate the probability that a component will fail in that interval. More formally, we define the **hazard rate $h(t)$** as:

$$h(t) = \frac{f(t)}{R(t)}$$

$h(t)\delta t$ is the probability that the component will fail during the interval $[t, t+\delta t]$, given that it had not failed before t.

EXAMPLE 10.8: The hazard rate for the important exponential pdf of Example 10.2 is λ.

So far, we have been concerned only with the uncertainty surrounding the time at which the system fails for the first time. But in many cases, systems fail repeatedly (not always from the same cause), and we want to understand the behavior of all of these failures collectively. Thus, suppose that a system fails at time t_1. We attempt to fix it (for example, by replacing a particular component that has failed), and the system runs satisfactorily until it fails at time t_2. We fix this new problem, and again the system runs until the next failure. After a series of $i-1$ failures, we want to be able to predict the time of the ith failure. This situation is represented in Figure 10.5.

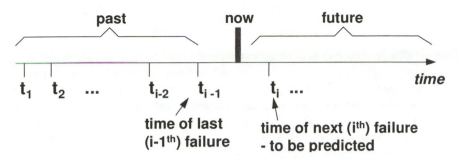

Figure 10.5: Reliability problem for the scenario of attempting to fix failures after each occurrence

For each i, we have a new random variable t_i representing the time of the ith failure. Each t_i has its own probability density function f_i, (and so of course also its own F_i and R_i). In classical hardware reliability, where we are simply replacing failed components with identical working components, we might expect the series of probability density functions to be identical. However, sometimes we can replace each failed component with one of superior quality. For example, we may be able to make a design change to minimize the likelihood of recurrence of the fault that caused the previous one to fail. Here, we expect the probability density function of t_{i+1} to be different from that of the probability density function of t_i. In particular, we would expect the mean of f_{i+1} to be greater than that of f_i; in other words, the new component should fail less often than the old one. In such a situation, we have **reliability growth**: successive observed failure times tend to increase. This situation is not normally considered in hardware reliability, but reliability growth is a goal of software maintenance, so we assume it in our study of software reliability.

In this scenario, there are several other measures that may be useful to us. The hazard rate helped us to identify the likely occurrence of a first failure in an interval. We can define a similar measure to tell us the likelihood of any failure, whether or not it is the first one. The **rate of occurrence of failures** (ROCOF) $\lambda(\tau)$ is defined so that $\lambda(\tau)\delta t$ is the probability of a failure, not necessarily the first, in the interval $[t, t+\delta t]$. ROCOF can be quite difficult to compute in practice. For this reason, ROCOF is often crudely (but wrongly) defined as the number of failures in a unit interval.

A system runs successfully for a time, and then it fails. The measures we have introduced so far have focused on the interruption to successful use. However, once a failure occurs, there is additional time lost as the faults causing the failure are located and repaired. Thus, it is important to know the mean time to repair (MTTR) for a component that has failed. Combining this time with the mean time to failure tells us how long the system is unavailable for use: the **mean time between failures (MTBF)** is simply

$$MTBF = MTTF + MTTR$$

These measures tell us about when the system is available for use. **Availability** is the probability that a component is operating at a given point in time. Pressman, 1992 and others define availability as

$$\text{Availability} = \frac{\text{MTTF}}{\text{MTTF} + \text{MTTR}} \times 100\%$$

However, this formulation is not always meaningful for software.

In the discussion so far, we have assumed that time is measured as continuous operational time. Although we do not address it here, there is an analogous theory in which operational time is treated in discrete units that are normally regarded as **demands** on the system. (We can justify addressing only the continuous case; in practice, we can treat counts of demands as continuous variables with little error, since these inter-failure counts are usually very large.) For example, any control device (such as a simple thermostat) is called into action only when certain environmental conditions prevail. Every time this happens, we have a demand on the device, which is expected to operate in a certain way. It will either succeed or fail. In such situations, the most important measure of reliability may be the **probability of failure on demand**. In software, the discrete scenario is highly relevant when a program is regarded as executing a sequence of inputs or transactions.

10.2 THE SOFTWARE RELIABILITY PROBLEM

There are many reasons for software to fail, but none involves wear and tear. Usually, software fails because of a design problem. Other failures occur when the code is written, or when changes are introduced to a working system. These changes, resulting from new or changed requirements, revised designs, or corrections of existing problems, do not always create failures immediately (if they do at all); the failures are triggered only by certain states and inputs. Ideally, we want our changes implemented without introducing new faults, so that by fixing a known problem we increase the overall reliability of the system. If we can fix things cleanly in this way, we have **reliability growth**.

On the other hand, when hardware fails, the problem is fixed by replacing the failed component with a new or repaired one, so that the system is restored to its previous reliability. Rather than growing, the reliability is simply maintained. Thus, the key distinction between software reliability and hardware reliability is the difference between intellectual failure (usually due to design faults) and physical failure. Although hardware can also suffer from design faults, the extensive theory of hardware reliability does not deal with them. For this reason, the techniques we present represent a theory of **design reliability**, applicable equally to software and hardware. However, we discuss reliability solely in terms of software.

In the discussion that follows, we make two assumptions about the software whose reliability we wish to measure:

1. The software is operating in a real or simulated user environment.
2. When software failures occur, attempts are made to find and fix the faults that caused them.

Table 10.1: Execution times in seconds between successive failures, read left to right in rows

3	30	113	81	115	9	2	91	112	15
138	50	77	24	108	88	670	120	26	114
325	55	242	68	422	180	10	1146	600	15
36	4	0	8	227	65	176	58	457	300
97	263	452	255	197	193	6	79	816	1351
148	21	233	134	357	193	236	31	369	748
0	232	330	365	1222	543	10	16	529	379
44	129	810	290	300	529	281	160	828	1011
445	296	1755	1064	1783	860	983	707	33	868
724	2323	2930	1461	843	12	261	1800	865	1435
30	143	108	0	3110	1247	943	700	875	245
729	1897	447	386	446	122	990	948	1082	22
75	482	5509	100	10	1071	371	790	6150	3321
1045	648	5485	1160	1864	4116				

In the long run, we expect to see the reliability improve; however, there may be short-term decreases caused by ineffective fixes or the introduction of novel faults. We can capture data to help us assess the short- and long-term reliability by monitoring the time between failures. For example, we can track execution time, noting how much time passes between successive failures.

Table 10.1 displays this type of data, expressing the successive execution times, in seconds, between failures of a command-and-control system during in-house testing using a simulation of the real operational environment (Musa, 1979). This data set is unusual, in that great care was taken by Musa in its collection. In particular, it was possible to obtain the actual execution time, rather than merely calendar time (the relevance of which was described in Chapter 5). As we read across the columns and down the rows, our cursory glance detects improvement in reliability in the long run: later periods of failure-free working tend to be significantly longer than earlier ones. Figure 10.6 plots these failure times in sequence, and the improvement trend is clearly visible.

However, the individual times vary greatly, and quite short times are observed even near the end of the data set. Indeed, there are several zero observations recorded, denoting that the system failed again immediately after the previous problem was fixed. It is possible that the short inter-failure times are due to inadequate fixes, so that the same problem persists, or the fix attempt has introduced a new and severe problem. Musa claims that the zero times are merely short execution times rounded, as is all this data, to the nearest second.

We capture this data sequentially, and at any time we can ask several questions about it:

- How reliable is the software now?
- Is it sufficiently reliable that we can cease testing and ship it?
- How reliable will it be after we spend a given amount of further testing effort?
- How long are we likely to have to wait until the reliability target is achieved?

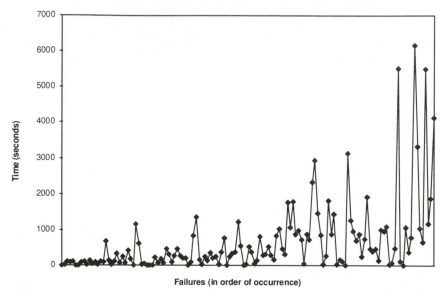

Figure 10.6: Plot of failure times in order of occurrence for the Musa dataset

Reliability measures address each of these questions. The remainder of this section explains how we can answer the first question.

Inherent in the data of Table 10.1 (and later in Table 10.5) is a natural uncertainty about the sequence of numbers: even if we had complete knowledge of all the faults in the software, we would not be able to state with certainty when next it would fail. This result may seem counter-intuitive, but it rests on the fact that we do not know with certainty what inputs will be supplied to the software and in what order, so we cannot predict which fault will be triggered next (and result in failure). In other words, at a given point in time, the time to the next failure is uncertain: it is a **random variable**. But the randomness means that we can apply the reliability theory and functions introduced earlier in this chapter.

Assume that we have seen $i-1$ failures, with recorded inter-failure times

$$t_1, t_2, \ldots, t_{i-1}$$

as illustrated by Musa's data. Fixes have been attempted to correct the underlying faults, and the program has just been set running. Denote by T_i the random variable that represents the yet-to-be-observed next time to failure. Note the convention that random variables are upper case, while observations of random variables (that is, data) are lower case. To answer our first question, the current reliability must be expressed in terms of probability statements about T_i. As we saw earlier, we can describe this probability by knowing any one of: the probability density function (f_i), the distribution function (F_i), or the reliability function (R_i); we have seen that once we know one of them, then we can easily compute the others. We can express the reliability function as:

$$R_i(t) = P(T_i > t) = 1 - F_i(t)$$

Recall that $R_i(t)$ is the probability that the program will survive for a time t before failing next, and $F_i(t)$ is the distribution function of the random variable T_i. We can now compute several measures of current reliability. For example, the mean time to failure is

$$E(T_i) = \int tf_i(t)dt$$

and the median time to failure is the value of m_i satisfying $F_i(m_i) = 1/2$. We can use similar measures to compute the reliability at some specified time in the future.

These theoretical measures answer our question, but in reality we are far from done. The actual functions f_i and F_i (for each i) are unknown to us, so we cannot compute numerical reliability measures. Instead, we must use the observed failure times together with an understanding of the nature of the failure process to obtain estimates $\hat{F}_i(t_i)$ of the unknown distribution functions $F_i(t_i)$. In other words, we are not computing an exact time for the next failure; we are using past history to help us make a prediction of the failure time. This point is quite important, so we emphasize it: *all attempts to measure reliability, however expressed, are examples of prediction.* Even the simplest questions about current reliability relate to a random variable, T_i, that we shall observe in the future. Thus, we are not assessing a product's reliability; rather, software-reliability measurement is a prediction problem, and we use the data we have available (namely $t_1, t_2, \ldots, t_{i-1}$) to make accurate predictions about the future $T_i, T_{i+1}, \ldots$

Chapter 2 tells us that to solve a prediction problem, we must define a prediction system. Consequently, we need:

1. a **prediction model** that gives a complete probability specification of the stochastic process (such as the functions $F_i(T_i)$ and an assumption of independence of successive times);
2. an **inference procedure** for the unknown parameters of the model based on realizations of $t_1, t_2, \ldots, t_{i-1}$
3. a **prediction procedure** that combines the model and inference procedure to make predictions about future failure behavior.

EXAMPLE 10.9: We can construct a crude prediction system in the following way:

1. **The model:** if we assume that failures occur purely randomly, then Example 10.2 tells us that the model is exponential. Thus, for each i, we can express the distribution function as:

$$F_i(t_i) = 1 - e^{-\lambda_i t_i}$$

2. **Inference procedure:** there is one unknown parameter for each i, namely λ_i. We have seen in Example 10.6 that, for this model, the

mean time to next failure is $1/\lambda_i$. A naive inference procedure for computing λ_i is to calculate the average of the two previously observed values of t_i. That is, we estimate that

$$\frac{1}{\lambda_i} = \frac{t_{i-2} + t_{i-1}}{2}$$

and solve for λ_i

$$\lambda_i = \frac{2}{t_{i-2} + t_{i-1}}$$

3. **Prediction procedure:** we calculate the mean time to i^{th} failure by substituting our predicted value of λ_i in the model. The mean time to failure is $1/\lambda_i$, so we have the average of the two previously observed failure times. Alternatively, we can predict the median time to i^{th} failure, which we know from Example 10.7 is equal to $1/\lambda_i \log 2$.

We can apply this prediction system to the data in Table 10.1. When $i = 3$, we have observed $t_1 = 3$ and $t_2 = 30$. So we estimate the mean of the time to failure T_3 to be $33/2 = 15.5$. We continue this procedure for each successive observation, t_i, so that we have:

- for $i = 4$, we find that $t_2 = 30$ and $t_3 = 113$, so we estimate T_4 to be 71.5;
- for $i = 5$, we have $t_3 = 113$ and $t_4 = 81$, so we estimate T_5 to be 97;
- and so on.

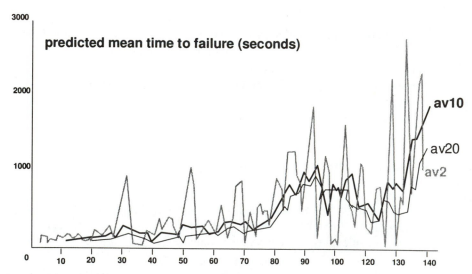

Figure 10.7: Plots from various crude predictions using data from Table 10.1 (The x-axis shows the failure number, and the y-axis is the predicted mean time to failure (in seconds) after a given failure occurs.)

The results of this prediction procedure are depicted as the light gray line in Figure 10.7. Many other, more sophisticated procedures could be used for the prediction. For example, perhaps our predictions would be more accurate if, instead of using just the two previous observed values of t_i, we use the average of the 10 previously observed t_i. A plot for this variation, and another for using the previous 20 observed t_i, are also shown in Figure 10.7.

For predicting the median time to next failure, our procedures are similar. For this distribution, the median is $1/\lambda_i \log_e 2$ and the mean is $1/\lambda_i$, so the procedure is the same, except that all the results above are multiplied by $\log_e 2$ (that is, by a factor of about 0.7).

Many prediction systems have been proposed, some of which use models and procedures far more sophisticated than Example 10.9. We as users must decide which ones are best for our needs. In the next section, we review several of the most popular models, each of which is parametric (in the sense that it is a function of a set of input parameters). Then, we can turn to questions of accuracy, as accuracy is critical to the success of reliability prediction.

10.3   PARAMETRIC RELIABILITY GROWTH MODELS

Suppose we are modeling the reliability of our program according to the assumptions of the previous sections, namely that the program is operating in a real or simulated user environment, and that we keep trying to fix faults after failures occur. We make two further assumptions about our program:

1.   Executing the program involves selecting inputs from some space I (the totality of all possible inputs).
2.   The program transforms the inputs into outputs (comprising a space O).

This transformation is shown schematically in Figure 10.8, where P is a program transforming the inputs of I to outputs in O. For a typical program, the input space is extremely large; in most cases, a complete description of the input space is not available. Also, different users may have different purposes in using the program, or they may have different habits, so the probability that one user will select a given input may be different from the probability for another user. For example, in a word-processing program, one user may move from one page to another by using function keys, while a second may use the mouse and click on buttons. Thus, we make a simplifying assumption that a single user is running and using the program.

The output space consists of two types of outputs: those that are acceptable (the program runs as it should), and those that are not (a failure occurs). In other words, a program fails when an input is selected that cannot be transformed into an acceptable output. The totality of inputs leading to unacceptable outputs is labeled I_F in Figure 10.8. In practice, a failure is detected when the output obtained by processing a particular input is compared with the output that ought to have been produced

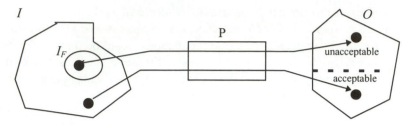

Figure 10.8: Basic model of program execution

according to the program's specification. Detection of failures is, of course, no trivial task, and we do not address this problem here.

Given these assumptions, there are two sources of uncertainty in the failure behavior:

1. *Uncertainty about the operational environment.* Even if we were to know I_F completely, we cannot know when next we will encounter it.
2. *Uncertainty about the effect of fault removal.* We do not know whether a particular attempt to fix a fault has been successful. And even if the fix is successful, we do not know how much improvement has taken place in the failure rate. That is, we do not know whether the fault that has been removed causes a large or small increase in the resulting reliability.

Good reliability models must address both types of uncertainty. Modeling type-1 uncertainty is easiest, as it seems reasonable to assume that the set I_F is encountered purely randomly during program execution. That is, the time to next failure (and so the inter-failure times) has, conditionally, an exponential distribution. As we saw in Example 10.9, if $T_1, T_2, \ldots$ are the successive inter-failure times, then we have a complete description of the stochastic process if we know the rates $\lambda_1, \lambda_2, \ldots$

Thus, the most difficult problem is to model type-2 uncertainty: the way in which the value of λ changes as debugging proceeds. The popular software reliability models can be characterized by the way they handle this uncertainty. We present the details of each of several models, but we acknowledge that the mathematics can be daunting; complete understanding of the details is not necessary for comparing and contrasting the models. However, the details are useful for implementing and tailoring the models.

10.3.1 The Jelinski–Moranda model

The Jelinski–Moranda model (denoted JM in subsequent figures) is the earliest and probably the best-known reliability model (Jelinski and Moranda, 1972). It assumes that, for each i,

$$F_i(t_i) = 1 - e^{-\lambda_i t_i}$$

with

$$\lambda_i = (N - i + 1)\,\phi$$

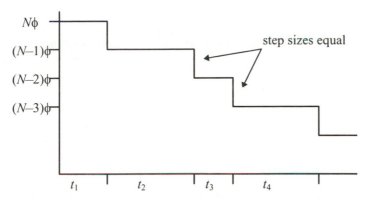

Figure 10.9: Jelinski–Moranda model hazard rate (y-axis) plotted against time (x-axis)

Here N is the initial number of faults, and ϕ is the contribution of each fault to the overall failure rate. Thus, the underlying model is the exponential model, so that the type-1 uncertainty is random and exponential. There is no type-2 uncertainty in this model; it assumes that fault detection and correction begin when a program contains N faults, and that fixes are perfect (in that they correct the fault causing the failure, and they introduce no new faults). The model also assumes that all faults have the same rate. Since we know from Example 10.8 that the hazard rate for the exponential distribution is λ, it follows that the graph of the Jelinski–Moranda hazard rate looks like the step function in Figure 10.9. In other words, between the $(i-1)^{st}$ and i^{th} failure, the hazard rate is $(N - i + 1)\, \phi$.

The inference procedure for Jelinski–Moranda is called **maximum likelihood estimation**; its details need not concern us here, but they may found in Cox and Hinckley (1982). In fact, maximum likelihood is the inference procedure for all the models we present. For a given set of failure data, this procedure produces estimates of N_i and ϕ_i. Then, t_i is predicted by substituting these estimates in the model. (We shall see the Jelinski–Moranda median time to failure predictions in Figure 10.10, based on the data of Table 10.1.)

EXAMPLE 10.10: We can examine the reliability behavior described by the Jelinski–Moranda model to determine whether it is a realistic portrayal. Consider the successive inter-failure times where $N = 15$ and $f = 0.003$. Table 10.2 shows both the mean time to the ith failure and also a simulated set of failure times (produced using random numbers in the model). In the simulated data, the nature of the exponential distribution produces high variability, but generally there is reliability growth. Notice that as i approaches 15, the failure times become large. Since the model assumes there are no faults remaining after $i = 15$, the mean time to the sixteenth failure is said to be infinite.

There are three related criticisms of this model.

Table 10.2: Successive failure times for Jelinski–Moranda when $N = 15$ and $\phi = 0.003$

i	Predicted mean time to ith failure	Simulated time to ith failure
1	22	11
2	24	41
3	26	13
4	28	4
5	30	30
6	33	77
7	37	11
8	42	64
9	48	54
10	56	34
11	67	183
12	83	83
13	111	17
14	167	190
15	333	436

1. The sequence of rates is considered by the model to be purely deterministic. This assumption may not be realistic.
2. The model assumes all faults contribute equally to the hazard rate. The Adams example in Chapter 9 provides empirical evidence that faults vary dramatically in their contribution to program unreliability.
3. We will show that the reliability predictions obtained from the model are poor; they are usually too optimistic.

10.3.2 Other models based on Jelinski–Moranda

Several models are variations of Jelinski–Moranda. **Shooman's model** is identical (Shooman, 1983). The **Musa model** (one of the most widely used) has Jelinski–Moranda as a foundation but builds some novel features on top. It was the first model to insist on using execution time to capture inter-failure times. However, it also includes a model of calendar time, so that we can make project management estimates, such as the time until target reliability is achieved (Musa, 1975). By tying reliability to project management, Musa encouraged the widespread use of reliability modeling in many environments, particularly telecommunications.

10.3.3 The Littlewood model

The **Littlewood model** (denoted LM in subsequent figures) attempts to be a more realistic finite fault model than Jelinski–Moranda by treating the hazard rates (corresponding to the different faults) as independent random variables. Thus, whereas Jelinski–Moranda is depicted with equal steps, Littlewood has steps of differing size.

In fact, these rates are assumed to have a *gamma* distribution with parameters (α, β). Unlike the Jelinski–Moranda model, Littlewood introduces two sources of uncertainty for the rates; thus, we say that the model is *doubly stochastic*. In this model, there is a tendency for the larger-rate faults (that is, the faults with larger "steps," and so larger contribution to unreliability) to be encountered (and so removed) earlier than the smaller ones, but this sequence is itself random. The model therefore represents the diminishing returns in improved reliability that come from additional testing.

Both the Jelinski–Moranda and Littlewood models are in a general class called **exponential order statistic models** (Miller, 1986). In this type of model, the faults can be seen as competing risks: at any point in time, any of the remaining faults can cause a failure, but the chance that it will be a particular fault is determined by the hazard rate for that fault. It can be shown that the times, X_j, at which the faults show themselves (measured from when observation of the particular program began) are independent, identically distributed random variables. For the Jelinski–Moranda model, this distribution is exponential with parameter ϕ. For the Littlewood model this distribution has a Pareto distribution:

$$P(X_j < x) = 1 - \left(\frac{\beta}{\beta + x}\right)^{\alpha}$$

10.3.4   The Littlewood–Verrall model

The Littlewood–Verrall model (denoted LV in subsequent figures) is a simple one that, like the Littlewood model, captures the doubly-stochastic nature of the conceptual model of the failure process (Littlewood and Verrall, 1973). Here we make the usual assumption that the inter-failure times, T_i, are conditionally independent exponentials with probability density functions given by:

$$\text{pdf}\,(t_i | \Lambda_i = \lambda_i) = \lambda_i e^{-\lambda_i t_i}$$

The λ_i are assumed to be independent gamma variables:

$$\text{pdf}\,(\lambda_i) = \frac{\psi(i)^{\alpha-1} e^{-\psi(i)\lambda}}{\Gamma(\alpha)}$$

In this model, reliability growth (or decay) is controlled by the sequence $\psi(i)$. If this sequence is an increasing function of i, it can be shown that the λ_is are stochastically decreasing and hence the T_is stochastically increasing. The user chooses the ψ family; usually $\psi(i) = \beta_1 + \beta_2 i$ works quite well. The sign of β_2 then determines whether there is growth or decay in reliability; therefore, the data themselves are allowed to determine whether the reliability is increasing, decreasing or constant via the estimate of β_2.

10.3.5   Non-homogeneous Poisson process models

Consider again the Musa data in Table 10.1. It consists of a sequence of "point events," where each point has no "memory." In other words, the future of the process is statistically independent of the past. We call this behavior **non-stationary**, and it can be modeled by what is called a **non-homogeneous Poisson process (NHPP)** (Cox and Iham, 1980). The behavior of the process is in a sense completely random, determined entirely by the rate at which failures are occurring. A minor drawback to this approach is that most such processes have rate functions that change continuously in time. This behavior may not be realistic for software reliability; it can be argued that, for software, the only changes that take place are the jumps in reliability occurring when a fix is made. However, one way of constructing a non-homogeneous Poisson process is to assume that N (the total number of initial faults) is Poisson-distributed; we can use this process as the probability specification in models such as Jelinski–Moranda and Littlewood (Miller, 1986).

The *Goel–Okumoto model* (denoted GO in subsequent figures) is a NHPP variant of Jelinski–Moranda (Goel and Okumoto, 1979). Similarly, the *Littlewood NHPP model* (denoted LNHPP in subsequent figure) is a NHPP variant of the original Littlewood model. Numerous other rate functions have been proposed for non-homogeneous Poisson process models, including the *Duane model* (DU), originally devised for hardware reliability growth arising from burn-in testing (eliminating faulty components in complex systems by forcing them to fail early in testing) (Duane, 1964).

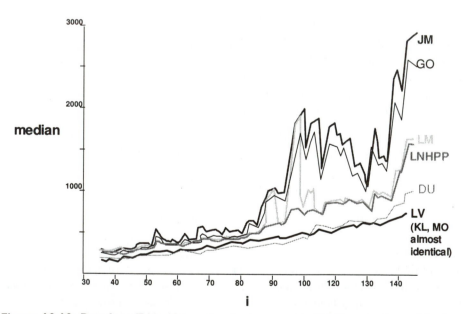

Figure 10.10: Data from Table 10.1 analyzed using several reliability-growth models; the current median time to next failure is plotted on the *y*-axis against failure number on the *x*-axis. We use the model abbreviations introduced in the previous sections; two additional models are considered here: KL (Keiller–Littlewood) and MO (Musa–Okumoto)

10.3.6   General comments on the models

We have introduced only a few of the many models proposed over the years. All above are parametric models, in the sense that they are defined by the values of several parameters. For example, the Jelinski–Moranda model is defined by the values of ϕ and N. As we have noted, using a model involves a two-step process: selecting a model, and then estimating the unknown parameter values from available data. You can think of this estimation as computing the likely values of the parameters, and in fact you calculate the maximum likelihood estimates. Fortunately, practitioners can avoid the intimidating mathematics, as there is commercially-available software to perform the extensive calculations (Reliability and Statistical Consultants, 1988).

Some researchers prefer a different approach to estimating the parameters. They suggest finding the *Bayesian posterior distribution* of the unknown parameters (de Groot, 1970), and from this compute the Bayesian predictive distribution of T_i (Aitchison and Dunsmore, 1975). However, this procedure can be extremely computationally intensive.

For the rest of this chapter, we shall assume that you have access to a tool or spreadsheet in order to perform the calculations necessary to use the various reliability models. The next step in choosing an appropriate reliability model is evaluating model accuracy. We assist your evaluation by describing a formal procedure for determining which models perform best on a given set of data. In fact, our technique is useful regardless of the models' assumptions.

10.4   PREDICTIVE ACCURACY

Experience reveals great variation in the accuracy of software-reliability prediction models (Abdel-Ghaly, Chan, and Littlewood, 1986). Certainly, no single method can be trusted to give accurate results in all circumstances. In fact, accuracy is likely to vary from one data set to another, and from one type of prediction to another.

Figure 10.10 displays the results of applying several models to the data of Table 10.1; it clearly illustrates the variability of prediction. Each model is used to generate 100 successive estimates of current reliability, expressed as the median time to next failure. Although all models agree that reliability is increasing, there is considerable disagreement about what has actually been achieved, particularly at later stages of testing. Not only are some models more optimistic in their estimates of reliability than others, but some are also more "noisy," giving highly fluctuating predictions as testing proceeds.

Results like these are typical, and they can be disappointing for potential users of the techniques. Users want trustworthy predictions, so we must question predictive accuracy and devise means of detecting inaccurate results.

There are two main ways in which reliability predictions can be inaccurate:

- Predictions are **biased** when they exhibit a reasonably consistent departure from the truth (that is, the true reliability). We will see that the most optimistic of the predictions in Figure 10.10, Jelinski–Moranda's, are indeed truly optimistic in comparison with the true median, and the most pessimistic, Littlewood–Verrall's, are truly pessimistic.
- Predictions are **noisy** when successive predictions of, say, the median times to next failure fluctuate in magnitude more than is the case for the true medians.

To see the difference between bias and noise, consider reliability estimates with fluctuations centered approximately on the truth. That is, the positive and negative errors have about the same magnitude. This consistency of departure means that the estimates are not biased. However, there is a great deal of noise, so no single prediction can be trusted, since it may exhibit a large error.

It is common for poor predictions to exhibit both bias and unwarranted noise. The difficulty we face in detecting bias and noise is that, of course, we do not know the true reliabilities against which the predictions are to be judged. There is no evidence merely from Figure 10.10 to indicate which, if any, of the series of predictions is accurate. In particular, we must bear in mind that the figure shows only a simple summary (the medians) of the successive reliability predictions; usually, we are interested in bias or noise in the complete sequence of predictive distribution functions $\hat{F}_i(t_i)$.

To address this problem, we introduce some formal techniques for analyzing the accuracy of reliability predictions. The techniques emulate how users would actually behave (similar to the descriptions in Examples 10.9 and 10.10). Typically, users make a prediction, observe the actual outcome of the predicted event, and repeat this process several times to obtain a sequence of predictive and actual data. Finally, they evaluate this evidence to determine whether the actual observations differ significantly from what had been predicted.

10.4.1   Dealing with bias: the u-plot

We consider first the problem of bias. To detect bias in the medians (as plotted in Figure 10.10), we can count the number of times the observed t_i is smaller than the (earlier) predicted median. If, for n observations, this count differs significantly from $n/2$, then we are likely to have bias. For example, in the data plotted in Figure 10.10, the Jelinski–Moranda model (JM) has 66 of 100 instances where the actual observations are smaller than the predicted median. The predicted medians are consistently too large, confirming that Jelinski–Moranda is too optimistic in its portrayal of the software-reliability growth, as expressed by the medians. If we consider only the last 50 predictions in the data, we find the effect to be even more dramatic: 39 out of the 50 observations are smaller than the corresponding predicted medians. Thus, the clear increase in reliability predicted by Jelinski–Moranda and displayed in Figure 10.10 (about half-way through the plot) is misleading. Yet this result is quite surprising. Intuitively, we would expect a model to produce more accurate answers later (when more data are available) than earlier (with less data). Similarly, the medians of the Littlewood–Verrall model show that the model is actually too pessimistic in its median predictions. On the other hand, there is no evidence here to suggest that the medians of LNHPP are biased.

Of course, lack of bias in the median does not guarantee lack of bias in other reliability measures. What we really seek is evidence of consistent differences between the sequences of functions $\hat{F}_i(t_i)$ (the predictions) and $F_i(t_i)$ (the actual values). To tackle this problem, we introduce the notion of the u-plot.

To construct a **u-plot** for a reliability model, we begin by computing the sequence of numbers $\{u_i\}$ given by

$$u_i = \hat{F}_i(t_i)$$

Each element of the sequence is simply the estimate of $P(T_i < t_i)$ (the probability that the observed inter-failure time is less than the previously predicted probability). In other words, we are estimating the likelihood that the actual observation was less than what we had predicted it would be.

EXAMPLE 10.11: In Example 10.9, we defined a crude prediction system in which the mean time to next failure (based on the exponential model) was the average of the two previously observed failure times. If we apply this prediction system to the successive failure time data of the Musa data, we generate the predictions shown in the third column of Table 10.3.

In this case, the estimated distribution function is

$$\hat{F}_i(t_i) = 1 - e^{-\hat{\lambda}_i t_i}$$

where

$$\hat{\lambda}_i = \frac{1}{\text{predicted mean time to } i\text{th failure}}$$

Table 10.3: Generating u_i values for the crude prediction system of Example 10.9 (based on the Musa data)

i	t_i	Predicted mean time to ith failure	$\hat{\lambda}_i$	u_i
1	3			
2	30	16.5	0.061	0.84
3	113	71.5	0.014	0.79
4	81	97	0.010	0.57
5	115	98	0.010	0.69
6	9	62	0.016	0.14
7	2	5.5	0.182	0.30
8	91	46.5	0.022	0.86
9	112	101.5	0.010	0.67
10	15	63.5	0.016	0.21

From this information, we can compute the sequence of u_is. For example:

$$u_2 = \hat{F}_2(t_2) = \hat{F}_2(30) = 1 - e^{-\frac{1}{16.5}30} = 0.84$$

Similarly, we compute the rest of the u_is as shown in the final column of Table 10.3.

Next, we construct the u-plot, shown in Figure 10.11, by placing the values of the u_is along the horizontal axis (which runs from 0 to 1) and then drawing the step function where each step has height $1/(n+1)$ (assuming there are n u_is).

A set of predictions is said to be **perfect** if:

$$\hat{F}_i(t_i) - F_i(t_i)$$

for all i. If we have perfect predictions, then the set of u_i will look like realizations of independent random variables with a uniform distribution on the interval (0, 1) (Dawid, 1984). Thus, we draw the uniform distribution (which is the line of unit slope) on the u-plot and compare the two. Any significant difference between them indicates a deviation between predictions and observations. We measure the degree of deviation by using the **Kolmogorov distance** (the maximum vertical distance), as shown in Figure 10.11.

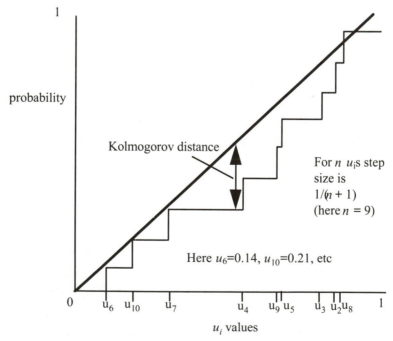

Figure 10.11: The u-plot (computed for the first 9 values of Example 10.11)

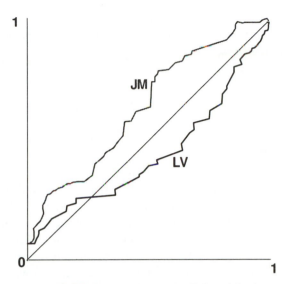

Figure 10.12: Jelinski–Moranda (JM) and Littlewood–Verrall (LV) *u*-plots for 100 predictions of the one-step-ahead predictions

EXAMPLE 10.12: Figure 10.12 shows two *u*-plots for the most extreme reliability models of Figure 10.10: Jelinski–Moranda (JM) and Littlewood–Verrall (LV), using the data of Table 10.1. To see whether the two plots differ significantly from the line of unit slope, we measure the Kolmogorov distance (the greatest vertical distance) of a plot from the line of unit slope. For JM, this distance is 0.190, which is statistically significant at the 1% level; for LV, the distance is 0.144, which is significant at the 5% level. Thus, this data set provides very strong evidence against the accuracy of the JM predictions, and quite strong evidence against those from LV.

The plots show us something more important than the simple evidence of inaccuracy; they tell us about the detailed nature of the prediction errors. The plot for JM is always above the line of unit slope, indicating that there are too many small *u* values. That is, the model tends to underestimate the probability of failure before t_i (the later, actual, observed failure time) and so is too optimistic. Conversely, there is evidence that LV is largely below the line of unit slope and so is too pessimistic in its predictions. These conclusions certainly agree with Figure 10.10, where we saw that JM was relatively more optimistic than LV, and the earlier analysis in terms solely of the medians. We now have evidence that JM is objectively optimistic when compared with the truth, and this optimism exists in all measures of current reliability (that is, not only in the median, but also in other percentiles of the time to failure distribution). A user might reasonably conclude from this analysis that the truth lies somewhere between LV and JM predictions. For example, in Figure 10.10, we might expect the LNHPP predictions to be better than LV and JM. In fact, a *u*-plot of these predictions is very close to uniform (the Kolmogorov distance, 0.098, is not statistically significant), which generalizes the result we have already seen for the median predictions.

10.4.2 Dealing with noise

As we have seen, the other major source of inaccuracy in predictions is *noise*. In fact, it is quite easy to obtain predictions that are close to being unbiased but are useless because of their excessive noise.

> **EXAMPLE 10.13:** If we seek an unbiased estimate of the median of T_i, we can use the median value of the preceding three observed inter-event times t_{i-1}, t_{i-2}, and t_{i-3}. For example, consider the data in Table 10.1. Using the three previous inter-event times, we predict the median of T_4 to be 30, the median of T_5 to be 81, the median of T_6 to be 113, and so on. There is only a slight pessimistic bias here if the true reliability of the software is changing slowly. However, the individual median estimates obtained this way are likely to be very far from the true values, and they will fluctuate wildly even when the true median sequence is changing smoothly.

Informally, we can think of noise as the fluctuation we find in predictions. We must consider whether the underlying true reliability is also fluctuating in a similar way. If the true reliability is not fluctuating, then any noise in the predictions is **unwarranted**. On the other hand, if the true reliability really is fluctuating, then any accurate prediction should also fluctuate. For example, the true reliability of a system or program may in fact suffer reversals of fortune, with frequent decreases corresponding to the introduction of new faults during attempts to fix old ones. In this case, what appears to be noise in the prediction is actually there for good reason, and we want the predictions to track these reversals; if they do so, the predictions exhibit **absolute noise**.

It is possible to devise a measure of absolute noise in a sequence of predictions. Then, using such a measure, we might expect the median predictions of Jelinski–Moranda in Figure 10.10 to be more noisy than those of Littlewood–Verrall, which exhibits quite smooth growth. Similarly, we might find that the simple-minded medians proposed in Example 10.13 (based on only three data points) would be even noisier. However, looking at absolute noise can be misleading. It is really unwarranted noise that affects the quality of prediction.

So far, no one has been able to devise a test that is sensitive solely to such unwarranted noise. Instead, we use a more general tool, responsive to inaccuracies of prediction of all types, including unwarranted noise and bias.

10.4.3 Prequential likelihood function

We have seen that different prediction models can generate vastly different predictions for the same set of data. We can characterize the differences in terms of noise and bias, but so far we have seen no way of selecting the best model for our needs. However, help is at hand. We can use the *prequential likelihood function* to compare several competing sets of predictions on the same data source, and to select the one that produces the "globally most accurate" predictions. Details of the mathematical theory behind prequential likelihood can be found in Dawid (1984); the following is an informal and intuitive interpretation. (The word "prequential", commonly used in the statistical community, was introduced by Phil Dawid, who defined the prequential likelihood technique. It is a merger of the two words, "predicting" and "sequential".)

Assume, as before, that we want to estimate $F_i(t)$, the distribution of T_i, on the basis of the observed $t_1, t_2, \ldots, t_{i-1}$. Using a prediction system, A, we make predictions for a range of values of i, say from $i = m$ to $i = n$. After each prediction, we eventually observe the actual t_i.

The **prequential likelihood function** for these predictions, coming from model A, is defined as:

$$PL = \prod_{i=m}^{i=n} \hat{f}_i(t_i)$$

where $\hat{f}_i(t_i)$ is the estimate of the probability density function of T_i.

Notice how this estimating technique works. We begin by estimating the probability density function of the random variable T_i, using the observations of previous times between failures. Then, when the actual t_i is observed, we substitute the actual observations in the probability density function. This procedure is similar to the way in which we formed the u-plot from the distribution function.

EXAMPLE 10.14: In Example 10.9, we built a crude prediction system by using an exponential model in which we estimated the mean time to next failure by simply computing the average of the two previously observed values. In this situation, the estimated probability density function is described by the equation:

$$\hat{f}_i(t_i) = \hat{\lambda}_i e^{-\hat{\lambda}_i t_i}$$

where $1/\hat{\lambda}_i$ is the average of t_{i-2} and t_{i-1}. Using the data of Table 10.1 and a spreadsheet package, we can easily compute the sequence of prequential likelihood functions. Table 10.4 shows the results of these calculations for i ranging from 1 to 13. In the table, the right-hand column contains the prequential likelihood values. For instance, when $i = 5$:

$$PL = \prod_{i=3}^{i=5} \hat{f}_i(t_i) = \hat{f}_3(t_3) \times \hat{f}_4(t_4) \times \hat{f}_5(t_5)$$

Table 10.4: Computing the sequence of prequential likelihood functions for the crude prediction system of Example 10.9

i	t_i	T_i	$\hat{\lambda}_i$	$\hat{f}_i(t_i)$	PL
3	113	16.5	0.060606	0.0000643	6.43E-05
4	81	71.5	0.013986	0.0045050	2.9E-07
5	115	97	0.010309	0.0031502	9.13E-10
6	9	98	0.010204	0.0093087	8.5E-12
7	2	62	0.016129	0.0156170	1.33E-13
8	91	5.5	0.181818	0.0000000	1.57E-21
9	112	46.5	0.021505	0.0019342	3.04E-24
10	15	101.5	0.009852	0.0084987	2.59E-26
11	138	63.5	0.015748	0.0017923	4.64E-29
12	50	76.5	0.013072	0.0067996	3.15E-31
13	77	94	0.010638	0.0046894	1.48E-33

Similarly, we can compute the sequence of prequential likelihood values of other prediction systems. For example, an exercise at the end of this chapter asks you to calculate PL for the prediction system where the estimate of the mean time to next failure is the average of the three previously-observed values.

To see how prequential likelihood allows us to compare models, suppose we have two candidate sets of predictions, from prediction systems A and B. For each prediction system, we compute the respective prequential likelihood functions, denoting them as PL_A and PL_B. The major theoretical result in Dawid (1984) states that if

$$\frac{\text{PL}_A}{\text{PL}_B} \to \infty \text{ as } n \to \infty$$

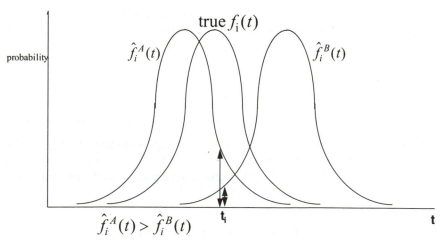

Figure 10.13: How prequential likelihood works

then model A discredits model B, in the sense that model B can be rejected. In a looser interpretation of this result, we can say that if $\dfrac{\text{PL}_A}{\text{PL}_B}$ increases consistently as n increases, then A is producing more accurate predictions than B.

Figure 10.13 is an intuitive justification for this looser result. Here we examine a single prediction of T_i. We show the true probability density function, $f_i(t)$, and two predictions of it. Clearly the prediction system for A is closer to the "truth" and is thus more accurate. When we eventually see the actual t_i, it is most likely to lie in the central body of the true probability density function $f_i(t)$, from which it is sampled. The body of this probability density function covers the tails of both the predictive probability density functions. The further away that a prediction is from the truth, the smaller will be the height of this predictive probability density function at this point. In other words,

$$f_i^B(t)$$

will be small compared to

$$f_i^A(t)$$

(which in turn is smaller than the true value). For a consistently poor set of predictions, this effect will tend to occur for each of the terms making up the product in the PL equation. Thus, if model B is giving consistently worse results than A, the ratio

$$\frac{\text{PL}_A}{\text{PL}_B}$$

will increase.

This technique is responsive to the various ways in which predictions can be inaccurate. For instance, if a set of predictions were consistently optimistic (a special case of what we have called bias), the predictive probability density function would

Table 10.5: Prequential likelihood analysis of LNHPP and JM predictions for the data of Table 10.1

n	Prequential likelihood ratio LNHPP:JM
10	1.28
20	2.21
30	2.54
40	4.55
50	2.14
60	4.15
70	66.0
80	1516
90	8647
100	6727

tend to be displaced to the right in comparison with the true probability density function. If predictions were noisy but unbiased, the sequence of successive predictive probability density functions would be randomly displaced to left and right. In these cases, and for other kinds of departure from accuracy, the prequential likelihood will detect when one series of predictions is inferior to another.

> **EXAMPLE 10.15:** Table 10.5 shows a prequential likelihood comparison of the predictions made by the LNHPP and JM models on the data of Table 10.1. Here, n is the number of predictions on which the prequential likelihood ratio (PLR) is based. Thus, when $n = 10$, the PLR involves predictions of T_{35}, ..., T_{44}; when $n = 15$, it involves T_{35}, ..., T_{49}, and so on. From this analysis, there is little difference between the models for about the first 60 predictions (that is, until about T_{95}), but thereafter there is strong evidence of the superiority of LNHPP to JM. This comparison confirms the earlier analysis, since it was precisely after this late stage that the JM predictions become too optimistic.

Of course, the fact that a particular model has been producing superior predictions in the past is no guarantee that it will continue to do so in the future. However, experience suggests that such reversals on a given data source are quite rare. Certainly, if method A has been producing better predictions than method B in the recent past, then it seems sensible to prefer A for current predictions.

10.4.4   Choosing the best model

We have presented several ideas for contrasting models, including examining basic assumptions, degree of bias and noise, and prequential likelihood. These techniques may help you to decide whether one model is less plausible than another, but they do not point to a definite best model. The behavior of models depends greatly on the data to which they are applied, and we have seen how several models can produce dramatically different results even for the same data set. In fact, the accuracy of models also varies from one data set to another (Abdel-Ghaly, Chan, and Littlewood, 1986; Littlewood, 1988). And sometimes no parametric prediction system can produce reasonably accurate results!

> **EXAMPLE 10.16:** Table 10.6 shows another of Musa's data sets. Using this data, we can plot the median time to failure for several different prediction systems, shown in Figure 10.14. There is clear and profound disagreement among the predictions: all but two sets are in close agreement with one another, but differ by an order of magnitude from the remaining two (Littlewood–Verrall (LV) and Keillor–Littlewood (KL)), which are close to one another. Advocates of majority voting might believe that the truth probably lies closer to the more optimistic sets of predictions, but in fact this is not so. Prequential likelihood analysis shows that the pair of more pessimistic prediction systems is performing significantly better than the others. However, the u-plot analysis in Figure 10.15 shows that all are extremely poor: six are grossly optimistic, and two are very pessimistic.

Table 10.6: Musa SS3 data: execution time to failure in seconds; read from left to right

107400	17220	180	32880	960	26100	44160	333720	17820
40860	18780	960	960	79860	240	120	1800	480
780	37260	2100	72060	258704	480	21900	478620	80760
1200	80700	688860	2220	758880	166620	8280	951354	1320
14700	3420	2520	162480	520320	96720	418200	434760	543780
8820	488280	480	540	2220	1080	137340	91860	22800
22920	473340	354901	369480	380220	848640	120	3416	74160
262500	879300	360	8160	180	237920	120	70800	12960
300	120	558540	188040	56280	420	414464	240780	206640
4740	10140	300	4140	472080	300	87600	48240	41940
576612	71820	83100	900	240300	73740	169800	1	302280
3360	2340	82260	559920	780	10740	180	430860	166740
600	376140	5100	549540	540	900	521252	420	518640
1020	4140	480	180	600	53760	82440	180	273000
59880	840	7140	76320	148680	237840	4560	1920	16860
77040	74760	738180	147000	76680	70800	66180	27540	55020
120	296796	90180	724560	167100	106200	480	117360	6480
60	97860	398580	391380	180	180	240	540	336900
264480	847080	26460	349320	4080	64680	840	540	589980
332280	94140	240060	2700	900	1080	11580	2160	192720
87840	84360	378120	58500	83880	158640	660	3180	1560
3180	5700	226560	9840	69060	68880	65460	402900	75480
380220	704968	505680	54420	319020	95220	5100	6240	49440
420	667320	120	7200	68940	26820	448620	339420	480
1042680	779580	8040	1158240	907140	58500	383940	2039460	522240
66000	43500	2040	600	226320	327600	201300	226980	553440
1020	960	512760	819240	801660	160380	71640	363990	9090
227970	17190	597900	689400	11520	23850	75870	123030	26010
75240	68130	811050	498360	623280	3330	7290	47160	1328400
109800	343890	1615860	14940	680760	26220	376110	181890	64320
468180	1568580	333720	180	810	322110	21960	363600	

The situation in Example 10.16 presents us with a serious problem: we can try all available prediction techniques, but we can demonstrate that none of them produces trustworthy reliability measures. Indeed, it is possible for all of them to be very inaccurate. In the next section, we examine a recalibration technique that can rescue us in many cases.

10.5 THE RECALIBRATION OF SOFTWARE-RELIABILITY GROWTH PREDICTIONS

So far we have been using the models to make predictions about reliability as we observe and record failure data for a given system. Each time a new failure is observed, we have applied the models in the same way, regardless of the known inaccuracies that we have discussed. Now we turn to improving predictions as we examine the

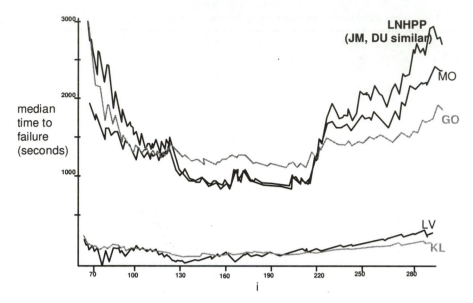

Figure 10.14: Raw predictive median time to failure of T_{106} through T_{278} for eight models, using the data of Table 10.6 (X-axis displays failure number)

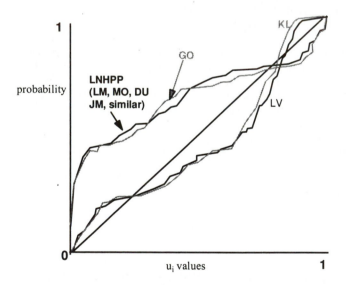

Figure 10.15: u-plots for raw predictions of T_{106} through T_{278} for eight models, using the data of Table 10.6

current data. In other words, if we can learn about the nature of the inaccuracies of reliability prediction at the early stages of observation, then we can use this knowledge to improve future predictions on the same data source. We call this process **recalibration**, and our recalibration technique involves the u-plot.

Consider a prediction $\hat{F}_i(t_i)$ of the random variable T_i, when the true (unknown) distribution is $F_i(t_i)$. Let the relationship between these be represented by the function G_i where:

$$F_i(t) = G_i\left[\hat{F}_i(t)\right]$$

Example 10.17: Suppose that the true distribution $F_i(t_i)$ is the one based on the Jelinski–Moranda model in Example 10.10, with $N = 15$ and $\phi = 0.003$. In this case,

$$F_i(t_i) = 1 - e^{-(15-i+1)0.003t_i} = 1 - e^{(i-16)0.003t_i}$$

Suppose that our estimate has $N = 17$ and $\phi = 0.003$. Then:

$$\hat{F}_i(t_i) = 1 - e^{(i-18)0.003t_i} = 1 - e^{(i-16)0.003t_i}e^{(-2)0.003t_i} = 1 - e^{(-2)0.003t_i}F_i(t_i)$$

These results tell us that we have:

$$F_i(t_i) = e^{0.006t_i}\left(1 - \hat{F}_i(t_i)\right)$$

Thus, the function G_i is defined by:

$$G_i(x) = e^{0.006t_i}(1 - x)$$

By knowing G_i, we can recover the true distribution of T_i from the inaccurate predictor, $\hat{F}_i(t_i)$. In fact, if the sequence $<G_i>$ were completely stationary (that is, $G_i = G$ for all i), then G would characterize the notion of consistent bias discussed earlier. In this case, we could also estimate G from past predictions and use it to improve the accuracy of future predictions.

Of course, in practice it is unlikely that the sequence $<G_i>$ will be completely stationary. But in many cases the sequence changes slowly as i increases, so in some sense it is "approximately stationary." This characteristic is the key to our recalibration approach.

We want to approximate G_i with an estimate G_i^* and so form a new prediction:

$$\hat{F}_i^*(t_i) = G_i^*\left[\hat{F}_i(t_i)\right]$$

If we look at how G_i is defined, we observe that it is the distribution function of $U_i = \hat{F}_i(T_i)$. Therefore, we can base our estimate G_i^* on the u-plot, calculated from predictions that have been made prior to T_i. The new prediction recalibrates the raw

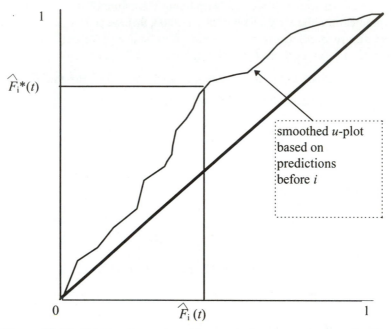

Figure 10.16: Using u-plot analysis of past predictions to improve future predictions

model output, $\hat{F}_i(t_i)$, in the light of our knowledge of the accuracy of past predictions for the data source under study. The new procedure is a truly predictive one, "learning" from past errors.

The simplest form for G_i^* is the u-plot with steps joined up to form a polygon. For technical reasons, it is usually best to smooth this polygon, as shown in Figure 10.16; see Brocklehurst *et al.* (1990) for details.

Thus, we can describe a complete procedure for forming a recalibrated prediction for the next time to failure, T_i:

1. Check that error in previous predictions is approximately stationary. (See Abdel-Ghaly, Chan, and Littlewood (1986) for a plotting technique, the y-plot, that detects non-stationarity.)

2. Obtain the u-plot for predictions made before T_i, that is, based on $t_1, t_2, \ldots, t_{i-1}$. Join up the steps to form a polygon, and smooth it to form G_i^*, as shown in Figure 10.16.

3. Use the basic prediction system to make a "raw" prediction, $\hat{F}_i(t_i)$.

4. Recalibrate the raw prediction using $\hat{F}_i^*(t_i) = G_i^*[\hat{F}_i(t_i)]$.

The procedure can be repeated at each stage, so that the functions G_i^* used for recalibration are based on more information about past errors as i increases. This technique is not computationally daunting; by far the greatest computational effort is needed for the statistical inference procedures used to obtain the raw model predictions. Most importantly, this procedure produces a genuine prediction system in the sense described earlier: at each stage we are using only past observations to make predictions about unobserved future failure behavior.

EXAMPLE 10.18:   Consider the u-plots of Figure 10.15. The most notable feature of each prediction system is its extreme optimism or pessimism. However, the extreme nature is not the simple effect of a single characteristic of the system. For example, in Jelinski–Moranda, the behavior of the plot at each extremity suggests too many very small u values and too many very large ones. For Littlewood–Verrall, there seem to be too many fairly large us and too few us near to 1. Thus, although the statements about optimism and pessimism are correct at first glance, a more detailed look reveals that the u-plots present precise information about the incorrect shapes of the complete predictive distributions.

The recalibration technique works dramatically well here for all eight models discussed so far. All eight raw u-plots have Kolmogorov distances that are significant well beyond the 1% level, which is the most extreme value in the tables of this statistic. After recalibration, all the distances are more than halved, and none is significant at this high level. Figure 10.17 shows the dramatic improvement resulting from recalibrating the u-plots in comparison with the raw predictions of Figure 10.15. The differences in the detailed median predictions can be seen by comparing Figure 10.14 and Figure 10.18. We have much closer agreement among the recalibrated models than among the raw ones.

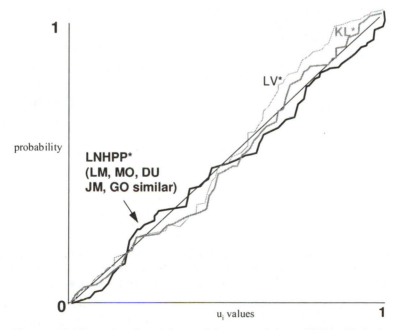

Figure 10.17: u-plots for eight models using of data of Table 10.6 after recalibration (Note the improvement over raw u-plots of Figure 10.15.)

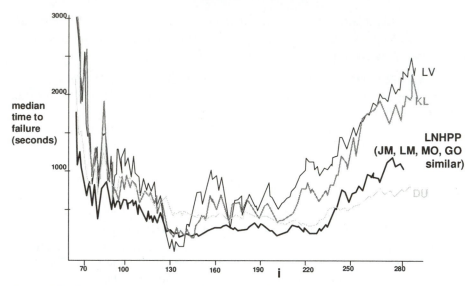

Figure 10.18: Medians of recalibrated predictions from eight models, using data of Table 10.6 (Note how these are now in close agreement compared with the great disagreement shown in the raw predictions of Figure 10.15.)

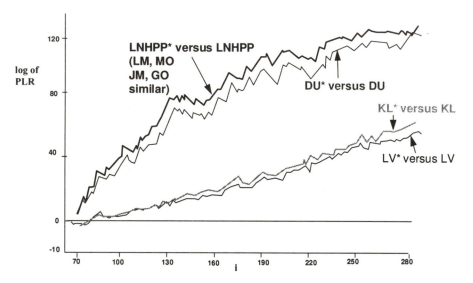

Figure 10.19: Prequential likelihood analysis of recalibrated versus raw predictions, using the data of Table 10.6 (Note that, since this is a plot of log of the prequential likelihood ratio, the results give strong evidence for the superiority of the recalibrated results.)

Example 10.18 provides evidence that prediction systems that were in disagreement have been brought into closer agreement by the recalibration technique. Much more important, however, is that we have objective evidence (by comparing the u-plot with the u^*-plot) that the recalibrated predictions are less biased than the raw ones. The prequential likelihood analysis confirms that the recalibration is working dramatically well in this case. We see the effects of recalibration in Figure 10.19, which shows the evolution of the prequential likelihood ratios for the recalibrated predictions against raw model predictions.

There is, for example, overwhelming evidence that the prequential likelihood ratio, LV*:LV, is increasing rapidly; it has reached more than e^{40} during these predictions. Therefore, we can be very confident that the LV* predictions here are more accurate than the LV ones. A comparison of JM* and JM is even more dramatic: the prequential likelihood ratio reaches e^{90} over the range of predictions shown. This result is due in part to the fact that raw JM predictions are significantly less accurate than those of raw LV (although both are bad from u-plot evidence). Thus, JM starts off with more room for improvement. In fact, after recalibration, the two predictors LV* and JM* have comparable accuracy on the prequential likelihood evidence, with slight evidence of superiority for JM*.

The recalibration technique described works well in most situations. We can evaluate its performance directly: it creates a genuine prediction system when it operates on a raw model, so we can apply the usual analytic techniques to examine predictive accuracy.

10.6   THE IMPORTANCE OF THE OPERATIONAL ENVIRONMENT

We have seen how to investigate the accuracy of predictions of software reliability growth emanating from several models on a single data set. Of course, there is no guarantee of future accuracy from a model that was accurate in the past. Intuitively, we assume that the model will be accurate again if its conditions of use are the same as in the past. However, Example 10.19 shows us the difficulty of assuring this similarity.

> **EXAMPLE 10.19:**   Suppose we have developed a software system, and we seek to predict its reliability in operation. Usually, our prediction will be based on observations of failures occurring during testing. Unfortunately, our testing environment may not reproduce the typical use of the system in actual operation. Thus, our reliability prediction may be an inaccurate reflection of the reliability as seen by the user.

The problem of realism is even more difficult when there are different modes of system use, different user experience levels, and different environments in which the system will be placed. For example, a novice user of a word-processor system is not likely to use the same short-cuts and sophisticated techniques as an experienced user, so the failure profiles for each are likely to be quite different.

John Musa recognized these differences and pioneered an approach to address this problem by devising a scheme to anticipate typical user interaction with the system. The typical use is captured in an **operational profile**, a description of likely user input over time. Ideally, the operational profile is a probability distribution of inputs. The testing strategy is based on the operational profile, and test data reflect the probability distribution.

> **Example 10.20:** An operational profile is often created by dividing the input space into a number of distinct classes, and assigning to each class a probability that an input from that class will be selected. For example, suppose a program allows you to run one of three different menu options: f, g, and h. We determine from tests with users that option f is selected twice as often as g or h (which are selected equally often). We can assign a probability of: 0.5 to f, 0.25 to g and 0.25 to h. Then, our testing strategy is to select inputs randomly so that the probability of an input's being an option on f is 0.5, on g is 0.25 and on h is 0.25.

Such a test strategy is called **statistical testing**, and it has at least two benefits:

1. Testing concentrates on the parts of the system most likely to be used, and hence should result in a system that the user finds more reliable.
2. Using the techniques described in this chapter, we have confidence that reliability predictions based on the test results will give us an accurate prediction of reliability as seen by the user.

It is not easy to do statistical testing properly. There is no simple or repeatable way of defining operational profiles. Mills' Cleanroom technique incorporates statistical testing, and the results of Cleanroom provide a body of empirical evidence to show that statistical testing can be applied practically and effectively (Linger, 1994).

10.7 Wider Aspects of Software Reliability

We have presented the software reliability growth problem in some detail, as it has the most complete solution. However, there are many more aspects of software reliability to be considered. In particular, measuring and predicting reliability cannot be separated from the methods for achieving it.

Testing addresses the dual role of achievement and assessment. We have discussed the difficulty of constructing testing strategies to emulate operational environments, allowing estimates of user-perceived reliability. In addition, some practitioners argue that statistical testing is an inefficient means of removing faults and hence of achieving reliability. More conventional test strategies, it is claimed, allow testers to use their knowledge of the likely types of faults present in order to remove them more efficiently. However, the conventional techniques do not produce data suitable for software reliability measurement. There is thus an apparent conflict between testing as a means of achieving reliability, and testing as a means of evaluation. We must resolve the conflict by developing new testing strategies.

Ideally, we want to test in an environment that supports fault-finding, so that we can increase the likelihood of achieving reliability, and then use the collected data to estimate and predict operational reliability. In classical hardware reliability, this is accomplished by **stress testing**. A component is tested in an environment that is more stressful, in a measured way, than that in which it will operate. For example, the component may be subjected to high temperature, more vibration, or greater pressure than normal. The survival times of stressed components can then be used to estimate the survival times of items in operational use. Unfortunately, the notion of stress is not well-understood for software, and stress is not likely to be described as a simple scalar quantity, as it is with hardware. However, some attempts have been made. Several software researchers have characterized the environment in terms of module call frequencies and sojourn times (Littlewood, 1979; Cheung, 1980)

Perhaps one of greatest and most surprising gaps in our knowledge concerns the relationship between process and product. That is, we do not understand how the nature of the software-development process affects the characteristics (including operational reliability) of the final product. As we will see in Chapter 15, there is little rigorous investigation of the efficacy of different development methods, so we do not know how much each contributes to product reliability.

As we increase our use of software in safety-critical systems, we commonly require measurement of the achievement and assurance of very high software reliability.

EXAMPLE 10.21: Rouquet and Traverse report that the reliability requirement for the fly-by-wire computer system of the Airbus A320 is a failure rate of 10^{-9} per hour, because loss of this function cannot be tolerated (Rouquet and Traverse, 1986). Since this reliability constraint is the system requirement, the software requirement must be even more restrictive.

Example 10.21 describes **ultra-high reliability**, where the system can tolerate at most one failure in 10^9 hours. Since this constraint translates to over 100 000 years of operation, we cannot possibly run the system and observe the failure times to measure reliability. Thus, the reliability growth techniques described in this chapter are of little help here.

Figure 10.20 illustrates this problem of assuring ultra-high reliability. The figure depicts an analysis of the failure data from a system in operational use, for which software and hardware design changes were being introduced as a result of the failures. Here the current rate of occurrence of failures (ROCOF) is computed at various times in the history, using the Littlewood–Verrall model. The dotted line is fitted manually to give a visual impression of what seems to be a very clear law of diminishing returns: later improvements in the MTTF are brought about through proportionally longer testing. It is by no means obvious how the details of the future reliability growth of this system will look. For example, it is not clear to what the curve is asymptotic: will the ROCOF approach zero, or is there an irreducible level of residual unreliability reached when the effects of correct fault removal are balanced by those of new fault insertion? Clearly, even if we were sure that the system would

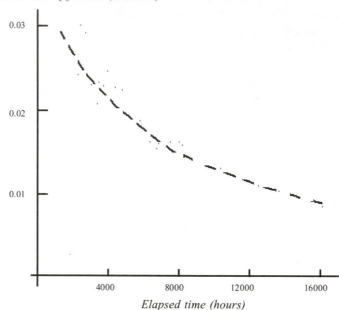

rate of occurrence of failures (hours −1)

Elapsed time (hours)

Figure 10.20: Successive estimates of the rate of occurrence of failures for the data of Table 10.6. The broken line here is fitted by eye.

achieve a particular very high reliability figure, the time needed to demonstrate and measure it would be very high.

In fact, even if a program is tested for a very long time and never fails, we still do not have the level of assurance we need.

EXAMPLE 10.22: Littlewood has shown that if a program has worked failure-free for x hours, there is about a 50:50 chance that it will survive the next x hours before failing. To have the kind of confidence apparently needed for the A320 airplane would require a failure-free performance of the software for several billion hours (Littlewood, 1991). It is easy to see, therefore, that even in the unlikely event that the system had achieved such a reliability, we could not assure ourselves of that achievement in an acceptable time.

Assuring software to very high levels of reliability is one of the most difficult, yet important challenges confronting the software industry (Littlewood and Strigini, 1993). Mathematical verification techniques may eventually become available for large control programs, but they cannot address the problem of faults in the specification. And we can always make mistakes in proofs, so formal proof methods are not foolproof. Most of the research addressing ultra-high reliability involves one of three techniques: *design diversity*, *testability*, and *program self-checking*.

Design diversity for fault tolerance: Design diversity has been advocated as a means of achieving high reliabilities cost effectively (Avizienis and Kelly, 1984). The technique involves building the same system several independent ways, each involving a different design, to decrease the likelihood that all versions will fail at the same time. Several systems have been built using such techniques, including the Airbus A320 (Rouquet and Traverse, 1986). Unfortunately, evidence suggests that independently-developed software versions will not fail independently, and so will not deliver dramatic increases in reliability over single versions. For example, Knight and Leveson report an experiment in which 27 versions were developed independently but contained a high incidence of common faults (Knight and Leveson, 1986). Eckhardt and Lee present a theoretical scenario, based on the notion of varying the difficulty of different inputs, that supports these empirical findings (Eckhardt and Lee, 1985). These problems of dependence make design diversity an untrustworthy technique for achieving ultra-high reliability. More importantly, they make the assurance problem essentially impossible. Even in the unlikely event of our having successfully built a system with such an extremely high reliability, we would never be able to assure ourselves or others of this success. We cannot appeal to simple hardware-like theories of redundancy with independent failures; we must try to estimate the dependence between versions. This problem has been shown to be as difficult as the problem of simply testing the complete fault-tolerant system as a black box, and so is essentially impossible (Miller, 1986).

Testability: Recent work by Voas and his colleagues has attempted to extend the traditional reliability modeling approach to tackle the ultra-high reliability problem (Hamlet and Voas, 1993; Voas and Miller, 1995). The authors introduce the notion of **testability**, the probability that the software will fail if is faulty. They propose methods for improving program testability as a way of improving reliability. The simple idea behind this approach is that if a highly testable program has revealed no failures during testing, then we have increased confidence that the software is truly fault-free. However, there are potential dangers. By making a program highly testable, you may increase the probability that the program is fault-free, but you also increase the probability that failures will occur if faults do remain. Bertolino and Strigini address this and other concerns about testability (Bertolino and Strigini, 1995).

Program self-checking: Blum and colleagues describe a theory of program self-checking, in which programs can be shown to be correct with a probability arbitrarily close to 1. The drawback of their approach is that it is restricted to a narrow class of mathematical-type problems (Blum *et al.*, 1993).

In the absence of proven methods of assuring ultra-high software reliability levels, it is surprising to find that systems are being built whose safe functioning relies upon their achievement.

10.8   Summary

Software reliability is a key concern of many users and developers of software. Because reliability is defined in terms of failures, it is impossible to measure before development is complete. However, if we carefully collect data on inter-failure times, we can make accurate predictions of software reliability. There are several software reliability growth models to aid the estimation, but none can be guaranteed to produce accurate predictions on all data sets in all environments. On the other hand, we can analyze objectively the predictive accuracy of the models and select those that are working best for the given data. Moreover, we can then get improved predictions using a technique known as recalibration. In this way, we make predictions in whose accuracy we can be confident. Tools exist to automate these computationally intense procedures.

Unfortunately, these techniques work effectively only if the software's future operational environment is similar to the one in which the failure data was collected. If we must predict reliability for a system that has not yet been released to a user, then we must simulate the target operational environment in our testing. (Otherwise, we cannot be confident in our predictions). The Cleanroom method embodies a testing strategy called statistical testing, which is based on this very idea.

Worse still, there are no current methods that can feasibly assure software systems with ultra-high reliability requirements. The techniques described in this chapter should be restricted to systems with relatively modest reliability requirements. However, most software requires modest reliability, so the techniques in this chapter are useful.

10.9   Exercises

1   Consider the functions $f(t)$, $F(t)$, and $R(t)$ defined in this chapter. Redefine each in terms of the others.

2   For the probability density function of Example 10.4, show that the median time to failure is 5 hours.

3   For the probability density function of Example 10.5, compute the median time to failure when $\lambda = 4$.

4   Draw the u-plot for the sequence of u_is calculated in Example 10.11. On the same chart, plot the true values of the $F_i(t_i)$. (You can calculate these values using Table 10.2, which gives the true means $1/\lambda_i$ of the distribution.) Compare the true values with the uniform distribution.

5   Imagine that your job is to evaluate the reliability of the software produced by your company. This task involves establishing an in-house testing service, whereby test cases would be generated to provide input to the reliability growth models described in this chapter. How would you accomplish this when the software in question is:

- a word-processing system
- an air-traffic control system
- a car engine management system
- a controller for a domestic washing machine

In each case, discuss whether you can justify the test procedure you are advocating as the only testing to be carried out on the particular product, bearing in mind that there is a fixed budget from which all testing must be funded.

6   Using the data of Table 10.1 and one of the more accurate sets of predictions from the median plots of Figure 10.10, obtain an approximate plot of achieved median against total elapsed test time. Comment on the shape of this graph. You have been asked to continue testing until you are confident that the median time to failure is 1000 hours (remember that the raw data is in seconds); comment on the feasibility of this approach.

7   Look at the crude prediction system described in Example 10.9 (the exponential model in which we estimate the mean time to next failure by simply computing the average of the two previously observed values). Using a spreadsheet, compute successive mean and median time to next failure for the data of Table 10.6 (up to about $i = 20$). Analyze informally the accuracy of this prediction system on this data (if you wish, you could do this formally by carrying out u-plot and prequential likelihood analyses), and try to address the issues of bias and noise as they are defined in the chapter. Does the situation improve if you change the prediction system by:

- basing your prediction of the mean on the average of the three previously observed t_is ?
- basing your prediction of the mean on just the one previously observed t_i?

8   Example 10.14 shows how to compute the sequence of prequential likelihood values for the prediction system of Example 10.9 using the data in Table 10.1. Call this prediction system A. Repeat the computations for the prediction system B where the estimate of the mean time to next failure is the average of the three previously observed values. Now you can compute both PL(A)/PL(B) and PL(B)/PL(A) for a number of values of i and see what happens as i increases. Does this give you any evidence of which of A or B is superior?

9   When faults are found and fixed in a program, we observe reliability growth. Specifically, we see a sequence of times between successive failures $t_1, t_2, \ldots, t_n$ which tend to increase in magnitude. Explain carefully the underlying failure process, identifying the sources of uncertainty that require us to adopt a probabilistic approach when we wish to predict the future failure behavior of the program.

10   Many different probability models have been proposed to represent the growth in reliability as fault detection and correction progress. Unfortunately, it is not

possible to select one of these *a priori* and be confident that it will give accurate predictions. Imagine that you are responsible for making reliability predictions from the failure data coming from a particular program under test. What could you learn from the *u*-plots and prequential likelihood functions about the accuracy of the predictions coming from the different models? How could you use the *u*-plot to improve the accuracy of predictions?

11   Figures 10.17, 10.18 and 10.19 show, successively, one-step-ahead median predictions, *u*-plots and prequential likelihood functions for several models operating upon some software-failure data obtained in the testing of a telephone switch. State, very briefly, what you would conclude from these figures. (Hint: there is no need to give a detailed analysis of each model's performance individually.) Suggest how the analysis might be continued.

12   You are part of a team that is to build a critical system, the safety of which depends upon the correct functioning of its software. Your responsibility will be to assess the system, and in particular the software, to decide whether it is sufficiently safe to use. In discussion with your colleagues responsible for building the system, several sources of evidence arise that might be relevant to your eventual assessment of the software. Comment briefly on the strengths and weaknesses of the following:

- failure data from debugging in operational testing
- observation of long periods of failure-free working
- design diversity, such as three versions with 2-out-of-3 voting at run-time
- formal verification
- quality of the development process

13   Why is reliability an external attribute of software? List three internal software product attributes that could affect reliability.

14   Suppose you can remove 50% of all faults resident in an operational software system. What corresponding improvements would you expect in the reliability of the system?

15   Consider a design or programming methodology with which you are familiar. List the ways in which this methodology influences the documents produced, and propose ways in which they can increase external quality. How can you determine that an actual increase had been achieved?

10.10 FURTHER READING

An exceptionally comprehensive account of the whole software reliability area may be found in Lyu's book which includes contributions from all of the leading researchers.

Lyu, M. (ed.). *Handbook of Software Reliability Engineering*, IEEE Computer Society Press, 1996.

The extensive theory of hardware reliability is described in this textbook:

Barlow, R.E. and Proschan, F., *Statistical Theory of Reliability and Life Testing*, Holt, Rinehart and Winston, New York, 1975.

For a detailed treatment of the underlying statistics needed for the reliability models (notably how to compute maximum likelihood estimates) see this textbook:

Cox, D.R. and Hinkley, D.V., *Theoretical Statistics*, Chapman & Hall, London, 1982.

Mellor presents a good overview of software-reliability modeling. Goel and Musa describe details of particular software-reliability models.

Mellor, P., "Software reliability modelling: the state of the art," *Journal of Information and Software Technology*, 29(2), pp. 81–98, 1987.
Goel, A.L., "Software reliability models: assumptions, limitations and applicability," *IEEE Transactions on Software Engineering*, 11(12), pp. 1411–23, 1985.
Musa, J., Iannino, A. and Okumoto, K., *Software Reliability: Measurement, Prediction and Application*, McGraw-Hill, New York, 1987.

For full details of the method used for analyzing the predictive accuracy of models, see these papers by Littlewood and his colleagues.

Abdel-Ghaly, A.A., Chan, P.Y. and Littlewood, B., "Evaluation of competing software reliability predictions," *IEEE Transactions on Software Engineering*, SE-12(9), pp. 950–67, 1986.
Littlewood, B., "Predicting software reliability," *Philosophical Transactions of the Royal Society of London*, A 327, pp. 513–27, 1989.
Brocklehurst, S. and Littlewood, B., "New ways to get accurate software reliability modeling," *IEEE Software*, 9(4), July 1992.

Brocklehurst and her research team describe the details of the recalibration techniques for improving predictions.

Brocklehurst, S., Chan, P.Y., Littlewood, B. and Snell, J., "Recalibrating software reliability models," *IEEE Transactions on Software Engineering*, SE-16(4), pp. 458–70, 1990.

The July 1992 issue of *IEEE Software* was devoted to software reliability. In that issue, Schneidewind and Keller applied reliability models in a realistic setting, and Hamlet critiqued the assumptions usually made in reliability modeling.

Schneidewind, N.F. and Keller, T.W., "Applying reliability models to the space shuttle," *IEEE Software*, 9(4), pp. 28–33, July 1992.
Hamlet, D., "Are we testing for true reliability?" *IEEE Software,* 9(4), pp. 21–7, July 1992.

Veevers and Marshall link reliability to the test coverage metrics described in Chapter 9.

Veevers, A. and Marshall, A.C., "A relationship between software coverage metrics and reliability," *Journal of Software Testing, Verification and Reliability*, 4, pp. 3–8, 1994.

Both Dyer and Mills present a comprehensive treatment of Cleanroom. Curritt describes a successful application of Cleanroom, and Linger provides empirical evidence from a number of projects that confirm the effectiveness of Cleanroom in improving reliability.

Dyer, M., *The Cleanroom Approach to Quality Software Development*, Wiley, New York, 1992.

Mills, H., Dyer, M. and Linger, R., "Cleanroom software engineering," *IEEE Software*, 4(5), pp. 19–25, September 1987.

Curritt, P.A., Dyer, M. and Mills, H.D., "Certifying the reliability of software," *IEEE Transactions on Software Engineering*, SE-12(1), pp. 3–11, 1986.

Linger, R., "Cleanroom process model," *IEEE Software*, 11(2), March 1994.

Littlewood and Strigini provide an excellent discussion of the limitations of assuring software systems with ultra-high reliability requirements.

Littlewood, B. and Strigini, L., "Validation of ultra-high dependability for software-based systems," *Communications of the ACM*, 36(11), 1993.

11 Resource measurement: productivity, teams, and tools

Software developers are a diverse and flexible group. Some of us have backgrounds in computer science or software engineering, while others have migrated to software from literature and language, anthropology, mathematics, psychology, or the physical, biological or even secretarial sciences. Thus, each of us brings to our job a different set of skills and experience. This diversity enriches our profession, but it makes it difficult to study our characteristics and their effects on the products we build and maintain. In this chapter, we turn to measuring ourselves as we try to understand how to improve our personal contributions to quality software. In particular, we look at how to measure our productivity, and how productivity and quality are affected by our teams and tools.

In 1975, Brooks observed that "If you throw more people on to a late software project, you will make it later" (Brooks, 1975). Many who have worked on large projects agree. Brooks' wisdom reflects our frequent emphasis on productivity. Because we do not always understand how to get the most and best from ourselves and others, we sometimes treat software production as if it were much like other production: by speeding up the assembly line or adding more personnel, we somehow expect to finish on time. We think of productivity as the production of a set of components over a certain period of time, and we want to maximize the number of components built for a given duration. But in fact, individual programmer productivity (measured in lines of code per person month) usually decreases as we add people to our projects. And the added personnel can affect quality, too, and not always positively.

We begin our investigation of productivity in a rigorous way, consistent with the measurement framework introduced in Chapter 2. That is, we ask ourselves what attribute we are measuring, and what intuitive properties it has that must be preserved by any measurement we make. Next, we ask which entities have the attribute. Only then can we address specific measures of productivity. The final sections of this chapter turn from the external attribute of productivity to several internal resource attributes. We consider ways to measure team structure, experience, methods, tools, and hardware, so that we can determine their effects on productivity and quality.

11.1   THE MEANING OF PRODUCTIVITY

In economics, productivity is defined in a straightforward way:

> The rate of output per unit of input used especially in measuring capital growth, and in assessing the effective use of labour, materials and equipment.
>
> Oxford English Dictionary, 2nd edition

The idea of comparing input with output is useful for software developers, too. Intuitively, the notion of productivity involves the contrast between what goes into a process and what comes out. Somehow, increasing the inputs should increase the outputs. Or improving the process for the same inputs should increase the outputs. However, measuring the productivity of a software engineer, or of a software-engineering process, is not at all intuitive. We do not understand what constitutes the set of inputs, and we do not know how process changes affect the relationship of input to output. What we find instead is that software engineers define productivity in terms of a measure, rather than considering carefully what attribute is being captured (as we recommended in Chapter 2). The measure most commonly used is one of size over effort. That is, the size of the output is compared with the amount of effort input to yield a **productivity equation**:

$$productivity = \frac{size}{effort}$$

Size is usually measured as lines of code (but can be any size measure, including those described in Chapter 7), and effort is measured in person-days or person months. Thus, software developers often calculate productivity as

$$\text{productivity} = \frac{\text{lines\_of\_code}}{\text{person\_months}}$$

In Chapter 2, we highlighted the danger of allowing the measurement definition to divert us from the meaning of the natural language concepts. The productivity equation is no exception, as it takes no account of the "effective use" of labor and resources identified in the economic definition.

The equation's simplicity hides the difficulty of measuring effort. Effort is not something that can be recorded as easily as an odometer reading. Indeed, many projects that have reached completion cannot report actual expended effort. When a person spends a day working on a project, the "day" measure does not reflect whether the day consisted of 8, 12 or 16 hours. More importantly, as some of us are more effective on some days than on others, one eight-hour day of work can mean eight hours of productive effort for one person but only two hours for another. Similarly, we often count two half-time workers to be the equivalent of one full-time worker. But the contributions of a half-time worker may be very different from 50% of a full-timer. Other effort considerations involve the contributions of support staff whose hours are charged directly to the project, and of corporate staff (such as researchers or librarians) whose time is paid from non-project funds but who nevertheless make a significant contribution to the project's output.

The numerator presents problems, too. The productivity equation views output only in terms of size, so that the value of the output is ignored. We must consider productivity in light of the benefit we deliver, not just the size of the code. It does no good to be very effective at building useless products. And we shall see in Chapter 14 that benefit is in the eye of the beholder.

There are other concerns about the productivity equation and its underlying assumptions. By considering output solely in terms of the number of components produced, this view of productivity treats software development to be much like any traditional manufacturing process. For example, consider automobile manufacture. Designing a car is clearly similar to designing a complex software system, and both design processes involve prototyping and choosing among several alternatives. However, for automobile manufacture, the primary focus of the implementation process is replication: building many copies of the same item, perhaps with mild variations (such as paint color, trim, or radio type). Here, it is customary and reasonable to measure productivity in terms of the number of items produced per person month. Each item has a clearly understood utility in terms of a known market price, and this measure of productivity corresponds well with our intuition about the effectiveness of the manufacturing process.

By contrast, there is usually little or no replication in software development. And even when replication is required (as, for example, in producing "shrink-wrapped" software), the cost of each copy is generally minimal in comparison with the cost of building the original. This small replication cost is a key feature that distinguishes software "manufacture" from more traditional manufacturing. Another is the role of the creative process. Just as it would be silly to measure the productivity of poets by computing the number of words or lines they produce and dividing by the number of hours they spend writing, it may be equally inappropriate to measure software productivity using the productivity equation. Instead, we need a measure of productivity that has a more direct relationship to quality or utility. Similarly, we need to measure input by more than effort or time, as other resources (such as tools and training) are "consumed" during the production process.

11.2 PRODUCTIVITY OF WHAT?

The discussion above shows us that we must take care to distinguish the productivity of a process from the productivity of the resources. In many instances, we are more concerned about the latter: we want to know how productive are the developers, so that we can take steps to improve their productivity. This need to measure and understand personnel productivity has its drawbacks, though; when people feel they are being monitored and measured, they may become suspicious and resentful, and they may supply poor-quality data as a result. By relying on a goal-driven approach to measurement, and by making clear the likely benefits to all concerned, a measurement program can avoid this problem.

Of course, there are other resources whose productivity we can measure. For example, we may evaluate the productivity of a compiler, measured in terms of the attributes listed in Table 11.1. Even in this relatively simple example, people may confuse product or resource attributes with process attributes. Although the productivity of a compiler (a product or a resource, depending on whether we are building it or using it) must take into account the process of compilation (that is, running it on some source code), it is incorrect to talk of the productivity of the compilation process.

In the discussion that follows, we do not differentiate clearly between product, process, and resource productivity, as they are in fact intertwined. We can meaningfully refer to personnel productivity during a given process while working on a particular product, and it is in this sense that productivity is an external resource attribute. That is, we need a context for measuring and assessing productivity. For example, consider

Table 11.1: Sieve benchmark (extracted from comparison between two C compilers running on microcomputers)

Attribute	Compiler 1	Compiler 2
Compile time	3.15	22.41
Compile and link time	6.55	22.49
Execution time	6.59	10.11
Object code size	239	249
Execution size	5748	7136
Price	$ 99.95	$ 450.00

the productivity of an individual programmer during the coding (that is, the process) of a program (the product). Any measure of the programmer's productivity must reference the coding activity, as opposed to design or testing. Table 11.2 shows some examples of typical processes and products we should consider when measuring the productivity of certain typical resources. We have also added a column for relevant resources used, since they may also be important.

Table 11.2 highlights several possible limitations of the productivity equation. Notice how the formula addresses only the first four examples; that is, it can be used only to measure the productivity of programmers during coding. It is irrelevant for assessing the productivity of other software personnel performing other development tasks. In fact, whether the formula actually measures programmer productivity during software development in the intuitive sense discussed earlier is also highly questionable.

We are not suggesting that the productivity equation should never be used. Rather, we suggest that the equation should not be defined and used as the only measure of (personnel) productivity, as it captures only a narrow sense of what we mean intuitively about productivity.

We have mentioned code reuse in earlier chapters, and we have discussed the difficulty in measuring the size of reused code. From the perspective of productivity, we must also consider the impact of reuse. The inclusion of previously constructed code will certainly increase the value of the productivity equation, but unless the code is executed, we have no real increase in productivity. Thus, productivity as a measure defined by the productivity equation fails to satisfy the representation condition for measurement. We can demonstrate this failure with an example.

Table 11.2: Productivity of resources

Resource (whose productivity we wish to assess)	Process	Product	Examples of resources used
Programmer	Coding	Program	Compiler
Programmer	Coding	Set of programs	Compiler and static analyzer
Programming team	Coding	Program	Compiler
Programming team	Coding	Set of programs	Compiler and LAN
Programmer	Testing	Program	Debugger
Programmer	Coding and documenting	Program, documentation, and user manual	Compiler and word-processor
Designer	Developing	Set of detailed module designs	CASE tool
Designer	Reviewing	Specification	CASE tool
Specifier	Constructing	Formal specification	Theorem prover
Programmer	Maintaining	Set of programs documentation	Program
Programmer	Maintaining	Set of programs plus documentation	Reverse-engineering tools
Super-programmer	Full life cycle	Specification, design, test cases, programs, and documentation	Compiler
Compiler	Compiling	Source-code program	Microprocessor

EXAMPLE 11.1:   When we measure programmer productivity, our entities are individuals producing specific programs. Suppose that P is the entity "Fred producing program A," that it takes Fred 100 days to complete A, and that A is 5000 lines of code. According to the productivity equation,

$$\text{Productivity}(P) = 50 \text{ LOC per day}$$

Does this proposed measure capture our intuition about productivity in the sense of satisfying the representation condition? To see that it does not, suppose that Fred adds another copy of program A to the original one, in such a way that the second copy is never executed. This new program, A', has 10 000 lines of code but is functionally equivalent to the old one. Moreover, since the original version of A was already tested, the incremental development time is nil, so the total time required to create A' is essentially equal to the time required to create A.

Intuitively, we know that Fred's productivity has not changed. However, let P' be the entity "Fred producing program A'". The productivity equation tells us that

$$\text{Productivity}(P') = 100 \text{ LOC per day}$$

This significant increase in productivity (according to the measure) is a clear violation of the representation condition, telling us that the productivity equation does not define a true measure, in the sense of measurement theory.

You may protest, saying that we can still use the productivity equation if we do not count reused code. However, consider the situation in which a programmer decides to remove a block of code from his program. Has his productivity suddenly decreased? We think not.

11.3   MEASURING PRODUCTIVITY

Despite its theoretical problems, the productivity equation will continue to be used for many years. Its appeal derives from its simplicity and ease of automatic calculation. Moreover, because productivity (as defined by the productivity equation) is a ratio scale measure, we can perform all reasonable statistical analyses on it. In particular, we can meaningfully compute arithmetic means, yielding information about average team productivity across people in a given process, or average programmer productivity across a number of different projects. We can also have meaningful discussions about proportional increases, decreases or comparisons in productivity.

Nevertheless, many pragmatic problems remain. First, to make effective use of the productivity equation, we must solve the problem of variations in the definition of lines of code. We saw in Chapter 7 that, for a given language, one lines-of-code count can be as much as five times another, depending on the counting technique. An organization's standard definition can address this problem, as can an automatic code counter. But a second problem rests with the variation in expressiveness of different languages. For example, the equivalent functionality of a single statement coded in a fourth-generation language like Dbase may require dozens of statements in a language like COBOL or Pascal; likewise, a single statement in Pascal may require dozens of Assembler statements. At the same time, programmers have wide variation in their programming styles. We must accept the fact that program size (in different languages) does not capture information about program utility. Thirdly, we must count comments and reused code separately.

These problems stem from using lines of code not as a measure of length (as we proposed in Chapter 7) but as a measure of effort, utility, or functionality. If lines of code truly measured effort, utility, or functionality, then the measure ought to be indifferent to variations in counting convention and expressive power. In fact, it was precisely this problem which lead Albrecht to formulate function points as a measure of functionality. As a result, some researchers have proposed that we measure programmer productivity as:

$$\frac{number\_of\_function\_points\_implemented}{person\_months}$$

If function points really do capture functionality, then this measure is attractive for several reasons:

- The function-points-based measure more accurately reflects the value of output.
- It can be used to assess the productivity of software-development staff at any stage in the life cycle, from requirements capture onwards. For example, to measure the productivity of the architectural designers, we need only compute the number of function points for those parts of the system for which architectural design has been completed.
- We can measure progress by comparing completed function points with incomplete ones.

EXAMPLE 11.2: In his book on software measurement, Jones reports on the US averages for software productivity and quality. He categorizes US software projects in terms of their size in function points, as shown in Figure 11.1. Then, he presents productivity ranges and modes for selected project sizes, as listed in Table 11.3.

Many managers refuse to use function points because they find lines of code to be more tangible. That is, they understand what a line of code means, but they have at best an intuitive grasp of the meaning of function points. Such managers prefer to "translate" function-point counts to lines of code counts. Both Albrecht and Gaffney (1983) and Behrens (1983) have investigated the empirical relationship between function points and lines of code, and they have published tables showing the correspondence. For example, Table 11.4 relates the average number of source

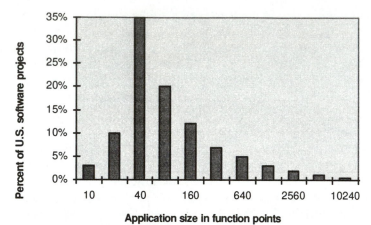

Figure 11.1: Distribution of US software project sizes, in function points (Jones, 1991)

statements per function point for various languages, based on Behrens' empirical study. Some cost-estimation tools, such as Before You Leap, calculate function points and translate them to lines of code automatically, for use as input to a lines-of-code-based cost model such as COCOMO.

A drawback of function points is their computational difficulty, compared with lines of code. For this reason, many practitioners prefer an alternative measure of functionality, such as DeMarco's bang, that can be extracted automatically by certain CASE tools. However, many of these automatic extractions depend on the use of a particular notation. For example, to extract DeMarco's bang automatically, the design must be expressed using DeMarco's structured specification technique.

Measures of length do not capture information about the quality and utility of software; neither do measures of functionality. Ideally, we want to relate our measures of productivity to the quality of the products, wherever possible and relevant. To do so, some of the measures discussed in Chapters 9 and 10 may be helpful. For example,

Table 11.3: Productivity ranges and modes for selected software project sizes (Jones, 1991)

Productivity rates in function points per person month	100 function points	1000 function points	10 000 function points
> 100	1.0%	0.01%	0.0%
75–100	3.0%	0.1%	0.0%
50–75	7.0%	1.0%	0.0%
25–50	15.0%	5.0%	0.1%
15–25	40.0%	10.0%	1.4%
5–15	25.0%	50.0%	13.5%
1-5	10.0%	30.0%	70.0%
< 1	4.0%	4.0%	15.0%

Table 11.4: Approximate number of source statements required to code one Albrecht Function Point (Behrens, 1983)

Language	Source statements per function point
Assembler	320
C	150
ALGOL	106
COBOL	106
FORTRAN	106
Pascal	91
RPG	80
PL/1	80
Modula-2	71
Prolog	64
LISP	64
BASIC	64
4-GL for databases	40
APL	32
Smalltalk	21
Query languages	16
Spreadsheet languages	6

if test or operational failure data are available, then we can compute the operational reliability. This measure is relevant to a particular programmer's productivity only if the failures counted are attributable to errors made by an individual programmer; if we are measuring the productivity of the whole software-development team, our data need not have such a fine granularity. If the software is to have a long life span, then we might measure maintainability as well. Again, to assess individual programmers, we must be sure that the data can be related to individuals.

When it is not possible to compute external quality attributes directly, we can turn to the internal attributes described in Chapter 8. In particular, we are forced to make this compromise when we investigate the productivity of specifiers and designers. A designer may rapidly transform specifications into detailed designs; if the specifications are thereby poorly structured, we can relate the designer's productivity to quality for a more complete picture of design effectiveness.

EXAMPLE 11.3: Table 11.5 presents an example that compares the productivity of two designers. The data include important information about structure. Although designer A is delivering more output (in terms of size and functionality) than designer B, the structure of A's output is poor; it has high coupling, low cohesion, and high tree impurity. On the other hand, A has been able to reuse more of an existing design than B. A comparison based strictly on size or functionality would not have revealed these related aspects of each designer's efforts.

Table 11.5: Measuring designer productivity

Designer	Productivity (per month)		Reuse proportion	Structure		
				coupling level	cohesion ratio	tree impurity
A	25 pages 350 modules	200 function points	20%	3.1	0.2	0.8
B	15 pages 250 modules	150 function points	10%	1.4	0.9	0.3

The notion of productivity incorporates the concept of output of some kind. For specifiers, designers, and programmers, the nature of that output is quite clear. For instance, we can measure reviewer productivity in terms of the number of specification, design, or code pages reviewed per person month. Similarly, we can measure inspector productivity by calculating the number of modules inspected per person month. But there are many other personnel involved in software development and maintenance for whom the output is not as obvious. For example, what is the output of project managers, test teams, the quality assurance staff, or even the measurement staff? Surely we do not want to measure project-manager productivity by the number of milestones on progress charts, or the number of reports produced each week or month! Some seemingly reasonable measures of productivity may in fact be misleading.

> **EXAMPLE 11.4:** Suppose two software testers, Ben and Jerry, are testing the same piece of code. We might measure their productivity in at least two ways: by calculating the number of lines of code tested per month, or by counting the number of defects discovered per month. The first measure tells us about the progress made by each tester, but it tells us nothing about the quality of testing. The second measure considers "discovered defects" as the output of testing, and it captures information about test quality; however, it may be misleading. Even assuming that the definition of "defect" is well-defined and clearly understood, the Adams results discussed in Chapter 9 caution us that defect discovery does not always lead to improved reliability. In other words, if Ben finds more defects in the code than Jerry, Ben may be more effective at locating defects, but not necessarily more effective at improving reliability.

11.4 TEAMS, TOOLS, AND METHODS

We have examined the need to measure productivity, and looked at the benefits and drawbacks of several possible measures. But measuring productivity is not an end in itself. As we saw in Chapter 3, a good Goal–Question–Metric analysis generates questions we want to answer, based on our overriding goals. Thus, we are likely to be measuring productivity because we want to assess its current value, understand what contributes to its increase, and then monitor that increase as we make improvements. Several types of resources have been touted as productivity enhancers: team structure, tools, and methods. For the remainder of this chapter, we examine ways to measure each one.

11.4.1   Team structure

For many years, team structure has been regarded as a key factor in determining team productivity. As early as the 1970s, both Brooks and Weinberg cautioned us that team organization and dynamics contribute more to productivity than fancy tools and techniques (Brooks, 1975; Weinberg, 1971). They presented empirical results indicating that high "complexity" of the team structure leads to low staff "productivity" and poor output quality. The concept of Chief Programmer Teams, developed at IBM, was based on this idea that complexity be kept to a minimum (Baker, 1972).

Rook draws an analogy between the benefits of certain structural attributes of software products and the benefits of structural attributes of development and management teams. These incisive analogies are shown in Table 11.6 (Rook, 1990).

There is little published evidence of the actual link between team structure and productivity or quality. Thus, we must continue to accept anecdotal evidence and expert recommendation until we can properly investigate the team factors that improve process and product.

One factor hypothesized to affect productivity is the complexity of communication among team members, first introduced by Grady and Caswell at Hewlett-Packard. (We will learn more about Hewlett-Packard's measurement program in Chapter 14.) In particular, they identified "communications complexity" as the complexity caused by the number of individuals involved or the method of communications required among members of a project (Grady and Caswell, 1987). However, just as we rejected the notion of a single complexity measure for software products, we also reject a similar measure for team communication. We prefer to consider the important distinct attributes that underlie the complexity and seek measures for each of them.

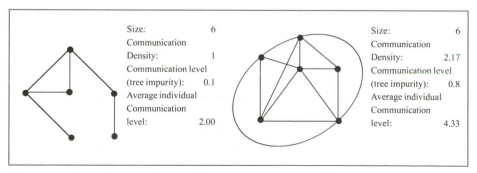

Figure 11.2: Team communication structures with some measures

Table 11.6: Rook's analogies between software structure and team structure

Software structure	Team structure
Each software unit should be so small that it can be easily understood. Each software unit should be only loosely coupled to other software units.	Each software team should be so small that is can be effectively controlled. Each software team should be assigned units of work that minimize unnecessary communication among software teams.
Each software unit should be highly cohesive. The scope of effect of a software unit should be a subset of the scope of control.	Each software team should be assigned work units that are highly cohesive. Software teams should be grouped together under one manager in such a way that the decisions made within the managerial group have minimal effect on the work of other managerial groups.
As software is decomposed into a hierarchy of units, higher-level units perform decision making and lower-levels units do the work. Pathological connections (that is, communication links not following the hierarchical software structure) should be avoided, or at least fully documented.	In the software company hierarchy, high-level management makes the decisions and the lower organizational levels perform the production work. Organizations should not have to rely on pathological connections, such as dependence on arbitrary communications among programming teams, to find out the consequences of design decisions.

An intuitively appealing model for team structure communication is a graph where the nodes correspond to individuals in the team and arcs to a possible direct (work-related) communications path between the corresponding two individuals. Figure 11.2 shows two examples of this type of graph. Using this model, we can identify several relevant measures:

- The **size** of the structure is the number of nodes in the graph.
- The **communication density** is the arc-to-node ratio.
- The **communication level** is the tree impurity measure.
- The **individual communication level** is the degree of the corresponding node (that is, the sum of fan-in and fan-out for the node).
- The **average individual communication level** is the average node degree.

Examples of these measures are indicated on Figure 11.2.

By contrast, Grady and Caswell initially interpreted communication in terms of the "amount of time spent on the phone," but they decided that such data were too difficult to collect. Instead, they defined communication complexity as "the number of interfaces that a lab project team has." After trying to implement this measure, they reported that:

> It was very difficult for projects to precisely count communications, especially because the required communications changed throughout the life-cycle. We believed that communications overhead had a profound impact on schedules, and we also learned that a project manager could not control the dependencies of the project. As a result few people filled out the communication form, and it was eliminated (Grady and Caswell, 1987).

Our proposed, graph-based measures avoid these problems, as they require only a simple project staff audit but yield a good overview of the team structure. On projects where the personnel change, it might be useful to record this picture over repeated, short intervals, and compare the change in communication as a result of the team variability.

11.4.2   Personnel experience

Although most of us would agree that experience is a key contributor to productivity, we find it difficult to measure and record experience in a meaningful way. Whatever way we choose, we must distinguish experience of individuals from experience of the team. Within those categories, we also must consider experience with the project, the environment (that is, the underlying hardware being used), the tools, the methods, and the languages. We can use a simple ordinal measure for each, derived from an objective, orthogonal classification like this one:

0. No previous experience at all.
1. Familiarity (through course or book) but no working experience.
2. Working experience on one previous project or up to 20 worked hours of use.
3. Working experience on several previous projects or between 21 and 100 worked hours of use.
4. Thoroughly experienced.

Because this scale is ordinal, we can define a valid measure of team experience by taking the median of the experience measures of the individuals on the team.

A measure of experience may be misleading if the experience is out of date. Thus, we may want to define a companion measure to capture information about up-to-date training. We can use a simple count of the number of days spent attending relevant courses, a ratio-scale measure that can be calculated by category (training on a particular tool, on a particular language, and so on) over a given period of time (such as the last three years).

EXAMPLE 11.5:   Both the original COCOMO model and COCOMO 2.0 effort estimation models (to be described in detail in Chapter 12) use a necessarily less objective ordinal-scale measure for each of the (more general) personnel attributes "applications experience" and "programming language experience". For example, "applications experience" is rated "low" if the staff has between four and twelve months of experience with the particular application, and "high" if it has approximately six years of experience. By contrast, "analyst capability" is measured on an ordinal scale based on percentile ranges. For instance, the rating is "very high" if the analyst is in the ninetieth percentile, and "nominal" for the fifty-fifth percentile. Unfortunately, COCOMO provides no guidelines for performing the necessary measurement to determine the percentiles into which people fall.

The experience of a team working together on a project can enhance or deflate productivity dramatically. Some teams stay together from project to project, building up a team spirit that makes it the envy of other projects. Other teams simply do not function well, and productivity lags because of lack of enthusiasm and communication. There have been few software-engineering studies to help us understand how the collaborative nature of what we do can make our jobs more interesting, thereby making us more enthusiastic and productive. DeMarco and Lister suggest several ways to enhance team interaction and trust, including non-traditional events such as cooking a spaghetti dinner (DeMarco and Lister, 1987).

For many years, sociologists have studied personnel attributes, both as individuals and teams, and their effect on productivity and products. These characteristics include age, level and type of education, intelligence, gender, marital status, type of remuneration, and more. Although we do not yet measure these aspects of software developers and their work habits, it is clear that when researchers find them relevant to other professions, they are likely to be relevant to ours.

11.4.3   Methods and tools

Many tool and technology vendors claim that methods and tools can increase productivity dramatically, and many practitioners feel likewise. But in fact, there have been few attempts to quantify the extent to which tools and methods have been used, and there is little evidence that this use supports the claims and beliefs. Often, tool and method use is rated simply as a binary nominal scale: used or not used.

However, since effort is a key component of productivity, effort-estimation models need to measure tool and method use in a more sophisticated way. The original COCOMO model included two cost drivers: "use of software tools" and "use of modern programming practices", with measurement scales shown in Tables 11.7 and 11.8.

The left-hand column in each table is a simple ordinal scale for the attribute, defined subjectively (and not always clearly) in the corresponding right-hand column.

Table 11.7: Use of software tools (from the original COCOMO model)

Category	Value	Meaning
Very low	1.24	Basic microprocessor tools
Low	1.08	Basic minicomputer tools
Nominal	1.00	Basic midi- or maxi-computer tools
High	0.91	Strong maxi programming, test tools
Very high	0.83	Requirements, design, management, documentation tools

Table 11.8: Use of modern programming practices (from the original COCOMO model)

Category	Value	Meaning
Very low	1.24	No use
Low	1.08	Beginning use
Nominal	1.00	Some use
High	0.91	General use
Very high	0.82	Routine use

The central column is the factor for each level of the attribute. For example, if your project is rated "low" in use of software tools, COCOMO includes an 8% increase in project effort compared to the "nominal" use of software tools.

COCOMO 2.0 tries to eliminate some of the ambiguity of the original version. For example, the five categories of tool use are more clearly defined, as shown in Table 11.9.

Although a clear improvement over the used/not-used measure, the COCOMO approach is also problematic. Its assertions about effort increases or decreases are not meaningful (in the formal sense of Chapter 2), since the scale is only nominal; either a ratio or interval scale is required.

Table 11.9: Tool use categories (from COCOMO 2.0)

Category	Meaning
Very low	Edit, code, debug
Low	Simple front-end, back-end CASE, little integration
Nominal	Basic life-cycle tools, moderately integrated
High	Strong, mature life-cycle tools, moderately integrated
Very high	Strong, mature, proactive life-cycle tools, well-integrated with processes, methods, reuse

EXAMPLE 11.6: COCOMO 2.0 incorporates productivity in its initial effort estimate. The baseline object-count procedure computes a weighted object count, as described in Chapter 7. But the object count is then divided by a productivity factor that is chosen based on the categories listed in Table 11.10. For example, if the developer experience and capability are rated low, and the ICASE (integrated computer-assisted software engineering tools) maturity and capability are rated low, then the productivity factor is seven, so the number of person months required is the weighted object count divided by seven. When the two ratings are not equal, the productivity factor is a weighted average of the factors corresponding to each rating.

Effort and cost estimation are not the only reasons why we should measure the degree to which we use certain kinds of software tools. By tracking tool use carefully and examining its relationship with other project variables, we can judge the efficacy of our tools in terms of quality, timeliness of delivery, and the productivity of personnel using them. For these reasons, it may be enough to arrive at an objective nominal scale (rather than the subjective scales above) for each tool or method (or class of tools or methods).

EXAMPLE 11.7: To evaluate the level of use of CASE tools on a given project, we can define a rating scheme such as the one below, applied to each designer on the project:

0. Tools not used at all.
1. Tools used only as an aid to less than 20% of documentation.
2. Tools used for documenting at least 50% of the high-level design.
3. Tools used for documenting at least 50% of the high-level and detailed design.
4. Tools used for design and automatic code generation of at least 50% of the system.
5. Tools used for design and automatic code generation of at least 90% of the system.

Since this is an ordinal scale, a valid measure of overall level of tool use can be derived by taking the median computed value of the set of designers on the team.

EXAMPLE 11.8: A similar ordinal scale can be used to measure the level of use of fault detection tools by programmers:

Table 11.10: Productivity estimate calculation (from COCOMO 2.0)

	Very low	Low	Nominal	High	Very high
Developers' experience and capability	Very low	Low	Nominal	High	Very high
ICASE maturity and capability	Very low	Low	Nominal	High	Very high
Productivity factor	4	7	13	25	50

0.   No fault detection tool used at all, other than editor.
1.   Editor with trace aid used.
2.   Editor with trace and flow aid used.
3.   Editor with trace, flow, and cross-reference used.

Examples 11.7 and 11.8 show how simple ordinal measures based on objective classifications can be used. But this approach is applicable for quantifying a wide range of other resources, including:

- homogeneity and compatibility of equipment in project;
- use of electronic mail and other communications facilities;
- level of secretarial and administrative support;
- availability, reliability, efficiency, and operating speed of key support equipment such as photocopiers;
- attributes of the office environment, such as levels of temperature, noise, and space, amount and type of furniture;
- level of information resources, such as library and reference facilities.

Jones has examined the effects of a great many factors on programmer productivity. For many of the factors, he defines detailed classification schemes that provide useful nominal (and at times ordinal measures) for many of the above resource attributes (Jones, 1986).

11.5 SUMMARY

On many software projects, we are interested in the productivity of particular project members, rather than in the productivity of the process as a whole. Thus, we wish to measure productivity as a resource attribute, rather than as a process attribute. The productivity equation, dividing lines of code by person months to yield a measure of productivity, should be used with caution. Its relevance applies only to programmers, not to the other team members, so it paints only a partial picture of team productivity. Moreover, it does not capture the intuitive notion of utility of output, and it is easy to manipulate to provide misleading results. Although more difficult to compute, a productivity measure using function points as a size measure addresses the intuitive relationship of productivity to utility. In addition, such a measure can be used to assess productivity of all software development staff.

Productivity measurement should also take account of the quality of output. For example, the reliability of code produced (as measured in Chapter 10) should be considered in assessing programmer productivity. Even quality of work for other development staff can be assessed. Designers' work may be measured directly in terms of number of changes requested to design, or indirectly in terms of internal attributes of design documents (such as coupling and cohesion).

The structure of software teams and the internal attributes that describe them can reveal important information about what makes projects successful. Team structure is of particular interest, but a single measure of structural "complexity" is inappropriate. Instead, we can model the structure as a graph, and then derive a combination of graph measures to describe the meaningful aspects of overall complexity. Together, the morphological measures paint a more useful picture of complexity than a single measure alone. Moreover, since the graph measures are easily computed, they can be recorded at regular intervals, so that the effect of team structure and change can be monitored objectively.

Reasonable ordinal scale measures of individual and team experience can be computed by considering simple objective classifications. It is possible to define objective nominal scale measures for the extent of use of tools and methods on projects. Unless we record such information, we will never be able objectively to determine the efficacy of applying technology.

11.6   Exercises

1   Suppose you want to assess the productivity of a software tester on your project. How would you define the tester's productivity, and what data would you collect? At what point in the development process would you collect the data?

2   Other than personnel, which software-development resources can be assessed in terms of their productivity? How would you define and measure productivity for these entities?

3   Suggest some possible measures of productivity for personnel performing software maintenance. Explain how the productivity measure is different from that of a developer.

4   Table 11.5 illustrates a method for measuring designer productivity. Using a similar approach, devise a scheme for measuring the productivity of software maintainers.

5   Draw a graph of the team structure for one of your sports teams (or for a team with which you are familiar, if you do not participate in sports). Then, draw a second graph for a project team with which you have worked, either in school or on the job. For each of the team structures, compute the graph measures listed in Figure 11.2. Do the measures help characterize differences in the success of the teams?

6   List resource-related factors that might affect the productivity of a software-development team. Then, consider them from the perspective of Chapter 4: how might you measure and control each factor so that you can determine its effect on productivity?

11.7 FURTHER READING

This chapter has referred to several factors that affect productivity, many of which were introduced in earlier chapters. For a good overview of productivity in the context of cost and schedule, consult Boehm's book:

Boehm, B.W., *Software Engineering Economics*, Prentice Hall, Englewood Cliffs, NJ, 1981.

Jones has performed an in-depth study of factors affecting programmer productivity:

Jones, C., *Programmer Productivity*, McGraw-Hill, New York, 1986.

Chapter 5 of Conte, Dunsmore, and Shen's book addresses productivity factors:

Conte, S.D., Dunsmore, H.D. and Shen, V.Y., *Software Engineering Metrics and Models*, Benjamin-Cummings, Menlo Park, CA, 1986.

Thadhani looks at productivity factors at IBM:

Thadhani, A.J., "Factors affecting programmer productivity during application development," *IBM Systems Journal*, 23(1), pp. 19–35, 1984.

Klepper and Bock investigate the effects of language type on productivity, concluding that productivity is significantly higher with 4GLs than with 3GLs.

Klepper, R. and Bock, D., "Third and fourth generation language productivity differences," *Communications of the ACM*, 38(9), pp. 69–79, 1995.

12 Making process predictions

Including contributions from the first edition by Barbara Kitchenham (University of Keele)

We saw in Chapter 3 that software process concepts can guide us in selecting and organizing our measurement program. Process often provides a structure or overview of the elements about which we hope to learn. Thus, measuring aspects of software process can present a high-level view of what is happening during software development.

In particular, we would like to make process predictions. We can capture information about past processes and use it to help us make judgments about existing or future ones. Likewise, we can measure attributes during early stages of a current process and use the data to predict what is likely to happen later on.

There are many processes suitable for measurement, from the overall development process on a single project to the reuse process over a large collection of projects. Similarly, we can consider subprocesses by themselves: the configuration management process, the re-engineering process, the design process, the requirements capture process, and so on. Rather than examine all possible processes and their prediction opportunities, we focus in this chapter on estimating cost and effort during the development process. Cost and effort estimation spawned some of the first attempts at rigorous software measurement, so it is in a sense the oldest, most mature aspect of software metrics. But, as you will see, we are far from expert at cost and effort prediction, and the lessons learned in this narrow aspect of process prediction have wide application across other attempts at process prediction.

We begin the chapter by looking at what we mean by a good estimate, and we propose several measures of estimation accuracy. In Section 12.2, we focus on cost estimation, identifying key problems and summarizing the current approaches. In Section 12.3, we describe some popular models of cost and effort, including COCOMO and SLIM. After a discussion of the problems with existing modeling methods in Section 12.4, we present several possible solutions in Section 12.5. Finally, we point out how the lessons learned in analyzing cost estimation apply more generally to process prediction.

12.1 GOOD ESTIMATES

Our process predictions guide our decision-making, from before the development begins, through the development process, during the transition of product to customer, and while the software is being maintained. Figure 12.1 illustrates some of the predictions that guide us through the life cycle.

A prediction is useful only if it is reasonably accurate. We do not expect our predictions to be exact, but we expect them to be close enough to the eventual actual numbers that we can make sound judgments. For example, we may not be able to predict exactly how long it will take to complete a task, but on a three-month project, we would like to be able to predict the task length within about a week's time.

12.1.1 What is an estimate?

It is important to think of a prediction as a range or window, rather than as a single number. An estimate or prediction is not a target; rather, an estimate is a probabilistic assessment, so that the value produced as an estimate is really the center of a range. Let us explore the meaning and implications of this notion.

DeMarco was one of the first to explain that an estimate is a prediction that is equally likely to be above or below the actual result (DeMarco, 1982). To understand what this means, consider a situation in which we want to estimate (from a given set of requirements) the time it will take for a project to finish. Imagine that we could record the actual completion times of a large number of projects, all trying to implement the same set of requirements. Then we would be able to graph the probability density function of the time t to complete the project from the stated requirements; an example is shown in Figure 12.2. (The probability density function in the figure is a normal distribution, but in reality it need not be normal). From such a graph, we can compute the probability that any project based on the given requirements will be completed within a time interval $[t_1, t_2]$; the probability is simply the area under the curve between t_1 and t_2. For example, the probability that the project will be completed between months 8 and 16 is about 0.9, and the probability that the project will be done in less than 12 months is 0.5. Usually, we are interested in the probability that a project will be completed by some time t, so we are interested

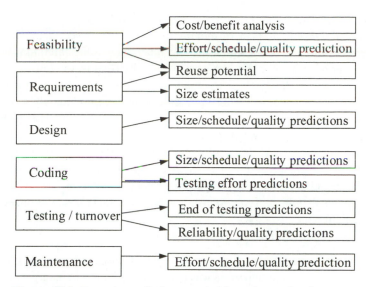

Figure 12.1: Example predictions needed for software development decision-making

in the interval [0, *t*]. (Because the graph is continuous, and the probability is defined as the area under the curve, it is not meaningful to talk about a point probability. In other words, it is meaningless to try to compute the probability of a project's completing in exactly 12 months, as all such point values must have zero probability; the probability makes sense only for intervals of non-zero length.)

In reality, we do not know the distribution of Figure 12.2, but we must still make an estimate of the completion time. Formally, an **estimate** is defined as the median of the (unknown) distribution. Thus, the estimate should divide the area under the curve into two equal parts, so area A is equal to area B. In other words, the actual value is just as likely to be less than the estimate than greater than the estimate.

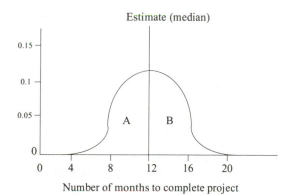

Figure 12.2: An estimate as the median of the probable results

Software engineers often misconceive an "estimate," regarding it (incorrectly) as the smallest defensible number of months in which the project can be completed. This interpretation points not to the median but rather to the minimum value t for which an interval $[t, t + \varepsilon]$ has a non-zero probability (that is, the left-most non-zero point on the curve). This minimum value is the shortest possible time in which the project can be completed; in Figure 12.2, this value is approximately 4. As a result, the probability of the project's finishing in a time greater than t is very large, and project managers decry the overrun.

Even when the meaning of "estimate" is understood correctly, many software engineers create estimates and then set them as targets. By designating the median of the probability distribution as the target for project completion, we know that there is a 50% chance that the project will take longer. Thus, there is a 50% chance that the target will be missed.

Targets can be dangerous for another reason:

EXAMPLE 12.1: A study by Jeffery and Lawrence (reported in DeMarco (1987)) found that productivity was worse on projects where targets were set by supervisors than when they were set by independent third parties. Productivity was best for projects that had no formally set targets at all.

Responsible project managers understand that the estimate is the center of a window in which the project can be completed, and they plan for the likely cases where the project will take less time or more time than was estimated.

Thus, to indicate this window, estimates should ideally be presented as a triple: the most likely value (that is, the median of the distribution), plus upper and lower bounds on the value. (In probability theory we refer to these bounds as confidence intervals.) A good estimate is phrased as a number plus or minus a certain amount of variation.

EXAMPLE 12.2: For the project represented by Figure 12.2, the true probability density function tells us that the project will complete in 12 plus or minus 4 months with a probability of about 0.9. Therefore, an estimate that asserts that the project will complete in 12 plus or minus 4 months is likely to prove correct. An estimate that asserts that the project will complete in 12 plus or minus 1 month is likely to prove incorrect, since this interval has a probability of about 0.2.

12.1.2 Evaluating estimation accuracy

Once our project is ongoing, we have the opportunity to compare actual values with the estimates we had made earlier. Conte, Dunsmore, and Shen suggest several ways to measure estimation accuracy (Conte, Dunsmore, and Shen, 1986). Suppose E is our estimate of a value, and A is the actual value. The **relative error** in our estimate is computed to be

$$RE = \frac{A - E}{A}$$

Thus, if the estimate is greater than the actual value, the relative error is negative. Likewise, if the estimate is less than the actual value, the relative error is positive. When the relative error is greater than zero, then it must be between 0 and 1.

Often, we need to compute the relative error of a collection of estimates, not for a single estimate. For example, we usually want to know if our effort predictions are accurate for a large group of development projects. Here, we define the **mean relative error** for n projects to be:

$$\overline{RE} = \frac{1}{n} \sum_{i=1}^{n} RE_i$$

It is possible for small relative errors on some projects to balance out large ones in the formula, so we consider the magnitude of the error. That is, we define the **magnitude of the relative error** to be the absolute value of RE, and we denote it as MRE. Then, for a set of n projects, the **mean magnitude of relative error** is:

$$\overline{MRE} = \frac{1}{n} \sum_{i=1}^{n} MRE_i$$

If the mean magnitude of relative error is small, then our predictions are generally good. Conte, Dunsmore, and Shen suggest that an acceptable level for mean magnitude of relative error is something less than or equal to 0.25.

They use this notion to define a measure of **prediction quality**. Of a set of n projects, let k be the number of them whose mean magnitude of relative error is less than or equal to q. We let:

$$PRED(q) = k/n$$

For example, if $PRED(0.25) = 0.47$, then 47% of the predicted values fall within 25% of their actual values. Conte, Dunsmore, and Shen suggest that an estimation technique is acceptable if $PRED(0.25)$ is at least 0.75. We use these measures later in this chapter to evaluate several cost estimation models.

DeMarco suggests the use of an **estimating quality factor** (EQF) in assessing the accuracy of the prediction process (DeMarco, 1982). In his technique, estimates are made repeatedly throughout the process, as more information is known about the final products. Ideally, the estimates should get closer to the actual figure as the project progresses. Figure 12.3 shows a graph of several such effort estimates, compared with the actual effort value. The hatched region of the figure represents the difference between estimates and actuals. If we divide the area of the hatched region by $D \times A$, we have a gross measure of the effectiveness of the estimating process, in terms of how well the estimates converge on the actual value.

The EQF varies from zero to infinity. For a series of estimates, DeMarco suggests that a value of 4 (which corresponds to estimates being within 25% of the actual project effort over the period of product development) should be relatively easy to

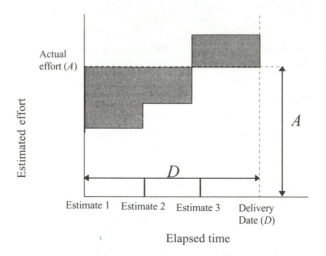

Figure 12.3: Estimating quality factor

achieve, and that cost estimators should aim to achieve values of 8 and above.

12.2 COST ESTIMATION: PROBLEMS AND APPROACHES

We turn next to a closer look at cost estimation, to see what lessons we can learn about it in particular and process prediction in general. When software engineers and project managers talk of "cost estimation," they usually mean predictions of the likely amount of effort, time, and staffing levels required to build a software system. Because staff costs often dominate overall project cost, the terms "cost estimation" and "effort estimation" are sometimes used interchangeably. In this chapter, we use cost estimation in this way, as an umbrella term for several types of estimation.

Cost estimates are needed throughout the life cycle. Preliminary estimates are required when bidding for a contract or determining whether a project is feasible in terms of a cost–benefit analysis. However, preliminary estimates are the most difficult to obtain, and they are often the least accurate, because very little detail is known about the project and the product at its start. We try to generate gross estimates of effort, and we hope that we can partition the total effort into effort by activity. Such predictions support planning and resource allocation; feasibility studies investigate not only whether a project can be done at reasonable cost, but also whether the key resources will be available at the required time.

Once a project has begun, more detailed estimates are needed to assist with project planning. Throughout the project, and within particular activities, the actual effort and duration for individual tasks must be compared with estimated and planned values. A natural part of project control, this step enables project managers and planners to re-estimate periodically, and to re-allocate resources when necessary.

12.2.1 Problems with cost estimation

As a profession, we are notoriously inaccurate when estimating cost and schedule. Other professions take advantage of the repeatability of their tasks. For example, construction estimators have a handbook that suggests effort and timing, based on materials, size, and other considerations. Rarely is there a radical difference in building the next building from building the last few. So construction estimators use their experience and expertise in combination to make their predictions. On the other hand, our next software project is likely to be considerably different from the last few we developed. The application domain may be different, the hardware and supporting tools may have changed, and the techniques and staff may be new.

Moreover, the novelty of the application plays a big part in our estimation difficulties. Often, we are solving a problem that has never been solved before. Such novelty introduces far more uncertainty into our predictions than in other fields. In fact, we are more creators than constructors, so we need to be able to take into account the likelihood of change in the requirements and design during development.

The nature of the problem is not the only reason for inaccurate estimates. Some estimating problems are political, as when managers convert estimates to targets, or when they manipulate the estimation parameters to fit an already-given outcome. For example, some managers practice what is called "price-to-win"; they determine the price needed to under-bid their competitors (regardless of the feasibility of completing the project for that price), and then select parameters to force the price to be the output of an estimation technique. In other words, when an organization is willing to invest only certain resources in a project, the estimate is sometimes forced to match the given resource values.

There are also technical problems with the estimating process itself. Most good estimates are based on an understanding of current productivity, as well as an assessment of the size of the ultimate product. But as practitioners, we are not encouraged to collect data about our processes or products, so we have very few historical records from which to make judgments and predictions. Indeed, many organizations invest a great deal of time and effort in estimation at the beginning of a project, but they do not reflect on a completed project to determine if the estimates were accurate and how the process could be tailored to improve them. Without such data, we have no sound basis for estimation.

12.2.2 Current approaches to cost estimation

Most software engineers use one of four techniques for estimating effort and schedule:

1. expert opinion
2. analogy
3. decomposition
4. models

Expert opinion takes advantage of a mature developer's personal experience. To use this technique, a developer or manager describes the parameters of the project to be undertaken, and experts make predictions based on their past experience. The experts may in fact use tools, models, or other methods to generate the estimates, but these supporting techniques are not made visible to the requester. Instead, the strength of the estimate relies on the quality of the experts and their breadth of experience.

Analogy is a formal, more visible approach to expert opinion. Here, the estimators compare the proposed project with one or more past projects. They try to identify particular similarities and differences. Then, the differences are used to adjust the actual effort value for a past project, based on its differences from the current one. This technique forces the estimators to describe a project in terms of key characteristics, so the underlying model of effort begins to appear. Moreover, this analysis is usually documented, so it is available for use with subsequent estimates; it can be reviewed to find reasons why the estimate may not have been as accurate as was hoped.

Decomposition is more formal still, in that it involves a more thorough analysis of the project characteristics that affect cost. The analysis is focused either on the products to be delivered or on the tasks required to build the software. In the first case, the software is described in terms of its smallest components, and then estimates are made for the effort required to produce each component. In the second case, the activities are decomposed into low-level tasks, and effort estimates are made for each of these. The low-level estimates are usually based on an "average" case, or on some measure of product or task complexity based on past experience.

In both cases, the low-level estimates are then combined to produce a complete project estimate. For simple projects, the low-level estimates are summed. But for more complex projects, there may be sophisticated compositional rules, to take into account the interfaces between components or the interactions among task participants.

Models of effort are techniques that identify key contributors to effort, generating mathematical formulae that relate these items to effort. Size is often a major determinant of effort, but many models include other input variables, such as experience of the developers, implementation language, degree of reuse, and so on. The models are usually based on past experience, and their input values may require some decomposition. We discuss some of these models later in this chapter.

12.2.3 Bottom-up and top-down estimation

Each of the four techniques described above can be applied in one of two ways: bottom-up or top-down. **Bottom-up estimation** begins with the lowest-level parts of products or tasks, and provides estimates for each. Much like decomposition, the bottom-up approach then combines the low-level estimates into higher-level ones. However, bottom-up is not restricted to decomposition. Models can be built by combining several smaller, partial models, or analogies can be applied by amalgamating analogous estimates for each of the parts of the larger process or product.

On the other hand, **top-down estimation** begins with the overall process or product. A full estimate is made, and then the estimates for the component parts are calculated as relative portions of the larger whole. This approach also applies to all four estimation techniques.

> **EXAMPLE 12.3:** As we see later in this chapter, the original COCOMO model involves an effort estimate that is computed for the entire project, based on an equation requiring inputs about size, application type, and several cost factors. The resulting effort prediction is then partitioned into effort for each of the development activities, based on a percentage of the total effort for each activity (Boehm, 1981).

12.3 MODELS OF EFFORT AND COST

Most organizations prefer the decomposition or modeling approach to expert opinion or analogy. By documenting the effort relationships among the lower-level activities or products (as with decomposition), or by building a model of the parameters contributing to effort or cost (as with more general modeling), software engineers have something to examine when they compare the estimated to the actual values. That is, the object of making predictions is not just to provide an estimate; rather, it is to provide a process by which accurate estimates can be generated. By incorporating a model in the process, estimators can examine the relationship between the model and its accuracy, so that they can fine-tune it to improve accuracy for future projects. In this sense, even decomposition is a modeling technique, in that it captures relationships; summing the individual attributes according to the decomposition model is a primitive form of modeling equation.

There are two types of models that have been used to estimate effort: cost models and constraint models. **Cost models** provide direct estimates of effort or duration. Most cost models are based on empirical data reflecting factors that contribute to overall cost. Often, these models have one primary input (usually a measure of product size) and a number of secondary adjustment factors (sometimes called cost drivers). The **cost drivers** are characteristics of the project, process, products, or resources that are expected to influence effort or duration in some way. The driver values are used to adjust the preliminary estimate provided by the primary factor. As we shall see, COCOMO is such an empirical cost model.

By contrast, **constraint models** demonstrate the relationship over time between two or more parameters of effort, duration, or staffing level. The Rayleigh curve is used as a constraint model in several commercial products, including Putnam's (Putnam, 1978).

> **EXAMPLE 12.4:** In the early 1960s, Norden examined the rate of staff buildup and decline in many of IBM's engineering (but not necessarily software) projects. He graphed the staffing profiles for these projects, noting that projects tended to be

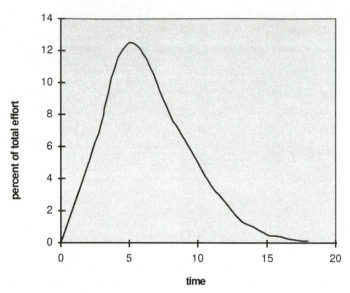

Figure 12.4: A Rayleigh curve

assigned staff according to the curve depicted in Figure 12.4 (Norden, 1963). Although these observations were empirical, this curve has been used as the basis for the relationship between effort and time in many effort and duration models.

12.3.1   Regression-based models

The earliest attempts at building cost models used regression techniques, as described in Chapter 6. By collecting data from past projects and examining relationships among the attribute measures captured, software engineers hypothesized that some factors could be related by an equation. Once the basic equation is defined, the estimate can be adjusted by other, secondary cost factors.

Figure 12.5 illustrates how such a regression equation might be derived. Each data point represents a project. As noted in Chapter 6, the regression has been performed using the logarithm of project effort (measured in person months) on the y-axis and the logarithm of project size (measured in thousands of lines of code) on the x-axis, to highlight the linearity of the relationship and minimize the residuals.

Transforming the linear equation

$$\log E = \log a + b \log S$$

from the log–log domain to the real domain yields an exponential relationship of the form:

$$E = aS^b$$

If size were a perfect predictor of effort, then every point of the graph would lie on the line of the equation, with a residual error of 0. In reality, there is usually a significant residual error.

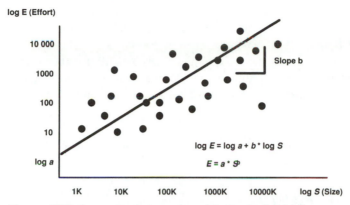

Figure 12.5: Regression line generated for cost model

Thus, the next step in regression-based modeling is identifying the factors that cause variation between predicted and actual effort. For example, you may find that 80% of the variation in required effort for similar-sized projects is explained by the experience of the programming team. A factor analysis can help you identify these additional parameters. You can then add these parameters to your model as cost drivers, and assign weighting factors to model their effects. For instance, if most of your developers have 8 to 10 years of experience, then you may define a weight for "low" experience (under 8 years) as 1.3, "medium" (8 to 10 years) as 1.0, and "high" (more than 10 years) as 0.7. The weights should be based on empirical data, not simply on expert judgment. Similarly, you can assign weights for other significant factors. These weights are applied to the right-hand side of the effort equation, yielding a model of the form

$$E = (aS^b) F$$

where F is the effort adjustment factor, computed as the product of the cost driver (effort multiplier) values. This computation of F is valid only when the individual adjustment factors are independent (Pfleeger, 1991a).

EXAMPLE 12.5:   The intermediate and advanced versions of Boehm's original COCOMO model contain 15 cost drivers, for which Boehm provides the relevant multiplier weights.

Bailey and Basili suggest a technique for deriving a cost model from your own data. When they applied the technique to data collected at NASA–Goddard Space Flight Center, they produced a model that is one of the most accurate reported in the literature.

EXAMPLE 12.6:   The Bailey–Basili approach minimizes the standard error estimate in the data. They demonstrated how it works by applying it to information from 18 large, similar projects involving scientific software written in FORTRAN (Bailey and Basili, 1981). The basic effort equation from this data is

$$E = 5.5 + 0.73 \ S^{1.16}$$

and is adjusted according to the ratio between predicted and actual values. Then, a technology adjustment factor is used, based on the attributes in Table 12.1.

Each entry in the table is given a score, from 0 (not present) to 5 (very important), as judged by the project manager. Then, each column is summed, and the sums are used in a least-squares regression to fit the equation

$$\text{Adjusted effort} = a\ METH + b\ CPLX + c\ EXP + d$$

Bailey and Basili stress that it is the technique that is transferrable to other development environments, not the model itself.

12.3.2   COCOMO

In the 1970s, Barry Boehm investigated data from a large set of projects at TRW, a consulting firm based in California. Using this data, he derived the **constructive cost model (COCOMO)**. Boehm was the first researcher to look at software engineering from the point of view of economics, and his book describing COCOMO is still a useful reference for understanding cost models. He and his colleagues have since revised COCOMO, suggesting an updated version, COCOMO 2.0, that takes advantage of technological changes over the fifteen years between the two models (Boehm *et al.*, 1995). In this section, we look at the original COCOMO; later in the chapter, we describe some of the changes.

12.3.2.1   Original COCOMO: effort

The original COCOMO is actually a collection of three models: a basic model that can be applied when little about the project is known, an intermediate model that is

Table 12.1: Technology adjustment factors for the Bailey–Basili model

Total methodology (METH)	Cumulative complexity (CPLX)	Cumulative experience (EXP)
Tree charts	Customer interface complexity	Programmer qualifications
Top-down design	Application complexity	Programmer machine experience
Formal documentation	Program flow complexity	Programmer language experience
Chief programmer teams	Internal communication complexity	Programmer application experience
Formal training	Database complexity	Team experience
Design formalisms	External communication complexity	
Code reading	Customer-initiated program design changes	
Unit development folders		
Formal test plans		

applied after requirements are specified, and an advanced model that is applied when design is complete. All three take the same form,

$$E = aS^b F$$

where E is effort in person months, S is size measured in thousands of delivered source instructions (KDSI), and *F is an adjustment factor* (equal to 1 in the basic model). The values of a and b, listed in Table 12.2, depend on the development mode, determined by the type of software under construction. An **organic system** involves data processing; it tends to use databases and focus on transactions and data retrieval. A banking or accounting system is usually organic. An **embedded system** contains real-time software that is an integral part of a larger, hardware-based system. For example, a missile guidance system or a water temperature sensing system are embedded. A **semi-detached system** is somewhere between organic and embedded.

By selecting a development mode and applying the appropriate effort equation, COCOMO yields a preliminary estimate of effort.

> **EXAMPLE 12.7:** To predict the effort required to implement the software for a major telephone switching system, we are told that the system will require approximately 5000 KDSI. The software is embedded, since it is a real-time system that is part of a large, complex hardware system. The initial effort estimate using COCOMO is:
>
> $$E = 3.6 \, (5000)^{1.2}$$
>
> or approximately 100 000 person months of effort.

As noted above, this **basic** model of COCOMO is used at the beginning of development, when little is known about a project except its mode and likely size. When more is known about who will work on the project, what language will be used, what tools will be involved, and so on, then an estimator can apply the **intermediate** model of COCOMO. Here, estimators select a rating for each of fifteen cost drivers, listed in Table 12.3. (There is also a version of COCOMO tailored specifically for Ada development; it has 18 cost drivers.)

The importance to the project of each cost driver is rated on an ordinal scale with at most six points: very low, low, nominal, high, very high, and extra high. To each point corresponds an adjustment factor value. For example, very high reliability has an adjustment factor of 1.40, and the basic effort equation is multiplied by 1.40 to yield the adjusted effort estimate. In other words, a system with a requirement for

Table 12.2: Effort parameters for three modes of COCOMO

Mode	a	b
Organic	2.4	1.05
Semi-detached	3.0	1.12
Embedded	3.6	1.20

Table 12.3: Cost drivers for original COCOMO

Product attributes:	Required software reliability	
	Database size	
	Product complexity	
Process attributes:	Use of modern programming practices	
	Use of software tools	
	Required development schedule	
Resource attributes:	**Computer attributes**	**Personnel attributes**
	Execution time constraints	Analyst capability
	Main storage constraints	Applications experience
	Virtual machine volatility	Programming capability
	Computer turnaround time	Language experience
	Virtual machine experience	

very high reliability should require 40% more effort than an otherwise identical one with no such reliability requirement. Because Boehm assumed that the cost factors are independent, the final effort estimate is found by multiplying the basic effort estimate by the 15 cost driver values. The "average" project (that is, the one in which all factors are nominal and are therefore set to 1) can use the basic COCOMO model; all other projects have an adjustment factor that reflects the way in which the project differs from the "average" case. The adjustment factors for each cost driver were derived for Boehm's development environment at TRW; the model must be "calibrated" to reflect your own development environment, which is likely to be substantially different from Boehm's.

Once individual software modules have been identified, estimators can apply their better understanding of the system by using the **detailed** COCOMO model. Here, the intermediate version of COCOMO is applied at the component level, and then a phase-based model is used to build up an estimate of the complete project.

12.3.2.2   Original COCOMO: duration

To see how COCOMO predicts duration, suppose that we have estimated the effort for an embedded project to be E person months. For estimating duration, COCOMO contains a constraint model that predicts elapsed time from effort. The duration model has a form similar to the effort model, namely:

$$D = aE^b$$

where D is duration in months, and E is effort in person months. The coefficient and exponent depend on the development mode, as shown in Table 12.4.

This duration equation is intended to give the optimal estimate of project duration for a given effort. A cost driver assesses the effect of artificially reducing or increasing project duration, so that total project effort changes accordingly when project duration is decreased or increased in comparison to the optimal value.

Table 12.4: Duration parameters for three modes of COCOMO

Mode	a	b
Organic	2.5	0.38
Embedded	2.5	0.35
Semi-detached	2.5	0.32

EXAMPLE 12.8: The development time for a 3000 person month embedded project is predicted by COCOMO to be:

$$2.5 \, (3000)^{.38} = 52 \text{ months}$$

Thus, we can calculate that the project requires 58 staff working for 52 months to complete the software.

12.3.2.3 COCOMO 2.0

Over the years since COCOMO was developed, software-engineering technology has changed. New life-cycle processes have been implemented that make it difficult to use the phased approach of COCOMO's detailed model. Increased use of tools, reengineering, applications generators, object-oriented approaches, and more have shown COCOMO to be inflexible and inaccurate for these new techniques. Consequently, Boehm and his colleagues have defined an updated COCOMO, called COCOMO 2.0, that is useful for a much wider collection of techniques and technologies. In addition, COCOMO 2.0 permits us to use different sizing models as we know more about the system during development (Boehm *et al.*, 1995). In this section, we highlight some of the key differences between the old and new COCOMO models.

The COCOMO 2.0 estimation process is based on three major stages of any development project. Whereas the original COCOMO model used delivered source lines of code as its key input, the new model acknowledges that lines of code are impossible to know early in the development cycle. In stage 1, the project usually builds prototypes to resolve high-risk issues involving user interfaces, software and system interaction, performance, or technological maturity. Here, little is known about the likely size of the final product under consideration, so COCOMO 2.0 estimates size in object points. This technique, described in Chapter 7, captures size in terms of high-level effort generators, such as number of server data tables, number of client data tables, and the percentage of screens and reports reused from previous projects.

At stage 2, a decision has been made to move forward with development, but the designers must explore alternative architectures and concepts of operation. Again, there is not enough information to support fine-grained effort and duration estimation, but far more is known than at stage 1. For stage 2, COCOMO 2.0 employs function

Table 12.5: Comparison of original and new COCOMO models

Model aspect	Original COCOMO	COCOMO 2.0 Stage 1	COCOMO 2.0 Stage 2	COCOMO 2.0 Stage 3
Size	Delivered source instructions (DSI) or source lines of code (SLOC	Object points	Function points (FP) and language	FP and language or SLOC
Reuse	Equivalent SLOC	Implicit in model	% unmodified reuse, % modified reuse (determined by function)	Equivalent SLOC as function of other variables
Breakage	Requirements volatility	Implicit in model	% breakage	% breakage
Maintenance	Annual change traffic (ACT) = % added + % modified	Object point ACT	Reuse model	Reuse model
Scale (b) in nominal effort equation	Organic: 1.05 Semi-detached: 1.12, Embedded 1.20	1.0	1.02 to 1.26 depending on precedent, conformity, early architecture, risk resolution, team cohesion, SEI process maturity	1.02 to 1.26 depending on precedent, conformity, early architecture, risk resolution, team cohesion, SEI process maturity
Product cost drivers	Reliability, database size, product complexity	None	Complexity, required reusability	Reliability, database size, documentation needs, product complexity
Platform cost drivers	Execution time constraints, main storage constraints, virtual machine volatility, computer turnaround time	None	Platform difficulty	Execution time constraints, main storage constraints, virtual machine volatility
Personnel cost drivers	Analyst capability, applications experience, programmer capability, virtual machine experience, programming language experience	None	Personnel capability and experience	Analyst capability, applications experience, programmer capability, programmer experience, language and tool experience, personnel continuity
Project cost drivers	Use of modern programming practices, use of software tools, required development schedule	None	Required development schedule, development environment	Use of software tools, required development schedule, multisite development

points as a size measure. As we saw in Chapter 7, function points estimate the functionality captured in the requirements, so they offer a richer system description than object points.

By stage 3, development has begun, and far more information is known. This stage corresponds to the original COCOMO model, in that sizing can be done in terms of lines of code, and many cost factors can be estimated with some degree of comfort.

There are many other differences among the three stages besides size, and Table 12.5 summarizes them. COCOMO 2.0 incorporates models of reuse, takes into account maintenance and breakage (that is, the change in requirements over time), and more. Cost drivers are similar to those in original COCOMO, but some are new, and others have recalculated values. Because COCOMO 2.0 is new, there are no published data on its accuracy.

12.3.3 Putnam's SLIM model

In 1978, the US Army needed a method for estimating the total effort and delivery time for very large projects. To address this need, Putnam developed a constraint model called SLIM, to be applied to projects exceeding 70 000 lines of code (Putnam, 1978). The basic SLIM equations can be adjusted for smaller projects. Putnam's model assumes that effort for software-development projects is distributed similarly to a collection of Rayleigh curves, one for each major development activity, as shown in Figure 12.6.

Putnam used some empirical observations about productivity levels to derive his "software equation" from the basic Rayleigh curve formula. This equation relates size (measured as lines of code) to several variables: a technology factor, C, total project effort measured in person years, K (which includes maintenance effort), and elapsed time to delivery, t_d, measured in years. The relationship is expressed as:

$$\text{Size} = CK^{\frac{1}{3}}t_d^{\frac{4}{3}}$$

In theory, t_d is the point at which the Rayleigh curve reaches a maximum. In practice, however, this technology factor (which is a composite cost driver involving 14 components) can take on up to 20 different values, and the equation cannot be used unless size can be estimated, the technology factor agreed upon, and either K or t_d held constant. The equation relating them allows you to assess the effect of varying delivery date on the total effort needed to complete the project.

Because the SLIM software equation includes a fourth power, it has strong implications for resource allocation on large projects. The relationship between effort and duration says that effort is inversely proportional to the fourth power of delivery time.

EXAMPLE 12.9:   The SLIM software equation implies that a 10% decrease in elapsed time results in a 52% increase in total life-cycle effort.

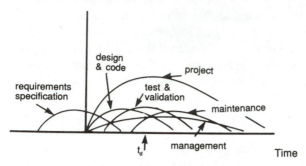

Figure 12.6: Collection of Rayleigh curves for SLIM model

To allow effort or duration estimation, Putnam introduced another equation:

$$D_0 = \frac{K}{t_d^3}$$

D_0, a constant called **manpower acceleration**, takes on a specific value for a particular type of project. For example, the manpower acceleration is 12.3 for new software with many interfaces and interactions with other systems, 15 for stand-alone systems, and 27 for re-implementations of existing systems. Putnam obtained these values from studies of existing systems. Using these two equations, we can solve for effort or duration. For instance, we can derive:

$$K = (S / C)^{\frac{9}{7}} D_0^{\frac{4}{7}}$$

These equations demonstrate an underlying similarity in most cost models, despite different derivation techniques. For example:

- The duration equation shows that delivery time is proportional to the cube root of effort, which is similar in format to Boehm's duration equation.
- The effort equation shows that effort is proportional to size to the power 1.286, which is similar to Boehm's effort equation.

SLIM uses separate Rayleigh curves for

1. design and code
2. test and validation
3. maintenance
4. management

Development effort is assumed to be only 40% of the total life-cycle costs represented by K. In addition, requirements specification is not included in the model, and so is not included in life-cycle costs. We assume that estimation using SLIM is not expected to take place until the start of design and code.

Several researchers have criticized the use of a Rayleigh curve as a basis for cost estimation. Many have pointed out that Norden's original observations were empirical, and not based on a sound theory. Moreover, his data reflected non-software projects, leaving room for doubt that software projects are staffed in the same way. Parr suggested that design and code do not normally start from a zero staffing level, and he proposed adjusting the curve to a positive start (Parr, 1980). Jeffery showed that a number of the underlying assumptions of the Rayleigh curve model do not hold. In particular, he found no evidence of the relationship between difficulty and productivity that Putnam used to construct the software equation. Neither did he find that productivity necessarily decreased when elapsed time was decreased below its optimal value (Jeffery, 1987).

12.3.4 Multi-project models

All of the models discussed so far deal with one project at a time. But often the effort estimates are affected by other projects, especially when reuse is involved. Several researchers have taken a multi-project focus. For example, Pfleeger uses average productivity, rather than size, as the primary parameter of an effort-estimation model (Pfleeger, 1989; 1991). In her approach, she notes that models such as Bailey and Basili's are accurate because they are applied in organizations that tend to develop the same type of software repeatedly. This being the case for many organizations, the effort can be estimated based on what has usually happened in the past, adjusted by cost factors to account for differences between the "usual" project and the current one. Pfleeger also notes that any costs can be amortized over several upcoming projects. For example, the cost of training a staff member in a new technique or tool should not be applied to a single project if the technique or tool will be used on several subsequent projects; instead, the costs should be amortized over the number of projects that are likely to take advantage of this new knowledge. Similarly, cost factors usually affect part of a project, rather than the whole thing; if only half of a product is written in C, then the effects of using C tools should be applied only to half of the effort estimate.

Because reuse naturally involves multiple projects, there are several reuse cost models that consider groups of projects. Bollinger and Pfleeger present a reuse model that treats reuse cost much like any other corporate investment. Estimates are made based on likely reuse over several projects, and investment decisions require understanding of cost-sharing among projects (Bollinger and Pfleeger, 1992; Pfleeger and Bollinger, 1995). Lim has developed a multiple-project model for Hewlett-Packard's reuse investments, using accounting notions familiar to the financial community (Lim, 1994). As organizations recognize that projects are interdependent, there is likely to be increased interest in more general cost models that take into account the collections of projects that are affected by cost decisions.

12.4 PROBLEMS WITH EXISTING MODELING METHODS

Conte, Dunsmore, and Shen (1986) and Pfleeger (1989) have surveyed the effort prediction literature, only to find disappointing reports of model accuracy. The Conte group suggests that a model be considered acceptable when $PRED(0.25)$ exceeds 0.75; sadly, that rarely happens. Bredero and his colleagues cite almost two dozen studies of model accuracy, noting that these evaluations take one of two forms (Bredero *et al.*, 1989):

1   The study applied a model to past project data from a number of projects, and compared the actual effort with predicted effort.
2.   The study used a selection of models to estimate effort (or duration) for a particular project or product.

In the first case, actual values are usually very different from the predicted values, even when all the input values are known. (That is, the number of lines of code is known precisely, not estimated, as it would be for a genuine effort estimate.) In the second case, the different models give very different results for the same inputs.

All of the studies paint a clear picture of model insufficiency. There are many reasons why existing modeling methods have fallen short of their goals.

12.4.1   Model structure

Most researchers and practitioners agree that product size is the key determinant of the effort required to build the product. But the exact relationship between effort and size is far from clear. Empirical studies have confirmed that the relationship can be modeled as a function of size with an exponent *b* and a multiplicative term *a*. However, the values of *a* and *b* differ from data set to data set. That is, most models suggest that effort is approximately proportional to size, but they include an adjustment for diseconomy of scale (*b* is slightly greater than 1), so that larger projects are less productive than small ones.

In practice, there is little evidence to suggest that the exponent, *b*, is different from 1. Banker and Kemerer analyzed seven data sets, finding that only one data set had an exponential value significantly different from 1 (with a level of significance of $p = 0.05$) (Banker and Kemerer, 1989).

Similarly, many model builders feel that the optimal duration for a project is proportional approximately to the cube root of effort.

> **EXAMPLE 12.10:**   Table 12.6 summarizes the empirical results from seven different published data sets: Bailey and Basili (1981), Belady and Lehman (1976), Yourdon (reported in Conte, Dunsmore, and Shen (1986)), Wingfield (reported in Conte, Dunsmore, and Shen (1986)), Kemerer (1987), Boehm (1981), and Kitchenham and Taylor (1985). Most of the data sets produced a significant non-linear relationship between effort and duration, and in most cases the exponential term was not significantly different from 0.333 (using $p = 0.05$ as the level of significance).

However, there is little consensus about the effect of reducing or extending duration. Putnam's model implies that decreasing duration increases effort, but increasing duration decreases effort. At the same time, Boehm's schedule cost driver assumes that increasing or decreasing duration increases project effort.

Table 12.6: Exponential term in effort–duration models

Dataset	b	se(b)	> 0	= 0.333	Projects
Bailey–Basili	0.167	0.076	yes	no	19
Belady–Lehman	0.420	0.046	yes	yes	33
Yourdon	0.252	0.080	yes	yes	17
Wingfield	1.016	0.625	no	–	15
Kemerer	0.315	0.158	no	–	15
Boehm					
– All	0.375	0.031	yes	yes	63
– Organic	0.438	0.074	yes	yes	23
– Semi-detached	0.458	0.054	yes	no	12
– Embedded	0.400	0.057	yes	yes	28
Kitchenham–Taylor	0.262	0.262	yes	yes	33

Empirical results reported by Jeffery have added to the confusion. He calculated the extent of schedule compression and effort compression for a number of projects, and then constructed a scatter plot comparing the two. The resulting graph included schedule-compressed projects that were also effort-compressed, contradicting both the Boehm and Putnam models (Jeffery 1987; 1987a). Results similar to Jeffery's were reported by researchers on the MERMAID project doing a similar analysis (Kitchenham, 1992). Thus, although single models can work well in the environments for which they are derived, it appears unlikely that a simple model of cost parameters can be valid universally.

Moreover, most general models perform poorly because they were developed from *post hoc* analysis of a particular data set. They incorporate the particular characteristics of the data, often including input parameters that would have been difficult to assess accurately at the start of a project. Thus, the first step in building better models is taking care to include parameters known early on.

12.4.2   Overly complex models

It is clear that an organization's particular characteristics can influence its productivity. For this reason, many models include adjustment factors, such as COCOMO's cost drivers and SLIM's technology factor, to provide the flexibility needed to capture these differences. Such simple techniques attempt to avoid the need for extensive calibration, where adjustment factors would have to be derived from an extensive database of information particular to the organization's past projects. However, this generalized approach has fallen short of its promise.

- Application of the COCOMO cost drivers does not always improve the accuracy of estimates (Kemerer, 1987; Kitchenham and Taylor, 1985).
- It is not easy to obtain an accurate estimate of the technology factor (Kemerer, 1987), and SLIM estimates are extremely sensitive to the technology factor (Kitchenham and Taylor, 1985).

- The cost drivers are not independent (Subrahmanian and Brelawski, 1989; Pfleeger, 1989), but they are treated as if they were by COCOMO and similar models. This situation leads to inappropriate multiplication of cost drivers, and equations that are likely to be unstable when applied to data sets other than the ones from which they were derived.

- Cost driver values are usually based on subjective assessments of the influence of some factor (such as staff experience or problem complexity) on overall project effort. It is difficult to ensure that different people assess the factors consistently and that the factors are assessed by the model user in the way that was intended by the model producer (Cuelenaere, van Genuchten, and Heemstra 1987).

- Current models include many adjustment factors, allowing the estimator to cope with many different types of project. However, the projects undertaken by a single development group are often quite similar, and only a few factors need be considered (Pfleeger, 1989; 1991).

12.4.3 Product size estimation

As we have seen, most models require an estimate of likely product size. But this variable is not measurable early in the life cycle (for example, during bid assessment or initial project planning). Models such as COCOMO and SLIM require size in lines of code (LOC), but LOC cannot be measured from a requirements document or an invitation to tender. Furthermore, evidence suggests that estimates of lines of code can be very inaccurate.

> **Example 12.11:** Conte, Dunsmore, and Shen report an unpublished study by Yourdon Inc. that examined the accuracy of size estimates produced by experienced managers. Several managers were asked to look at the complete specifications of 16 projects, and from them to estimate their size in LOC. Then, the average size estimate for each project was compared with the actual size. The average deviation between actual and estimate was 64% of the actual size, and only 25% of the estimates were within 25% of the actual size (that is, *PRED* (0.25) = 0.25) (Conte, Dunsmore, and Shen, 1986).

The current crop of sizing tools does not appear to help:

> **Example 12.12:** A study performed for the US Air Force found that, for a single example product, only two of the tools tested produced size estimates within 30% of the actual, while estimates produced by other tools were 100–200% different from the actual (IIT, 1987).

Finally, we must remember that, in the effort equation, the values of a and b are affected by the organization's counting rules for size and effort. Unless the counting rules in the model are the same as those used in practice, the model will not yield accurate results.

12.5   DEALING WITH PROBLEMS OF CURRENT ESTIMATION METHODS

There are several steps we can take to improve the accuracy of our predictions.

12.5.1   Local data definitions

The first and most important method of improving cost estimation in a particular environment is to use size and effort measures that are defined consistently across the environment. The measures must be understandable by all who must supply or use them, and two people measuring the same product should produce essentially the same number or rating. Tools can help in this regard, as they institutionalize commonly understood measurement definitions. Then, either existing models can be calibrated to the characteristics of your organization, or organization-specific models can be developed.

12.5.2   Calibration

Extensive evidence suggests that calibration significantly improves the accuracy of all models (Kemerer, 1987; Miyazaki and Mori, 1985). The **calibration process** involves two procedures:

1. Ensuring that values supplied to the model are consistent with the model requirements and expectations.
2. Readjusting model coefficients using data about past projects to reflect the basic productivity found in the new environment. It may also be necessary to exclude certain cost drivers from the model, tailor existing ones, or introduce new ones that reflect the needs and concerns of your organization.

Only after the second stage in this process can genuine improvements in accuracy be expected. In addition, calibration cannot be regarded as a one-time activity. The model must be re-evaluated and re-calibrated periodically, so that it remains up to date (Jeffery and Low, 1990).

12.5.3   Independent estimation group

DeMarco suggests that it is useful, although difficult, to assign estimating responsibility to a specific group of people. This group provides estimates to all projects, storing the results of all data capture and analysis in a historical database (DeMarco, 1982). There are several advantages to this approach. First, the group members are familiar with the estimation and calibration techniques, so they are likely to be consistent from one project to another. Second, their estimating experience gives them a better sense of when a project is deviating from the "average" or "standard" one, so that the adjustment factors are realistic. Third, by monitoring the database, the group can identify trends and perform analyses that are impossible for single projects. Finally, by being separated from the project staff, the estimating group can re-estimate periodically, based on data elicited from project members.

12.5.4 Reduce input subjectivity

We have seen how subjectivity of ratings and early estimates of code size can add to the inaccuracy of estimates. There is a great deal of interest in alternative size measures that better reflect the likely size of the final product. We explored some of these alternatives in Chapter 7.

In addition, empirical evidence suggests that local estimation models based on fairly homogeneous data sets are more accurate than more general, complex models. These local models are less likely to need a large number of adjustment factors, thereby reducing subjectivity.

12.5.5 Preliminary estimates and re-estimation

Early estimates necessarily require use of incomplete information. Thus, estimation is likely to be improved by taking two related steps: basing preliminary estimates on measures of available products, and re-estimating as more information becomes available and more products (such as specifications and designs) are produced.

It is likely that the first estimates will be based at least in part on expert judgment and analogy. There are several techniques available to improve the results of such techniques.

12.5.5.1 Group estimates

One simple technique is to derive preliminary estimates from a group, rather than relying on an individual. By using group estimates, individuals get experience with a wider variety of projects, and the resulting estimates are less likely to reflect personal bias.

Group estimating can be done in an organized way using the **Wideband Delphi technique** (Boehm, 1981). The basic procedure is as follows:

1. A coordinator presents each expert with a specification of the proposed project, as well as any other relevant information (such as data on similar projects that have been completed in the past).
2. The coordinator calls a group meeting, where experts ask questions and discuss estimation issues.
3. Each of the experts provides an initial estimate anonymously, indicating judgment of the total project effort and total development effort. The estimate is provided as a range, with most likely value set between upper and lower bounds.
4. The coordinator prepares and circulates a summary report, indicating the individual estimates and the average of the group's estimates.

5. Then, the coordinator holds a meeting at which the experts discuss their current estimates, this time considering them in the context of other estimates and the reasons for them.

6. Finally the experts provide (perhaps revised) anonymous estimates, and steps 2 through 6 are repeated until the group decides that the average is representative and satisfactory.

Putnam and Fitzsimmons suggest that the group estimate should not be the simple average of individual estimates (Putnam and Fitzsimmons, 1979). Rather, it should be the average of weighted individual estimates obtained from the formula:

$$\text{estimate} = \frac{\text{lower\_bound} + 4(\text{most\_likely}) + \text{upper\_bound}}{6}$$

That is, the group estimate is the average of the individual weighted estimates. The variance of an individual estimate can be derived using the formula:

$$\text{variance} = \frac{\text{upper\_bound} - \text{lower\_bound}}{6}$$

The group variance is the average of the individual variances, and the standard deviation is the square root of the variance.

12.5.5.2   Estimation by analogy

Actual effort and duration for similar, completed projects are useful as input for preliminary estimates of a new project. Then values should be adjusted in light of a subjective assessment of the differences between the new project and the old ones. Thus, if the new project is believed to be 10% larger than the old project, the effort estimate can be increased by 10%. For each cost factor (for example, stringency of reliability or performance requirements, or extent of reuse), the new project is compared with past project data, and adjustments are made to the estimate, if necessary.

Effort adjustments can be treated linearly, but duration adjustment should not be. Instead, you can make a subjective assessment of duration based on the duration of the analogous project, or you can use one of the existing effort–duration models.

If enough data are available, you can improve the preliminary estimate by selecting two similar projects: one larger and one smaller than the new project. Then, you can interpolate between the two to obtain an initial estimate of the effort and duration for the new project.

12.5.5.3   Re-estimation

As more information becomes available, we can re-assess the model inputs and re-estimate our outputs. This approach, advocated in DeMarco (1982), is the basis of COCOMO 2.0 and the Pfleeger model (Pfleeger, 1989). The estimation process can in fact use different models at different stages in the life-cycle, so that each estimate takes advantage of equations, size measures, adjustment factors, and other data that are appropriate to the information available. The MERMAID project used this approach, with phased-based equations and input variables based on early available measurements (not estimates) (Kitchenham, Kok, and Kirakowski, 1990).

Note that expert opinion or analogy estimates may still be necessary if the project being undertaken is not similar to projects commonly developed. For example, if an unusual application is being developed, or if a new development method is adopted, then expert opinion may be involved in assessing similarities or differences with other, completed projects. These subjective estimates can also provide an additional perspective with which to check a more formal cost model's estimate.

12.5.6   Alternative size measures for cost estimation

We have noted the difficulty of predicting eventual code size from early life-cycle products. Several models have adopted techniques that use measurements of early products. We described some of these measures in detail in Chapter 7; here, we present evidence that alternative size measures can yield more accurate estimates.

Function points, a weighted sum of counts of user-visible product features, can be derived from a requirements specification. They are viewed by many estimators as a useful alternative to estimating lines of code. Some cost estimation tools use function points as a "front end" to COCOMO or other models, where the number of function points is converted to lines of code based on factors derived from historical data. Some companies collect data to determine the average effort required to implement a single function point; this information is then supplied to a model to estimate likely effort on a proposed project.

> **EXAMPLE 12.13:**   The US Air Force investigated function-point-based tools, including ASSET-R and Before You Leap (BYL). ASSET-R has a function point extension that is used for scientific programs, while BYL has a function points front end to a COCOMO tool. Each was applied to scientific programs. The first ASSET-R estimate was within 28% of the actual value, and the other was 30% of the actual. BYL produced an estimate within 144% of the actual. (We have been informed that the current version of BYL has been updated; the Air Force evaluation reported here refers to an older, outdated version.)

Specification weight metrics (originally called bang metrics) are based on DeMarco's structured analysis and design notation (DeMarco, 1978). DeMarco suggested two types of bang metric: one for function strong systems, where functionality guides development, and one for data strong systems, where data structures and transaction processing guide development. The **function bang** measure is based on the number of functional primitives (that is, bubbles) in a data-flow diagram. The basic functional primitive count is weighted according to the type of functional primitive and the number of data tokens used by the primitive. The **data bang measure** is based on the number of entities in the entity-relationship model. The basic entity count is weighted according to the number of relationships involving each entity.

The bang measures have been used on some projects, but no results are reported in the literature, and the technique has not been subjected to any independent validation. However, as CASE tools can generate the values automatically, bang measures offer promise as an alternative specification measure.

Other researchers have tailored their size measures to development type as well as specification needs. Verner and Tate report success in using a function-points-like approach in estimating the size of fourth-generation languages (Verner and Tate, 1992). Olsen applied the Pfleeger model, using a count of objects and methods for object-oriented development; he reports that the estimate was within 3% of the actual (Olsen, 1993).

EXAMPLE 12.14:   British Aerospace's Military Aircraft Division, in seeking an alternative to function points, derived its own specification measures:

- number of diagrams
- number of processes (including terminal processes)
- number of terminal processes
- amount of data (critical and non-critical)
- number of pages in issued documents

An estimation model was then developed using historical data, and the model was applied to eleven projects. The number of terminal processes was found to be the best predictor of lines of code, with a mean magnitude of relative error equal to 0.17 and *PRED*(0.25) equal to 0.91 (Mason, 1994).

12.5.7   Locally developed cost models

We have noted how locally developed cost models appear to have higher accuracy than more general ones, since they reflect the particular characteristics of an organization's typical applications and development environment. Often, local cost models use different equations or techniques at different phases of the project, in order to reflect the different size measures available during development. This flexibility contrasts with the rigidity of most commercial models, which force the use of predefined size measures (usually lines of code or function points).

DeMarco suggests five steps in defining a local cost model (DeMarco, 1982):

1.   Decompose cost elements

Begin by identifying the phases and activities that are to be included as part of the software-development process. That is, decide just which activities' effort and duration comprise the project estimate. For some organizations, the effort estimate involves requirements elicitation and specification, while others consider the project to begin only after the specification is completed and approved. Likewise, some effort estimates include maintenance activities, while others do not. Once the activities are identified, they suggest the number of cost models required, and they form the basic sources of data for them.

2. Formulate cost theory

Each cost model must be based on a theory of which inputs affect the output and in what way. The most common cost theory is that size is the main cost driver; a local cost model based on this theory must next identify a suitable size measure as appropriate input for each stage of the project. In general, the cost theory must describe the relationship between inputs and outputs, and an overall model must describe how the individual models are related. For example, an estimate made during the requirements phase might be input to the estimating process at design; the cost theory must explain how the requirements-based estimate relates to the design-based one.

Local cost models and equations often include cost drivers and adjustment factors, as well as effort expended on completed tasks. Several researchers have noted that effort on completed tasks is highly correlated with the effort remaining to complete the entire project (Kitchenham and Taylor, 1985; Grady, 1987).

It is important to remember that the collection of cost models, although linked, need not be the same. In particular, the size measure at each stage of development may be different.

> **EXAMPLE 12.15:** We have seen that COCOMO 2.0 takes advantage of different size measures for different stages of development. Its cost theory links the three COCOMO stages, explaining how object points and function points are related to lines of code.

3. Collect data

To check the validity of the cost theory, we must collect data on projects that have already been completed in the particular environment represented by the local model. Chapter 5 presented the key issues to be addressed in collecting such data. You should take care in attempting to reconstruct information about completed projects that had no formal data collection system, as such data may be inaccurate or biased; formal data collection is usually much more reliable.

The number of past projects required to test a cost theory depends on the number of input variables included in the cost equation. Theoretically, three projects are sufficient to test a cost theory based on one input variable, and in general, $n+2$ projects are needed to test a theory involving n input variables. However, in practice, seven to ten projects should be used for each input variable, because it is likely that the natural variability of the data will be too great to detect any underlying relationships with a smaller number of data points.

The collection of cost models, and the theories that support them, are aimed at producing more accurate predictions. We want to be able to test the prediction accuracy as soon as actual data become available on a project. And we want to be able to apply the cost equations and models simply and quickly. Thus, we recommend beginning with simple models and equations, and testing them on actual projects. These equations and models can be refined as accuracy is evaluated.

4.   Analyze data and evaluate model

Regression analysis should be used to analyze the past project data and test the significance of the results. Statistically derived models have an advantage over deterministic models, because they provide a measure of their own accuracy that can be expressed in terms of upper and lower bounds on predictions (that is, with 95% confidence limits).

5.   Check model

Statistical significance is not sufficient to give a good predictor. Assessment measures such as mean magnitude of relative error, *PRED*(0.25) and EQF should be used to determine if the models are producing estimates with acceptable accuracy. If not, the models should be examined carefully, their inputs checked, and these five steps revisited to adjust the cost models and the theories on which they are based.

Step 5 is particularly important, as continuous feedback is necessary not just to check the model but also to reflect changing processes, resources, and techniques. Local models may be refined each time a new project is completed. This refinement may include the introduction of new input variables, or a more accurate assessment of the variability of the data. In addition, individuals taking part in early group estimation exercises should always examine actual project results in a *post mortem* review of the project and estimation process. The estimation process may require revision, as well as the models and theories.

12.6   IMPLICATIONS FOR PROCESS PREDICTION

In earlier chapters, we have seen many examples of process prediction. For instance, Chapter 10 examined techniques for predicting reliability, while Chapters 8 and 9 offered measures that were useful in predicting the effort and duration required for the testing process. There are many other opportunities to make predictions throughout the software development and maintenance processes. We may want to predict how many requirements will change during development (an outcome that may depend on the customer, the application domain, and the novelty of the application, among other things), or the number of requirements faults we can expect to find during inspections. Similarly, we may want to predict the size or complexity of the design from the requirements, the amount of design that can be reused from past projects, the number of design faults, or the amount of time needed for design review and rework. During coding, we often need to predict when coding will be complete, how much code will be reusable on future projects, or when integration and system testing

Table 12.7: Questions to be answered in process prediction

Question	Possible relevant factors
When will it start?	Resources
	Size
	Previous activity
When will it end?	Resources
	Size
	Novelty
	Application type
How many staff will it require?	Resources
	Size
	Novelty
	Application type
	Experience
How many faults will be injected?	Size
	Novelty
	Application type
	Experience
How many faults can we expect to find?	Application type
	Novelty
	Size
	Experience
	Quality measures of previous activities
How sensitive is it to change?	Novelty
	Application type
	Quality measures of previous activities

can begin. And during testing, we predict when testing will be complete and when the product can be turned over to the customer. We can identify similar needs in the maintenance process, the reuse process, the configuration management process, and more.

All of these processes have characteristics similar to the ones examined in this chapter. Each is a collection of activities with a clear starting and ending point. And each involves a degree of uncertainty, making the accuracy of prediction a challenging but necessary part of software engineering. Table 12.7 lists some of the prediction questions that must be answered for any process.

Our examination of the cost estimation process offers several lessons for general process prediction. We have seen the need to view prediction in terms of models and theories. We identify key variables that affect the attribute we wish to predict, and we formulate a theory of how the variables relate to each other and to the attribute. Then we build a model that reflects that relationship. Sometimes, we describe a collection of relationships, which in turn are related to one another. Where possible, we express these models and relationships as equations, which we then use to calculate our estimates. Figure 12.7 illustrates this prediction process.

Recall that the estimates are not single-point items; rather, they are expressed in a window, with some level of confidence in the prediction. And the estimates are not static; as predictions, they change as we gather more information about the process and its completed tasks and products. Thus, preliminary estimates, usually involving some subjective judgment, give way to more formal and objective predictions as more data are available.

We have noted that locally derived models are usually more accurate than universal models; this result is true for most prediction, not just for cost and effort estimation. The same techniques described for constructing local cost models can be applied more generally to any process prediction.

12.7 SUMMARY

Prediction is a necessary part of any good process, whether it be design, testing, or software development as a whole. In this chapter, we have seen that estimates can be assessed by looking at the mean magnitude of relative error, at the percentage of time that the estimate is within 25% of the actual value, and at the way in which successive estimates narrow the gap between estimate and actual (EQF). We have examined cost estimation as a particular example, noting that the creative, rather than manufacturing, aspects of software development make cost and effort especially difficult to estimate.

The current approaches to cost estimation involve a large degree of subjectivity, especially when we rely on expert judgment and analogy for the size estimate, the cost driver settings, or even for the entire effort estimate. The currently available models are designed to be general, and their accuracy is usually far less than locally

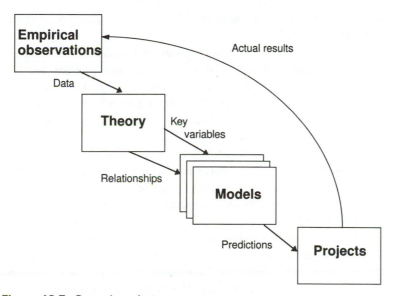

Figure 12.7: General prediction process

developed models that are tailored to particular development environments. We have suggested several techniques, including calibration, repeated estimation, and alternative size measures, to help improve the accuracy of existing models or newly developed ones. And we have noted that a collection of related models, each based on measurable data available at a given stage of development, is likely to be more accurate than a single, generic model.

Finally, we have noted that the lessons learned in estimating cost also apply more generally to process prediction. Any prediction technique should:

- allow the use of different estimation methods;
- use measures, not estimates, as input to the models;
- support periodic re-estimation; and
- provide feedback to improve the skill of estimators and the accuracy of estimation models.

12.8 EXERCISES

1. Find out what Parkinson's Law is. Explain why this law is not really a cost estimation method.

2. What activities might be overlooked when using bottom-up estimation?

3. What might lead to underestimating effort using top-down estimation?

4. Using the semi-detached model, what is the basic COCOMO estimate of the effort to produce 5000 delivered source instructions? Does this seem reasonable? Notice that COCOMO estimates include project management, quality assurance, configuration management, and documentation.

5. According to the Rayleigh curve model, what is the effect of extending the delivery date by 20%?

6. Assume that a very good development environment leads to a technology factor of 46 369, and suppose that you have a five-year timescale for delivery. How much development effort does the Rayleigh curve model predict for a ten thousand KDSI space-based missile systems project? What happens to the estimate if the development environment is not as good as expected, so that the technology factor is really 10 946?

7. What features need to be considered when you define a line of code?

8. What measures can be used to assess product size at the design stage?

9. What are the advantages and disadvantages of developing an environment-specific cost estimation process compared with calibrating an existing cost estimation model?

10. Suppose that you are developing the software for a nuclear power plant control system. Select the most appropriate mode for the project, and use the COCOMO model to give a crude estimate of the total number of person months required for the development, assuming that the estimated software size is 10 000 delivered source instructions.

11 Describe three essentially different methods that could be used to estimate the cost of a software project.

12 Compare Conte, Dunsmore, and Shen's *PRED* measure with DeMarco's EQF. When is each one used? What values indicate a good estimate? Is there a relationship between the two measures?

13 Explain why an average project using the COCOMO model for estimation can use the basic model instead of the intermediate one.

12.9 FURTHER READING

Boehm's book is a classic and useful reference, and it contains a complete derivation of the original COCOMO model.

Boehm, B.W., *Software Engineering Economics*, Prentice Hall, Englewood Cliffs, NJ, 1981.

Conte, Dunsmore, and Shen present a good overview of the history and theory behind most commercial cost estimation models.

Conte, S., Dunsmore, H. and Shen, V., *Software Engineering Metrics and Models*, Benjamin-Cummings, Menlo Park, CA, 1986.

COCOMO 2.0 is described by the team that updated it and developed tools to support it.

Boehm, B.W., Clark, B., Horowitz *et al.*, "Cost models for future life cycle processes: COCOMO 2.0," *Annals of Software Engineering* 1(1), pp. 1–24, November 1995.

PART III
MEASUREMENT AND MANAGEMENT

13 Planning a measurement program

In previous chapters, we have explored the reasons for establishing a metrics program, the ways of deriving metrics from goals, and the myriad possibilities for choosing particular metrics. For the remainder of the book, we consider measurement as a management tool. We begin in this chapter by discussing how to plan and establish a measurement program in your organization. In Chapter 14, we look at measurement in practice: what other organizations are doing, and what makes them successful. Finally, in Chapter 15, we return to the role of measurement in empirical research, where we study several examples of experiments and case studies to see how measurement supports informed decision making.

In this chapter, we turn to packaging a comprehensive measurement program. We look at how to put the pieces together, doing so in a manner that is sensitive to the managerial and organizational issues that are likely to be involved. This chapter lays out the steps in devising a measurement plan; after reading it, you should be able to plan a measurement program tailored to your organization's needs. When, in the next chapter we describe several examples of measurement in practice, you can compare your plans with the actual experiences of other organizations.

Many software project managers acknowledge that measurement helps them understand and guide the development of their projects. They want to select particular metrics, perhaps as part of an overall development plan, but they do not know how to begin. The answers to a manager's metrics questions should appear in the project's metrics plan, so that managers and developers know what to collect, when to collect it, and how the data relate to management decisions. The plan enables managers to establish a flexible and comprehensive metrics program as part of a larger process or product improvement program.

We begin by describing the contents of a metrics plan, outlining the types of information that such a plan should include. Then, we explain how the techniques described earlier in this book, from the GQM approach to notions of process maturity, can be interwoven in the plan. Throughout the discussion, we present examples of how the techniques have been used in real projects to decide how to begin metrics collection and analysis.

13.1 What is a Metrics Plan?

A metrics plan is much like a newspaper article: it must describe the who, what, where, when, how and why of metrics. With answers to all of these questions, whoever reads the plan knows exactly why metrics are being collected, how they are used, and how metrics fit into the larger picture of software development or maintenance.

The plan usually begins with the **why**. It is in this introductory section that the plan lays out the goals or objectives of the project, describing what questions need to be answered by project members and project management. For example, if reliability is a major concern to the developers, then the plan discusses how reliability will be defined and what reporting requirements are imposed on the project; later sections of the plan can then discuss how reliability will be measured and tracked.

Next, the plan addresses **what** will be measured. In many cases, the measures are grouped or related in some way. For instance, productivity may be measured in terms of two component pieces, size and effort. So the plan will explain how size and effort are defined and then how they are combined to compute productivity.

At the same time, the plan must lay out **where** and **when** during the process the measurements will be made. Some measurements are taken once, while others are made repeatedly and tracked over time. The time and frequency of collection are related to the goals and needs of the project, and those relationships should be made explicit in the plan.

How and **who** address the identification of tools, techniques, and staff available for metrics collection and analysis. It is important that the plan discusses not only what measures are needed but also what tools will be used for data capture and storage, and who is responsible for those activities. Often, metrics plans ignore these crucial issues, and project members assume that someone else is taking care of metrics business; the result is that everyone agrees that the metrics are important, but no one is actually assigned to get the data. Likewise, responsibility for analysis often slips through the project cracks, and data pile up but are never used in decision making. The plan must state clearly what types of analysis will be carried out with the data, who will do the analysis, how the results will be conveyed to the decision makers, and how they will support decisions.

Thus, the metrics plan paints a comprehensive picture of the measurement process, from initial definition of need to analysis and application of the results. The remainder of this chapter discusses how the techniques introduced in earlier chapters can be used to answer the questions addressed in the metrics plan.

13.2 WHY AND WHAT: DEVELOPING GOALS, QUESTIONS, AND METRICS

A manager or developer may find a particular measurement useful when the measure helps in understanding a process, its resources, or one of its resultant products. However, the utility derives from knowing how the process, product, or resource relates to overall project goals. Thus, recognizing improvement can occur only when the project has clearly defined goals for process and products. The Goal–Question–Metric (GQM) approach to process and metrics, described in Chapter 3, provides a structure from which managers and developers can derive a set of crucial project goals, plus the questions that must be answered in order to tell if the goals have been met. Recall that GQM begins by identifying the overall organizational goals. From each goal, questions are identified, whose answers help managers know if progress is being made toward reaching the goal. Then, each question is analyzed in terms of what measurements are needed to help decide the answer to each question. In this way, an understanding of goals is used to generate suggested metrics for a given project.

> **EXAMPLE 13.1:** The US National Aeronautics and Space Administration's Goddard Space Flight Center has been using metrics for many years as part of a larger program to understand and improve their products and processes. Their Software Engineering Laboratory has published several documents to guide developers in the major activities of software production. The *Manager's Handbook for Software Development* contains a chapter on verification, testing and certification, organized along a GQM-like framework (SEL, 1990). Each major verification or testing method is described in five ways: purpose, plan, participants, activities, and monitoring. The purpose and plan address the goals, and the participants and activities generate questions. Monitoring suggests metrics.

The GQM templates provided by Basili and Rombach encourage managers to consider the context in which a question is being asked, as well as the viewpoint of the questioner. For example, a programmer is likely to ask different questions about productivity or quality from a corporate vice-president. The programmer may want to know productivity to be able to project when she will finish designing or coding a module, while the vice-president may want to know if productivity has been improved by a recent investment in tools. The viewpoint can affect the way a metric is defined (by the programmer on a module-by-module basis, or by the vice-president on a project-by-project basis) and used. By deriving measurements from goals and questions, it is clear how the resulting data points will be related to one another and used in the larger context of the project.

Once these questions are identified, each question is analyzed to determine what must be measured in order to answer the question.

EXAMPLE 13.2: In Chapter 11, we saw the importance of understanding the effects of tool use on productivity. Suppose that evaluating tool use is one of our major goals. Several questions arise from that goal, including:

- Which tools are used?
- Who is using each tool?
- How much of the project is affected by each tool?
- How much experience do developers have with the tool?
- What is productivity with tool use? Without tool use?
- What is product quality with tool use? Without tool use?

What is not evident from the GQM tree is the model needed to combine the measurements in a sensible way so that the questions can be answered. For example, coder productivity may be measured in terms of effort per line of code, but that relationship is not explicit in the tree. Thus, the GQM approach must be supplemented by one or more models that express the relationships among the metrics.

EXAMPLE 13.3: A project involves developing a complex piece of software, including a large database of sensor data. The sensor data capture routines are being written in C, while the data storage and manipulation routines are being written in Smalltalk. The project manager wants to track coder productivity. Her metrics plan includes a GQM-derived question: is the productivity for C development the same as for Smalltalk development? Productivity will be measured as size per person day, where size is measured in three ways: as a count of objects and methods, as a count of lines of code, and as function points. The metrics plan also depicts a model of productivity for the entire project, showing how the different programmer productivity measures are combined into a project productivity measure. The project measure weights the individual measures by experience with the language and experience with the application.

Thus, the goals tell us why we are measuring, and the questions, metrics, and models tell us what to measure.

13.2.1 Other measurement frameworks

In Chapter 3, we described how process visibility, combined with the GQM approach, can be used to suggest what kind of measurement is appropriate for your process and project. The concept of visibility was summarized in terms of five levels of maturity, based loosely on the Software Engineering Institute's original notion of process maturity. We saw how the degree of visibility or maturity could influence the choice of measurement; for example, a low maturity project might count only number of requirements, while a high maturity project could count requirements by type, track changes, and relate them to design and code. However, there are several other frameworks for discussing process improvement, and each can be combined with the GQM approach to provide a context for measurement. Measurement is intricately intertwined with the process improvement approach, as can be seen in this definition of process assessment by an international standards committee:

> The disciplined examination of the processes used by an organisation against a set of criteria to determine the capability of those processes to perform within quality, cost and schedule goals. The aim is to characterise current practice, identifying strengths and weaknesses and the ability of the process to control or avoid significant causes of poor quality, cost and schedule performance (ISO/IEC, 1992).

In this section, we look at several of the more popular process assessment frameworks. Because many of these approaches are being mandated by corporations or governments, it is important to understand them and to be aware of measurement's role within them.

13.2.1.1 Capability maturity model

The **capability maturity model** (CMM) was developed by the US Software Engineering Institute (SEI) to assist the Department of Defense in assessing the quality of its contractors. The CMM, inspired by Deming's work (Deming, 1989), had its beginning as the **process maturity model**, where an organization was rated on an ordinal scale from 1 (low) to 5 (high), based on the answers to 110 questions about its development process. Table 13.1 lists the twelve questions required for a level 2 (repeatable) assessment; if any of these questions is answered "no," then the organization was automatically assessed at a level 1, regardless of the answers to the 98 other questions.

There were many problems with this approach, and the CMM was developed to address them and replace the process maturity model. However, many of the basic principles of the original process maturity approach remain: the CMM uses a questionnaire to assess the maturity of a developer, supplements the questionnaire with requests for evidence to verify the answers, and generates a rating on a five-point scale (as we saw in Chapter 3). That is, the CMM describes principles and practices that are assumed to lead to better software products, and the model organizes them in five levels, providing a path to more process visibility and control, and to the improved products that result. The model is used in two ways: by potential customers, to identify the strengths and weaknesses of their suppliers, and by software developers themselves, to assess their capabilities and set a path toward improvement.

Table 13.1: Required questions for level 1 of process maturity model

Question number	Question
1.1.3	Does the Software Quality Assurance function have a management reporting channel separate from the software development project management?
1.1.6	Is there a software configuration control function for each project that involves software development?
2.1.3	Is a formal process used in the management review of each software development prior to making contractual commitments?
2.1.14	Is a formal procedure used to make estimates of software size?
2.1.15	Is a formal procedure used to produce software development schedules?
2.1.16	Are formal procedures applied to estimating software development cost?
2.2.2	Are profiles of software size maintained for each software configuration item over time?
2.2.4	Are statistics on software code and test errors gathered?
2.4.1	Does senior management have a mechanism for the regular review of the status of software development projects?
2.4.7	Do software development first-line managers sign off on their schedule and cost estimates?
2.4.9	Is a mechanism used for controlling changes to the software requirements?
2.4.17	Is a mechanism used for controlling changes to the code?

Each of the five capability levels is associated with a set of key process areas on which an organization should focus as part of its improvement activities. The first level of the maturity model, **initial**, describes a software development process that is *ad hoc* or even chaotic. Few processes are defined, and the success of development depends on individual efforts, not on team accomplishments. As shown in Table 13.2, there are no key process areas at this level.

The next level is **repeatable**, where basic project management processes track cost, schedule and functionality. There is some discipline among team members, so that successes on earlier projects can be repeated with similar, new ones. Here, the key process areas are primarily management activities that help to understand and control the actions and outcomes of the process.

Improving the repeatable process leads to a **defined** process, where management and engineering activities are documented, standardized and integrated; the result is a standard process for everyone in the organization. Although some projects may differ from others, the standard process is tailored to these special needs, and the adaptation must be approved by management. At this level of maturity, the key process areas have an organizational focus.

Table 13.2: Key process areas in the capability maturity model (Paulk, 1995)

CMM level	Key process areas
Initial	none
Repeatable	Requirements management
	Software project planning
	Software project tracking and oversight
	Software subcontract management
	Software quality assurance
	Software configuration management
Defined	Organization process focus
	Organization process definition
	Training program
	Integrated software management
	Software product engineering
	Intergroup coordination
	Peer reviews
Managed	Quantitative process management
	Software quality management
Optimizing	Defect prevention
	Technology change management
	Process change management

A **managed** process directs its efforts at product quality. By introducing detailed measures of process and product quality, the organization focuses on using quantitative information to make problems visible and to assess the effect of possible solutions. Thus, the key process areas address quantitative software management as well as software quality management.

The most desirable level of capability maturity is **optimizing**, where quantitative feedback is incorporated in the process to produce continuous process improvement. In particular, new tools and techniques are tested and monitored to see how they affect the process and products. Key process areas include defect prevention, technology change management, and process change management.

Table 13.2 summarizes the maturity levels and process areas. But the capability maturity model has another level of granularity not shown in the table: each process area is composed of a set of key practices whose presence indicates that the developer has implemented and institutionalized the process area. The key practices are supposed to provide evidence that the process area is effective, repeatable, and long-lasting (Paulk, 1995).

The key practices are organized by these common features:

- **Commitment to perform:** what actions ensure that the process is established and will continue to be used? This category includes policy and leadership practices.
- **Ability to perform:** what preconditions ensure that the organization is capable of implementing the process? Practices here address resources, training, orientation, tools, and organizational structure.

Table 13.3: Measurement changes with growth in maturity

Metric category	Measurement	Level 1 % usage	Level 2 % usage	Level 3 % usage	Level 4 %usage
Process	Compliance	0	43	50	100
	Resources	0	14	25	100
Stability	Software requirements tracking	0	25	75	100
Quality	PR status	100	86	100	100
	Statistics on development defects	40	71	100	100
	Defect profile	20	71	75	100
	Product quality (defects/KDSLOC)	0	14	50	100
	% defects found in inspections	0	14	50	100
Cost	Cost data	25	100	100	100
Staffing	Personnel trends	100	100	100	100
Productivity	Delivered LOC	20	86	75	100
	New LOC	40	86	100	100
	% of reused code	0	71	75	100
Effort	Estimate to complete	80	71	50	100
	Rework effort and time	0	29	50	–
Schedule	Variance	20	100	100	100
	Milestones	100	100	100	100
Progress	Module development	80	86	75	100
	Design	60	57	100	100
	Test	80	86	100	100
	Rework	–	14	–	–
	Earned value	0	57	75	100

- **Activities performed:** what roles and procedures are necessary to implement a key process area? This category includes practices on plans, procedures, work performed, corrective action, and tracking.
- **Measurement and analysis:** what procedures measure the process and analyze the measurements? The practices in this category include process measurement and analysis.
- **Verifying implementation:** what ensures that activities comply with the established process? The practices include management reviews and audits.

An organization is said to satisfy a key process area only when the process area is both implemented and institutionalized. Implementation is determined by the answers to the "activities performed" questions; the other practices address institutionalization.

The implications for measurement are clear. The capability maturity model emphasizes quantitative control of the process, and the higher levels direct the

Table 13.4: Average number of metrics across maturity levels

Level number	Average number of metrics
1	11
2	19
3	22
4	26
5	31

organization to use measurement and quantitative analysis. A GQM analysis of a project using the CMM framework can derive many of its goals and questions directly from the key process areas and practices. In fact, such an analysis has been performed; the Software Engineering Institute provides a technical report that discusses the metrics implications of the CMM (Baumert and McWhinney, 1992).

EXAMPLE 13.4: Brodman and Johnson surveyed 33 companies to determine the impact of the CMM on several aspects of company business (Brodman and Johnson, 1995). Among other things, they tracked the measurements used by each company and grouped them by maturity level. Table 13.3 shows the results. It is clear that the degree of measurement increases with maturity, and Table 13.4 summarizes that growth. However, the metrics captured at higher levels are not necessarily the same as the ones at lower levels.

13.2.1.2 SPICE

The capability maturity model spawned a proliferation of process assessment methods, from Trillium (produced by Canadian telecommunications companies) to Bootstrap (an extension of the CMM developed by a European Community ESPRIT project). This growth, and the application of process assessment techniques to products that were commercially sensitive, led the UK Ministry of Defence to propose an international standard for process assessment (Rout, 1995). The new standard, called SPICE (for Software Process Improvement and Capability dEtermination), is intended to harmonize and extend the existing approaches. Similar to the Capability Maturity Model, SPICE is recommended both for process improvement and capability determination. The framework is built on an assessment architecture that defines desirable practices and processes.

There are two different types of practices:

- **Base practices** are essential activities of a specific process.
- **Generic practices** institutionalize or implement a process in a general way.

Figure 13.1 illustrates how the SPICE architecture ties the two together and includes actual ratings for each.

The left-hand side of the diagram represents functional practices involved in software development. This functional view considers five activities:

1. **customer-supplied:** processes that affect the customer directly, support development and delivery of the products to the customer, and ensure correct operation and use;
2. **engineering:** processes that specify, implement, or maintain the system and its documentation;
3. **project:** processes that establish the project, coordinate or manage resources, or provide customer services;
4. **support:** processes that enable or support performance of the other processes;

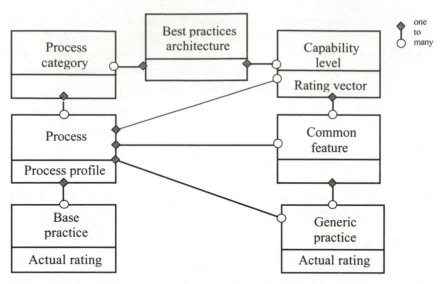

Figure 13.1: SPICE architecture for process assessment (Rout, 1995)

5. **organization:** processes that establish business goals, and develop assets to achieve those goals.

The right-hand side of Figure 13.1 shows a picture of management; the generic practices, applicable to all processes, are arranged in six levels of capability:

0. **not performed:** fails to perform, and no identifiable workproducts;
1. **performed informally:** not planned and tracked, depends on individual knowledge, identifiable workproducts;
2. **planned and tracked:** verified according to specified procedures, workproducts conform to specified standards and requirements;
3. **well-defined:** well-defined process using approved, tailored versions of standard, documented processes;
4. **quantitatively controlled:** detailed performance measures, prediction capability, objective management, workproducts evaluated quantitatively;
5. **continuously improving:** quantitative targets for effectiveness and efficiency based on business goals, quantitative feedback from defined processes plus trying new ideas.

An assessment report is a **profile**; each process area is evaluated and reported to be at one of the six capability levels. Figure 13.2 is an example of how the profile is reported. The shading indicates the degree to which the activities were satisfied at each level.

Thus, whereas the CMM addresses organizations, SPICE addresses processes. As with the CMM, a SPICE assessment is administered in a carefully prescribed way, to minimize subjectivity in the ratings.

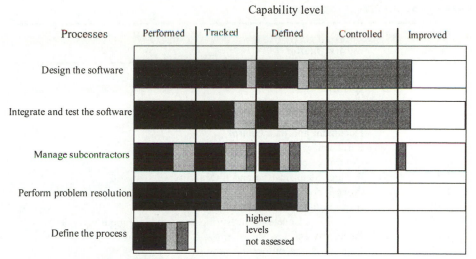

Figure 13.2: SPICE assessment profile (Rout, 1995)

13.2.1.3 ISO 9000

ISO, the international standards organization, has produced a series of standards that collectively are known as ISO 9000. The standards specify actions to be taken when any system (that is, not necessarily a software system) has quality goals and constraints. In particular, ISO 9000 applies when a buyer requires a supplier to demonstrate a given level of expertise in designing and building a product. The buyer and supplier need not belong to separate companies; the relationship can exist even within the same organization.

Among the ISO 9000 standards, standard 9001 is most applicable to the way we develop and maintain software (ISO, 1987). It explains what a buyer must do to ensure that the supplier conforms to design, development, production, installation and maintenance requirements. Table 13.5 lists the clauses of ISO 9001. Since ISO 9001 is quite general, there is a separate document, ISO 9000-3, that provides guidelines for interpreting ISO 9001 in a software context (ISO, 1990a).

EXAMPLE 13.5: Clause 4.2 of ISO 9001 requires an organization to have a documented quality system, including a quality manual, plans, procedures, and instructions. ISO 9000-3 interprets this clause for software, explaining how the quality system should be integrated throughout the software development process. For instance, clause 4.2.3 discusses quality planning across projects, and 5.5 addresses it within a given development project.

Similarly, clause 4.4 of ISO 9001 requires establishing procedures to control and verify design, including

- planning, design, and development activities
- defining organizational and technical interfaces

Table 13.5: ISO 9001 clauses

Clause number	Subject matter
4.1	Management responsibility
4.2	Quality system
4.3	Contract review
4.4	Design control
4.5	Document and data control
4.6	Purchasing
4.7	Control of customer-supplied product
4.8	Product identification and traceability
4.9	Process control
4.10	Inspection and testing
4.11	Control of inspection, measuring and test equipment
4.12	Inspection and test status
4.13	Control of nonconforming product
4.14	Corrective and preventive action
4.15	Handling, storage, packaging, preservation and delivery
4.16	Control of quality records
4.17	Internal quality audits
4.18	Training
4.19	Servicing
4.20	Statistical techniques

- identifying inputs and outputs
- reviewing, verifying, and validating the design
- controlling design changes

Then, ISO 9000-3 maps these activities to a software context. Clause 5.3 addresses the purchaser's requirements specification, clause 5.4 looks at development planning, 5.5 at quality planning, 5.6 at design and implementation, 5.7 at testing and validation, and 6.1 at configuration management.

The ISO 9000 standards are used to regulate internal quality and to assure the quality of suppliers. Typically, a contractor will subcontract for part of a system, based on the supplier's ISO 9000 certification. The certification process has a defined scope and is carried out by quality-system auditors. In the UK, ISO 9000 certification is performed under the auspices of the TickIT program, and there is a comprehensive TickIT guide to interpret and elaborate on the concepts and application of ISO 9000 (DTI, 1992).

Measurement is also part of ISO 9000, but it is not as explicit as in SPICE or the CMM. In particular, the strong emphasis on statistical process control found in SPICE and CMM is missing in ISO 9000. However, as with the other frameworks, the goals of the framework can easily be mapped to questions and metrics.

13.2.1.4 The reliability of measuring maturity

The maturity models and their assessment methods are becoming *de facto* standards in many organizations. For example, minimum CMM scores are expected to be required for some US Air Force software contracts (Saiedian and Kuzara, 1995), and the scores have a significant effect on US Navy contract decisions. Rugg points out that "software capability – as measured in the submitted proposal and on site – counted as one third of the weight for consideration to award the contract' (Rugg, 1993). But ever since the introduction of the Software Engineering Institute's original process maturity model, there have been objections to its application and use. Bollinger and McGowan noted many problems with the use of the original process maturity questionnaire; in particular, they pointed out that limited questions captured only a small number of the characteristics of good software practice, and their yes/no answers made partial compliance impossible to measure. They also noted that the process maturity model assumes a manufacturing paradigm for software; as we discussed in Chapter 12, manufacturing and replication may be inappropriate analogies for software development (Bollinger and McGowan, 1991).

> **EXAMPLE 13.6:** We saw in Table 13.1 that level 2 (repeatable) requires a "yes" answer to the question, "Do software development first-line managers sign off on their schedule and cost estimates?" This question means that a level-2 project must be managed by those who are willing to take responsibility for their estimates. However, the question does not force the managers to assess the accuracy of their estimates, or to improve the estimation process as more is learned about estimation modeling. The danger in taking this type of question-based approach with yes/no answers is that it may paint a misleading picture of the project and its management. In this case, inappropriate models and inaccurate measurement are missed, and the management may be "rewarded" with a level 2 assessment nevertheless.

The CMM and other models try to address these issues, and their popularity continues to grow. As the models help to identify strengths and weaknesses, organizations make major business and technical decisions based on the assessment results. However, if the models and measurements are incorrect or misguided, the result can be misallocation of resources, loss of business, and more. Card reported that inconsistent results were obtained from CMM assessments of the same organization by different teams, thus raising the issue of reliability of assessments shortly after the CMM was introduced (Card, 1992). Here, **reliability** refers to the extent to which the same measurement procedure yields the same results on repeated trials (Carmines and Zeller, 1979). We discussed in Chapter 3 the notion of measurement validity; reliability is a necessary (but insufficient) condition for validity.

El Emam and Madhavji have further investigated reliability, asking:

- How reliable are such assessments?
- What are the implications of reliability for interpreting assessment scores?

They built a model of organizational maturity based on the CMM, Trillium, and several other popular models, and performed a case study to address these questions. They found clear evidence of unreliability, when measured along four dimensions: standardization, project management, tools and organization. Moreover, when they investigated the relationship between organizational maturity and other attributes of process and product, they found a small, significant relationship between maturity and quality of service, but "no relationship was found with quality of products" and "a small negative correlation between the standardization and project management dimensions and the quality of projects" (El Emam and Madhavji, 1995).

Thus, there are serious measurement questions to be addressed in considering the use of these process and organizational frameworks. We must ensure that the models are appropriate, in the sense described in Chapter 2. That is, we must understand how reliable and valid the measurements and models are. We must know what entities and attributes are being measured, and we must test the relationships between the maturity scores and the behaviors that "maturity" is supposed to produce or enhance.

13.3 WHERE AND WHEN: MAPPING MEASURES TO ACTIVITIES

Business goals and questions suggest why you should measure, and process maturity suggests both what can be measured and where in the process it can be captured. The metrics plan must make the measurement activities more explicit, by describing exactly how measurement will be integrated with normal development activities.

EXAMPLE 13.7: In Example 13.1, we saw that NASA identifies five aspects of each of its major activities. For instance, integration testing is described as follows (SEL, 1990):

1. **Purpose:** integration testing verifies the internal integrity of a collection of logically related units (called a module) and checks the module's external interfaces with other modules, data files, external input and output, etc.
2. **Plan:** although a formal test plan is generally not required, integration testing is more carefully controlled than unit testing.
3. **Participants:** integration testing is usually performed by the members of the development team responsible for the modules being integrated.
4. **Activities:** during integration testing, the software is slowly built up by adding a few units at a time to a core of modules that have already been integrated. Integration may follow a top-down approach, in which lower-level modules are added to the top-level driver level by level. Alternatively, an end-to-end functional path, or thread, may be constructed, to which other modules are then added.
5. **Monitoring:** use number of units planned versus number successfully integrated to measure progress; track number of errors found to gauge software reliability.

By associating metrics with each aspect, the developers know exactly when in the process the measurement will take place. NASA has produced a Measurement Handbook as companion to its management document, to explain how measurement should be done relative to each major activity (Software Productivity Consortiumn, 1995).

For some organizations, a process model is useful to provide a context for measurement, allowing developers to determine the when, who, and how. For instance, we saw in Example 5.11 that a simple process model for reuse was employed for understanding where measurements should be made. This approach should be taken for any kind of measurement in any process and documented in the metrics plan. Using a model of the process being measured, you should:

- find the place in the process where the measurement should be made;
- record who will make it;
- record when and how often to measure;
- record where result will be stored and who can access it.

By identifying this information early, the participants in the process will know who is responsible and how the measurement process is integrated within the larger process.

13.4   How: measurement tools

Once we know what data to collect and where in the process to collect them, we must decide how to collect them. But the mechanics of collection must be considered in concert with data quality; if the right data are not collected, then analysis will be meaningless, and the objectives of the measurement program cannot be met. Thus, we must invest time up front in planning for good data collection, and follow that with time throughout development in actually performing collection activities.

In Chapter 5, we described the general principles of good data collection; other chapters suggested detailed ways to collect specific data. The principles should be summarized and reiterated in the metrics plan, so that those involved in the project are aware of how data-collection procedures address the goals of the metrics program. Data collection will be a familiar task to many on the project, as those involved in configuration management or project management are accustomed to capturing status and progress information. In fact, it may be desirable to expand current data collection and storage capabilities to accommodate new metrics; the configuration management or project management databases can be expanded or linked to other data, so that a larger project or organizational database is formed.

No matter how data collection is implemented, it must adhere to two important principles:

1. it must be sufficiently simple so as to minimize disruption to normal working patterns; and
2. the data must ultimately be included in a metrics database.

The first principle suggests using tools and standard forms wherever possible. Automatic counting or capture minimizes subjectivity and avoids misinterpretation of counting rules.

There are many types of tools available, not all of which are directed primarily at metrics programs.

- **Planning tools:** a few packages are available to help you in planning your overall program, including deriving questions and metrics from goals. For example, the ami tool and accompanying handbook implement the GQM and process maturity approach (Pulford *et al.*, 1995). One advantage of doing metrics planning in an automated way is that the plan is easy to revise and update as the project or organization goals change.

- **Forecasting tools:** many tools are available to help forecast likely effort, schedule, or defect information. Cost estimation packages abound, many of which implement function points counting, public models such as COCOMO, or proprietary models such as SLIM. Reliability modeling tools help to track defect information, and test support tools use defect discovery histories to forecast when testing will be complete.

- **Data collection:** static and dynamic code analyzers can be used to measure size and structure, as well as to find latent errors not discovered using other techniques. Other tools can compare files, track change histories, count requirements and design components, and more.

- **Data analysis:** the data can be analyzed using sophisticated metrics tools, computing control flow paths or identifying testing coverage. But a great deal of analysis can be done using simple spreadsheets and statistical packages. The spreadsheets can examine trends, generate histograms and pie charts, and do simple data analysis. Statistical packages can generate classification trees, draw box plots, and perform standard analyses to test hypotheses.

- **Data storage:** data can be stored in a conventional database management system (DBMS) or as an extension to a configuration or project management system. The DBMS can provide a degree of confidentiality not always available on other storage media; it can also support combining data from multiple projects to permit an organizational or corporate view of project results and trends.

Unfortunately, not all data collection can be automated. Thus, standard forms are critical to good data, and the forms should be easy to use and validate. Any new forms should be tried on a pilot project, to determine the form's clarity, correctness and completeness; then, a corrected form can be made a standard for a wider audience.

The metrics database acts not only as the key source of information for monitoring and prediction, but also as a common cultural focus within an organization. In some sense, the database holds all that the project considers important, as an organizational history and legacy to future projects.

EXAMPLE 13.8:   At the Contel Corporation, data collection was performed using a Metrics Toolkit. Based on an IBM PC, the toolkit included a function points front-end to a COCOMO cost estimation package, a static code analyzer, and a spreadsheet. Custom code was written so that the metrics tool output was automatically transferred to the spreadsheet. Standard project management forms were included in the spreadsheet, as were customized macros to allow the toolkit user to view graphs and charts of project data automatically, and to track trends over time. Thus, the toolkit became a project metrics database for each project in the company. And the contents of each project database formed a project history for a separate corporate database (Pfleeger, 1993).

13.5   WHO: MEASURERS, ANALYSTS, AND AUDIENCE

The success of the metrics program ultimately depends on the people who plan and implement it. So the metrics plan should take great care in considering the needs of all who will be involved with it. There are many more people involved in measurement than just the collectors and analysts of the data. The metrics plan must address the people who perform each of these tasks:

- capturing data
- formatting data
- validating data
- analyzing data
- presenting data
- using data (with respect to the project whose goals are addressed by the program)
- evaluating data (with respect to the effectiveness of the metrics program)

The variety of tasks are married to a variety of perspectives, so that different people may do different things with the same data.

13.5.1   Different perspectives

We began our metrics plan by examining a set of goals, and then generating questions and metrics. The measurements needed to address the goals fall into two broad classes: technical and managerial. The **technical measures** address the needs of software developers and maintainers as they analyze a problem and generate a software-based solution. The **managerial measures** address the questions of understanding, control, and forecasting. Together, the measures allow developers and managers to build the best product they can, given the constraints under which they are working. But the goals must also be viewed in terms of the perspectives of the people who are working on the project. There are many kinds of developers and managers, and each has different needs and interests.

EXAMPLE 13.9: Theofanos and Pfleeger documented the typical goals of a reuse process in the US Department of Defense (Theofanos and Pfleeger, 1993). Then, using a GQM approach, they identified likely questions to be answered and the measurements that will aid in answering them. For example, storing and managing components is a major goal of reuse. The goal is viewed from five different perspectives: that of software developer (the staff who build and maintain the library), project manager (the person who oversees a particular library), the program manager (the manager of the libraries related to a single domain), the department manager (who oversees a collection of distributed libraries) and the corporate executive (who is interested in the costs and benefits of reuse from a corporate perspective). Within each perspective, questions are listed that reflect the concerns of that perspective. Thus, the developer asks questions such as:

- How much effort is involved in certifying, maintaining, and cross-referencing components?
- How much effort is involved in supplying components to requesters?

While the project manager asks:

- How efficient is the library system in terms of speed and disk space?

The program manager wants to know:

- What is the usage profile of components, and how can it be improved?
- What criteria are used to decide whether a component should be removed from the library?

The department manager is interested in:

- What trends of component characteristics promote reuse across domains?

While the corporate executive asks:

- What are the costs and benefits of reuse for this corporation?

By taking into account as many perspectives as possible, you ensure that as many people as possible have a stake in the success of the measurement program. Indeed, the success of the projects and organizations is tied to successful measurement.

13.5.2 Roles and responsibilities

It is easy to see that, once data are captured and validated, the goals and questions direct us to appropriate analysis. In other words, once we collect the data, we must evaluate it in a way that gives us answers to the questions we posed. However, who handles the data and when are not always so clear. So the metrics plan must identify the paths taken by each data element. As we shall see in Chapter 14, metrics programs are most successful when the data is kept close to the people who need it. For example, static code analysis is more useful to the coder as he or she is coding than it is to a manager several levels above. Similarly, the data should be provided as feedback to its provider as soon as possible; code structure and size measurements are useless to a coder two weeks after they have been gathered, as the code has probably changed in the interim.

Thus, the metrics plan should organize roles and responsibilities according to these guidelines:

- The people who generate the measures should be able to view and analyze them as soon as possible.
- Global validation and analysis of the data should be performed by personnel separate from the data provider, both to ensure objectivity and to relieve the provider of any additional burden; the primary job of developers should be development, not measurement.
- Data and results should be made available only to the people who need to see them.

Usually, a separate measurement team is formed. The team can work at the project level, but, as we shall see in Chapter 14, it often works best at an organizational or corporate level. The team members assist developers and managers in understanding the definitions and usage of metrics, as well as in interpreting the results. At the same time, the team has a broader perspective than an individual or project, and so can place the data in the larger context of division and organizational goals. It is the measurement team, not the project members, that are responsible for the care and feeding of the organizational or corporate database, tracking trends and taking action in anticipation of likely results.

In particular, the measurement team can evaluate metrics definitions, revising them to reflect the results of validation efforts and changing goals. The team can also assess commercial tools or develop custom tools to aid data collection and analysis. Most important, the team can perform vital data analysis, allowing project team members to concentrate on their primary development tasks.

Recall that the metrics plan is generated with a process focus, where process visibility and process models help to determine what to measure and when. The measurement team must encourage this process focus as well, using measures to understand and improve the process, not particular people. If metrics are viewed to be supporting the assessment of individuals, the developers may feel threatened; the result may be carelessly gathered data or even refusal to participate in the measurement program. However, if measurement is viewed as part of a larger team effort, where everyone on the team has a stake in improving processes and products, then measurement is a welcome part of development and maintenance.

What are the characteristics of measurement team members? It is useful to have most of the team consist of people who have a long history as developers. This development experience gives the team credibility; then, measurement is viewed not as an academic exercise but as in integral part of the project. It is also helpful to have a team member who understands statistics and experimental design, or at least has access to such a person. When measurement is part of an organization- or corporation-wide effort, it is also essential that the measurement team leader (if not all team members) understand the primary business problems related to software development. Measurement results are presented to upper-level managers, many of whom are familiar with the company's business but not necessarily with software development. For example, the president of a telecommunications company may be a whiz at understanding what the customers want, but she may have a background in finance or engineering, not in software development. So the measurement team must be able to speak the language of the managers, not just the language of software engineering. Conversely, the team members must be able to translate business needs, as articulated by management, into measurable goals in ways that help the developers understand why certain kinds of data are being collected.

13.6   REVISING THE PLAN

To stay successful, businesses should be flexible and grow. So too should metrics programs. Like anything else that is important to a company, the metrics program requires strategic planning. In particular, the measurement plan should be revisited periodically to decide if changes are in order:

- **Are the goals the same?** If the business goals have changed, then metrics program's goals may need to change with them. For example, initial goals may involve establishing a baseline for the organization or company. Once that is accomplished, goals relating to increased productivity may supersede them. Similarly, once productivity is increased, the company or division may want to focus on improving quality.
- **Are the priorities of the goals the same?** As one type of improvement is implemented successfully, other types may be selected for the next initiative. For example, initial high priorities may be assigned to goals involving test tool usage. But once test tool usage becomes part of the corporate development culture, requirements and design activities may become the focus of understanding and improvement.
- **Are the questions the same?** Questions that are relevant for the first stages of a metrics program (such as, how much should we invest in metrics tools?) may be replaced by questions of maturation (such as, how much money and time are we saving by using metrics?). Similarly, projects that are implemented by beginning with pilot projects may eventually generate new questions related to technology transfer (such as, what costs from the pilot project are likely to be incurred again when we introduce metrics company-wide?).

- **Are the metrics the same?** As the process matures, the richness of the measurements increases. At the same time, some metrics may no longer be necessary to collect, and they may be replaced by new ones. For instance, initial collection of size measures may be replaced by some kind of functionality measure. Similarly, as reuse becomes a widely accepted practice in the corporation, measures of reliability, availability, and maintainability may be collected to determine the effect of reuse on corporate product quality. Metrics related to customer satisfaction may also grow, from measures of the number of services requested and used to measures of interface and customer service quality.

- **Is the maturity the same?** The maturity of the metrics process may improve, and with it the visibility needed to measure new items. For example, initial attempts at data capture may not be automated, and the data may be stored in a simple spreadsheet. But as the metrics program grows and with it the size of the metrics database, an automated system may be developed to support it. With automation comes a finer level of granularity, as measurements can be made repeatedly over time and progress tracked.

- **Is the process the same?** The development process itself may change dramatically over time. Feedback loops may be added as measurement data are used in decision making. Or prototyping may change the way in which products are developed and assessed. Each change has important implications for measurement, as even the type and magnitude of the change may be candidates for measurement.

- **Is the audience the same?** Many metrics programs start small, often as a pilot in a department or division, and expand to the corporation slowly and carefully. As they do, the audience for measurement changes from the programmers, managers, and department heads to the division heads and corporate executives. That is, the audience changes with the impact of the measurement. It is important for the measurements to change, too, to reflect the questions and interests of the audience.

EXAMPLE 13.10: NASA's Goddard Space Flight Center views its measurement program as part of a feedback and control system. As a manager changes the development process, measures are adjusted and plans revised. Figure 13.3 shows how measurement and management interact (SEL, 1990).

13.7 SUMMARY

This chapter has described the elements of a measurement plan, based on the principles introduced in earlier chapters. By blending a top-down analysis of goals to be met and questions to be answered with a process maturity framework that allows more to

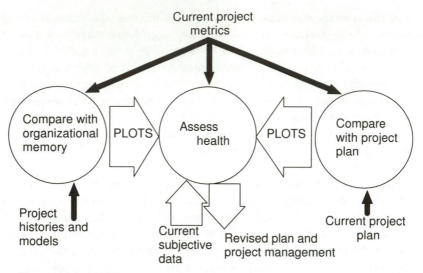

Figure 13.3: NASA's management and measurement

be measured as the process elements are made more visible, the planning approach allows a project to start small (with key goals) and grow a metrics program as time and resources permit.

Unlike previous approaches to measurement, the plan also includes a process model and multiple viewpoints to help assure that the metrics program will be practical. The modeling forces the project manager to understand the component activities of the development or maintenance process and thereby learn where measurement will fit in. The model also helps managers to identify who will collect the measurements and who will analyze them. Then, the multiple viewpoints ensure that all who need to understand the project will be able to do so.

Automated data collection, standardized forms, and metrics databases should be described in the measurement plan. In addition, the roles of the measurement team members should be made clear. In particular, the measurement team should take responsibility for validating data, analyzing results, and presenting them to upper levels of management.

In the next chapter, we will look closely at measurement in practice. We examine the actual measurement programs of several organizations, and we identify key practices that help to assure the success of the measurement program.

13.8 Exercises

1 Suppose you are developing a measurement plan for your development project. Your chief goal is determining the effectiveness of defect detection and prevention. What are the questions you might ask? What measures would you

need to answer the questions? Develop a brief measurement plan to describe where the measurements would be taken, how often, and in what manner. What analysis techniques might you use for the data, and how would you present the results to upper management?

2   DeMarco suggests that a cost estimation team spend only half its time on estimation activities. Discuss whether this idea should apply to a measurement program; should members of the measurement team work only half-time on metrics activities?

3   What are the implications for a metrics database in a company where many measurement programs take place independently?

4   Some developers prefer to remain anonymous; they do not want their names associated with their data. Describe situations where this anonymity would prevent the metrics program from being effective. Suggest a situation where the anonymity would not affect the success of the metrics program.

5   Compare the five levels of the capability maturity model with Pfleeger and McGowan's five levels of process visibility described in Chapter 3. How are they different? What are the implications of these differences for measurement?

6   Identify the activities likely to be performed by a measurement team. How many people are needed on the team to accomplish them?

13.9   FURTHER READING

DeMarco's classic text on controlling software projects has inspired many to develop metrics plans and programs.

> DeMarco, T., *Controlling Software Projects*, Yourdon Press, New York, 1982.

Humphrey's book presents an overview of the process maturity model. Criticism of the model, and a rebuttal of the criticism, are in *IEEE Software*'s July 1991 special issue on process assessment.

> Humphrey, W., *Managing the Software Process*, Addison-Wesley, Reading, MA, 1989.

The updated capability maturity model is available as an SEI technical report.

> Paulk, M. *et al. Capability Maturity Model for Software, Version 1.1*, SEI Technical Report SEI-CMU-93-TR-24, Software Engineering Institute, Pittsburgh, PA, 1994.

The pilot issue of *Software Process: Improvement and Practice* (1995) contains several articles describing alternatives to the CMM, including SPICE and ISO 9000. Hetzel's book represents the view that measurement should be done from the bottom up, rather than as part of a process improvement effort.

> Hetzel, W.C., *Making Software Measurement Work: Building an Effective Software Measurement Program*, QED Publishing Group, Wellesley, MA, 1993.

Theofanos and Pfleeger have produced a technical report describing a framework for a reuse measurement plan.

Theofanos, M.F. and Pfleeger, S.L., *A Framework for Creating a Reuse Measurement Plan*, Martin Marietta Technical Report, Martin Marietta Energy Systems – Data Systems Research and Development Division, Oak Ridge, TN, 1993.

14 Measurement in practice

In previous chapters, we have introduced principles of measurement, frameworks for selecting metrics, examples of particular metrics, and guidelines for writing a measurement plan. In this chapter, we look at real-world examples of measurement to see what organizations, large and small, are measuring. We begin by considering two measurement programs, one driven by product goals and the other by process goals, to see how measurement programs differ. Then, we consider success criteria for measurement programs, so that we can build and refine our program using a goal-and-question approach much like GQM.

Next, we present two case studies of measurement in the small: using measurement to solve particular problems in a small part of an organization. From that, we turn to measurement in the large, where measurement is used throughout the company or agency. Finally, we look at lessons learned from many different kinds of measurement programs, and we suggest guidelines for making your metrics program a success.

14.1 SUCCESS CRITERIA

Not all measurement programs are the same. We saw in Chapter 3 and again in Chapter 13 that different goals can lead to different measurement programs. In fact, even when the measurements are the same, they can be put to different uses, depending on goals and organizational philosophy. To see how, consider two different attitudes toward quality. In the USA, the Malcolm Baldrige National Quality Award is given to companies who demonstrate significant improvements in product quality. Both Motorola and AT&T have won the award by instituting aggressive methods for finding and eliminating sources of defects, as well as for improving quality and turnaround time. But each has taken a very different approach.

EXAMPLE 14.1: In 1987, Motorola declared total customer satisfaction to be its primary corporate goal. Quality was the "linchpin" of the strategy for attaining that goal, and quality performance was measured by the total number of defects per unit of finished product throughout the process (where "unit" was defined appropriately for each type of product that Motorola produces) (Smith, 1993). Thus, the quality goal was expressed in a well-defined and measurable way, and quality improvement was monitored carefully.

The Motorola improvement program was based on several key principles:

- A product is built in the shortest time and at lowest cost if no mistake is made in the process.
- If no defect can be found anywhere in the development process, then the customer is not likely to find one either.
- The more robust the design, the lower the inherent failure rate.

Motorola measured **robustness** by using the ratio of the maximum allowable range of a characteristic to a normal variation of up to three standard deviations from the mean. In terms of defects, this constraint meant that there could be no more than 27 defects per unit of a part containing 10 000 characteristics. However, in 1987, this ratio was extended to six standard deviations, leading to the program's name, *six sigma*, and allowing only 3.4 defects per million characteristics.

To reach this goal, every Motorola project was managed in a quantitative fashion. Project activities were defined in terms of deliverables that had to meet rigid quality and reliability goals. The result of this program was a dramatic improvement in all Motorola products (Smith, 1993).

Motorola used a product improvement approach, implemented and monitored with clearly defined measurements. By contrast, AT&T took a process improvement approach.

EXAMPLE 14.2: AT&T turned to **total quality management** (TQM) to improve its product quality. TQM, originally proposed by W. Edwards Deming as a series of fourteen points for management, became popular in the USA in 1980 (Deming, 1989). The goal of TQM is to create a system of management procedures that focus on customer satisfaction. The corporate culture and practices are revised to focus on the customer, and all activities are aligned to improve quality, service and cost. Thus, three critical elements of TQM are customer expectations, full participation, and continuous process improvement.

To implement TQM, AT&T used a quality planning matrix; Table 14.1 shows an example. The matrix is created by top management, with input from the entire organization. Then, it is sent to all teams, so that team efforts will address business goals.

Table 14.1: Part of a quality planning matrix (Bellefeuille, 1993)

Direction	Detailed objective	Individual project	Indicator	1992 Goals	Long-term goals
2.0 Enhancing quality	2.1 Improving key processes	2.1.1 Manufacturing processes	% processes in beta sites at 6 sigma	Improve by 1 sigma from end of 1991	100% by (year)
		2.1.2 Office support	% customer-identified impactors at 6 sigma	Reduce by 1 sigma from end of 1991	90% by (year)

To implement the goals, each team follows a plan–do–check–act cycle. First, team members gather preliminary data and identify the root causes of defects they would like to eliminate. Then, they implement countermeasures and monitor the results to determine if performance has improved. Finally, they standardize their process steps. When one goal has been met, they move on to the next one, continuing to improve the process.

Thus, it is clear that there is more than one path to the same place, and good measurement plays a vital role in each approach. But how do we know that a measurement program is successful? By answering questions about its goals.

There are at least four key goals for any measurement program: understanding, control, forecasting, and business value. For each one, we must ask questions to help us decide if the measurement program is effective. These questions are shown in Table 14.2.

We can evaluate and measure a measurement program, just as we can any other aspect of business. If the answers we get are satisfactory, then the measurement program is successful; if not, we can change the program to address the goals in a more suitable manner.

Table 14.2: Success questions for a measurement program

Goal	Questions
Understanding	What are the key characteristics of our business that keep us competitive, and can we measure them? Can we present these characteristics to all interested parties in ways they can understand? Are these characteristics useful? Are we measuring the characteristics directly/ indirectly? at the appropriate level of granularity?
Control	For each key characteristic, are there trends by project/department/organization? Are the characteristics useful for setting targets and tracking progress?
Forecasting	Are measures accurate and useful in predicting future behavior of product, project, process, or resource characteristics?
Business value	How much are we investing in the metrics program, and what is our return on investment?

EXAMPLE 14.3: Brodman and Johnson investigated the use of **return on investment (ROI)** for evaluating process improvement programs, and their results raise issues for measurement programs as well (Brodman and Johnson, 1995). They note that the textbook definition of return on investment, derived from the financial community, describes the investment in terms of what is given up for other purposes. That is, the "investment must not only return the original capital but enough more to at least equal what the funds would have earned elsewhere, plus an allowance for risk" (Putnam and Myers, 1992). Economists use three models to assess ROI: a payback model, an accounting rate-of-return model, and a discounted cash flow model. However, for software, the US government and US industry interpret ROI in a very different way.

The government views ROI in terms of dollars, looking at reducing operating costs, predicting dollar savings, and calculating the cost of employing new technologies. Investments are also expressed in dollars, such as the cost of introducing new technologies or process improvement initiatives.

Industry views investment in terms of effort, rather than cost or dollars, while return is expressed in terms of:

- training
- schedule
- risk
- quality
- productivity
- process
- customer
- costs, and
- business

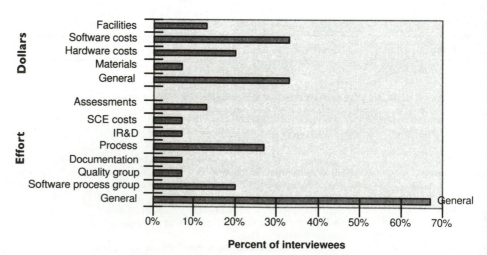

Figure 14.1: Industry definition of items included in investment (Brodman and Johnson, 1995)

Here, the cost issues involve meeting cost predictions, improving cost performance, and staying within budget, rather than reducing operating costs or streamlining the project or organization. Figure 14.1 shows a summary of how many organizations included an investment item in its definition of ROI. For example, about 5% of those interviewed included a quality group's effort in the ROI effort calculation, and approximately 35% included software costs when considering number of dollars invested.

There are good reasons for these differing views. Dollar savings from reduced schedule, higher quality and increased productivity are returned to the government rather than the contractor. On the other hand, contractors look for a competitive edge and increased work capacity as well as greater profit; the ROI is more effort- than cost-based. In particular, more accurate cost and schedule estimation can mean customer satisfaction and repeat business. And decreased time to market, as well as improved product quality, offer business value, too.

Example 14.3 illustrates the importance of interpreting measurements in the context of organizational and business goals. Here, the government is looking for a different kind of return from the contractors, but both use return as a measure of program success. Similarly, measurement programs must be measured in terms of characteristics that make sense for the business context of the program. On the other hand, it is worrying that software technology return on investment is not the same as financial ROI. At some point, program success must be reported to higher levels of management, many of which are related not to software but to the main company business, such as telecommunications or banking. Much confusion will result from the use of the same terminology to mean vastly different things. Thus, our success criteria must make sense not only for software projects and processes, but also for the more general business practices they support.

14.2 MEASUREMENT IN THE SMALL

Not every use of measurement in practice is part of a large, organization-wide measurement program. More often, measurement is used to help answer a particular question on a given project or within a specific organization.

EXAMPLE 14.4: Pfleeger, Fenton, and Page used metrics to evaluate reliability and maintainability at Company X in the UK under the auspices of the SMARTIE project (Pfleeger, Fenton, and Page, 1994). The first goal, reliability, required information about actual operational failures, as we saw in Chapter 10. The second, maintainability, required data on discovering and fixing faults. The company made available all of its data relating to a large system essential to its business; begun in November 1987, the system had 27 releases between 1987 and the end of 1992. Its 1.7 million lines of code involved two programming languages, COBOL (both batch COBOL and CICS COBOL) and Natural (a 4GL), with significant growth (15.2%, almost all of it in Natural) in only a year's time.

The system under scrutiny runs continually. Users report problems to a help desk, whose staff determines whether the problem is a user error or a failure of the system to do something properly. Thus, all the data related to software (rather than documentation) failures, and the research team concentrated on the 481 software failures recorded and fixed in 1992.

The maintenance group at Company X periodically grouped problems into a single "fault" report and assigned a number to it. We use "fault" in quotation marks, since the group labels failures as faults. A typical fault report consisted of a "fault" number, the week it was reported, the system area and fault type, the week the underlying cause was fixed and tested, and the actual number of hours to repair the problem (that is, the time from when the maintenance group decides to clear the "fault" until the time when the fix is tested and integrated with the rest of the system).

There were 28 system areas, designated by the maintenance group to describe where in the system the underlying fault had been traced. Each system area name referred to a particular function of the system, rather than to the system architecture. There was no documented mapping of programs or modules to system areas. A typical system area involved 80 programs, with each program consisting of 1000 lines of code. The fault type indicated one of 11, many of which were overlapping. In other words, the classes of faults were not orthogonal, so it was possible to find more than one fault class appropriate for a given fault. In addition, there was no direct, recorded link between "fault" and program in most cases. Neither was there information about program size or complexity.

There was neither mean-time-between-failures nor operational usage information available, so reliability could not be evaluated directly. As an approximation, the trend in the number of "faults" received per week was graphed, as illustrated in Figure 14.2. There was great variability in the number of "faults" per week, suggesting no general improvement in system reliability.

Figure 14.3 contrasts the "faults" received with the "faults" addressed and resolved ("actioned") in a given week. Notice that there is wide variation in the proportion of "faults" actioned each week. In spite of the lack of improvement trend, this chart provides managers with useful information; they can use it to begin an investigation into which "faults" are handled first and why.

The number of "faults" per system area is shown in Figure 14.4. However, there is not enough information to know why particular system areas generate more "faults" than others. In the absence of information such as size, complexity and operational usage, we can draw no definitive conclusions.

Pfleeger, Fenton, and Page recovered size information that was missing from the original data. By using the size to normalize the existing information, many

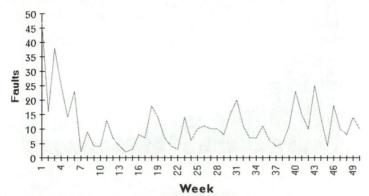

Figure 14.2: Reliability trend: Faults received per week

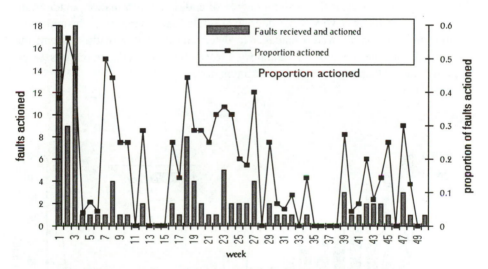

Figure 14.3: Dealing with failures: Faults actioned and received in same week

of the reliability problems were made more visible. For example, Figure 14.5 shows the startling result that C2, one of the smallest system areas (with only 4 KLOC), had the largest number of "faults." (Size information was not known for C1, T, and U, with 15, 21, and 5 faults, respectively.)

Similarly, if the fault rates are graphed by system area, as in Figure 14.6, it is easy to see that C2 dominates the chart. Without size information, this important information would not be visible.

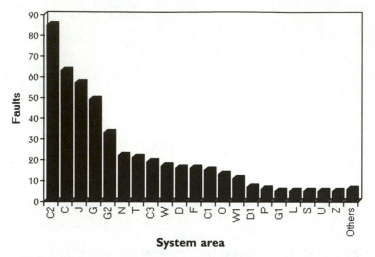

Figure 14.4: Fault-prone system areas: Number of faults per system area (1992)

This example makes clear that a small degree of additional information, made more explicit, can result in a very large degree of additional management insight. The existing information allowed a manager to determine the status of the system; the additional data made visible explanatory information, allowing managers to be proactive rather than reactive during maintenance.

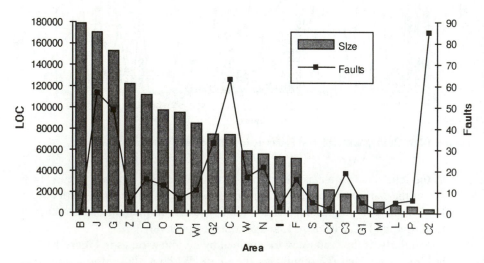

Figure 14.5: Reliability and size: System area size versus faults

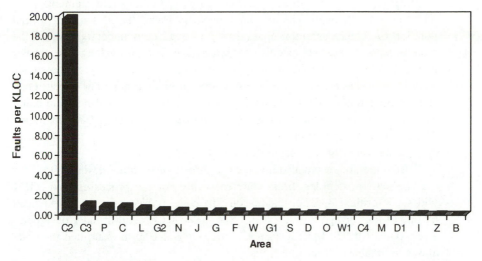

Figure 14.6: Normalized fault rates per system area

Sometimes, companies make large investments in technology, when they believe it holds real promise of improving some aspect of software development. As practitioners and researchers, we continue to look for methods and tools that help us to improve our software development processes and products. Articles in software engineering periodicals focus on candidate technologies that promise increased productivity, better quality, lower cost or enhanced customer satisfaction. But these methods and tools can be tested empirically and rigorously to determine if they make a quantifiable difference to software we produce. Often, such evaluation is not considered until after the technology has been used, making careful, quantitative analysis difficult if not impossible. However, when evaluation planning is incorporated in overall project planning, the result can be a rich record of the effectiveness of the tool or technique.

EXAMPLE 14.5:   A major British developer built an information system to support a safety-critical system in the early 1990s using a variety of formal methods. The developer had used formal methods before, but not to the extent used in this system, and they wanted to assess the effect of formal methods on the ultimate quality of the system (Pfleeger and Hatton, 1996).

Several different formal methods were involved in the development. The functional requirements were developed using three techniques:

- an entity-relationship analysis to describe the real-world objects, their properties, and interrelationships (such as arrivals, departures, workstations, plasma display screens);
- a real-time extension of Yourdon's structured analysis to define the processing requirements
- a formal specification language, to define the data and operations.

A complete, top-level formal specification of critical system elements used VDM (Jones, CB, 1986). The development team found that this use of formal notation to capture essential operations improved their understanding of the requirements. An abstract specification was written in a formal language, similar to VDM. The user interface definitions, derived from a prototyping exercise, were expressed as pictures, text, and state-transition diagrams. The concurrency specification was a mixture of data flow diagrams and formal notation using Milner's calculus of **communicating sequential processes** (CCS) technique. The abstract specification was by far the largest document, and all other documents were linked to its definitions.

Formal methods were also involved in three places in the design: VDM for the application modules, finite state machines for the processes, and VDM with CCS for the LAN. For this reason, any code in the system was influenced by one of four design types: VDM, FSM, VDM/CCS or informally designed.

As part of the SMARTIE project, Pfleeger and Hatton examined the code and data to answer three questions:

1. Did the formal methods make a quantitative difference to the code quality?
2. Was one formal method superior to another?
3. How could data collection and analysis be improved to make quality questions easier to answer?

They looked at the more than three thousand fault reports that were generated from the end of 1990 to the middle of 1992, when the software was delivered, and they classified each module and document by the type of design that influenced it: VDM, VDM/CCS, FSM or informal methods. Table 14.3 presents an overview of the results.

The second column quantifies the number of code changes resulting from fault reports that affected code of each type. That is, if a single fault report resulted in a change to each of several modules, then each module change was considered a fault and counted separately. Consequently, the total number of faults (that is, code changes) exceeds the total number of fault reports. Then, the third column divides the second column by the number of thousands of

Table 14.3: Relative sizes and faults reported for each design type in delivered code

Design type	Total lines of delivered code	Number of fault report-generated code changes in delivered code	Code changes per KLOC	Number of modules having this design type	Total number of delivered modules changed	Percentage of delivered modules changed
FSM	19 064	260	13.6	67	52	78%
VDM	61 061	1539	25.2	352	284	81%
VDM/CCS	22 201	202	9.1	82	57	70%
Formal	102 326	2001	19.6	501	393	78%
Informal	78 278	1644	21.0	469	335	71%

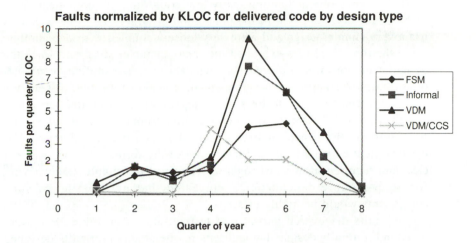

Figure 14.7: Faults reported by quarter, normalized by size of code

lines of code in that design type to yield a normalized measure of the relative number of faults in each design category. Although VDM/CCS-designed code has fewer changes than the others, the changes to informally designed delivered modules are not substantially different from those of the aggregated formally designed ones.

The last three columns look at the same data in terms of number of modules. Here, VDM/CCS still produces the best results; fewer VDM/CCS modules were changed overall, but code developed using VDM alone required the most module changes.

Figure 14.7 shows the result of a trend analysis to determine how design type affected the number of faults reported per quarter. Once again, VDM/CCS modules exhibited the best quality.

The analysis of fault records was supplemented by a static analysis of the delivered code using QAC, an automated inspection toolset for the C language. The code was audited as three packages under the following categories, and compared with Programming Research Ltd's database of millions of lines of code:

- syntax and constraint violations
- in-line and interface faults
- reliance on imprecisely defined features of C
- potential reliance on uninitialized variables
- reliance on implicit narrowing conversions and implicit conversions between signed and unsigned behavior
- clutter
- component and system complexity
- C++ compatibility

The system contained an unusually low proportion of components with high complexity compared to the population at large. The three packages had a very simple design and were very loosely coupled with one another. Since the three packages exhibited the same characteristics, and since the design techniques were different for each package, the simplicity could not be attributed to a particular design method, formal or informal. Instead, the simplicity seemed likely to be a direct legacy of the specification rather than the design. Whether the simplicity resulted from using a formal method for specifying the system or from a more thorough than usual analysis of the specification (that is, an indirect result of the formal method) was not clear and required further investigation. However, the simple modules with few inter-module dependencies suggested that unit testing of such components would be highly effective.

The faults discovered during unit testing, shown in Table 14.4, were found in informally designed modules more often than in formally designed ones; this relationship persisted even when the number of faults was normalized by dividing by the number of modules in a given design type, suggesting that formal design may have helped to minimize errors or to aid discovery early in development.

The thoroughness of pre-delivery testing was borne out by the differences in failures reported before and after release; only 273 problems were reported between delivery in 1992 and the end of the dataset in June 1994 (of which 147 were actual code faults), so the delivered code was approximately ten times less fault-prone after system testing. Moreover, far fewer changes were required to formally designed parts of the delivered system than to informally designed parts. As shown in Table 14.5, the code compared favorably with others reported, confirming the favorable profile presented by the static code audit's comparison with the larger Programming Research population.

As a result, Pfleeger and Hatton drew these conclusions about the effects of formal methods:

Table 14.4: Faults discovered during unit testing

Design type	Number of faults discovered	Number of modules having this design type	Number of faults normalized by number of modules
FSM	43	77	0.56
VDM	184	352	0.52
VDM/CCS	11	83	0.13
Formal	238	512	0.46
Informal	487	692	0.70

Table 14.5: Post-delivery problem rates reported in the literature (adapted from (Hatton, 1995))

Source	Language	Failures per KLOC	Formal methods used?
Siemens operating system	Assembly	6–15	No
NAG scientific libraries	Fortran	3	No
Information system support	C	0.81	Yes
Lloyd's language parser	C	1.4	Yes
IBM cleanroom development	Various	3.4	Partly
IBM normal development	Various	30	No
Satellite planning study	Fortran	6–16	No
Unisys communications software	Ada	2–9	No

1. There was no compelling quantitative evidence that formal design techniques alone were responsible for producing code of higher quality than informally designed code, since the pre-delivery fault profile showed no difference between formally designed and informally designed code. On the other hand, the unit testing data showed fewer errors revealed in formally designed code, and post-delivery failures were significantly less for formally designed code. Thus, formal design together with other techniques led to code that was highly reliable.

2. Because the high-quality audit profile was uniform and independent of design type, it was likely that it was the formal specification that led to components that were relatively simple and independent, making them relatively easy to unit-test.

The software engineering literature contains many other examples that illustrate how measurement, applied to a particular problem, can make the problem – and its solution – more visible.

14.3 MEASUREMENT IN THE LARGE

Many organizations begin measuring in the small, by applying measurement to a "hot spot" or difficulty, or by measuring to quantify the improvement in a process, product, or resource. Eventually, as staff become more comfortable with measurement, the small pockets of measurement spread to encompass most or all of an organization's software activities. This bottom-up approach to a measurement program is both popular and effective, as staff "buys in" to the value of measurement one project or problem at a time.

However, there are many organizations that prefer a top-down approach, where a measurement program is implemented company- or organization-wide. Often, the corporate measurement program is sponsored by, or even initiated by, someone very high in the organization who recognizes the value of measurement. But this sponsorship is not always enough to convince the developers of measurement's importance. Since organizational and corporate cultures differ drastically from one development to another, it is important to tailor the metrics implementation approach to the needs and expectations of those involved in and affected by it. In this section, we examine several top-down programs, looking in particular at how they were designed to fit the context in which they were implemented.

14.3.1   NASA–Goddard Space Flight Center

The most well-known large-scale measurement program in America was implemented at the National Aeronautical and Space Administration's (NASA's) Goddard Space Flight Center in Greenbelt, Maryland. In 1973, NASA established a Software Engineering Laboratory as a collaborative effort with Computer Sciences Corporation (a software developer) and the University of Maryland. The Software Engineering Laboratory (SEL) focused first on understanding software development and then on improving it. The overriding goal of the measurement program was to assess the effects of various methods, tools and models on the software process, and to identify and apply the best practices.

Initially, it was difficult for the program to provide rapid feedback to the developers. But as measurement was used increasingly in decision making, it became more acceptable. At the same time, the measurement team tailored the metrics to the realities of development. For example, initial attempts to collect effort data were revised as it was found that too much precision at a local level tended to mask long-term trends. In fact, the program collects only about half as much data now as it did when the program began;

> "too much data without strong drivers as to the reasons for collecting them [had] camouflaged the real issues" (Rifkin and Cox, 1991).

The current focus is on incremental improvement, rather than rapid feedback, and the GQM paradigm is used to identify measures for new studies. Measurement is now an integral part of the recommended practices at NASA Goddard, and Table 14.6 summarizes the measures that are included in the management guidelines.

The cost of collection has been minimized to 1–2% of the cost of development. Data-processing, including data validation and database maintenance, costs approximately 6–9% of development. However, analysis costs can run as high as 20%, and the total cost of the measurement program is 20 to 30% of development costs.

But the return on investment justifies the expense. The measurement effort has led to institutionalization of code reviews, testing methods and design techniques that have improved software quality. And the data have enabled groups to tailor practices to take advantage of local applications, environments, and processes. For

Table 14.6: SEL recommended metrics (SEL, 1990)

Metric	Source	Frequency (collect/analyze)	Typically used in determining ...
Changes (to source)	Tool	Weekly/weekly	Quality of configuration control,stability of specifications/design
Changes (to specifications)	QM	By event/biweekly	Quality of specifications, the need to replan
Changes (classes of)	Developers	By event/monthly	'Gold plating,' design instability, specifications volatility
Computer usage	Tool	Biweekly/biweekly	Progress, design instabilities, process control
Discrepancies (reported/open)	Testers and developers	By event/biweekly	Areas of staffing needs, reliability of software, schedules
Effort (total)	Time accounting	Weekly/weekly	Quality of planning/managing
Effort (per activity)	Developers and managers	Weekly/monthly	Schedules, the need to replan
Effort (to repair/to change)	Developers	Weekly/monthly	Quality of design, cost of future maintenance
Errors (per inspection)	Developers	By event/monthly	Quality of software, lack of desk work
Errors (classes of)	Developers	By event/monthly	Specific design problems
Errors (total)	Developers	By event/monthly	Software reliability, cost of future maintenance
Size (modules planned/ designed/inspected/coded)	Managers	Biweekly/biweekly	Progress
Size (manager's estimate of total)	Managers	Monthly/monthly	Stability of specifications, the need to replan
Size (source growth)	Tool	Weekly/weekly	Quality of progress, design completeness/quality
Items to-be-done (TBD) (specifications/design)	Managers	Biweekly/biweekly	Level of management control
Tests (planned/ executed/passed)	Testers	Weekly/weekly	Completion schedules, progress

example, independent verification and validation were dropped when they were shown not to be cost effective. And when an error analysis revealed an excessive number of interface errors, an interface checking tool was purchased; measurement verified that the benefits of the tool exceeded its cost.

14.3.2   Hewlett-Packard

Hewlett-Packard, a market leader in electronics, is also a pioneer in software measurement. In 1983, in response to the recommendations of a task force that focused on software productivity and quality, the company set up teams to address short-term productivity improvements through tools as well as long-term improvements through the use of a common development environment. Hewlett-Packard created a Software Engineering Laboratory, which in turn created a Software Metrics Council. The Metrics Council, representing the major divisions of the company, proposed a set of metrics standards that addressed five issues (Grady and Caswell, 1987):

1. **Size:** how big is the software that is produced?
2. **People, time and cost:** how much does it cost to produce a given piece of software and associated documentation?
3. **Defects:** how many errors are in the software?
4. **Difficulty:** how complex is the software to be produced, and how severe are the constraints on the project?
5. **Communications:** how much effort is spent in communicating with other entities?

Then, metrics were recommended to address each issue:

1. **Size:** non-comment source statements;
2. **People, time and cost:** payroll month;
3. **Defects:** problem or error in the software;
4. **Difficulty:** a number between 35 and 165, with 165 being the most difficult; the number is determined by answers to a questionnaire;
5. **Communications:** number of interfaces that a lab team project has.

Over time, the defect measurements have expanded to include number of defects, defect severity, duplicate reports for the same defect, and efficiency of testing in defect removal. Also, user satisfaction has been monitored by looking at user defect reports and the number of user requests for enhancement.

This program helped Hewlett-Packard address the corporate goals put forth by its president, John Young, in 1986: a tenfold improvement in two key software quality measures in the next five years:

- post-release defect density (measured as the total number of defects reported from any source during the first twelve months of shipment divided by the size of the product in non-comment source statements);
- open critical and serious problem reports (measured as the number of defects reported and classified critical or severe but not closed at the end of each month).

To ensure that the program addressed needs throughout the company, it was directed at all three levels of management. High-level measurement was provided to group managers and above, where a group manager has responsibility for 3 000 to 10 000 employees. In addition to measures relating to Young's goals, the managers set an objective in terms of break-even time: the length of time it takes Hewlett-Packard to recover its investment. The long-term goal was to cut product development time in half, so that break-even time was halved as well. Other high-level measures included ten research-and-development metrics, such as measuring the effectiveness of development by tracking the number of discontinued, continuing, and released projects. All strategic measures were supported by automated internal tools. Young's "10X" measures were supported by a corporate defect tracking and reporting system, while the others were supported by PC tools (Cox, 1991).

Middle-level measurement addressed the needs of division managers and research-

and-development lab managers. It added to the high-level measures a software quality and productivity analysis, assessing the state of each division and lab and comparing it with others inside and outside of the company. The analysis examined eight major areas that affect software development, such as methodologies and staff characteristics. A second set of measures looked at annual productivity and quality, including size, effort and defect density. The middle-level managers also used lab-specific measures, such as the amount of reused code being integrated into products.

Low-level measurement was used by project managers for specific project needs. Here, complexity measures and software reliability growth models supplemented the basic corporate measures to provide information about particular product requirements and capabilities.

Each organization within Hewlett-Packard tailors these recommendations to meet its own needs. For example, some sites measure cyclomatic number, while others track the rate of change of source lines of code. Still others measure the DeMarco EQF introduced in Chapter 12. Grady has reported significant measurement efforts to assess the effectiveness of inspections at Hewlett-Packard (Grady and van Slack, 1994), and Lim describes a quantitative investigation of reuse in the corporation (Lim, 1994).

EXAMPLE 14.6: Lim reports the effects of reuse on software quality and productivity at two divisions of Hewlett-Packard. Figure 14.8 shows how reuse

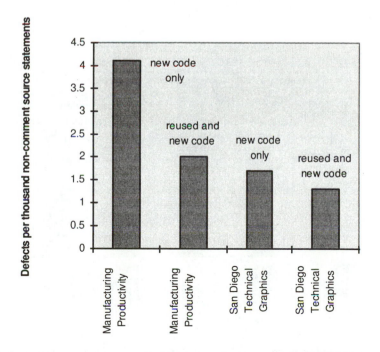

Figure 14.8: Effects of reuse on software quality at Hewlett-Packard

affected the defect density at each division, while Figure 14.9 illustrates the effect on productivity. The data were collected during a formal process called a reuse assessment. By implementing reuse, the Manufacturing Productivity division exhibited a 51% defect reduction and a 57% increase in productivity. Similarly, the San Diego Technical Graphics division reduced its defects by 24% and increased productivity by 40%; it also reduced time to market by 42%.

14.3.3 Contel

In 1989, Contel, a US telecommunications firm, instituted a corporate measurement program. Like many large American companies, Contel had grown by acquiring smaller businesses, so not only were the products diverse, but so also were the cultures developing the software to support them. There were no standard development environment, language, staff profile, or methodology. As a result, Pfleeger and McGowan used process visibility as the guiding principle for suggesting appropriate metrics, as well as for general process improvement (Pfleeger, 1993).

In addition, as we saw in Example 13.8, a standard metrics toolkit was built, to provide services and a project database, and to act as a bridge to a corporate historical database. The vice president for technology supported these efforts, and he prepared a corporate policy to encourage every project to participate.

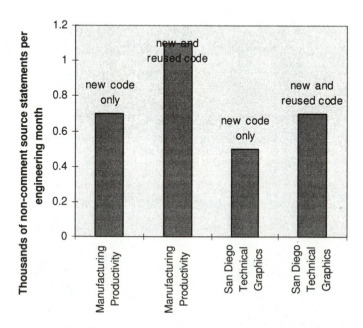

Figure 14.9: Effects of reuse on software productivity at Hewlett-Packard

Although the metrics program took a company-wide approach, the metrics collection was implemented by helping the most problematic projects first. Then, as measurement made problems visible and the effectiveness of solutions easier to see, the results were disseminated using employee newsletters and development seminars. Thus, eager participants became metrics advocates, and the program grew as more projects requested help from the metrics team.

The Contel metrics team developed presentation techniques to address the different cultures in the corporation. Many of the high-level managers had financial or telecommunications backgrounds, but they knew very little about software. The metrics team illustrated improvement in a general way, so that the managers need not become experts in software or software measurement. They used a multiple metrics graph, depicted in Figure 14.10, to show the effects of several measurements at once and in context, while preserving the individual measurements (Pfleeger *et al.*, 1992). In the figure, three measures are shown, with A more important than C, which in turn is more important than B. Only measure C is within its target, since the representation of C is within the "goal circle" in the center of the graph.

EXAMPLE 14.7: Contel purchased its telephone software switches from three different vendors and needed a way of comparing competing products. A multiple metrics graph was constructed using eight vendor-supplied measurements, as shown in Figure 14.11. The measures were weighted according to importance, and the size of the "pie slice" in the graph represented the relative importance of each measure. The central circle represented an acceptable or target level for the measure, and each measure was plotted with respect to it in each pie slice. The area of the polygon (formed by connecting the representations of each measure) reflected the overall quality of the switch, and the graphs could be overlaid to compare two switches in each dimension.

One of the key principles of the Contel program was its focus on the process. Using process models and process visibility, the metrics team framed its evaluation in terms of process improvement. This approach was successful in keeping the program from threatening individuals; any recommendations for additional training or skills

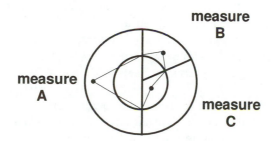

Figure 14.10: Multiple metrics graph

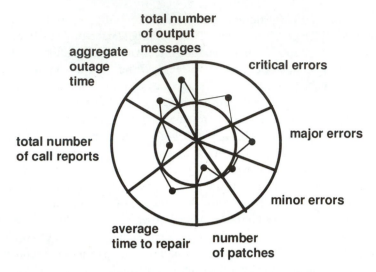

Figure 14.11: Multiple metrics graph for evaluating switch software

were part of overall process improvement.

14.3.4 Siemens

Siemens, a multinational corporation based in Germany, has implemented measurement as part of a larger best-practices program. Moeller and Paulish report the results of several Siemens measurement efforts; we summarize their discussion here (Moeller and Paulish, 1993). In October 1990, the data and information systems group of Siemens AG was merged with a similar group at Nixdorf AG, and the best practices of both groups were evaluated and merged, too. As a result, a measurement program was established, one of the earliest documented metrics efforts in Europe. The program was directed at systems software development; that is, it addressed the operating systems, compiler, communications, database and utility software developed for Siemens and Nixdorf computers. Typical products ranged from ten thousand to five million lines of code, developed in languages such as C, SPL, and assembler. The 3000 software engineers developing and maintaining these systems were located primarily in Germany, Belgium, and Austria.

The software development process was documented in a methodology handbook. The process phases included actions or process steps, with fixed starting and ending points accompanied by quality assurance actions. Table 14.7 shows the key process phases and steps.

The recommended metrics measured the quality of products, as well as the productivity and profitability of the software development and maintenance processes. Metrics for current projects were used to assess whether the project was on target, while metrics for completed projects formed an empirical history used for estimating

Table 14.7: Siemens process phases and steps (Moeller and Paulish, 1993)

Process phase	Process steps
Planning and high-level design	Requirements study
	Solution study
	Functional design
	Interface design
	Detailed project plan
Detailed design and implementation	Component design
	Code design
	Coding
	Component test
	Functional test
Quality control	Product test
	System test
Installation and maintenance	Pilot installation and test
	Customer installation

costs and expected defects and for guiding process improvement.

The metrics were derived from project artifacts:

- problem reports and defects counted during implementation, quality control, pilot test, and first year of installation;
- development costs in Deutschmarks (DM) and staff months (SM);
- maintenance costs in DM;
- sales in DM;
- product size in gross lines of code (BLOC), net lines of code without comments and blank lines (NLOC), and newly developed or changed net lines of code as compared to a prior release (DLOC).

Table 14.8 lists the quality, productivity, and profitability metrics calculated from these counts.

These measures were not collected in isolation. Rather, they formed an integral part of several key activities. For example, the top management of the Systems Software Division explicitly set as its goal the development of systems software "with outstanding quality, on time, and with minimal cost to reach high customer acceptance" (Moeller and Paulish, 1993). A quality deputy was identified to report to top management and support this goal. Measurement data were reported to management in the annual quality report, making metrics and improvements highly visible, and a limited version of the report was produced mid-year. In addition, statistics on defects and quality costs were reported to management weekly or monthly, and summaries of metrics progress were described in employee newsletters and meetings.

The program resulted in a focus on quality, improved customer satisfaction, and continued growth of sales and profit margins. Moreover, the systems software metrics program has acted as a model for other divisions of Siemens. For example, the Siemens Nixdorf applications software division has defined a master software process,

Table 14.8: Siemens metrics

Metric type	Metric definition
Quality metrics	Number of defects counted during code review, component, and functional test divided by number of thousands of lines of code
	Number of defects counted during quality control divided by number of thousands of lines of code
	Number of defects counted during pilot test divided by number of thousands of lines of code
	Number of defects counted during first year of customer installation divided by number of thousands of lines of code
	Total number of defects received per fiscal year from the field after customer installation divided by number of thousands of lines of code for the latest version in the field
	Total number of field problem reports received after customer installation divided by half the sum of the number of thousands of lines of code delivered within two years
	Number of defects counted after customer installation divided by the total gross number of delivered lines of code by fiscal year for each product profit group and for the overall system software development organization
Productivity metrics	Development costs divided by number of thousands of lines of code
	Maintenance costs divided by number of defects after customer delivery for every fiscal year and for each product line
	Total gross lines of code delivered to customers divided by total staff months expended for system software development for every fiscal year
	Number of thousands of lines of code divided by development effort in staff months
	Number of thousands of lines of code divided by development time in months
Profitability metrics	Sales in DM divided by software development costs in DM for every fiscal year for each product line
	Sales in DM divided by total cost for development, maintenance, and marketing for every fiscal year for each product line

documented in a Process Engineering Handbook. The process involves preliminary cost estimation, including effort estimates for each work package based on size, staffing requirements, and other resources. The metrics data from past projects are used to help estimate effort for current projects. Other measurement includes project management (planned versus actual milestone results, planned versus actual product quality assessment, fault statistics by phase, and planned versus actual costs) and quality metrics (fault profiles and qualitative fitness-for-use ratings). As a result of this program, substantial quality improvements have been documented, and the measurements are used to help set targets, motivate developers, and improve customer satisfaction.

EXAMPLE 14.8: Siemens Medical Electronics has defined five measures for research-and-development performance:

- **S-measure:** a measure of development schedule adherence, comparing achieved schedule with project plan reviewed at the beginning of the development phase;
- **C-measure:** a measure of customer complaint activity in units of complaints per thousand units installed;
- **M-measure:** a measure of mean-time-between-failures for device hardware;
- **B-measure:** the total number of software problems reported by quality assurance divided by the number of thousands of lines of delivered source code for each product for each release (a measure of software quality and testing effectiveness);
- **D-measure:** the number of change requests made by customers for the first year of field use of a given release divided by the number of thousands of lines of delivered source code for that release (a measure of pre-release testing and overall software product quality).

Siemens claims that the benefits of its metrics program include:

- improved quality
- improved productivity
- increased pride and improved staff motivation
- better business decisions
- better technology decisions
- improved communication
- improved team cooperation

14.3.5   Hitachi

In 1969, Hitachi Ltd established the Hitachi Software Engineering (HSE) company to support its mainframe software. Within ten years, HSE was the largest software house in Japan. As HSE grew, so too did its product range, and it expanded from operating systems to application systems development, maintenance and consulting. To manage its costs, schedules, and quality, HSE instituted a measurement program. Tajima and Matsubara reported that the most important goal of the program was to detect problems at the earliest possible stage. Using a diagram similar to Figure

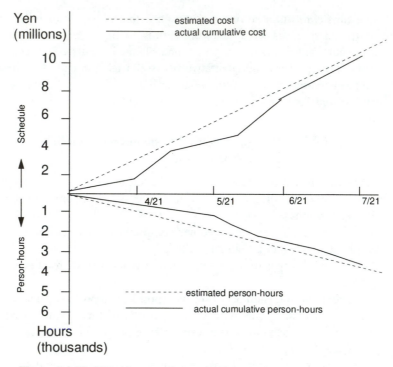

Figure 14.12: Hitachi cost–process diagram

14.12, project leaders compared estimated to actual staff hours, estimated to actual machine hours, and estimated to actual costs; then, they updated their initial estimates and summarized their progress (Tajima and Matsubara, 1981). As a result, 98% of the projects were completed on time, and 99% of the projects cost between 90 and 110% of the original estimate.

Once cost and schedule were under control, team efforts turned to improving productivity and quality. To assure quality for its users, Hitachi used statistical testing during module and integration testing. Based on empirical data and statistical analysis, certain types of tests were enhanced, and a product was not approved by the division until quality goals were met. Before coding began, developers compiled a quality checklist to apply to the code. Then, project leaders drew a quality-progress diagram that included a comparison of the expected conditions and the number of faults to be detected with the actual number of unchecked conditions and faults found, respectively. As testing took place, the diagram depicted progress against both the checklist and expectations.

After delivery, metrics analysis continued as the accounting division investigated **spoilage**: the cost to fix problems once the product is being used by the customer. The ratio of aggregate spoilage to aggregate project cost is used as a measure of software quality; Figure 9.8 in Chapter 9 shows how the ratio improved from 1976 to 1979.

14.4 LESSONS LEARNED

As software becomes more pervasive and software quality more critical, measurement programs will become more necessary. In 1990, Rubin reported that 300 major US information technology companies (that is, companies having at least 100 information technology staff) had implemented measurement programs (Rubin, 1990). Of these, he determined that sixty were successful, where "success" means that:

- the measurement program results were actively used in decision making;
- the results were communicated and accepted outside of the information technology department; and
- the program lasted longer than two years.

Rubin's colleague, Verdugo, suggests several reasons for failure in the remaining 240 companies:

1. Management did not clearly define the purpose of the program and later saw the measures as irrelevant.
2. Systems professionals resisted the program, perceiving it as a negative commentary on their performance.
3. Already burdened project staff were taxed by extensive data-collection requirements and cumbersome procedures.
4. Program reports failed to generate management action.
5. Management withdrew support for the program, perceiving it to be mired in problems and "no-win" situations.

We have suggested criteria for evaluating measurement programs, and we have seen many examples of how measurement is used in practice. But what do successful programs have in common? That is, what lessons can you learn from other organizations when you are designing a measurement program for yours?

In 1991, Rifkin and Cox of the Software Engineering Institute identified the eleven best measurement programs in the US, including the NASA, Contel and Hewlett-Packard examples described in this chapter (Rifkin and Cox, 1991). Each organization lauded by the SEI has its own character, and its measurement program is carefully tailored to the organizational culture. And each organization has its own perception of what makes a measurement program succeed.

> **EXAMPLE 14.9:** Grady and Caswell list ten steps to success for a measurement program, based on their experience at Hewlett-Packard (Grady and Caswell, 1987).
>
> 1. Define the company and project objectives for the program.
> 2. Assign responsibilities to each activity.
> 3. Do research.
> 4. Define the initial metrics to collect.
> 5. Sell the initial collection of these metrics.
> 6. Get tools for automatic data collection and analysis.

7. Establish a training class in software measurement.
8. Publicize success stories and encourage exchange of ideas.
9. Create a metrics database.
10. Establish a mechanism for changing the standard in an orderly way.

Similarly, Pfleeger lists ten lessons learned in the Contel program (Pfleeger, 1993).

1. Begin with the process.
2. Keep the metrics close to the developers.
3. Start with the people who need help; then let them do your advertising for you.
4. Automate as much as possible.
5. Keep things simple and easy to understand.
6. Capture whatever you can without burdening developers.
7. If developers don't want to collect data, don't make them.
8. Using some metrics is better than using no metrics.
9. Use different strokes for different folks.
10. Criticize the process and the product, not the people.

Rifkin and Cox extracted common elements from the eleven diverse programs, suggesting that there are persistent patterns that may lead to success. Two items were common to all the programs: decriminalization of errors, and the fact that measurement is part of something larger. That is, the organizations seek to identify and eliminate faults:

> Defects were made public. No one was surprised by them. Everyone was working to eliminate them. Errors were talked about in the hallways and around the water coolers. These organizations believe that if you cannot see errors, you cannot eliminate them (Rifkin and Cox, 1991).

And measurement was carried out as part of a larger focus on software (but not necessarily process) improvement. Measurement was only one aspect of a more general culture of quality; it did not stand alone.

There are other patterns that, though not common to all eleven, were consistent throughout many of the organizations. They fell into four categories: the content of the measures, human issues, the measurement program itself, and program implementation.

14.4.1 Measures

Most of the organizations advocated starting with a small set of measures, and in fact some focused only on defects. All emphasized measures that were practical, required little cost and effort, and could be presented simply. At the same time, the required measures were defined rigorously, and many were collected in an automated way.

14.4.2 People

The managers were motivated to collect and use measurements, and emphasis was placed on support for decision making. Expectations were set, so that measurement teams were careful not to "over-promise" the benefits of data collection and analysis. By emphasizing data that could be used for a clear purpose, measurement became part of the developers' standard practice, rather than an added burden.

Because measurement is used in different ways by different levels of management, all levels were invited to discuss goals, uses, and definitions. This broad involvement, combined with training and lack of blame, earned the trust of all participants and helped to overcome any negative earlier experiences with measurement.

14.4.3 Program

The most successful programs took an evolutionary approach, similar to that advocated at the end of Chapter 13. The goals, audience, and implementation were continually evaluated, and the program changed to match the needs of the organization. Some metrics and approaches were pilot-tested and discarded when deemed inappropriate. At the same time, it was important to stress early successes. Care was taken to choose for pilots those projects where metrics were likely to be beneficial.

The value of a good metrics program evaporates quickly if essential information is not reported to the people who need it. Thus, measurement reports must be relevant, timely and limited to what the recipient needs.

14.4.4 Implementation

The measurement program added value to the existing effort, enabling smarter and better management and development. Part of this value involved empowerment, where individuals had more control over what they did and how they did it. A "whole process" view was important here, so that the implications of measurement and action could be viewed in a global context. Finally, it was essential that participants understand that measurement effectiveness takes time, as good programs require a change in attitude or a shift in culture.

Table 14.9 summarizes their recommendtions. Rifkin and Cox also noted that measurement programs have three key benefits:

1. They support management planning by providing insight into product development and by quantifying trade-off decisions.
2. They support understanding of both the development process and development environment.
3. They highlight areas of potential process improvement and characterize improvement efforts.

Table 14.9: Recommendations for successful metrics program (Rifkin and Cox, 1991)

Pattern type	Recommendation
Measures	Start small.
	Use a rigorously defined set.
	Automate collection and reporting.
People	Motivate managers.
	Set expectations.
	Involve all stakeholders.
	Educate and train.
	Earn trust.
Program	Take an evolutionary approach.
	Plan to throw one away.
	Get the right information to the right people.
	Strive for an initial success.
Implementation	Add value.
	Empower developers to use measurement information.
	Take a 'whole process' view.
	Understand that adoption takes time.

14.5 SUMMARY

This chapter has examined several measurement programs to determine what makes measurement successful. We have learned that programs vary, with the best ones tailoring their metrics and activities to the culture and context in which they are placed. Some programs implement measurement in the small, where a particular problem is addressed on a project or within a small part of a larger organization. Other programs work in the large, from the top down, using corporate goals or business objectives to suggest measurement activities throughout a large organization or company.

Most successful corporate programs define their measurements carefully, automate wherever possible, and focus on criticizing the process or product rather than the people. An evolutionary approach, allowing the program to change as different techniques and measurements are tried out, seems to work well. And measurement must be addressed to all levels of the company or organization, with techniques that keep ideas and results simple and direct.

This chapter's guidelines, coupled with the principles introduced in earlier chapters and an understanding of your organization or project, give you what you need to design a measurement program that is likely to be powerful and effective. In the next chapter, we look at particular examples of how sophisticated measurement programs have used empirical research to examine important problems in software engineering.

14.6 EXERCISES

1   Are Rubin's success criteria relevant for all types of programs? Compare them with our success criteria based on the goals of measurement programs.

2   Consider a measurement program whose objective is improving the reliability of accounts system software. Describe how you would avoid Verdugo's five problems.

3   Suppose Hewlett-Packard produces a set of products that is widely purchased but rarely used. How is this situation treated by the company's "10X" measures?

4   Baumert and McWhinney have analyzed the capability maturity model and identified software measures that would be appropriate at each level and for each key process area (Baumert and McWhinney, 1992). Discuss the pros and cons of such an approach. In particular, would this approach discourage early measurement of a characteristic, or would it encourage measurement only when appropriate?

5   Name four different audiences for measurement data and analysis. Explain how multiple metrics graphs can be used for each level to present results simply.

6   The US Software Engineering Institute has prepared several documents that describe four recommended measures: size, effort, quality and schedule. Should everyone measure these four items? Why or why not?

7   Jeffery and Berry have examined much of the literature on measurement in practice. From the recommendations of many successful programs, they have compiled a checklist for program assessment. Table 14.10 lists the questions of their checklist. Compare the entries in this table with the recommendations of Rifkin and Cox in Table 14.9. How are they alike? How are they different? Do they address the same problem?

14.7 FURTHER READING

There is limited information in the literature about successful, comprehensive measurement programs. Grady and Caswell describe the origins of the Hewlett-Packard program in their book, and Grady's subsequent book on practical software metrics contains many additional examples from that program. Moeller and Paulish describe their experiences with Siemens in their metrics book, which also contains information about several European metrics-based projects.

Grady, R.B. and Caswell, D., *Software Metrics: Establishing a Company-wide Program*, Prentice Hall, Englewood Cliffs, NJ, 1987.

Grady, R.B., *Practical Software Metrics for Project Management and Process Improvement*, Prentice Hall, Englewood Cliffs, NJ, 1992.

Moeller, K.H. and Paulish, D., *Software Metrics: A Practitioner's Approach to Improved Software Development*, Chapman & Hall, and IEEE Computer Society Press, Los Alamitos, CA, 1993.

The Contel program is described in Pfleeger's *IEEE Software* article, and Tajima and Matsubara explain the Hitachi program in the context of the state of the art of Japanese software development.

Table 14.10: Jeffery-Berry checklist (Jeffery and Berry, 1993)

Area addressed	Question
Context	Were the goals of the measurement program congruent with the goals of the business?
	Could the measured staff participate in the development of the measures?
	Had a quality environment been established?
	Were the processes stable?
	Could the required granularity be determined and were the data available?
	Was the measurement program tailored to the needs of the organization?
	Was senior management commitment available?
	Were the objectives and goals clearly stated?
	Were there realistic assessments of payback period?
Inputs	Was the program resourced properly?
	Were resources allocated to training?
	Were at least three people assigned to the measurement program?
	Was research done?
Process motivation and objectives	Was the program promoted through the publication of success stories and encouraging exchange of ideas?
	Was a firm implementation plan published?
	Was the program used to assess individuals?
Process responsibility and metrics team	Was the metrics team independent of the software developers?
	Were clear responsibilities assigned?
	Was the initial collection of metrics sold to the data collectors?
Process data collection	Were the important initial metrics defined?
	Were tools for automatic data collection and analysis developed?
	Was a metrics database created?
	Was there a mechanism for changing the measurement system in an orderly way?
	Was measurement integrated into the process?
	Were capabilities provided for users to explain events and phenomena associated with the project?
	Was the data cleaned and used promptly?
	Did the objectives determine the measures?
Process training and awareness	Was adequate training in software metrics carried out?
	Did everyone know what was being measured and why?

Area addressed	Question
Products	Were the measures clear and of obvious applicability? Did the end result provide clear benefits to the management process at the chosen management audience levels? Was feedback on results provided to those being measured? Was the measurement system flexible enough to allow for the addition of new techniques? Were measures used only for predefined objectives?

Pfleeger, S.L., "Lessons learned in building a corporate metrics program," *IEEE Software,* 10(3), May 1993.

Tajima, D. and Matsubara, T., "The computer software industry in Japan," *IEEE Computer,* 14(5), pp. 89–96, 1981.

Rifkin and Cox describe eleven programs in detail in their SEI technical report. The front part of the report is a summary of the common practices among the eleven, as described in this chapter. The remainder of the document is a discussion of each program: its origins, measurements, benefits, problems and lessons learned.

Rifkin, S. and Cox, C., *Measurement in Practice,* SEI technical report SEI-CMU-91-TR-16, Software Engineering Institute, Pittsburgh, PA, 1991.

The US Software Engineering Institute has recommended metrics in two contexts: as a part of the capability maturity model (as described by Baumert and McWhinney) and as a set of four generally recommended measurements (called core measures). The technical report by Rozum and Florac describes the four, recent experiences with using them, and recommendations for changes to their definitions.

Baumert, J.H. and McWhinney, M.S., *Software Measures and the Capability Maturity Model,* SEI technical report, CMU/SEI-92-TR-25, ESC-TR-92-0, Software Engineering Institute, Pittsburgh, PA, 1992.

Rozum, J.A. and Florac, W.A., *A DoD Software Measurement Pilot: Applying the SEI Core Measures,* SEI technical report CMU/SEI-94-TR-016, Software Engineering Institute, Pittsburgh, PA, May 1995.

15 Empirical research in software engineering

This book has discussed measurement in many forms, from assessing current status to setting goals for future performance, from building models to building experiments and case studies. In each chapter, we have set forth a theoretical basis for our discussion, and then provided examples of how to put the theory into practice. So it is fitting for us to end the book with a look at how measurement is applied to empirical research in software engineering.

Recall that in Chapter 2 we showed how measures map entities and attributes in the real world to the formal, mathematical world. In that formal setting, we manipulate the formal objects to make judgments about them. Eventually, we must return to consider the real world and decide what the mathematically based judgments mean about the original entities and objects with which we started. In other words, our measurement activities must be practical; we must understand the implications of measurement for our products, processes, and resources.

Empirical research builds this practical link by focusing on hypotheses in the real world and testing them with empirical data. Many scientific disciplines are more mature than software engineering, so the body of empirical research is rich and varied.

Throughout this book, we have seen many empirically based software engineering examples that help us to understand the effects of what we do and how we do it. But there are too many examples of inadequate empirical research in software engineering. In this chapter, we examine some of these inadequacies to determine how we can improve the quality of our research and thus of our discipline's techniques and products.

We begin by examining some of the problems encountered in performing empirical research, and we suggest guidelines for evaluating the quality of the research you perform and read about. Then, we present several examples of empirical research, looking at product, resource, and process investigations. We end with a discussion of the state of measurement today.

15.1 PROBLEMS WITH EMPIRICAL RESEARCH

In Chapter 4, we discussed the issues involved in performing software engineering surveys, case studies, and experiments. The information in that chapter is useful not only for designing your own investigations but also for evaluating the investigations of others.

The literature is full of claims about new products, methods, and techniques. But we must question whether the claims are backed up by data and investigation.

> Little is known [of] the impact of software engineering practices and processes. While much is written about the topic in qualitative terms, little quantitative information is available. In many ways, the software engineering process is an informational "black hole" – it draws in money and resources like a magnet but little data emerges (Rubin, 1993).

Because it is important to base your technology and business decisions on fact, not opinion we recommend that you ask the following questions about each claim you hear:

- Is it based on empirical evaluation and data rather than intuition and advocacy?
- Does it have a good experimental design?
- Is it a toy situation or a real situation?
- Are the measurements appropriate to the goals of the experiment?
- Was the experiment run long enough to evaluate the true effects of the change in practice?

For the remainder of this section, we look at the implications of each question.

15.1.1 Empiricism versus advocacy

In many instances, software engineering techniques and tools are adopted because of the credibility of the seller or advocate. In other words, if someone you trust tells you

Table 15.1: Comparison of testing efficiency (Grady, 1992)

Testing type	Efficiency (defects found per hour)
Regular use	0.21
Black box	0.282
White box	0.322
Reading/inspections	1.057

a new technique will help, you consider using it. But adopting a new technique can involve much time and expense. Rather than rely on advocacy, an investigation based on empirical evidence can help you to decide whether to take the plunge throughout your organization.

Suppose you want to reduce the number of defects in the code you produce. When faced with that problem at Hewlett-Packard, Grady compared the efficiency of different kinds of testing techniques, as shown in Table 15.1 (Grady, 1992). This experiment and similar research results confirm one of the few consensus views to emerge in empirical studies: inspections are the cheapest and most effective testing techniques for finding faults. Even here, it is important to keep the objective of the experiment in mind. The table shows overall testing efficiency, but it does not report efficiency with respect to particular kinds of faults. Nevertheless, analysis of empirical data in the context of a rigorous investigation provides a sounder basis for change in practice than mere anecdote or intuition.

15.1.2   Good experimental design

Even when empirical data are collected and analyzed, the experimental design must be correct for the hypothesis being tested. Some of the best-publicized studies have led to results and decisions that have subsequently been challenged on the basis of inappropriate experimental design. For example, the results of an experiment by Shneiderman and his colleagues (Shneiderman *et al.*, 1977) led to the widely held view that pseudocode should replace the use of structured flowcharts as a means of program and design documentation. Specifically, Shneiderman's study showed that flowcharts were no greater an aid to comprehension than pseudocode. As a result, flowcharts were subsequently shunned in the software engineering community. Highly influential practitioners referred to Shneiderman's experiment in asserting that

> "flowcharts are to be avoided as a form of program documentation" (Martin and McClure 1985).

As a result of the Shneiderman research, software engineering and computing textbooks almost invariably used pseudocode rather than flowcharts to describe specific algorithms. However, in a follow-on experiment some years later, Scanlan demonstrated that structured flowcharts are preferable to pseudocode for program documentation (Scanlan, 1989). He compared flowcharts and pseudocode with respect to the relative time needed to understand the algorithm and the relative time needed to make (accurate) changes to the algorithm. In both dimensions, flowcharts were clearly superior to pseudocode. Although some of Scanlan's criticisms of Shneiderman's study are controversial, Scanlan appears to have exposed a number of experimental flaws that explain the radically different conclusions about the two types of documentation. In particular, Scanlan demonstrated that Shneiderman overlooked several key variables in his experimental design.

A classic Weinberg–Schulman experiment on meeting goals provides another example of how careful we must be in experimental design (Weinberg and Schulman, 1974). The experiment shows that if attributes for determining success are not chosen carefully, then it is easy to maximize any single one as a success criterion. Each of six teams was given a different programming goal in the experiment, and each optimized its performance with respect to that goal – but was poor in terms of the other five goals. We can expect to see similar results if we run our experiments out of context, in the sense that we define "success" narrowly by using only one aspect or attribute.

15.1.3   Toy versus real situations

Because of the cost of designing and running large-scale studies, exploratory research in software engineering is all too often conducted on artificial problems in artificial situations. Practitioners refer to this body of research as "toy" projects in "toy" situations. The number of software research studies using experienced practitioners (rather than students or novice programmers) on realistic projects is minuscule.

The problem is particularly noticeable in investigations of programmers, where evaluative and experimental research is the norm. Many findings reported in the literature involve small, student projects; because of constraints on cost and time, researchers refrain from doing large-scale, realistic studies.

To be sure, evaluative research in the small is better than no evaluative research at all. And a small project may be appropriate for an initial foray into testing an idea or even a research design. For example, Vessey and Conger present an interesting experiment that indicates that object orientation is not the natural approach to systems analysis and design that its advocates claim it to be (Vessey and Conger, 1993). The study subjects were students, and the subject problems assigned were small. The results may not be conclusive, especially for experienced practitioners on real software projects, but Vessey and Conger's work indicates directions for further investigation.

In another small-scale but valuable study, Soloway, Bonar and Ehrlich examined which looping constructs are most natural for novice programmers (Soloway, Bonar, and Ehrlich, 1983). As a result of popular assumptions about structured programming, many languages have available a *while-do* type of loop (with an exit at the top) or a *repeat-until* loop (with an exit at the bottom). The researchers discovered that the most natural looping structure was neither of these; rather, the participants preferred a "middle exit" loop, which is generally excluded as a built-in structure. This observation, which is contrary to recommended practice based on "common wisdom," may imply that the structural decisions made by programming language designers may inadvertently make programming tasks more difficult than they need to be.

Thus, it is natural for us to ask how the studies and results from toy situations scale up to larger, more realistic ones. The best that we can say is that, just as software in the small has different characteristics from software in the large, research in the small may not be representative of research in the large. There is something about the nature of software tasks and the required communication among team members that means that an understanding of small-scale work does not always yield an understanding of large-scale work.

Obviously, there is no easy solution to this problem. But it is something of which you should be aware, both when conducting your own studies and reading the results of others.

15.1.4   Bad measurement versus good

Sometimes, an experiment is designed properly, but the researchers measure and analyze insufficient data or even the wrong data. In earlier chapters, we suggested guidelines for evaluating whether the data are appropriate for the question being answered:

- correct analysis for the measurement scale
- appropriate definition of entity and attribute
- internal versus external attribution
- related to key goals and questions
- appropriate for the process maturity
- subjective versus objective
- represents an appropriate population with an appropriate sample size

These issues can help you to decide whether the conclusion is based on reasonable data or not.

15.1.5   Short-term versus long-term view

Sometimes, journals report on research that is designed and measured properly but just is not carried on long enough. Short-term results masquerade as long-term effects. For example, speakers at the annual NASA–Goddard Software Engineering Conference often point out that the NASA Software Engineering Laboratory (SEL) investigated the benefits of using Ada as opposed to FORTRAN. In examining a set of new Ada projects, the researchers found that the productivity and quality of the resulting Ada programs fell short of their typical counterparts in FORTRAN. However, the SEL did not stop there and report that Ada was a failure. Instead, they continued to develop programs in Ada, so that eventually the project teams each had experience with at least three major Ada developments. The results indicated that there were indeed significant benefits of Ada over FORTRAN. What the SEL concluded was that the learning curve for Ada is long, and that the first set of projects represented programmers' efforts to code FORTRAN-like programs in Ada. By the third time around, the programmers were taking advantage of Ada characteristics that are not available in FORTRAN, and these characteristics had measurable benefits. Thus, the long-term view led to conclusions very different from those with merely a short-term view.

Similarly, the CASE Research Corporation has considered the empirical evidence supporting the use of CASE tools (CASE, 1990). They note that, contrary to the revolutionary improvements invariably claimed, there is normally a decrease in productivity in the first year followed by eventual modest improvements. These observations have been confirmed in studies of other technologies. They demonstrate again that the short-term assessment yields conclusions opposite to a long-term analysis.

Thus, it seems clear that we must take a long-term view of proposed practices that promise to have a profound effect on software development and maintenance. The resistance of personnel to new techniques, coupled with the difficulty in making radical changes quickly, can mislead us if we take only a short-term view.

15.2 INVESTIGATING PRODUCTS

One of the key goals of any business is to produce high-quality products and services. Thus, evaluating product quality – and knowing what contributes to it – are important. In this section, we explore several studies that have investigated the assessment of product quality.

15.2.1 Software structure and maintenance

Many organizations are interested in knowing how maintainable their software is. Several studies have been reported in the literature, some more careful than others about defining their objectives, collecting their data, and analyzing the results. How do you know which studies apply to your situation? In the examples that follow, we consider this question.

> **EXAMPLE 15.1:** Between 1986 and 1988, the UK Government funded a collaborative project (as part of its Alvey research program) to look at how the theory of software structure could help assess software maintainability (Fenton, 1990). The research group defined measures of various internal structural attributes, and data were collected from several projects. Without considering whether these measures were valid, and without any hypotheses or proper experimental framework, the team attempted to correlate values of the measures for specific modules or programs against historically collected process data (such as cost and number of module changes) that happened to be available for the modules and programs. Not surprisingly, the results echoed those of many

previous studies: all the measures correlated reasonably well with each other, and none correlated significantly better than lines of code.

The lack of validation and experimental structure means that the results are hard to interpret. The study would have been more meaningful if two preparatory steps had been taken. First, the team should have proposed specific hypotheses as the basis for a prediction system using the defined measures. Second, by relying on team knowledge of the measures' applications, the team should have shown that a number of measures of different structural properties were related specifically to the maintainability of the resulting code. To do this, the team needed data that were specifically related to maintainability, such as the time to find and repair faults. This emphasis on maintenance was considered negative, so the appropriate hypothesis was never properly articulated.

EXAMPLE 15.2:   Henry, Henry, Kafura, and Matheson worked with Martin Marietta Corporation to improve software maintenance (Henry *et al.*, 1994). They sought to answer three questions:

- How can we quantitatively assess the maintenance process?
- How can we use that assessment to improve the maintenance process?
- How do we quantitatively evaluate the effectiveness of any process improvements?

They used a process modeling technique based on control flow diagrams to define the maintenance process. Then, they captured and analyzed data about upgrade items for, and upgrade specification changes to, the largest program in the system during product enhancement. They validated their results by cross-referencing data, performing automated analysis of the delivered source code, and interviewing people.

They had several hypotheses to test. One suggested that the number of defects found before delivery had a significant effect on reliability. They defined reliability to be the error-proneness of functional groups, measured as defects detected per functional group. Henry and his colleagues collected this data over a nine-month period, plus information about upgrades and changes, lines of code added, changed or deleted, effort spent implementing upgrades, and the number of pre-delivery defects. Rank correlations were used to investigate the association between upgrade impact and number of defects detected after delivery, and there were strong correlations between post-delivery defects detected, functional upgrades, upgrade specification changes, lines of code added, and pre-delivery defects detected. To improve the quality of the software, the organization added walkthroughs at the module level, and they focused testing activities on those functional groups affected by the upgrades. Although the median number of defects per functional group remained steady across programs, the mean showed a significant reduction, and the standard deviation decreased significantly, showing less variation across functional groups.

This example contrasts sharply with the previous one. The researchers established a hypothesis, defined goals and measures, collected data, and performed appropriate analysis. One important difference between the two is that Alvey researchers used historical data that could not be validated and might not have been relevant to the goals of the research. By contrast, Henry and his colleagues collected data after the problem and measurements were defined, and they validated the data before analysis. Thus, we should have more confidence in the results of Example 15.2 than in those of 15.1.

15.2.2   Size, structure, and quality

Many studies reported in the literature have focused on predicting fault density. As we have seen in earlier chapters, fault density is considered to be an indicator of likely product quality after delivery, so this prediction can be useful in deciding when testing can end and the product turned over to the users. Most of the fault density prediction studies have involved size or structure metrics as prediction variables.

> **EXAMPLE 15.3:**   One of the earliest studies of fault density was performed by Akiyama at Fujitsu in Japan (Akiyama, 1971). Akiyama generated a typical regression-based data-fitting model that predicted the total number of faults. Here, the set of faults included both faults found during testing as well as faults found up to two months after release. The model included four equations. For example, the equation:
>
> $$d = 4.86 + 0.018L$$
>
> predicted faults, d, from size, L, measured in lines of code, so that a module of 1000 lines of code was expected to have approximately 23 faults. The other equations predicted faults from the number of decisions, number of subroutine calls, and a composite metric of decisions and subroutine calls.

The fundamental problem with this type of prediction is its lack of transferability. The conditions under which Akiyama's study took place bear no relationship to modern programming environments. Humphrey reports that even within the same environment, there can be variations in fault densities of ten to one (Humphrey, 1989). Moreover, the prediction model assumes a linear relationship between size and faults, and the relationship may be more complex than that. Thus, many researchers have taken context and other variables into account.

> **EXAMPLE 15.4:**   Lipow used Halstead's theory to define a relationship between fault density and size that took into account differences among languages (Lipow, 1982). He proposed that the relationship takes the form:
>
> $$d/L = A_0 + A_1 \ln L + A_2 \ln^2 L$$
>
> where d is number of faults, L is size in lines of code, and each of the A_i depends on the average number of uses of operators and operands per line of

code for a particular language. For example, for FORTRAN, $A_0 = 0.0047$, $A_1 = 0.0023$ and $A_2 = 0.000043$; for an assembly language, $A_0 = 0.0012$, $A_1 = 0.0001$ and $A_2 = 0.000002$.

Gaffney argued that the relationship between d and L was not language-dependent (Gaffney, 1984). He used Lipow's own data to deduce the prediction:

$$d = 4.2 + 0.0015 \, (L)^{4/3}$$

This equation suggests that there is an optimal size for a module, relative to fault density. In this case, the optimal size is 877 lines of code, but other researchers have reported dramatically different optimal sizes. For example, at Unisys, Compton and Withrow's polynomial regression equation:

$$d = 0.069 + 0.00516 \, L + 0.00000047 \, (L)^2$$

plus contextual information suggest that the optimal size for an Ada module with respect to fault density is 83 source statements (Compton and Withrow, 1990).

There are several case studies that suggest that our intuition about module size is wrong: they show that larger modules may be of higher quality (in terms of fault density) than smaller ones (Basili and Perricone, 1984; Shen *et al.*, 1985). Basili and Perricone explain that there are a large number of faults caused by problems with the programmer-to-programmer interface and distributed evenly across modules, and that larger modules tend to be developed more carefully. Moeller and Paulish provide further convincing evidence, based on data gathered at Siemens (Moeller and Paulish, 1993).

EXAMPLE 15.5: Moeller and Paulish investigated the effects of modification and reuse on fault density. They discovered that:

- Code including modifications that are introduced at a later stage (especially as corrections) has a much greater fault density than code with early corrections and modifications.
- Reused modules in which up to 25% of the lines of the original module have been modified have four to eight times more faults than newly written modules.
- Modules having at least 70 lines of code have similar fault densities. When modules are smaller than 70 lines of code, they tend to have far higher fault densities than the larger modules.
- Regardless of programming language used, smaller modules generally had higher fault densities than larger modules. Compared to assembly languages, the high-level language SPL appeared to perform better with smaller modules.

Similar experiences are reported by Hatton and Roberts (Hatton, 1993; Hatton and Roberts, 1994).

In general, size and context are not enough to produce good predictions of faults. Many researchers have turned to structural measures to help explain fault behavior.

EXAMPLE 15.6: Pickard and Kitchenham examined the relationship between the changes in two subsystems and a number of metrics, including cyclomatic number (Kitchenham, Pickard and Linkman, 1990). Two different regression equations resulted:

$$c = 0.042 \ MCI - 0.075 \ N + 0.00001 \ HE$$
$$c = 0.25 \ MCI - 0.53 \ DI + 0.09 \ V$$

The first equation represents behavior in the first subsystem; there, changes to the system, c, were found to be dependent on machine code instructions, MCI, the total number of operators and operands, N, and Halstead's effort metric, HE. The second equation reflects behavior in the other subsystem; c was partially explained by cyclomatic number, V, machine code instructions, MCI, and data items, DI.

Although there is no convincing evidence that any of the hundreds of published complexity metrics are good predictors of fault density, there is a growing body of evidence that some of these metrics may be useful in outlier analysis (especially when grouped together); they can be used to predict which of a set of modules is likely to be especially fault-prone (Bache and Bazzana, 1993; Hatton, 1993).

Code is not the only object of investigation. Many researchers have examined requirements and design to find relationships between their characteristics and resulting quality.

EXAMPLE 15.7: We noted in Section 8.3.6 that Troy and Zweben investigated the relationship between coupling and quality (Troy and Zweben, 1981). Based on the data they used to perform validation, we can reconstruct their implicit hypothesis:

Designs (programs) with high coupling contain more faults than designs (programs) with low coupling. In other words, quality measured by number of discovered program faults is inversely proportional to the level of coupling.

However, Troy and Zweben did not propose a specific measure of coupling; without such a measure, the hypothesis is untestable. Instead, they identified the various characteristics that might contribute to coupling, such as number of modules and total number of module connections. Then, they demonstrated a linear correlation of each against the number of faults recorded for various programs. As we know from the principles discussed in Chapter 4, this approach does not test their hypothesis. Our proposed measure of coupling in Chapter 8 may be useful in testing the Troy–Zweben hypothesis.

Some researchers focus on measuring and evaluating products, claiming that they are easier to assess than resources and processes. But, as these examples make clear, we need more rigor in our product investigations, as well as more repetition to confirm the results of reported case studies. The product studies reported in the literature suffer from the following problems:

- The hypothesis is not clearly defined.
- There is no defined measure of the independent variable.
- The results are not transferable.
- There is no underlying explanatory theory of behavior.

15.3 INVESTIGATING RESOURCES

There are very few studies of resources, in part because human characteristics are difficult to control in experimental investigation. Most researchers acknowledge that social and organizational issues play a large role in determining the quality of products and processes. Somehow, we must discover the best ways to communicate among project members, to maintain motivation, and to promote those conditions that make developers productive and effective. Some surveys have revealed the spread between best and worst; for example, Jones reports on the effects of various factors on programmer productivity (Jones, C., 1986), and Boehm reports a difference of ten to one in programmer productivity for programmers working on similar projects (Boehm, 1981). But we need more systematic studies of people and their effects on products; while process automation will help make development more consistent, we can never eliminate the role of fault discovery and correction, which must be performed by humans.

Curtis points out that most investigations of the human role in development use student programmers or artificial tasks in laboratory settings (Curtis, 1986). It is not always clear that these toy results apply to actual development situations. Perry, Staudenmayer, and Votta suggest using iterative exercises to address problems in real development environments, rather than constructing toy ones. They have begun a series of studies to examine what happens now in the development process and what blocks progress. By understanding the impediments, we can then make process changes that enable developers to be more productive (Perry, Staudenmayer, and Votta, 1994).The Japanese used this approach in the 1960s, when developers gathered information on existing processes before attempting to change or improve them (Cusumano, 1991).

> **EXAMPLE 15.8:** Perry, Staudenmayer, and Votta conducted two experiments to determine how developers spend their time; this work was part of a long-term effort to help reduce time to market. In the first experiment, programmers kept time diaries of their activities, and in the second, direct observation validated the diary entries (Perry, Staudenmayer, and Votta, 1994).
>
> To control as much variability as possible while keeping the sample representative, the researchers selected participants at random but stratified along certain key project dimensions (organization, phase, and type) and personnel dimensions (age, gender, race, personality, and years of experience).

Although their sample was small, we can think of the investigation as a case study, suggesting what may happen on a broader scale. Using time diaries (that had been pre-tested and revised) and direct observation, they verified the reliability of their findings by randomly comparing reports prepared by independent observers. Among the findings were the following:

- The waterfall model does not reflect what really happens during development; neither does an iterative or cyclical model. Instead, many iterative, evolutionary processes are performed concurrently.
- The ratio of elapsed time to time spent in actual work was roughly 2.5 to 1. In other words, developers spent only 40% of their time actually working on development. The rest of the time, they were either waiting or doing other work.
- Coding exhibited the least amount of blocking; that is, it was impeded least by other activities, reflecting low dependence on outside organizations or resources.
- The amount of rework was approximately 20%.
- Each developer spent on average 75 minutes of unplanned interpersonal communication each day.
- On average, work was performed in two-hour chunks.

This study demonstrates several important points about empirical investigation of resources. First, it shows that people are willing to be observed, and that the observations are not so intrusive as to keep work from being done. Although the researchers gave the participants the option of dropping out of the study, no one exercised the option. Second, time diaries are useful for capturing global information about activities. However, only direct observation enabled the researchers to note and understand unplanned activities, such as the unplanned interpersonal interactions. Third, such investigation provides a better understanding of how we work, generating a rich set of hypotheses for future research.

EXAMPLE 15.9: Weller collected measurements from more than 6000 inspection meetings at Bull HN Information Systems to help the company understand how to make inspections effective (Weller, 1993). One focus of his work was to determine how the number of people on each inspection team affected the results. Using data from over 400 code inspections that discovered defects, he found that four-person teams were twice as effective, and more than twice as efficient, as three-person teams.

Figure 15.1 illustrates some of Weller's other findings. He examined the rate at which each inspector prepared for an inspection, measuring the preparation rate in lines per hour. By this definition, someone preparing at a rate less than 200 lines per hour spends more time getting ready to inspect a given program than a colleague whose rate is greater than 200 lines per hour for the same program. Thus, a "lower" preparation rate (using Weller's measure) meant more preparation time. Inspection performance was measured in terms

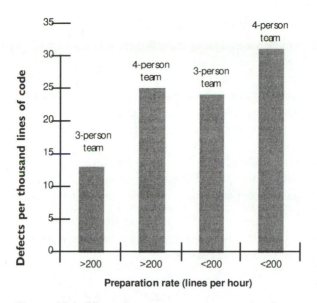

Figure 15.1: Effect of team size on inspection results

of faults discovered per thousand lines of code. Note that four-person teams always outperformed three-person teams, and teams with lower preparation rates (that is, that spent more time preparing) detected more defects than those with higher preparation rates. In particular, a three-person inspection team with a low preparation rate seems to do as well as a four-person team with a higher rate.

In his article, Weller claims that there are two reasons for the effect of team size that he observed. First, the code producer represents a smaller portion of a larger team, and so the larger remainder of the larger team is looking at the code with fresh eyes. Second, the fourth inspector is a good indication that team members as a whole have a higher level of product knowledge. He concludes that "an inspection team"s effectiveness and efficiency depend on how familiar they are with the product and what their inspection-preparation rate is." However, Weller uses no measures of expertise, experience, or understanding of the product, so his explanation of the effects is speculative. If Weller"s hypothesis is that a larger team size results in more effective and efficient inspections, then his study is a valid one. But if his hypothesis is that the effectiveness and efficiency depend on familiarity with product, then he has not measured the independent variable (familiarity) and assessed its effects on the dependent variables (effectiveness and efficiency).

15.4 INVESTIGATING PROCESSES

A great deal of recent research has focused on process, mainly because of heightened interest generated by the process improvement community. In this section, we examine several process investigations to see whether they have incorporated solid research principles.

15.4.1   Cleanroom research

The best available evidence evaluating the effects of process methods on fault densities concerns the Cleanroom method, which we introduced in Chapter 10. For example, Linger reports that, for 17 relatively small projects (averaging 60 000 lines of code), the use of Cleanroom resulted in an average of 2.7 faults per thousand lines of code found in all testing (Linger, 1994). This fault density is exceptionally low, compared with traditional development post-delivery defect densities of 5–10 defects per thousand lines of code.

Studies at NASA–Goddard's Software Engineering Laboratory, done in conjunction with the University of Maryland Computer Science Department and Computer Sciences Corporation (CSC), help us to understand Cleanroom's impact.

> **EXAMPLE 15.10:**   The Cleanroom fault detection and testing methodology
> was examined in three successive contexts:
>
> * using student subjects on small projects;
> * using NASA staff members on small but real projects;
> * using experienced industry practitioners on a sizable, real project.
>
> Findings involved the use of data collected both pre-study and in each context,
> and there was baseline data from prior projects not using the Cleanroom
> approach. For instance, non-Cleanroom fault density was 6 per thousand lines
> of code, and productivity was 24 lines of code per day. The data for the NASA
> staff using Cleanroom showed 4.5 faults per thousand lines of code and
> productivity of 40 lines of code per day. And on the industry practitioners"
> Cleanroom project, there were 3.2 faults per thousand lines of code and
> productivity of 26 lines of code per day. Notice that, whereas fault density
> improved significantly as the use of the Cleanroom approach was scaled up to
> a large program, productivity did not (Kouchakdjian and Basili, 1989).

This study included nearly all of the criteria for good software engineering research:

* It involved empirical evaluation and data.
* The experimental design was reasonable, given that the projects were "real."
* It involved both toy and real situations.
* The measurements were appropriate to the goals.
* The experiment was conducted over a period of time sufficient to encompass the effects of change in practice.

There is another significant finding from this study. Although the Cleanroom approach calls for the use of formal verification techniques prior to any testing, the study found the use of formal verification impractical, substituting rigorous inspections instead. Exploring the viability of techniques is, of course, one of the important reasons for software engineering evaluative research. And this kind of finding might not be possible without research involving empirical evaluation on real projects.

15.4.2   Object orientation

A more mixed example of good software engineering research has also evolved from the Software Engineering Laboratory. In this case, the study examined the benefits of the object-oriented (OO) approach to building software.

> **EXAMPLE 15.11:**   Data had been gathered on eight major software projects using the OO approaches over a period of several years and were reported in the annual proceedings of the NASA–SEL workshops. However, even before the scaled-up study was performed and research was complete, the preliminary results showed that OO represented "the most important methodology studies by the SEL to date": the amount of reuse had risen dramatically, from 20–30% before OO to 80% with OO, and OO programs were about 75% the length (in lines of code) of comparable traditional solutions (Stark, 1993). SEL researchers also learned some negative lessons: OO projects had reported performance problems (although it was unclear how much was the result of OO), and success with OO required significant domain analysis and project tailoring.

There is a serious problem with these OO studies. The technologies studied were not limited to OO. Projects using the approach under study were also using the Ada language, and the studies did not separate the effects of OO from those of Ada. Further, many of the gains appeared to come from the heavy reuse achieved. Thus, it was not clear which gains are due to Ada, OO, or reuse. In other words, although these experiments involve empirical evaluation and data in real situations, the experimental design is questionable, in that the effects of OO, Ada, and reuse are confounded.

15.4.3   Inspections

There are a great many studies that investigate the effects of inspections on code quality. (One such study was shown in Table 5.1.) Their different designs and approaches provide a rich literature of examples of empirical research.

> **EXAMPLE 15.12:**   Kitchenham and her colleagues at ICL performed a case study of a single project to see whether Fagan inspections would increase software quality without decreasing productivity (Kitchenham, Kitchenham, and Fellows, 1986). Forty-three of the project's 73 programs were given detailed design inspections, but the rest were not. The research team compared the post-design fault profile of the inspected programs with the profile of the uninspected ones, and they tracked fault counts, total project effort, inspection

Table 15.2: Fault profile of inspected and uninspected code

Test method	Faults per 100 lines of inspected code (13 334 lines total)	Faults per 100 lines of uninspected code (8852 lines total)
Code reading	0.97	0.45
Unit test	0.82	0.68
System test	0.20	0.36
Customer	0.012	0.043
Overall	2.0	1.54

effort, and the place in the process where faults were discovered (including post-release).

The study design ensured that several productivity and quality measurements were made. The researchers found that design inspections detected half of all faults found up to nine months after release, while accounting for 6% of the total development costs. The fault detection rate was 1.2 hours per fault. However, since there was no project or organizational baseline, the researchers were unable to determine if these results were better or worse than usual.

Table 15.2 compares the fault profile of inspected with uninspected code.

The results of Example 15.12 might lead you to believe that inspections actually lowered the quality of the code. However, as Kitchenham, Pickard, and Pfleeger point out, it is important to know how modules were selected for inspection or not (Kitchenham, Pickard, and Pfleeger, 1995). In fact, modules were assigned to be inspected only if they were thought to be difficult; otherwise, the modules were not inspected. Thus, the lower fault density for uninspected programs is likely to be a result of their simplicity. On the other hand, note that the inspected programs reveal their faults earlier in the development process than uninspected ones; by the time the modules entered system test, the inspected ones were of higher quality than the uninspected ones.

Another problem with this case study is the choice of project. There was no formal selection process to ensure that this project was representative of typical ICL projects. Instead, the project was chosen because the team wanted to participate. Not only did this volunteer effort affect the representativeness, it probably also biased the team members in favor of inspection.

This study illustrates a common problem with empirical research. The choice of modules for inspection made a great deal of sense for the project but invalidated the results of the case study. We saw in Chapters 3 and 13 that measurement must reflect different goals and perspectives; this example shows us how goals and perspectives can conflict. Had the allocation of modules to inspection been random, the researchers could have performed an analysis of variance on the results and revealed any significant differences. But since the difficulty of modules confounds the results, the best that can be said is that there is a significant difference in post-design fault activity.

15.5 MEASUREMENT TODAY AND TOMORROW

In spite of the problems with many empirical studies today, the state of measurement looks promising. Most practitioners and researchers are convinced of measurement's value, and many are paying attention to the principles we have discussed in this book. In this section, we discuss several trends in measurement research, so that you can see how measurement is likely to affect your software engineering activities.

15.5.1 *Reducing large numbers of measures*

Developers report dissatisfaction with measurement because they sometimes feel overwhelmed with data. That is, the developers get quantitative feedback on a variety of attributes, and it is not always clear which attributes should change in order to improve the overriding goal of productivity or quality. Hence, there have been many efforts to combine measures into a single, summary measure.

> **EXAMPLE 15.13:** Evanco and Agresti examined information about software project complexity. They suggest that complexity has at least two dimensions: design complexity and development environment complexity. They built a defect model based on a categorical multivariate regression analysis that incorporated these dimensions, showing how relevant empirical measures can be combined in a single composite complexity measure that is manifested as software defects (Evanco and Agresti, 1994).

Often, the contributing measures capture radically different attributes. For example, measures of test coverage are different from measures of intra-module information flow, which in turn are different from measures of inter-module control-flow complexity. Since all of these attributes can contribute to fault density, some researchers have developed multilinear regression models based on multiple metrics. One of the goals of this combinational approach is to ensure that the accuracy of prediction with a large number of measures is not diminished when the measures are collapsed to a smaller set (Munson and Khoshgoftaar, 1990). This goal is not difficult to attain, because many popular metrics capture the same underlying attribute. For example, several of the more popular code "complexity" metrics are really measuring size, so the reduced set of metrics has the same information content as the original set (Neil, 1992). Consequently, much work has concentrated on how to select those metrics that are most powerful or representative. We have seen in Chapter 6 how principal component analysis (Manly, 1986) is used in some studies to reduce the dimensionality of many related metrics to a smaller set of "principal components," while retaining most of the variation observed in the original metrics.

> **EXAMPLE 15.14:** Neil determined that 38 metrics, collected on approximately 1000 modules, could be reduced to six orthogonal dimensions that account for 90% of the variability. The most important dimensions, size, nesting,

and prime (the latter two being defined as in Chapter 8), were then used to develop an equation to discriminate between low and high maintainability modules (Neil, 1992).

Munson and Khoshgoftaar use a similar technique, *factor analysis*, to reduce the dimensionality to a number of independent factors (Khoshgoftaar and Munson, 1990; Munson and Khoshgoftaar, 1990; 1992). The name of each factor represents the underlying attribute being measured, such as control, volume and modularity. One benefit of this approach is its avoidance of regression analysis in the presence of multicolinearity.

However, the multivariate approach to modeling size and complexity metrics is questionable on two counts. First, the application of multivariate techniques, like factor analysis, produces metrics that cannot be easily nor directly interpretable in terms of program features. For example, Khoshgoftaar and Munson calculate a factor dimension metric, *control*, using a weighted sum:

$$control = a_1 HNK + a_2 PRC + a_3 E + a_4 VG + a_5 MMC + a_6 error + a_7 HNP + a_8 LOC$$

where *HNK* is Henry and Kafura's information flow complexity metric, *PRC* is a count of the number of procedures, *E* is Halstead's effort metric, *VG* is McCabe's cyclomatic number, *MMC* is Harrison's complexity metric, *error* is the number of defects, and *LOC* is lines of code (Khoshgoftaar and Munson, 1990). Although this equation avoids multicolinearity, it is hard to advise a programmer or designer in how to redesign the program to achieve a better value of *control* for a given module. Likewise, the effect of such a change on faults is not clear.

Second, it is tempting but misleading to use these techniques to generate an ultimate or relative complexity metric (Khoshgoftaar and Munson, 1992). The simplicity of a single number, though appealing, is not based on a key principle of measurement: identifying differing well-defined attributes with single standard measures (Fenton, 1992). The clear role for data reduction and analysis techniques analysis should not be confused with or used instead of measurement theory. For example, statement count and lines of code are highly correlated, because programs with more lines of code typically have a higher number of statements. But the true size of programs is not necessarily a combination of the two metrics; they are alternative measures of the same attribute.

15.5.2   *Measuring the effects of technology insertion*

As software becomes pervasive, its costs and benefits receive more and more attention. Many organizations need to estimate the likely cost of introducing a new technology, as well as assessing the effects of previous technology insertion. We saw in Chapter 14 how Brodman and Johnson looked at return on investment for several American companies. Others have taken similar approaches for examining the effects of technology. For instance, Lim has framed reuse benefit in financial terms, as have Pfleeger and Bollinger (Lim, 1994; Pfleeger and Bollinger 1990; 1994).

EXAMPLE 15.15: Pfleeger and Cline evaluated the effects of technology at the Tennessee Valley Authority. They built a model of benefits based on how the nature of work changed after office automation was introduced. For example, if the Authority paid more for technical work than administrative work, an increase in the amount of technical work was modeled as an increase in the dollar benefit of that work. They demonstrated that the increase in valued work was greater than the cost of hardware, software and training, so that office automation yielded substantial net benefit (Pfleeger and Cline, 1985; Pfleeger, 1988).

In this study, Pfleeger and Cline captured "before" and "after" information using a survey. It was impossible to take a one-time universal snapshot of activity, as installation of the system took over a year; the time lag between first users and last users of the system would have skewed the results. The subjectivity of their survey was acceptable in this instance, as the goal of the study was to assess global change rather than exact dollar value.

Other benefit analyses show how technology change affects the products and processes of software development.

EXAMPLE 15.16: Herbsleb and his colleagues at the US Software Engineering Institute collected data from thirteen organizations representing a variety of levels of the capability maturity model. By examining the changes in performance over time as software process improvement activities were implemented, the research team identified benefits in productivity, early defect detection, time to market, and quality. The results are shown in Table 15.3 (Herbsleb *et al.*, 1994).

Table 15.3: Aggregate results from SEI benefits study

Category	Range	Median
Total yearly cost of software process improvement activities	$49 000 to $1 202 000	$245 000
Years engaged in software process improvement	1 to 9	3.5
Cost of software process improvement per engineer	$490 to $2004	$1375
Productivity gain per year	9% to 67%	35%
Early detection gain per year (defects discovered pre-test)	6% to 25%	22%
Yearly reduction in time to market	15% to 23%	19%
Yearly reduction in post-release defect reports	10% to 94%	39%
Business value of investment in software process improvement (value returned on each dollar invested)	4.0 to 8.8	5.0

This study paints a very positive picture of software process improvement. However, you must be cautious about the applicability of the results to your own environment. The participating organizations volunteered to take part in the study; thus, this group did not form a random sample of the larger population. Moreover, the organizations volunteered projects, some of which had implemented process improvement and some which had not. Although some pairs of projects may have shared common features (such as type of application or experience level of personnel), there was no measurement done to assure that the projects were pairwise comparable; nor was there measurement to determine how representative were the projects. Hence, although we can see that software process improvement was beneficial for this sample, we cannot conclude that software process improvement is beneficial in general.

On the other hand, the study introduces some useful measures of benefit. Productivity and early defect detection are calculated using the notion of **percentage gain per year**:

$$percentage\_gain\_per\_year = 100 \sqrt[i]{overall\_gain\_ratio} - 1$$

where the overall gain ratio is the ratio of the baseline value to the final value. For example, if productivity increases from 1 unit to 1.8 units over a period of five years, then i is 5, the overall gain ratio is 1.8, and the resulting percentage gain per year is 12%. For decreasing quantities, the percentage reduction per year is based on a similar calculation.

15.5.3   Organizing the body of empirical research

As developers and researchers realize the value of empirical research, both in evaluating their own work and the work of others, they have created an infrastructure to assist them in organizing the existing body of results. In the USA, the Center for High Integrity Software Systems Assurance (part of the National Institute of Standards and Technology in Rockville, Maryland) is building a database of information about empirical research. The database will allow you to search for reported results on the effects of a particular technology. For example, if you want to know what is reported in the literature about reuse repositories, you can search the CHISSA database to get a list of existing empirical results.

At the same time, an international group has formed to discuss and promote the use of empirical research in software engineering. The International Software Engineering Research Network (ISERN) publishes technical reports and holds workshops on defining data, storing it, retrieving it, and discussing the results. For example, Kamsties and Lott have evaluated the use of three defect detection techniques at the University of Kaiserslautern in Germany; their results have been published as an ISERN technical report (Kamsties and Lott, 1995).

The software engineering literature has also recognized the role of empirical research. A journal, *Empirical Software Engineering*, has been created to report on recent results, and many other publications require data and analysis to support the claims of any papers submitted to them.

15.6 SUMMARY

This chapter has looked in depth at some of the empirical results reported in the literature. Beginning with guidelines for good empirical research, we have shown that there is a considerable body of work investigating products, processes, and resources. This work is to be applauded, as it attempts to assess current practices by evaluating real data in real situations. However, we have a great deal of room for improvement, and there is an infrastructure developing to support careful, evaluative research. As software engineering embraces more empirical research, we can make better decisions about technology and its impact. This trend can lead only to better practices and more powerful techniques.

We hope that this book has taught you to be skeptical and thorough, and to involve measurement in your work when it is appropriate, tailored to your needs and based on a solid theoretical framework. We encourage you to participate in the growing network of empirical research, and to use measurement to question what you do, why you do it, and how it affects your resources, processes and products.

15.7 EXERCISES

1. There is an abundance of papers describing the use of inspections and their effect on defect detection and product quality. Find two of the papers and analyze them in terms of appropriateness of measures, experimental design, and representativeness of the sample. Do they meet the five criteria for empirical research suggested at the beginning of the chapter?

2. It is not always possible to do a controlled experiment in a real development setting. Describe how you can use measurement to control variables by determining how representative the projects, staff, and processes are.

3. Examine the latest three issues of *IEEE Software*. How many articles involve measurement? How many articles make claims that would be stronger if measurement were involved?

4. Explain why duration of a practice has bearing on its effectiveness. That is, explain why you cannot make judgments about a new technique from having used it only once.

15.8 FURTHER READING

In recent years, there have been several projects promoting the use of empirical research in software engineering. In the early 1990s, the UK Department of Trade and Industry sponsored a project called DESMET that described the role of various kinds of analysis in software engineering research. DESMET produced a series of reports, each one addressing aspects of research such as case studies, experiments, and feature analysis. Since 1994, the DESMET results have been published in abbreviated form in ACM SIGSOFT *Software Engineering Notes*. The full DESMET reports are available from the National Computing Centre.

> Pfleeger, S.L.,"Experimental design and analysis in software engineering," parts 1 to 5, ACM SIGSOFT *Software Engineering Notes*, October 1994 to January 1995.
> Kitchenham, B., and Pickard, L.,"Experimental design and analysis in software engineering," parts 6 to 20, ACM SIGSOFT *Software Engineering Notes*, March 1995 to mid-1998.
> DESMET technical reports, National Computing Centre, Oxford House, Oxford Road, Manchester, UK.

A good analysis of the problems with multivariate assessment can be found in Neil's paper.

> Neil, M.D., "Multivariate assessment of software products," *Journal of Software Testing, Verification and Reliability*, 1(4), pp. 17–37, 1992.

The Center for High Integrity Software Systems Assurance produces technical reports about its database as well as empirical research in general.

> Center for High Integrity Software Systems Assurance, National Institute of Standards and Technology, Rockville, MD, USA.

Technical reports from the International Software Engineering Research Network are available from the University of Kaiserslautern.

> Universität Kaiserlautern, Postfach 3049, D-67653 Kaiserslautern, Germany.

Appendix A: Solutions to selected exercises

Chapter 2: The basics of measurement

2   I. Nominal, ordinal, interval, ratio and absolute are the five scale types.

      II. The scale type for the complexity measure is ordinal, because there is a clear notion of order, but no meaningful notion of "equal difference" in complexity between, say, a trivial and simple module and a simple and moderate module. A meaningful measure of average for any ordinal-scale data is the median. The mode is also meaningful, but the mean is not.

3   The answer is given in Table A.1.

14 A statement about measurement is meaningful if its truth value is invariant of the particular measurement scale being used.

Table A.1: Examples of useful software measurements

Scale type	Software measure	Entity	Entity type	Attribute
Nominal	Classification C, C++, Pascal, ...	Compiler	Resource	Language
Ratio	Lines of Code	Source code	Product	Length
Absolute	Number of defects found	Unit testing	Process	Defects found

The statement about Windows is meaningful (although probably not true) assuming that by size we mean something like the amount of code in the program. To justify its meaningfulness, we must consider how to measure this notion of size. We could use lines of code, thousands of lines of code, number of executable statements, number of characters, or number of bytes, for example. In each case, the statement's truth value is unchanged; that is, if a Windows program is about four times as big as the DOS program when we measure in lines of code, then it will also be about four times as big when we measure in number of characters. We can say this because the notion of size is measurable on a ratio scale.

The rating scale for usability in the second statement is (at best) ordinal, so there is no way to say that the difference in usability from 1 to 2 is the same as from 2 to 3. Therefore, if "average" refers to the mean, then the statement is not meaningful; changing to a different ordinal scale does not necessarily preserve the order of the mean values. However, if "average" refers to the median, then the statement is meaningful.

17 We must assume that the complexity ranking is ordinal, in the sense that the individual categories represent (from left to right) notions of increasing complexity.

i. You can use the median of the M values. This choice is meaningful, because the measure M is an ordinal scale measure. Mode is also acceptable.

ii. Consider the following statement A: "The average complexity of modules in system X is greater than the average complexity of modules in System Y." We must show that A is not meaningful when "average" is interpreted as mean. To do this, we show that the truth value of the statement is not invariant of the particular measure used. Thus, consider the two valid measures M and M' in Table A.2.

Suppose that the complexities of the modules in X are given by:

x_1 trivial, x_2 and x_3 simple, x_4 moderate, x_5 incomprehensible

while the complexities of the modules in Y are given by:

y_1 simple, y_2, y_3 and y_4 moderate, y_5, y_6, and y_7 complex.

Under M, the mean of the X values is 2.6, while the mean of the Y values is 3.1, so statement A is false under the measure M. However, under M', the mean of the X values is 3.6, while the mean of the Y values is 3.1. Thus, statement A is true under M'. From the definition of meaningfulness, it follows that the mean is not a meaningful average measure for this (ordinal scale) data.

iii Your answer might include a crude criterion based on some metric value, such as McCabe's cyclomatic number, v. For example, if $v(x) \leq 2$, we assign x as trivial; if $2 < v(x) < 5$ we assign x as simple, and so on. Finally, if $v(x) > 100$, we assign x as

Table A.2: Example measures

	trivial	simple	moderate	complex	very complex	incomprehensible
M	1	2	3	4	5	6
M'	1	2	3	4	5	10

incomprehensible. A more sophisticated criterion might be based on some measurable notion that closely matches our intuition about complexity. For example, complexity of software modules is (intuitively) closely related to the difficulty of maintaining the modules. If maintenance data were available, such as Mean Time to Repair faults for each module, then we could base our criterion on it. For example, if $MTTR(x) < 30$ minutes, then we assign x as trivial; if 30 minutes$\leq MTTR(x) <$ 90 minutes, we assign x as simple, and so on, until if $MTTR(x) >$ 5 days, we assign x as incomprehensible.

21   The only way to report "number of bugs found" is to count number of bugs found. The answer to the second part depends very much on how you define program correctness. If you believe that a program is either correct or not, then correctness is measurable on a nominal scale with two values, such as (yes, no) or (1, 0). Or you may decide that correctness is measurable on a ratio scale, where the notion of zero incorrectness equals absolute correctness. (In this case, the number of bugs found could be a ratio-scale measure of program correctness.) In either of these cases, the number of bugs found cannot be an absolute-scale measure for the attribute. Moreover, if "correctness" is taken to be synonymous with reliability, then counting bugs found may not be a measure of correctness at all, since we may not be finding the bugs that cause actual failures.

CHAPTER 3: A FRAMEWORK FOR SOFTWARE MEASUREMENT

5   GQM means Goal–Question–Metric, and it is based on the notion that measurement activities should always be preceded by identifying clear goals for them. To determine whether you have met a particular goal, you ask questions whose answers will tell you if the goal has been met. Then, you generate from each question the attributes you must measure in order to answer the questions.

Goal-oriented measurement is common sense, but there are many situations where some measurement activity can be beneficial even though the goals are not clearly defined. This situation is especially true where a small number of metrics address several different goals, such as monitoring quality changes while predicting testing effort, for example. Also, GQM introduces the problem of determining who sets the goals. High-level managers may be bad at identifying goals, or they may have goals for which no metrics can be practically computed at the engineering level. Because of this mismatch between goals and practicality, some people have proposed the need for bottom-up measurement, where the engineers collect metrics data that are useful and practical.

A typical GQM tree may resemble Figures A.1 and A.2.

The trees depict only direct measures. Questions such as, "what is the reliability requirement?" are answered in terms of indirect measures derived from the direct ones, and the tree can be extended to include both types. For example, the reliability requirement might be expressed as an average number of failures per 100 hours of use, or a number of defects per KLOC. Similarly, current reliability might be measured by number of defects per test case. It might also be useful if failures and defects were partitioned into two categories, "serious" (that is, really affecting reliability) and "not serious," since many anomalies found during testing may be benign.

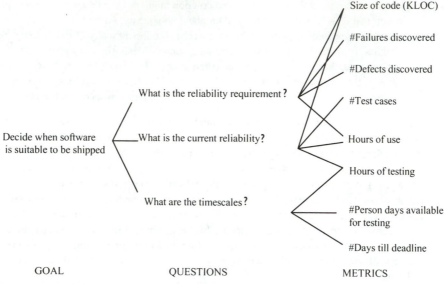

Figure A.1: GQM tree on software reliability

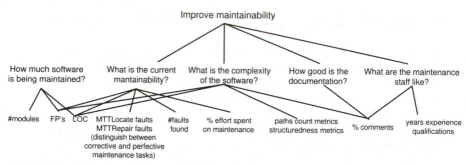

Figure A.2: GQM tree on improving maintainability of software

7   A typical GQM tree may resemble Figure A.2.

CHAPTER 5: SOFTWARE-MEASUREMENT DATA COLLECTION

1   An error is a mistake made by a human designer. A fault is the encoding of an error in the software. A failure is the manifestation of a fault during software execution.

5   i.   Note first that only project-wide issues can be addressed because of the data's coarse granularity. Moreover, only goals and questions relating to project-wide comparisons are reasonable. Some possibilities are:

- General project-wide trends or comparisons in *productivity*, measured as the ratio of effort and lines of code. An example goal might be: "Improve project productivity," and a question might be: "What is current best, average, and worst productivity?" The well-known problems with this particular productivity measure should be cited here. (For example, lines of code do not really measure utility or even size of output or there are problems with the definition of the lines of code measure itself.)

- General project-wide trends or comparisons in quality, measured as the ratio of faults with lines of code. An example goal might be: "Improve product quality," and a question might be: "What gave current best, average, and worst quality?" Note problems with the lines of code measure again, but the real limitation is the use of faults. Total number of faults recorded may be more an indication of differences in recording or testing practice than of genuine quality. It does not reflect quality of the end product.

- Providing you have data from a reasonable number of similar projects, it is possible to use the measures to improve project forecasting (that is, effort estimation). You achieve this goal by using regression analysis on effort and lines-of-code data from the past projects.

- Providing you have data from a reasonable number of similar projects, you can use the measures for outlier analysis. For example, your goal may be to identify those projects having unusual productivity or quality values. However, all the limitations noted above still apply. To address this goal, you can use boxplots, two-dimensional scatter diagrams, etc.

ii. You must collect data at the module level, rather than only at the project level. In particular, size, effort, and fault data should be available for each module. For each module, you must also identify the specific quality-assurance techniques that were used. (Ideally, you would know the extent of such use, measured by effort.) It would be helpful if the effort data per module could be partitioned into effort by activity, such as design, coding, testing, and so on.

To get a more accurate perspective on whether a particular method has been effective, we need an external quality measure for each module. The number of faults discovered during testing is weak (and totally dependent on the level of testing and honesty of the tester). It would be better to obtain data on operational failures, where the failure can be traced back to individual modules.

To overcome the problems of lines of code as a poor size measure, it may be useful to collect other size data for each module. Static analysis tools or metrics packages offer inexpensive ways to collect structural metrics, which at least will indicate differences in structural complexity between modules (a difference not highlighted by lines of code). It may even be useful (although not as inexpensive) to use function-point analysis.

6 i. There are several important aspects of dependability:

1. **Safety** must be the main concern, since lives are endangered if the system malfunctions.

2. **Availability** is important, since it contributes to safety. Long or frequent "outages" will require personal supervision of patients by nursing staff, and drugs will have to be administered by hand.

3. **Reliability** is similarly important. Safety will be adversely affected by frequent failure, and frequent false alarms will cause unnecessary work for the medical staff, and maybe complacency, which could mean that a genuine warning is

ignored. This and the following attributes may be considered to be of equal importance.

4. **Recoverability** is important since it contributes to high availability.
5. **Maintainability** also contributes to high availability, and (in the case of removal of design faults) to growth in safety and reliability.
6. **Usability** is important from the point of view of the nursing staff, mainly because it contributes to safety by reducing the probability of human error, for example, in missing an indication that a patient requires attention.

It is important to recognize that death or deterioration in a patient's condition are worse than those resulting only in inconvenience to staff or financial loss to the hospital. A case may be made for maintainability or recoverability being more important than availability or reliability. Security is of relatively minor concern, since the system is unlikely to be open to potential external interference. Features such as "fault tolerance" assist reliability and safety, but are not themselves dependability attributes.

ii. Any of the following are acceptable:

1. **Location:** identity of the installation and piece of equipment on which the incident was observed.
2. **Timing(1):** when did the incident occur in real time?
3. **Timing(2):** when did the incident occur in relation to system operational time, or software execution time?
4. **Mode(1):** type of symptoms observed.
5. **Mode(2):** conditions of use of system.
6. **Effect:** type of consequence. This attribute will partly determine whether the incident affects safety, availability, or reliability.
7. **Mechanism:** how did the incident come about?
8. **Cause(1):** type of trigger, such as physical hardware failure, operating conditions, malicious action, user error, erroneous report, "unexplained." This attribute will determine whether the incident is classified as relevant to usability or reliability.
9. **Cause(2):** type of source, such as physical hardware fault, unintentional design fault, intentional design fault, usability problem, "no cause found."
10. **Cause(3):** identity of source (mode of failure and component in the case of physical failure, identity of fault in the case of design failure).
11. **Severity(1):** categorization of how serious the effect of the incident was. This will determine whether the incident affects safety.
12. **Severity(2):** cost to user (nursing staff or hospital) in terms of time lost, inconvenience, or extra effort incurred.
13. **Cost:** how much effort and other resources were expended by the vendor in order to diagnose and respond to the report of the incident?
14. **Count:** how many incidents occurred in a given time interval?

iii. These are examples of types of data that might be needed:

1. records of design faults and design modifications; operating time of each part of the system, and (ideally) execution;
2. time of each software module;

3. the operational profile of the various parts of the system must also be recorded, since this will affect the levels of safety and reliability;

4. to measure availability, recoverability or maintainability, the time to restore service and the effort to diagnose and repair faults must be recorded;

5. to measure operating time and mode of operation accurately, it will be necessary to instrument the system, and write the data automatically to a file.

It is important to distinguish clearly between operating time and real time (calendar, or wall-clock, time), and to note that the operating time-base for the BED computer and for PAN computers (which execute many copies of the same code simultaneously) are different.

iv. Five possible modes are the following:

1. PAN sends signal to operate drug pump when not required. Affects safety. **Effect:** Pump administers overdose. **Severity:** critical/major (depending on the drug).

2. BED software crashes. Affects availability, possibly safety. **Effect:** loss of patient status information to nurse. **Severity:** critical/major (depending on length of outage).

3. PAN software does not detect that a sensor has failed. **Effect:** relevant vital sign not monitored. **Severity:** major.

4. BED software indicates emergency although PAN has not reported deviation of vital signs. Affects reliability. **Effect:** nurse visits patient unnecessarily. **Severity:** minor.

5. "Wake up" signal not sent to junior doctor sufficiently often. Affects reliability, possibly safety. **Effect:** delay in response of doctor to emergency. **Severity:** major/minor.

7 i. For each failure, it will be necessary to record:

- **Time:** both calendar time of the failure and total execution time of the software up to the failure (or, alternatively, the total execution time on all instances of the software during a given calendar time period) are required.

- **Location:** the particular instance of the software that failed, identified by the installation on which it is running. In this case, the control room will operate one (or more) instance(s) of the CAM software, and each taxi will operate an instance of the COT software.

- **Mode:** what symptoms were observed? That is, what was the system seen to do that was not part of its required functions?

- **Effect:** what were the consequences of the failure for the driver of the taxi and for the whole of the SCAMS operation?

- **Severity:** how serious were these consequences? (This may be expressed either as a classification into major/minor/negligible, or in terms of the cost of lost business, or of the time that CAM or COT were out of action.)

- **Reporter:** person making the report (taxi driver, control room operator, customer).

The following are five examples of software failure modes:

1. CAM software crashes

    -   **Time:** date and time; hours and minutes CAM was running until failure.
    -   **Location:** control room.
    -   **Mode:** loss of all screen displays, keyboard unresponsive, all COT systems lose contact with control room.
    -   **Effect:** loss of central control and guidance for all vehicles until CAM is rebooted and re-establishes contact with COT systems.
    -   **Severity:** major. Disruption of service for all drivers and passengers, with considerable inconvenience and loss of business.
    -   **Reporter:** control room operator.

2. COT software crashes

    -   **Time:** date and time; hours and minutes all COT systems have been running until failure (alternatively, if that is not possible, total running hours on all COT systems on that date).
    -   **Location:** number of the taxi whose COT failed, and where it was at the time. (The latter might be useful if the COT failure was in response to certain geographical data being input.)
    -   **Mode:** driver's display blank, driver's control console unresponsive, loss of communication of CAM with that vehicle.
    -   **Effect:** loss of central control and guidance for the affected vehicle until the driver could restart the COT.
    -   **Severity:** minor. Disruption of service for one driver and (possibly) passenger. Some loss of business (for instance, if driver could not pick up a passenger at the agreed place and time).
    -   **Reporter:** driver.

3. CAM sends incorrect directions to COT

    -   **Time:** date and time. Hours and minutes CAM was running until failure.
    -   **Mode:** directions displayed on driver's screen are inconsistent with the actual position of the vehicle as observed by the driver.
    -   **Effect:** driver confused, and possibly gets lost.
    -   **Severity:** minor, unless the same CAM failure affects many vehicles.
    -   **Reporter:** driver or control room operator (depending on who first notices the incompatibility).

4. COT reports incorrect location to CAM

    -   **Time:** date and time. Operating time of all COT systems.
    -   **Mode:** apparent discontinuity in vehicle movement as tracked by CAM.
    -   **Effect:** CAM cannot send correct directions to COT. Driver confused or lost.
    -   **Severity:** minor. Affects one vehicle only.
    -   **Reporter:** driver or control room operator.

5. Journey time is calculated by CAM to be shorter than it should be

- **Time:** date and time. Hours and minutes CAM was running until failure.
- **Mode:** estimated arrival time displayed by CAM is found to be inaccurate when compared to driver's actual reported journey time.
- **Effect:** driver arrives to pick up passenger later than arranged.
- **Severity:** minor, unless the inaccuracy affects many journeys.
- **Reporter:** driver.

ii. There are several important dependability attributes.

- **Safety:** the only critical failure mode is the failure of the silent alarm. Target: 1 failure per thousand demands (maximum).
- **Reliability:** targets will differ for different modes of failure:

  - for crash of COT software: 1 per 1000 operating hours.
  - for crash of CAM software: 1 per 10 000 operating hours.
  - for wrong directions: 1 per 5000 CAM operating hours, etc.

- **Recoverability:** target is to have the software recover after crash or error in an acceptable time. Different targets will apply to CAM and COT:

  - CAM: reload and resume service after crash within 1 minute on average.
  - COT: reload and resume service after crash within 10 seconds on average.
  - Other targets may be set for recovery from lesser error conditions; for example, detection of CAM that it has given wrong directions, and alerting driver.

- **Availability:** target is to have the whole system up and running for an acceptable proportion of real time. Subsidiary targets may be set for individual subsystems; for example:

  - CAM: 99.8% up time
  - COT: 98% up time

- **Maintainability:** target can be set for diagnosing and fixing a software fault.

iii. Reliability, usability, safety, and security all relate to our expectation that certain types of events will not occur in operation. They can be measured by "the probability that the system will deliver a required service, under given conditions of use, for a given time interval, without relevant incident."

Reliability relates to departures of any kind from the required service. Usability relates to difficulties experienced by a human user attempting to operate the system, and roughly equates to "user-friendliness." Safety is concerned only with incidents that can result in death, injury, or other catastrophic damage. Security relates to incidents that result in unauthorized disclosure or alteration of sensitive information, or in denial of service to legitimate users by unauthorized persons.

It is therefore necessary to record all incidents, and measure their location, time of occurrence, the execution time over which they occur, mode, effect, and severity. Once again, it is necessary to record the execution time for CAM and COT software separately. COT execution time will need to be totaled over all vehicles, and this will probably mean that only "failure count" data is available for COT, whereas "time to failure" data can be obtained fairly easily for CAM.

Once an incident has been shown to be a genuine failure and diagnosed as being due to a software fault, the identity of the fault responsible should be recorded. The type of fault can be used to establish to which attribute a given incident is relevant. The fault identity and cross-reference from each record of a failure in which it manifested itself can be used to extract "execution time up to first manifestation of each fault" (for CAM), or "count of faults manifest and total execution time in a given period" (for COT).

Measurement of maintainability requires the recording of the effort to diagnose and repair each fault. Recoverability requires records of time to restore service after each failure. A measure of availability can be derived from reliability and recoverability.

Chapter 6: Analyzing software-measurement data

10   i.   The standard quality measure in this context is defect density, calculated as number of defects divided by thousands of lines of code. The defect density for each system is in Table A.3:

Table A.3: Defect densities

System	A	B	C	D	E	F	G	H	I
defect density	0.88	0	19.0	0.7	0.46	0.57	0.92	0.4	1.125

   ii.   Box plots reveal that the defect metric has two outliers: one high (system C, with 95 defects) and one low (system B, with no defects). The lines of code metric has no outliers. The defect density metric has one outlier (over 15 times bigger than any other), namely system C at 19 defects/KLOC.

   iii. Clearly subsystem C is the problem area. Despite the fact that it is exceptionally small (just 4 KLOC), it contains an abnormally high number of defects. You would be well advised to investigate this subsystem further to determine why. Is it exceptionally complex? Is it the part of the system most used? Has it the worst programmers or tools? There is also something unusual about subsystem B. Although large, this subsystem had no defects. Are there positive lessons to learn from it (for example, was it developed with the best programmers or tools?), or is it simply that this subsystem was not used?

   iv.   A major weakness is that there is no notion of usage; subsystem C may be used much more than others, and system B may be never used. There are also no notions of severity of defects nor of complexity of subsystems. (KLOC is just a crude measure of size.) There is a blurring of the key distinction between fault and failure. Why should a failure always be due to a single defect in a single subsystem?

   v.   It would be extremely useful to get some measure of usage for each subsystem, since this would enable us to use the existing data to produce genuine reliability assessments of the different subsystems. Since system users are already logging failures as they occur, it should not be too difficult to get them to log the way they use the system. We should at least be able to get some estimate of the relative calendar time spent using the different subsystems. It would not be too difficult to insert some monitoring code into the system so that this can be done automatically. Another addition to the data collection should be the measurement of actual time to locate and fix faults. This would reveal important maintainability information. Given the size of the system and the number of defects per year, maintainability is a major concern.

11   The outliers for CFP are modules R and P. The outliers for Faults are P, Q and R. So the outliers for CFP and Faults are more or less the same, whereas LOC has none. This result suggests that a high CFP is a more reliable indicator of a faulty module than high LOC. Thus, it would be a wise testing strategy to compute CFP for each module in a system and devote more time to testing, or redesigning, those that are outliers. Contrary to what many will say, there may be no point at all in redesigning modules R and P to lower their CFP, as the faults have already occurred!

12   The outliers of MOD and FD are the same, namely systems A, D, and L. Systems A and D are outliers of MOD because they have exceptionally low average module size, while system L is an outlier because it has exceptionally high average module size. Each of these three systems also had abnormally high fault density. This suggests that those systems in which average module size is either very high or very low are likely to be the most fault-prone. On the basis of this data, the outliers of MOD are excellent predictors of the high outliers of FD. A reasonable quality-assurance procedure would therefore be to restrict module sizes (on average) to between 16 and 88 LOC. This procedure should avoid systems whose fault-proneness is explained by module size. A stricter quality procedure might focus on values between the upper and lower quartiles. In other words, we should restrict module sizes (on average) to between 43 and 61 LOC. From the data, we can also conclude that size of a system alone (measured by KLOC) gives no indication of its fault proneness, nor of its likely average module size. For example, the only outlier for KLOC – the exceptionally large system R – has neither an unusual average module size nor an unusually high fault density.

CHAPTER 7: MEASURING INTERNAL PRODUCT ATTRIBUTES: SIZE

7   Function points are a measure of the functionality of a software system. The unadjusted function count UFC is derived from counting system inputs, outputs, enquiries and files. A technical complexity factor, F, is then computed for the system, and the function-point count is FP = UFC × F.

The main applications of FPs are:

- sizing for purposes of effort/cost estimation (providing that you have data about previous projects that relates the number of FPs in a system to the actual cost/effort);
- sizing for purposes of normalization; thus, FPs are used to compute quality density (defects/FP), productivity (person months/FP), and so on.

Comparing FPs with LOC:

- Unlike LOC, FPs can be extracted early in the software life cycle (from the requirements definition or specification) and so can be used in simple cost-estimation models where size is the key parameter.

- FPs, being a measure of functionality, are more closely related to utility than LOC.
- FPs are language-independent.
- FPs can be used as a basis for contracts at the requirements phase.

However:

- FPs are difficult to compute, and different people may count FPs differently.
- Unlike LOC, FPs cannot be automatically extracted.
- There is some empirical evidence to suggest that FPs are not very good for predicting effort. Empirical evidence also suggests that FPs are unnecessarily complex.

8 i. Function points are supposed to measure the amount of functionality in a software "product," where product can mean any document from which the functional specification can be extracted: the code itself, the detailed design, or the specification. Function points are defined in a language-independent manner, so the number of function points should not depend on the particular product representation. Function points are also commonly interpreted as a measure of size.

Drawbacks:

- The main drawback of function points is the difficulty in computing them. You must have at least a very detailed specification. This task is not easily automated or even repeatable. Different people will generally arrive at a different FP count for the same specification, although the existence of standards helps minimize the variance.
- The definition of function points was heavily influenced by the assumption that the number should be a good predictor of effort; in this sense, the function point measure is trying to capture more than just functionality. Thus, FPs are not very well-defined from the measurement theory perspective.
- FPs have been shown to be unnecessarily complicated. In particular, the TCF appears to add nothing in terms of measuring functionality, nor does it help to improve the predictive accuracy when FPs are used for effort prediction.

ii. Most common answers will be:

- FPs can be used as the main input variable in an effort-prediction system. Traditionally, LOC (or some similar code-based metric) has been used. The advantage of FPs is that they can be computed directly from the specification, so you need not predict LOC early in development.
- Function points can be used in any application where you need to normalize by size. So if you measure productivity traditionally by LOC/effort, it would be advantageous to use FPs instead of LOC, since FPs are more obviously related to the utility of output, and they are independent of the language used. You could also use FPs in this same equation to measure designer (or even specifier) productivity and not just coder productivity.
- You could use FPs to measure defect density as defects/FP, rather than defects/ LOC.

Table A.4:

External inputs		
coursework marks	simple	3
exam marks	simple	3
menu-selection: course choice	simple	3
menu-selection: operation choice	simple	3
External inquiries		
average	simple	3
letter grade	average	4
External outputs		
List of student marks, etc.	average	5
External files		
None.		
Internal file		
Course file database: this contains the course list, student lists, and all known marks, and grades.	complex	10

iii. There is no single correct answer here. However, good answers should contain similar information.

We identify the items in Table A.4 and their associated "complexity," weighting them as shown (using the table for UFC weighting factors).Then UFC = 35. To compute the Technical Complexity Factor (TCF), we consider the 14 listed factors in the Albrecht model. We assume that all but the following are irrelevant:

F6   online data entry
F7   operational ease
F9   online update
F13 multiple sites

Each of these is rated essential and hence get a weighting of 5.

Therefore TCF = 0.65 + 0.01 × (4 × 5) = 0.85

Thus FP = UFC × TCF = 30.

CHAPTER 8: MEASURING INTERNAL PRODUCT ATTRIBUTES:
STRUCTURE

21 Coupling is a property of pairs of modules, while cohesion is a property of individual modules. Coupling between modules is the extent of interdependence between modules, whereas cohesion of a module is the extent to which the elements of the module have a common purpose, that is, are part of the same function.

It is generally believed that if a design is made up of a number of related modules, then there should be (as far as possible) a low level of coupling; this way, errors made in any one module should affect a minimum number of others. Also, low coupling should help keep independent the implementation of the modules. On the other hand, high cohesion of each module may be desirable for conceptual simplicity and ease of testing. The lowest level of coupling can be achieved by having a single module for the whole system, but such a module will have very low cohesion. Analogously, we could ensure the highest level of cohesion of each module at the expense of very high coupling, namely where each individual statement corresponds to a module. Therefore we have to find an optimal balance of low coupling and high cohesion.

22 Types of cohesion:

1. Functional: the module performs a single well-defined function.
2. Sequential: the module performs more than one function, but these occur in an order described in the specification.
3. Communicational: the module performs more than one function, but these are all on the same body of data (which is not organized as a single type or structure).
4. Procedural: the module performs more than one function, and these are related only to a general procedure affected by the software.
5. Temporal: the module performs more than one function, and these are related only by the fact that they must occur within the same time span.
6. Logical: the module performs more than one function, and these are related only logically.
7. Coincidental: the module performs more than one function, and these are unrelated.

The software entity is source code (or the flowgraph representation of source code). The attribute is, strictly speaking, the number of linearly independent paths through the code, or the number of decisions plus one. The attribute is internal.

23 The statement coverage strategy is a form of white-box testing. The tester must select inputs so that, when the program is executed, enough paths are executed for each statement of the program to lie on at least one path.

26 A procedure is D-structured, formally, if its decomposition tree contains only primes of the form P_n, D_0, D_1, D_2, or D_3, which is true in this case (Figure A.3).

27 The key thing to note about this algorithm is that its underlying flowgraph is the double-exit loop shown in Figure A.4.

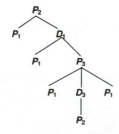

Figure A.3:
Decomposition loop

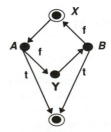

Figure A.4: Double-exit loop

In the strict interpretation of structured programming, only certain single-exit loops are allowed as building blocks. The two-exit loop is a prime structure that cannot be structured in terms of other such loops. Thus, in the strict sense, the algorithm is unstructured. But this example highlights the limitations of the strict view. Any attempt to rewrite the algorithm in "structured form" requires the introduction of new dummy variables that mar the simple and intuitive structure of the original algorithm. More liberal views of structured programming allow primes such as the two-exit loop, which is very natural in any control environment.

CHAPTER 9: MEASURING EXTERNAL PRODUCT ATTRIBUTES

3 The measure is quite useful for developers but is almost useless for users or potential purchasers. For developers who measure both LOC and faults found (in the code) in a consistent manner, the measure will indicate:

- broad differences in quality among different modules, systems, and teams;
- trends that can aid quality-control efforts;
- potential troublespots in the system;
- when the developers have reached the point of diminishing returns on testing.

However, the measure is of limited usefulness to the user, as it:

- gives no real indication of reliability (since faults may not be good predictor of failures, as shown in the Adams data);
- gives no indication at all of usability;
- gives no indication of the severity of the faults;
- cannot be used compare products from different producers; the producers may count LOC differently, and they may have different definitions or classifications of faults;
- may say more about the rigor of the testing process (or of the tester) than about the quality of the code; clearly, the testing strategy influences how many faults are found;
- invites abuse by programmers who may artificially increase the length of a program in order to be seen to be producing higher-quality code;
- is irrelevant for assessing quality before coding has begun;
- cannot be used comparatively with earlier products whose system size is not LOC;
- does not take account of reused code.

4 To compare projects with a given measure, it must be either normalized using size or type of project or independent of size/type of project. None of the measures here is normalized. Therefore, the only ones of value for comparative purposes are:

- mean time to failure, for all projects at beta-test phase (a good measure of system reliability);
- mean time to repair reported defects (a reasonable measure of maintainability);
- maximum cyclomatic number (a very crude measure of system structuredness, and much less useful than the previous two measures);
- average number of function points produced per month of programmer effort (a crude measure of programmer productivity; it would be dangerous to use this if the projects involved vastly different applications).

Each of the other measures, although useful for tracking and quality control purposes within a project, cannot be used sensibly for cross-project comparisons unless normalized.

- Total number of user-reported failures: for this to be used as a comparative measure of quality, it should be normalized against both system size and usage time. The former could be measured by total number of function points in the system (presumably already collected) or a simple measure like LOC. The latter would be much more difficult to measure, since it can be done only by the system users.
- Total number of defects found during system testing: at the very least, this measure should be normalized against size (as above). It may also need normalization against amount of testing.
- Total number of changes made during development: if this measure is normalized against size (preferably measured by function points), it may be a measure either of system volatility (if the changes are being suggested by customers) or quality (if the changes are being made as a result of discovering faults).
- Total project overspend/underspend: this measure should be normalized against actual expenditures to yield a measure of the accuracy of the cost predictions.

Chapter 10: Software reliability: measurement and prediction

8 Both prequential likelihood ratios actually converge at around $i = 10$ for this particular data set. This result suggests that neither one is better than the other. (In fact, neither is particularly good.)

9 The totality of all possible inputs forms an input space. A fault can be thought of as a collection of points in the input space, each of which, when executed, results in output that is regarded as failed. (The decision to label an output failed will depend upon a comparison of what was required with what was produced.) Execution of the program involves the successive execution of a sequence of inputs. This sequence will be a random walk in the input space – random because the selection of future inputs is unpredictable and determined by the outside world. Such a trajectory through the input space will fall over the fault regions and so cause failures randomly.

There is a further source of randomness (or uncertainty) when a fix is carried out. If the fix is successful, we are uncertain of the magnitude of the effect of its removal on the unreliability. There will be a tendency for high-rate faults to be encountered, and removed, earlier than low-rate ones. In addition, there is the possibility that a fix is not perfect. In this case, the effect on the program may be to increase the unreliability by an unknown amount.

10 The u-plot essentially detects consistent bias in predictions of reliability: the magnitude of the maximum departure from unit slope can be used to test whether the bias is statistically significant. The precise shape of the u-plot gives information about the nature of the errors. For example, a plot that is consistently above the line of unit slope tells us that the predictions are too optimistic.

The prequential likelihood ratio allows us to compare the accuracies of prediction of model A with model B on the same data. If the prequential likelihood ratio is consistently increasing as the data vector increases in dimension, the model in the numerator can be said to be more accurate than the model in the denominator. The prequential likelihood ratio is sensitive to all kinds of departure from the truth, and not just bias, but it is only a comparative analysis.

The smoothed u-plot of previous predictions can be used to modify the current prediction as follows:

$$F_i^*(t) = G_{i-1}\{F_i(t)\}$$

where $F_i(t)$ is a raw estimate from a particular model of $P(T_i < t)$, G_{i-1} is the smoothed u-plot based on predictions of … t_{i-2}, t_{i-1}, and $F_i^*(t)$ is the modified – recalibrated – prediction of $P(T_i < t)$.

11 The results clump into two groups: six model predictions in one group, two in the other. There is reasonable agreement of the median predictions within each group, but big differences between groups. From the u-plot, all predictions are bad: six too optimistic, two too pessimistic. From the prequential likelihood ratio, the two pessimistic ones are not as bad as the six optimistic ones. None of the predictions can be trusted as they are; they should be recalibrated.

12
- **Debugging data**: use a reliability growth model, but you can get only quite modest reliability because of the law of diminishing returns. You must also worry about the efficacy of fixes, since models tend to assume fixes are correct and do not introduce new faults; this is not a conservative assumption in the case of safety-critical systems.
- **Failure-free working**: this is quite weak evidence of reliability. Roughly, we can expect there to be a 50:50 chance of working failure-free for a time t when we have seen a time t of failure-free working.
- **Diversity**: there are experimental and theoretical reasons to doubt that the versions will fail independently. There is some evidence that this approach does deliver improvements over a single version, but the improvement is hard to quantify. Evaluating a particular diverse system is equivalent to treating it as a black box, and thus the previous two paragraphs apply.
- **Verification**: this technique addresses consistency with formal specification, but does not always address the issue of whether this is complete and accurate representation of the informal engineering requirements. There are practical difficulties with verification for any except small programs, because of resource constraints.
- **Process**: there is very weak evidence to show a link between process and product.

14 Unless you know a lot about the faults you have removed, there is very little you can say about the improvements to reliability. It might be tempting to assume a proportional improvement in reliability, but on the basis of the Adams data, you could actually remove 95% of all faults and yet see no perceptible reliability improvements; this is because a very small proportion of faults cause almost all the common failures.

CHAPTER 12: MAKING PROCESS PREDICTIONS

10. The system type must be "embedded mode," since the power plant will be controlled by software. Hence we must choose the model

$$E = 3.6 \, S^{1.2}$$

where E is effort (in person months) and S is size (in thousands of delivered source instructions). We must assume that a line of code corresponds to a delivered source instruction (DSI). Then, the model predicts that:

$$E = 3.6 \, (10 \, 000)^{1.2} = 227 \, 145 \text{ person months}$$

Appendix B: Metrics tools

The book has mentioned numerous metrics tools. The contact details for some of these are listed below.

Before You Leap
Gordon Group,
San Jose
California
USA

Function Point Workbench
Macloud Group
11–15 High Street
Marlow
Bucks SL7 1AU
UK
tel +44 (0)1628 890313
fax +44 (0)1628 890198
The same company is also the UK distributor for SPR's estimation tool, Checkmark.

LDRA Testbed
Program Analyzers
56 Northbrook Street
Newbury, Berkshire
RG13 1AN
UK

Logiscope
Verilog
3010 LBJ Freeway, Suite 900
Dallas
Texas 75234
USA

M-BASE
National Computing Centre
Oxford Road
Manchester M1 7ED
UK

McCabe's ACT (Analysis of Complexity Tool), Battlemap
McCabe & Associates
5501 Twin Knolls Rd, Suite 111
Columbia, MD 21045
USA
Tel +1 800-683-6316

Metrics Advisor
MITRE Corporation
7525 Colshire Drive
McLean, Virginia
USA
tel +1 703 883-6000

PC Metric
SET Laboratories
PO Box 868
Mulino
Oregon 97042
USA

QAC, QAC Dynamic, QAC++ and QA Fortran
Programming Research Ltd (PR:QA)
Glenbrook House
1/11 Molesey Road
Hersham
Surrey KT12
UK
Tel +44 (0)1932 888080

QA Manager
Programming Research Corporation
6401 Golden Triangle Drive, Suite 450
Greenbelt, MD 20770
USA

QUALMS
CSSE
South Bank University
Borough Road
London SE1 0AA
UK

Slim
Quantitative Software Management
2000 Corporate Ridge
Suite 900
McLean, Virginia 22102
USA
tel +1 703 790-0055
Fax +1 703 749-3795

SoftCost
RCI,
25550 Hawthorne Blvd, Suite 112
Torrance
California 90505
USA
tel +1 310 373-8728

Appendix C: Acronyms and glossary

ami: *Application of Metrics in Industry*. ESPRIT metrics technology transfer project (1991–3) based on CMM and GQM

Bootstrap: ESPRIT project resulting in a framework for assessing software process maturity

BSI: *British Standards Institute.*

BS 5750: BSI standard equivalent to ISO 9001

COCOMO: *COnstructive COst MOdel.* Software cost estimation model developed by Boehm

CMM: *Capability Maturity Model.* Five-level model of a software-development organization's process maturity

CSR: *Centre for Software Reliability* (at City Universityin London). Organizers of workshops on software-related issues; also the umbrella organization for the UK national clubs on safety critical systems and reliability and metrics

DOD: *Department of Defense* (USA).

DSI: *Delivered Source Instructions.* Measure of software code size

ESPRIT: *European Strategic Programme of Research and Development in Information Technology*

FP: *Function Point.* Measure of software size extractable from specification

FPA: *Function Point Analysis.* Process by which FP measure for a software system is computed

GQM: *Goal–Question–Metric.* Rigorous goal-oriented approach to measurement developed by Basili and colleagues at University of Maryland, USA

IEEE: *Institute of Electrical and Electronic Engineers* (USA).

IEEE 1061: IEEE standard for a software quality metrics methodology (finalized in 1992)

IFPUG: *International Function Point Users Group.*

ISO: *International Standards Organisation.*

ISO 9001: General quality management standard

ISO 9003: Quality management standard specific to software

ISO 9126: Standard for software product evaluation based on SQM ideas; approved 1992

KDSI: *Kilobyte Delivered Source Instructions* (thousands of delivered source instructions). Measure of software code size

KLOC: *Kilobyte Lines Of Code* (thousands of lines of code).

KPA: *Key Process Area or Key Process Activity.* Component of the CMM

LOC: *Lines Of Code.*

MOD: *Ministry of Defence* (UK).

NASA: National Aeronautics and Space Administration, US government organization that funds a software engineering laboratory

NCLOC: *Non-Comment Lines Of Code.*

QA: *Quality Assurance.*

QC: *Quality Control.*

QFD: *Quality Function Deployment.* Technique that evolved from TQM principles that aims at deriving indicators from the user's point of view

QUANTUM: A measurement-based framework for software quality developed by Praxis, commissioned by the UK Department of Trade and Industry (1992)

SEI: *Software Engineering Institute* (at Carnegie–Mellon University, Pittsburgh, Pennsylvania, USA).

SQM: *Software Quality Metrics.* Framework for software quality assessment based on a set of quality factors that are refined into a set of criteria, which are further refined into a set of metrics

SPC: *Statistical Process Control.*

SPICE: *Software Process Improvement and Capability dEtermination.* International project whose aim is to develop a standard for software process assessment, building on the best features of the CMM, Bootstrap, and ISO 9003

TCF: *Technical Complexity Factor* (in Function Point Analysis).

TickIT: Software quality initiative sponsored by the UK Department of Trade and Industry, based on ISO 9003 principles

TQC: *Total Quality Control.*

TQM: *Total Quality Management.*

UFC: *Unadjusted Function Count* (in Function Point Analysis).

Annotated bibliography

Abdel-Ghaly, A.A., Chan, P.Y. and Littlewood, B., "Evaluation of competing software reliability predictions," *IEEE Transactions on Software Engineering*, SE-12(9), pp. 950–67, 1986.
Original source for the work on analysis of predictive accuracy of software reliability growth models as described in Chapter 10. It introduces u-plots, y-plots, prequential likelihood and measures of noisiness of predictions, and gives examples involving several real-life data sets.

Abreu, F.B. and Carapuca, R., "Candidate metrics for object-oriented software within a taxonomy framework," *Journal of Systems and Software*, 23(1), pp. 87–96, July 1994.

Aczel, J., Roberts, F.S. and Rosenbaum, Z., "On scientific laws without dimensional constants," *Journal of Mathematical Analysis and Applications*, 119, pp. 389–416, 1986.

Adam, M.F., Le Gall. G., Moreau, B. and Valette, N., "Towards an observatory aiming at controlling the software quality," *Proceedings of the IEE/BCS Software Engineering Conference*, pp. 50–4, 1988.
Describes a study to measure software quality factors over a range of systems. A number of tools were used for measurement, and one is descibed in some detail: Logiscope. Because of the nature of the tools used, only internal attributes were measured, and the only analysis performed was correlation against each other. With such an approach, it is not surprising that the authors concluded that software quality cannot be defined using quantitative criteria alone.

Adams, E., "Optimizing preventive service of software products," *IBM Journal of Research and Development*, 28(1), pp. 2–14, 1984.
Important paper. Analyzes a number of large software systems and shows that many software faults rarely lead to failures, while a small proportion causes the most frequent failures. See Section 9.1 for fuller description.

Adams, G. and Brewer, M., *Introduction to the Requirements of a Central Certification Database System, Software Certification Programme in Europe (SCOPE)*, Project 2151, Report SC92/106/AEA.ga.mb/T2.4.2/RP/01, 1992.

Agresti, W.W., Quality Time column, *IEEE Software*, 8(6), November 1991.

Agresti, W.W. and Evanco, W.M., "Projecting software defects from analyzing Ada designs," *IEEE Transactions on Software Engineering*, 18(11), pp. 988–97, 1992.
Interesting study that describes models to predict defect density based on product and process attributes. The product attributes were all internal, measured by a static code analyzer. The models explain 63–74% of the variation in defect density.

Aho, A.V., Hopcroft, J.E. and Ullman, J.D., *The Design and Analysis of Computer Algorithms*, Addison-Wesley, Reading, MA, 1974.

Aitchison, J. and Dunsmore, I.R., *Statistical Prediction Analysis*, Cambridge University Press, 1975.

Akao, Y. (ed), *Quality Function Deployment: Integrating Customer Requirements Into Product Design*, Productivity Press, Cambridge, MA, 1990.

Akiyama, F., "An example of software system debugging," *Information Processing*, 71, pp. 353–79, 1971.
One of the earliest papers proposing a defect prediction model based on software size.

Al-Janabi, A. and Aspinwall, E., "An evaluation of software design using the DEMETER tool," *Software Engineering Journal*, 8(6), pp. 319–24, 1993.

Albrecht, A.J., "Measuring application development," *Proceedings of IBM Applications Development* Joint *SHARE/GUIDE Symposium*, Monterey, CA, pp. 83–92, 1979.
The seminal paper on function points.

Albrecht, A.J. and Gaffney, J., "Software function, source lines of code and development effort prediction," *IEEE Transactions on Software Engineering*, SE-9(6), pp. 639–48, 1983.
Describes relationship between function points and Halstead's size and effort measures.

Alexander, C., *Notes on Synthesis of Form*, Harvard University Press, Cambridge, MA, 1964.

Anderson, B. and Gossain, S., "Software re-engineering using C++," *Proceedings of the Spring 1988 European UNIX Systems User Group*, pp. 213–18, 1988.
A generic C program was rewritten in C++. There is a real attempt to quantify the differences in the two versions.

Anderson, T., *Software Requirements Specification and Testing*, Blackwell, 1985.

Arthur, L.J., *Measuring Programmer Productivity and Software Quality*, Wiley, New York, 1985.
A powerful argument in support of measurement in software engineering, aimed mainly at software managers. Provides a useful introduction to a range of topics, including quality models, function points, and system-type metrics. Suffers from the lack of a coherent framework. For example, the chapter on productivity contains a description of all popular product measures. The book's structure is built around the author's own quality model.

Ashcroft, E. and Manna, Z., "The translation of GOTO programs to WHILE programs," in Frieman, C.V. (ed.): *Information Processing 71* Vol. 1 (North Holland), pp. 250–55, 1972.
Authors show how an arbitrary algorithm can be restructured into sequence, selection, and iteration; this is done by "breaking" loops and inserting flag variables which are used to direct the flow of control accordingly.

Ashley, N., "METKIT: Training in how to use measurement as a software management tool," *Software Quality Journal*, 3(3), pp. 129–36, 1994.

Ashley, N., *Measurement as a Powerful Software Management Tool*, McGraw-Hill, 1995.

AT&T, *Process Quality Management and Improvement Guidelines*, AT&T Quality Steering Committee, Issue 1.1, 1988.

Atkins, R.K. and Spence, D., "The development of the software product assurance requirements of the European Space Agency," *Proceedings of the 22nd Hawaii International Conference on Systems Science* (ed. Shriver, B.), IEEE Computer Society Press, Vol. 2, pp. 320–9, 1989.
Powerful argument that use of "good practice" methods alone provides no direct guide to the likely behavior of a system in operation. Authors argue that quantification (notably of reliability) is essential if we are to have true confidence. Also contains a useful classification of hazards and failures.

Auer, A., "A judgment and decision-making framework," SHIP document, SHIP/T/013/v02, 1994.
Describes an approach to safety assessment based on the Analytic Hierarchy Process.

Austin, S. and Parker, G.I., *Formal Methods: A Survey*, National Physical Laboratory, crown copyright, 1993.
Results of a survey of both industry and academia done in 1992 about the benefits, limitations and barriers to formal methods.

Avison, D.E., Shah, H.U. and Wilson, D.N., "Software quality standards in practice: the limitations of using ISO-9001 to support software development," *Software Quality Journal*, 3(2), pp. 105–12, 1994.

Avizienis, A. and Kelly, J.P.J., "Fault tolerance by design diversity: concepts and experiments," *IEEE Computer*, 17(8), pp. 67–80, 1984.

Azuma, M., *Information Technology – Software Product Evaluation – Indicators and Metrics*, ISO/JTC1/SC7/WG6 Project 7.13.3, working draft, 1993.

Baber, R.L., *Error-Free Software: Know-how and Know-why of Program Correctness*, Wiley, New York, 1991.

Bache, R., *Graph Theory Models of Software*, PhD thesis, South Bank University, London, 1990.
Fully exploits the notion of structural decomposition (as described in Chapter 8) at both the inter- and intra-modular level. Major source for axiom scheme described in Chapter 8, as well as the family of VINAP measures.

Bache, R., *Prometrix Tool Guide*, Infometrix Software, 141 St. James St., Glasgow, Scotland, 1993.

Bache, R. and Bazzana, G., *Software Metrics for Product Assessment*, McGraw-Hill, New York, 1993.
Very useful book that describes the practical results of the CEC-funded SCOPE project on software product certification.

Bache, R. and Mullerburg, M., "Measures of testability as a basis for quality assurance," *Software Engineering Journal*, 5(2), pp. 86–92, 1990.
A definitive treatment of measuring test coverage as described in Chapter 8. The prime decomposition of a program is used as the basis for automatically computing the number of tests required to satisfy a range of white box test strategies.

Bache, R. and Neil, M., "Validating technologies for software certification," *Proceedings of the Conference on Approving Software Products*, Garmisch, Germany, 1990.

Bache, R. and Neil, M., "Introducing metrics into industry: a perspective on GQM," in *Software Quality Assurance and Metrics: A Worldwide Perspective* (eds Fenton, N.E., Whitty, R.W. and Iizuka, Y.), International Thomson Press, pp. 59–68, 1995.
Makes a very reasonable argument against the GQM approach, proposing instead that in many situations a bottom-up approach may be better. They propose MQG, which seeks to exploit existing data collection practices within an organization.

Bache, R. and Tinker, R., "A rigorous approach to metrication: A field trial using KINDRA," *Proceedings of the IEE/BCS Software Engineering*, pp. 28–32, 1988.
Interesting validation study of a number of the structural measures described in Chapter 8. A large number of programs developed at British Telecom were analyzed using the QUALMS tool. The resulting measures (including, notably, the VINAP measure) were compared against historical data collected for the programs (like fault data). Unfortunately, no data relating to maintenance difficulty had been recorded. Thus, although the study showed significant correlations between certain measures and the number of faults, the crucial hypothesis that VINAP was a better predictor of maintenance effort than other measures was never tested.

Bailey, J.W. and Basili, V.R., "A meta-model for software development resource expenditure," *Proceedings of the 5th International Conference on Software Engineering*, IEEE Computer Society Press, pp. 107–16, 1981.
Gives a procedure for developing a local cost estimation model.

Bailey, C. and Dingee, W., "A software study using Halstead metrics," *ACM SIGMETRICS Performance Evaluation Review*, 10, pp. 189–97, 1981.

Baker, A.L. and Zweben, S.H., "The use of software science in evaluating modularity concepts," *IEEE Transactions on Software Engineering*, SE-5(3), pp. 110–20, 1979.

Baker, A.L. and Zweben, S.H., "A comparison of measures of control flow complexity," *IEEE Transactions on Software Engineering*, SE-6(6), pp. 506–12, 1980.

Baker, A.L., Bieman, J.M., Gustafson, D.A. and Melton, A.C., "Modelling and measuring the software development process," *Proceedings of the Hawaii International Conference on Systems Science*, 20(2), pp. 23–30, 1987.
Describes a rigorous approach to software measurement throughout the life cycle. The products of software are considered to be a set of documents (at all phases in the life cycle). The paper defines a product-based model of the software-development process, called the Software Project Model (SPM). The view of software development is one of transforming representations of a system; the process is time-dependent and so a real-time clock is a component of the model. The SPM is a set of document histories, which are represented as acyclic digraphs whose nodes are document versions.

Baker, A.L., Bieman, J.M., Fenton, N.E. *et al.*, "A philosophy for software measurement", *Journal of Systems and Software*, 12, pp. 277–81, July 1990.
Short summary of the formal approach to software measurement that is recommended in this book. In particular, it describes how the basic principles of measurement theory should be applied, and the minimal obligations for attempting to construct predictive measures.

Baker, F.T., "Chief programmer team management of production programming," *IBM Systems Journal*, 11(1), 1972.

Ballotta, M., La Manna, M., Lancellotti, R. and Ratt, A., "Proposta di introduzione di un sistema di metriche software in Necsy," Necsy Internal Report, October, 1991.

Banker, R.D. and Kemerer, C.F., "Scale economies in new software development," *IEEE Transactions on Software Engineering*, SE-15(10), 1989.
Suggests that organizations have a critical product size such that products smaller than the critical value exhibit economies of scale, while products larger than the critical value exhibit diseconomies of scale. However, the authors place rather too much credence in the moderate support for their theories available from existing published data.

Banker, R.D., Chang, H. and Kemerer, C.F., "Evidence on economies of scale in software development," *Information and Software Technology*, 36(5), pp. 275–82, 1994.

Banker, R.D., Datar, S.M. and Kemerer, C.F., "A model to evaluate variables impacting productivity on software maintenance projects," *Management Science*, 37(1), pp. 1–18, 1991.

Banker, R.D., Datar, S.M., Kemerer, C.F. and Zweig, D., "Software complexity and software maintenance costs," *Communications of the ACM*, 1993.

Banker, R.D., Kauffman, R.J., Wright, C.W. and Zweig, D., "Automating output size and reuse metrics in a respository-based CASE environment," *IEEE Transactions on Software Engineering*, 20(3), pp. 169–87, 1994.
Concentrates on automating function points and software reuse measures.

Banker, R.D., Kauffman, R.J. and Kumar, R., "An empirical test of object-based output measurement metrics in a computer-aided software engineering (CASE) environment," *Journal of Management Information Systems*, 8(3), pp. 127–50, 1991.

Banville, C. and Landry, M., "Can the field of MIS be disciplined?," *Communications of the ACM*, 32(1), pp. 48–60, 1989.

Barford, N.C., *Experimental Measurements: Precision, Error and Truth*, Addison-Wesley, Reading, MA, 1967.
Good description and examples of issues involved in deciding which of two data sets is a better representation of the truth.

Barlow, R.E. and Proschan, F., *Statistical Theory of Reliability and Life Testing*, Holt, Rinehart and Winston, New York, 1975.

Barnard, J. and Price, A., "Managing code inspection information," *IEEE Software*, 11(2), pp. 59–69, March 1994.
Extensive quantitative study into the effectiveness of Fagan inspections based on metrics collected over many years at AT&T. Also good example of use of GQM in real case study.

Basili, V.R., "Data collection, validation and analysis," in *Tutorial on Models and Metrics for Software Management and Engineering*, IEEE Computer Society Press, 1981.

Basili, V.R. and Hutchens, D.H., "An empirical study of a syntactic complexity family," *IEEE Transactions on Software Engineering*, SE-9(6), pp. 652–63, 1983.
Contains a description of a generic schema for defining structural metrics, and describes the statistical validation of a particular instance of a metric defined by this schema, namely SynC. The class of metrics defined by the Basili–Hutchens schemas has been shown to be a subclass of the hierarchical metrics described in Chapter 10.

Basili, V.R. and Perricone, B.T., "Software errors and complexity: an empirical investigation," *Communications of the ACM*, 27(1), pp. 42–52, 1984.
Analyzes distributions and relationships derived from software changes data.

Basili, V.R. and Reiter, R.W., "A controlled experiment quantitatively comparing software development approaches," *IEEE Transactions on Software Engineering*, SE-7(3), 1981.

Basili, V.R. and Rombach, H.D., "The TAME project: Towards improvement-oriented software environments," *IEEE Transactions on Software Engineering*, 14(6), pp. 758–73, 1988.
Provides a fairly comprehensive description of the Goal-Question-Metric paradigm. Basili's experience in software engineering experimentation is summarized as a set of 10 software-engineering and 14 measurement principles. Half of the software-engineering principles address the need for developing quality *a priori*, and half address the need for tailoring the process for different environments. The TAME model is based on improvement by learning.

Basili, V.R. and Weiss, D., "A methodology for collecting valid software engineering data," *IEEE Transactions on Software Engineering*, SE-10(6), pp. 728–38, 1984.
This article is directed at large-scale data collection. The original source of the Goal–Question–Metric paradigm, the paper describes a goal-oriented methodology for evaluating software development methodologies and for studying the software development process.

Basili, V.R., Selby, R.W. and Hutchens, D.H., "Experimentation in Software Engineering," *IEEE Transactions on Software Engineering*, 12(7), pp. 733–43, 1986.
One of the first papers to point out the need for a rigorous experimentation framework in software engineering was published by Basili and his colleagues. It presents a suggested framework for analyzing experimental work performed in software engineering. It describes a variety of actual experiments in terms of the framework, explaining their contribution to the software engineering discipline.

Basili, V.R., Selby, R.W. and Phillips, T.Y., "Metric analysis and data across FORTRAN projects," *IEEE Transactions on Software Engineering*, SE-9(6), pp. 652–63, 1983.
Some "complexity" metrics (Halstead's, McCabe, LOC) were correlated against data like effort and errors, as well as against each other.

Basso, L., Winterbottom, A. and Wynn, H.P., "A review of the Taguchi methods for off-line quality control," *Quality and Reliability Engineering International*, 2, pp. 71–9, 1986.

Baumert, J.H. and McWhinney, M.S., *Software Measures and the Capability Maturity Model*, Software Engineering Institute Technical Report, CMU/SEI-92-TR-25, ESC-TR-92-0, 1992.

Bazzana, G., Zontini, G., Damele, G. and Maiocchi, M., "Applying software reliability models to a large industrial dataset," *Information and Software Technology*, Vol. 35 No. 11/12, pp. 669–76, 1993.

Bazzana, G., Caliman, P., Gandini, D. *et al.*, "Software management by metrics: practical experiences in Italy," in *Software Quality Assurance and Measurement* (eds. Fenton, N.E., Whitty, R.W. and Iizuka, Y.), International Thomson Computer Press, London, pp. 185–94, 1995.
Interesting report with some good data.

Beane, J., Giddings, N., and Silverman, J., "Quantifying software designs," *Proceedings of the 7th International Conference on Software Engineering*, pp. 314–22, 1984.

Behrens, C.A., "Measuring the productivity of computer systems development activities with function points," *IEEE Transactions on Software Engineering*, SE-9(6), pp. 648–52, 1983.

Beizer, B., *Software Testing Techniques*, 2nd edn, Van Nostrand Reinhold, New York, 1990.
Second edition of one of the few comprehensive texts on software testing. Contains detailed descriptions of many specific strategies, and takes the issues of measurement seriously.

Belady, L.A. and Lehman, M.M., "A model of large program development," *IBM Systems Journal*, 15(3), pp. 225–52, 1976.

Belady, L.A. and Lehman, M.M., "The characteristics of large systems," in *Research Directions in Software Technology* (ed. Weger, P.), MIT Press, Cambridge, MA, 1979.
Contains gross statistics on 37 projects, 33 of which included measures of product size, development effort, and duration. Precise definitions of the measures were not provided.

Belford, P.C. and Berg, R.A., "Central flow control software development: a case study of the effectiveness of software engineering," *Proceedings of the 4th International Conference on Software Engineering*, IEEE Computer Society Press, pp. 85–93, 1979.

Bellcore (Bell Communication Research), *Reliability and Quality Measurements for Telecommunications Systems (RQMS)*, Technical reference: TR-TSY-000929, 1990.

Bellefeuille, J., "Total quality management," *IEEE Spectrum*, pp. 47–50, September 1993.

Belton, V., "A comparison of the analytic hierarchy process and a simple multi-attribute utility function," *European Journal of Operational Research*, 26, pp. 7–21, 1986.

Benford, S., Burke, E. and Foxley, E., "Learning to construct quality software with the Ceilidh system," *Software Quality Journal*, 2(3), pp. 177–97, 1993.
Describes an automated teaching assistant tool that supports software quality measurement.

Bennett, P.A., "Software development for the channel tunnel: a summary," *High Integrity Systems*, 1(2), pp. 213–20, 1994.
Rather vague overview that presents an unconvincing case for the safety of the channel tunnel software. Logiscope was used to ensure that the cyclomatic complexity of each module was less than 20, and statement count no more than 50.

Benyon-Tinker, G., "Complexity measures in an evolving large system," in *Proceedings of the Workshop on Quantitative Software Models*, IEEE Computer Society Press, New York, pp. 117–27, 1979.

van den Berg, K.G. and van den Broek, P.M., "Static analysis of functional programs," *Information and Software Technology*, 37(4), pp. 213–24, 1995.
Describes a flowgraph-type model for functional programs and applies the theory of decomposition as described in Chapter 8.

Berka, K., *Measurement: its Concepts, Theories and Problems*, Boston Studies in the Philosophy of Science, Boston, MA, Vol. 72, 1983.
Anyone who still thinks that measurement is a very clear-cut subject should read this book. A penetrating, philosophical report on the subject.

Berlack, H.R., "How not to write commercial standards," *IEEE Computer,* pp. 79–81, May 1990.
Nice article that emphasizes that it is the "what" rather than the "how" that is important in software development standards.

Bern, G.M., "Assessing software maintainability," *Communications of the ACM,* 27(1), pp. 14–23, 1984.

Bernot, G., Gaudel, M.C. and Marre, B., *Software Testing Based on Formal Specifications: a Theory and a Tool,* research report 581, Université de Paris-Sud, 91405 Orsay, France, 1990.
Generates test cases from algebraic specifcations.

Berry, R.E. and Meekings, B.A.E., "A style analysis of C programs," *Communications of the ACM,* 28(1), pp. 80–8, 1985.

Bertolino, A. and Marre, M., "Automatic generation of path covers based on the control flow analysis of computer programs," *IEEE Transactions on Software Engineering,* 20(12), pp. 885–99, 1994.

Bertolino, A. and Marre, M., "How many paths are needed for branch testing?," *Journal of Systems and Software,* 1995.
Excellent paper that explains the practical problems with the branch coverage metric. It proposes an alternative strategy for branch coverage based on covering the "weakly incomparable" unconstrained edges. This results in a set of paths that provide reasonable coverage in a very intuitive sense and are much more likely to be feasible. The authors provide a hierarchical definition of the minimal number of paths needed to satisfy their testing strategy. This metric is more closely aligned to minimum practically feasible paths. The paper also shows how the metric can be formulated using the prime decomposition approach.

Bertolino, A. and Strigini, L., "On the use of testability measures for dependability assessment," *IEEE Transactions on Software Engineering,* 22(2), pp. 97–108, 1996.
Authors look at the ideas of testability promoted by Voas *et al.* They point out that there are potential dangers in this approach. By making a program highly testable, you may increase the probability that the program is fault-free, but you also increase the probability that failures will occur if faults do remain. Authors address this concern and also propose an improved model for testability that takes account of the fact that a fault may trigger an error but still not lead to a failure.

Bertolino, A., Mirandola, R. and Peciola, E., "A case study in branch testing automation," in "Achieving Quality in Software" (Eds Bologna, S. and Bucci, G.) Chapman & Hall, London, pp. 369–80, 1996.
Describes a method for automatically generating likely feasible paths to satisfy the branch coverage criteria.

Bevan, N., "Measuring usability as quality of use," *Software Quality Journal,* 4(2), pp. 115–30, 1995.
Describes work from the MUSiC project. Quality of use is measured by the extent to which specific goals can be achieved with effectiveness, efficiency and satisfaction by specified users carrying out specified tasks.

Bhandari, I., Halliday, M., Tarver, E. *et al.,* "A case study of software process improvement during development," *IEEE Transactions on Software Engineering,* 19(12), pp. 1157–70, 1993.
Interesting case study based on analyzing defect data. Includes a defect classification.

Bhandari, I., Ray, B., Wong, M.Y. *et al.,* "An inference structure for process feedback: technique and implementation," *Software Quality Journal,* 3(3), 1994.
Quite an interesting paper that describes an automatic technique using defect data to make predictions about the software development process. The paper also contains an orthoganal defect classification scheme.

Bicego, Kuvaia and members of the BOOTSTRAP project team, "BOOTSTRAP: Europe's assessment method," *IEEE Software*, 10(3), pp. 93–5, May 1993.
The BOOTSTRAP method evolved from a CEC-funded project on process improvement and assessment. The method is proposed as a refinement of CMM.

Bieman, J.M. and Debnath, N.C., "An analysis of software structure using a generalized program graph," *Proceedings of the IEEE-CS 9th International Computer Software and Applications Conference* (COMPSAC 85), pp. 254–9, 1985.

Bieman, J.M. and Ott, L.M., "Measuring functional cohesion," *IEEE Transactions on Software Engineering*, 20(8), pp. 644–57, 1994.
Serious attempt to measure functional cohesion based on the notion of program slices. Scale types of proposed measures are analyzed using measurement theory.

Bieman, J.M. and Schultz, J.L., "An empirical evaluation (and specification) of the all-*du*-paths testing criterion," *Software Engineering Journal*, 7(1), pp. 43–51, 1992.
Very interesting empirical study that is described in detail in Chapter 8.

Bieman, J.M., Baker, A.L., Clites, P.N. *et al.*, "A standard representation of imperative language programs for data collection and software measures specification," *Journal of Systems and Software*, 8(1), pp. 13–37, January 1988.
Describes a generic model (and modeling procedure) for capturing structural aspects of imperative language programs, for the purpose of their input into measurement and analysis tools. VDM is used to specify the model. The language Pascal is provided as an example of the approach.

Bieman, J., Fenton, N.E., Gustafson, D. *et al.*, "Moving from philosophy to practice in software measurement," in *Formal Aspects of Software Measurement* (eds Denvir, T., Herman, R. and Whitty, R.), Chapman & Hall, London, 1992.

Biggerstaff, T.J. and Perlis, A.J., "Reusability framework, assessment and directions," *IEEE Software*, 4(2), pp. 3–11, March 1987.

Bishop, P.G., Esp, D.G., Barnes, M. *et al.*, "PODS – an experiment in software reliability," *IEEE Transactions on Software Engineering*, 12(9), pp. 929–40, 1986.
Interesting empirical study.

Blackburn, J.D., Scudder, G.D., van Wassenhove, L.N. and Hill C., "Time-based software development," *European OMA Conference*, Cambridge, England, 1994.

Bloomfield, R., de Neumann, B., Littlewood, B. *et al.*, (eds), *Software Safety*, Elsevier, Holland, 1992.

Blum, B.I., "Some very famous statistics," *The Software Practitioner* 3(2), March 1991.

Blum, M., Luby, M. and Rubinfield, R., "Self-testing/correcting with applications to numerical problems," *Journal of Computer and Systems Sciences*, 47, pp. 549–95, 1993.

Blumenthal, S.C., *Management Information Systems: A Framework for Planning and Development*, Prentice Hall, Englewood Cliffs, NJ, 1969.

Boehm, B.W., *Software Engineering Economics*, Prentice Hall, Englewood Cliffs, NJ, 1981.
This book is one of the first to approach software engineering from an "engineering" point of view. Boehm discusses the derivation and application of the COCOMO model for software effort and schedule estimation. It is of particular interest because Boehm based COCOMO on a large set of data from TRW, a defense contractor.

Boehm, B.W., "A spiral model of software development and enhancement", *IEEE Computer* 21(5), pp. 61–72, May 1988.

Boehm, B.W., *Software Risk Management*, IEEE Computer Society Press, Los Alamos, 1989.

Boehm, B.W., Brown, J.R. and Lipow, M., "Quantitative evaluation of software quality," *Proceedings of the Second International Conference on Software Engineering*, 1976.

Boehm, B.W., Brown, J.R., Kaspar, J.R. *et al.*, *Characteristics of Software Quality*, TRW Series of Software Technology, Amsterdam, North Holland, 1978.
Proposes definitions and measures for a range of quality attributes. This book describes a "model" of software quality that has since been referred to as Boehm's quality model.

Boehm, B.W., Clark, B., Horowitz, E. *et al.*, "Cost models for future life cycle processes: COCOMO 2.0," *Annals of Software Engineering* 1(1), pp. 1–24, November 1995.
This paper describes the problems perceived in using the original COCOMO model and the techniques used to address them in a revised version of COCOMO.

Böhm C., and Jacopini, G., "Flow diagrams, Turing machines and languages with only two formation rules," Communications of the ACM 9(5), pp. 366–71, 1966.
An important paper in the history of structured programming. It shows that any algorithm can be implemented using only sequence, selection, and iteration.

Bollinger, T.B. and McGowan, C., "A critical look at software capability evaluations," *IEEE Software*, 8(4), pp. 25–41, July 1991.
Interesting critique of the Software Engineering Institute's process maturity model. Humphrey and Curtis' response appeared in the same issue of the journal.

Boloix, G. and Sorenson, P.G., "Software metrics using a metasystem approach to software specification," technical report, Department of Computer Science, University of Alberta, Canada, 1992.
Describes a tool for extracting metrics from diagrammatic specification and design documents.

Bowen, J.P. and Hinchley, M.G., "Ten commandments of formal methods," *IEEE Computer*, 28(4) pp. 56–63, April 1995.

Bowen, J.P. and Hinchley, M.G., "Seven more myths of formal methods," *IEEE Software*, 12(4), 34–41, July 1995.

Bowen, J.P. and Stavridou, V., "Safety critical systems, formal methods and standards," *Software Engineering Journal*, 8(4), pp. 189–209, 1993.
Very useful survey paper, including a review of industrial practice of formal methods.

Bradley, D., "Play defect tracking and win," *Proceedings of the Third International Conference on Applications of Software Measurement*, pp. 2.136–51, 1992.

Brazendale, J. and Bell, R., "Safety-related control and protection systems: standards update," *Computing and Control Engineering Journal*, 5(1), pp. 6–14, 1994.

Bredero, R., Caracoglia, G., Jaggers, C. *et al.*, "Comparative evaluation of existing cost estimation tools," MERMAID report D7.1Y, 1989.
This report from the ESPRIT MERMAID project provides a summary of empirical studies of cost estimation models and tools, and software sizing models and tools. In addition, it includes a report of a study of six cost estimation tools undertaken by the MERMAID project.

Brehmer, C. and Carl, J.R., "Incorporating IEEE Standard 1044 into your anomaly tracking process," *Proceedings of the Third International Conference on Applications of Software Measurement*, 1.108–23, 1992.

Briand, L.C., Basili, V.R. and Thomas, W.M., "A pattern recognition approach for software engineering data analysis," *IEEE Transactions on Software Engineering*, 18(11), pp. 931–42, 1992.

Brilliant, S., Knight, J.C. and Leveson, N., "Analysis of faults in an *n*-version software experiment," *IEEE Transactions on Software Engineering*, 16(2), 1990.

British Standards Institute, *Guide to Assessment of Reliability of Systems Containing Software*, British Standards Institute, Draft DD198 (to become BS5760 part 8), 1991.

British Standards Institute, *Reliability of Systems, Equipment and Components: Guide to the Assessment of Reliability*, British Standards Institute, BS5760 (part 2), 1993.

Brocklehurst, S. and Littlewood, B., "New ways to get accurate software reliability modeling," *IEEE Software*, 9(4), July 1992.
Comprehensive discussion of the statistical techniques that enable us to get improved reliability predictions using existing models.

Brocklehurst, S., Chan, P.Y., Littlewood, B. and Snell, J., "Recalibrating software reliability models," *IEEE Transactions on Software Engineering*, SE-16(4), pp. 458–70, 1990.
This paper describes in detail the work on recalibration of software reliability growth predictions that is outlined in Chapter 12. Details are given of the methods of calculating the recalibrated predictions from smoothed versions of the u-plot. Several real data sets are analyzed, and the effect of recalibration on the shape of the predictive distribution is shown.

Brodman, J.G. and Johnson, D.L., "Return on investment (ROI) from software process improvement as measured by US industry," *Software Process – Improvement and Practice*, 1(1), pp. 35–47, 1995.
Interesting study to show that the use of ROI by the software community is very different from ROI as used by the financial community. The variation in interpretation can lead to trouble as results are presented to higher levels of management.

van den Broek, P.M. and van den Berg, K.G., "Generalised approach to software structure metrics," *Software Engineering Journal*, 10(2), pp. 61–8, 1995.
Generalizes the Fenton-Whitty decomposition of flowgraphs by allowing arbitrary decomposition operations.

Broekstra, G., "Organizational humanity and architecture," *Cybernetics and Systems*, 17, pp. 13–41, 1986.

Brooks, F.P., *The Mythical Man-Month: Essays on Software Engineering*, 2nd edn, Addison-Wesley, Reading, MA, 1995. (Originally published in 1975.)
This book remains a classic text describing the problems of controlling large software projects.

Brown, P.J., "Assessing the quality of hypertext documents," *Hypertext: Concepts, Systems and Applications, Proceedings of the European Conference on Hypertext*, pp. 180–93, 1990.

Bryan, E.G., "CP-6: quality and productivity measures in the 15-year life cycle of an operating system," *Software Quality Journal*, 2(2), pp. 129–44, 1993.
Contains some very interesting defect data collected over many years for a large system (Bull HW, Los Angeles).

Buck, R.D. and Robbins, J.H., "Application of software inspection methodology in design and code," in *Software Validation* (ed. Hausen, H.-L.), Elsevier Science, pp. 41–56, 1984.
Describes the results of applying Fagan's inspection principle to software developed at IBM in Manassas, Virginia. Authors report on some remarkably consistent "metric" values across different types of software projects (which apparently also hold in different IBM sites). For new code developed (presumably with Fagan's method), the number of defects discovered per 1000 LOC settles to a number between 8 and 12. There is no such consistency for old code. Also, the number of person hours expended in the inspection process per major defect is always between 3 and 5. The authors are sufficiently confident of the consistency of these values to call them the natural numbers of programming, believing that they are "inherent to the programming process itself." They go so far as to suggest that it would take radically new development tools to alter these values.

Bunge, M., *Treatise on Basic Philosophy: Ontology II: The World of Systems*, Riedel, Boston, MA, 1979.
Deals with the meaning and definition of representations of the world. Since these are precisely the goals of the object-oriented approach, Bunge's ontological principles have been used by researchers on object-oriented design. In particular, they have been used as the basis for defining metrics of object-oriented designs.

Burke, M.M. and Wall, D.N., "The FRIL Model approach for software diversity assessment" in *Software Fault Tolerance: Achievement and Assessment Strategies* (ed Kerstan, M., and Saglietti, F.), Springer-Verlag, pp. 147–76, 1991.

Burlando, P., Gianetto, L. and Mainini, M.T., "Functional diversity", in *Software Fault Tolerance: Achievement and Assessment Strategies*, Springer-Verlag, pp. 33–48, 1991.

Bush, M. and Fenton, N.E., "Software measurement: a conceptual framework," *Journal of Systems and Software*, 12, pp. 223–31, July 1990.
Concise description of the classification and framework presented in Chapter 3.

Butler, R.W. and Finelli, G.B., "The infeasibility of quantifying the reliability of life-critical real-time software," *IEEE Transactions on Software Engineering*, 19(3), pp. 3–12, 1993.
Explains formally why it is impossible to certify software at utlra-high levels of reliability. Effectively produces the same results as done independently (but earlier) by Littlewood.

Campbell, N.R., *Physics: The Elements*, Cambridge University Press, Cambridge, MA, 1920. Reprinted as *Foundations of Science: The Philosophy of Theory and Experiment*, Dover, New York, 1957.
The earliest reference within measurement theory. Campbell introduces the notions of fundamental and derived measurement. His intention was to characterize the difference between those attributes like mass and length which can be measured without reference to any other measures (and hence are deemed to be fundamental), and attributes like density whose measurement depends on two or more other measures, in this case on both volume and mass (and hence are deemed to be derived). However, many attributes (e.g. temperature) may be measured by reference to only one other attribute. Thus, the definition of direct measurement given in Chapter 2 is the same as Campbell's fundamental measurement, but the definition of indirect measurement is more general than his notion of derived measurement.

Campbell, D.T. and Stanley, J., *Experimental and Quasi-Experimental Designs for Research*, Rand McNally, Chicago, IL, 1966.
Practical industrial experimental design.

Card, D.N., "The role of measurement in software development," *Proceedings of the IEE/BCS Software Engineering Conference*, 1988.
Touches on many of the issues addressed in this book. Card argues that practitioners have not adopted results of researchers because there are too many competing measures, not substantiated by significant data, and difficult to collect. On the other hand, managers resist measurement for fear of evaluation and cost. Suggests some guidelines for setting up a metrics program.

Card, D.N., "Software quality engineering," *Information and Software Technology*, 32(1), pp. 3–10, 1990.
Software quality engineering encompasses: product inspection, process control and design improvement.

Card, D.N., "Capability evaluations rated highly variable," *IEEE Software*, 9(5), pp. 105–107, September 1992.

Card, D.N. and Agresti, W.W., "Measuring software design complexity," *Journal of Systems and Software*, pp. 185–97, 1988.
Useful paper that describes some measures that can be extracted from software designs. Includes empirical results that show the proposed measures could be useful for predicting error rate and productivity.

Card, D.N., Church, V.E. and Agresti, W.W., "An empirical study of software design practices," *IEEE Transactions on Software Engineering*, SE-12(2), pp. 264–71, 1986.

Card, D.N. and Glass, R.L., *Measuring Software Design Quality*, Prentice Hall, Englewood Cliffs, NJ, 1990.

Card, D.N., McGarry, F. and Page, G.T., "Evaluating software engineering technologies," *IEEE Transactions on Software Engineering*, 15(7), 1987.

Card, S.K., Moran, T.P. and Newell, A., "The keystroke-level model for user performance time with interactive systems," *Communications of the ACM*, 23(7), pp. 396–409, 1980.

Carmines, E. and Zeller, R., *Reliability and Validity Assessment*, Sage Publications, 1979.

Carver, D.L., "Comparison of the effect of development paradigms on increases in complexity," *Software Engineering Journal*, 3(6), pp. 223–8, 1988.

CASE Research Group, *The Second Annual Report on CASE*, Bellevue, Washington, DC, 1990.

Caulcutt, R., *Statistics in Research and Development*, Chapman & Hall, London, England, 1991.

Catuneanu, V.M. and Mihalache, A.N., *Reliability Fundamentals*, Elsevier, Amsterdam, 1989.
Good theoretical treatment of reliability of general systems. Requires reasonable understanding of probability theory.

CCTA, *SSADM Version 4 Reference Manual*, CCTA, published by NCC Blackwell, ISBN 1-85554-004-5, 1992.

Channon, R.N., "On a measure of program structure," *Proceedings of the Programming Symposium*, Springer-Verlag, pp. 9–18, 1974.

Chapin, N., "A measure of software complexity," *Proceedings of the National Computer Conference*, pp. 995–1002, 1977.

Chatfield, C., *Statistics for Technology*, Chapman & Hall, London, England, 1993.

Chen, E.T., "Program complexity and programmer productivity," *IEEE Transactions on Software Engineering*, SE-4(3), pp. 187–94, 1978.

Cheng, J. and Bishop, P., *SHIP (Assessment of the Safety of Hazardous Industrial Processes in the Presence of Design Faults)*, State of the Art Report, Adelard, Deliverable 2.1.1, 1993.

Cheon, M. J., Grover, V. and Sabherwal, R., "The evolution of empirical research in information systems: A study in information systems maturity," *Information and Management*, 24, 1993, North Holland, pp. 107–9.
Data are collected on past empirical work and evaluated with respect to a set of defined criteria. The authors use the results to recommend the direction in which empirical study should go.

Cherniavsky, J.C. and Smith, C.H., "On Weyuker's axioms for software complexity measures," *IEEE Transactions on Software Engineering*, 17(6), pp. 636–8, 1991.

Cheung, R.C., "A user-oriented software reliability model," *IEEE Transactions on Software Engineering*, SE-6(3), pp, 118–25, 1980.

Chevalier, M. and Bergerand, J.L., "A complexity measure for data-flow language programs," *Proceedings of IFAC Safecomp '89*, Vienna, Austria, pp. 117–21, 1989.

Chidamber, S.R. and Kemerer, C.F., "Towards a metrics suite for object-oriented design," *Proceedings of 6th ACM Conference on Object Oriented Programming, Systems, Languages and Applications (OOPLSLA)*, Phoenix, AZ, pp. 197–211, 1991.

Chidamber, S.R. and Kemerer, C.F., "A metrics suite for object oriented design," *IEEE Transactions on Software Engineering*, 20(6), pp. 476–98, 1994.

Chillarege, R., Bhandari, I.S., Chaar, J.K. *et al.* "Orthogonal defect classification: A concept for in-process measurements," *IEEE Transactions on Software Engineering*, 18(11), pp. 943–56, November 1992.
A good description of fault classification and its application at IBM. However, the classification may not be truly orthogonal, as, for example, documentation appears as a category of defect type.

Christensen, K., Fitsos, G.P. and Smith, C.P., "A perspective on software science," *IBM Systems Journal*, 20(4), pp. 372–87, 1981.

Churcher, N.I. and Shepperd, M.J., "Comments on "A metrics suite for object oriented design"," *IEEE Transactions on Software Engineering*, 21(3), pp. 263–5, 1995.

Churchman, C.W., *The Systems Approach*, Dell, New York, 1968.

Clapp, J.A. and Stanten, S.F., *A Guide to Total Software Quality Control*, vols. 1 and 2, Rome Laboratory, Air Force Materiel Command, Griffiss Air Force Base, New York, RL-TR-92-316, 1992.

Clark, J.A. and Pradhan, D.K., "Fault injection: a method for validating computer-system dependability," *IEEE Computer*, 28(6), pp. 47–56, June 1995.

Coad, P. and Yourdon, E., *Object-Oriented Design*, Prentice Hall, Englewood Cliffs, NJ, 1991.

Cobb, R.H. and Mills, H.D., "Engineering software under statistical quality control," *IEEE Software*, 7(6), pp. 44–54, November 1990.
    Contains information about defect rates on Cleanroom projects as well as a discussion of Adams' failure and fault data.

Cochran, W.G., *Sampling Techniques*, 2nd edn, Wiley, New York, 1963.
    Discussion of methodological issues of surveys. In particular, how to sample a finite population so that survey results can be generalized.

Coehn, L., "Quality function deployment: An application perspective from Digital Equipment Corporation," *The National Productivity Review*, pp. 197–208, 1988.

Cohen, B., "Justification of formal methods for system specification," *Software Engineering Journal*, 4(1), pp. 26–35, 1989.

Cohen, B., Harwood, W.T. and Jackson, M.I., *The Specification of Complex Systems*, Addison-Wesley, Reading, MA, 1986.
    Reasonable introduction to a number of formal specification notations.

Cohn, A., "The notion of proof in hardware verification," *Journal of Automated Reasoning*, 5, pp. 127–39, 1989.
    A watershed paper for the formal verification community. The author describes her experiences of working on the verification of the VIPER microprocessor. She shows that the commercial claims of a "fully verified" chip are highly dubious.

Coleman, D., Ash, D., Lowther, B. and Oman, P., "Using metrics to evaluate software system maintainability," *IEEE Computer*, 27(8), pp. 44–9, August 1994.

Collins, B.P. and Nix, C.J., "The use of software engineering, including the Z notation, in the development of CICS," *Quality Assurance*, 14(2), pp. 103–10, September 1988.

Collofello, J.S. and Balcom, L.B., "A proposed causative software error classification scheme," *Proceedings of the National Computer Conference*, pp. 537–45, 1985.

Comer, P., Bradley, P. and Ross, N., *Software Data Collection Manual*, Issue 2, report produced by ALV/PRJ/SE/078: Software Data Library Project, 1987.

Commission of European Communities, *ESSI: The European System and Software Initiative*, 200, rue de la Loi, B-1049, Brussels, Belgium, 1993.

Compton, J. and Withrow, C., "Prediction and control of Ada software defects," *Journal of Systems and Software*, 12, pp. 199–207, 1990.
    Fascinating empirical study. Looks at optimal size of modules with respect to defect density. Concluded that the optimal size for an Ada module with respect to error density is 83 source statements. First appeared in the 1990 Oregon Workshop proceedings.

Connell, J.L. and Shafer, L.B., *Structured Rapid Prototyping*, Yourdon Press, New York, 1989.

Conte, S.D., Dunsmore, H.D. and Shen, V.Y., *Software Engineering Metrics and Models*, Benjamin-Cummings, Menlo Park, CA, 1986.

The first textbook on software metrics. Contains excellent sections on experimental design, cost-estimation models, productivity models and defect models, but is now rather dated.

Conway, R., *A Primer on Disciplined Programming*, Winthrop Publishers, Cambridge, MA, 1978.

Cook, M., "Software metrics: an introduction and annotated bibliography," *ACM SIGSOFT Software Engineering Notes*, 7(2), pp. 41–60, 1982.

Cook, T.D. and Campbell, D.T., *Quasi-Experimentation: Design and Analysis Issues for Field Settings*, Houghton-Mifflin, Boston, MA, 1979.
This book discusses many of the issues involved in doing experiments where it is difficult to control all of the variables. It presents a solid overview of the issues involved in conducting experiments in the field, as opposed to the laboratory. Includes experimental design and statistical analysis protocols for use in different contexts. Numerous examples from many disciplines help to ensure effective communication of complicated ideas.

Coulter, N., "Software science and cognitive psychology," *IEEE Transactions on Software Engineering*, SE-9(2), pp. 166–71, 1983.
Discusses how the psychological underpinnings of Halstead's measures are misinterpreted.

Courtney, R.E. and Gustafson, D.A., "Shotgun correlations in software measures," *Software Engineering Journal*, 8(1), pp. 5–13, 1993.
Excellent critique of software metrics validation. Shows theoretically that use of correlation analysis on many metrics will inevitably throw up spurious "significant" results.

Cox, D.R. and Hinkley, D.V., *Theoretical Statistics*, Chapman & Hall, London, 1982.

Cox, D.R. and Isham, V., *Point Processes*, Chapman & Hall, London, 1980.

Cox, G., "Sustaining a metrics programme in industry," in *Software Reliability and Metrics* (eds Fenton, N.E. and Littlewood, B.), Elsevier, London, pp. 1–15, 1991.
Describes how the Hewlett-Packard metrics program evolved in its first seven years.

Craigen, D., Gerhart, S. and Ralston, T., "Formal methods reality check: industrial usage," *IEEE Transactions on Software Engineering*, 21(2), pp. 90–8, 1995.

Cuelenaere, A.M.E., van Genuchten, M.J.I. and Heemstra, H.J., "Calibrating a software estimation model: why and how," *Journal of Information and Software Technology*, 29(10), 1987.
Points out the difficulties of using commercial cost estimation tools from the viewpoint of understanding what it is necessary to input. It highlights the problems involved in standardizing subjective classifications and ratings.

Cullyer, W.J. and Storey, N., "Tools and techniques for the testing of safety-critical software," *Computing and Control Journal*, 5(5), pp. 239–44, October 1994.

Cullyer, W.J., Goodenough, S.J. and Wichmann, B.A., "The choice of computer languages for use in safety-critical systems," *Software Engineering Journal*, 6(2), 1991.

Curritt, P.A., Dyer, M. and Mills, H.D., "Certifying the reliability of software," *IEEE Transactions on Software Engineering*, SE-12(1), pp. 3–11, 1986.
Describes the IBM Cleanroom approach to the design and validation of software. The Cleanroom approach involves an evaluation of the operational reliability of the software via testing in a real or simulated operational environment. Such testing is carried out by a special team with sole responsibility for this evaluation, independent of the system developers.

Curtis, B., "Measurement and experimentation in software engineering," *Proceedings of the IEEE*, 68(9), September 1980, pp. 1144–57.
Curtis was probably the first software engineer to address the need for measurement and experimentation. His paper discusses the role of measurement in developing theoretical models, stressing concern for reliability and validity. It uses then-current examples of software measurement, including control flow, module interconnectedness, and Halstead's Software Science measures. Curtis argues that many advances

in software engineering will be related to improvements in the measurement and experimental evaluation of software techniques and practices.

Curtis, B., "By the way, did anyone study any real programmers?" in *Empirical Studies of Programmers* (eds Soloway, R. and Iyengar, S.), Ablex Publishing, Norwood, NJ, pp. 256–62, 1986.

Curtis, B., Sheppard, S.B., Milliman, P. *et al.*, "Measuring the psychological complexity of software maintenance tasks with the Halstead and McCabe metrics," *IEEE Transactions on Software Engineering*, SE-5 (2), pp. 96–104, 1979.

Important paper because it describes a carefully constructed experiment that had the right hypothesis for "complexity" metrics, namely: they correlate with difficulty of maintenance. Maintenance was measured in terms of time to understand and implement changes. Experiment found little difference between the complexity metrics with respect to time and accuracy of maintenance, and they had most significance with unstructured code.

Cusumano, M.A., *Japan's Software Factories*, Oxford University Press, New York, 1991.

Damele, G., Bazzana, G., Giunchi, M. and Rumi, G., "Setting-up and using a metrics program for process improvement," *Proceedings of AQUIS Conference*, Venice, Italy, 1993.

Daroczy, Z. and Varga, L., "A new approach to defining software complexity measures," *Acta Cybernetica*, 8(3), pp. 287–91, 1988.

Theoretical paper describing a method to generate complexity metrics.

Daskalantonakis, M.K., "A practical view of software measurement and implementation experiences within Motorola," *IEEE Transactions on Software Engineering*, 18(11), pp. 998–1010, 1992.

Data Analysis Center for Software (DACS), *A Descriptive Evaluation of Software Sizing Models*, report prepared for Headquarters USAF/Air Force Cost Center (AFCCE), IIT Research Institute, Lanham, MD, 1987.

Davies, G., "Software metrics and software engineering," in *Software Engineering: The Decade of Change* (ed. Ince, D.), pp. 27–39, 1986.

A basic introduction to software metrics.

Davis, A. *et al.*, "Identifying and measuring quality in a software requirements specification," *Proceedings of the First International Software Metrics Symposium*, Baltimore, MD, IEEE Computer Society Press, pp. 141–52, 1993.

Defines 24 quality attributes that are relevant for requirements specifications, and proposes simple metrics for each of them.

Davis, J.S. and LeBlanc, R.J., "A study of the applicability of complexity measures," *IEEE Transactions on Software Engineering*, 14(9), pp. 1366–72, 1988.

Dawid, A.P., "Statistical theory: the prequential approach," *Journal of the Royal Statistical Society*, A147, pp. 278–92, 1984.

Dawid was responsible for developing the innovative statistical techniques that have come to be called the prequential approach to statistics. It is novel in as much as emphasis is placed upon prediction of future behavior of a system, rather than estimation of system attributes and parameters. Most of the literature on this subject requires a fair degree of statistical knowledge on the part of the reader, and this paper is no exception. But Dawid writes well, and in this review the important themes can be appreciated even if the technical details are skipped.

de Groot, M.H., *Optimal Statistical Decisions*, McGraw-Hill, New York, 1970.

de Neumann, B., (ed.), *Software Certification*, Elsevier, London, 1989.

de Neumann, B., "The application of mathematical axiomatics to software engineering," IMA Bulletin 26, pp. 47–9, March 1990.

Nice paper that explains the infeasibility of using formal specifications for complex systems.

De Young, G.E. and Kampen, G.R., "Program factors as predictors of program readability," *Proceedings of the Computer Software and Applications Conference (COMPSAC)*, IEEE Computer Society Press, pp. 668–73, 1979.

Debou, C., Haux, M. and Jungmayr, S., "A measurement framework for improving verification processes," *Software Quality Journal*, 4(3), pp. 227–42, 1995.
Descibes an application of the ami approach. The application focuses on the identification of defects.

Deharnais, J.-M., "Analyse statistique de la productivité des projets de développement en informatique a partir de la technique des points de fonction," Université du Quebec à Montreal, Masters thesis, 1989.

Delic, K.A., Mazzanti, F. and Strigini, L., *Formalising a Software Safety Case Via Belief Networks*, SHIP/T046, City University, London EC1V 0HB, 1995.

DeMarco, T., *Structured Analysis and System Specification*, Yourdon Press, New York, 1978.

DeMarco, T., *Controlling Software Projects*, Yourdon Press, New York, 1982.
A practical and powerful book about how to use simple measures to understand what is happening and predict the likely outcome of software projects. Lots of common sense. Lots on cost models and their problems.

DeMarco, T. and Lister, T., *Peopleware*, Dorset House, New York, 1987.
An extremely amusing and readable book about the sociological side of the software industry. It is anecdotal in style but backed up with the results of a variety of empirical investigations.

DeMillo, R.A. and Lipton, R.J., "Software project forecasting," in *Software Metrics* (eds Perlis, A.J., Sayward, F.G., and Shaw, M.), MIT Press, Cambridge, MA, pp. 77–89, 1981.
Excellent article describing why software measurement has much to learn from measurement theory. Inspired some of the work described in this book.

Deming, E., *Out of Crisis*, MIT Centre for Advanced Engineering Study, Cambridge, MA, 1989.

Denvir, T., Herman, R. and Whitty, R.W. (eds), *Formal Aspects of Software Measurement*, Springer-Verlag, Berlin, 1992.
Interesting collection of papers arising out of a British Computer Society – FACS workshop in London.

Deutsch, M. and Willis, R., *Sofware Quality Engineering*, Prentice Hall, Englewood Cliffs, NJ, 1988.

Devine, C., Fenton, N.E. and Page, S., "Deficiencies in existing software engineering standards as exposed by SMARTIE," in *Safety Critical Systems* (eds Redmill, F. and Anderson, T.), Chapman & Hall, London, pp. 255–72, 1993.

Dobson, A.J., *An Introduction to Generalized Linear Models*, Chapman & Hall, London, 1990.
Good introduction to the principles of generalized linear models which allow regression analysis to cope with many different underlying distributions. Not suitable for non-statisticians.

Doerflinger, C. and Basili ,V., "Monitoring software development through dynamic variables," *IEEE Transactions on Software Engineering*, SE-11(9), pp. 978–85, 1985.

Draper, N. and Smith, H., *Applied Regression Analysis*, Wiley, New York, 1966.
A sound introduction to classical regression analysis (single and multivariate). It includes information on testing the significance of the Pearson correlation coefficient and regression coefficients.

Drapkin, T. and Forsyth, R., *The Punter's Revenge*, Chapman & Hall, London, 1987.

Dromey, R.G., "Cornering the chimera", *IEEE Software*, 13(1), 33–43, 1996.
Attempts to define software quality in terms on internal attributes.

Drummond-Tyler, E., "Software metrics: an international survey of industrial practice," ESPRIT 2 Project METKIT, Sema Group, London, 1989.

DTI, *TickIT Guide to Software Quality Management, System Construction and Certification Using ISO 9001/EN 29001/BS 5750 Issue 2.0*, available from TickIT Project Office, 68 Newman Street, London W1A 4SE, 1992.

Duane, J.T., "Learning curve approach to reliability monitoring," *IEEE TransAerospace*, 2, pp. 563–6, 1964.

Dubois, D. and Prade, H., *Possibility Theory: An Approach to Computerized Processing of Uncertainty*, Plenum Press, New York, 1988.

Dunham, J.R., "Software errors in experimental systems having ultra-reliability requirements," *Proceedings of the Fault-Tolerant Computer Science Conference*, pp. 158–64, 1986.

Dunham, J.R. and Kruesi, E., "The measurement task area," *IEEE Computer*, pp. 47–54, November 1983.
Nice paper that makes a convincing case for using measurement in software engineering.

Dunsmore, H.E., "Software metrics," *Information Processing and Management*, 20(1/2), pp. 183–92, 1984.

Dyer, M., *The Cleanroom Approach to Quality Software Development*, Wiley, New York, 1992.

Ebenau, R.G., "Managing program development with software inspections," *Proceedings of the Third International Conference on Applications of Software Measurement*, pp. 1.240–9, 1992.

Ebert, C., "Visualization techniques for analyzing and evaluating software measures," *IEEE Transactions on Software Engineering*, 18(11), pp. 1029–34, 1992.
Some interesting and unusual ideas for presenting and analyzing software measurement data.

Ebert, C. and Oswald, H., "Complexity measures for the analysis of specifications of (reliability-related) computer systems," *Proceedings of the IFAC SAFECOMP*, pp. 95–100, Pergamon Press, London, 1991.

Ebert, C. and Riegg, A., "A framework for selecting system design metrics," *Proceedings of the International Symposium on Software Reliability Engineering*, pp. 12–19, IEEE Computer Society Press, Los Alamitos, CA, 1991.

Eckhardt, D.E. and Lee, L.D., "A theoretical basis for the analysis of multi-version software subject to coincident errors," *IEEE Transactions on Software Engineering*, SE-11(12), pp. 1511–17, 1985.
A seminal paper on the efficacy of software diversity. Eckhardt and Lee show that, even in the unlikely event that several versions are truly statistically independent (and they give a precise definition of this, for the first time), the versions will fail dependently. This result implies that not merely is it very hard to develop software versions independently of one another (something that is widely acknowledged), but that even if we were successful in this task, we could not aspire to the improvements in reliability that we have come to expect in the case of hardware redundancy.

Eick, S.G., Steffan, J.L. and Sumner, E.E., "Seesoft – a tool for visualizing line-oriented software statistics," *IEEE Transactions on Software Engineering*, 18(11), pp. 957–68, 1992.
Describes an interesting visualization tool that allows you to analyze up to 50000 LOC simultaneously by mapping each line into a thin row. The color of each row indicates statistic of interest, e.g. red rows are those most recently changed.

Ejiogu, L.O., "Beyond structured programming: an introduction to the principles of applied software metrics," *Structured Programming*, 11(1), pp. 27–43, 1990.
Interesting formal treatment of a range of structural measures. Uses classical measure theory (as distinct from measurement theory).

El Emam, K., and Madhavji, N.H., "The reliability of measuring organizational maturity," *Software Process Improvement and Practice*, 1(1), pp. 3–25, 1995.

Elliott, J.J., *Data complexity aspects of software*, Alvey Project SE/69, PRRM/002/01, South Bank Polytechnic, London, 1988.

Ellis, B., *Basic Concepts of Measurement*, Cambridge University Press, Cambridge, UK, 1966.
Ellis stresses a slightly different emphasis to measurement than that described in Chapter 2. He notes that we are generally interested in knowing if the axioms and relations are satisfied before we can assume that they are. Bearing in mind the observation that no procedure of measurement is perfectly accurate, we arrive at the experimental focus of measurement. This is concerned with the practical questions of devising scales and making measurements; it makes use of and depends on the structures explored by the mathematicians, and the raw materials are forced to fit some relatively familiar structure. It is also worth noting that Ellis noted the problems with Campbell's notions of fundamental versus derived measurement, and it is his preferred ideas of direct and indirect measurement that we use in Chapter 2.

Emerson, T.J., "A discriminant metric for module cohesion," *Proceedings of the 7th International Conference on Software Engineering*, pp. 194–203, 1984.

Endres, A., "An analysis of errors and their causes in system programs," *IEEE Transactions on Software Engineering*, SE-1(2), pp. 140–9, 1975.

Eriksson, I. and Torn, A., "A model for IS quality," *Software Engineering Journal*, 6(4), pp. 152–8, 1991.

Eskenasi, A. and Angelova, V., "A new method for software quality evaluation," *Journal of New Generation Computer Systems*, 3(1), pp. 47–53, 1990.
The method is based on classification procedures (rather than the hierarchical-type models of Boehm and McCall). The idea is that experts determine a set of binary characteristics.

Evanco, W.M. and Agresti, W.W., "A composite complexity approach for software testing," *Software Quality Journal*, 3(1), pp. 45–58, 1994.
A defect model based on a categorical multivariate regression analysis. Authors argue that no single complexity metric is adequate: a software project is characterized by both measures of design complexity and development environment complexity. However, they show these empirical measures can be combined into a single composite complexity metric which is manifested as software defects.

Evangelist, W.M., "Software complexity metric sensitivity to program restructuring rules," *Journal of Systems and Software*, 3, pp. 231–43, 1983.
Highlights the danger of trying to equate low values of complexity metrics with high quality. Analyzes a range of complexity metrics and a range of standard program restructuring rules (like use indentation, meaningful variable names, etc.), and shows that the value of many complexity metrics stays the same or increases when these rules are applied.

Evangelist, W.M., "Complete solution to the software measurement problem," *IEEE Software*, 5(1), pp. 83–4, January 1988.
An amusing critique of the worst kinds of practices in software measurement.

Fagan, M.E., "Design and code inspections to reduce errors in program development," *IBM Systems Journal*, 3, pp. 182–211, 1976.
Original paper on Fagan inspections.

Fagan, M.E., "Advances in software inspections," *IEEE Transactions on Software Engineering*, SE-12 (7), pp. 744–51, 1986.
An updated description of the classical Fagan inspection approach.

Fairley, R., "Risk management for software projects," *IEEE Software*, 11(3), pp. 57–67, May 1994.
Contains a good overview of software cost modeling.

Falmagne, J.-C. and Narens, L., "Scales and meaningfulness of quantitative laws," *Synthese*, 55, pp. 287–325, 1983.
Discusses the notion of meaningfulness.

Farbey, B., "Software quality metrics: considerations about requirements and requirement specifications," *Information and Software Technology*, 32(1), pp. 61–4, 1990.
Very useful paper that looks at attributes of good specifications as well as measures that can be extracted for predictive purposes.

Feldman, J.A. and Sutherland, W.R., "Rejuvenating experimental computer science," *Communications of the ACM*, 22(9), pp. 497–502, 1979.
Very interesting paper that highlights the paucity of experimental work done in computer science compared with other disciplines and proposes some solutions. It is doubtful whether things have improved very much over the subsequent 17 years.

Felician, L. and Zalateu, G., "Validating Halstead's theory for Pascal programs," *IEEE Transactions on Software Engineering*, SE-15(12), pp. 1630–2, 1989.
The authors claim that Halstead's formula for program length is underestimated for Pascal programs because of the lack of operators. Hence they attempt to modify the formula in order to get a better correlation.

Fenton, N.E., "The structural complexity of flowgraphs," in *Graph Theory and Its Applications to Algorithms and Computer Science* (eds Alavi, Y., Chartrand, G., Lesniak, L., *et al.*), Wiley, New York, pp. 273–82, 1985.

Fenton, N.E. (ed.), *Structure-Based Software Metrics: Collected Papers of Alvey Project SE/ 69*, South Bank University, CSSE, Borough Road, London SE1 0AA, 1988.

Fenton, N.E., "Software measurement: theory, tools and validation," *Software Engineering Journal*, 5(1), pp. 65–78, 1990.
Provides a comprehensive summary of Alvey project SE/69, Structure-Based Software Metrics. In particular it describes how the notion of prime decomposition was built into a software analysis and measurement tool called QUALMS.

Fenton, N.E., "The mathematics of complexity in computing and software engineering," in *The Mathematical Revolution Inspired by Computing* (eds Johnson, J.H. and Loomes, M.), Oxford University Press, Oxford, UK, pp. 243–56, 1991.
Complexity of programs-in-the-small is traditionally synonymous with algorithmic efficiency. Measurement has always been central in this work, although it is not clear that it is true measurement in the sense of measurement theory. This chapter describes how such measurement does satisfy the representation condition. The chapter then discusses the role of measurement in controlling complexity of programs-in-the-large.

Fenton, N.E., "When a software measure is not a measure," *Software Engineering Journal*, 7(5), pp. 357–62, 1992a.

Fenton, N.E., "How effective are software engineering methods?," *Journal of Systems and Software* 20, pp. 93–100, 1993.

Fenton, N.E., "Objectives and context of measurement and experimentation," in *Experimental Software Engineering Issues* (eds Rombach, H.D., Basili, V.R. and Selby, R.W.), Springer-Verlag, Berlin, pp 82–6, 1993a.

Fenton, N.E., "Software measurement: a necessary scientific basis," *IEEE Transactions on Software Engineering*, 20(3), pp. 199–206, 1994.

Fenton, N.E., *Guidelines for Interpreting Standards*, CAS/CITY/D212, CASCADE project, Lloyds Register, Croydon, England, 1994b.

Fenton, N.E., *Multi-Criteria Decision Aid; With Emphasis on its Relevance in Dependability Assessment*, DATUM/CSR/02, CSR, 1995.

Fenton, N.E. and Hill, G., *Systems Construction and Analysis: A Mathematical and Logical Approach*, McGraw-Hill, New York, 1992.

Textbook that provides a comprehensive coverage of the discrete mathematics basis for computer science. Has detailed chapters on measurement theory and the structural decomposition methods outlined in Chapter 8.

Fenton, N.E. and Kaposi, A.A., "Metrics and software structure," *Journal of Information and Software Technology*, pp. 301–20, July 1987.
Provides a detailed description of program decomposition and how it may be used to define recursive measures. Shows how many popular measures fit into this framework.

Fenton, N.E. and Kitchenham, B.A., "Validating software measures," *Journal of Software Testing, Verification and Reliability*, 1(2), pp. 27–42, 1991.

Fenton, N.E. and Littlewood, B. (eds), *Software Reliability and Metrics*, Elsevier, 1991.
ISBN 1-85166-675-3 (now available from Chapman & Hall, UK). This book is the edited Proceedings of the Centre for Software Reliability Conference, Garmisch-Partenkirchen, Germany, 12–14 September 1990.

Fenton, N.E. and Melton, A., "Deriving structurally based software measures," *Journal of Systems and Software*, 12, pp. 177–87, 1990.

Fenton, N.E. and Mole, D., "A note on the use of Z for flowgraph decomposition," *Journal of Information and Software Technology*, 30(7), pp. 432–7, 1988.
The QUALMS system for program analysis was initially specified in the Z notation. This paper descibes the main part of the specification.

Fenton, N.E. and Whitty, R.W., "Axiomatic approach to software metrication through program decomposition," *Computer Journal* 29(4), pp. 329–39, 1986.
Original source for the prime decomposition theorem and its proof. Also introduces the notion of structural measures via axioms for sequence and nesting, which Prather subsequently characterized as recursive and hierarchical.

Fenton, N.E. and Whitty, R.W., "Program structures: some new characterizations," *Journal of Computer and System Sciences*, 43(3), pp. 467–83, 1991.

Fenton, N.E., Iizuka, Y. and Whitty, R.W. (eds), *Software Quality Assurance and Measurement: A Worldwide Perspective*, International Thomson Computer Press, London, 1995.
This book provides a comprehensive review of current leading-edge industrial activities in software quality assurance and measurement. The carefully edited work contains contributions from many of the world's leading experts in the subject. The book is unique in its international coverage, and its insight into Japanese practice is possibly the most extensive ever published in the West.

Fenton, N.E., Littlewood, B. and Page, S., "Evaluating software engineering standards and methods," in *Software Engineering: A European Perspective* (eds Thayer, R. and McGettrick, A.D.), IEEE Computer Society Press, pp. 463–70, 1993.

Fenton, N.E., Neil, M. and Ostralenk, G., *Metrics and Models to Predict Software Fault Rates*, DATUM/CSR/10, Centre for Software Reliability, 1995.

Fenton, N., Pfleeger, S.L. and Glass, R.L., "Science and substance: A challenge to software engineers," *IEEE Software*, 11(4), July 1994.
The authors suggest that software engineering research be read and conducted with an eye toward rigor and careful planning. They list several considerations, and then judge some existing research according to the list.

Fenton, N.E., Whitty, R.W. and Kaposi, A.A., "A generalized mathematical theory of structured programming," *Theoretical Computer Science*, 36, pp. 145–71, 1985.
Provides a detailed and formal treatment of the theory of irreducible program structures, and how these may be used in structured programming. Contains a number of results concerning program restructuring.

Ferdinand, A.E., "A theory of system complexity," *International Journal of General Systems*, 1, pp. 19–33, 1974.

Argues that the expected number of faults increases with the number *n* of code segments; a code segment is a sequence of executable statements which, once entered, must all be executed. Specifically the theory asserts that for smaller numbers of segments, the number of faults is proportional to a power of *n*; for larger numbers of segments, the number of faults increases as a constant to the power *n*.

Ferrari, D., *Computer System Performance Evaluation*, Prentice Hall, Englewood Cliffs, NJ, 1978.
Useful book for finding out about an important area of measurement in computing not covered in this book.

Ferrari, D., Serazzi, G. and Zeigner, A., *Measurement and Tuning of Computer Systems*, Prentice Hall, New York, 1983.

Fetzer, J.H., "Program verification: the very idea," *Communications of the ACM*, 31(9), pp. 1048–63, 1988.
As the title suggests, this is a highly critical appraisal of the notion of program verification, which the author suggests is completely infeasible. This paper sparked a storm of reaction and subsequent issues of the *Communications of the ACM* contained numerous letters, many of them critical of Fetzer's views. Many people felt that he completely misrepresented verification.

Finkelstein, L., "Representation by symbol systems as an extension of the concept of measurement," *Kybernetes*, 4, pp. 215–23, 1975.

Finkelstein, L., "What is not measurable, make measurable," *Measurement and Control*, 15, pp. 25–32, 1982.

Finkelstein, L., "A review of the fundamental concepts of measurement," *Measurement*, 2(1), pp. 25–34, 1984.
A good introduction to the theory of measurement and the representation condition.

Fleming, P.J. and Wallace, J.J., "How not to lie with statistics," *Communications of the ACM*, 29, pp. 218–21, 1986.

Flood, R.L. and Carson, E.R., *Dealing with Complexity*, Plenum Press, New York, 1988.
This book explains the role of measurement in dealing with system complexity and contains a nice introductory chapter on measurement theory.

Florac, W.A., *Software Quality Measurement: A Framework for Counting Problems, Failures and Faults*, CMU/SEI-92-TR-22, ESC-TE-92-22, Pittsburgh, PA, Software Engineering Institute, Carnegie Mellon University, September 1992.

Frank, M.V., "Choosing among safety improvement strategies: a discussion with examples of risk assessment and multi-criteria decision approaches for NASA," *Reliability Engineering and System Safety*, 49, pp. 311–24, 1995.

Frankl, P.G. and Weiss, S.N., "An experimental comparison of the effectiveness of branch testing and data-flow testing," *IEEE Transactions on Software Engineering*, 19(3), pp. 774–87, 1993.
Compares the all-uses (data-flow) strategy and the all-branches strategy. Experiment could not confirm the hypothesis that all-uses was more likely to expose errors than all-branches.

Frankl, P.G. and Weyuker, E.J., "A formal analysis of the fault-detecting ability of testing methods," *IEEE Transactions on Software Engineering*, 19(3), 1993.
Compares different testing criteria with respect to their ability to detect faults.

Freeman, P., "Reusable software engineering: Concepts and research directions," in *ITT Proceedings of the Workshop on Reusability in Programming*, 1983, pp. 129–37, 1983.

Freeman, P., *Reusability: Progress or Repetition?*, Keynote Address at the First International Workshop on Software Reusability, at Dortmund, Germany, July 3–5, 1991.

Fuchs, E. and Chappell, S.G., "Software quality and productivity at AT&T Bell Laboratories," *Proceedings of the 22nd Hawaii International Conference on Software Systems,* Vol. 2 (ed. Shriver, B.), pp. 330–6, 1989.

Fujitsu, *Practice of Software Quality Assurance in Fujitsu Corporation,* Japanese Union of Software Engineering Press, Japan, 1989.

Funami, Y. and Halstead, M.H., "A software physics analysis of Akiyama's debugging data," *Proceedings of the Symposium on Computational Software Engineering,* pp. 133–8, 1976.

Furuyama, T., Arai, Y. and Iio, K., "Fault generation model and mental stress effect analysis," *Journal of Systems and Software,* 26, pp. 31–42, 1994.

Furuyama, T., Arai, Y. and Iio, K., "Metrics for measuring the effect of mental stress on fault generation during software development," *International Journal of Reliability, Quality and Safety Engineering,* 1(2), pp. 257–75, 1994a.

Gaffney, J.E., "Estimating the number of faults in code," *IEEE Transactions on Software Engineering,* SE-10 (4), pp. 459–65, 1984.
Argued that the relationship between number of defects and size was not language-dependent. Produced a new model.

Gaffney, J.E., Jr and Cruickshank, R.D., "A general economic model of software reuse," in *Proceedings of the Fourteenth International Conference on Software Engineering,* pp. 327–37, 1992.

Galbraith, J.R. (1973), *Designing Complex Organizations,* Addison-Wesley, Reading, MA, 1973.

Galliers, R.D., "Choosing appropriate information systems research approaches: a revised taxonomy," in *Information Systems Research: Contemporary Approaches and Emergent Traditions* (eds Nissen, H.E., Klein, H.K. and Hirshheim, R.), Elsevier Science Publishers, B.V. (North Holland), pp. 327–45, 1991.
This article reviews the range of approaches suitable for research in information systems, assessing the strengths and weaknesses of each. The approaches are placed in two categories: empirical and interpretive. Galliers suggests that we rethink the view that only the empirical approach is useful. He also presents a taxonomy of information systems research methods, identifying situations for which each method is best suited.

Gannon, J.D., Katz, E.E. and Basili, V.R., "Metrics for Ada packages; an initial study," *Communications of the ACM,* 29(7), 1986.

Gansner, E.R., Koutsofios, E., North, S.C. and Vo, K.-P., "A technique for drawing directed graphs," *IEEE Transactions on Software Engineering,* 19(3), pp, 214–30, 1993.

Garey, M.R. and Johnson, D.S., *Computers and Intractability,* W.H. Freeman, San Francisco, CA, 1979.
Still the definitive text and reference source for the topic of computational complexity.

Garvin, D.A., "What does "product quality" really mean?," *Sloan Management Review,* pp. 25–45, Fall 1984.

Gasston, J.L. and Rout, T.P., "Can the effectiveness of software processes be assessed?," *Software Quality Journal,* 3(3), pp. 153–66, 1994.

Gerhart, S., Craigen, D. and Ralston, T., "Observation on industrial practice using formal methods," *Proceedings of the 15th International Conference on Software Engineering,* IEEE Computer Society, pp. 24–33, 1993.

Gibbs, N.E., "The SEI education program: Strategy and accomplishments," *Information Processing '89,* pp. 863–6, Elsevier, 1989.

Gibson, V.R. and Senn, J.A., "System structure and software maintenance performance," *Communications of the ACM*, 32(3), pp. 347–58, 1989.
Very interesting paper. Argues that claims made by zealots about the effectiveness of particular methods/ theories have "rarely been subjected to empirical testing." Specifically assesses the effect of structuredness on the maintainability of COBOL systems, and also looks to see if any internal attribute measure captures system differences. Some sound experimental design. The conclusions are that structure is important and that measures of internal attributes have management potential. However, it is particularly relevant that programmers were very unreliable in assessing their own performance; for each maintenance task they were asked to rate subjectively how well they had done on a simple ordinal scale. Their own ratings in no way correlated with their actual performance measured in terms of the accuracy of their work. This highlights the dangers of using subjective measurement in this way.

Gilb, T., *Software Metrics*, Chartwell-Bratt, Cambridge, MA, 1976.
Early pioneeering book (unfortunately now out of print). Numerous informal ways of measuring product attributes are suggested.

Gilb, T., *Principles of Software Engineering Management*, Addison-Wesley, Reading MA, 1988.
This highly entertaining book describes an evolutionary approach to software and systems design based on the measurement of quality attributes. Specifically, a project's quality objectives should be broken down until measurable components are identified and agreed between customer and developer. There is much common sense and pragmatism, and it is a usable approach for project managers. The only drawback is there is little or no theoretical basis to any of the measurement techniques proposed.

Gilb, T. and Graham, D., *Software Inspections*, Addison-Wesley, Reading, Massachusetts, 1994.
Excellent account of the modern-day Fagan inspection approach. Contains a wealth of measurement information and stresses the central role of measurement in inspections.

Gill, G.K. and Kemerer, C.F., "Cyclomatic complexity density and software maintenance productivity," *IEEE Transactions on Software Engineering*, 17(12), pp. 1284–8, 1991.
Provides empirical evidence that cyclomatic complexity divided by size (measured in source statements) is a useful predictor of maintenance productivity.

Glass, R.L., "Persistent software errors," *IEEE Transactions on Software Engineering*, SE-7(2), March 1981.

Glass, R.L., *Building Quality Software*, Prentice Hall, Englewood Cliffs, NJ, 1992.

Glass, R.L., "Do the measuring advocates measure up?," *Proceedings of the Third International Conference on Applications of Software Measurement*, pp. 1.02–12, La Jolla, CA, 1992a.

Glass, R.L., "The software research crisis," *IEEE Software*, 11(12), pp. 42–7, November 1994.
Nice paper that argues that software "crisis" has been grossly exaggerated by researchers, and that it is research that is really in crisis. Glass is particularly critical of "advocacy" research that is not supported by empirical results.

Glass, R.L., "A tabulation of topics where software practice leads software theory," *Journal of Systems and Software*, 25, pp. 219–22, 1994.
Highlights the tremendous gap, especially between theory and practice in software metrics.

Goel, A.L., "Software reliability models: assumptions, limitations and applicability, *IEEE Transactions on Software Engineering*, 11(12), pp. 1411–23, 1985.
Contains a good overview and critique of a number of models.

Goel, A.L. and Okumoto, K., "Time-dependent error-detection rate model for software reliability and other performance measures," *IEEE Transactions on Reliability*, R-28, pp. 206–11, 1979.

Goldschlager, L. and Lister, A., *Computer Science: a Modern Introduction*, Prentice Hall, Englewood Cliffs, NJ, 1981.
Well-known and highly respected textbook with a very good section on measuring algorithmic complexity.

Gordon, R.D., "Measuring improvements in program clarity," *IEEE Transactions on Software Engineering*, SE-5(2), pp. 79–90, 1979.

A Halstead-type measure is shown to correlate closely with subjective views of program clarity.

Grady, R.B., "Measuring and managing software maintenance," *IEEE Software,* 4(3), pp. 35–45, 1987.

Grady, R.B., *Practical Software Metrics for Project Management and Process Improvement,* Prentice Hall, Englewood Cliffs, NJ, 1992a.

Grady, R.B., "What do you need to be successful?," *Proceedings of the Third International Conference on Applications of Software Measurement,* 1.163–79, 1992.

Grady, R.B., "Successfully applying software metrics," *IEEE Computer,* 27(9), pp. 18–25, September 1994.

Grady, R.B. and Caswell, D., *Software Metrics: Establishing a Company-wide Program,* Prentice Hall, Englewood Cliffs, NJ, 1987.
Important book that describes the implementation of a metrics program at Hewlett-Packard. Anyone considering such a program should consult this book. In many ways, our book was inspired by this one, because we felt that a more rigorous approach to measurement could help future metrics programs overcome some of the difficulties reported by Grady and Caswell.

Grady, R.B. and Van Slack, T., "Key lessons in achieving widespread inspection use," *IEEE Software,* 11(4), pp. 46–57, July 1994.

Green, J. and d'Oliveira, M., *Units 16 & 21 Methodology Handbook (part 2),* Open University, Milton Keynes, England, 1990.
Overview of experimental design and analyis, with many good examples.

Gremillion, L.L., "Determinants of program repair maintenance requirements," *Communications of the ACM,* 27(8), pp. 826–32, 1984.

Gunning, R., *The Technique of Clear Writing,* McGraw-Hill, New York, 1968.

Haase, V., Messnarz, R., Koch, G., *et al.*, "Bootstrap: fine-tuning process development," *IEEE Software,* 11(4), pp. 25–35, July 1994.

Hall, J.A., "Seven myths of formal methods," *IEEE Software,* 7(5), September 1990.

Hall, N.R. and Preiser, S., "Combined network complexity measures," *IBM Journal of Research and Development,* 23(1), pp. 15–27, 1984.

Hall, T. and Fenton, N.E., "Implementing software metrics – the critical success factors," *Software Quality Journal,* 3(4), pp. 195–208, 1994.

Hall, T. and Fenton, N.E., "Software practitioners and software quality improvement," *Proceedings of the 5th International Conference on Software Quality,* pp. 313–23, 1995.

Halstead, M., *Elements of Software Science,* Elsevier, North Holland, 1977.
Source of the Halstead family of metrics. The emphasis is on establishing that there are certain natural laws of programming as there are laws of physics. Classical scientific methods are used to "discover" these laws. Unfortunately, changes in programming techniques, together with many subsequent empirical studies, have resulted in many of Halstead's theories being shown to be questionable or irrelevant.

Hamer, P. and Frewin, G., "Halstead's software science: a critical examination," *Proceedings of the 6th International Conference on Software Engineering,* pp. 197–206, 1982.
One of several studies that has discredited some of Halstead's theories. The results indicate that most represent neither natural laws (this was always dubious) nor (more worryingly) useful engineering approximations.

Hamlet, D., "Are we testing for true reliability?" *IEEE Software,* 9(4), pp. 21–7, July 1992.
Criticizes the assumptions that are made for software reliability modeling.

Hamlet, D. and Voas, J., "Faults on its sleeve: amplifying software reliability testing," *Proceedings of the ISSTA '93,* Boston, MA, pp. 89–98, 1993.

Hansen, W.J., "Measurement of program complexity by the pair (cyclomatic number, operator count)," *ACM SIGPLAN*, vol. 3, pp. 29–33, 1978.
Example of a hybrid complexity measure.

Harel, D., *Algorithmics*, 2nd edn, Addison-Wesley, Reading, MA, 1992.
Superb book covering many important topics in computer science. Based on a radio series in Israel, the book manages to explain extremely difficult ideas with almost no prerequisites. If you are without a computing background but want to find about the measurement of algorithmic efficiency and computational complexity, then this is the book for you.

Harrison, R., "Quantifying internal attributes of functional programs," *Journal of Information and Software Technology*, 35(10), pp. 554–60, 1993.

Harrison, W.A., "Software complexity metrics: a bibliography and category index," *SIGPLAN Notices*, 19(2), pp. 17–27, 1984.

Harrison, W.A., "An entropy-based measure of software complexity," *IEEE Transactions on Software Engineering*, 18(11), pp. 1025–9, 1992.

Harrison, W.A. and Magel, K., "A topological analysis of the complexity of computer programs with less than three binary branches," *ACM SIGPLAN Notices*, 16(4), pp. 51–63, 1981.

Harrison, W.A. and Magel, K.I., "A complexity measure based on nesting level," *ACM SIGPLAN Notices*, 16(3), pp. 63–74, 1981a.

Harrison, W.A., Magel, K.I., Kluczny, R. and DeKock, A., "Applying software complexity metrics to program maintenance," *IEEE Computer*, 15(9), 65–79, 1982.

Harvey, D.A., "Software metrication – an aid to software project management," *GEC Journal of Research*, 12(1), pp. 26–32, 1995.

Hatton, L., "The automation of software process and product quality," in Ross, M., Brebbia, C.A., Staples, G. and Stapleton, J. (eds), *Software Quality Management*, Southampton: Computation Mechanics Publications, Elsevier, pp. 727–44, 1993.

Hatton, L., "Static inspection: tapping the wheels of software," *IEEE Software*, 12(3), pp. 85–7, May 1995.

Hatton, L. and Hopkins, T.R., "Experiences with Flint, a software metrication tool for Fortran 77," *Symposium on Software Tools*, Napier Polytechnic, Edinburgh, Scotland, 1989.

Hatton, L. and Roberts, A., "How accurate is scientific software?," *IEEE Transactions on Software Engineering*, 20(10), pp. 785–97, 1994.
Describes an experiment in *n*-version programming. Authors comment that about 6 in every 1000 lines of commercially released Fortran code contain statically detectable faults, like overwriting DO loop variables through a calling sequence, or relying on uninitialized varaibles having sensible values.

Hatton, L. and Safer C., *Developing Software for High-integrity and Safety-critical Systems*, McGraw-Hill, New York, 1995.

Hausen, H.-L., "Yet another model of software quality and productivity," in *Measurement for Software Control and Assurance* (ed Littlewood, B.), Elsevier, London, 1989.
Covers a lot of ground, including a quite general approach to evaluation, measurement and assessment, taking into account different conceptual levels of software systems. Contains schemas for defining measures of many different types of structural (and other) attributes of software.

Hecht, M.S., *Flow Analysis of Computer Programs*, Elsevier, North Holland, 1977.
The source of several ideas and algorithms concerning post-dominators in flowgraphs which have been extensively exploited in our own work and tools outlined in Chapter 8.

Heitkoetter, U., Helling, B., Nolte, H. and Kelly, M., "Design metrics and aids to their automatic collection," *Journal of Information and Software Technology*, 32(1), pp. 79–87, 1990.

Nice paper describing work on the ESPRIT project MUSE. Motivates the need for system design metrics, and defines a generic representation for designs. The idea is that, like the flowgraph model for source code, this model can be used to capture the salient features of designs written in a range of popular notations. A metrics tool evaluates designs in the generic representation. Potentially, this technique could be used to automate the measurement of many of the design measures described in Chapter 8. Of course, the obligation is to write a design language "front-end" that can automatically translate a design in a given language into the generic representation.

Henderson-Sellers, B. and Tegarden, D., "The theoretical extension of two versions of cyclomatic complexity to multiple entry/exit points," *Software Quality Journal*, 3(4), pp. 253–69, 1994.

Henhapl, W. and Jones, C.B., "A formal description of ALGOL 60 as described in the 1975 Modified Report," in *The Vienna Development Methods: The Meta-language* (eds Bjorner, D. and Jones, C.B.), Springer-Verlag, Lecture Notes in Computer Science 61, pp. 305–36, 1978.

Henry, J., Henry, S.H., Kafura, D. and Matheson, L., "Improving software maintenance at Martin Marietta," *IEEE Software*, 11(4), pp. 67–75, July 1994.
An interesting measurement-based study.

Henry, S. and Goff, R., "Complexity measurement of a graphical programming language," *Software Practice and Experience*, 19(11), pp. 1065–88, 1988.

Henry, S. and Kafura, D., "Software structure metrics based on information flow," *IEEE Transactions on Software Engineering*, SE-7(5), pp. 510–8, 1981.
Source of the now well-known Henry–Kafura metric. Authors argue that controlling system structure improves external quality, hence supporting the assumptions of Chapter 8. A model for information flow between modules is proposed from which the complete structure of information flow is derived. Unfortunately the details are sufficiently vague to enable numerous interpretions; this means that different people may construct different models for the same system with correspondingly different measures. Also the measures are unfortunately called "complexity" measures (described in Chapter 8). Even procedure length is referred to as procedure complexity.

Henry, S. and Kafura, D., "The evaluation of software systems structure using quantitative software metrics," *Software Practice and Experience*, 14(6), pp. 561–73, June 1984.

Henry, S. and Lewis, J., "Integrating metrics into a large scale software development environment," *Journal of Systems and Software*, 13, pp. 89–95, 1990.

Henry, S. and Selig, C., "Design metrics which predict source code quality," *IEEE Software*, 7(2), March 1990.

Herbsleb, J., Carleton, A., Rozum, J. *et al.*, *Benefits of CMM-based Software Process Improvement: Initial Results*, Technical Report CMU/SEI-94-TR-13, Software Engineering Institute, Pittsburgh, PA, August 1994.

Hetzel, W.C., *Making Software Measurement Work: Building an Effective Software Measurement Program*, QED Publishing Group, Wellesley, MA, 1993.
A very well-written book that provides an excellent, pragmatic introduction to software metrics. One theme of the book is the author's objections to the principles of GQM. He argues that GQM can lead to unreasonable and impractical data-collection requirements.

Hoaglin, D.C., Mosteller, F. and Tukey, J.W., *Understanding Exploratory Data Analysis*, Wiley, New York, 1983.
Collection of articles addressing exporatory data analysis, including box plots.

Hoare, C.A.R., "Maths adds safety to computer programs," *New Scientist*, pp. 53–6, September 1986.

Hoel, P. G., *Introduction to Mathematical Statistics*, 3rd edn, Wiley, New York, 1962.
Good introduction to the basics of statistics.

Hollecker, C., *Software Reviews and Audits Handbook*, Wiley, New York, 1990.

Hollom, J.H. and Pulford, K.J., "Experience of software measurement programmes and application of the ami method within GEC," *GEC Journal of Research*, 12(1), pp. 17–25, 1995.

Horgan, J.R., London, S. and Lyu, M.R., "Achieving software quality with testing coverage measures," *IEEE Software,* 11(4), pp. 60–70, July 1994.
Investigates relationship between the quality of dataflow testing and the subsequent detection of failures.

Houston, I. and King, S., "CICS project report: experiences and results from the use of Z," *Lecture Notes in Computer Science*, vol. 551, Springer-Verlag, pp. 588–96, 1991.
One of the few published studies on the use of Z in CICS which actually provides some information on the measurements that were used to assess cost-effectiveness. However, there is insufficient detail to check that the popular claims are valid.

Howden, W.E., "Methodology for the generation of test data," *IEEE Transactions on Computing*, 24, pp. 554–60, May 1975.

Huff, K.E., Sroka, J.V. and Struble, D.D., "Quantitative models for managing software development processes," *Software Engineering Journal*, 1(1), pp. 17–23, 1986.

Humphrey, W.S., *Managing the Software Process*, Addison-Wesley, Reading, MA, 1989.
Major source of the CMM. Stresses the importance of measurement for controlling the software process.

Humphrey, W.S., Snyder, T.R. and Willis, R.R., "Software process improvement at Hughes Aircraft," *IEEE Software,* 8(4), pp. 11–23, July 1991.
Describes how Hughes went from level 2 to level 3 (CMM).

Humphrey, W.S., *A Discipline for Software Engineering*, Addison-Wesley, Reading, MA, 1995.
This book describes Humphrey's Personal Software Process and how it was applied to a large number of developers to improve the way they produced software.

Iannino, A., Musa, J.D., Okumoto, K. and Littlewood, B., "Criteria for software reliability model comparisons," *IEEE Transactions on Software Engineering*, 10(6), pp. 687–91, 1984.
Proposes a set of criteria that is intended to help potential users of models in their selection.

IEEE, *IEEE Standard 729: Glossary of Software Engineering Terminology*, IEEE Computer Society Press, 1983.

IEEE (ed.), "Software Engineering Standards," (3rd edn) Institute of Electrical and Electronics Engineers, New York, 1989.

IEEE, *Software Quality Metrics Methodology Standard P-1061/D20*, IEEE Computer Society Press, 1989.
Based on the McCall approach to measuring software quality attributes. Very fragmented with many deficiencies. For example, in its introductory list of definitions, the word metric is not defined!

IEEE, "Standard 1061: Software Quality Metrics Methodology," IEEE Computer Society Press, 1992.

IEEE P1044, *A Standard Classification for Software Anomalies* (draft), IEEE Computer Society Press, 1992a.
Extremely useful document, discussed in Chapter 5 .

IFPUG 1990, *Function Point Counting Practices Manual – Release 3.1*, The International Function Point Users Group, Westerville, OH, 1990.

IIT Research Institute, "*A Descriptive Evaluation of Software Sizing Models,*" Data Analysis Center for Software, RADC/COED, Griffiss Air Force Base, New York 13441, USA, 1987.

Ince, D., "Software Metrics," in *Measurement for Software Control and Assurance* (eds Kitchenham, B. and Littlewood, B.), Elsevier, pp. 27–62, 1989.
Nice tutorial introduction to the subject, with some of its history.

Ince, D.C. and Hekmatpour, S., "An approach to automated software design based on product metrics," *Software Engineering Journal*, 3(2), pp. 53–6, March 1988.

Ince, D.C. and Shepperd, M.J., "A review of software system design metrics," *Proceedings of the Second IEE/BCS Software Engineering Conference*, IEE, London, 1988.
Good review including discussion of software tools and empirical validation. Concludes by stating the need for a proper theoretical basis.

Ince, D.C. and Shepperd, M.J., "An empirical and theoretical analysis of an information-flow based system design metric," *Proceedings of the European Software Engineering Conference*, 1989.

Incorvaia, A.J. and Davis, A.M., "Case studies in software reuse," in *Proceedings of COMPSAC '90*, pp. 301–6, 1990.

Inglis, J., "Standard software quality metrics," *AT&T Technical Journal*, 65(2), pp. 113–18, 1985.

International Standards Organisation, *The C Programming Language*, ISO 9899, 1990.

International Standards Organisation, *Quality Management and Quality Assurance Standards – Part 3: Guidelines for the Application of ISO 9001 to the Development, Supply and Maintenance of Software*, ISO/IS 9000-3, Geneva, Switzerland, 1990.

International Standards Organisation, *Information Technology – Software Product Evaluation – Quality Characteristics and Guide Lines for their Use*, ISO/IEC IS 9126, Geneva, Switzerland, 1991.

International Standards Organisation, *ISO 9001: Quality Systems – Model for Quality Assurance in Design, Development, Production, Installation and Servicing*, International Standards Organisation, 1987.

International Standards Organisation, *The Need and Requirements for a Software Process Assessment Standard*, study report, Issue 2.0, JTC1/SC7 N944R, 1992.

International Standards Organisation, *SPICE Baseline Practice Guide, Product Description*, Issue 0.03 (Draft), July 1993.

International Standards Organisation, *Capability Maturity Model. New Work Item to Develop A Standard for Software Process Assessment*, ISO/IEC JTC1/SC7 N986, 1994.

Isoda, S., "SoftDA – A Computer-Aided Software Engineering System," in *Proceedings of Fall Joint Computer Conference*, pp. 147–51, 1987.

Isoda, S., "Experience report on software reuse project: its structure, activities and statistical results," in *Proceedings of the Fourteenth International Conference on Software Engineering*, pp. 320–6, 1992.

Jackson, M.A., *System Development*, Prentice Hall, Englewood Cliffs, NJ, 1984.
Although of no direct relevance to measurement, this is a superbly written book on software and systems, that describes a reasonably high-level graphical system design method which is potentially amenable to structural analysis and measurement.

Jacky, J., "Specifying a safety critical control sysem in Z," *IEEE Transactions on Software Engineering*, 21(2), pp. 99–106, 1995.

Jeffery, D.R., "Time-sensitive cost models in commercial MIS environment," *IEEE Transactions on Software Engineering*, SE-13(7), 1987.
Jeffery investigated a number of assumptions underlying the Rayleigh curve model and found little empirical support for them. He also demonstrated that all the simplistic models relating effort and duration were invalid.

Jeffery, D.R., "The relationship between team size, experience, and attitude and software development productivity," *Proceedings of the COMPSAC*, IEEE Computer Society Press, 1987a.

Jeffery suggested that relationships between productivity and project duration can be modeled accurately if staffing levels are included in the model. However, he also pointed out that issues such as staff experience and motivation could have a significant impact on such relationships.

Jefferey, D.R. and Berry, M., "A framework for evaluation and prediction of metrics program success," *Proceedings of the First International Software Metrics Symposium*, Baltimore, MD, IEEE Computer Society Press, pp. 28–39, 1993.
Interesting paper. The framework for evaluation resulted from the authors' experience with three company metrics programs (having varying degrees of success).

Jeffery, D.R. and Low, G., "Calibrating estimation tools for software development," *Software Engineering Journal*, (5)4, pp. 215–21, 1990.
Authors checked a cost estimation model that had been fully calibrated some years earlier against new project data. The model was very inaccurate on the new data. This paper provides strong evidence of the need for continually evolving (or self-calibrating) models.

Jeffery, D.R., Low, G.C. and Barnes, M., "A comparison of function point counting techniques," *IEEE Transactions on Software Engineering*, 19(5), pp. 529–32, 1993.
Empirical study that suggests the adjusted function point measure is no better at predicting effort than the cruder unadjusted version.

Jelinski, Z. and Moranda, P.B., "Software reliability research," in *Statistical Computer Performance Evaluation* (ed. Freiberger, W.), Academic Press, New York, pp. 465–84, 1972.
One of the earliest papers on software reliability growth modeling. While the model's assumptions would now be regarded as overly simplistic, this has been a very influential model, largely in its guise as the Musa model.

Jensen, H.A. and Vairavan, K., "An experimental study of software metrics for real-time software," *IEEE Transactions on Software Engineering*, SE-11(2), pp. 231–4, 1985.

Jensen, R.W., "A comparison of the Jensen and COCOMO schedule and cost estimation models," *Proceedings of the of International Society of Parametric Analysis*, pp. 96–106, 1984.

Joergensen, A.H., "A methodology for measuring the readability and modifiability of computer programs," *BIT*, vol. 20, pp. 394–405, 1980.

Johnson, M.A., "A case study of tracking software development using quality metrics," *Software Quality Journal*, 4(1), pp. 15–32, 1995.
Interesting account of metrics program at Mentor Graphics. Focuses on defect density tracking.

Johnson, S.C., *YACC – Yet Another Compiler Compiler*, Bell Labs, Murray Hill, New Jersey, CSTR 32, 1979.

Jones, C., *Programmer Productivity*, McGraw-Hill, New York, 1986.

Jones, C., *A Short History of Function Points and Feature Points*, Software Productivity Research Inc., USA, 1987.

Jones, C., *Applied Software Measurement*, McGraw-Hill, New York, 1991.

Jones, C., *Software Productivity and Quality Today: The Worldwide Perspective*, Preprint, IS Management Group, 5841 Edison Place, Carlsbad, CA 92008, 1993a.

Jones, C., "Software quality: what works and what doesn"t?," *Proceedings of the Fourth International Conference on Applications of Software Measurement*, pp. 72–96 (also available as preprint), 1993b.

Jones, C., *Assessment and Control of Software Risks*, Prentice Hall, Englewood Cliffs, NJ, 1994.

Jones, C.B., *Systematic Software Development Using VDM*, Prentice Hall, Englewood Cliffs, NJ, 1986.
Definitive VDM reference.

Jones, D., "Bugs in the C Standard," *EXE*, pp. 12–15, November 1993.

Jones, G.W., *Software Engineering*, Wiley, New York, 1990.

Jorgensen M., "Experience with the accuracy of software maintenance task effort prediction models," *IEEE Transactions on Software Engineering*, 21(8), pp. 674–81, 1995.
Reports on experiences with 11 different models developed applying regression analysis, neural networks and pattern recognition. Most accurate predictions were achieved applying models based on multiple regression and on pattern recognition.

Kada, S., Woods, D. and Cole, R.J., "Design methods and code structure: a comparative case study," *Software Quality Journal*, 2(3), pp. 163–76, 1993.

Kafura, D. and Canning, J., "A validation of software metrics using many metrics and two resources," *Proceedings of the Eighth International Conference on Software Engineering*, London, IEEE Computer Society Press, pp. 378–85, 1985.
Some large systems are analyzed. A number of complexity metrics are correlated against historically collected resource expenditure data.

Kafura, D. and Henry, S., "Software quality metrics based on interconnectivity," *Journal of Systems and Software*, 2, pp. 121–31, 1981.

Kafura, D. and Reddy, G.R., "The use of software complexity metrics in software maintenance," *IEEE Transactions on Software Engineering*, SE-13(3), pp. 335–43, 1987.

Kamsties, E. and Lott, C.M., *An Empirical Evaluation of Three Defect-Detection Techniques*, ISERN technical report ISERN-95-02, International Software Engineering Research Network, University of Kaiserslautern, Germany, May 1995.

Kan, S.H., *Metrics and Models in Software Quality Engineering*, Addison-Wesley, Reading, MA, 1995.

Kano, N., Nobuhiro, S., Takahashi, F. and Tsuji, S., "Attractive quality and must be quality," *Quality*, 14(2), pp. 39–48, 1989.

Kanoun, K. and Sabourin, T., "Software dependability of a telephone switching system," *Proceedings of FTCS 17*, IEEE Computer Society Press, pp. 236–41, 1987.

Kaposi, A.A., "Measurement theory," in *Software Engineer's Reference Book* (ed. McDermid, J.), Butterworth Heinemann, 1991.

Kaposi, A.A. and Kitchenham, B.A., "The architecture of systems quality," *Software Engineering Journal*, 2(1), pp. 2–8, 1987.

Kaposi, A.A. and Myers, M., *Systems, Models and Measures*, Springer-Verlag, Berlin, 1993.

Karam, G.M. and Casselman, R.S., "A cataloging framework for software development methods," *IEEE Computer*, pp. 34–46, February 1993.
Useful qualitative framework for comparing and evaluating software development methods. Provides 21 characterizing properties of methods. Of these, fourteen are technical, such as life-cycle coverage, five are usage properties, such as ease of instruction, and two are managerial properties, such as ease of integration.

Kauffman, R. and Kumar, R., *Modeling Estimation Expertise in Object Based CASE Environments*, Stern School of Business Report, New York University, January 1993.

Kearney, J.K., "Total Quality: time to take off the rose-tinted spectacles," *The TQM Magazine*, February 1992.

Kearney, J.K., Sedlmeyer R.L., Thompson W.B. *et al.*, "Software complexity measurement," *Communications of the ACM*, 29(11), pp. 1044–50, 1986.
Discusses both the benefits and dangers of using software metrics, as well as some obligations for validation of measures in general.

Keller, T., "Measurement's role in providing "error-free" onboard shuttle software," *Third International Applications of Software Metrics Conference*, La Jolla, CA, pp 2.154–66. Proceedings available from *Software Quality Engineering*, 1992.

Kemerer, C.F., "An empirical validation of software cost estimation models," *Communications of the ACM*, 30(5), pp. 416–29, 1987.
This empirical study of cost estimation models not only looked at COCOMO and the Rayleigh curve model, but also looked at function points and one of the tools that uses function points as one of its input parameters. The paper confirms the need for calibration, and questions the need for the COCOMO cost drivers and the function point "technology factor adjustment."

Kemerer, C.F, "Reliability of function points measurement: a field experiment," *Communications of the ACM*, 36(2), pp. 85–97, February 1993.

Kemerer, C.F. and Porter, B., "Improving the reliability of function points measurement: an empirical study," *IEEE Transactions on Software Engineering*, 18(10), pp. 1011–24, 1992.

Kernighan, B.W. and Plauger, P.J., *The Elements of Programming Style*, McGraw-Hill, New York, 1974.

Kernighan, B. and Ritchie, D., *The C Programming Language,* 2nd edn, Prentice Hall, Englewood Cliffs, NJ, 1988.

Kersken, M. and Saglietti, F. (eds), *Software Fault Tolerance: Achievement and Assessment Strategies*, Springer-Verlag, Berlin, 1991.
Based on ESPRIT project 300 REQUEST. Contains some interesting papers about measuring software diversity.

Keyes, J., "Gather a baseline to assess CASE impact," *Software Magazine*, pp. 30–43, August 1990.
Very good paper because it emphasizes the importance of measurement in evaluating technologies (CASE here). This paper is also a very good introduction to software metrics.

Khoshgoftaar, T.M. and Allen, E.B., "Applications of information theory to software engineering measurement," *Software Quality Journal*, 3(2), pp. 105–12, 1994.

Khoshgoftaar, T.M. and Munson, J.C., "Predicting software development errors using complexity metrics," *IEEE Journal of Selected Areas in Communications*, 8(2), pp. 253–61, 1990.

Khoshgoftaar, T.M. and Szabo, R.M., "Investigating ARIMA models of software system quality," *Software Quality Journal*, 4(1), pp. 33–48, 1995.
Describes an approach for predicting faults in future software releases based on complexity metrics and fault counts from previous releases.

Khoshgoftaar, T.M., Munson, J.C., Bhattacharya, B.B. and Richardson, G.D., "Predictive modeling techniques of software quality from software measures," *IEEE Transactions on Software Engineering* 18(11), pp. 979–87, 1992.
Describes some statistical techniques that enable software complexity metrics to be good predictors. The dependent variable (the surrogate quality measure) was number of changes.

Khoshgoftaar, T.M., Szabo, R.M. and Woodcock, T.G., "An empirical study of program quality during testing and maintenance," *Software Quality Journal*, 3(3), pp. 137–51, 1994.

Kincaid, J.P., Aagard, J.A., O"Hara, J.W. and Cottrell, L.K., "Computer readability editing system," *IEEE Transactions on Professional Communication*, PC-24(1), pp. 38–41, March 1981.

Kirk, R.E., *Experimental Design Procedures For the Behavioral Sciences*, 2nd edn, Brooks Cole, Belmont, CA, 1982.
An advanced text describing theory and methods of analysis of variance. Should only be approached by those with a solid understanding of experimental design and statistical analysis.

Kirkman, J., *Good Style: Writing for Science and Technology*, Spon, London, 1992.

Kitchenham, B.A., "Measures of programming complexity," *ICL Technical Journal*, pp. 298–316, May 1981.

Kitchenham, B.A., "Towards a constructive quality model," *Software Engineering Journal*, 2(4), pp. 105–13, 1987.
Contains a useful overview of work in the area of software quality modeling.

Kitchenham, B.A., "An evaluation of software structure metrics," *Proceedings of the COMPSAC 88*, Chicago, IL, 1988.

Kitchenham, B.A., "Measuring software quality," *Proceedings of the First Annual Software Quality Workshop*, Rochester Institute of Technology, Rochester NY, 1989.

Kitchenham, B.A., "Empirical studies of assumptions that underlie software cost-estimation models," *Information and Software Technology*, 34(4), pp. 211–18, 1992.

Kitchenham, B.A., "Using quantitative case studies to evaluate software engineering methods and tools," *Proceedings of the Third Software Quality Workshop*, Napier University, Scotland, pp 1–37, July 1993 .

Kitchenham, B.A., "Using function points for software cost estimation," in *Software Quality Assurance and Measurement* (eds Fenton, N.E., Whitty, R.W. and Iizuka, Y.), International Thomson Computer Press, pp. 266–80, 1995.
Powerful critique of function points. For example, highlights empirical data that show that the "Technical Complexity Factor" does not improve the predictive ability of function points.

Kitchenham, B.A., "Series on experimentation in software engineering," *ACM Software Engineering Notes*, 1996.
Pfleeger described experiments in this series from 1994 to 1995. Kitchenham extends it to case studies, feature analysis, and others.

Kitchenham, B.A. and Känsälä, K., "Inter-item correlations among function points," *Proceedings of the IEEE Software Metrics Symposium*, Baltimore, MD, IEEE Computer Society Press, pp. 11–15, 1993.

Kitchenham, B.A. and Littlewood, B. (eds), *Measurement for Software Control and Assurance*, Elsevier, London, 1989.
The Proceedings of the 1987 CSR Workshop. Contains a number of interesting papers on software measurement, which provide further reading for much of the material presented here.

Kitchenham, B.A. and McDermid, J.A., "Software metrics and integrated project support environments," *Software Engineering Journal*, 1(1), pp. 58–64, 1986.

Kitchenham, B.A. and de Neumann, B., "Cost modelling and estimation," in *Software Reliability Handbook* (ed. Rook, P.), Elsevier Applied Science, pp. 333–76, 1990.

Kitchenham, B.A. and Pickard, L.M., "Towards a constructive quality model. Part II: statistical techniques for modelling software quality in the ESPRIT REQUEST project," *Software Engineering Journal*, 2(4), pp. 114–26, July 1987.

Kitchenham, B.A. and Taylor, N.R., "Software project development cost estimation," *Journal of Systems and Software*, 5(4), pp. 267–78, 1985.
Further empirical investigations of project data. This study noted that the effort–time profiles of small projects did not correspond to a Rayleigh curve. The paper also pointed out that, as a project progresses, a good estimation model should make use of data available about project progress (such as effort on completed tasks).

Kitchenham, B.A. and Walker, J.G., "A quantitative approach to monitoring software development," *Software Engineering Journal*, 4(1), pp. 2–13, 1989.

Kitchenham, B.A., Kitchenham, A.P. and Fellows, J.P., "The effects of inspections on software quality and productivity," *ICL Technical Journal*, pp. 112–22, May 1986.

Kitchenham, B.A., Kok, P.A.M. and Kirakowski, J., "The MERMAID approach to software cost estimation," *ESPRIT '90*, pp. 296–314, Kluwer Academic Press, 1990.

Kitchenham, B.A., Pfleeger, S.L. and Fenton, N.E., "Towards a framework for software measurement validation," *IEEE Transactions on Software Engineering*, 21(12), 929–44, 1995.
Describes a formal model of measurement attributes, tools, etc., and proposes it as the basis for validating that a measure represents what it should in the real world.

Kitchenham, B.A., Pickard, L.M. and Linkman, S.J., "An evaluation of some design metrics," *Software Engineering Journal*, 5(1), pp. 50–8, 1990.

Kitchenham, B.A., Pickard, L. and Pfleeger, S.L., "Case studies for method and tool evaluation," *IEEE Software*, 12(4), pp. 52–62, July 1995.
This article discusses the issues that should be considered in designing and carrying out a case study for software-engineering research. The principles are illustrated with critiques of the authors' own previously-published case study work.

Kleinrock, L., *Queueing Systems, Volume 1: Theory, and Volume 2: Computer Applications*, Wiley, New York, 1975.

Klepper, R. and Bock, D., "Third and fourth generation language productivity differences," *Communications of the ACM*, 38(9), pp. 69–79, 1995.
Interesting empirical study (from a single company) that looks at the effect of language type on productivity measured by function points per programming hour. Concludes that productivity is significantly higher when using 4GLs than 3GLs. It is also significantly higher when 4GLs are used in combination with 3GLs.

Knight, J.C., and Leveson, N.G., "An empirical study of failure probablities in multi-version software", in *Digest 16th International Symposium on Fault-tolerant Computing*, IEEE Press, 165–70, 1986.
Describes a large experiment to examine the efficacy of software diversity, and thus, by extension, software fault tolerance. 27 teams of programmers in Virginia and California were given the task to solve a particular problem. The 27 versions were tested on a very large set of test cases and several faults were found to be common to several versions. The authors carried out a statistical test to see whether these results could have occurred by chance, and this hypothesis was decisively rejected. On the evidence of this experience, not merely cannot it be asumed that versions will fail independently, but the degree of dependence appears to be very large. Although there has been some controversy about these results, mainly about the use of student programmers, the experiment itself was conducted very carefully and it now seems incumbent on those who advocate methods of fault tolerance based on diversity to present empirical results demonstrating the degree to which it can be effective.

Knuth, D.E., *The Art of Computer Programming*, vol. 3, Addison-Wesley, Reading, MA, 1973.

Knuth, D.E., "The Errors of TEX," *Software Practice and Experience*, 19(7), pp. 607–85, 1989.

Koga, K., "Software reliability design method in Hitachi," *Proceedings of the Third European Conference on Software Quality*, Madrid, 1992.

Kogure, M. and Akao, Y., "Quality function deployment and CWQC in Japan," *Quality Progress*, 16(10), pp. 25–29, October 1983.

Kohlas, J., "The reliability of reasoning with unreliable arguments," *Annals of Operations Research*, 32(1–4), pp. 67–113, July 1991.

Kohoutek, H.J., *Worldwide Review of Practices in Software Quality Assurance*, Hewlett-Packard, Fort Collins, CO, 80525-9599, 1990.
Looks at SQA practices at different companies around the world.

Kosaraju, R.S., "Analysis of structured programs," *Journal of the CSS*, 9, pp. 232–255, 1974.
Contains an important theoretical result of structured programming. Although it is known that every algorithm can be "encoded" using just sequence, selection, and iteration (the "D-structures" – see Bohm reference above), achieving this can involve the introduction of many new variables. The functionally equivalent structured program may be far more unwieldy than its unstructured predecessor. This paper provides a graph theoretic characterization of those programs which necessarily require the introduction of new variables to make them "D-structured." Essentially the program flowgraph must not contain a cycle which has two or more exits. This result was subsequently generalized by Fenton and Whitty.

Kouchakdjian, A. and Basili, V.R., "Evaluation of the cleanroom methodology in the SEL," *Proceedings of the Software Engineering Workshop*, NASA Goddard, Greenbelt, MD, 1989.

Krantz, D.H., Luce, R.D., Suppes, P. and Tversky, A., *Foundations of Measurement*, vol. 1, Academic Press, New York, 1971.
This book contains numerous representation theorems, that is, theorems that assert necessary and sufficient conditions for empirical relation systems to be representable on a specific scale.

Kraut, R.E. and Streeter, L.A., "Coordination in software development," *Communications of the ACM*, 38(3), pp. 69–81, 1995.
Gives the results of a very extensive survey assessing which formal and informal techniques seem to work.

Krekel, D, "Zur konzeptionellen Lueke zwischen Problembeschreibung und Programmier-spracheneinsatz," *Angewandte Informatik*, pp. 424–33, 1983.

Kuntzmann-Combelles *et al.*, *ami Handbook: a Quantitative Approach to Software Management*, ami consortium, ISBN 0-9522262-0-0, 1992.
The source text for the ami approach. Obtainable from the ami User Group, CSSE, School of Computing, Information Systems and Mathematics, South Bank University, London SE1 0AA. A revised version of the ami Handbook was subsequently published as Pulford *et al.*, 1995.

Kuvaja, P. and Bicego, A., "BOOTSTRAP: a European assessment methodology," *Software Quality Journal*, 3(3), pp. 117–28, 1994.

Kyburg, H.E., *Theory and Measurement*, Cambridge University Press, Cambridge, 984.
An excellent, thought-provoking text that provides a different perspective from that presented in Chapter 2. Kyburg (like Ellis) notes that, in addition to the mathematical and experimental focus, there is a need to focus on the relation between the acceptability of a theory and the concrete results of measurement. In particular, he is concerned about the consequences of and responses to actual measurements and comparative judgments that contradict assumed axioms. His approach to dealing with this is to account for both the desirability of remaining loyal to our observations and pay homage to the elegant and useful structures and axioms which in some degree conflict with our judgment. The balance is achieved by the introduction of a theory of errors of measurement. Kyburg is quite rightly worried by the apparent lack of reference to the notion of errors in the literature. It is our assumption that a complete rigorous study of measurement would take full account of Kyburg's approach (or something similar), building on the approach described in Chapter 2. An important notational difference between our approach and Kyburg's is that he talks about quantities to mean both the attribute and the proposed assignment of numbers (function); thus a quantity is an attribute together with a function proposed to capture it.

Lackshmanan, K.B., Jayaprakesh, S. and Sinha, P.K., "Properties of control-flow complexity measures," *IEEE Transactions on Software Engineering*, 17(12), pp. 1289–95, 1991.
Interesting paper. It extends the Weyuker properties but concentrates on a set of properties that are specific to control-flow complexity. The properties focus on the effects of sequence and nesting.

Lanergan, R.G. and Grasso, C.A, "Software engineering with reusable design and code," *IEEE Transactions on Software Engineering*, 10(5), pp. 498–501, 1984.

Lanning, D.L. and Khoshgoftaar, T.M., "Modeling the relationship between source code complexity and maintenance difficulty," *IEEE Computer*, 27(9), pp. 35–40, September 1994.
Canonical correlation analysis is used as an exploratory tool to help understand the relationships.

Laprie, J.-C. (ed.), *Dependability: Basic Concepts and Terminology*, Springer-Verlag, Vienna, 1992.
Contains a comprehensive set of definitions of terms relevant to dependability assessment, notably faults, errors and failures. The framework is applicable to systems generally (it is not restricted to software). The book contains translations of the framework in five languages (English, French, German, Italian and Japanese).

Lauterbach, L. and Randall, W., "Experimental evaluation of six test techniques," *Proceedings of the Compass 89*, 1989.

Law, D., *Methods for Comparing Methods*, NCC Publications, Manchester, England, 1988.
Takes a serious look at the important question of how to assess and compare different software methods. The approach is based almost entirely on checklists and subjective opinion.

Lawrence, P.R. and Lorsch, J.W., *Organization and Environment*, Harvard Business School, 1967.

Leach, R.J., "Software metrics and software maintenance," *Journal of Software Maintenance, Research and Practice*, 2(2), pp. 113–42, 1990.

Ledgard, H.F. and Marotty, M., "A genealogy of control structures," *Communications of the ACM*, 18(11), pp. 629–39, 1975.

Lee, W., *Experimental Design and Analysis*, Freeman, San Francisco, CA, 1975.

Lesk, M.E. and Schmidt, E., *LEX – A Lexical Analyzer Generator*, Bell Laboratories, Murray Hill, NJ, CSTR 32, 1979.

Leveson, N., *Safeware: System Safety and Computers*, Addison-Wesley, Reading, MA, 1995.

Leveson, N.G. and Harvey, P.R., "Analyzing software safety," *IEEE Transactions on Software Engineering*, SE-9(5) pp. 569–79, 1983.

Leveson, N.G. and Turner, C.S., "An investigation of the Therac-25 accidents," *IEEE Computer*, 26(7), pp. 18–41, July 1993.
Definitive analysis of a famous software failure that resulted in loss of life.

Lew, K.S., Dillon, T.S. and Forward, K.E., "Software complexity and its impact on software reliability," *IEEE Transactions on Software Engineering*, SE-14(11), pp. 1645–55, 1988.

Lewis, J.A. and Henry, S.M., "On the benefits and difficulties of a maintainability via metrics methodology," *Software Maintenance: Research and Practice*, 2, pp. 113–31, 1990.
Shows how to integrate metrics into a maintenance strategy. For example, includes "Alarm" threshold figures for a number of metrics.

Lewis, T.G., *Software Engineering: Analysis and Verification*, Reston Publishing Company, Reston, VA, 1982.

Lewis, T.G., *CASE: Computer Aided Software Engineering*, Van Nostrand Reinhold, New York, 1991.

Li, H.F. and Cheung, W.K., "An empirical study of software metrics," *IEEE Transactions on Software Engineering*, 13(6), 1987.

Li,W. and Henry, S., "Object oriented metrics that predict maintainability," *Journal of Systems and Software*, 23, pp. 111–22, 1993.

Li, W. and Henry, S., "Maintenance metrics for the object oriented paradigm," *Proceedings of the First International Software Metrics Symposium*, Baltimore, MD, IEEE Computer Society Press, pp. 52–60, 1993a.

Ligier, Y., *A Software Complexity Metrics System Based on Intra- and Inter-Modular Dependencies*, RC 14832, IBM Research Divison, Yorktown Heights, NY 10598, 1989.

Lim, W.C., "Effects of reuse on quality, productivity and economics," *IEEE Software,* 11(5), pp. 23–30, September 1994.

Good measurement-based assessment at Hewlett-Packard.

Linger, R.C., "Cleanroom process model," *IEEE Software,* 11(2), March 1994.
Good tutorial on Cleanroom. Also contains case study results with defect densities.

Linger, R.C., Mills, H.D. and Witt, R.L., *Structured Programming: Theory and Practice*, Addison-Wesley, Reading, MA, 1979.
Textbook describing an approach to structured programming based on principles similar to the general notion of structuredness and decomposition described in Chapter 8. The notion of a prime flowgraph originates from here, although the definitions (including the flowgraph model) must be changed to get the unique prime decomposition.

Lipow, M., "Number of faults per line of code," *IEEE Transactions on Software Engineering*, 8(4), pp. 437–9, 1982.
Proposes a prediction system for fault density based on Halstead's metrics.

Lister, A., "Software science – the Emperor's new clothes?," *Australian Computer Journal*, pp. 66–70, May 1982.

Littlewood, B., "A software reliability model for modular program structure," *IEEE Transactions on Reliability*, R-28(3), pp. 241–6, 1979.

Littlewood, B., "Stochastic reliability growth: a model for fault removal in computer programs and hardware designs," *IEEE Transactions on Reliability*, R-30, pp. 313–20, 1981.

Littlewood, B. (ed.), *Software Reliability: Achievement and Assessment*, Blackwell Scientific Publications, Oxford, UK, 1987.

Littlewood, B., "Predicting software reliability," *Philosophical Transactions of the Royal Society of London*, A 327, pp. 513–27, 1989.
Provides a good summary of the material covered in Chapter 11.

Littlewood, B., "Limits to evaluation of software dependability," in *Software Reliability and Metrics* (eds Fenton, N., and Littlewood, B.) Elsevier, 1991.
Provides a convincing formal argument about why it is infeasible to certify ultra-high levels of reliability.

Littlewood, B. and Miller, D.R., "Conceptual modeling of coincident failures in multiversion software," *IEEE Transactions on Software Engineering*, 15(12), pp. 1596–614, 1989.
Shows that the use of diverse methodologies decreases the probability of simultaneous failure. Hence this paper offers some comfort to the software fault tolerance community, especially as an earlier paper by Eckhardt and Lee showed that independently developed program versions will fail dependently.

Littlewood, B. and Miller, D.R., *Software Reliability and Safety*, Elsevier, 1991.

Littlewood, B. and Strigini, L., "Validation of ultra-high dependability for software-based systems," *Communications of the ACM*, 36(11), 1993.

Littlewood, B. and Verrall, J.L., "A Bayesian reliability growth model for computer software," *Journal of the Royal Statistical Society*, C22, pp. 332–4, 1973.

Littlewood, B., Brocklehurst, S., Fenton, N.E. *et al.*, "Towards operational measures of security," *Journal of Computer Security*, 2, pp. 211–29, 1993.
Defines measures of operational security that are the analogues of reliability measures.

Liu, S., Stavridou, V. and Dutertre, B., "The practice of formal methods in safety critical systems," *Journal of Systems and Software*, 28, pp. 77–87, 1995.

Lockart, R. and Whitty, R., *Testability Metrics*, COSMOS project GC/WPR/TEC/57.2, 1991.
Looks at white box testability metrics that can be generated by flowgraph decomposition. Concludes that in some cases exact calculation of the minimum number of test cases is infeasible.

Lockhart, R., "On statistics in software engineering measurement," *Software Quality Journal*, 2(1), 1993.
Excellent article that complements the approach described in this book.

Lohse, J.B. and Zweben, S.H., "Experimental evaluation of software design principles: an investigation into the effect of module coupling on system and modifiability," *Journal of Systems and Software*, 4, pp. 301–8, 1984.

Lorenz, M., *Object-Oriented Software Development: A Practical Guide*, Prentice Hall, Englewood Cliffs, NJ, 1993.

Lott, C.M., "Measurement support in software engineering environments," *International Journal of Software Engineering and Knowledge Engineering*, 4(3), pp. 409–26, 1994.
Surveys the trend toward supporting measurement in software-engineering environments and gives details about several existing research and commercial systems.

Lutz, R.R., "Targeting safety-related errors during requirements analysis," *Proceedings of the First ACM SIGSOFT Symposium* (ed. Notkin, D.), *ACM Software Engineering Notes* 18(5), pp. 99–105, 1993.

Lytz, R., "Software metrics for the Boeing 777: a case study," *Software Quality Journal*, 4(1), pp. 1–14, 1995.
Interesting case study (of a very large system, approximately two million lines of code). The data relate mainly to problem reports during test, and code size and utilization.

Lyu, M.R. (ed), "*The Handbook of Software Reliability Engineering*", McGraw Hill, New York, 1996.
Comprehensive and well edited collection of papers by leading authorities in the field.

Lyu, M.R. and Nikora, A., "Applying reliability models more effectively," *IEEE Software*, 9(4), pp. 43–52, July 1992.
Looks at how combining the results of individual models may give more accurate predictions.

MacDonnell, S.G., "Rigor in software complexity measurement experimentation," *Journal of Systems and Software*, 16, pp. 141–9, 1991.
The lack of rigor in experimentation is blamed for some of the lack of acceptance of complexity research. This article examines 13 areas in which empirical problems have arisen, and recommends procedural improvements.

MacDonell, S.G., "Comparative review of functional complexity assessment methods for effort estimation," *IEEE Software Engineering Journal*, 9(3), pp. 107–16, 1994.
Qualitative assessment of bang, function points, and more, based on six criteria: automation, comprehensive assessment, objectivity, specification basis, testing and validity.

Macro, A. and Buxton, J., *The Craft of Software Engineering*, Addison-Wesley, Reading, MA, 1987.

Madhavji, N.H. and Schafer, W., "Prism – Methodology and process-oriented environments," *IEEE Transactions on Software Engineering*, 17(12), pp. 1270–83, 1991.

Maiden, N.A. and Sutcliffe, A.G., "Exploiting reusable specifications through analogy," *Communications of the ACM*, 35(4), 1992.

Maier, H.H., "Die Prufung des Software–QualitatsmerkmalsBenutzungsfreundlichkeit," *QZ Management der Qulaitatssicherung* 1(28), 1983.
A specific attempt to define a measure of usability which takes account of both ease of use and user satisfaction.

Manly, B.F., *Multivariate Statistical Methods: A Primer*, Chapman & Hall, London, 1986.

Markusz, Z. and Kaposi, A.A., "Complexity control in logic-based programming," *Computer Journal*, 28(5), pp. 487–96, 1985.

Martin, J., *Information Engineering: Planning and Analysis*, Prentice Hall, Englewood Cliffs, NJ, 1990.

Martin, J. and McClure, C., *Diagramming Techniques for Analysts and Programmers*, Prentice Hall, Englewood Cliffs, NJ, 1985.

Martin, R., "Evaluation of current software costing tools," *ACM Sigsoft Notes*, 13(3), pp. 49–51, 1988.

Mason, M.D., "Estimating Ada lines of code from CORE using a MERMAID-style approach," *Proceedings of the European Cost Modeling Conference*, Italy, 1994.

Massey, B.S., *Measures in Science and Engineering: Their Expression, Relation and Interpretation*, Ellis Horwood, 1986.

Matson, J.E., Barrett, B.E. and Mellichamp, J.M., "Software development cost estimation using function points," *IEEE Transactions on Software Engineering*, 20(4), pp. 275–87, 1994.

Matsumoto, K., Kusumoto, S., Kikuno, T. and Torii, K., "A new framework of measuring software development processes," *Proceedings of the First International Software Metrics Symposium*, Baltimore, MD, IEEE Computer Society Press, pp. 108–19, 1993.
Uses a Petri net model as the basis for modeling software processes. Process measures are then defined on the Petri net.

Matsumoto, Y. and Ohno, Y., *Japanese Perspectives in Software Engineering*, Addison-Wesley, Reading, MA, 1989.

Mayer, A. and Sykes, A.M., "Probability model for analysing complexity metrics data," *Software Engineering Journal*, 4(5), 1989.
Good example of the use of generalized linear modeling techniques to investigate relationships between software attributes.

Mayer, A. and Sykes, A.M., "Statistical methods for the analysis of software metrics data," *Software Quality Journal*, 1(4), pp. 209–24, 1992.

Mays, R.G., Jones, C.L., Holloway, G.J. and Studinski, D.P., "Experiences with defect prevention," *IBM Systems Journal*, 1991.

McCabe, T., "A software complexity measure," *IEEE Transactions on Software Engineering* SE-2(4), pp. 308–20, 1976.
One of the most referenced papers in software engineering. This is the source for both the cyclomatic complexity metric and the essential complexity metric (although the definition of the latter is ambiguous).

McCabe, T. and Butler, C.W., "Design complexity measurement and testing," *Communications of the ACM*, 32(12), pp. 1415–25, 1989.

McCall, J.A., Richards, P.K., and Walters, G.F., "Factors in Software Quality", RADC TR-77-369, 1977. Vols I, II, III, US Rome Air Development Center Reports NTIS AD/A-049 014, 015, 055, 1977.
This work contains one of the early and much referenced Software Quality Models. It was used as the basis for the first international standard for software quality measurement (ISO 9126).

McClure, C.L., "A model for program complexity analysis," *Proceedings of the Third International Conference on Software Engineering*, pp. 149–57, 1978.

McCracken, D.D., Denning, P.J. and Brandin, D.H., "An ACM executive committee position on the crisis in experimental computer science," *Communications of the ACM*, 22(9), pp. 502–4, 1979.
This was the broadly supportive response to the Feldman and Sutherland (1979) report.

McDermid, J.A., "Safety-critical software: a vignette," *Software Engineering Journal*, 8(1), pp. 2–3, 1993.

McGowan, C.L. and Bohner, S., "Model-based process assessment," *Proceedings of the 15th International Conference on Software Engineering*, Baltimore, MD, IEEE Computer Society Press, pp. 202–11, May 1993.

Mellor, P., "Field monitoring of software maintenance," *Software Engineering Journal*, 1(1), pp. 43–9, 1986.

Mellor, P., "Software reliability modelling: the state of the art," *Journal of Information and Software Technology*, 29(2), pp. 81–98, 1987.

Mellor, P., "Failures, faults and changes in dependability measurement," *Information and Software Technology*, 34(10), pp. 640–54, 1992.

Mellor, P., "CAD – Computer Aided Disaster," *High Integrity Systems Journal*, 1(2), pp. 101–56, 1994.
Excellent analysis of a number of well-known (and less well-known) failures dues to (or conjectured to be due to) computers and software.

Melton, A. (ed.), *Software Measurement*, International Thomson Computer Press, 1995.
Well edited collection of metrics paper that focus on the formal foundations of software measurement. Based on an earlier metrics workshop.

Melton, A.C., Bieman, J.M., Baker, A. and Gustafson, D.A., "Mathematical perspective of software measures research," *Software Engineering Journal*, 5(5), pp. 246–54, 1990.
Intelligent paper which reiterates the view that there is an implicit hierarchy of orders on software products (documents) throughout the life cycle, and describes the subsequent obligations for real measures. Also contains a good discussion on the perils of equating structural complexity with psychological complexity.

Meyer, C., "More software failure analysis," *Proceedings of the Third International Conference on Application of Software Measurement*, pp. 2.181–206, 1992.

Miller, D.R., "Exponential order statistic models of software reliability growth," *IEEE Transactions on Software Engineering*, SE-12(1), pp. 12–24, 1986.

Miller, E., "Coverage measure definitions reviewed," *Testing Technologies Newsletter*, 3, p. 6, November 1980.

Mills, E., *Software Metrics: SEI Curriculum Module SEI-CM-12-1.1*, Software Engineering Institute, Carnegie Mellon University, Pittsburgh, PA, 1988.

Mills, H.D., *On the Statistical Validation of Computer Programs*, FCS-72-6015, IBM Federal Systems Division, 1972.

Mills, H.D., "Structured programming: retrospect and prospect," *IEEE Software,* 3(6), pp. 58–66, November 1986.

Mills, H.D., Dyer, M. and Linger, R., "Cleanroom software engineering," *IEEE Software*, 4(5), pp. 19–25, September 1987.

Ministry of Defence Directorate of Standardization, *Interim Defence Standard 00–55: The Procurement of Safety Critical Software in Defence Equipment; Parts 1–2*, 1991.
High profile draft standard that mandates the use of formal specification techniques.

Mintzberg, H., *The Structure of Organizations*, Prentice Hall, Englewood Cliffs, NJ, 1979.

Mitchell, J. and Welty C., "Experimentation in software engineering: an empirical view," *International Journal of Man–Machine Studies*, 29, pp. 613–24, 1988.
Fascinating study which reveals that there is much less published empirical work in computer science than in many other disciplines.

Mitchell, J., Urban, J.E. and McDonald, R., "The effect of abstract data types on program development," *IEEE Computer*, pp. 85–8, August 1987.

Authors attempted to establish the effectiveness of the use of ADTs by showing that productivity was increased with their use. Even with our poor understanding of productivity it is clear that this was not an appropriate attribute to choose; even worse was that productivity was measured by lines of code. Not surprisingly the results of the study were inconclusive.

Miyazaki, Y. and Mori, K., "COCOMO evaluation and tailoring," *Proceedings of the Eighth International Conference Software Engineering*, IEEE Computer Society Press, 1985.
Provides a detailed report on how COCOMO was calibrated to a Japanese company (Fujitsu).

Miyoshi, T. and Azuma, M., "An empirical study of evaluating software development environment quality," *IEEE Transactions on Software Engineering*, 19(5), pp. 425–35, 1993.

Moeller, K.-H. and Paulish, D., *Software Metrics: A Practitioner's Approach to Improved Software Development*, Chapman & Hall, and IEEE Computer Society Press, Los Alamitos, CA, 1993.
Useful book that describes (at a high level) some metrics programs in European companies. Unfortunately, almost no data are presented.

Moeller, K.-H. and Paulish, D., "An empirical investigation of software fault distribution," in *Software Quality Assurance and Measurement* (eds Fenton, N.E., Whitty, R.W. and Iizuka, Y.), International Thomson Computer Press, pp. 242–53, 1995.
Very interesting study that throws up some counter-intuitive findings such as: large modules tend to have lower defect densities.

Mohammed, W.-E.A. and Sadler, C.J., "Methodology evaluation: a critical survey," *Eurometrics '92*, pp. 101–12, 1992.
Takes a critical look at a number of published case studies and experiments from the viewpoint of good design.

Moher, T. and Schneider, G.M., "Methodology and experimental research in software engineering," *International Journal of Man–Machine Studies*, 16(1), pp. 65–87, 1982.

Moroney, M.J., *Facts from Figures*, Penguin Books, London, 1950.

Mosteller, F. and Tukey, J.W., *Data Analysis and Regression*, Addison-Wesley, Reading, MA, 1977.
Provides useful information on transforming data and the analysis of residuals. Also includes a good discussion of cross-validation (checking the accuracy of a regression equation using data which was not used to construct the equation) and jackknife estimates (which are useful for reducing bias in estimates obtained from small datasets).

Mukhopadhyay, T. and Kekre, S., "Software effort models for early estimation of process control applications," *IEEE Transactions on Software Engineering*, 18(10), pp. 915–24, 1992.

Munson, J.C. and Khoshgoftaar, T.M., "Regression modeling of software quality: an empirical investigation," *Information and Software Technology*, 32(2), pp. 106–14, 1990.

Munson, J.C. and Khoshgoftaar, T.M., "The detection of fault-prone programs," *IEEE Transactions on Software Engineering*, 18(5), pp. 423–33, 1992.

Musa, J.D., "A theory of software reliability and its application," *IEEE Transactions on Software Engineering*, SE-1, pp. 312–27, 1975.

Musa, J.D., *Software Reliability Data*, technical report available from Data Analysis Center for Software, Rome Air Development Center, New York, 1979.
Still one of the most extensive single collections of software failure data available. Musa was project manager of some of the projects, and could thus exercise complete control over the quality of the data collected. All others were projects within the same organization, and thus Musa had extensive quality control.

Musa, J.D. and Ackerman, A.F., "Quantifying software validation: when to stop testing?," *IEEE Software,* 6(3), pp. 19–27, May 1989.
Describes how statistical testing works.

Musa, J.D., Iannino, A. and Okumoto, K., *Software Reliability: Measurement, Prediction and Application*, McGraw-Hill, New York, 1987.
One of the few books that describes some of the reliability growth techniques in detail. There is a tendency for a single model to be recommended, rather than the more pragmatic approach described in Chapter 10.

Myers, G.J., *Reliable Software through Composite Design*, Van Nostrand Reinhold, Wokingham, UK, 1975.

Myers, G.J., *Software Reliability, Principles and Practices*, Wiley Interscience Publication, New York, 1976.

Myers, G.J., "An extension to the cyclomatic measure of program complexity," *SIGPLAN Notices*, 12(10), pp. 61–4, 1977.

Myers, G.J., "A controlled experiment in program testing and code walkthroughs/inspections," *Communications of the ACM*, 21(9), pp. 760–8, 1978.

Myers, G.J., *Composite Structured Design*, Van Nostrand Reinhold, New York, 1978a.

Myers, M., *Quality Assurance of Specification and Design of Software*, PhD thesis, South Bank University, 103 Borough Road, London, SE1 0AA, 1990.

Myrvold, A., "Data anaysis for software metrics," *Proceedings of the Annual Oregon Software Metrics Symposium*, 1990.
Describes some useful analysis techniques, and explains the dangers of not transforming skewed data.

Nadler, G., "System methodology and design," *IEEE Transactions on Systems, Man and Cybernetics*, SMC-15(6), pp. 685–97, 1985.

NAG (Numerical Algorithms Group), *The GLIM System Release 3.77 Manual* (ed. Payne, C.D.), Oxford, UK, 1985.

Nakajo, T. and Kume, H., "A case history analysis of software error cause–effect relationships," *IEEE Transactions on Software Engineering*, 17(8), pp. 830–8, 1991.

Nakimura, E. (ed.), *AYUMI: Continuous Improvement of Software Quality is Key at Fujitsu in Japan,* Fujitsu, 1992.

Narens, L., *Abstract Measurement Theory*, MIT Press, Cambridge, MA, 1985.

Natale, D., "On the impact of metrics application in a large scale software maintenance environment," *Proceedings of the Conference on Software Maintenance*, IEEE Computer Society Press, pp. 114–18, 1991.
Interesting study of "complexity metrics" in a large COBOL system, although the empirical details are sketchy. Shows that maintenance time for "unstructured" programs (as characterized by the metrics) is greater than for structured ones. Also "availability time" (meaning time between interventions) is greater for the structured programs. Metrics tool used was METCOB (Static Analyzer for Cobol Program Metrics) developed by CRIAI as part of the SOGEI research project.

National Computing Centre, *Data Collection and Storage System (DCSS) User Manual, Version 2*, National Computing Centre Ltd, Oxford Road, Manchester, UK, 1992.

National Physical Laboratory, *Software Metrics and Security Standard Conformance Testing*, NPL report DITC 176/91, Teddington Physical Laboratory, Middlesex TW11 0LW, UK, 1991.
Very useful document giving a good overview of metrics "for confidence building" and test coverage metrics.

Naur, P., "Formalisation in program development," *BIT* 22, pp. 437–52, 1982.

Naur, P., "Understanding Turing's Universal Machine – personal style in program description," *Computer Journal*, 36(4), pp. 351–71, 1993.
Very interesting study that suggests some fundamental limitations of formal notations. Specifically the benefits of using formal notations are shown to be highly sensitive to individual differences.

Navlakha, J.K., "A survey of system complexity metrics," *Computer Journal*, (30)3, pp. 233–8, 1987.
Provides a reasonable survey (up to 1983) of those "complexity" metrics (of the graph-theoretic nature) which may be applied to system designs where the latter are expressed in graphical notation.

Nippon Electric Corporation, *Total Quality Control of Software – SWQC Activity in NEC Corporation*, JUSE Press, 1990.

Neil, M.D., "Multivariate assessment of software products," *Journal of Software Testing, Verification and Reliability*, 1(4), pp. 17–37, 1992.

Neil, M.D., "Measurement as an alternative to bureaucracy for the achievement of software quality," *Software Quality Journal*, 3(2), pp. 65–78, 1994.

Neil, M.D. and Bache, R.M., "Data linkage maps," *Journal of Software Maintenance*, 5(3), 1993.

Nejmeh, B.A., "NPATH: A measure of execution path complexity and its applications," *Communications of the ACM*, 31(2), pp. 188–200, 1988.

NetFocus: Software Program Managers Network, 207, Department of the Navy (US), January 1995.
This newsletter describes the derivation of a metrics "dashboard" that depicts a small number of key measures. The dashboard is to be used by project managers to "drive" a software development project, telling the manager when the products are ready for release to the customer.

Neumann, P.G., *Computer-Related Risks*, Addison-Wesley, Reading, MA, 1994.

Norden, P., "Useful tools for project management," *Operations Research in Research and Development* (ed. Dean, B.V.), Wiley, New York, p. 4, 1963.

O"Brien, S.J. and Jones, D.A., "Function points in SSADM," *Software Quality Journal* 2(1), 1–12, 1993.

O"Connor, M., *Writing Successfully in Science*, Chapman & Hall, London, 1991.

Ohlsson, N. and Alberg, H., *Predicting Error-Prone Software Modules in Telephone Switches*, to appear *IEEE Transactions on Software Engineering*, 1996.

Ohmori, A., "Software quality deployment approach: framework design, methodology and example," *Software Quality Journal*, 3(4), pp. 209–40, 1994.

Ohno, Y., "Current status of software engineering in Japan," *Journal of Information Processing*, 14(3), pp. 232–6, 1991.

Oivo, M. and Basili, V.R., "Representing software engineering models: the TAME goal oriented approach," *IEEE Transactions on Software Engineering*, 18(10), pp. 886–98, 1992.

Olsen, N. "The software rush hour", *IEEE Software*, 10(5), pp. 29–37, September 1993.

Oman, P.R. and Cook, C.R., "A paradigm for programming style research," *SIGPLAN Notices*, 23(12), pp. 69–78, December 1988.

Onvlee, J., "Use of function points for estimation and contracts," in *Software Quality Assurance and Measurement* (eds Fenton, N., Whitty, R.W. and Iizuka, Y.), pp. 88–93, 1995.
Describes the role of FPA in the Netherlands. Author claims that 50–60% of the fixed price contracts there are costed on the basis of FPA, and that the FPA is included in the contract.

Ostle, B. and Malone, L.C., *Statistics in Research*, 4th edn, Iowa State University Press, Ames, IA, 1988.

Ostralenk, G., Southworth, M., Tobin, M. and Neil, M., *SREDM Formal Method Analysis*, IED/4/1/3029 SREDM, TP04/02, Lloyds Register, 1994.
Case study that shows that the use of formal methods on a medium scale development led to very low defect density in the resulting code.

Ostrand, T.J. and Weyuker, E.J., "Collecting and categorizing software error data in an industrial environment," *Journal of Systems and Software*, 4, pp. 289–300, 1984.

Ottenstein L.M., "Quantitative estimates of debugging requirements," *IEEE Transactions on Software Engineering*, 5(5), pp. 504–14, 1979.
Study based on Halstead metrics.

Ould, M.A., *Strategies for Software Engineering: The Management of Risk and Quality*, Wiley, New York, 1990.

Oulsnam, G., "Cyclomatic numbers do not measure complexity of unstructured programs," *Information Processing Letters*, pp. 207–11, December 1979.
Theoretical demolition of McCabe's cyclomatic number as a complexity measure.

Oviedo, E.I., "Control flow, data flow, and program complexity," *Proceedings of COMPSAC 80*, IEEE Computer Society Press, New York, 1980, pp. 146–52, 1980.

Park, R., *Software Size Measurement: A Framework for Counting Source Statements*, CMU/SEI-92-TR-20, Software Engineering Institute technical report, Pittsburgh, PA, 1992.
This report provides extensive checklists intended to guide the reader in deciding what to include when measuring a line of code. It distinguishes physical lines from logical, and it includes considerations such as reuse, automatic generation of code, and use of purchased or supplied code.

Parnas, D.L., "On the criteria to be used in decomposing systems into modules," *Communications of the ACM*, 15(12), pp. 1052–8, 1972.

Parnas, D.L., "Education for computing professionals," *IEEE Computer*, 23(1), pp. 17–22, January 1990.

Parnas, D.L., "Predicate logic for software engineering," *IEEE Transactions on Software Engineering*, 19(3), 1993.

Parnas, D.L., Madey, J. and Iglewski, M., "Precise documentation of well-structured programs," *IEEE Transactions on Software Engineering*, 20(12), pp. 948–76, 1994.

Parr, F.N., "An alternative to the Rayleigh curve model for software development effort," *IEEE Transactions on Software Engineering*, SE-6(3), 1980.
Parr pointed out that most projects do not start their design and code activities with zero staff. He proposed an alternative to the Rayleigh curve which allowed a non-zero staffing level at the start of the design phase.

Paulish, D.J. and Carleton, A.D., "Case studies of software process-improvement measurement," *IEEE Software*, 11(4), pp. 50–9, July 1994.

Paulk, M.C., "Comparing ISO 9001 and the capability maturity model for software," *Software Quality Journal*, 2(4), pp. 245–56, 1993.

Paulk, M.C., "How ISO 9001 compares with the CMM," *IEEE Software*, 12(1), pp. 74–83, January 1995,

Paulk, M.C., Curtis, B., Chrissis, M.B. and Weber, C.V., *Capability Maturity Model for Software, Version 1.1*, SEI technical report SEI-CMU-93-TR-24, Software Engineering Institute, Pittsburgh, PA, 15213-3890, USA, 1993.

Paulk, M.C., Curtis, B., Chrissis, M.B. and Weber, C.V., *Key Practices of the Capability Maturity Model, Version 1.1*, SEI technical report SEI-CMU-93-TR-25, Software Engineering Institute, Pittsburgh, PA, 15213-3890, USA, 1993.

Paulk, M.C., Weber, C.V. and Curtis, B., *The Capability Maturity Model for Software: Guidelines for Improving the Software Process*, Addison-Wesley, Reading, MA, 1994.

Pearl, J., *Probabilistic Reasoning in Intelligent Systems*, Morgan Kaufmann, Palo Alto, CA, 1988.

Pengelly, A., Performance of effort estimating techniques in current development environments, *Software Eng. J.*, 10(5), pp. 162–70, 1995.

Perlis, A.J., Sayward, F.G. and Shaw, M. (eds), *Software Metrics: An Analysis and Evaluation*, MIT Press, Cambridge, MA, 1981.
Much underused (and in many cases sadly forgotten) book covering a wide range of topics in software measurement. The book is actually the proceedings of a conference on software metrics held in Washington in 1980, with the papers organized into appropriate sections. The papers are followed by the transcripts of the discussions which took place after their presentation. Some of these are illuminating, and the book is worth getting just for some of the amusingly inept contributions from well known "experts." There is an extensive annotated and classified bibliography by Mary Shaw on all work in software metrics through 1980. Excellent papers by Browne and Shaw (an "ahead-of-its-time" discussion of a scientific basis for software evaluation), by Sayward (design of software experiments), DeMillo and Lipton (software project forecasting) and many others (including papers by Curtis and Basili). The contributions of Mary Shaw are excellent. Many of these papers contain material that has been reinvestigated many times in the ensuing sixteen years. All too often the subsequent material has been inferior and offered no new insights.

Perrow, C., *Normal Accidents: Living with High-Risk Technologies*, Basic Books, New York, 1984.

Perry, D.E., Staudenmayer, N.A. and Votta, L.G., "People, organizations and process improvement," *IEEE Software*, 11(4), pp. 36–45, July 1994.

Peterson, W.W., Kasami, T. and Tokura, N., "On the capabilities of While, Repeat and Exit statements," *Communications of the ACM*, 16(8), pp. 503–12, 1973.

Petrova, E. and Veevers, A., "Role of non-stochastic-based metrics in quantification of software reliability," *Information and Software Technology*, 32(1), pp. 71–8, 1990.
Highlights the weakness of static metrics as predictors of operational reliability.

Pfleeger, S.L., "Measuring improved productivity," *Journal of the Office Systems Research Association*, 6(2), pp. 1–5, Spring 1988.

Pfleeger, S.L., *An Investigation of Cost and Productivity for Object-Oriented Development*, PhD dissertation, George Mason University, Fairfax, VA, 1989.
Contains a history of cost models, including comparison and critique. Suggests new model based on average productivity, adjusted by user-created cost factors. For object orientation, shows that a count of objects and methods as size measure yields more accurate estimate than COCOMO or Ada-COCOMO.

Pfleeger, S.L., *Software Engineering: The Production of Quality Software*, 2nd edn, Macmillan, New York, 1991.
Contains history of cost estimation, including comparisons of several of the major cost estimation models. Also contains information about Contel's measurement program, and about the relationship between process and measurement.

Pfleeger, S.L., "Model of software effort and productivity," *Information and Software Technology*, 33(3), pp, 224–31, April 1991.
Summarizes key findings of Pfleeger (1989), presenting comparison of Pfleeger model with COCOMO and Ada-COCOMO.

Pfleeger, S.L., "Lessons learned in building a corporate metrics program," *IEEE Software*, 10(3), May 1993.
A description of a measurement program for a large telecommunications company.

Pfleeger, S.L. and Bollinger, T. "The economics of reuse: issues and alternatives," *Information and Software Technology*, 32(10), pp. 643–52, December 1990.

Pfleeger, S.L. and Bollinger, T., "The economics of reuse: new approaches to modelling cost," *Information and Software Technology*, 36(8), pp. 475–84, August 1994.

Pfleeger, S.L. and Cline, J.N., "A model of office automation benefits," *Journal of the Office Systems Research Association*, 3(2), pp. 51–6, Spring 1985.

Pfleeger, S.L. and Hatton, L., "How do formal methods affect code quality?," *IEEE Computer*, May 1996.

Pfleeger, S.L. and McGowan, C.L., "Software metrics in a process maturity framework," *Journal of Systems and Software*, 12(3), pp. 255–61, 1990.
Describes the connection between process maturity and measurement, so that process visibility suggests what to measure.

Pfleeger, S.L. and Palmer, J.D., "Software estimation for object-oriented systems," *Proceedings of the International Function Point Users Group Fall Conference*, San Antonio, TX, pp. 181–96, 1990.
Similar to Pfleeger (1991a), but with comments about object orientation and function points.

Pfleeger, S.L., Fenton, N.E. and Page, S., "Evaluating software engineering standards," *IEEE Computer*, 27(9), pp. 71–9, September 1994.
Summarizes preliminary findings of SMARTIE project, showing that standards are not defined well. Suggests guidelines for evaluating standards, and presents a case study showing how to improve data collection standards.

Pfleeger, S.L., Fitzgerald, J.C. Jr., and Rippy, D.A., "Using multiple metrics for analysis of improvement," *Software Quality Journal*, 1(1), pp. 27–36, 1992.
Contains a description of the use of multiple metrics graphs at Contel, with an example of using the graph to evaluate telephone switch software.

Phillips, M., "CISC/ESA 3.1 experiences," *Proceedings of the Z User Group Workshop* (ed. Nicholls, J.E.), pp. 179–85, 1989.
Contains quantified claims of the effectiveness of the use of Z but no data to back it up (only a graph without scales) and no explanation of what data was actually gathered.

Porter, A. and Selby, R., "Empirically-guided software development using metric-based classification trees," *IEEE Software*, 7(2), pp. 46–54, March 1990.

Porter, A.A., Votta, L.G. and Basili, V.R., "Comparing detection methods for software requirements inspections: a replicated experiment," *Proceedings of the 18th International Conference on Software Engineering*, Sorrento, Italy, IEEE Computer Society Press, 1994.
Nice study comparing search-for-all-problems inspections with scenario inspections, where scenarios assign certain problem classes to each inspector (so that each inspector looks for different things). Shows that scenarios are more effective, but also shows that there is "meeting loss:" some problems found by individuals are not reported at collective meeting.

Potier, D., Albin, J.L., Ferreol, R. and Bilodeau, A., "Experiments with computer software complexity and reliability," *Proceedings of the Sixth International Conference on Software Engineering*, IEEE Computer Society Press, pp. 94–103, 1982.

Potter, M., *Software Reliability Modelling Database: User Manual*, report produced under ALV/PRJ/SE/072: Software Reliability Modelling Project, 1989.

Potts, C. and Bruns, G., "Recording the reasons for design decisions," in *Proceedings of Tenth International Conference on Software Engineering*, IEEE Computer Society Press, 1988.

Prasad, D., McDermid, J. and Wand, I., "Dependability terminology: similarities and differences," *Proceedings of COMPASS '95*, 1995.

Prather, R.E., "An axiomatic theory of software complexity measure," *Computer Journal*, pp. 340–47, 1984.
Inspired the axiomatic approach to software measurement in Fenton and Whitty (1986) and the notion of hierarchical measures. Prather proposed a set of specific axioms which captured intuitive notions of complexity for the structural relationships between D-structured programs.

Prather, R.E., "On hierarchical software metrics," *Software Engineering Journal*, 2(2), pp. 42–5, 1987.

In this paper, Prather consolidated and extended the work in Fenton and Whitty (1986) on the classification and axiomatization of structural metrics. He provided a classification of metrics axiomatically into those which are recursive and those which are hierarchical. He showed that although Fenton and Whitty had implicitly defined the larger of these classes (recursive) by their axioms, all examples which they had cited actually fell into the smaller class (hierarchical) which could be characterized by restricting the axiom for nesting functions. The value of making the distinction is described in this paper, and this is emphasized by the axiomatic construction of an interesting metric which is recursive but not hierarchical, namely the number-of-paths metric.

Prather, R.E., "Hierarchical metrics and the prime generation problem," *Software Engineering Journal*, 8(5), pp. 246–52, 1993.

Interesting theoretical paper that describes a method for generating prime flowgraphs.

Prather, R.E. and Giulieri, S.G., "Decomposition of flowchart schemata," *Computer Journal*, 24(3), pp. 258–62, 1981.

Important paper that describes a formal decomposition of flowgraphs into primitive components. Some of the ideas contained in the algorithm presented here were ultimately incorporated into the implementation of the QUALMS decomposition algorithm.

Pressman, R.S., *Software Engineering: A Practitioner's Approach*, 3rd edn, McGraw-Hill, New York, 1992.

Useful software-engineering text book. It is one of the few to pay more than mere lip service to measurement, with sections on measurement in quality assurance and productivity, and cost estimation.

Prieto-Diaz, R., "Domain analysis for reusability," in *Proceedings of COMPSAC'87*, pp. 23–9, 1987.

Prieto-Diaz, R., "Making software reuse work: an implementation model," *ACM SIGSOFT Software Engineering Notes*, 16(3), pp. 61–8, 1991.

Program Analysers, *TESTBED*, Program Analysers Ltd, Newbury, Berkshire, UK, 1990.

Pulford, K., Kuntzmann-Combelles, A. and Shirlaw, S., *A Quantitative Approach to Software Management*, Addison-Wesley, Reading, MA, 1995.

An updated version of the ami handbook, the primary product of the ESPRIT-funded ami (applications of measurement in industry) project.

Putnam, L.H., "A general empirical solution to the macrosoftware sizing and estimating problem," *IEEE Transactions on Software Engineering*, SE-4(4), pp. 345–61, 1978.

Putnam, L.H., "The value of process improvement: does it pay off?," *Proceedings of the Fourth International Conference on Applications of Software Measurement*, pp. 304–31, 1993.

Putnam, L.H. and Fitzsimmons, A., "Estimating software costs," *Datamation*, September, October and November 1979, pp. 312–15.

This series of papers discuss the Rayleigh curve approach to cost estimation. They also discuss the problem of obtaining a good estimate of size.

Putnam, L.H. and Myers, W., *Measures for Excellence: Reliable Software on Time, Within Budget*, Yourdon Press, Englewood Cliffs, NJ, 1992.

Pyramid Consortium, *Quantitative Management: Get a Grip on Software!*, technical reference: EP-5425 Y 91100-4, 1991.

Rade, A. and Richter, L., "A proposal for measuring the structural complexity of programs," *Journal of Systems and Software*, pp. 55–70, September 1980.

Ramamoorthy, C.V. and Bastani, F.B., "Software reliability: status and perspectives," *IEEE Transactions on Software Engineering*, SE-8 (4), pp. 354–71, July 1982.

Rambo, R., Buckley, P. and Branyan, E., "Establishment and validation of software metrics factors," *Proceedings of the Seventh Annual Conference of the International Society of Parametric Analysts*, pp. 406–17, 1985.

Rapp, W., "RCA PRICE parametric sizing software sizing," *Proceedings of the Seventh Annual Conference of the International Society of Parametric Analysts*, 4(1), 1985.

Rapps, S. and Weyuker, E.J., "Selecting software test data using data flow information," *IEEE Transactions on Software Engineering,* 11(4), pp. 367–75, 1985.

Ratcliffe, B. and Rollo, A.L., "Adapting function point analysis to Jackson System Development," *Software Engineering Journal*, 5(1), 1990.
Provides a strong case for the function point concepts but refutes the belief that function points are independent of development method.

Ravn, A.P. and Stavridou, V., "Specification and development of safety critical software: an assessment of MOD Draft Standard 00–55," *International Conference on Software Engineering 12, Workshop on Industrial Use of Formal Methods*, 1990.

Redish, K.A. and Smyth, W.F., "Evaluating measures of program quality," *The Computer Journal*, 30(3), 1987.

Redmill, F. and Anderson, T. (eds), *Safety Critical Systems*, Chapman & Hall, London, 1993.

Rees, C. and Oddy, G., "Safety critical software for defence systems: requirements of interim defence standards 00–55," *GEC Journal of Research*, 12(1), pp. 43–9, 1995.

Rees, M.J., "Automatic assessment aid for Pascal programs," *SIGPLAN Notices*, 17(10), pp. 33–42, October 1982.

Reifer, D.J., "Asset-R: A function point sizing tool for scientific and real-time systems," *Journal of Systems and Software*, 11, pp. 159–71, 1990.

Reliability and Statistical Consultants Ltd, *"Software Reliability Modelling Programs,"* Available from RSC Ltd., 5 Jocelyn Road, Richmond, Surrey, TW9 2TJ, UK, 1988.
Commercially available software that performs the calculations needed to apply several models (described in Chapter 10) to particular data and analyzes their predictive accuracy. Runs on IBM PC and some workstations.

Reynolds, R.G., "The partial metrics system: modeling the stepwise refinement process using partial metrics," *Communications of the ACM*, 30(11), pp. 956–63, 1987.

Richardson, D.J. and Thompson, M.C., "An analysis of test data selection criteria using the RELAY model of fault detection," *IEEE Transactions on Software Engineering*, 19(3), pp. 533–53, 1993.

Rifkin, S. and Cox, C., *Measurement in Practice*, SEI technical report SEI-CMU-91-TR-16, Software Engineering Institute, Pittsburgh, PA, 1991.

Riley, P., "Towards safe and reliable software for Eurostar," *GEC Journal of Research*, 12(1), pp. 3–12, 1995.
Fascinating account of the role of software (and how it was assessed) in the Channel Tunnel and Eurostar trains. Particularly interesting account of the testing process (including residual error analysis) and data collection.

Roberts, F.S., *Measurement Theory with Applications to Decision Making, Utility, and the Social Sciences*, Addison-Wesley, Reading, MA, 1979.
This excellent text provides a natural next step for readers of a mathematical disposition who enjoyed Chapter 2. Half of the book is devoted to applications of measurement theory to areas where measurement was traditionally considered impossible. It is these applications which should convince you that it is possible to obtain formal objective measures for many software attributes often considered unmeasurable.

Roberts, F. S., "Applications of the theory of meaningfulness to psychology," *Journal of Mathematical Psychology*, 29, pp. 311–32, 1985.

Robillard, P. and Boloix, G., "The interconnectivity metrics: a new metric showing how a program is organized," *Journal of Systems and Software*, 10, pp. 29–39, October 1989.

Robinson, R., "Measuring six sigma quality in software," *Proceedings of the Third International Conference on Applications of Software Measurement*, pp. 1.30–52, 1992.

Rollo, T., Steven, C. and Shoostarian, C., "Function points reliability: a laboratory experiment," *Proceedings of European Software Cost Modelling Conference* (ESCOM), 1993.

Rombach, H.D., "A controlled experiment on the impact of software structure on maintainability," *IEEE Transactions on Software Engineering*, SE-7(5), pp. 510–18, 1987.

Rombach, H.D., Basili, V.R. and Selby, R.W. (eds), *Experimental Software Engineering Issues*, Springer-Verlag, Berlin, 1993.
Contains a number of papers from leading experts who gathered in Dagstuhl to discuss experimental software engineering issues.

Rooijmans, J., Aerts, H. and van Genutchen, M., "Software quality in consumer electronics products," *IEEE Software*, 13(1), 55–64, January 1996.
Fascinating case study from Phillips giving the measurement results from three projects. Focuses on the data that shows the effectiveness of Fagan inspections.

Rook, P. (ed.), *Software Reliability Handbook*, Elsevier North Holland, 1990.
An exceptionally well coordinated collection of papers that addresses all key concepts relating to software reliability, namely the different methods of achievement and assessment. There are good sections and appendices on software metrics and cost estimation.

Ross, N., "The collection and use of data for monitoring software projects," in *Measurement for Software Control and Assurance* (eds Kitchenham, B.A. and Littlewood, B.), Elsevier, pp. 123–54, 1989.

Ross, N., "Using metrics in quality management," *IEEE Software*, 7(4), pp. 80–5, July 1990.

Rossetti, D.J. and Iyer, R.K., *Software Related Failures on the IBM 3081: A Relationship with System Utilisation*, T-R 82-8 (CSL TN No. 209), Center for Reliable Computing, Stanford University, CA, 1982.

Rouquet, J.C. and Traverse, P.J., "Safe and reliable computing on board the Airbus and ATR aircraft," in *Proceedings of the 5th IFAC Workshop on Safety of Computer Control Systems* (ed. Quirk, W.J.) Pergamon Press, Oxford, UK, pp. 93–7, 1986.

Rout, T.P., "SPICE: A framework for software process assessment," *Software Process – Improvement and Practice*, 1(1), pp. 57–66, August 1995.

Roy, B., "Decision aid and decision making," *European Journal of Operational Research*, 45, pp. 324–31, 1990.

Rozum, J.A. and Florac, W.A., *A DoD Software Measurement Pilot: Applying the SEI Core Measures*, Software Engineering Institute technical report CMU/SEI-94-TR-016, Pittsburgh, PA, May 1995.
Describes the use of SEI core measures in the US Department of Defense, and suggests changes to the core definitions based on these experiences.

Rubey, R.J., Dana, J.A. and Biche, P.W., "Quantitative aspects of software validation," *IEEE Transactions on Software Engineering*, SE-1, pp. 150–5, 1975.
Stresses the need for, and approaches to, careful data collection.

Rubin, H.A., "A comparison of cost estimation tools," *Proceedings of the International Conference on Software Engineering*, IEEE Computer Society Press, 1985.

Rubin, H.A., *The Rubin Review*, vol. III (3), July 1990.

Rubin, H.A., "Software process maturity: measuring its impact on productivity and quality," *Proceedings of the First International Software Metrics Symposium*, Baltimore, MD, IEEE Computer Society Press, pp. 28–39, 1993.
Contains some interesting benchmarking data.

Rubin, L.F., "Syntax-directed pretty printing: a first step towards a syntax-directed editor," *IEEE Transactions on Software Engineering*, SE-9(2), pp. 119–27, 1983.

Rudolph, E. and Bremerhaven, H., "Precision of function point counts," *Proceedings of European Software Cost Modelling Conference* (ESCOM), 1993.

Rugg, D., "Using a capability evaluation to select a contractor," *IEEE Software*, 10(4), pp. 36–45, July 1993.

Russell, M., "International survey of software measurement education and training," *Journal of Systems and Software*, 12, pp. 233–41, July 1990.
A remarkable survey for two reasons: (1) the exceptionally high target and response rate – every university and polytechnic in the UK and Germany with over 50% response (due partly to the tenacity of the author), and (2) the surprisingly large amount of metrics teaching reported. There was also found to be a desperate need for better quality teaching materials.

Ryder, B.G., "Constructing a call graph of a program," *IEEE Transactions on Software Engineering*, SE-5(3), pp. 216–26, 1979.
Describes and verifies an algorithm for producing call graphs. Very useful paper for people wanting to automate the measures described in Chapter 9.

Rydstrom, L. and Viktorrson, O., "Software reliability prediction for large and complex telecommunications systems," *Proceedings of the 22nd Hawaii International Conference on System Science*, IEEE Computer Society Press, pp. 312–19, 1989.

Saaty, T., *The Analytic Hierarchy Process*, McGraw-Hill, New York, 1980.
Definitive reference for this increasingly popular approach to assessment.

Saiedian, H. and Kuzara, R., "SEI Capability Maturity Model's impact on contractors," *IEEE Computer*, 28(1), pp. 16–26, January 1995.

Saglietti, F., "Software diversity metrics quanitifying dissimilarity in the input partition", *Software Engineering Journal*, 5(1), 59–63, 1990.

Samson, W.B., Nevill, D.G. and Dugard, P.I., "Predictive software metrics based on a formal specification," *Software Engineering Journal*, 5(1), 1990.
Describes the results of a project that attempted to derive metrics from formal specifications. In this case, the formal specifications were actually written in OBJ which is an executable specification language. The nature of OBJ is such that specs are amenable to being modeled by flowgraphs, and thus structural metrics may be derived. Some very simple metrics (McCabe's, Halstead, LOC) were thus derived and compared with the metrics derived from programs written in languages like Pascal and Ada which "implemented" the OBJ "specifications."

Sanders, J. and Curran, E., *Software Quality: A Framework For Success in Software Development and Support*, Addison-Wesley, Reading, MA, 1994.

Sayet, C. and Pilaud, E., "An experience of a critical software development," *Proceedings of the FTCS'90*, pp. 36–45, 1990.

Scacchi, W., "Understanding software productivity: a comparative empirical review," *Proceedings of the Hawaii International Conference on Systems Science '89*, IEEE Computer Society Press, Vol. 2, pp. 969–77, 1989.
Interesting paper that focuses on the difficulties of measuring productivity. Looks at a number of studies to highlight the factors affecting productivity.

Scanlan, D.A., "Structured flowcharts outperform pseudocode: an experimental comparison," *IEEE Software*, 6(5), pp. 28–36, September 1989.

Classic (carefully designed and implemented) experiment that debunked a popular myth. Showed that in every reasonable respect, people performed better with flowcharts than with pseudocode.

Schein, E.H., *Organizational Psychology*, Prentice Hall, Englewood Cliffs, NJ, 1965.

Schick, G.J. and Wolverton, R.W., "An analysis of competing software reliability models," *IEEE Transactions on Software Engineering*, SE-4, pp. 104–20, 1978.

Schneidewind, N.F., "Application of program graphs and complexity analysis to software development and testing," *IEEE Transactions on Reliability*, R-28, pp. 192–8, 1979.
Useful tutorial in graph-type concepts.

Schneidewind, N.F., "Controlling and predicting the quality of space shuttle software using metrics," *Software Quality Journal*, 4(1), pp. 49–68, 1995.
This is essentially a study in metrics validation using data from the space shuttle software development. A range of metrics is validated against an indirect measure of quality "drcount" (deviations from requirements).

Schneidewind, N.F., "Methodology for validating software metrics," *IEEE Transactions on Software Engineering*, 18(5), pp. 410–22, 1992.
Defines six validity criteria, mostly based on the idea that the metric has to predict some quality attribute. The criteria are: association (meaning that the metric has to correlate well with a particular quality factor), consistency, discriminative power, tracking, predictability and repeatability.

Schneidewind, N.F., "Validating metrics for ensuring space shuttle flight software quality," *IEEE Computer*, 27(8), pp. 50–8, August 1994.

Schneidewind, N.F. and Keller, T.W., "Applying reliability models to the space shuttle," *IEEE Software*, 9(4), pp. 28–33, July 1992.
Describes the successful use of software reliability models at IBM to the space shuttle's on-board software.

Schreiber, B. and Zwegers, A., "Software cost data collection," *Proceedings of the European Software Cost Modelling Conference*, 1992.
Describes the European Space Agency metrics program.

Schulmeyer, G.G. and McManus, J.I., *Handbook of Software Quality Assurance*, Van Nostrand Reinhold, New York, 1987.

Schulmeyer, G.G. and McManus, J.I., *Total Quality Management for Software*, Van Nostrand Reinhold, New York, 1992.

Segot, J. and Lechevallier, M., "Software metrics action plan in the Thomson-CSF Group," *Proceedings of Eurometrics 92*, Commission of the European Community, Brussels, Belgium, pp. 163–70, 1992.

SEL, *Manager's Handbook for Software Development, Revision 1*, Software Engineering Laboratory Series SEL-84-101, November 1990.

Selby, R.W., "Extensible integration frameworks for measurement," *IEEE Software*, 7(6), pp. 83–4, November 1990.
Contains examples of GQM and metric-driven classification trees.

Shaw, M., "Annotated bibliography on software metrics," in *Software Metrics* (eds Perlis, A.J., Sayward, F.G. and Shaw, M.) MIT Press, Cambridge, MA, 1981.

Shaw, M., "Prospects for an engineering discipline of software," *IEEE Software*, 7(6), pp. 15–24, November 1990.
Excellent article that looks at the evolution of engineering disciplines and compares them to software engineering.

Sheldon, F.T., Krishna, K.M., Tausworthe, R.C. *et al.*, "Reliability measurement: from theory to practice," *IEEE Software*, 9(4), pp. 12–20, July 1992.
Nice general overview of software reliability that emphasizes why it must be taken seriously.

Shen, V.Y., Conte, S.D. and Dunsmore, H.E., "Software science revisited: a critical analysis of the theory and its empirical support," *IEEE Transactions on Software Engineering*, 9(2), pp. 155–65, March 1983.
This paper reviews the underpinnings of Halstead's work and examines the experimental results published about it since 1977.

Shen, V.Y., Yu, T., Thebaut, S.M. and Paulsen, L.R., "Identifying error-prone software – an empirical study," *IEEE Transactions on Software Engineering*, SE-11(4), pp. 317–23, 1985.

Shepperd, M.J., "A critique of cyclomatic complexity as a software metric," *Software Engineering Journal*, 3(2), pp. 30–6, 1988.
Shepperd does a convincing demolition job on the theoretical and practical basis of McCabe's metric, as well as addressing a number of issues relating to the theoretical basis of "complexity" metrics in general (including the axiomatic approach).

Shepperd, M.J., *Software Engineering Metrics, Volume 1: Measures and Validations*, McGraw-Hill, New York, 1993.
Shepperd has collected together what he considers are sixteen key representative papers (dating from 1976 to 1990) which chart the evolution of the subject area. Papers are arranged into three parts, dealing respectively with: the Beginnings (code complexity measures); Early life-cycle metrics; and Validations. Each part is preceded by an overview by Shepperd that attempts to relate the individual papers and draw some general conclusions. Additionally, the author has written his own 11-page introductory section to describe his own view of the past, present, and future of software metrics.

Shepperd, M.J. and Ince, D., "Metrics, outlier analysis and the software design process," *Information and Software Technology*, 31(2), pp. 91–8, 1989.

Shepperd, M.J. and Ince, D.C., "The use of metrics in the early detection of design errors," *Proceedings of the European Software Engineering Conference '90*, pp. 67–85, 1990.

Shepperd, M.J. and Ince, D., *Derivation and Validation of Software Metrics*, Clarendon Press, Oxford, UK, 1993.
This book concentrates on metrics that can be determined in the software-development life cycle, specifically metrics that can be computed from designs and specifications. The authors are especially looking for metrics that can provide early feedback on future maintenance and implementation costs. This is one of their key criteria for metric validity, which must be demonstrated empirically. The book starts with a historical review and then looks in detail at the validation of three very well-known metrics: Halstead, McCabe and Henry and Kafura's information flow measure. The authors conclude that the three chosen metrics are bad, not by bad luck but by carelessness of approach and poor awareness of measurement. To address these problems, the authors suggest three issues that need to be addressed: the meaning of metrics (via measurement theory), model evaluation (both empirical and theoretical via axioms), and the need to tailor metrics for different goals. The book contains chapters to deal with each of these issues in turn. The authors propose their own formal models of designs and define measures which can be extracted from these. The two types of validation (via axioms and empirically) are performed, and the results of these lead to model refinement and ultimately to increasingly promising results. This book will appeal primarily to people who already have some experience of software metrics. Because of the central role of the notion of formal models and axioms, readers need some mathematical maturity if they are to really benefit from it.

Shepperd, M.J. and Turner, R., "Real time function points: an industrial validation," *Proceedings of European Software Cost Modelling Conference* (ESCOM), 1993.

Sherif, Y.S., Ng, E. and Steinbacher, J., "Computer software quality measurements and metrics," *Microelectronics and Reliability*, 25(6), pp. 1105–50, 1986.
Very good survey paper. Because it appeared in such an unusual source, it has been largely overlooked by the software metrics community. The survey is based on a classification of attributes that appears to amount to a new quality "mode." Also contains a good bibliography.

Shneiderman, B., Mayer, R., McKay, D., and Heller, P., "Experimental investigations of the utility of detailed flowcharts in programming," *Communications of the ACM*, 20(6), pp. 373–81, June 1977.

Shneiderman, B., "Measuring computer program quality and comprehension," *International Journal of Man–Machine Studies*, 3, pp. 465–78, 1984.

Shooman, M.L., *Software Engineering: Design, Reliability and Management*, McGraw-Hill, New York, 1983.

Siegel, S. and Castellan, N.J., Jr., *Nonparametrics Statistics for the Behavioral Sciences*, 2nd edn, McGraw-Hill, New York, 1988.
A classic text with a lot of material about measurement scales, and the types of operations that may be performed on them. This most recent edition describes non-parametric statistical tests. The popularity of this text stems from the worked examples that help clarify when a test is appropriate, and show the student how to actually calculate the value of the statistic.

Simon, H., *Science of the Artificial*, MIT Press, Cambridge, MA, 1980.

Smith, B., "Six-sigma design," *IEEE Spectrum*, 30(9), pp. 43–7, September 1993.

Smith, J.E., "Characterizing computer performance with a single number," *Communications of the ACM*, 31, pp. 1202–6, 1988.

Sneed, H. and Merey, A., "Automated software quality assurance," *IEEE Transactions on Software Engineering*, 11(9), pp. 909–16, 1985.

Software Metrics Laboratory, *SML-QUALMS user manual, version 4.0*, Software Metrics Laboratory, Glasgow Caledonian University, Scotland, 1992.

Software Productivity Consortium, *Software Measurement Guidebook* (main contributors Bassman, M.J., McGarry, F. and Pajesrki, R.), International Thomson Computer Press, London, 1995.
An excellent practical overview of software measurement using extensive examples drawn from many years of experience on major collaborative projects. This was formerly published as Software Engineering Laboratory Series SEL-94-002, Software Engineering Branch, Code 552, Goddard Space Flight Center, Greenbelt, MD 20771.

Soloway, E., Bonar, J. and Ehrlich, K., "Cognitive strategies and looping constructs: an empirical survey," *Communications of the ACM*, 26(11), pp. 853–60, 1983.
Describes some experiments undertaken to assess the relative "cognitive complexity" associated with the use of different looping structures in languages like Pascal. For example, their experimental evidence suggests that in many situations a middle-exit loop – the D4 prime (not available in standard Pascal) – would be far more natural to use than a *repeat* or *while* loop. Particularly relevant further reading for Chapter 8, where we argued the need for a more flexible approach to structured programming.

Sommerville, I., *Software Engineering* (4th edn), Addison-Wesley, Reading, MA, 1993.

Song, X. and Osterweil, L.J., "Experience with an approach to comparing software design methodologies," *IEEE Transactions on Software Engineering*, 20(5), pp. 364–84, May 1994.
A systematic and defined process (CDM) is introduced to objectively compare software design methods. CDM is tried out experimentally.

Soong, N.L., "A program stability measure," *Proceedings of the ACM Annual Conference*, pp. 163–73, 1977.

Souter, J.B. and Cheney, D.P., "Information technology quality system certification in Europe," *Proceedings of the Third European Conference on Software Quality*, Madrid, 3–6 November 1992.

Spivey, J.M., *The Z Notation: A Reference Manual*, Prentice Hall, Englewood Cliffs, NJ, 1993.
There is more than one dialect of the Z specification notation. This book is widely considered to be the most standard Z description.

Sprent, P., *Applied Nonparametric Statistical Methods*, Chapman & Hall, London, 1989.
Gives details of robust correlation and Theil's method of robust regression. It is a very readable modern text.

Srimani, P.K. and Malaiya, Y.K., "Steps to practical reliability measurement," *IEEE Software*, 9(4), pp. 10–12, July 1992.
This is actually the guest editors' introduction to a special issue of *IEEE Software* devoted to software reliability measurement. It makes the case for using software reliability models.

Stark, M., "Impact of object-oriented technologies: Seven years of software engineering," *Journal of Systems and Software*, November 1993.

Stark, G., Durst, R.C. and Vowell, C.W., "Using metrics in management decision making," *IEEE Computer*, 27(9), pp. 42–9, September 1994.
Describes the metrics program in NASA's Mission Operation Directorate. Contains some very interesting data on size, defect density, and cyclomatic number. Emphasizes how the metrics program removed the inherent optimism of engineering judgment.

Stark, G., Kern, L.C., Durst, R.C. and Vowell, C.W., "Establishing a software metrics program: approach and observations," *Proceedings of the 10th Annual Software Reliability Symposium*, Denver, CO, pp. 52–8, 1992.
Describes early results from the metrics program at NASA Mission Operations Directorate.

Stetter, F., "A measure of program complexity," *Computer Languages*, 9(3), pp. 203–10, 1984.

Stevens, D.F., "Attributes of good measures," *The Software Practitioner*, 5(1), pp. 11–13, January 1995.
Nice little paper. The attributes are trustworthiness, timeliness, simplicity, directness.

Stevens, S.S., "On the theory of scale types and measurement," *Science*, 103, pp. 677–80, 1946.
This appears to be the origin of the definition of the hierarchy of measurement scale types (nominal, ordinal, interval, and ratio).

Stevens, W., Myers, G. and Constantine, L., "Structured design," *IBM Systems Journal*, 13(2), 1974.
Classic paper that introduces notions of coupling and cohesion.

Stricker, C., "Evaluating effort prediction systems," in *Software Quality Assurance and Measurement* (eds Fenton, N.E., Whitty, R.W. and Iizuka, Y.), International Thompson Computer Press, pp. 281–93, 1995.
Empirical study that casts grave doubts on the accuracy of function points and COCOMO.

Subrahmanian, G.H. and Brelawski, S.A., *A Case for Dimensionality Reduction in Software Development Effort Estimation*, TR-89-02, Department of Computer Science, Temple University, Philadelphia, PA, 1989.
The authors reanalyzed the COCOMO database and found that the large number of cost drivers proposed by Boehm were unnecessary.

Sullivan, M. and Chillarege, R., "Software defects and their impact on system availability – A study of field failures in operating systems," *Proceedings of the Fault Tolerant Computing Symposium*, 1991.

Swanson, E.B. and Beath, C.M., "The use of case study data in software management research," *Journal of Systems and Software*, 8, pp. 63–71, 1988.
The authors describe an illustrative multiple-case study of application software maintenance that combines quantitative with qualitative data. Among the topics discussed are research context and design, data collection, analysis and synthesis, and the sharing of data and results. They conclude with methodological lessons learned.

Swanson, M.E. and Curry, S.K., "Implementing an asset management program at GTE Data Services," *Information and Management*, 16, 1989.
Describes the use of incentives to encourage reuse at GTE Data Services.

Sydenham, P.H. (ed.), *Handbook of Measurement Science*, vol. 1, Wiley, New York, 1982.
Contains a number of papers on applications and nature of measurement in a number of scientific disciplines. Includes a chapter by Finkelstein with a comprehensive introduction to measurement theory.

Symons, C.R., "Function point analysis: Difficulties and improvements," *IEEE Transactions on Software Engineering*, 14(1), pp. 2–11, 1988.
Symons proposed a a new method of counting function points based on transactions. This approach fits well with some methods of system specification.

Symons, C.R., *Software Sizing and Estimating: Mark II Function Point Analysis*, Wiley, New York, 1991.

Tai, K.C., "A program complexity metric based on data flow information in control graphs," *Proceedings of the 7th International Conference on Software Engineering*, pp. 239–48, 1984.

Tajima, D. and Matsubara, T., "The computer software industry in Japan," *IEEE Computer*, 14(5), pp. 89–96, 1981.

Takahashi, M. and Kamayachi, Y., "An emprirical study of a model for program error prediction," *IEEE Transactions on Software Engineering*, 5(1), pp. 82–6, 1989.

Tamine, J., "On the use of tree-like structures to simplify measures of complexity," *ACM SIGPLAN Notices*, 18(9), pp. 62–9, 1983.

Tanik, M.M. and Chan, E.S., *Fundamentals of Computing for Software Engineers*, Van Nostrand Reinhold, New York, 1991.

Tausworthe, R.C., *Deep Space Network Software Cost Estimation Model*, Publication 81–7, Jet Propulsion Laboratory, Pasadena, CA, 1981.

Tervonen, I., "Support for quality-based design and inspection", *IEEE Software*, 13(1), 44–54, 1996.

Thadhani, A.J., "Factors affecting programmer productivity during application development," *IBM Systems Journal*, 23(1), pp. 19–35, 1984.

Thayer, R.H., "Software engineering project management: a top-down view," in *Tutorial: Software Engineering Project Management*, (ed. Thayer, R.H.), IEEE Computer Society Press, 1990.

Thayer, T.A., Lipow, M. and Nelson, E.C., *Software Reliability*, North-Holland, New York, 1978.

Theofanos, M.F., and Pfleeger, S. L., "CIM Reuse Metrics Plan, version 2.3", Martin Marietta Technical Report K/DSRD-1231,Oak Ridge National Laboratory, Oak Ridge, Tennessee, 13 November, 1992.

Theofanos, M.F. and Pfleeger, S.L., *A Framework for Creating a Reuse Measurement Plan*, Martin Marietta Technical Report, Martin Marietta Energy Systems – Data Systems Research and Development Division, Oak Ridge, TN, 1993.

Tian, J. and Zelkowitz, M.V., "A formal program complexity model and its applications," *Journal of Systems and Software*, 17, pp. 253–66, 1992.

Tian, J. and Zelkowitz, M.V., "Complexity measure evaluation and selection," *IEEE Transactions on Software Engineering*, 21(8), pp. 641–50, 1995.

A number of basic axioms for complexity measures are proposed, together with means for evaluating measures in a particular application domain. The approach is used to select measures in an empirical trial, with quite promising results.

Torn, A.A., "Models of software accumulation," *Journal of Systems and Software*, 12, pp. 39–42, 1990.

Trachtenberg, M., "Validating Halstead's theory with system 3 data, *"IEEE Transactions on Software Engineering*, SE-12(4), p. 584, 1986.

Tracz, W., "Software reuse myths," *Software Engineering Notes*, 13(1), pp. 18–22, January 1988.

Troy, D.A. and Zweben, S.H., "Measuring the quality of structured design," *Journal of Systems and Software*, 2, pp. 113–20, 1981.

Tsai, W.T., Lopez, M.A., Rodriguez, W. and Volovik, D., "An approach to measuring data structure complexity," *Proceedings of IEEE COMPSAC 86*, IEEE Computer Society Press, pp. 240–6, 1986.

Tsalidis, C., Christodoulakis, E. and Maritsas, D., "Athena: A software measurement and metrics environment," *Journal of Software Maintenance: Research and Practice*, 4(2), pp. 61–81, 1992.

Tse, T.H., "Towards a single criterion for identifying program unstructuredness," *Computer Journal*, 30(4), pp. 378–80, 1987.

Turk, C. and Kirkman, J., *Effective Writing: Improving Scientific, Technical and Business communication*, Spon, London, 1989.

Turner, J., "The structure of modular programs," *Communications of the ACM*, 23(5), pp. 272–7, 1980.

Vaisanen, A., Auer, A. and Korhonen, J., *Assessment of the Safety of PLCs: Janiksenlinna Water Plant Study*, SHIP/T/033, VTT, Finland, 1994.
Uses the analytical hierarchy process to do a real safety assessment.

Van Emden, M.H., *An Analysis of Complexity*, Mathematical Centre Tracts, 35 Mathematical Centre, 49 2e Boerhaavestraat, Amsterdam, 1971.
Provides a comprehensive and formal treatment of the notion of complexity in systems. This book was sadly ignored by many subsequent works on measuring complexity.

Van Verth, P.B., *A System for Automatically Grading Program Quality*, SUNY–Buffalo technical report, 1985.

Veevers, A. and Marshall, A.C., "A relationship betwen software coverage metrics and reliability," *Journal of Software Testing, Verification and Reliability*, 4, pp. 3–8, 1994.
Presents an argument for an inverse logarithmic relationship between test coverage and reliability. This relationship depends on the structure of the software and the strength of the coverage metric.

Velleman, P.F. and Wilkinson, L., "Nominal, ordinal, interval and ratio typologies are misleading," *The American Statistician*, 47(1), pp. 65–72, February 1993.
Refutes some of the arguments made by measurement theorists.

Verner, J.M. and Tate, G., "Estimating size and effort in fourth generation language development," *IEEE Software*, 5(4), pp. 173–7, July 1988.

Verner, J.M. and Tate, G., "A software size model," *IEEE Transactions on Software Engineering*, 18(4), pp. 265–78, 1992.
Describes a function-points-like approach to estimating size for 4GLs that produces reasonable accuracy.

Vessey, I. and Conger, S., "Requirements specification: Learning object, process and data methodologies," *Communications of the ACM*, 37(5), pp. 102–13, 1994.

Vessey, I. and Weber, R., "Research on structured programming: An empiricist's evaluation," *IEEE Transactions on Software Engineering*, 10(4), pp. 397–407, July 1984.
This paper reviews the empirical studies that have been undertaken to evaluate structured programming, critiquing each in terms of the soundness of the methodology and the ability to contribute to scientific understanding. The authors conclude that the evidence supporting structured programming is weak, and they outline a framework for an ongoing research program.

Vincke, P., *Multicriteria Decision Aids*, Wiley, New York, 1992.
Excellent text on a fast-growing subject.

van Vliet, J.C., *Software Engineering: Principles and Practice*, Wiley, New York, 1993.
Very interesting approach that is quite different from other text books on software engineering. Measurement is taken seriously throughout. Highly recommended.

Voas, J.M. and Miller, K.W., "Software testability: the new verification," *IEEE Software*, 12(3), pp. 17–28, May 1995.
Discussed in Chapter 10.

Waguespack, L.J. and Badlani, S., "Software complexity assessment: an introduction and annotated bibliography," *ACM SIGSOFT Software Engineering Notes*, 12(4), pp. 52–71, 1987.

Walker, J.G. and Kitchenham, B.A., "The architecture of an automated quality management system," *ICL Technical Journal*, pp. 156–70, May 1988.
Reference to the COQUAMO tools.

Wallace, D.R. and Fujii, R.U., "Software verification and validation: an overview," *IEEE Software*, 6(3), pp. 10–17, May 1989.
Useful survey paper.

Wallace, D.R., Ippolito, L.M. and Kuhn, D.R., *High Integrity Software Standards and Guidelines*, NIST SPEC PUB 500–201, US Department of Commerce/National Institute of Standards and Technology, September 1992.

Walston, C.E. and Felix, C.P., "A method of programming measurement and estimation," *IBM Systems Journal*, 16(1), pp. 54–73, 1977.

Watson, S., "The meaning of probability in probabilistic safety analysis," *Reliability Engineering and System Safety 45*, pp. 261–9, 1994.

Watts, R., *Measuring Software Quality*, NCC Publications, Manchester, UK, 1987.
Useful booklet describing the then state of the art of software quality measurement.

Weerahandi, S. and Hausman, R.E., "Software quality measurement based on fault-detection data," *IEEE Transactions on Software Engineering*, 20(9), 1994.
Uses (field) fault discovery data for previous versions of a system to predict fault density next time round.

Wegbreit, B., "Verifying program performance," *Journal of the ACM*, 23(4), pp. 691–9, 1976.

Weiderman, N.H., Haberman, A.N., Borger, M.W. and Klein, M.H., "A methodology for evaluating environments," *ACM SIGPLAN Notices*, pp. 199–207, 1986.

Weinberg, G., *The Psychology of Computer Programming*, Van Nostrand Reinhold, New York, 1971.

Weinberg, G.M., *Quality Software Management Volume 2: First-Order Measurement*, Dorset House, New York, 1993.

Weinberg, G.M. and Schulman, E.L., "Goals and performance in computer programming," *Human Factors*, 16(1), pp. 70–7, 1974.
Describes a classic experiment that showed that programming teams could always optimize their performance with respect to a single success criterion, but always at the expense of the other goals.

Weiss, D.M. and Basili, V.R., "Evaluating software development by analysis of changes: some data from the Software Engineering Laboratory," *IEEE Transactions on Software Engineering*, SE-11(2), pp. 157–68, 1985.

Weller, E.F., "Lessons learned from two years of inspection data," *Proceedings of the Third International Conference on Applications of Software Measurement*, pp. 2.57–69, 1992.

Weller, E.F., "Lessons from three years of inspection data," *IEEE Software*, 10(5), pp. 38–45, September 1993.
Excellent empirical study showing data from more than 6000 inspection meetings. For example, compares defect detection rates for different sized teams and different types of code.

Weller, E.F., "Using metrics to manage software projects," *IEEE Computer*, 27(9), pp. 27–34, September 1994.
Looks at the successful results arising from Bull's (Arizona) project-management program that included software metrics and inspections.

Weyuker, E.J., "On testing non-testable programs," *The Computer Journal*, 25(4), pp. 465–70, 1982.

Weyuker, E.J., "Axiomatizing software test data adequacy," *IEEE Transactions on Software Engineering*, SE-12(12), pp. 1128–38, 1986.

Weyuker, E.J., "Evaluating software complexity measures," *IEEE Transactions on Software Engineering*, SE-14(9), pp. 1357–65, 1988.

Weyuker, E.J., "Can we measure software testing effectiveness?" *Proceedings of the First International Software Metrics Symposium*, Baltimore, MD, IEEE Computer Society Press, pp. 100–7, 1993.
Argues that comparison rather than measurement of effectiveness of different testing criteria is possible.

Weyuker, E.J., "More experience with data-flow testing," *IEEE Transactions on Software Engineering*, 19(3), pp. 912–19, 1993a.
Demonstrates the cost-effectivenss of the Rapps–Weyuker testing strategy.

Whitty, R.W., *The Flowgraph Model of Sequential Processes*, Alvey Project SE/69, Report GCL/004/01, South Bank Polytechnic, London, 1987.

Whitty, R.W. and Lockhart, R., *Structural Metrics*, ESPRIT 2 project COSMOS, document GC/WP1/REP/7.3, Goldsmiths' College, London, 1990.

Whitty, R.W., Fenton, N.E. and Kaposi, A.A., "A rigorous approach to structural analysis and metrication of software," *IEEE Software and Microsystems*, 4(1), pp. 2–16, 1985.

Wichmann, B.A., *Why Are There No Measurement Standards for Software Testing?*, National Physical Laboratory, Teddington, Middlesex, TW11 0LW, UK, 1993.

Wichmann, B.A. and Cox, M.G., "Problems and strategies for software component testing standards," *Journal of Software Testing, Verification and Reliability*, 2, pp. 167–85, 1992.

Wiener, L.R., *Digital Woes: Why We Should Not Depend on Software*, Addison-Wesley, Reading, MA, 1993.

Williams, J.D., "Metrics for object oriented projects," *Proceedings of OOP-94*, Munich, pp. 253–8, 1994.

Wilson, L. and Leelasena, L., *The QUALMS Program Documentation*, Alvey Project SE/69, SBP/102, South Bank Polytechnic, London, 1988.

Wilson, R.J., and Watkins, J.J., *Graphs: An Introductory Approach*, John Wiley & Sons, New York, 1990.
Solid, standard text on graph theory. More than adequate background for Chapter 8.

Wingfield, C.G., *USAACSC Experience with SLIM*, Report IAWAR 360–5, US Army Institute for Research in Management Information and Computer Science, Atlanta, GA, 1982.
Provides product size, project effort and duration data on 15 projects.

Wingrove, A., "Software certification," in *Software Reliability and Metrics* (eds Fenton, N. and Littlewood, B.), Elsevier, London, 1991.

Wirth, N., "Program development by stepwise refinement," *ACM Computing Surveys*, 6, pp. 247–59, 1974.

Wirth, N., "A plea for lean software," *IEEE Computer,* 28(2), pp. 64–8, February 1995.
Excellent article that argues the case against large software systems.

Woda, H. and Schynoll, W. (eds), "Lean Software Development," *ESPRIT BOOTSTRAP conference proceedings*, Stuttgart, Germany, 1992.

Wohlin, C. and Ahlgren, M., "Soft factors and their impact on time to market," *Software Quality Journal*, 4(3), pp. 189–206, 1995.
Based on data collection from 12 large projects, the authors describe a procedure for predicting time to market. There are 10 soft factors, including "competence," "product complexity" and "requirements stability."

Wohlwend, H. and Rosenbaum, S., "Schlumberger's software improvement program," *IEEE Transactions on Software Engineering*, 20(11), pp. 833–9, 1994.
Authors report that the defect rate (meaning density) went from 0.22 per KNCSS (for 400 000 NCSS) to 0.13 per KNCSS (for 700 000 NCSS). At the end, fewer than 10% of defects were post-release customer-reported.

Wolverton, R.W., "The cost of developing large-scale software," *IEEE Transactions on Computers*, 23(6), pp. 615–36, 1974.

Wong, W.E. and Mathur, A.P., "Fault detection effectiveness of mutation and data flow testing," *Software Quality Journal*, 4(1), pp. 69–93, 1995.

Woodfield, S., "An experiment on unit increase in problem complexity," *IEEE Transactions on Software Engineering*, SE-5(2), pp. 76–8, 1979.

Woodfield, S.N., Dunsmore, H.E. and Shen, V.Y., "The effect of modularization and comments on program comprehension," *Proceedings of the Fifth International Conference on Software Engineering*, IEEE Computer Society Press, pp. 213–23, 1979.
Authors chose comprehensibility as a quality attribute conjectured to be improved in programs constructed using modularization. A controlled experiment (where comprehensibility was measured by the results of carefully defined tests) appeared to confirm the conjecture.

Woodfield, S.N., Shen, V. and Dunsmore, H.E., "A study of several metrics for programming effort," *Journal of Systems and Software*, 2(2), pp. 97–103, 1981.

Woods, D. and Cole, R.J., *Observation Model First Report, Measurement-based Experiment for Techniques Assessment* (META), Project IED P3155, Report R1.2.1, p. 103, 1992.

Woodward, M.R., "Difficulties using cohesion and coupling as quality indicators," *Software Quality Journal*, 2(2), pp. 109–28, 1993.
Based on a case study using a medium-sized FORTRAN program. Shows that many of the coupling and cohesion metrics proposed in the literature are so subjective that there is little agreement on the values.

Woodward, M.R., Hennell, M.A. and Hedley, D., "A measure of control flow complexity in program text," *IEEE Transactions on Software Engineering*, SE-5(1), pp. 45–50, 1979.

Woodward, M.R., Hedley, D. and Hennell, M.A., "Experience with path analysis and testing of programs, *IEEE Transactions on Software Engineering*, 6(5), pp. 278–86, 1980.
Main reference for the LCSAJ testing strategy discussed in Chapter 8.

Wynekoop, J.L. and Conger, S.A., "A review of computer-aided software engineering research methods," in *Information Systems Research: Contemporary Approaches and Emergent Traditions* (eds Nissen, H.E., Klein, H.K. and Hirshheim, R.), Elsevier Science Publishers, B.V. (North Holland), pp. 301–25, 1991.

The authors examine computer-aided software engineering (CASE) research, noting the general lack of action research, case studies, field studies, and experiments. They suggest that this lack hinders further development of useful tools.

Yand, Y. and Weber, R., "An ontological model of an information system," *IEEE Transactions on Software Engineering*, 16, pp. 1282–92, 1990.

Was the model used by Chidamber and Kemerer for their metrics of object-oriented designs.

Yasuda, K., "Software quality assurance activities in Japan," in *Japanese Perspectives in Software Engineering* (eds Matsumoto, Y., and Ohno, Y.), pp. 187–205, Addison-Wesley, Reading, MA, 1989.

Yates, D.F. and Malevris, N., "The effort required by LCSAJ testing: an assessment via a new path generation strategy," *Software Quality Journal*, 4(3), pp. 227–42, 1995.

Interesting experimental study. The new path selection strategy makes it easier to identify infeasible paths. The results are that a good LCSAJ coverage ratio of 0.85 can be achieved with an acceptable level of effort.

Yau, C. and Gan, L.-Y., "Comparing the top-down and bottom-up approaches of function point analysis," *Software Quality Journal*, 4(3), pp. 175–88, 1995.

Comparative empirical study that shows that a top-down approach to function point analysis is superior to a bottom-up approach.

Yau, S.S. and Collofello, J.S., "Some stability measures for software maintenance," *IEEE Transactions on Software Engineering*, 6(6), pp. 545–52, 1980.

A design stability measure for a given module M is defined by considering control and information flow knowledge about the system to determine the likely "ripple effect" to other modules of changes to M.

Yau, S.S. and Collofello, J.S., "Design stability measures for software maintenance," *IEEE Transactions on Software Engineering*, 11(9), pp. 849–56, 1985.

Yin, B.H. and Winchester, J.W., "The establishment and use of measures to evaluate the quality of system designs," *Proceedings of the Software Quality and Assurance Workshop*, pp. 45–52, 1978.

Yoshida, T., "Attaining higher quality in software development evaluation in practice," *Fujitsu Science and Technology Journal*, 21(3), pp. 305–16, 1985.

Youll, D.P., *Making Software Development Visible*, Wiley, New York, 1990.

Yourdon, E. and Constantine, L.L., *Structured Design*, Prentice Hall, Englewood Cliffs, NJ, 1979.

Zadeh, L.A., "Fuzzy sets as a basis for a theory of possibility," *Fuzzy Sets and Systems*, 1, pp. 3–28, 1978.

Definitive reference on fuzzy sets.

Zage, W.M. and Zage, D.M., "Evaluating design metrics on large-scale software," *IEEE Software*, 10(4), pp. 75–81, July 1993.

Zave, P., "An operational approach to requirements specification for embedded systems," *IEEE Transactions on Software Engineering*, SE-8(3), pp. 250–69, 1982.

Zhuo, F., Lowther, B., Oman, P. and Hagemeister, J., "Constructing and testing maintainability assessment models," *Proceedings of the First International Software Metrics Symposium*, Baltimore, MD, IEEE Computer Society Press, pp. 61–70, 1993.

Describes a number of regression-based maintainability models that were validated against subjective assessments of maintainability for 14 systems.

van Zijp, W. and van der Pol, J.J.M., *Project management: models in practice*, Cap Gemini Publishing (in Dutch), 1992.

Zuse, H., *Software Complexity: Measures and Methods*, De Gruyter, Berlin, 1991.

This book provides a very thorough treatment of how measurement theory can be used to assess software complexity metrics. The book analyzes just about every published complexity measure (which may be derived from a flowgraph) and considers the different assumptions that must hold for the metrics to be used on various scales. Provided you can understand the mathematics, you should never use a complexity metric wrongly again once you have read this book!

Zuse, H., "Properties of software measures," *Software Quality Journal* 1(4), 225–60, 1992.

Zuse, H., "Support of experimentation by measurement theory," *Experimental Software Engineering Issues* (eds Rombach, H.D., Basili, V.R. and Selby, R.W.) Lecture Notes in Computer Science, 706, pp. 137–40, Springer-Verlag, Berlin, 1993.

Zweben, S.H., Edwards, S.H., Weide, B.W. and Hollingsworth, J.E., "The effects of layering and encapsulation on software development cost and quality," *IEEE Transactions on Software Engineering*, 21(3), pp. 200–8, March 1995.

This paper discusses some of the problems involved in using parametric and non-parametric statistical tests and suggests how to deal with some aspects of software engineering data.

Index